Fodor's

D0444342

NOVA SCOTIA &
ATLANTIC CANADA

WELCOME TO NOVA SCOTIA & ATLANTIC CANADA

Bordered by the sea, Canada's easternmost provinces share an appealing, low-key vibe as well as some striking natural beauty. Nova Scotia's capital, Halifax, is the region's one larger city. Elsewhere, coastal towns dot the landscape, adding mellow charm with weathered wharves and lighthouses. You can visit Prince Edward Island's Green Gables sites, hike around New Brunswick's Bay of Fundy, or marvel at Newfoundland's spectacular parks. Wherever you go, lobster suppers and traditional music sessions are signs of the region's unique maritime and cultural history.

TOP REASONS TO GO

★ **Marine marvels:** Whales, seabirds, icebergs, and the planet's highest tides.

★ **Coastal scenery:** Drives such as the Cabot Trail reveal beautiful ocean vistas.

★ **Historic sites:** The Vikings, French, and British all left their mark here.

★ **Beaches:** Sandy strands for swimming, pebble-strewn coves, surfers' favorites.

★ **Succulent seafood:** Lobster, oysters, salmon, and scallops don't come any fresher.

★ **Traditional music:** Listening to Celtic or Acadian tunes is a memorable experience.

12
TOP EXPERIENCES

Nova Scotia & Atlantic Canada offer terrific experiences that should be on every traveler's list. Here are Fodor's top picks for a memorable trip.

1 Lunenburg, Nova Scotia

"Timeless" is a word that's justifiably applied to the South Shore's signature port town. Hundreds of colorful 18th- and 19th-century buildings line the steep streets of its historic core, a UNESCO World Heritage Site. *(Ch. 2)*

2 Gros Morne National Park, Newfoundland

The stellar scenery encompasses a fjord, glacier-carved Western Brook Pond, and the Tablelands, a rock massif created millions of years ago. *(Ch. 5)*

3 Bay of Fundy, New Brunswick

Fundy's phenomenal tides—the highest in the world—rise and fall twice daily with dramatic results. For proof, you can watch the waters peak and ebb at the Hopewell Rocks. *(Ch. 3)*

4 Anne's Land, Prince Edward Island

On PEI it's hard to avoid a certain redheaded orphan. For fans of the 1908 novel *Anne of Green Gables*, the sites around Cavendish are much-loved ground. *(Ch. 4)*

5 Beaches, Prince Edward Island

Lapped by the warmest waters north of the Carolinas, PEI's pebbly shores and sandy crescents attract swimmers, sun worshippers, and bird-watchers. *(Ch. 4)*

6 Cabot Trail, Nova Scotia

Cape Breton's winding highway by the ocean proves the journey is more important than the destination: it's often called one of the most gorgeous roads on earth. *(Ch. 2)*

7 Seafood Feasts

Lobster, scallops, oysters, salmon, and more: whether you dine at casual waterfront shacks or in fine dining rooms, sublime fresh seafood tops the menu. *(Ch. 2–5)*

8 Halifax, Nova Scotia

The province's capital manages to feel at once traditional and trendy. Atlantic Canada's largest city is built around the world's second-largest natural harbor. *(Ch. 2)*

9 Confederation Trail, Prince Edward Island

Following a former railroad bed, this gently graded bike path crosses the island, winding past green fields, red clay cliffs, sandy beaches, and the blue sea. *(Ch. 4)*

10 Golf Courses, Prince Edward Island

PEI is said to have more golfing options per square mile than anywhere else in Canada, with 30-plus courses, some quite scenic, open from May through October. *(Ch. 4)*

11 Notre Dame Bay, Newfoundland

Spectacular icebergs weighing 100,000 to 200,000 tons serenely float offshore from June through early July. Humpback whales frolic near Twillingate until September. *(Ch. 5)*

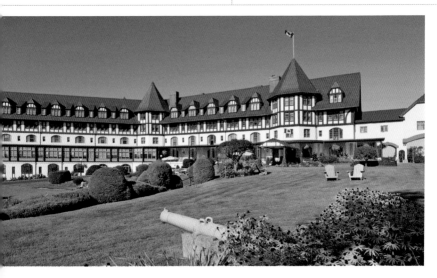

12 St. Andrews-by-the-Sea, New Brunswick

Century-old homes and manicured gardens give this resort village a genteel vibe, but proximity to the Bay of Fundy means there are options for outdoor adventure as well. *(Ch. 3)*

CONTENTS

1 EXPERIENCE NOVA SCOTIA AND ATLANTIC CANADA 11
What's Where 12
When to Go 14
Province Picker 15
Nova Scotia and Atlantic Canada Today 16
If You Like 18
Quintessential Nova Scotia & Atlantic Canada 20
Nova Scotia and Atlantic Canada with Kids 22

2 NOVA SCOTIA 23
Welcome to Nova Scotia 24
Halifax 31
South Shore and Annapolis Valley ...48
The Eastern Shore and Northern Nova Scotia 80
Cape Breton Island 97

3 NEW BRUNSWICK 119
Welcome to New Brunswick 120
Saint John 126
The Fundy Coast 137
The Acadian Coast 161
St. John River Valley 174
Fredericton 182

4 PRINCE EDWARD ISLAND 191
Welcome to Prince Edward Island 192
Charlottetown 198
Central Coastal Drive 211
Points East Coastal Drive 222
North Cape Coastal Drive 229

5 NEWFOUNDLAND AND LABRADOR 237
Welcome to Newfoundland and Labrador 238

St. John's, Newfoundland 246
Avalon Peninsula 263
Eastern Newfoundland 271
Gander and Around 279
Western Newfoundland 284

UNDERSTANDING NOVA SCOTIA AND ATLANTIC CANADA 297
Books and Movies 298
French Vocabulary 299
Menu Guide 302

TRAVEL SMART NOVA SCOTIA AND ATLANTIC CANADA 305

INDEX 318

ABOUT OUR WRITERS 336

MAPS

Halifax 35
South Shore and Annapolis Valley 50
The Eastern Shore and Northern Nova Scotia 81
Cape Breton Island 98
Saint John 128
The Fundy Coast 138
Fundy National Park 151
The Acadian Coast and The St. John River Valley 162
Fredericton 183
Charlottetown 201
Central Coastal Drive 212
Points East Coastal Drive 223
North Cape Coastal Drive 230
St. John's 249
Avalon Peninsula 265
Eastern Newfoundland and Gander 273
Western Newfoundland 285

ABOUT THIS GUIDE

Fodor's Recommendations

Everything in this guide is worth doing—we don't cover what isn't—but exceptional sights, hotels, and restaurants are recognized with additional accolades. Fodor'sChoice★ indicates our top recommendations. Care to nominate a new place? Visit Fodors.com/contact-us.

Trip Costs

We list prices wherever possible to help you budget well. Hotel and restaurant price categories from $ to $$$$ are noted alongside each recommendation. For hotels, we include the lowest cost of a standard double room in high season. For restaurants, we cite the average price of a main course at dinner or, if dinner isn't served, at lunch. For attractions, we always list adult admission fees; discounts are usually available for children, students, and senior citizens.

Hotels

Our local writers vet every hotel to recommend the best overnights in each price category, from budget to expensive. Unless otherwise specified, you can expect private bath, phone, and TV in your room. For expanded hotel reviews, facilities, and deals visit Fodors.com.

Restaurants

Unless we state otherwise, restaurants are open for lunch and dinner daily. We mention dress code only when there's a specific requirement and reservations only when they're essential or not accepted. To make restaurant reservations, visit Fodors.com.

Credit Cards

The hotels and restaurants in this guide typically accept credit cards. If not, we'll say so.

Top Picks		Hotels & Restaurants	
★	Fodor'sChoice	🏨	Hotel
Listings		⬎	Number of rooms
⊠	Address	❙○❙	Meal plans
⊠	Branch address	✕	Restaurant
☎	Telephone	⌂	Reservations
🖷	Fax	🏛	Dress code
⊕	Website	⊟	No credit cards
✎	E-mail	$	Price
🎟	Admission fee		
⊙	Open/closed times	**Other**	
Ⓜ	Subway	⇨	See also
✛	Directions or Map coordinates	☞	Take note
		🏌	Golf facilities

EXPERIENCE NOVA SCOTIA AND ATLANTIC CANADA

WHAT'S WHERE

The following numbers refer to chapters.

2 Nova Scotia. Nova Scotia is the land of lighthouses and lobster traps: throw a dart at the map and you'll likely hit one or the other. But there are inland highlights, too, like sylvan orchards and dramatic highlands. If you're looking for urban amenities, the capital—hip, historic Halifax— is the largest city in Atlantic Canada and has the region's broadest range of dining and nightlife options.

3 New Brunswick. Fronted by the Bay of Fundy, New Brunswick is a fine place to witness the action of the planet's highest tides as they rise and fall a phenomenal 14.5 meters (48 feet) twice daily. Beyond the bay, the province boasts rivers, mountains, and dense forests—all of which offer abundant adventure opportunities—plus two rich cultures (English and French) and more than four centuries of history.

4 Prince Edward Island. PEI is rightly nicknamed "The Gentle Island" because it's generally prettier and more pastoral than its neighbors. PEI's rich red soil supports thriving farms, while its sandy warm-water beaches and nostalgia-inducing towns are a magnet for vacationers. Being largely flat, Canada's smallest province is also hugely popular with cyclists and golfers.

5 Newfoundland and Labrador. This province is rugged and remote (Newfoundland sits alone in the North Atlantic; Labrador is tucked into northern Québec). It's also relatively cold, which allows for iceberg-watching in summer, great snow sports in winter, and wildlife-viewing year-round. Nevertheless, a warm welcome is assured: people here have been greeting visitors since the Vikings arrived 1,000 years ago.

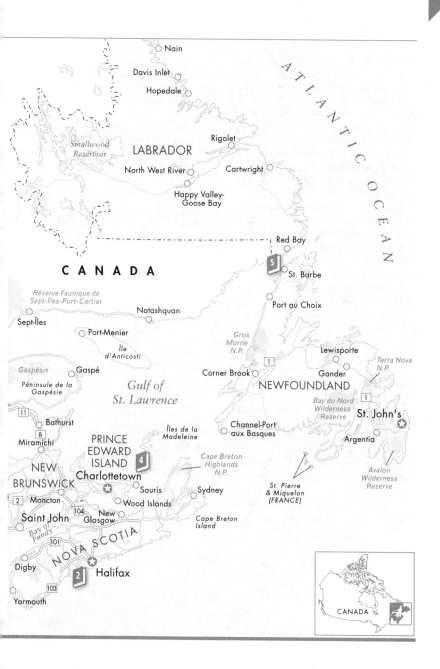

WHEN TO GO

July and August, when long, warm days let you fully enjoy attractions and activities, are the most popular months to visit Atlantic Canada. Beaches beckon in summer, sites open their doors for extended hours, and outfitters go full tilt, offering both soft and extreme outdoor adventures. As an added bonus, the seafood is freshest during those sunny days (or at least it seems so when you're eating at a waterside café) and the calendar is packed with festivals. Fall brings bountiful harvests, excellent whale-watching, and, of course, brilliant foliage. The trees, which start turning in late September, are at their most dazzling in October, and events like Cape Breton's Celtic Colours International Festival are scheduled to coincide with the vivid display.

Although many outlying inns and eateries close for the coldest months, there is a lot to do in Atlantic Canada during the winter. Snowmobilers and skiers, for example, can chill in northern New Brunswick, which gets as much as 400 centimeters (157 inches) of snow annually. March and April are the months for maple syrup and north-bound migratory birds, but travelers typically avoid this time as the weather is often frosty and wet. Late spring, though, is delightful. Apple trees bloom, wildflowers reappear, seasonal tourism operations reopen, and the visitor-to-local ratio remains low.

Climate

As a general rule, spring arrives later in coastal regions than inland, and nights are cool by the water even in summer. The balmiest land temperatures are recorded in July and August, while the ocean is at its warmest in August and early September. Autumn can last well into November, with warm, clear days and crisp nights. Most of Atlantic Canada is blanketed by snow in winter.

As far as main cities go, it may be handy to note that St. John's is uncommonly cold and Halifax, due to the Gulf Stream, is relatively moderate in winter.

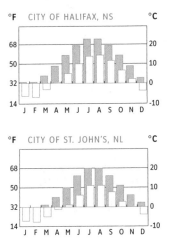

PROVINCE PICKER

Not sure which of the four Atlantic provinces is right for you? All have hospitable people and stunning scenery, but not every one might offer that unique mix of attributes that makes it ideal for your trip. Use this chart to compare how each province will measure up to your idea of the perfect vacation. Remember, if you're looking for big cosmopolitan cities and TMZ-worthy nightlife, you'd be better off in a different part of the world.

	Nova Scotia	New Brunswick	Prince Edward Island	Newfoundland and Labrador
Cold-water beaches	◑	◑	○	●
Warm-water beaches	◑	●	●	○
Water sports	●	●	●	●
Snow sports	◑	●	○	●
Golfing	●	◑	●	◑
National parks	●	●	●	●
Rugged coastline	●	●	◑	●
Scenic drives	●	●	●	●
Lighthouses	●	●	●	●
Lobster	●	●	●	●
Iceberg-watching	○	○	○	●
Whale-watching	●	●	○	●
Bird-watching	●	●	●	●
Historic sites	●	●	◑	◑
Museums	●	●	◑	◑
Arts and crafts	●	●	●	●
Wineries and distilleries	●	○	◑	○
Spas	◑	◑	◑	◑
Cool capitals	●	◑	◑	◑

● = Noteworthy, ◑ = Some, ○ = Little or none

NOVA SCOTIA AND ATLANTIC CANADA TODAY

Canada's east coast is justifiably famous for its natural beauty—after all, its photogenic headlands, highlands, and harbors provide endless Instagram opportunities. However, it is the people who live here that really set this place apart. These days Atlantic Canadians

. . . are dealing with the economy

Thanks to off-shore oil, St. John's (Newfoundland and Labrador's largest city) is booming. The economic outlook in Halifax is bright, too, as demonstrated by the amount of construction downtown. Being the de facto capital of Atlantic Canada, Halifax is the regional center for health and education (which gives it a strong white-collar presence); plus the Canadian navy's Atlantic fleet is based here (adding a lot of "sailor blue"). As a port city, Halifax is further benefiting from a multiyear, $25-billion shipbuilding contract awarded in 2011.

But here, as elsewhere in North America, rural areas are struggling. Heritage industries still form the economic backbone: farming is one, forestry and its offshoots (like the pulp-and-paper business) is another. Fishing, of course, also counts because seafood isn't just a menu staple: along much of the coast, it provides livelihoods. Not surprisingly, tourism in such spots is especially important. So while Atlantic Canadians are genuinely happy to see you, the cash visitors inject into the economy offers them an added incentive to be friendly.

. . . are proud of their roots

In today's fast-changing world locals might not be sure where they are going, but they remain very conscious of where they came from. Mi'Kmaq communities here continue to honor traditions handed down from the original inhabitants, and the legacy of early European settlers is equally apparent. Witness the living culture of Francophone Acadians, who proudly fly their own Stella Maris flag in parts of Nova Scotia, New Brunswick, and PEI. Their *joie de vivre* tinges everything from the instruments they play to the delicacies they devour (think spoons and *rappie* pie respectively). On Cape Breton, conversely, descendants of Scots who arrived centuries ago nibble oatcakes, step-dance to Celtic fiddle music, and enliven conversations with the odd Gaelic phrase. Newer immigrant groups have also staked their claim, showcasing their own contributions to the region at events such as the annual Nova Scotia Multicultural Festival.

. . . are enjoying the great outdoors

Urban sprawl is virtually unheard of around here, and huge tracts of land—particularly in Newfoundland and Labrador and central New Brunswick—remain undeveloped. Generously sized civic green spaces (picture Halifax's Point Pleasant Park or Saint John's Rockwood Park) are plentiful as well, so it's easy for outdoorsy sorts to find a place to play. Fresh-air fans regularly lace up hiking boots, pick up paddles, hop on bikes, lob golf balls, and grab fishing gear. All of their energy isn't expended on exercise, though. Atlantic Canadians also work hard to preserve their natural heritage for future generations. This explains why they have successfully lobbied to protect Sable Island (which was being threatened by the off-shore oil industry) as a national park, and to win UNESCO Biosphere Reserve status for both the Bay of Fundy and more than 13,770 square km (5,316 square miles) of pristine southwest Nova Scotian terrain.

. . . are being creative

Atlantic Canada is home to a disproportionate number of high-quality artisans and craftspeople: some are native born, others are CFAs ("come from aways") drawn by inspiring vistas and a comparatively low cost of living. The region abounds with potters, painters, and pewtersmiths, as well as practitioners of folk disciplines such as quilting, wood carving, and rug hooking—many of whom give traditional motifs an updated twist. These creative types can be found in city centers and quiet rural locales. Notable among the latter is Newfoundland's remote Fogo Island, where an extraordinary, über modern arts colony featuring studios and residency programs has just been built from scratch by the Shorefast Foundation. But they can also be found in postsecondary institutions because several schools (including a New Brunswick craft college and a Nova Scotia university devoted to art and design) lend the scene academic cred and added prestige.

. . . are eating well

Long before the Slow Food and Eat Local movements gained momentum, folks here tended to be locavores. Now a matter of preference, it was once a matter of necessity. In cities, "local" was all that you could buy fresh. In the countryside, where people fished, raised, picked, or otherwise procured their own food, it was all that was available. Yet the downhome diet has never presented any great hardship since stellar seafood is prevalent across all four provinces; and, in Newfoundland and Labrador especially, game gets added to the list (if you have never tried moose burgers or caribou medallions, here's your chance!). Factor in a cornucopia of farm produce, plus a bounty of wild berries, and you have the makings for memorable meals. Visitors can sample these at a range of innovative eateries and old-school restaurants. Want to learn to prepare them yourself? Nova Scotia's award-winning Trout Point Lodge has gourmet cooking vacations.

. . . are raising the bar

Like all Canadians, those in the Atlantic region are crazy about Tim Hortons coffee. (Forget that mocha-choca latte: the standard order here is Timmie's large double-double—shorthand for a big cup of Joe with two creams and two sugars.) Residents, however, are always ready to imbibe something stronger. And they don't just drink it: they make it. Take Nova Scotian wine: Samuel de Champlain and his thirsty French crew planted the former colony's first grapevines in 1611. Today the wine industry adds $196-million a year to the provincial economy, with the number of grape growers and boutique wine producers increasing almost annually. In 2012, Nova Scotia even introduced its own appellation: Tidal Bay, a crisp white. Thanks to a mild micro-climate, most wineries are concentrated in the Annapolis Valley, and several (including Wolfville's Domaine de Grand Pré and Falmouth's Sainte Famille) offer tours and tastings.

IF YOU LIKE

On-the-Water Activities

PEI and Newfoundland are both islands; and Nova Scotia is almost one. New Brunswick, meanwhile, is cut by mighty rivers and boasts three coasts that extend for a collective 2,250 km (1,398 miles). That's good news for beachgoers, as well as for travelers eager to try something more adventurous than sunbathing or sandcastle building.

■ **Beach Bumming.** Prince Edward Island tops most beach lovers' lists. It has classic crescents and several variations on the theme, including shores backed by rare parabolic dunes and ones composed of "singing sand" that squeaks when you walk on it (check out Basin Head for that).

■ **Surfing.** The water may be frigid, but that doesn't deter surfing devotees who routinely head to Nova Scotia's Eastern Shore to indulge their passion. Lawrencetown Beach and Martinique Beach have the best breaks, especially in late summer when the tail-ends of hurricanes whip up waves.

■ **Salmon Fishing.** Grab your rod and hip waders. The Miramichi in New Brunswick, the Margaree in Nova Scotia, and the Humber in Newfoundland and Labrador are legendary salmon rivers. Pulling a trophy-sized specimen from one is the Alpha and Omega-3 of fishing experiences.

■ **Riding the Tide.** When incoming Fundy tides meet an outflowing river in Saint John, New Brunswick, the former pushes the latter backward, creating a phenomenon known as the Reversing Rapids. Slicker-clad thrill seekers can brave the resulting whitewater on a wild jet boat ride.

Scenic Drives

It's no surprise that Atlantic Canada earns an A+ for scenery. Crashing surf, craggy headlands, forest-clad mountains, rolling farmland, meandering rivers: they're all here. Each of the four provinces has designated camera-ready drives (Nova Scotia alone has 11 so-called Scenic Travelways); and these showcase the best of the best, making auto touring easy.

■ **Cabot Trail,** Nova Scotia. This renowned 298-km (185-mile) road ranks among the region's most dramatic. Timid motorists should note that tackling its vertiginous, ocean-hugging turns is no easy task: sound brakes and steady nerves are required. Yet its sheer beauty rewards the effort.

■ **Central Coastal Drive,** Prince Edward Island. Compact PEI is a driver's dream. Highlighting the province's midsection, this route loops through top sites (including Cavendish, the island's national park, and Charlottetown), taking in vintage Victoria and other pretty villages.

■ **River Valley Scenic Drive,** New Brunswick. Discover a more bucolic side to New Brunswick by veering inland from the wave-lashed Fundy coast and following the St. John River. The route's southern portion, with its covered bridges and little cable ferries, is particularly picturesque.

■ **Road to the Isles,** Newfoundland and Labrador. This 172-km (107-mile) stretch of the Kittiwake Coast focuses on Notre Dame Bay. Stop at Twillingate, where summertime visitors can ogle icebergs and watch for whales—specifically the supersized "Humpbacks of Notre Dame."

National Parks

With the addition of Sable Island in 2013, Atlantic Canada now has nine national parks. Several are hard to miss: for example, Fundy National Park (one of New Brunswick's big draws) sits between Saint John and Moncton, while the famed Cabot Trail runs right through Cape Breton Highlands National Park.

- **Gros Morne National Park,** Newfoundland and Labrador. Notable for geologic features that date back almost 500,000,000 years, Gros Morne wears its age well. Recreational opportunities in the rugged park include hiking, fishing, and boat tours on glacier-sculpted Western Brook Pond.

- **Prince Edward Island National Park,** Prince Edward Island. More than a playground for the sun-and-sand set, this park—running from Cavendish to Dalvay, with a Greenwich Peninsula adjunct—also appeals to bird-watchers and, since Green Gables sits on its property, Anne fans.

- **Kejimkujik National Park,** Nova Scotia. Both a National Park and a National Historic site, "Keji" combines natural splendor with a rich Aboriginal heritage. Today you can paddle through pristine woodlands using the same canoe routes that the ancient Mi'Kmaq people once followed.

- **Kouchibouguac National Park,** New Brunswick. Washed by the warm Northumberland Strait, the beaches here provide a quiet counterpoint to busy Parlee Beach in nearby Shediac. The park's lagoons shelter sea life and dune grasses protect birds such as the endangered piping plover.

Living History

With all due respect to Columbus, it was actually Viking explorer Leif Eriksson who "discovered" the New World when he landed on Newfoundland's Great Northern Peninsula in AD 1000. By the 1600s, French and English forces were duking it out in the rest of the region; and, in the next century, war in America and poverty in Europe brought waves of immigrants. Hence there is area is rife with history, and there are many places where you can step back in time.

- **L'Anse aux Meadows,** Newfoundland and Labrador. The Viking settlement, unearthed in the 1960s, is now a UNESCO World Heritage Site with excavated and replicated sod huts, plus an artifact-filled visitor center. Activities range from guided walks to weaving lessons.

- **Fortress of Louisbourg,** Nova Scotia. Return to the 1700s, when France fought for control of the continent, at North America's largest historical reconstruction. Costumed interpreters lend an air of authenticity to the 12-acre property.

- **Highland Village Museum,** Nova Scotia. Honor the area's Scottish immigrants (remember, Nova Scotia is Latin for "New Scotland") by learning a thing or two about Celtic culture at this engaging, open-air attraction in Cape Breton.

- **Kings Landing Historical Settlement,** New Brunswick. History buffs can hit the pause button at this sprawling riverfront site, which re-creates life among the United Empire Loyalists (also known as the Tories, depending which side of the American Revolution you supported).

QUINTESSENTIAL
NOVA SCOTIA & ATLANTIC CANADA

Succulent Seafood

Atlantic salmon, Digby scallops, Malpeque Bay oysters—this part of Canada is nirvana for seafood connoisseurs. Nothing, however, makes true aficionados swoon like fresh local lobster. Fast-food junkies can try a McLobster while Food Channel fans can buy lobster right off the wharf and boil it themselves. In some places, visitors curious about crustaceans can learn how to haul in traps before devouring the catch. Want to get right down to business? You'll find lobster ready to eat in simple dockside eateries and haute-cuisine restaurants almost everywhere. Perhaps the most satisfying feasts are the communal lobster suppers hosted each summer by rural churches and community centers: look for signs posted in coastal areas. At these unpretentious gatherings tables are long, prices are low, and the ambience is unforgettable.

Illuminating Lighthouses

Nowhere is the seafaring heritage of Atlantic Canada more evident than in the 400-plus lighthouses that stand sentry on the coast. Each has its own claim to fame. Newfoundland's Cape Spear Light, for instance, marks North America's most easterly point; the one at Peggy's Cove, near Halifax, is one of the continent's most photographed. Amazing views of ferries, fishing boats, and, occasionally, spouting whales set New Brunswick's Swallowtail Light apart. But PEI's Cape Bear beacon has a sadder distinction: it received the first SOS from the *Titanic* as she sank in 1912. Though designed to be seen from afar, many lighthouse facilities now offer visitors up-close experiences. Some house museums, crafts shops, or restaurants. A few—like Newfoundland's Quirpon, Nova Scotia's Cape d'Or, and PEI's West Point—even offer accommodations.

If you want to genuinely *experience* Atlantic Canada, as opposed to merely seeing it, you must first learn what makes Atlantic Canadians tick. Sampling these tried-and-true activities will give you the inside track.

Lively Languages

Canada's multicultural model isn't a melting pot so much as a simmering stew that enables each group to maintain its distinctive character. In this region one result is a unique linguistic mélange. For most folks English is the mother tongue, yet in northern New Brunswick (Canada's only officially bilingual province), French predominates. Ditto for Nova Scotia's Acadian Coast and parts of PEI, so you may want to practice your *bonjour* and *merci* before arriving. Gaelic is added to the mix in Cape Breton, which is home to North America's only Gaelic college: you won't be on the island long before someone wishes you *ciad mille failte* (a hundred thousand welcomes). Newfoundland famously has a lingo all its own. You best twig to it, too, or you might be a chucklehead and decline if invited out for a scoff and a scuff (dinner and a dance).

A Slower Pace

You might as well ease your foot off that gas pedal because in Atlantic Canada no one's in a hurry to get anywhere. Despite their quick wits, people here choose to move at a slower pace and will happily interrupt almost any activity to chat with a friend, a neighbor—or you, if given a chance. Such behavior can frustrate travelers intent on sticking to a strict itinerary. If you're open to opportunities, though, you'll not only see firsthand how friendly Atlantic Canadians are, you will likely also come away with in-the-know info on hidden back roads, undiscovered eateries, and one-of-a-kind events. Taking time out may mean you have to pare back the destinations you cover or drop some attractions from your sightseeing checklist. Well, so be it. After all, this is a vacation, not *The Amazing Race*. Slow down and savor the experience.

NOVA SCOTIA AND ATLANTIC CANADA WITH KIDS

Traveling with kids? Here's the lowdown on what to do where.

Prince Edward Island

PEI is so compact that you can do it all. Most families, however, home in on the central section. It's a buffet for beach lovers because you can enjoy the unspoiled splendor of **Prince Edward Island National Park** as well as the kitschy seaside amusements around **Cavendish**, including **Shining Waters Family Fun Park** and **Ripley's Believe It or Not!** Of course, this is also L. M. Montgomery's native turf and two *Anne* sites—**Green Gables** plus a replica of **Avonlea Village** appeal to young fans. If your children weren't raised on "Anne with an E," brush up by seeing **"Anne of Green Gables—The Musical"** at the Confederation Centre in **Charlottetown**. The tuneful tearjerker has played to packed houses every summer since 1965. While in the city, also take in **Founders' Hall**, where state-of-the-art technology explains how Canada was created during the Charlottetown Conference of 1864.

Nova Scotia

In Nova Scotia, make **Halifax** your base. Aside from the amenities you'd expect in Atlantic Canada's largest urban center, Nova Scotia's capital has standout attractions, such as the historic Halifax Citadel (where reenactors drill daily in summer) and bustling **Waterfront Boardwalk.** On or near the latter you can visit a pair of cool, kid-centric museums (the **Maritime Museum of the Atlantic** and the **Canadian Museum of Immigration at Pier 21**), before choosing one of the many boat tours that operate out of **Cable Wharf.** For a taste of traditional coastal life, spend a morning scrambling over the rocks at the **Peggy's Cove Lighthouse**; or a full day exploring time-warped South Shore towns (most notably **Lunenburg**) with a beach break in between.

New Brunswick

Although New Brunswick is relatively large, you can tick off many family-oriented sites if you focus on the Moncton area. The city itself is home to **Crystal Palace** (an indoor amusement park), **Magic Mountain Water Park**, the **Magnetic Hill Zoo**, and **TreeGO Aerial Adventures** (an overhead obstacle course for Tarzan wannabes). Moreover, it puts you in easy shooting distance of both **Fundy and Kouchibouguac National Parks,** as well as the fabled **Hopewell Rocks.** As an added bonus, **Parlee Beach** is about 20 minutes away in **Shediac**. The 3-km (2-mile) expanse of sand—complete with tempting tidal pools—draws big crowds. Shediac also bills itself as "The Lobster Capital of the World," and kids can see how they're caught on a fun Lobster Tales Cruise.

Newfoundland and Labrador

National parks like **Gros Morne** engage kids through dedicated programs; ditto for National Historic Sites like **L'Anse aux Meadows**—a visit to which can be combined with one to nearby **Norstead,** a re-created Norse village featuring costumed staffers and a full-scale Viking ship. The downside is that vast distances separate many attractions and, frankly, the province's simple charms are often lost on children. **St. John's** is an exception to the rule. Clusters of houses are painted in Crayola colors, and spots like the geology-themed **Johnson GEO CENTRE** will score points with your offspring. Be sure to hike up **Signal Hill** and make the short drive to **Cape Spear:** from either you might spot whales or icebergs. For a different perspective, hop a harbor tour boat.

NOVA SCOTIA

WELCOME TO NOVA SCOTIA

TOP REASONS TO GO

★ **See the Coast:** There are postcard-perfect fishing villages and sprawling sandy beaches. The water is inviting, too, for kayaking, sailing, or whale-watching.

★ **Dine on Crustaceans:** This province is shaped liked a lobster claw, a happy coincidence because the lobster here is so delicious. Mussels and oysters are also plentiful, and Digby lays claim to the world's finest scallops.

★ **Shop for Crafts:** Nova Scotians—from the quilters at Suttles and Seawinds in Mahone Bay to the students of Halifax's Centre for Craft & Design—create high-quality products.

★ **Experience the Culture:** Cape Breton "kitchen parties" combine music and dancing, allowing you to sample the region's rich Celtic culture. For a French-tinged alternative, substitute a rollicking Acadian *soirée*.

★ **Enjoy the Camaraderie:** Bluenosers (the long-standing nickname for Nova Scotians) are famously friendly and very social. So be responsive—with a little encouragement you'll likely be embraced like long lost kin.

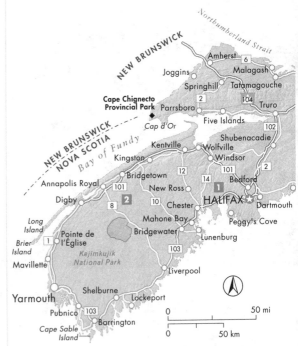

1 **Halifax.** The Halifax Regional Municipality is Atlantic Canada's biggest city and—as Nova Scotia's capital—has been a military, commercial, political, and cultural powerhouse for more than 250 years. Its downtown showcases the best of old and new through waterfront restaurants, pubs, galleries, heritage properties, and modern office towers.

2 **South Shore and Annapolis Valley.** The South Shore, on the Atlantic coast, is "classic" Nova Scotia, complete with weathered fishing villages, craggy coves, and white-sand beaches. The Annapolis Valley, on the Bay of Fundy side, is more pastoral and better known for orchards, vineyards, and picturesque farming villages.

QUEBEC

2

GETTING ORIENTED

Nova Scotia is all but surrounded by water, save for the narrow stretch of land that links it to the rest of Canada. Secondary highways hug the coastline and meander through historic, small towns, while "100-series" arterial highways offer the fastest travel routes. Halifax, the capital, sits on the eastern coast, roughly in the middle of the province's mainland. Southwest of the city, the South Shore runs all the way to Yarmouth. The Annapolis Valley, beside the Bay of Fundy, is the eastern spine of Nova Scotia. The central and northern areas lie beside Northumberland Strait (on a fine day you can see across to Prince Edward Island); while the northernmost region, Cape Breton Island, is connected to the remainder of the province by a 1.6-km (1-mile) causeway.

Map labels

Bay St. Lawrence
Pleasant Bay
Cape North
Cape Breton ◆ Highlands N. P.
Chéticamp
Ingonish
Margaree Harbour
Englishtown
4
St. Ann's
Glace Bay
19
Baddeck
Sydney
Mabou
105
Iona
Port Hood
Louisbourg
Big Pond
Bras d'Or Lake
4
PRINCE EDWARD ISLAND
NOVA SCOTIA
Gulf of St. Lawrence
St George's Bay
Pictou
Antigonish
Judique
104
New Glasgow
Guysborough
Arichat
3
Canso
Sherbrooke Village
Tangier
7
Musquodoboit Harbour
Atlantic Ocean

3 **Eastern Shore and Northern Nova Scotia.** The area east and north of Halifax reveals remarkable variety within a relatively short distance. The sparsely populated Eastern Shore has pounding surf, thick forests, and remote cranberry barrens, while Northumberland Strait boasts hiking trails and sandy warm-water beaches.

4 **Cape Breton.** The Island of Cape Breton is the Celtic heart of Nova Scotia, where music and dancing are a part of daily life. The gritty, industrial past of its towns and cities is a sharp contrast to the unspoiled natural beauty that defines the rural areas. The island is home to the Cabot Trail, a spectacular drive through the Cape Breton Highlands.

Updated by
Penny Phenix

For many, Nova Scotia evokes images of seascapes. To the south and east, the Atlantic crashes against rocky outcrops or washes placidly over white sand. To the northwest, Fundy tides recede to reveal mud flats, then rush back in, raising the sea level by more than 15 meters (50 feet). To the north, warm, relatively shallow Northumberland Strait flows between Nova Scotia and Prince Edward Island, providing a livelihood for fishermen on both sides. Nova Scotia is one of the world's largest exporters of seafood, particularly lobsters.

It was Thomas Chandler Haliburton who first said "seeing is believing," and the observation applies to his home province because it's hard to fathom such a variety of cultures and landscapes packed into an area smaller than West Virginia without witnessing it firsthand. Within the perimeter drawn by that convoluted coastline, lie the rolling farmlands of the Annapolis Valley, which yields vintner's grapes, apples, corn, peaches, and plums. In the middle of the province, dense forests are interspersed with blueberry patches, cranberry bogs, and, in spring and summer, open fields of wildflowers—purple and blue lupines, yellow coltsfoot, pink fireweed—that blanket the ground with color. In Cape Breton are highlands that rival Scotland's, rugged rock-rimmed inlets, woodlands that provide spectacular fall foliage, and mountains that plunge dramatically down to meet the waves. Throughout the province there is great biodiversity, including a number of endangered and threatened species that are being actively protected.

The people of Nova Scotia are equally diverse. The original inhabitants, the Mi'Kmaqs, have been here for 10,000 years and remain a major cultural presence. In the early days of European exploration, they were joined by the French and English who settled on the shores and harvested the sea. Later, waves of immigrants came: Germans in Lunenburg County; Highland Scots displaced by their landlords' preference for sheep; New England Loyalists fleeing the American Revolution; blacks arriving as freemen or escaped slaves; then Ukrainians, Poles, West Indians, Italians, and Lebanese drawn to the industrial centers of Halifax and Sydney.

That multicultural mélange accounts for the fact that you'll see Gaelic signs in Mabou and Iona, German sausage and sauerkraut prominently featured on menus in Lunenburg, and Francophones proudly flying their own tricolor flag in Acadian communities along the western Fundy coast and places such as Chéticamp in Cape Breton. It also helps explain why Nova Scotians, who originally hailed from so many different places themselves, are so famously hospitable to "people from away."

PLANNING

WHEN TO GO

Spring comes late in Nova Scotia: trees don't get leafy until mid-May, and it takes until mid-June for temperatures to heat up. As a result, many find July and August to be the ideal months here, but even then, come prepared. Bring a raincoat for morning fog and showers, a sweater to keep the ocean breezes at bay at night, and your bathing suit for the blazing sun in between. Autumn has its own charm: September has warm days, refreshingly cool nights, and hot events like Halifax's Atlantic Film and Atlantic Fringe festivals. From late September through October is peak time for foliage fans. The downside is that wildlife cruises, cycling tours, and kayaking outfitters generally only operate from mid-June through September. Keep in mind, too, that outside major tourist centers, many resorts, inns, and B&Bs close after Canadian Thanksgiving (Columbus Day in the United States) and don't reopen until Victoria Day in late May. Some shops, restaurants, and sites are also seasonal.

FESTIVALS

Nova Scotia hosts hundreds of festivals each year, and at first glance you might think most were devoted to food. Several coastal communities celebrate seafood, including Digby, Pictou, Shelburne, and Yarmouth, and the Annapolis Valley hosts events for apple-blossom time and the pumpkin harvest. Many events, though, highlight the diversity of the Nova Scotian people, from Halifax's multiculturalism to the Scottish heritage of Antigonish and Cape Breton to the North Shore's Acadian culture. Theater festivals range from Shakespeare to fringe, and music lovers will find much to choose from.

Multicultural Festival. A three-day celebration of Nova Scotia's multicultural mix, this late-June event takes place at Halifax Seaport near Pier 21, where many immigrants first set foot on Canadian soil. Music, arts and crafts, shopping, and the smells and tastes of world cuisines make for a lively scene. ⊠ *Halifax* ⊕ *www.multifest.ca.*

Pictou Lobster Carnival. Celebrating its 80th year in 2014, this three-day festival in early July marks the end of its region's fishing season with concerts, parades, lobster-boat racing, and a midway and other attractions. ⊠ *Pictou* ⊕ *www.pictoulobstercarnival.ca.*

Seafest. Yarmouth honors its seafaring roots with 11 days of festivities in late July. Highlights include a street parade, mackerel tossing, driftwood-art contests, beach parties, concerts, fireworks, and a parade of illuminated boats. ⊠ *Yarmouth* ⊕ *www.seafest.ca.*

Shelburne County Lobster Festival. The county celebrates the local lobster industry in early June with four days of events, entertainment, and lobster suppers. ⊠ *Shelburne* ⊕ *www.discovershelburnecounty.com/shelburnecountylobsterfestival.*

TD Halifax Jazz Festival. Musicians representing a variety of styles perform at this popular nine-day event held in early July. Some of the concerts are free. ⊕ *www.jazzeast.com.*

GETTING HERE AND AROUND

AIR TRAVEL

Halifax's Stanfield International Airport is Atlantic Canada's largest airport. Ground transportation into Halifax takes from 30 to 40 minutes. Limousine and taxi services, as well as car rentals, are available on-site. MetroTransit bus 320 serves the airport every 30 minutes at peak time, otherwise hourly; the fare is $3.25. Maritime Bus operates a shuttle service from the airport to downtown Halifax, including Dalhousie and St. Mary's universities and hotels in Halifax and Dartmouth (fare C$22 one way) and to other destinations in Atlantic Canada. Regular taxi fares into Halifax are C$63 each way. If you book ahead with Share-A-Cab, the fare is around C$32, depending on your time of arrival, but you must share your car with another passenger.

Visitors proceeding on to other Nova Scotian destinations can take shuttles to the South Shore, Annapolis Valley, and Cape Breton. Cape Breton–bound travelers short on time can also fly into Sydney's airport.

Contacts Halifax Stanfield International Airport ⊠ *1 Bell Blvd. Extension, Enfield* ☎ *902/873-4422* ⊕ *www.hiaa.ca.* **J.A. Douglas McCurdy Sydney Airport** ⊠ *280 Silver Dart Way, Sydney* ☎ *902/564-7720* ⊕ *www.sydneyairport.ca.* **Share-A-Cab** ☎ *902/429-5555, 800/565-8669* ⊕ *www.atyp.com/ashareacab.*

BUS TRAVEL

Long-distance bus service to Nova Scotia is limited. The nearest Greyhound stop is Montréal. Maritime Bus operates within Nova Scotia, New Brunswick, and Prince Edward Island; the company plans to expand its network, so it's worth checking the website for the latest developments. Cape Shuttle runs buses between Halifax and Sydney. Scotia Shuttle serves Yarmouth.

Contacts Cape Shuttle ☎ *902/539-8585, 800/349-1698* ⊕ *www.capeshuttleservice.com.* **Greyhound Canada** ☎ *800/661-8747* ⊕ *www.greyhound.ca.* **Maritime Bus** ☎ *902/429-2029 Halifax, 902/895-0313 Truro* ⊕ *www.maritimebus.com.* **Scotia Shuttle** ☎ *902/435-9686, 800/898-5883* ⊕ *www.scotiashuttle.ca.*

CAR TRAVEL

The only overland route to Nova Scotia crosses the Isthmus of Chignecto: a narrow neck of land that joins the province to New Brunswick. The Trans-Canada Highway (Highway 2 in New Brunswick) becomes Highway 104 in Amherst, the first town after the border. From there you can make it to Halifax, connecting to Highway 102 at Truro, in two hours. Alternately, you can opt for a scenic drive up Route 6, which runs along the coast of Northumberland Strait, or down Route 2, which hugs the Fundy Shore.

FERRY TRAVEL

Car ferries connect Nova Scotia with New Brunswick, Prince Edward Island, and Newfoundland (⇨ *See the Travel Smart chapter for specifics and timing*), and there is talk of the Yarmouth ferry from Portland, Maine being reinstated, though at the time of writing negotiations were still taking place.

Contacts **Bay Ferries Ltd.** ☎ *877/359–3760, 888/249–7245, 506/694–7777, 902/245–2116* ⊕ *www.ferries.ca.* **Cruise Halifax** ☎ *902/426–8222* ⊕ *www.cruisehalifax.ca.* **Marine Atlantic** ☎ *800/341–7981* ⊕ *www.marine-atlantic.ca.* **Port of Sydney** ☎ *902/564–0800* ⊕ *sydneyport.ca.*

BY TRAIN

Via Rail offers overnight service from Montréal to Halifax six times a week. The trip takes about 23 hours. An economy seat costs C$150.

Contacts **Via Rail** ☎ *888/842-7245* ⊕ *www.viarail.ca.*

DISCOUNTS AND DEALS

The Nova Scotia Museum Pass grants you admission to 27 facilities—including popular picks like Halifax's maritime museum, Lunenburg's fisheries museum, and Cape Breton's Highland Village—as many times as you want for a full year. Priced at C$43 for adults and C$85 for a family of four, the pass is an excellent value. Call ☎ *800/632–1114* or go to ⊕ *museum.novascotia.ca* for details.

OUTDOOR ACTIVITIES AND TOURS

Hiking, biking, and horseback riding routes make inland exploring a breeze; kayak and canoe routes let you splash out with ease; and there are snowmobile and cross-country skiing options, too. The province's trail site (⊕ *www.trails.gov.ns.ca*) will put you on the right path.

Motorists can sample Nova Scotia's sensational scenery by following any of the province's 11 Scenic Travelways. There are five in Cape Breton and six on the mainland, all clearly identified by roadside signs with icons that correspond to route names. Nova Scotia Tourism's encyclopedic *Doers and Dreamers Guide* has the lowdown (☎ *902/425–5781 or 800/565–0000* ⊕ *www.novascotia.com*). The two best places for whale-watching are on the Bay of Fundy, from Digby down to Digby Neck, or in Cape Breton on Pleasant Bay. There are other spots to go whale-watching (Halifax, for instance) but the chances of sightings aren't as great.

In addition to the commercial outdoor-activities outfitters listed throughout the chapter, the following organizations are also valuable resources: **Bicycle Nova Scotia** (☎ *902/425–5450 Ext. 316* ⊕ *www.bicycle.ns.ca*); **Canoe Kayak Nova Scotia** (☎ *902/425–5454 Ext. 316* ⊕ *www.ckns.ca*); **Golf Nova Scotia** (☎ *866/933-3217* ⊕ *www.golfnovascotia.com*); **Nova Scotia Golf Association** (☎ *902/468–8844* ⊕ *www.nsga.ns.ca*); **Surfing Association of Nova Scotia** (☎ *No phone* ⊕ *www.surfns.com*); **Nova Scotia Trails Federation** (☎ *902/425–5450 Ext. 325* ⊕ *www.novascotiatrails.com*); and **Nova Scotia Yachting Association** (☎ *902/425–5450 Ext. 312* ⊕ *www.nsya.ns.ca*).

Multiday packaged bus tours to and within Nova Scotia are available through Ambassatours Gray Line and Atlantic Tours.

Ambassatours Gray Line ☎ *902/423-6242, 800/565-7173* ⊕ *www.ambassatours.com.* **Atlantic Tours** ☎ *902/423-7172, 800/565-7173* ⊕ *www.atlantictours.com.*

NOVA SCOTIA GREAT ITINERARIES

Don't let the fact that Nova Scotia is Canada's second-smallest province fool you. Driving will likely take longer than you expect.

IF YOU HAVE 3 DAYS

Spend your first full day in **Halifax.** Explore downtown, leaving time to linger on the harbor-front boardwalk, and have a fun evening out in one of the many pubs and clubs. Don't stay out too late, though—you'll need to be up early to beat the crowds to **Peggy's Cove.** From there, head down to the "Holy Trinity" of South Shore towns: Chester, Mahone Bay, and Lunenburg. Take a coffee break in **Chester** before proceeding to lovely **Mahone Bay** for lunch and boutique browsing. In **Lunenburg** visit the Fisheries Museum and sign up for one of the boat tours departing from its dock. Next, drive on to the Liverpool area (an hour away), where you'll stop for the night. Depending on your preferences, you can dedicate the morning of Day 3 to blissful beaches or immediately veer northwest on Highway 8, which connects Liverpool to Annapolis Royal. Hikers can dally en route at **Kejimkujik National Park and Historic Site.** History buffs can drive 90 minutes straight through, thereby allowing more time to visit the heritage sites in and around **Annapolis Royal** and **Wolfville.** Given that Halifax is about 200 km (124 miles) from the former and 90 km (56 miles) from the latter, completing the loop and returning to the capital for your final night is easy.

IF YOU HAVE 5 DAYS

Stick to the above itinerary but, rather than returning to Halifax at the end of Day 3, bed down at a

Wolfville inn. As you've already seen the Atlantic and Bay of Fundy, it seems unsporting not to add Northumberland Strait to your itinerary. So, on the morning of Day 4, take the pretty three-hour drive cross country to **Pictou.** There you can visit Hector Heritage Quay, where the Scots landed in 1773, and take a dip in the strait's warm, salty water. On the morning of Day 5, explore a bit more of the **Sunrise Trail** by car or kayak, then make the two-hour trek back to **Halifax.**

IF YOU HAVE 7 DAYS

Cape Breton Island is a nice place to spend a week, or a lifetime, but you can cover the basics in two days. Follow the route above, but instead of spending Day 5 on the Sunrise Trail, head east via Antigonish to Port Hawkesbury. From here, follow the 107-km (67-mile) Ceilidh Trail passing through music-loving **Mabou** on the way to Chéticamp. Stop here for lunch, then take the **Cabot Trail** north, looping around **Cape Breton Highlands National Park.** The cliff-hugging trail ranks among the world's most dramatic drives. There should be time for a whale-watching trip or a scenic hike along the way. Spend the night at **Ingonish.** On Day 6, continue on the Cabot Trail to **Baddeck** to explore the Alexander Graham Bell site, the Highland Village, and perhaps get out on the lovely Bras d'Or Lakes. On Day 7, get an early start for the 80-minute drive to **Louisbourg.** Devote the morning to the reconstructed 18th-century French fortress. After lunch, backtrack to Sydney then follow Highway 4 along the southern shore of Bras d'Or Lake to Port Hawkesbury and return to Halifax, about a five-hour drive.

VISITOR INFORMATION

Nova Scotia Tourism ☎ *902/425–5781, 800/565–0000* ⊕ *www.novascotia.com.*

RESTAURANTS

The eating has always been good in Nova Scotia. The ocean's bounty lured the first Europeans across the Atlantic, and seafood remains a prime attraction for visitors today. From Halifax's high-end restaurants to the most casual coastal café, seafood is treated with the utmost respect. Many Nova Scotian chefs are committed to sourcing locally— you only have to visit one farmers' market here to appreciate the range and quality of the ingredients available to them. Generally speaking, eating out is not a stuffy affair in Nova Scotia. Even the finest dining destinations tend to be relatively casual, though you'd likely want to change out of your shorts before entering the swankiest places. One of the classic gastronomic experiences, of course, is to simply don a plastic bib and get to work on a fresh-cooked lobster within sight of the boat that delivered it from the sea.

Prices in the reviews are the average cost of a main course at dinner or, if dinner is not served, at lunch.

HOTELS

Nova Scotia is famous for its picturesque, historic bed-and-breakfast inns, of which there are many spread across the province's cities, towns, harbors, and countryside. Most B&Bs preserve the heritage and style of the building they occupy but come fully equipped with modern requirements such as Wi-Fi, flat-screen TVs, and updated bathrooms. It's worth doing some research, though, if mod-cons are important to you—there are a few establishments that really do want to transport you back in time. As for hotels, most major chains have a presence, including the outstanding Delta, and every town of any size will have an acceptable motel or two on the outskirts. Nova Scotia is also renowned for the friendly welcome it extends to visitors, and this holds true for all types of accommodations. Far from being a cliché, there is a widespread and genuine desire to please that goes well beyond issuing a routine "have a nice day."

Prices in the reviews are the lowest cost of a standard double room in high season. For expanded hotel reviews, facilities, and current deals, visit Fodors.com.

HALIFAX

1,240 km (770 miles) east of Montréal; 1,137 km (705 miles) northeast of Boston; 275 km (171 miles) southeast of Moncton, New Brunswick.

It was Halifax's natural harbor—the second largest in the world after Sydney, Australia's—that first drew the British here in 1749, and today most major sites are conveniently located either along it or on the Citadel-crowned hill overlooking it. That's good news for visitors because this city actually covers quite a bit of ground.

The old city manages to feel both hip and historic. Previous generations had the foresight to preserve much of it, culturally as well as architecturally, yet students from five local universities keep it from being stuffy. In addition to the energetic arts-and-entertainment scene the students help create, visitors also benefit from enviable dining, shopping, and museum-hopping options.

There's easy access to the water, too, and despite being the focal point of a busy commercial port, Halifax Harbour doubles as a playground. It's a place where container ships, commuter ferries, cruise ships, and tour boats compete for space, and where workaday tugs and fishing vessels tie up beside glitzy yachts. Like Halifax as a whole, the harbor represents a blend of the traditional and the contemporary.

GETTING HERE AND AROUND

For those not arriving by air into Halifax's Stanfield International Airport, public transportation to the city is somewhat limited. Via Rail offers "The Ocean" service from Montréal three times a week. The journey takes from 21 to 23 hours, and fares range from $136 for an economy seat to $1,150 per person for a double-bedroom suite. The closest you can get by Greyhound is Montréal, but Maritime Bus offers service to Halifax from New Brunswick and Prince Edward Island. It's a relatively new company and still developing its routes, so it's worth calling to check. By car, the Trans-Canada Highway heads south across the New Brunswick border, where it changes from Highway 2 to Highway 104. At Truro, Highway 102 branches off for Halifax. ⇨ *See Planning, above, for transportation contact information.*

Halifax is an intimate city that's large enough to have the trappings of a capital, yet compact enough to be explored with ease. Because most sites are comparatively close, walking is a good way to get around. The caveat is that streets connecting the waterfront to Citadel Hill are steep. If you're not prepared for a nine-block uphill hike, take a bus or grab a cab. Metro Transit operates comprehensive bus and ferry services. Fares are $2.50 per ride or $20 for 10 tickets. MetroLink ($3) and MetroX ($3.50) buses, which have limited stops, are designed for commuters. Taxi rates begin at C$3 and increase by $1.50 per kilometer (from 5% to 10% more if traffic is heavy; a crosstown trip should cost from C$7 to C$8, depending on traffic). You can usually hail a taxi downtown or pick one up at a hotel stand. Otherwise, call **Casino Taxi** or **Yellow Cab**.

TOURS

If you want to combine transportation with narration, **Ambassatours Gray Line** runs coach tours throughout Halifax, including ones aboard double-decker buses, as well as to outlying communities like Peggy's Cove and Lunenburg. Nearly every local cab company also provides customized driving tours.

Boat tours are popular, with the broadest selection being offered by **Murphy's Cable Wharf**. The company sails various vessels from mid-May to late October, among them a 23-meter (75-foot) ketch and a Mississippi-style sternwheeler. Murphy's even has an amphibious Harbour Hopper for those who want to tour by land *and* water. If you're traveling with kids, try a Big Harbour tour aboard Theodore Tugboat. Theodore is a seafaring version of Thomas the Tank Engine, and even children unfamiliar with the Canadian character will get a kick out of the tugboat's

Lodging Alternatives

Want to pretend that you're lucky enough to live in Nova Scotia? Consider opting for a vacation rental instead of a hotel room. You'll find anything from seaside cottages to UNESCO-protected heritage properties in the heart of town; choices are particularly plentiful on the South Shore and Cape Breton. Websites such as HomeAway (⊕ www.homeaway.com) and FlipKey (⊕ www.flipkey.com) are good places to start house hunting. A word to the wise, though: look carefully at a map before committing. Due to complicated coastal topography, neighboring communities can have quite different climates. Lunenburg and Mahone Bay, for example, are generally sunnier than nearby spots that sit on fog-trapping St. Margaret's Bay.

Cost-conscious visitors looking for a class act can book into a college dorm. From May through August, local universities—including **Dalhousie** (☎ 902/494–2429 ⊕ www.dal.ca), **King's** (☎ 902/422–1271 ⊕ www. ukings.ca), **St. Mary's** (☎ 902/420–5486 or 888/347–5555 ⊕ www. smu.ca), and **Mount St. Vincent** (☎ 902/457–6355 ⊕ www.msvu. ca)—rent out the no-frills rooms and apartments that students have vacated for the summer. For details, search "Conference Services" on the individual websites or call the universities directly. Prices range C$32–C$55 for single rooms to around C$110 for apartments, and perks like athletic center privileges, Wi-Fi, and cable TV are often included.

broad grin and bright red cap. A basic one-hour tour of Halifax Harbour costs about C$18. An affordable alternative to a Murphy's tour is to take the **Metro Transit Commuter Ferry** from the boardwalk terminal at Lower Water Street across the harbor to downtown Dartmouth. Inaugurated in 1752, it's North America's oldest saltwater ferry service and, at C$2.50 for a 20-minute ride, a real deal. Dartmouth—once Halifax's "Twin City" and now part of the HRM—is straight across the harbor and accessible from Halifax proper by passenger ferry or by car via the Angus L. Macdonald and A. Murray MacKay bridges. Motorists can avoid bridge traffic by taking a land route that loops around the Bedford Basin.

ESSENTIALS

Boat Tours Metro Transit Commuter Ferry ☎ 902/490–4000, 311 within Halifax ⊕ www.halifax.ca/metrotransit. **Murphy's Cable Wharf** ☎ 902/420–1015 ⊕ www.mtcw.ca.

Bus Tours Ambassatours Gray Line ☎ 902/423–6242, 800/565–7173 ⊕ www.ambassatours.com.

Taxi and Bus Contacts Casino Taxi ☎ 902/429–6666, 902/425–6666 ⊕ www.casinotaxi.ns.ca. **Metro Transit** ☎ 902/490–4000, 311 within Halifax ⊕ www.halifax.ca/metrotransit. **Yellow Cab** ☎ 902/420–0000 ⊕ yellowcabltd.ca.

Visitor Information Halifax Tourism ☎ 902/422–9334, 877/422–9334 ⊕ www.destinationhalifax.com.

EXPLORING

TOP ATTRACTIONS

Art Gallery of Nova Scotia. In an 1867 Italianate-style building that previously served as a post office, bank, and the headquarters of the Royal Canadian Mounted Police, this provincial art gallery has an extensive permanent collection of more than 14,000 works. Some are primarily of historical interest; others are major works by contemporary Canadian painters like Christopher Pratt, Alex Colville, and Tom Forrestall. In 2013 the gallery received a major donation of Annie Leibovitz photographs. The gallery's heart, however, is an internationally recognized collection of maritime folk art by artists such as woodcarver Sydney Howard and painter Joe Norris. The gallery also contains the actual home of the late painter Maude Lewis (Canada's answer to Grandma Moses), whose bright, cheery paintings cover the tiny structure inside and out. A guided tour of the collection is given daily at 2:30, with an extra one added on Thursday at 7. The gallery's gift shop carries an excellent selection of arts and crafts. ⊠ *1723 Hollis St.* ☎ *902/424–5280, 902/424–7542* ⊕ *www. artgalleryofnovascotia.ca* ⊠ *C$12; free Thurs. evening* ☉ *Mon.–Wed. and Fri.–Sun. 10–5, Thurs. 10–9; Nov.–Apr., closed Mon.*

FAMILY **Canadian Museum of Immigration at Pier 21.** Affectionately dubbed "Canada's Front Door," Pier 21 served as the entry point for nearly a million immigrants between 1928 and 1971. It's now a national museum where the immigrant experience is re-created. Several innovative exhibits make this well worth a stop, among them the holographic multimedia presentation, shown inside a faux ship, detailing the arrival of immigrants. The museum's many hands-on displays have built-in kid appeal, and special activities, like having "passports" stamped at various stations, are designed to engage young visitors. A research center, a gallery, a café, and a gift shop are on-site as well. ⊠ *1055 Marginal Rd.* ☎ *902/425–7770, 855/526–4721* ⊕ *www.pier21.ca* ⊠ *C$8.60* ☉ *May–Oct., daily 9:30–5:30; Nov., daily 9:30–5; Dec.–Mar., Tues.–Sat. 10–5; Apr., Mon.–Sat. 10–5.*

FAMILY
Fodor'sChoice
★
Halifax Citadel National Historic Site. You can't miss the Citadel, literally or figuratively. Erected between 1826 and 1856 on Halifax's highest hill, it still dominates the skyline and, as Canada's most-visited National Historic Site, remains a magnet for tourists. The present citadel, with its dry moat and stone ramparts, was the fourth defensive structure to be built on the site, and formerly was linked to smaller forts and gun emplacements on the harbor islands and the bluffs above the harbor entrance. A multimedia presentation that runs every 15 minutes recounts this story. You can visit the barracks, guard room, and powder magazine before heading for the parade ground to watch reenactors, sporting kilts and tall feather "bonnets," practice their drills. If you book ahead, you can participate in full uniform in the "Soldier for a Day" program ($199), which for adults includes learning how to handle and fire a weapon. Tours that help bring the history of both the fort and the city to life take place throughout the day in high season, but the best time to visit is just before noon when the Noon Gun is fired—a tradition since 1857. The Citadel is also home to the **Army Museum**, with excellent exhibits and a War Art Gallery. ■ **TIP→** Before leaving the Citadel, pause to enjoy the

Alexander Keith's
Nova Scotia
Brewery **10**

Anna Leonowens
Gallery **4**

Art Gallery of
Nova Scotia **7**

Canadian Museum
of Immigration
at Pier 21 ..... **14**

Government
House **11**

Halifax Citadel
National
Historic Site **3**

Halifax Public
Gardens **1**

Halifax Seaport
Farmer's
Market **12**

Halifax
Waterfront
Broadwalk **6**

Historic
Properties **5**

Maritime Museum
of the Atlantic .. **9**

Mary E. Black
Gallery **13**

Nova Scotia
Museum of Natural
History **2**

Point Pleasant
Park **15**

St. Paul's Anglican
Church **8**

view. In front of you are the spiky downtown buildings, crowded between the hilltop and the harbor; the wooded islands at the harbor's mouth; and the naval dockyard. Behind you is the 235-acre Halifax Common with its ball fields, tennis courts, playground, skateboard park, and open green. Worried about losing track of time while touring? Don't be. Simply keep an eye on Citadel Hill's **Town Clock.** Given to Halifax by Prince Edward, Duke of Kent (the military commander here from 1794 to 1800), it has ticked in its octagonal tower for more than 200 years. ⊠ *Citadel Hill, 5425 Sackville St.* 🕾 *902/426–5080* ⊕ *www.pc.gc.ca* ⊡ *June–mid-Sept. C$11.70; May and mid-Sept.–Oct. C$7.80; rest of yr free (grounds only)* ⊗ *May, June, Sept., and Oct., daily 9–5; July and Aug., daily 9–6.*

FAMILY

Fodor'sChoice

★

Halifax Waterfront Boardwalk. Running from Casino Nova Scotia to Pier 21, this photogenic 3-km (2-mile) footpath offers backdoor access to the Historic Properties and the Marine Museum of the Atlantic. Newer landmarks such as **Purdy's Wharf** (site of Halifax's two grandest skyscrapers) and **Bishop's Landing** (an attractive complex with condos and shops) are on the route; while others, including the Seaport Farmers' Market, Pier 21, and the cruise-ship terminal, are only a few minutes' walk away. The boardwalk has multiple entry points and many tourist-friendly amenities. Shops and restaurants line the section between Sackville Landing and the Historic Properties, and in peak season, bagpipers,

A GOOD WALK

Starting your walk at the **Halifax Citadel National Historic Site** is practical because, as the city's highest point, it puts you on a downhill course. More importantly, visiting the star-shaped fortress—built in the 1800s as an outpost for the then-expanding British Empire—is like taking a crash course in civic history. After exploring the site, descend the stairs (a more direct route for pedestrians than the road) to the **Town Clock**, which has been keeping time for more than two centuries.

From here, cross Brunswick Street and head down Carmichael, passing the Metro Centre (Halifax's main sporting venue) and the World Trade and Convention Centre en route to the Grand Parade. Once used for military drills, the leafy rectangle is now the setting for summertime picnics and free concerts. Anchoring its right end is **St. Paul's Church** (dating from 1750, it's the country's oldest Protestant church); the Second Empire–style stone building on the left end is **City Hall**. As you exit the park, Carmichael Street becomes St. George. Follow it two blocks down to Hollis, then make a short detour to see the impressive collection of folk art in the **Art Gallery of Nova Scotia**. **Province House**, Canada's oldest legislative building, is just across the street and is also open for tours. Walking down another two

blocks lands you on Water Street, where you'll find the **Historic Properties**, a cluster of restored warehouses linked by cobblestone lanes, that contain shops and eateries.

If you go straight through, you will reach the **Halifax Waterfront Boardwalk**, which runs all the way to Marginal Road. This is where decision-making gets difficult. Depending on your tastes (and budget) you might board a sightseeing boat at **Cable Wharf**, hop the **Metro Transit Commuter Ferry** to the Dartmouth side of the harbor, take in the action from a waterfront restaurant, or simply ogle the tugboats and transatlantic yachts that often tie up here. Whatever you choose, be sure to leave time for the **Maritime Museum of the Atlantic**, where you can learn about Nova Scotia's seafaring past. A final stop lies to the south, just off the boardwalk: the Port of Halifax seawall development, which includes the cruise ship terminal, the **Halifax Seaport Farmers' Market**, and **Pier 21**, a former immigration depot that now houses the **Canadian Museum of Immigration**. You could spend several hours in Pier 21 alone, so if you're staying in the city longer, save this for another day. Instead, cap your walking tour with a libation in a local pub. Halifax is said to have more pubs per capita than anywhere else in Canada.

ice-cream peddlers, and street performers do, too. The water, however, remains the real attraction. To get out on it, take one of the many boat tours that depart from the boardwalk's Cable Wharf.

Historic Properties. This series of restored waterfront warehouses dates from the days of yore, when trade and war made Halifax prosperous. They were built by such raffish characters as Enos Collins, a privateer, smuggler, and shipper whose vessels defied Napoléon's blockade to bring American supplies to the Duke of Wellington. The buildings have since been taken over by shops, offices, restaurants, and pubs including those in Privateer's Warehouse. Seven of them, all erected between the late 18th and early 19th century, have been designated as National Historic Sites. ☒ *1869 Upper Water St.* ☎ *902/429–0530* ⊕ *www.historicproperties.ca.*

FAMILY **Maritime Museum of the Atlantic.** The exhibits in this waterfront museum, housed partly in a restored chandlery, include small boats once used around the coast, as well as displays describing Nova Scotia's proud sailing heritage. The most memorable ones, though, are devoted to the *Titanic* and the Halifax Explosion. In the explosion exhibit, "Halifax Wrecked," newspaper accounts and quotes from survivors are poignantly paired with everyday objects recovered from the rubble, among them a schoolboy's book bag and a broken pocket watch that will forever record the time of impact. ☒ *1675 Lower Water St.* ☎ *902/424–7490* ⊕ *maritimemuseum.novascotia.ca* ☒ *May–Oct. C$9.25; Nov.–Apr. C$5* ⊙ *May–Oct., daily 9:30–5:30 (to 8 pm Tues.); Nov.–Apr., Tues. 9:30–8, Wed.–Sat. 9:30–5, Sun. 1–5.*

HALIFAX AND THE TITANIC

When the *Titanic* sank in 1912, Halifax became, in a sense, the fabled ship's final destination. Being the closest major port, it was the base for rescue and recovery operations, and 150 victims were ultimately buried in city cemeteries. Emergency response skills honed in the aftermath of the sinking were put to use five years later when tragedy struck again. In December 1917, two ships collided in Halifax Harbour, one of them loaded with explosives. The event sparked the greatest manmade explosion before Hiroshima, leveling 2 square miles of the city and claiming nearly 2,000 lives.

WORTH NOTING

Alexander Keith's Nova Scotia Brewery. Although Alexander Keith served three terms as mayor of Halifax, his political achievements are overshadowed by another accomplishment: he was colonial Nova Scotia's first certified brewmaster. Today, the popular beer is brewed in several modern facilities across Canada, but you can visit the original 1820 brewery building, a local landmark. On hour-long tours you can see how Keith's India Pale Ale was originally made, then sample a pint or two in the Stag's Head Tavern. (Nonalcoholic beverages are also available.) Actors in period outfits provide the explanations as well as old-fashioned maritime entertainment. ☒ *Brewery Market, 1496 Lower Water St.* ☎ *902/455–1474, 877/612–1820* ⊕ *keiths.ca* ☒ *C$19.95* ⊙ *June–Oct., Mon.–Sat. noon–8, Sun. noon–5; Nov.–May, Fri. 5–8, Sat. noon–8, Sun. noon–5.*

Anna Leonowens Gallery. Victorian wunderkind Anna Leonowens is famous for the time she spent as a royal governess in Thailand (then Siam), which inspired Rodgers and Hammerstein's musical *The King and I*. But she also spent two decades in Halifax, where she founded the Nova Scotia College of Art and Design; it later returned the favor by opening the Anna Leonowens Gallery. Its three exhibition spaces, which focus on contemporary studio and media art, serve as a showcase for the college faculty and students. The gallery mounts about 125 exhibitions a year. ☒ *1891 Granville St.* ☎ *902/494–8223* ⊕ *www.nscad.ca* ☒ *Free* ⊙ *Tues.–Fri. 11–5, Sat. noon–4.*

Government House. Built between 1799 and 1805 for Sir John Wentworth, the Loyalist governor of New Hampshire, and his racy wife, Fannie (Thomas Raddall's novel *The Governor's Lady* tells their story), this elegant house has since been the official residence of the province's lieutenant governor—the Queen's representative. It's North America's oldest consecutively occupied government residence because the White House, while older, was evacuated and burned during the War of 1812. Its construction of Nova Scotian stone was engineered by a Virginian Loyalist, Isaac Hildrith. ⊠ *1451 Barrington St.* ☎ *902/424–7001* ⊕ *www.lt.gov.ns.ca* 🖾 *Free* ☉ *Tours July and Aug., Fri. and Mon. 11–4, weekends 10–4.*

FAMILY **Halifax Public Gardens.** One of the oldest formal Victorian gardens in North America, this city oasis had its start in 1753 as a private garden. Its layout was completed in 1875 by Richard Power, former gardener to the Duke of Devonshire in Ireland. Gravel paths wind among ponds, trees, and flower beds, revealing an astonishing variety of plants from all over the world. The centerpiece is an ornate gazebo-like band shell, erected in 1887 for Queen Victoria's Golden Jubilee, where free Sunday afternoon concerts take place at 2 from mid-June through mid-September. The gardens are closed in winter, but you can still enjoy a pleasant stroll along the perimeter. ⊠ *Bounded by Sackville, Summer, and S. Park Sts. and Spring Garden Rd.* ⊕ *www.halifaxpublicgardens.ca* 🖾 *Free* ☉ *Mid-Apr.–Nov. (depending on weather), daily 8 am–dusk.*

Halifax Seaport Farmers' Market. Green in more ways than one, this waterfront market that hosts a few hundred local farmers, food producers, and artisans is one of Canada's most ecofriendly buildings. Noteworthy features include wind turbines, solar-energy and water-conservation systems, and a "biowall" that allows natural ventilation. There's a wonderful array of fresh produce, and sampling and shopping opportunities abound. ■TIP➔ **Don't confuse this venue with Brewery Square's Historic Farmers' Market, whose vendors didn't want to move here. Both claim to be the country's oldest farmers' market—and in a way, they both are.** ⊠ *1209 Marginal Rd.* ☎ *902/492–4043* ⊕ *www.halifaxfarmersmarket.com* ☉ *Weekdays 10–5, Sat. 7–3, Sun. 9–3.*

Mary E. Black Gallery. Between Pier 21 and the Seaport Farmers' Market, the exhibit space of the Nova Scotia Centre for Craft and Design, home of the Mary E. Black Gallery, presents shows of pottery, jewelry, textiles, metalwork, and other innovative, high-end crafts. The center itself holds classes, including one- and two-day workshops, from fall through spring. ⊠ *1061 Marginal Rd., Suite 140* ☎ *902/492–2522* ⊕ *www.craftdesign.ns.ca* 🖾 *Gallery free; workshops individually priced* ☉ *Weekdays 9–5, weekends 11–4.*

FAMILY **Nova Scotia Museum of Natural History.** This is the place to learn about fossils and dinosaurs, as well as the flora and fauna prevalent in Nova Scotia today. The Nature Centre is home to live snakes, frogs, insects, and other creatures. The museum also hosts major traveling exhibits as well as nature talks, walks, and workshops that appeal to all interests and ages. Returning visitors might miss the massive fiberglass model of a northern spring peeper (a frog) that once clung to the building's southeastern side—not gone, it has been moved indoors. ✉ *1747 Summer St.* ☎ *902/424–7353* ⊕ *naturalhistory.novascotia.ca* ✉ *C$6.25* ⊘ *Thurs.–Tues. 9–5, Wed. 9–8.*

Point Pleasant Park. Most of the city's former fortifications have been turned into public parks, including this one, which encompasses 186 wooded acres with walking trails and seafront paths. The city originally leased Point Pleasant from the British Crown for a shilling per year. The perfect vantage point from which to watch ships entering the harbor, in summer it's the site of Shakespeare by the Sea performances. ✉ *5718 Point Pleasant Dr.* ☎ *902/490–4700* ⊕ *www.pointpleasantpark. ca* ✉ *Free* ⊘ *6 am–midnight (parking lots close earlier).*

St. Paul's Anglican Church. Opened in 1750, this is Canada's oldest Protestant church and the burial site of many colonial notables. It played a pivotal role during the 1917 Halifax Explosion, as the vestry was used as a makeshift hospital. Evidence of the damage done to the building can be seen in the still-broken Explosion Window and debris embedded above the Memorial Doors. Designated as a National Historic Site, St. Paul's remains an active church. A pew is always reserved for Queen Elizabeth at Sunday morning services, and other out-of-town worshippers are welcome as well: there's a service each Wednesday at 11 am and Sunday services are at 9 and 11 from September through May and at 10 between June and August. ✉ *1749 Argyle St., on Grand Parade* ☎ *902/429–2240* ⊕ *www.stpaulshalifax.org* ⊘ *June–Aug., Mon.–Sat. 9–4:30; Sept.–May, weekdays 9–4:30.*

BEACHES

Rainbow Haven Beach Provincial Park. For ocean swimming, this sand and cobble beach is the closest serviced option to Halifax, but avoid the area near the channel when the tide is going out because currents make this section hazardous. Lifeguards, on duty in July and August, set out markers to indicate the dangerous areas. Elsewhere, Rainbow Haven is safe and great for families. The beach is free for day use, and there is a campground (fee) with its own swimming area. Change houses are available, and boardwalks aid accessibility. ⚠ **The beach's access road closes at 8 pm, so plan your time accordingly. Amenities:** food and drink; lifeguards; parking (free); showers; toilets. **Best for:** swimming; walking. ✉ *2248 Cow Bay Rd., off Bissett Rd., 8 km (5 miles) east of Cow Bay, Cole Harbour* ⊕ *www.novascotiaparks.ca.*

WHERE TO EAT

$$$
INTERNATIONAL
✕ **The Bicycle Thief.** Renowned Halifax restaurateurs Stephanie and Maurizio Bertossi opened this chic "casual fine-dining" place on the waterfront—look for the old bicycles parked outside. The lengthy menu (with courses labeled 1st Gear, 2nd Gear, and High Gear) slants Italian, incorporating the finest Nova Scotian ingredients. You could start

with local mussels or a generous salami board, then shift into second with authentic minestrone, a lobster and fish chowder, or one of the handmade pasta dishes. High Gear choices might include pistachio honey-crusted Atlantic salmon, local rabbit braised in Valpolicella and fresh herbs, or fall-off-the-bone ribs with polenta and wild mushrooms. ■ **TIP→ The lunch menu is equally interesting and more modestly priced.** [$] *Average main: C$25* ✉ *Bishop's Landing, 1475 Lower Water St.* ☎ *902/425–7993* 🌐 *bicyclethief.ca* 🕒 *Closed Sun.*

$$$ ECLECTIC 🍴 **Chives Canadian Bistro.** "Canadian" cuisine is broadly defined here (French, German, and Asian influences are all evident), but there is no mistaking the provenance of chef and cookbook author Craig Flinn's ingredients, which are invariably fresh and local. The menu adapts to whatever is available at the fishmongers' and farmers' markets, but each meal starts with Chives' signature buttermilk biscuits—and each *should* end with maple crème brûlée. Enjoy them in the main room, where planked-wood floors set a casual tone, or get intimate with a table for four in the former bank building's wine "vault." [$] *Average main: C$26* ✉ *1537 Barrington St.* ☎ *902/420–9626* 🌐 *www.chives.ca* 🕒 *No lunch.*

$$$$ ITALIAN 🍴 **Da Maurizio.** This northern Italian restaurant is a classic big-night-out choice. Subdued lighting, elegant furnishings, fresh flowers: all the decor details have been attended to, and ditto for the food, which is impressive and satisfying. Excellent seared foie gras is always on the menu, as is veal scaloppine sautéed with lobster and topped with a creamy garlic-and-cognac sauce. Prices on the specialty wine list go as high as C$600, but there are also fine bottles for under C$50. [$] *Average main: C$32* ✉ *1496 Lower Water St.* ☎ *902/423–0859* 🌐 *www.damaurizio.ca* 🕒 *Closed Sun. No lunch.*

$$ JAPANESE 🍴 **Dharma Sushi.** Tidy sushi, fresh sashimi, and feather-light tempura are artfully presented here, and although the service is fast-paced, the food doesn't suffer as a result. Lunchtime can be especially busy, so if you have trouble choosing from the long-as-your-arm menu, you might opt for a bento box or one of the daily specials. The latter—which can include California rolls, vegetable tempura, miso soup, and a popular chicken teriyaki—are a real deal and ready fast. Seating is available inside this pint-sized eatery and, in summer, on a small street-front patio. [$] *Average main: C$18* ✉ *1576 Argyle St.* ☎ *902/425–7785* 🌐 *www.dharmasushi.com* 🕒 *Closed Sun.*

$ ECLECTIC 🍴 **Economy Shoe Shop.** If you're looking for Birkenstocks, you're in the wrong place. But if you're hungry, that's another matter. Variety rules at this chaotic multiroom restaurant-*cum*-club. Start with an imported beer in the Belgian Bar, then head to Backstage to dine among the fake trees and other theatrical decorations before retiring to the private cave in the Diamond for after-dinner coffee. In summer there is also a street-front patio, which is invariably packed with locals. Although food at the "Shoe" isn't haute cuisine, portions are generous, and it's very hard to leave. There's regular live music too, including jazz on Monday evenings. [$] *Average main: C$12* ✉ *1661–1663 Argyle St.* ☎ *902/423–7463* 🌐 *www.economyshoeshop.ca.*

CLOSE UP

Local Flavors

Nova Scotia's verdant landscapes and churning seas provide a feast for the eyes and one for the table as well. Residents contend that the best meals are made using local ingredients—Lunenburg lobster, Digby scallops, Atlantic salmon, Annapolis Valley apples—and generations-old recipes. If you're serious about discovering down-home favorites, seek out dishes with curious names like Hodge Podge (a summer staple of beans, peas, carrots, and baby potatoes, cooked in cream), Solomon Gundy (a pickled-herring pâté), *rappie* pie (a hearty stew, usually of chicken, with dried, shredded potatoes), and blueberry grunt (a steamed pudding made with Nova Scotia's finest berries). For more sophisticated fare, check out the fine-dining establishments in Halifax and the southern part of the province that put their own spins on Nova Scotian classics, preparing time-honored dishes with contemporary flair. The province's annual *Taste of Nova Scotia: Culinary Adventure Guide* (🌐 *www.tasteofnovascotia.com*) will help you find them. A companion Adventures in Taste app is also available, free, at 🌐 *adventuresintaste.ca.*

For local libations, try a beer (or two) from the growing number of microbreweries. Propeller, Garrison, Keltic, and Rudder's all draw on the history of the region and produce distinctive ales, lagers, stouts, and other brews. Local wines are gaining in popularity and reputation as well. Try Jost from Malagash, Sainte Famille Winery from Falmouth, and Domaine de Grand Pré near Wolfville. And what better way to cap a Nova Scotian dinner than with a dram of the acclaimed Glen Breton, North America's original single-malt whiskey. (Nova Scotia may mean "New Scotland," but you still can't call it "Scotch" unless it's actually produced in Scotland.) In Gaelic, they call single-malt *Uisge beatha* ("the water of life"): sip some Glen Breton, and you'll know why.

$$$$ SEAFOOD 🍴 **Five Fishermen.** Installed in a heritage building across from the Grand Parade, this restaurant is splurge-worthy. Tables are backlit through a wall of stained glass, and the seafood is so good locals keep coming back. Main courses are pricey but each comes with complimentary salad and mussels. The three-course prix fixe (C$51) is an affordable alternative to à la carte choices, or you could go all out at one of the monthly dining events that feature a seven-course tasting menu with wine pairings (C$125). ■ TIP→ **For more modest, less pricey fare, head to the Five Fishermen Grill, downstairs from the main restaurant. Also open for lunch, it has an Oyster Happy Hour from 4:30 to 6:30 daily.** [$] *Average main: C$45* ✉ *1740 Argyle St.* ☎ *902/422–4421* 🌐 *www.fivefishermen.com* ⏲ *No lunch.*

$$ CANADIAN 🍴 **Hart & Thistle.** In a prime location on the waterfront part of the Historic Properties, this gastro brewpub pairs well-made food with beers crafted right on the premises. Huge wooden beams support cathedral ceilings in the lofty bar area, where patrons sip Hop Rock Candy Mountain IPA and other brews in view of gleaming copper brewery equipment. You'll find the requisite pub grub such as soups, sandwiches, pizza, pasta, and fish-and-chips, but the menu also includes more sophisticated fare—Jamaican curried chicken, perhaps, or filet mignon

with Blackpoint clams in red wine. The outdoor patio faces the board-walk; on a fine summer day few other spots in town provide better people-watching. On weekend evenings, the Hart & Thistle presents live entertainment. $\boxed{S}$ *Average main: C$15* ⊠ *1869 Lower Water St.* ☏ *902/407–4278* ⊕ *www.hartandthistle.com.*

$$
BRITISH

╳**Henry House.** Halogonian brewers uphold beer-making traditions dating back to 1754, and you can sample the results at this pub in what was once the house of William Alexander Henry, a prominent Canadian politician. Henry House serves five unpasteurized English-style ales crafted by Halifax's own Granite Brewery, plus special blends like Black Velvet (though cider is mixed with the stout here, rather than the usual champagne). The food is impressive, too—especially the fishcakes and homemade bread pudding. Best of all, the kitchen stays open late (until midnight from Thursday through Saturday, and until 10 on other nights). In winter fireplaces keep the ironstone building toasty, and in summer a tiered patio provides both access to the afternoon sun and shelter from the wind. $\boxed{S}$ *Average main: C$15* ⊠ *1222 Barrington St.* ☏ *902/423–5660* ⊕ *www.henryhouse.ca.*

$$
CANADIAN

╳**Lower Deck.** History surrounds you in Privateer's Warehouse, where two eateries share old stone walls and hand-hewn beams as well as a few menu items such as chicken-and-ribs or fish-and-chips. The main-floor pub sticks to pub grub, which is served at long trestle tables; the patrons here consider ale an entrée, so order a Keith's and join the fun. Holler "Sociable!" occasionally, and you'll be mistaken for a native in no time. The second-floor Beer Market is less casual and includes more refined dishes on the menu. The Lower Deck has nightly live music, including various festival events. $\boxed{S}$ *Average main: C$13* ⊠ *Historic Properties, 1869 Upper Water St.* ☏ *902/425–1501* ⊕ *www.lowerdeck.ca.*

$$$
SEAFOOD

╳**McKelvie's.** In a handsome 1906 firehouse across from the Maritime Museum of the Atlantic, McKelvie's is that rare find that hits the sweet spot between upmarket and down-home. Though all the menu main-stays are here, from oysters Rockefeller to surf and turf, the best bets are the contemporary twists on seafood classics, among them Caribbean-inspired calamari, lobster pot stickers, and Thai shrimp pasta. Although the restaurant has been in business for more than 25 years, its look is as fresh as the ingredients used here, and the service is always friendly. $\boxed{S}$ *Average main: C$25* ⊠ *1680 Lower Water St.* ☏ *902/421–6161* ⊕ *www.mckelvies.com* ☽ *No lunch weekends in July and Aug.*

$$
CONTEMPORARY

╳**Morris East.** Casually cool, yet somehow warm and intimate, Morris East stakes its reputation on locally sourced ingredients, many of them fresh from the Halifax Seaport Farmers' Market a few blocks away. Gourmet pizzas, topped with the region's best veggies, cheeses, and charcuterie and cooked in an oven that burns Annapolis Valley apple wood, are the house specialty. Libations have local flavor, too: spirits handcrafted in the province go into the artisanal cocktails made here. ■TIP➔ **The restaurant doesn't take reservations, so come early and take advantage of happy hour, from 5 to 6.** There's a second location in New Bedford. $\boxed{S}$ *Average main: C$17* ⊠ *5212 Morris St.* ☏ *902/444–7663* ⊕ *www.morriseast.com* ⟐ *Reservations not accepted* ☽ *Closed Mon. No lunch Sun. No brunch weekdays.*

2

$$$ SEAFOOD Fodor's Choice ★ 🍴 **The Press Gang.** Easily one of the city's hippest upscale establishments, the Press Gang prepares fish and meat with equal panache. You can start with crab dumplings or oysters on the half shell, complemented by a glass of muscadet from the well-stocked cellar, then tuck into prosciutto-wrapped halibut with roasted vegetables and a red-pepper jalapeño reduction, or herb-crusted rack of lamb. Or simply let the chef present his four-course tasting menu (C$150 for two). Thick, cold stone walls testify to the building's era (1759), but comfy seating and intimate lighting soften the effect. A trio plays classic rock, Motown, and New Orleans jazz on Friday and Saturday nights. [$] *Average main: C$30* ✉ *5218 Prince St.* ☎ *902/423–8816* 🌐 *thepressgang.net* 🕒 *No lunch.*

$$$ SEAFOOD 🍴 **Salty's.** Overlooking Privateer's Wharf and the rest of the harbor, this restaurant wins the prize for best location in Halifax. Steaming bowls of shellfish stew and curried scallops crown a menu that is sure to satisfy any seafood lover, though there are also meat and pasta options. Request a table with a window view and save room for the house dessert, Cadix (chocolate mousse over a praline crust). There is a less expensive Bar & Grill on the ground level. Salty's serves meals outside on the wharf in summer, but be warned: it can be very windy. [$] *Average main: C$28* ✉ *Historic Properties, 1869 Upper Water St.* ☎ *902/423–6818* 🌐 *www.saltys.ca.*

$$$ ECLECTIC 🍴 **The Wooden Monkey.** This fun, funky spot attracts health-conscious diners with its macrobiotic and organic food, locally brewed beer and wines, and fair-trade coffee. Aside from being good for you, though, the food here is also just plain good. Menu mainstays (the vegan dumplings, lentil-based veggie burger, free-range ginger beef, and chocolate tofu pie) are bound to win over skeptics. Don't believe us? Ask Oscar nominee Ellen Page. The *Juno* star is a native Haligonian—and a major Wooden Monkey fan. There's a second location on the Dartmouth waterfront. [$] *Average main: C$23* ✉ *1707 Grafton St.* ☎ *902/444–3844* 🌐 *www.thewoodenmonkey.ca.*

WHERE TO STAY

For expanded hotel reviews, visit Fodors.com.

$$ HOTEL FAMILY 🏨 **Cambridge Suites Halifax.** Homey comforts are a big selling point at this property, and the location—five blocks from the waterfront and one from the Spring Garden Road shopping district—is convenient. **Pros:** continental breakfast included; harbor views from some suites and the rooftop deck. **Cons:** the hill up is *steep*; some rooms billed as suites don't have separate sleeping areas. [$] *Rooms from: C$159* ✉ *1583 Brunswick St.* ☎ *902/420–0555, 800/565–1263* 🌐 *www.cambridgesuiteshalifax.com* 🛏 *115 rooms, 85 suites* 🍽 *Breakfast.*

$$$ HOTEL FAMILY 🏨 **Delta Halifax.** Though the Delta Halifax is a business-class hotel with spacious, attractive rooms, many vacationers choose it specifically for the water views: 126 rooms offer "premium" views and 80 have balconies. **Pros:** pleasant pool area; good setting for walkers; kids six and under eat free. **Cons:** awkward location for drivers; add-ons for phone calls, parking, and other amenities add up. [$] *Rooms from: C$179* ✉ *1990 Barrington St.* ☎ *902/425–6700, 888/890–3222* 🌐 *www.deltahotels.com* 🛏 *281 rooms, 15 suites* 🍽 *No meals.*

$$$ HOTEL **Halifax Marriott Harbourfront.** Built low to match the neighboring ironstone buildings, this waterfront hotel is convenient to the Historic Properties and the boardwalk. **Pros:** only hotel right on the harbor; deals and value-added packages available. **Cons:** parking is pricey; some rooms could use upgrading. [$] *Rooms from: C$200* ✉ *1919 Upper Water St.* ☎ *902/421–1700, 800/943–6760* 🌐 *www.marriott.com* 🛏 *333 rooms, 19 suites* 🍴 *Multiple meal plans.*

$$ HOTEL **The Halliburton.** Three early-19th-century town houses were cleverly combined to create Halifax's original boutique hotel, a couple of blocks from the waterfront and Spring Garden Road shopping. **Pros:** location means there's no climb uphill at the end of the day; quality linens; continental breakfast included. **Cons:** some parking is a block away; some rooms far from reception; no elevator. [$] *Rooms from: C$159* ✉ *5184 Morris St.* ☎ *902/420–0658, 888/512–3344* 🌐 *www.thehalliburton.com* 🛏 *25 rooms, 4 suites* 🍴 *Breakfast.*

$$$ HOTEL **Prince George Hotel.** Mahogany furnishings, vibrant draperies, and quality linens set the tone for rooms at this business-oriented hotel, while calm prevails in the public areas (garden patios offer a respite from downtown bustle). **Pros:** complimentary Wi-Fi; upgraded bathrooms. **Cons:** some find it stuffy; breakfast and parking not always included. [$] *Rooms from: C$189* ✉ *1725 Market St.* ☎ *902/425–1986, 800/565–1567* 🌐 *www.princegeorgehotel.com* 🛏 *186 rooms, 15 suites* 🍴 *No meals.*

$$ B&B/INN **Waverley Inn.** Like Oscar Wilde and P. T. Barnum, two of its former guests, the Waverley is best described as theatrical. **Pros:** an urban inn experience; has loads of character. **Cons:** "traditional" category rooms are small; front rooms get street noise. [$] *Rooms from: C$135* ✉ *1266 Barrington St.* ☎ *902/423–9346, 800/565–9346* 🌐 *www.waverleyinn.com* 🛏 *34 rooms* 🍴 *Breakfast.*

$$ HOTEL FAMILY **Westin Nova Scotian.** This imposing 1930s hotel sits beside the train station, with the harbor behind and Cornwallis Park in front, and though it provides top-notch business services, it also has a resort-y feel. **Pros:** half the rooms have harbor views; free downtown shuttle on weekdays. **Cons:** on southern edge of the action; some bathrooms are cramped. [$] *Rooms from: C$169* ✉ *1181 Hollis St.* ☎ *902/421–1000, 877/993–7846* 🌐 *www.thewestinnovascotian.com* 🛏 *310 rooms, 6 suites* 🍴 *No meals.*

NIGHTLIFE AND THE ARTS

There are up-to-date entertainment listings in the *Coast* (Halifax's free alternative newspaper); you can also log on to 🌐 *www.thecoast.ca.*

NIGHTLIFE

BARS **Bearly's House of Blues and Ribs.** This dimly lit tavern's name gives music and food equal billing, but the outstanding blues artists the place books makes clear where its loyalty lies. You can catch an act every day, except on Monday and Wednesday evenings (on the latter, stand-up comedy precedes killer karaoke). Bluegrass musicians perform on winter Saturday afternoons. ✉ *1269 Barrington St.* ☎ *902/423–2526* 🌐 *www.bearlys.ca.*

Old Triangle. A traditional Irish alehouse, the Old Triangle reels in patrons with better-than-average pub food and pints of Guinness, then keeps them fixated with live Celtic music on most nights. Traditional open sessions take place on Sunday afternoons and Tuesday evenings. ✉ *5136 Prince St.* ☎ *902/492–4900* 🌐 *www.oldtriangle.com.*

2

Reflections Cabaret. Consider this an alternative alternative. Though considered a gay hangout, Reflections is better described as an "anything goes" bar. Drag queens mingle with throngs of university students who hit the strobe-lit dance floor until 3:30 am. ⊠ *5184 Sackville St.* ☎ *902/422–2957* ⊕ *www.reflectionscabaret.com* ☺ *Mon. and Thurs.–Sat.*

Seahorse Tavern. The indie crowd gravitates here for late night music. The dark spot, below the Economy Shoe Shop café and bar, is a top venue for live funk and hip-hop, with some Motown thrown in for good measure. ⊠ *1663 Argyle St.* ☎ *902/423–7200* ⊕ *theeconomyshoeshopgroup.ca/seahorsetavern.*

The Split Crow. Halifax's oldest watering hole (its earliest incarnation opened in 1749) has an old-time ambience and a full menu heavy on finger foods and deep-fried seafood. Nevertheless, it's the beer/band combination—mostly classic rockers, nightly and on Saturday afternoons—that accounts for the bar's enduring popularity. ⊠ *1855 Granville St.* ☎ *902/422–4366* ⊕ *splitcrow.com.*

CASINO **Casino Nova Scotia.** Right on the waterfront, the casino has a full range of gaming tables and hundreds of slots, and is open around the clock in summer. There's entertainment, too, mostly provided by tribute bands and C-listers on their way up—or down. Patrons must be 19 or older. ⊠ *1983 Upper Water St.* ☎ *902/425–7777, 888/642–6376* ⊕ *www.casinonovascotia.com.*

ARTS

THEATER **Grafton Street Dinner Theatre.** Performances are staged here from three to six times weekly, depending on the season, and the lighthearted fun begins when you arrive in the lounge. ⊠ *1741 Grafton St.* ☎ *902/425–1961* ⊕ *www.graftonstdinnertheatre.com.*

Halifax Feast Dinner Theatre. The resident company specializes in musical comedies and spoofs of TV shows and movies. ⊠ *Maritime Centre, 1505 Barrington St., 1st fl.* ☎ *902/420–1840* ⊕ *www.feastdinnertheatre.com.*

Neptune Theatre. The country's oldest professional repertory playhouse—it opened in 1915—is also the largest in Atlantic Canada, with a main stage and studio theater under one roof. It presents year-round performances ranging from classics to comedy and contemporary Canadian drama. ⊠ *1593 Argyle St.* ☎ *902/429–7070, 800/565–7345* ⊕ *www.neptunetheatre.com.*

Shakespeare by the Sea. In July and August, actors perform works by the Bard and others in Point Pleasant Park, at the southern end of the Halifax peninsula. The natural setting—dark woods, rocky shore, and ruins of fortifications—provides a dramatic backdrop. Performances take place from Tuesday through Friday at 7 pm, and on weekends at 1 pm. Reserved seating is available (C$25) up to two hours before showtime, or you can arrive when you please and make a donation (C$20 is suggested). You can also rent chairs and blankets to sit on (C$2 and C$1 respectively). The nearby Park Place Theatre hosts performances during the shoulder months. ⊠ *Cambridge Battery, Point Pleasant Park, Point Pleasant Dr.* ☎ *902/422–0295* ⊕ *www.shakespearebythesea.ca.*

SPORTS AND THE OUTDOORS

CANOEING

St. Mary's Boat Club. Beautiful century-old homes dot the placid Northwest Arm, and the bench of a canoe is definitely the best seat from which to view them. On weekends from June through September, St. Mary's rents canoes by the hour to adults 18 years and older and to younger certified canoeists. ✉ *1641 Fairfield Rd., off Jubilee Rd., below Connaught* ☎ *902/490–4688* ⊕ *www.halifax.ca/smbc.*

GOLF

Glen Arbour. Natural features, including elevation changes and mature woodlands, lakes, and streams, make the 18-hole championship course here a scenic and memorable experience, culminating in the featured hole (the 18th), a 565-yard downhill par 5 with a dazzling view. The club also has a nine-hole, par-three course designed for novices. ✉ *40 Clubhouse La., Hammonds Plains* ☎ *902/835–4653, 877/835–4653* ⊕ *www.glenarbour.com* ⚲ *Championship course: 18 holes. 6800 yds. Par 72. Green Fee: C$79/C$105* ☉ *Closed early Oct.–Apr.* ☞ *Facilities: golf carts, pull carts, rental clubs, pro shop, restaurant, bar.*

Granite Springs Golf Club. This lush, semiprivate course, an easy drive west of downtown Halifax, overlooks Shad Bay. It progresses across rolling hillsides with granite outcroppings, water features, and sand traps. Fairways are narrow, calling for accurate shots, but four sets of tees cater to different levels of golfing ability. ✉ *4441 Prospect Rd., Bayside* ☎ *902/852–3419* ⊕ *www.granitespringsgolf.com* ⚲ *Course: 18 holes. 6401 yds. Par 72. Green Fee: C$51/C$60* ☉ *Apr.–mid-Oct.* ☞ *Facilities: driving range, putting green, pitching area, golf carts, pull carts, rental clubs, pro shop, lessons, restaurant, bar.*

HIKING

McNab's Island. At the mouth of Halifax Harbour, this island appeals to adventuresome spirits. Accessible only by boat, it has 14 km (9 miles) of wooded trails and birding sites, plus a 19th-century fort. Several companies provide water taxis or tours from different Halifax locations. The trip takes 25 minutes from the Halifax boardwalk and costs about C$20 for the round-trip. ⚠ **There is no drinking water available on the island, so you must bring your own.** ☎ *902/861–2560* ⊕ *www.mcnabsisland.ca.*

Point Pleasant Park. Free, easy to reach, and threaded with woodland and waterside trails, this park is popular with locals and visitors alike. ■**TIP**➔ **If you overstay and the parking lot is locked, call 311 to be let out.** ✉ *Point Pleasant Dr. and Tower Rd.* ☎ *902/490–4700* ⊕ *www. pointpleasantpark.ca.*

Sir Sandford Fleming Park. This park, free and very accessible, has a 2.8-km (1¾-mile) trail, with views across the Northwest Arm to Point Pleasant Park on the opposite shore. Marked by an impressive stone tower called

---

CRAFTY RESOURCES

If you're looking specifically for fine arts and crafts, pick up a free copy of the Halifax Art Map or download one at ⊕ *www. halifaxartmap.com.* It lists more than 50 shops and galleries around the city. For elsewhere in the province, try the Nova Scotia Centre for Craft and Design's annual guide (⊕ *www.craft-design.ns.ca/guide*) or Studio Rally's independently prepared Fine Art & Craft Studio Map (⊕ *www.studiorally.ca*).

the Dingle, it's named for the inventor of Standard Time, who summered on the property. ✉ *260 Dingle Rd., follow signs off Purcell's Cove Rd.*

HORSEBACK RIDING
Hatfield Farm Adventures. Horseback-riding experiences are available for all levels, including trail rides (C\$37–C\$51), lessons (C\$59 for two hours), summer camps, and pony rides (for kids; C\$8.70). ✉ *1840 Hammonds Plains Rd., Hammonds Plains* ☎ *902/835–5676, 877/835–5676* ⊕ *www.hatfieldfarm.com.*

SEA KAYAKING
East Coast Outfitters. About 31 km (19 miles) from downtown Halifax off Highway 333, this outfitter rents kayaking equipment and offers instruction and guided excursions from May through September. Half-day (C\$75), full-day (C\$135 with lunch), and shorter midday and sunset tours (C\$50 each) are available. Kayak rentals start at C\$20. ✉ *2017 Lower Prospect Rd., off Hwy. 333, Lower Prospect* ☎ *902/852–2567, 877/852–2567* ⊕ *www.eastcoastoutfitters.com.*

Mountain Equipment Co-op. Part of a small nationwide chain, this downtown sports store rents kayaks for C\$30 a day. ✉ *1550 Granville St.* ☎ *902/421–2667* ⊕ *www.mec.ca.*

SWIMMING
Chocolate Lake. In summer, lifeguards supervise this lake, just off the Northwest Arm, that's popular for swimming. The name doesn't mean that the water is delicious, but rather comes from a former chocolate factory on the site. ⚠ **Locals avoid swimming in Halifax Harbour or the Northwest Arm itself because of the dubious water quality.** ✉ *2 Melwood Ave.* ☎ *902/490–5458.*

SHOPPING

BOOKS

Woozles. The country's oldest children's bookshop is packed with books, many of them by Canadian and local authors. The store somehow manages to shoehorn a slew of toys amid the tomes. ✉ *1533 Birmingham St., near Spring Garden Rd.* ☎ *902/423–7626, 800/966–0537* ⊕ *www.woozles.com.*

CRAFTS AND GIFTS

Jennifer's of Nova Scotia. Tempting Jennifer's sells handmade soaps, hooked mats, ceramics, pewter, and other craft items made in Nova Scotia. ✉ *5635 Spring Garden Rd.* ☎ *902/425–3119* ⊕ *www.jennifers.ns.ca.*

NovaScotian Crystal. The boardwalk is *the* place to watch master craftsmen blowing glass into graceful decanters and bowls, which can be purchased in this shop's showroom. ✉ *5080 George St.* ☎ *902/492–0416, 888/977–2797* ⊕ *www.novascotiancrystal.com.*

Spring Garden Place. Accessories for you and your home (⇨ *See also Mills*) are the focus of this boutique-like downtown mall. ✉ *5640 Spring Garden Rd.* ☎ *902/420–0675* ⊕ *www.springgardenplace.ca.*

FOOD

Fodor'sChoice ★
Halifax Seaport Farmers' Market. Steps from the boardwalk's southern terminus, this eco-conscious venue is bright, airy, and contemporary. It's open daily, giving you ample opportunity to stock up on edibles and quality crafts from its more than 250 vendors—or to just indulge in the city's best people-watching. ✉ *Pier 20, 1209 Marginal Rd.* ☎ *902/492–4043* ⊕ *www.halifaxfarmersmarket.com.*

SHOPPING COMPLEXES

Bishop's Landing. An attractive complex of shops and condos, Bishop's Landing contains worth-a-peek jewelry, fashion, and other boutiques. ⊠ *1475 Lower Water St.* ☎ *902/422–6412* ⊕ *bishops landing.com.*

Historic Properties. A pleasant place to stroll through some of the city's oldest buildings, this delightful complex also houses interesting shops and restaurants. ⊠ *1869 Upper Water St.* ☎ *902/429–0530* ⊕ *www.historicproperties.ca.*

Mills. Still a local institution after relocating to an upscale mall, this small, nearly century-old department store contains two floors of fashions, footwear, accessories, perfumes, cosmetics, and gifts. ⊠ *Spring Garden Pl., 5640 Spring Garden Rd.* ☎ *902/429–6111, 800/465–1919* ⊕ *www.millshalifax.com.*

Park Lane. The shops at this specialty mall near the Halifax Public Gardens sell home furnishings, clothing, jewelry, gifts, and accessories. ⊠ *5657 Spring Garden Rd.* ☎ *902/420–0660* ⊕ *www.shopparklane.ca.*

OFF THE BEATEN PATH

Hydrostone Market. This block-long building lures shoppers to the city's North End with all sorts of one-of-a kind items. Flattened by the Halifax Explosion in 1917, the market site and surrounding area were rebuilt in a charming English-garden style using hydrostone—aka concrete. Shops of note include the **Bogside Gallery** for fine crafts, **Lady Luck** for jewelry and accessories, and **L.K. Yarns** for yarns and needlecraft accessories. After browsing, break for lunch at **Epicurious Morsels,** or grab "gourmet to go" at **Little Europe.** ⊠ *5515–5547 Young St., between Isleville and Gottigen Sts., North End* ☎ *902/454–2000* ⊕ *www.hydrostonemarket.ca.*

THE ACADIANS

The Acadians are descendants of French colonists who settled here in the 1600s. In 1755, they were expelled by the British for refusing to pledge allegiance to the crown. Some eluded capture and slowly crept back, many making new homes in New Brunswick and along this shore of Nova Scotia. Others, however, migrated south to another region held by France at the time: Louisiana, where their name was shortened to Cajun. (Say "Acadian" five times fast and the reason will be apparent!)

SOUTH SHORE AND ANNAPOLIS VALLEY

The South Shore is on the Atlantic side of the narrow Nova Scotia peninsula; the Annapolis Valley is on the Bay of Fundy side. Although they're less than an hour apart by car, the two seem like different worlds. The former, with its rocky coast, island-dotted bays, and historic fishing villages, has launched 1,000 ships—and 1,000 postcards. The latter is most notable for its fertile farmlands, vineyards, and orchards. Highway 103, Highway 3, and various secondary roads form the province's designated Lighthouse Route, which leads southwest from Halifax down the South Shore. It ends in Yarmouth, where the Evangeline Trail begins. This trail winds along St. Mary's Bay through a succession of Francophone communities collectively known as the Acadian Shore. The villages blend into one another for about 50 km (35 miles), each one, it seems, with its own wharf, fish plant, and Catholic church.

The verdant Annapolis Valley runs northeast, sheltered on both sides by the North and South mountains. Occasional roads over the South Mountain lead to the South Shore; short roads over the North Mountain lead to the Fundy Shore. Like the South Shore, the valley has numerous historic sites—some of Canada's oldest among them—and is punctuated by pleasant small towns with a generous supply of Victorian architecture.

PEGGY'S COVE

48 km (30 miles) southwest of Halifax.

Peggy's Cove is the home of Canada's most photographed lighthouse. As you wind along the edge of St. Margaret's Bay, woodlands eventually give way to rugged outcroppings that were deposited when the last glaciers swept through. On one side, massive granite boulders stand semi erect in scrubby fields; on the other, they lie prone, creating the granite shelf on which Peggy's Cove is perched. The hamlet itself consists of little more than a Lilliputian harbor with a tiny wooden church, a cluster of shingled houses, and some salt-bleached jetties. What distinguishes Peggy's Cove, though, is the solitary lighthouse towering over a slab of wave-blasted rock. Just don't be tempted to venture too close to the edge—many an unwary visitor has been swept out to sea by the mighty surf that sometimes breaks here. (Repeat this mantra: dark rocks are wet rocks, and must be avoided.) In addition to navigating the rugged terrain, you'll have to contend with the crowds in summer—750,000 tourists descend annually. To avoid them in July and August, plan to arrive early or late in the day.

GETTING HERE AND AROUND

There is no public transportation to Peggy's Cove. Travelers based in Halifax can drive here by taking either Exit 2 or Exit 5 from Highway 103 onto Highway 333. The former is mostly inland while the latter runs along St. Margaret's Bay. The ideal scenario, though, is to go via one and return via the other. At Peggy's Cove you can drive almost to the base of the lighthouse, but you'd do better to park in the spacious public lot below and make the three-minute walk up to this Canadian icon.

ESSENTIALS

Visitor Information Peggy's Cove Visitor Information Centre ⊠ *109 Peggy's Point Rd.* ☎ *902/823–2253, 902/823–2256* ⊕ *www.peggyscoveregion.com* ⊗ *May–Oct.*

EXPLORING

deGarthe Memorial. A local artist carved the striking 30-meter (100-foot) deGarthe Memorial, a bas-relief carved from local granite. The memorial commemorates fishermen who lost their lives here. ⊠ *109 Peggy's Point Rd., off Hwy. 333.*

Swissair Memorial. A tribute to Swissair Flight 111, which crashed into the waters off Peggy's Cove in 1998, this memorial commemorates the 229 casualties and honors the courageous local fisherfolk involved in

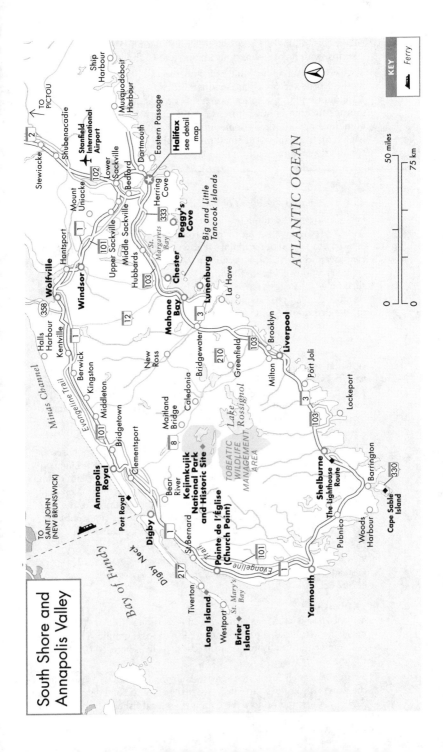

South Shore and Annapolis Valley

ATLANTIC OCEAN

KEY
▲—— Ferry

0 — 50 miles

0 — 75 km

TO PICTOU

Ship Harbour
Musquodoboit Harbour
Stanfield International Airport
Shubenacadie
Stewiacke
Eastern Passage
Dartmouth
Halifax see detail map
Bedford
Lower Sackville
Mount Uniacke
Herring Cove
Peggy's Cove
Big and Little Tancook Islands
Middle Sackville
Upper Sackville
Hantsport
Wolfville
Windsor
Hubbards
St. Margarets Bay
Chester
Lunenburg
Mahone Bay
La Have
Halls Harbour
Kentville
Berwick
Kingston
Middleton
New Ross
Evangeline Trail
Bridgewater
Greenfield
Brooklyn
Liverpool
Bridgetown
Caledonia
Maitland Bridge
Milton
Port Joli
Lockeport
Clementsport
Bear River
Kejimkujik National Park and Historic Site
TOBEATIC WILDLIFE MANAGEMENT AREA
Lake Rossignol
Shelburne
The Lighthouse Route
Barrington
Cape Sable Island
Port Royal
Annapolis Royal
TO SAINT JOHN (NEW BRUNSWICK)
Minas Channel
Digby
St. Bernard
Pointe de l'Église (Church Point)
Pubnico
Woods Harbour
Yarmouth
Bay of Fundy
Digby Neck
Tiverton
Westport
Long Island
Brier Island
St. Mary's Bay
Evangeline Trail

recovery efforts and comforting the grieving families. ✉ *Hwy. 333, 1.5 km (1 mile) north of village.*

WHERE TO EAT AND STAY

For expanded hotel reviews, visit Fodors.com.

$$ SEAFOOD 🍴 **Sou'wester Restaurant.** Poised on the rocks near the base of Peggy's Cove lighthouse, this sprawling 180-seat dining room serves a variety of seafood, including orange brandy shrimp and scallops, lobster dinners, and Down East specialties such as salt-fish hash and beans. There are also chicken, steak, and vegetarian options, and breakfast is served from 8:30 to 11 am. Sou'wester is a pleasant spot to linger over coffee and warm homemade gingerbread, provided the tour buses that regularly park out back haven't just disgorged hordes of hungry passengers. A large—generally kitschy—souvenir shop is on-site. [$] *Average main: C$20* ✉ *178 Peggy's Point Rd., off Hwy. 333* ☎ *902/823–2561* 🌐 *www.peggys-cove.com.*

$$ B&B/INN 🏨 **Oceanstone Seaside Resort.** Resembling a traditional seaside hamlet, Oceanstone's cluster of buildings sits picturesquely on the shore of St. Margaret's Bay, a short and peaceful distance from Peggy's Cove. **Pros:** most options have water views; eco-conscious owners. **Cons:** café only serves light fare and is closed on Monday from December through April; one cottage stands alone by the road. [$] *Rooms from: C$130* ✉ *8650 Peggy's Cove Rd., 3.5 km (2 miles) north of Peggy's Cove, Indian Harbour* ☎ *902/823–2160, 866/823–2160* 🌐 *www.oceanstoneresort.com* 🛏 *12 rooms, 2 suites, 8 cottages* 🍽 *No meals.*

SPORTS AND THE OUTDOORS

Boat excursions are available around Peggy's Cove spring through fall.

Four Winds Boat Charters. Based at Shining Waters Marine, about a 20-minute drive from Peggy's Corner, this company runs tours, weather permitting, in July and August aboard a Cape Islander. There's a two-hour scenic cruise, a three-hour nature cruise, and four-hour fishing trips, with prices starting at $25. ✉ *148 Nautical Way, Tantallon* ☎ *902/492–0022, 877/274–8421* 🌐 *www.fourwindscharters.com.*

SeaSun Kayak. Paddling tours, starting at $76 for a half-day, are available here, as well as kayak rentals—from $20 for an hour to $70 all day for a single kayak, and $30 to $90 for a double. Hiking tours cost from $55 to $70. ✉ *Shining Waters Marine, 148 Nautical Way, off Hwy. 333, 22 km (14 miles) north of Peggy's Cove, Tantallon* ☎ *902/850–7732, 866/775–2925* 🌐 *www.paddlenovascotia.com.*

SHOPPING

Beales' Bailiwick. Maritime-designed clothing, pewter, and jewelry are among the crafts sold here. The adjoining coffee shop affords one of the best photo ops in Peggy's Cove, and the renovated red schoolhouse next door is a venue for summertime theater and concerts. ✉ *124 Peggy's Point Rd.* ☎ *902/823–2099, 877/823–2099* 🌐 *www.beales.ns.ca* ⏲ *Closed early Nov.–Apr.*

CHESTER

64 km (40 miles) west of Peggy's Cove.

Although Chester is a short drive west of Peggy's Cove, you'll be forgiven for thinking you've taken a wrong turn and ended up in Maine or Massachusetts. New England planters settled the site in 1759, and their numbers were later bolstered by Loyalists escaping the American Revolution and Boston Brahmins who simply wanted to escape the city in summer. Thanks to the clapboard saltboxes and Cape Cod–style homes they left behind, Chester still calls to mind a classic New England community. Most visitors are content to explore its tree-shaded lanes or make forays into the surrounding countryside. Yachtsmen invariably stick close to the water.

GETTING HERE AND AROUND

There is no public transportation to Chester. From Halifax it's a 68-km (42-mile) drive via NS–103 and NS Trunk 3 W, or a slightly longer, much slower, meandering drive along St Margaret's Bay Road, NS–213, and NS Trunk 3 W.

ESSENTIALS

Visitor Information Chester Visitor Information Centre ⊠ *Old Train Station, 20 Smith Rd., Hwy. 3* ☎ *902/275–4616* ⊕ *www.chesterareans.ca* ☉ *May–Oct.*

EXPLORING

Big and Little Tancook islands. Out in Mahone Bay, 8 km (5 miles) out from Chester, these scenic islands have trails for hiking and biking, and provide great bird-watching and photography opportunities. There are sandy beaches, too, one of which is great for fossil hunting. Reflecting its part-German heritage, Big Tancook claims to have the best sauerkraut in Nova Scotia. The boat from Chester runs four times daily from Monday through Thursday, six times on Friday, and twice daily on weekends. The 50-minute ride costs C\$5.50 per adult or C\$21.75 for 10 tickets (cash only). ☎ *902/228–2927 Rec Centre, summer only, 902/275–7885 ferry information* ⊕ *www.tancookislandtourism.ca.*

FAMILY **Ross Farm Living Museum of Agriculture.** A restored 19th-century farm illustrates the evolution of agriculture from 1600 to 1925. The animals are those found on an 1800s farm—draft horses, oxen, and other heritage breeds—and traditional activities such as blacksmithing or spinning are demonstrated. Hands-on programs are regularly scheduled for kids who'd like to help out with the chores. The Peddler's Shop here sells items made in the community. ⊠ *4568 Hwy. 12, 30 km (18 miles) northwest of Chester via NS Trunk 3 E, New Ross* ☎ *902/689–2210, 877/689–2210* ⊕ *rossfarm.novascotia.ca* ⊠ *C\$6, free Sun. 9:30–11 am* ☉ *May–Oct., daily 9:30–5:30; Nov.–Apr., Wed.–Sun. 9:30–4:30.*

WHERE TO EAT AND STAY

For expanded hotel reviews, visit Fodors.com.

\$\$ × **Fo'c'sle Tavern.** This rustic midtown spot—a former store, stable, and CANADIAN inn dating to 1764—is full of natural pine and local art, and its staff and clientele treat regulars and newcomers like kin. In the windowed front section, a wood stove keeps things warm on chilly nights, and year-round you can order from a menu that's strong on seafood and comfort food—haddock stuffed with shrimp, scallops, tomato, and Parmesan, for instance, or liver, bacon, and onions with mashed potatoes. Lighter fare is also served, along with plenty of draft beers. Musicians perform on some nights, and there are pool tables and TVs. [$] *Average main: C$14* ✉ *42 Queen St.* ☎ *902/275–1408* 🌐 *www.focslechester.com* 🕒 *No brunch weekdays, except holidays.*

$ BAKERY Fodor's Choice ★ 🍴 **Julien's Pâtisserie, Bakery & Café.** The buttery croissants, brioches, and *pain de campagne* (country bread) made here are tasty testaments to its namesake owner's French roots. That's just the beginning, though. Savory homemade soups are also available, as are hefty deli sandwiches (the Knuckle & Claw lobster sandwich is justifiably famous in these parts). A slice of the fruity, brandy-doused Tart Pays d'Auge, named after an area in Normandy, makes a fine finish. Load up on lunchables for an impromptu picnic along Chester's scenic waterfront, or pull up a chair in the café section. [$] *Average main: C$10* ✉ *43 Queen St.* ☎ *902/275–2324* 🕒 *Closed Mon. early Sept.–mid-June. No dinner.*

$ B&B/INN 🏨 **Mecklenburgh Inn.** Nautical touches abound in this heritage B&B at the top of one of Chester's main streets. **Pros:** complimentary gourmet breakfast; claw-foot tubs in three rooms. **Cons:** two blocks from the water; books up a year ahead for Race Week; one bathroom, while private, is not en suite. [$] *Rooms from: C$135* ✉ *78 Queen St.* ☎ *902/275–4638, 866/838–4638* 🌐 *www.mecklenburghinn.ca* 🛏 *4 rooms* 🕒 *Closed Jan.–Apr.* 🍽 *Breakfast.*

NIGHTLIFE AND THE ARTS

Chester Playhouse. A summer theater season, spring and fall music seasons, movie screenings, and community-theater and other events keep this venue hopping. ✉ *22 Pleasant St.* ☎ *902/275–3933, 800/363–7529* 🌐 *www.chesterplayhouse.ca.*

SHOPPING

Amicus Gallery. Jewelry, stained glass, and other crafts by local artisans can be found here, along with the owner's own pottery. ✉ *20 Pleasant St.* ☎ *902/275–2496* 🌐 *www.amicusgallery.ca.*

Jim Smith Fine Studio Pottery. The earthenware pottery at this studio is as cheerful as the bright yellow-and-green building on the front harbor in which it's housed. From October through May it's open by chance or appointment. ✉ *Corner of Duke and Water Sts.* ☎ *902/275–3272* 🌐 *www.jimsmithstudio.ca.*

MAHONE BAY

24 km (15 miles) west of Chester.

Three vintage churches along a grass-fringed shoreline set a tranquil tone for this pastoral town that wraps around a sweeping curve of water. Of course, life here wasn't always so serene. Mahone Bay was once a thriving shipbuilding center. Before that, it was popular with pirates and privateers. In fact, Mahone Bay was named for the type of low-lying ship they used: it's a corruption of the French word *mahonne* (a low-lying barge-like boat).

GETTING HERE AND AROUND

There is no public transportation to Mahone Bay. To drive here, leave Highway 103 at Exit 10, turning onto NS–3.

ESSENTIALS

Visitor Information **Mahone Bay Visitor Information Centre** ✉ *165 Edgewater St.* ☎ *902/624–6151* 🌐 *www.mahonebay.com* 🕓 *May–Oct.*

EXPLORING

Mahone Bay's outdoor pleasures include kayaking into secret coves or around the many islands, including Oak Island, reputedly a favorite haunt of the notorious Captain Kidd. Modern-day treasure hunters are better off onshore, perusing the galleries and studios along Main Street and environs. Although Mahone Bay has a population of just 1,100, it supports an enviable assortment of craftspeople. ⇨ *See Shopping, below.*

WHERE TO EAT AND STAY

For expanded hotel reviews, visit Fodors.com.

$$ CANADIAN 🍴 **Kedy's Inlet Restaurant.** Diners at this chronically cute restaurant at Kedy's Landing—you'll see it just as you approach town off Exit 10—are treated to a fine view of Mahone Bay and the city's three charming churches. The Canadian-style menu emphasizes chowders and seafood, but there are meat and vegetarian options as well. The delicious Heavenly Chicken (in a white-wine and cream sauce) has been a mainstay for years, and the apple strudel, made in-house by the Bavarian-born chef, is alone worth a visit. [$] *Average main: C$18* ✉ *249 Edgewater St.* ☎ *902/624–6363* 🌐 *kedysinlet.com* 🕓 *Closed Jan.–mid-Mar. No breakfast weekdays.*

$$ CANADIAN FAMILY 🍴 **Mug & Anchor Pub.** Take in a view of the bay from inside this old, British-style alehouse, or enjoy waterside dining on the back deck. The menu includes basic pub fare, such as fish-and-chips and hamburgers, but you can also order fish cakes and other Lunenburg County favorites. Lunenburg scallops are a specialty, as is the Mug & Anchor meat pie, and there's a "tykes" menu that will please even the fussiest young diner. The pub swells with the sounds of live jazz, blues, and folk music on Thursday and Saturday evenings; in the off-season, Wednesday is Trivia Night. [$] *Average main: C$13* ✉ *643 Main St.* ☎ *902/624–6378* 🌐 *www.themugandanchorpubltd.com.*

$$ B&B/INN 🏨 **Amber Rose Inn.** The building dates from 1875 and is furnished with antiques, but you'll also find up-to-date creature comforts such as mini-refrigerators, coffeemakers, and whirlpool tubs. **Pros:** leafy grounds with a brook in back; quiet location. **Cons:** not on the water; off the main commercial stretch. [$] *Rooms from: C$125* ✉ *319 Main St.* ☎ *902/624–1060* 🌐 *www.amberroseinn.com* 🛏 *3 suites* 🍽 *Breakfast.*

SPORTS AND THE OUTDOORS

South Shore Boat Tours. Ninety-minute narrated nature cruises (C$40) around Mahone Bay depart three times a day, from June through October. A four-hour puffin-viewing trip (C$55) to Pearl Island and fishing charters are also available. ✉ *Mahone Bay Civic Marina, 683 Main St.* ☎ *902/527–8544* 🌐 *www.southshoreboattours.com.*

Sweet Ride Cycling. Before setting out on your ride, you can buy old-fashioned treats at this bicycle-slash-candy shop. Half-day rentals cost C$20, full-day ones C$30; child trailers and bikes run C$15 per day. Electric-assist bikes (C$30 half day, C$50 full day) are also available. ⊠ *523 Main St.* ☎ *902/531–3026* ⊕ *sweetridecycling.com* ⊙ *Closed Sun. and Mon. in winter.*

SHOPPING

Amos Pewter. Inside a former boat-building shop that dates to 1888, the artisans at Amos Pewter design and create pewter items using traditional methods. Jewelry, sculptures, tableware, and pewter renditions of shells and other natural objects are among the items for sale, along with a new original-design Christmas ornament each year. Interpretive displays explain the history of pewter and Amos Pewter's involvement with the "Economuseum Network," which emphasizes traditional skills. ■ TIP➡ **If watching the artisans at work gets your creative juices flowing, you can participate in the Hands-On Experience (C$5), and take home what you make.** ⊠ *589 Main St.* ☎ *902/624–9547, 800/565–3369* ⊕ *www.amospewter.com* ⊙ *Closed Sun. in Jan. and Feb.*

Spruce Top Rug Hooking Studio. Leave room in your luggage for the hooked rugs and hand-dyed woolens sold at this store, named after a popular rug pattern. You might see a "hooker" at work here, and classes are sometimes held. ⊠ *255 Main St.* ☎ *902/624–9312, 888/784–4665* ⊕ *www.sprucetoprughookingstudio.com* ⊙ *Closed Tues.*

Suttles and Seawinds. Renowned worldwide for its distinctively designed, high-quality quilts and clothing, the company displays its colorful goods on two floors of a heritage building. ⊠ *466 Main St.* ☎ *902/624–8375* ⊕ *www.suttles.ca.*

LUNENBURG

14 km (9 miles) south of Mahone Bay.

Fodor's Choice ★ This remarkably preserved town has a colorful past and some *very* colorful buildings, a combo that earned it a UNESCO World Heritage Site designation. The British probably had something more staid in mind when they founded Lunenburg in 1753, but the German, Swiss, and French Protestants recruited to settle here put their own stamp on it. The result? Rainbow-hued houses characterized by the "Lunenburg Bump": a detailed dormer over the front door. Naturally, locals didn't spend *all* their time on home improvements. By the 1850s they'd transformed the town into a world-class fishing and shipbuilding center. Today, blacksmiths and dory builders continue to work on the waterfront and, appropriately, the Fisheries Museum of the Atlantic is the top attraction. An in-the-middle-of-it-all location, plus a growing supply of fine lodging, dining, shopping, and touring options makes Lunenburg one of the best bases for a Nova Scotia vacation.

GETTING HERE AND AROUND

When the Beatles sang about "the long and winding road," they might have had the Lighthouse Route in mind. The curvy back roads that make up most of it hug the South Shore from Halifax to Yarmouth and are undeniably scenic, but a shorter option is to get to Lunenburg via Highway 103, using Exit 10 or Exit 11; they take about the same amount of time, but Exit 11 has nice views around Mahone Bay. Once you're in town, walking is the way to go, provided you're not daunted by the steep hill.

ESSENTIALS

Visitor Information Lunenburg Visitor Information Centre ⊠ *11 Blockhouse Hill Rd.* ☎ *902/634–8100, 902/634–3656, 888/615–8305* ⊕ *www.lunenburgns. com* ⊗ *May–Oct.*

EXPLORING

FAMILY

Fodor'sChoice

★

Fisheries Museum of the Atlantic. Flanked by sailing ships and painted a brilliant red, this museum on the Lunenburg waterfront strikes a dazzling pose, and the exhibits and activities experienced here more than live up to the initial impression. With aquariums devoted to native species, tidal touch tanks, themed films, and displays about shipbuilding, whaling, and other maritime endeavors, there's plenty to keep the whole gang happy. Demonstrations on topics such as sail making, boat building, and dory launching are also given, and dockside you can visit a restored saltbank schooner and a steel-hulled trawler and hear a few fish tales.

As if the comprehensive overview of Nova Scotia's fishing industry weren't enough, the *Bluenose II* (*902/634–4794 or 866/579–4909, www.bluenose.novascotia.ca*), the province's sailing ambassador, calls the museum home. Built in 1963, she's a faithful replica of the original *Bluenose,* the Lunenburg-built schooner that gained prominence during the 1920s and 1930s as the North Atlantic fleet's fastest vessel, which sank in 1946 after striking a reef. ■TIP➔ **If the Bluenose II isn't sitting pretty in port when you arrive, you can still get a glimpse of the famed ship by digging a Canadian dime out of your pocket—she's pictured on the back.** ⊠ *68 Bluenose Dr.* ☎ *902/634–4794, 866/579–4909* ⊕ *fisheries-museum.novascotia.ca* ⚑ *C$10 mid-May–mid-Oct., C$4 mid-Oct.–mid-May* ⊗ *Mid-May–mid-Oct., daily 9:30–5:30; mid-Oct.–mid-May, weekdays 9:30–4.*

Lunenburg Town Walking Tours. Landlubbers can get their exercise on one of the C$20 (cash only) guided strolls—ghostly ones among them—conducted year-round by this company. ■TIP➔ **The outfit's website has a link to an online waterfront tour.** ☎ *902/634–3848* ⊕ *www. lunenburgwalkingtours.com.*

WHERE TO EAT

$$$$

EUROPEAN

Fodor'sChoice

★

✕ **Fleur de Sel.** In-the-know foodies flock to this classy Continental alternative to the South Shore's dime-a-dozen fish joints. Tucked into a heritage home on Montague Street, the restaurant has an elegant, airy interior, and the food is superb, from the *tartare de boeuf* through the tuna Niçoise to the final bite of *fromage.* To try the chef's tasting menu—seven courses for C$90, plus C$58 to add wine pairings—you need to notify the restaurant ahead of your visit. ■TIP➔ **If you can't score one of the 35-odd seats at dinner, come for Sunday brunch, when stellar dishes such as lobster eggs Benedict and brioche French toast are served.** Ⓢ *Average main: C$34* ⊠ *53 Montague St.* ☎ *902/640–2121, 877/723–7258* ⊕ *fleurdesel.net* ⚑ *Reservations essential* ⊗ *Closed mid-Oct.–Mar. No lunch Mon.–Sat.*

2

$$ ECLECTIC 🍴 **Magnolia's Grill.** Exuberant and unabashedly eccentric, this place is the Auntie Mame of Lunenburg restaurants. The booths are close together and the walls cluttered with pictures, yet somehow the decor works and so does the menu, a Nova Scotian–Deep South hybrid featuring items such as fish cakes, creole peanut soup, and pulled pork. Once you see the key lime pie, you might want to skip straight to dessert. ■ TIP→ **The small space fills fast, so make a reservation or be prepared to wait.** [$] *Average main: C$20* ✉ *128 Montague St.* ☎ *902/634–3287* ✍ *Reservations essential* ⏲ *Closed late Oct.–Feb.*

$$$ SEAFOOD FAMILY 🍴 **Old Fish Factory Restaurant & Ice House Bar.** Lunenburg is riddled with seafood restaurants, but this one stands out for its location inside a former fish-processing plant at the Fisheries Museum of the Atlantic. The eatery overlooks Lunenburg Harbour and offers wharf-side dining in warm months. Seafood is the specialty, of course—try the lobster-and-crab-stuffed haddock—but you can also opt for chicken, steak, or vegetarian pasta. In summer the adjacent bar has a live jam on Tuesday nights and Gaelic folk music and dancing on Wednesday nights. [$] *Average main: C$23* ✉ *68 Bluenose Dr.* ☎ *902/634–3333, 800/533–9336* 🌐 *www.oldfishfactory.com* ⏲ *Closed mid-Oct.–mid-May.*

$$$ SEAFOOD 🍴 **Rum Runner Restaurant.** A wall of windows makes the most of this restaurant's Lunenburg Harbour location, creating an appropriately nautical setting for savoring the expertly prepared seafood the kitchen turns out. Thanks to its owners' German heritage, the Rum Runner has an attractive European-style dining room, where patrons enjoy bouillabaisse, seafood chowder, and mains that might include crab-stuffed local haddock or steamed Nova Scotia lobster. Ribs, steaks, and other meats are also on the menu, and there's usually a vegetarian option. ■ TIP→ **Though its main entrance is on a parallel street, this casual eatery can also be accessed on Bluenose Drive, opposite the Fisheries Museum.** [$] *Average main: C$25* ✉ *66 Montague St.* ☎ *902/634–8778* 🌐 *www.rumrunnerinn.com* ⏲ *Closed Nov.–Apr.*

WHERE TO STAY

For expanded hotel reviews, visit Fodors.com.

$ B&B/INN FAMILY 🏨 **Arbor View Inn.** Inside a grand early-20th-century house, Arbor View is secluded from Lunenburg's bustle but within walking distance of the town's attractions. **Pros:** idyllic grounds; books and board games for entertainment. **Cons:** no air-conditioning; only two rooms have TVs. [$] *Rooms from: C$120* ✉ *216 Dufferin St.* ☎ *902/634–3658, 800/890–6650* 🌐 *arborview.ca* 🛏 *3 rooms, 1 suite* 🍽 *Breakfast.*

$$ HOTEL 🏨 **Lunenburg Arms Hotel & Spa.** It's rare to find hotel-style amenities in small-town heritage properties, but this place has them—and not just an elevator and an ice machine. **Pros:** mid-hill location; complimentary use of spa's steam shower and hot tub. **Cons:** dining deck faces the street; free breakfast in the off-season only. [$] *Rooms from: C$169* ✉ *94 Pelham St.* ☎ *902/640–4040, 800/679–4950* 🌐 *www.eden.travel/lunenburg* 🛏 *22 rooms, 2 suites* 🍽 *Multiple meal plans.*

$$ B&B/INN 🏨 **Lunenburg Inn.** It's said that Joseph P. Kennedy Sr. was often a guest here during the prohibition era, when 13 cell-size rooms shared a single bathroom—if so, he wouldn't recognize the luxurious lodgings of today. **Pros:** free phone calls within Nova Scotia; fresh-baked cookies

in high season; guest take-one leave-one book exchange. **Cons:** street can be noisy; a bit outside the main tourist area. [$] *Rooms from: C$149* ✉ *26 Dufferin St.* ☎ *902/634–3963, 800/565–3963* 📠 *902/634–9419* 🌐 *www.lunenburginn.com* 🛏 *5 rooms, 2 suites* 🕒 *Closed late Nov.–Mar.* 🍴 *Breakfast.*

$ B&B/INN 🏠 **Pelham House Bed & Breakfast.** Close to downtown, with a veranda overlooking Lunenburg Harbour, this circa-1906 sea-captain's home is decorated in homey, country style. **Pros:** a sustaining breakfast is included; pleasant pets; discounts for multiple nights; suite works well for families. **Cons:** no grounds to speak of; not for people with pet allergies. [$] *Rooms from: C$99* ✉ *224 Pelham St.* ☎ *902/634–7113, 800/508–0446* 🌐 *www.pelhamhouse.ca* 🛏 *3 rooms, 1 suite* 💳 *No credit cards* 🍴 *Breakfast.*

SPORTS AND THE OUTDOORS

Lunenburg Bike Barn. Rentals start at C$25 at this friendly shop 2 km (1 mile) east of the town center. ✉ *579 Blue Rocks Rd.* ☎ *902/634–3426* 🌐 *www.bikelunenburg.com.*

Lunenburg Ocean Adventures. The thrill-seeker activities this outfitter makes possible include deep-sea fishing and shark-cage diving. The former costs C$55 per person, the latter C$600 (based on six divers) plus C$50 per extra person. Boats depart from the Fisheries Museum of the Atlantic. ✉ *68 Bluenose Dr.* ☎ *902/634–4833* 🌐 *www.lunenburgoceanadventures.com.*

Lunenburg Whale-Watching Tours. Whales, seals, and other marine life are the star attractions of these tours. The three-hour trips depart four times daily, from May through October, from the Fisheries Museum Wharf and cost C$52. You can arrange for bird-watching excursions and tours of Lunenburg Harbour, too. ☎ *902/527–7175* 🌐 *www.novascotiawhalewatching.com.*

Pleasant Paddling. Kayak rentals are priced from C$30 for a single kayak for two hours to C$90 per day for a double; the cost of guided excursions ranges from C$50 for two hours to C$125 for a day, including lunch. ✉ *221 The Point Rd., Blue Rocks* ☎ *902/541–9233* 🌐 *www.pleasantpaddling.com.*

Star Charters. From June through October, 90-minute daytime and sunset sailing trips (C$24 and C$27, respectively) take place aboard a 15-meter (48-foot) wooden ketch. ✉ *Fisheries Museum Wharf, Bluenose Dr.* ☎ *902/634–3535 June–Oct., 877/386–3535, 902/634–3537 Nov.–May* 🌐 *www.novascotiasailing.com.*

SHOPPING

Ironworks Distillery. Load up on liquid souvenirs here. Named for the old marine-blacksmith's shop it occupies, Ironworks produces hand-distilled vodka from Annapolis Valley apples and luscious liqueurs from local berries. ✉ *2 Kempt St.* ☎ *902/640–2424* 🌐 *www.ironworksdistillery.com.*

The Spotted Frog. This funky folk-art gallery represents three dozen or so artists from around the province. ✉ *125 Montague St.* ☎ *902/634–1976* 🌐 *www.spottedfrog.ca.*

Windbag Company of Nova Scotia. You can help save the earth *and* preserve a piece of Lunenburg's seafaring history by purchasing one of the company's terrific totes, made from recycled sails. The totes can also be found at other shops in the Maritimes and beyond. ⊠ *35 Falkland St.* ☎ *902/640–3555* ⊕ *www.windbagcompany.ca.*

EN ROUTE

Nearly every town on this storied stretch of coast has a museum or two, and **Bridgewater**, 18 km (11 miles) west of Lunenburg, is no exception. It has two, each worth a quick look. More people stop here, though, because the "Main Street of the South Shore," as Bridgewater is known, has the region's largest assortment of shops and services.

DesBrisay Museum. Artifacts dating back to the mid-19th century, including rare photographs of local shops, factories, and shipyards, are among the holdings of this museum of Lunenburg County history. There's also a folk-art gallery. ■ TIP➔ **Walking trails wind from behind the museum building through nearby parkland.** ⊠ *130 Jubilee Rd., Bridgewater* ☎ *902/543–4033* ⊕ *www.desbrisaymuseum.ca* ☎ *C$3.50, free on Sat.* ☉ *June–Aug., Tues.–Sat. 9–5; Sept.–May, Wed.–Sun. 1–5.*

Wile Carding Mill Museum. Life became easier for the locals after this mill opened that greatly reduced the time needed to card (process) wool. On a visit here you can view the restored mill and try your hand at carding wool and spinning yarn. ⊠ *242 Victoria Rd., Bridgewater* ☎ *902/543–8233* ⊕ *cardingmill.novascotia.ca* ☎ *C$3.50* ☉ *June–Sept., Mon.–Sat. 9:30–5:30, Sun. 1–5:30 (hrs subject to change).*

LIVERPOOL

69 km (43 miles) southwest of Lunenburg.

In recent years a paper mill has been Liverpool's economic mainstay, but between the American Revolution and the War of 1812, privateering was the most profitable pursuit. New Englanders who had turned on their former neighbors with a vengeance founded the town in 1759. Armed with a "Letter of Marque" from the British crown, they made a booming business out of seizing American ships and the valuable cargo they carried. Depending on which side you were on, such activity was interpreted as political expediency or legalized piracy. Each July, the town celebrates its notorious past with its Privateer Days festival (⇨ *See Planning, above*).

GETTING HERE AND AROUND
There is no public transportation to Liverpool. By road, it's off Highway 103 at the White PT Connector, then a left turn onto White Point Road. The town is small and easily walkable.

ESSENTIALS
Visitor Information Liverpool Visitor Information Centre ⊠ *28 Henry Hensey Dr.* ☎ *902/354–5421* ⊕ *www.regionofqueens.com/visit.*

EXPLORING
TOP ATTRACTIONS
Fort Point Lighthouse Park. The Port of the Privateers exhibit inside this structure—one of Canada's oldest surviving lighthouses—recounts its decades of stalwart service, from its completion in 1855 until 1989,

when operations ceased. Even if the lighthouse isn't open when you arrive, there are interpretive signs outside, and the views of Liverpool Harbour from the park are splendid. ✉ *21 Fort Point La., off Main St.* ☎ *902/354–5741* ✉ *Free* ⊗ *Daily.*

Kejimkujik National Park–Seaside. One of the last untouched tracts of coastline in Atlantic Canada, this park has isolated coves, broad white beaches, and imposing headlands, all of which are managed by Kejimkujik National Park and Historic Site (just plain "Keji" to locals or the linguistically challenged). A hike along the a 6-km (4-mile) trail reveals a pristine coast that's home to harbor seals, eider ducks, and many other species. ■ **TIP→ To protect nesting areas of the endangered piping plover, parts of St. Catherine's River beach (the main beach) are closed to the public from late April to early August.** ✉ *Off Hwy. 103, 25 km (16 miles) southwest of Liverpool, Port Joli* ☎ *902/682–2772* ⊕ *www.pc.gc. ca* ✉ *Free* ⊗ *Park daily, visitor center mid-May–Oct., daily from 8:30 am (closing times vary seasonally).*

FAMILY **Rossignol Cultural Centre.** A refurbished high school is now home to this eclectic center that contains three art galleries and five museums—including one devoted entirely to outhouses. Among the varied offerings are a trapper's cabin, an early-20th-century drugstore, 50 stuffed-wildlife exhibits, and a complete wood-paneled drawing room brought over from an English manor house. ✉ *205 Church St.* ☎ *902/354–3067* ⊕ *www.rossignolculturalcentre.com* ✉ *C$5* ⊗ *Mid-May–mid-Oct., Tues.–Sun. 10–5 (hrs and dates may vary).*

Sherman Hines Museum of Photography. Aside from showcasing the work of Sherman Hines and other renowned Canadian photographers, this museum traces the history of their chosen art form. Images ranging from daguerreotypes to holograms are on display, along with cameras, magic lanterns, and film boxes. There's even a mock-up of a Victorian studio. ✉ *219 Main St.* ☎ *902/354–2667* ⊕ *www. shermanhinesphotographymuseum.com* ✉ *C$5* ⊗ *Mid-May–mid-Oct., Tues.–Sat. 1–5.*

WORTH NOTING

Perkins House Museum. Built in 1766, this historic house was home to privateer-turned-leading-citizen Simeon Perkins, who kept a detailed diary about colonial life in Liverpool from 1760 until his death in 1812. Built by ships' carpenters, the intriguing structure gives you the illusion of standing in the upside-down hull of a ship. An interactive exhibit recounts the day-to-day lives of the Perkins family. ✉ *105 Main St.* ☎ *902/354–4058* ⊕ *perkinshouse.novascotia.ca* ✉ *C$5* ⊗ *June–mid-Oct., Mon.–Sat. 9:30–5:30, Sun. 1–5:30.*

Thomas Raddall Provincial Park. With four seabird sanctuaries nearby, this park is a great spot for birding, and it has some good hiking trails. Or you could just stretch out on one of the white-sand beaches. Occasional organized activities include family fun days and stargazing. ✉ *529 Raddall Park Rd.* ☎ *902/683–2664* ⊕ *www.novascotiaparks.ca* ✉ *Free* ⊗ *Mid-May–mid-Oct.*

BEACHES

Summerville Beach Provincial Park. The Liverpool area has easy access to some of the South Shore's best beaches, and this one has more than a kilometer of fine, pale-colored sand. Backing the beach is a dune system that shelters nesting sites for piping plovers—a clue to the location's uncrowded tranquility—and beyond this are salt marshes. The shallow water makes Summerville ideal for families, and near the beach is a picnic area with tables that have sunshades. **Amenities:** parking (free); toilets. **Best for:** solitude; sunsets; swimming; walking. ⊠ *7533 Hwy. 3, 14.5 km (9 miles) southwest of Liverpool, Summerville Centre* ⊕ *www.novascotiaparks.ca* ⊠ *Free* ☉ *Mid-May–mid-Oct.*

WHERE TO EAT AND STAY

For expanded hotel reviews, visit Fodors.com.

$ — B&B/INN — 🏨 **Lane's Privateer Inn.** Downtown Liverpool, though long on history, is short on accommodations, so this 200-year-old inn, once occupied by famed privateer Captain Joseph Barss, is a fortunate find, and most of its comfortable rooms have a river or harbor view. **Pros:** convenient location; pet-friendly; rate includes hot breakfast; some ground-floor rooms. **Cons:** room sizes vary; some rooms could use updating. $ *Rooms from: C$104* ⊠ *27 Bristol Ave.* ☎ *902/354–3456, 800/794–3332* ⊕ *lanesprivateerinn.wordpress.com* ⥏ *27 rooms* ⦿ *Breakfast.*

$$$$ — RENTAL FAMILY — 🏨 **Quarterdeck Beachside Villas & Grill.** Built just above the high-water mark, on the edge of the Summerville Beach Provincial Park, these quality villas make you feel like you're staying on a houseboat. **Pros:** terrific beach; baby-sitting service; restaurant offers room service and takeout; all units have whirlpool tubs. **Cons:** restaurant is closed from mid-October to mid-May. $ *Rooms from: C$349* ⊠ *7499 Hwy. 3, 15 km (10 miles) west of Liverpool, Port Mouton* ☎ *902/683–2998, 800/565–1119* ⊕ *www.quarterdeck.ns.ca* ⥏ *13 villas, 2 cottages* ⦿ *No meals.*

SPORTS AND THE OUTDOORS

Rossignol Surf Shop. The shop rents boards and wetsuits (C$25 each for half a day) and conducts two-hour surfing clinics (C$75) and guided kayak excursions (C$65 and up). Months and times vary. ⊠ *White Point Beach Resort, 75 White Point Beach Resort Rd., 10 km (6 miles) south of Liverpool, White Point* ☎ *902/354–7100* ⊕ *www.surfnovascotia.com.*

KEJIMKUJIK NATIONAL PARK AND HISTORIC SITE

67 km (42 miles) northwest of Liverpool; 45 km (28 miles) southeast of Annapolis Royal.

This inland woodsy area attracts campers, canoeists, hikers, bird-watchers, and cyclists.

GETTING HERE AND AROUND

You'll need a car to get to the park, which is off Highway 8 between Liverpool and Annapolis Royal. Just south of Maitland Bridge, the Kejimkujik Main Parkway heads east into the park from the highway.

EXPLORING

FAMILY **Kejimkujik National Park.** You'll have to veer inland to see this 381-square-km (147-square-mile) national park, which is about halfway between the Atlantic and Fundy coasts. The Mi'Kmaq used these gentle waterways for thousands of years, a fact made plain by the ancient petroglyphs carved into rocks along the shore. You can explore "Keji" on your own or take a guided interpretive hike—perhaps spying beavers, owls, loons, white-tailed deer, and other wildlife along the way. Guided paddles and children's programs are also available in summer, and leaf peepers can see the deciduous forests blaze with color in autumn. ■ TIP→ **Designated a Dark Sky Preserve by the Royal Astronomical Society of Canada, the park conducts nighttime programs for stargazers.** ✉ *Kejimkujik Main Pkwy., off Hwy. 8, Maitland Bridge* ☎ *902/682–2772* 🌐 *www.pc.gc.ca* 🎟 *C$5.80* ⏲ *Visitor Reception Centre late June–early Sept., daily 8:30–8; mid-May–mid-June and early-Sept.–Oct., Mon.–Thurs. 8:30–4:30, Fri. 8:30–6, and Sat. 8:30–5.*

WHERE TO STAY

For expanded hotel reviews, visit Fodors.com.

$ RESORT 🏨 **Mersey River Chalets and Nature Retreat.** Swimming, paddling, hiking, and bedtime bonfires fill the agenda at this 375-acre wilderness resort 5 km (3 miles) north of Kejimkujik National Park. **Pros:** pets welcome; snowshoeing and cross-country skiing offered in winter; excellent accessibility for wheelchair-bound guests. **Cons:** on-site restaurant only offers continental breakfast and snacks, and closes from October through April (though lodge room guests have use of shared kitchen). [$] *Rooms from: C$115* ✉ *322 Mersey River Chalets Rd. E, off Hwy. 8, 44 km (27 miles) south of Annapolis Royal, 75 km (47 miles) north of Liverpool, Caledonia* ☎ *902/682–2443, 877/667–2583* 🌐 *www.merseyriverchalets.ns.ca* 🛏 *9 chalets, 4 lodge rooms, 5 tents* 🍴 *Multiple meal plans.*

$ B&B/INN 🏨 **Whitman Inn.** Proximity to the Kejimkujik National Park is the big draw here, and the cozy lodgings at this friendly inn ensure that you can go wild without sacrificing creature comforts. **Pros:** pairs a B&B's intimacy with extra amenities; snow sports offered off-season. **Cons:** breakfast only included in a package; no air-conditioning; dinner orders must be made by 5 pm. [$] *Rooms from: C$79* ✉ *12389 Hwy. 8, Kempt* ☎ *902/682–2226, 800/830–3855* 🌐 *www.whitmaninn.com* 🛏 *8 rooms, 1 apartment* 🍴 *Multiple meal plans.*

SPORTS AND THE OUTDOORS

Whynot Adventure Outfitters. Also known as Keji Outfitters, this company inside Kejimkujik National Park rents bicycles, rowboats, kayaks, canoes, and camping gear from mid-May through mid-October. Prices for bikes and boats start at C$7 per hour, C$25 per day. ✉ *Kejimkujic National Park, Kejimkujik Main Pkwy., Jakes Landing* ☎ *902/682–5253* 🌐 *www.whynotadventure.ca.*

SHELBURNE

67 km (42 miles) southwest of Liverpool.

Shelburne, about two-thirds of the way down the Lighthouse Route, has a frozen-in-time appearance that many travelers love. It was settled after the American Revolution, when 10,000 Loyalists briefly made it one of the largest locales in North America—bigger than either Halifax or Montréal at the time. A smaller, temporary influx of Americans changed the face of Shelburne again in 1994, when film director Roland Joffe and crew arrived to shoot his version of *The Scarlet Letter*. The movie, starring Demi Moore, was an unequivocal mess, but the producers helped tidy up the town and raise awareness about its rich architectural heritage. Today's waterfront district looks much as it did when it was laid out in the 1780s, and many of the existing structures date from that period.

GETTING HERE AND AROUND

There is no public transportation to Shelburne. If you're driving from the Halifax direction, turn off Highway 103 at Exit 25 and follow Woodlawn Drive and then King Street. From the Yarmouth direction you can take Exit 27 or Exit 26. Once in Shelburne, you'll find it pleasant to stroll around.

ESSENTIALS

Visitor Information Shelburne Visitor Information Centre ✉ *43 Dock St.* ☎ *902/875–4547* ◷ *Mid-May–mid-Oct.*

EXPLORING

Black Loyalist Heritage Site. When Shelburne's population exploded after the Revolutionary War, Black Loyalists were relegated to land 7 km (4.5 miles) northwest of town. The community they created—Birchtown, named for the British general who oversaw their evacuation from New York—became the biggest free settlement of African Americans in the world. Birchtown's virtually forgotten story was told in Lawrence Hill's award-winning novel *The Book of Negroes*, and its founders are now honored at this site, which includes a national historic monument, a 1.5 km (1 mile) interpretive trail, and a small museum. A new larger museum and heritage center is expected to open in late 2014. ✉ *98 Old Birchtown Rd., off Hwy. 103, Birchtown* ☎ *902/875–1310, 888/354–0772* ⊕ *www.blackloyalist.com* ▱ *Monument and trail free; museum C$3* ◷ *Monument and trail daily year-round; museum June–Aug., daily 11–5; Sept.–May, weekdays by appointment.*

Shelburne Museum Complex. Shelburne's big-ticket attraction includes three properties operated by the Shelburne Historical Society. The **Ross-Thomson House and Store** is reputedly the oldest surviving (and from the looks of it, best stocked) general store in North America, restored to its 1820s appearance. Shelburne once had a thriving boat-building industry, turning out the traditional dories that were the mainstay of the fishing fleet. At the former waterfront workshop that houses the **J.C. Williams Dory Shop,** you can watch artisans craft new ones using old-fashioned techniques. Rounding out the trio, the **Shelburne County Museum** provides an overview of area history. ✉ *Dock St. and*

Charlotte La. ☎ *902/875–3141* 🌐 *www.historicshelburne.com* 🎟 *C$4 per museum, $10 for the whole complex* 🕒 *June–mid-Oct., daily 9:30–5:30. Shelburne County Museum also open mid-Oct.–May, weekdays 9:30–noon and 1:30–4:30. Off-season hrs may vary.*

AROUND SHELBURNE

Cape Sable Island—not to be confused with Sable Island, way out in the Atlantic—is a sleepy spot just off the beaten path, known for its contribution to the province's seafood harvest. Located 48 km (35 miles) south of Shelburne and accessed via the short Cape Sable Island Causeway (NS–330 South), it's Nova Scotia's southernmost point. You'll find colorful fishing boats afloat in Clark's Harbour. There are fine sandy beaches as well, one of which, Hawk Beach, offers excellent bird-watching and views of the 1861 Cape Sable Island Lighthouse.

Archelaus Smith Museum. Actual "sites" are hard to come by around here, but this museum, named for an early New England settler, is worth a gander. It recaptures late-1700s life with household items such as quilts and toys, plus fishing gear and information about shipwrecks and sea captains. ✉ *915 Hwy. 330, Cape Sable Island, Centreville* ☎ *902/745–2642* 🌐 *www.archelaus.org* 🎟 *Free* 🕒 *July and Aug., Mon.–Sat. 10–4:30, Sun. 1:30–4:30.*

Barrington museums. The town of Barrington, on the mainland side of the Cape Sable Island Causeway, has several old buildings near to each other along Highway 3 that are worth visiting. These include the self-explanatory **Barrington Woolen Mill,** at No. 2368; the **Old Meeting House Museum,** at No. 2408, where gatherings, elections, and religious services were held; the **Seal Island Light Museum,** at No. 2410, which occupies a replica lighthouse; and the **Western Counties Military Museum,** at No. 2401. ✉ *Hwy. 3, Barrington* ☎ *902/637–2185* 🌐 *capesablehistoricalsociety.com* 🎟 *$5 each museum (ask about discount if visiting 3 or more)* 🕒 *Military museum July and Aug., other museums at least mid-June–mid-Sept.; call for exact hrs, but all open daily.*

WHERE TO EAT AND STAY

For expanded hotel reviews, visit Fodors.com.

$$$ EUROPEAN Fodor's Choice ★

🍴 **Charlotte Lane Café.** Chef-owner Roland Glauser whips up creative seafood, meat, and pasta dishes in a restored building that started out as a butcher shop in the mid-1800s. The chowder is generous enough for a noon repast, and the rack of lamb with port-wine orange sauce and sun-dried berries is ideal at dinner, especially when capped with a refreshing lemon panna cotta. The café has a pleasant garden patio (a big plus, as there are only about 25 seats inside), plus a shop selling quality crafts. **TIP→ Reservations aren't accepted at lunch but are requested for dinner.** [$] *Average main: C$29* ✉ *13 Charlotte La.* ☎ *902/875–3314* 🌐 *www.charlottelane.ca* 🕒 *Closed Sun. and Mon. and mid-Dec.–early May. No brunch Tues.–Fri.*

$ B&B/INN

🏨 **Cooper's Inn.** Shelburne's historic waterfront was the site of a major Loyalist landing in 1783, and a year later the structure that now houses this inn went up. **Pros:** lovely location with water-view garden; some rooms have massage chairs. **Cons:** only breakfast is served on-site; no air-conditioning. $ *Rooms from: C$110* ✉ *36 Dock St.* ☎ *902/875–4656, 800/688–2011* 🌐 *www.thecoopersinn.com* 🛏 *7 rooms, 1 suite* ⏲ *Closed mid-Dec.–Apr.* 🍴 *Breakfast.*

SPORTS AND THE OUTDOORS

Shelburne Harbour Boat Tours. You can explore Shelburne's beautiful natural harbor aboard the MV *Brown Eyed Girl,* a 13-meter (44-foot) trawler. Day tours (at 9 am for 3 hours, at 2 pm for 3½ hours) cost C$35, and the 2½-hour evening tour (6 pm) costs C$25. Take the morning tour if you want to make a day of it and disembark at McNutt's Island to hike up to the Cape Roseway Lighthouse. ✉ *107 Water St.* ☎ *902/875–6521, 902/875–4439* 🌐 *www.shelburneharbourboattours.com* ⏲ *June–Sept.*

YARMOUTH

98 km (61 miles) west of Shelburne.

Yarmouth's status as a large port and its proximity to New England accounted for its early prosperity and today the town's shipping heritage is still reflected in its fine harbor, marinas, and museums. Since the discontinuation of ferry service from Maine, this isn't such an obvious destination for U.S. travelers. However, handsome Victorian architecture and a pleasantly old-fashioned main street make it worth a visit. Since the Evangeline Trail and Lighthouse Trail converge here, Yarmouth also allows easy access to the Acadian villages to the north or the Loyalist communities to the south.

GETTING HERE AND AROUND

If you're coming from or via Maine, it's worth finding out whether the Portland–Yarmouth ferry service has been reinstated. As of late 2013 negotiations were still underway. Within Nova Scotia, Bernie's Shuttle Service links Halifax to Yarmouth once a day (C$75 one-way), leaving Halifax (including pickups at and Stanfield International Airport) each afternoon between 2 and 4 pm for the 3½-hour journey. The trip back departs Yarmouth at 8 am. If you're driving, Yarmouth is at the eastern end of Highway 103 along the south shore and Highway 101 along the Fundy coast.

ESSENTIALS

Visitor Information **Yarmouth Visitor Information Centre** ✉ *228 Main St.* ☎ *902/742–5033, 902/742–6639* 🌐 *www.yarmouthandacadianshores.com* ⏲ *Mid-May–mid-Oct.*

EXPLORING

Art Gallery of Nova Scotia (Western Branch). This is the gallery's only satellite location. As with the flagship in Halifax, this one is housed in a heritage building and has a broad mandate, yet it's at its best when showcasing the works of regional artists. The branch exhibits art from the main gallery's permanent collection and mounts temporary shows of folk art and other disciplines. Family Sundays and children's workshops occasionally take place. ✉ *341 Main St.* ☎ *902/749–2248* 🌐 *www.artgalleryofnovascotia.ca* 🎟 *By donation* ⏲ *Thurs.–Sun. noon–5.*

Cape Forchu Lighthouse. It isn't the South Shore's most photogenic lighthouse—the one at Peggy's Cove wins that award—but this one finishes a close second, scoring points for its dramatic vistas and the dearth of other camera-clutching tourists. Erected in 1962 on the site of an earlier lighthouse, the concrete structure rises 23 meters (75 feet) above the entrance to Yarmouth Harbour. The adjacent keeper's quarters houses a small museum, a tearoom serving local treats, and a gift shop. ✉ *1856 Cape Forchu Rd., off Hwy. 304, Cape Forchu* ☎ *902/742–4522* 🌐 *www.capeforchulight.com* 🎟 *Donations accepted* 🕒 *June–late Sept., daily 11–5.*

FAMILY **Firefighters' Museum of Nova Scotia.** A good rainy-day destination, this museum recounts the history of fire fighting in the province through photographs, uniforms, and other artifacts, including vintage hose wagons, ladder trucks, and an 1863 Amoskeag Steamer. Kids will especially enjoy this spot—after checking out the toy engines, they can don a fire helmet and take the wheel of a 1933 Bickle Pumper. ✉ *451 Main St.* ☎ *902/742–5525* 🌐 *firefightersmuseum.novascotia.ca* 🎟 *C$4* 🕒 *July and Aug., Mon.–Sat. 9–5, Sun. 10–5; June and Sept.–mid-Oct., Mon.–Sat. 9–5; Nov.–May, weekdays 9–4, Sat. 1–4.*

Yarmouth County Museum & Archives. One of the largest collections of ship paintings in Canada resides here, along with exhibits of household items, musical instruments (including rare mechanical pianos and music boxes), and other items that richly evoke centuries past. There's even a Norse runic stone dating back to Viking transatlantic explorations around AD 1000. The museum has a preservation wing and an archival research area, where local history and genealogy are documented. Next door is the **Pelton-Fuller House,** summer home of the original Fuller Brush Man, which is maintained and furnished much as the family left it. The museum offers guided tours of a third building in high season: the **Killam Brothers Shipping Office.** Located at 90 Water Street, it recalls a long-standing family business that was established here in 1788. ✉ *22 Collins St.* ☎ *902/742–5539* 🌐 *yarmouthcountymuseum.ednet.ns.ca* 🎟 *Museum C$3, Pelton-Fuller House C$3, combined ticket C$5. Killam Brothers Shipping Office, call for details* 🕒 *Museum: mid-May–early Oct., Mon.–Sat. 9–5; early Oct.–mid-May, Tues.–Sat. 2–5. Pelton-Fuller House and Killam Brothers Shipping Office by guided tour only: June–Sept., weekdays 10–4 or by appointment.*

WHERE TO EAT AND STAY

For expanded hotel reviews, visit Fodors.com.

$ CANADIAN 🍴 **JoAnne's Quick 'n Tasty.** Laminated tables, vinyl banquettes, and bright lights greet you at this retro diner that still looks much as it did circa 1960. Options include fresh seafood and no-nonsense standbys like turkey burgers and club sandwiches. Devotees, however, swear by the hot lobster sandwich. Indeed, Haligonians have been known to make the three-hour trek just to dine on the creamed crustacean concoction that was supposedly invented here. [$] *Average main: C$10* ✉ *490 Hwy. 1, 4 km (2½ miles) northeast of Yarmouth, Dayton* ☎ *902/742–6606* 🕒 *Closed Dec.–Feb.*

$$ SEAFOOD 🍴 **Rudder's Seafood Restaurant and Brew Pub.** As its name implies this hopping waterfront spot serves the expected fish dishes and a few surprises (anyone for lobster poutine?) along with pub grub, all of which can be washed down with hand-crafted ales. Seating is inside a converted warehouse supported by 18th-century beams or, in fine weather, at picnic tables on the wraparound deck. Since Rudder's doubles as a microbrewery, you can also buy beer to go. Live entertainment on Wednesday, Friday, and Saturday evenings is good reason to linger. [$] *Average main: C$18* ✉ *96 Water St.* ☎ *902/742–7311* 🌐 *www.ruddersbrewpub.com.*

$$ B&B/INN 🏨 **Harbour's Edge Bed & Breakfast.** If you're looking for waterside gardens, appealing rooms, and welcoming hosts, you'll find them all at this 1864 home. **Pros:** the only Yarmouth lodging that's on the water; exemplary hosts; terrific French toast at breakfast. **Cons:** road outside can be busy; private bath for the "Clara Caie" room is down the hall (the other three rooms have en suite bathrooms). [$] *Rooms from: C$135* ✉ *12 Vancouver St.* ☎ *902/742–2387* 🌐 *www.harboursedge.ns.ca* 🛏 *4 rooms* 🍽 *Breakfast.*

$$$ RESORT Fodor's Choice ★ 🏨 **Trout Point Lodge.** Guests at this wilderness eco-resort can get away from it all without sacrificing luxury, excellent food, and top-drawer amenities. **Pros:** Relais & Chateaux property; hot tub, sauna, and in-room massages available. **Cons:** can be too secluded for some. [$] *Rooms from: C$239* ✉ *189 Trout Point Rd., off East Branch Rd. and Hwy. 203, 40 km (25 miles) northeast of Yarmouth, East Kemptville* ☎ *902/761–2142* 🌐 *www.troutpoint.com* 🛏 *11 rooms, 1 suite, 2 cottages* 🍽 *Multiple meal plans.*

SHOPPING

Hands On Crafts. Local artisans make all the cool jewelry, knitwear, birch-bark soap, and other items sold at this downtown co-op. ✉ *314 Main St.* ☎ *902/742–3515* 🌐 *www.handsoncrafts.ca.*

The Yarmouth Wool Shoppe. Whether you're looking for a gift or something to keep you warm on chilly Nova Scotian evenings, this local institution, open since 1883, has got you covered. Duffle coats, mohair throws, cashmere shawls, Guernsey fisherman-knit sweaters, and tartan robes are among the items for sale. ✉ *352 Main St.* ☎ *902/742–2255.*

POINTE DE L'ÉGLISE (CHURCH POINT)

70 km (43 miles) north of Yarmouth.

As small as they are, you still can't miss the communities that collectively make up the Acadian Shore. Each one on this stretch, beginning roughly in Beaver River and ending in St. Bernard, seems to have a surplus of Stella Maris flags, a disproportionately large Catholic church, and a French-speaking populace with an abiding passion for *rappie* pie, a hearty chicken stew with shredded potatoes. Church Point, called Pointe de l'Église by Francophones, tops the rest on all three counts.

GETTING HERE AND AROUND

There is no public transportation to Pointe de l'Église. By car, it's on Highway 1, the Evangeline Trail, which follows the coast parallel to Highway 101. Coming from the west, take Exit 29 onto Little Brook Road, then go north on the Evangeline; from the east, take Exit 28 onto the Evangeline at St. Bernard.

EXPLORING

Rendez-vous de la Baie. An arts and cultural complex that tries to be all things to all people—and succeeds—the Rendez-vous de la Baie serves locals, tourists, and students. Housed in a contemporary structure on the Université Sainte-Anne campus, the center has as its highlight the **Acadian Interpretive Centre and Museum,** whose exhibits provide an evocative overview of Acadian culture and history. The Rendez-vous complex also includes an art gallery that shows contemporary works, a theater for live and media presentations, an Internet café that hosts events, and a visitor information center. ■ TIP→ **The gift shop at the interpretive center carries an excellent selection of Acadian music.** ✉ *Université Sainte-Anne, 23 Lighthouse Rd, Unit 1, Pointe d'Église* ☎ *902/769–2345* 🌐 *rendezvousdelabaie.ca* 🕒 *Sept.–June, daily 7–4:30; July and Aug., daily 7–7.*

St. Mary's Church (Église Ste-Marie). The *église* for which this village is named stands proudly on the main road overshadowing everything around it. That's hardly surprising given that it is the largest wooden church in North America. Completed in 1905, St. Mary's is 58 meters (190 feet) long by 56 meters (185 feet) high, and the steeple, which requires 40 tons of rock ballast to keep it steady when ocean winds blow, can be seen for miles. The church is a registered museum with a stunning interior, two exhibit rooms housing a collection of vestments, and a souvenir shop that sells religious articles. Bilingual guides give tours regularly in summer and off-season by appointment. ✉ *1713 Hwy.1, Pointe d'Église* ☎ *902/769–2832* 🌐 *www.museeeglisesaintemariemuseum.ca* 🎟 *C$2 recommended donation* 🕒 *Mid-May–mid-Oct., Mon.–Thurs. noon–5; mid-Oct.–mid-May by appointment.*

WHERE TO EAT AND STAY

$$ SEAFOOD 🍴 **La Cuisine Robicheau.** Chef Scott Robicheau and his wife, Nadine, opened this restaurant specializing in seafood and Acadian cuisine in 2013, and it rapidly became *the* place to eat along this stretch of the coast. The excellent *pâté à la râpure* (rappie pie)—a traditional Acadian dish in this case containing grated potatoes and chicken or clams, all baked until brown—is usually the first thing to sell out. Come early if you'd like to sample it. Other good choices include the *fricot aux poutines râpées à la poule* (chicken soup with potato dumplings) and the haddock topped with lobster. The restaurant, which overlooks the ocean, occupies a restored and extended house whose five individually styled seating areas make for an intimate dining experience. ■ TIP→ **If you want wine with your meal, you'll need to bring your own.** [$] *Average main: C$20* ✉ *9651 Hwy. 1, Saulnierville* ☎ *902/769–2121* 🌐 *www.lacuisinerobicheau.com* ✍ *Reservations essential* 🕒 *Closed Mon.*

$ **Château d'la Baie.** Beautifully restored, this grand Victorian mansion

B&B/INN sits on the ocean side of the Evangeline Trail and offers large and sunny rooms furnished with antiques. **Pros:** exceptionally large rooms; convenient for the Université Sainte-Anne and Pointe de l'Église. **Cons:** some rooms don't have a sea view; not everyone cares for the communal breakfast-table concept. $ *Rooms from: C$95* ⊠ *959 Hwy. 1, Little Brook, Baie Sainte-Marie* ☎ *902/769–3113* ⊕ *www.havreducapitaine. ca/chateau* 🗫 *7 rooms* ⊙ *Closed Nov.–Apr.* ⦾ *Breakfast.*

$ **Havre du Capitaine.** Within easy reach of both Pointe de l'Église and

HOTEL Yarmouth, this low-rise lodging along the Evangeline Trail has sea views and modern, good-size rooms. **Pros:** friendly service; convenient location. **Cons:** breakfast a little disappointing. $ *Rooms from: C$100* ⊠ *9118 Hwy. 1, Meteghan* ☎ *902/769–2001* ⊕ *www.havreducapitaine. ca* 🗫 *18 rooms* ⦾ *Breakfast.*

THAT SOUNDS HEAVENLY!

Musique Saint-Bernard. The neo-Gothic St. Bernard Church, a stone structure famous for its acoustics, hosts classical concerts on some summer Sundays at 4 pm. Acclaimed artists from Canada and beyond perform here under the Musique Saint-Bernard banner. The church, a few miles north of Church Point, seats 1,000. Tickets are available at the door. ⊠ *Evangeline Trail, St. Bernard* ☎ *902/665–5103* ⊕ *www. musiquesaintbernard.ca* 🗫 *C$15 (cash only).*

DIGBY

35 km (22 miles) northeast of Pointe de l'Église/Church Point.

Digby is underappreciated: people tend to race to or from the ferry connecting it with Saint John, New Brunswick. Yet there is quite a bit to the town, including a rich history that dates to the 1783 arrival of Loyalists, and an appealing waterfront. Then, of course, there are the legendary Digby scallops. The world's largest in-shore scallop fleet docks in the harbor, and the plump, sweet "fruits of the sea" unloaded here are deemed to be delicacies everywhere. Come, if you can, for the Digby Scallop Days festival in early August. There *are* other fish in the sea, though, and while walking along the waterfront, you can buy ultra-fresh halibut, cod, and lobster—some merchants will even cook your purchase for you right on the spot. You can also sample Digby chicks (aka salty smoked herring) in local pubs or buy them from fish markets.

GETTING HERE AND AROUND

Bay Ferries Ltd. sails the *Princess of Acadia* between Saint John, New Brunswick, and Digby year-round. There is at least one round-trip per day—two in summer—and the crossing takes about three hours. If you are already in Nova Scotia, you'll need to drive here on Highway 1, the Evangeline Trail, or Highway 101 (which are the same road as you approach Digby). Take Exit 26. The town itself is easily explored on foot.

ESSENTIALS

Visitor Information Digby Tourist Bureau ⊠ *110 Montague Row* ☎ *888/463–4429, 902/245–5714* ⊙ *Mid-May–mid-Oct.* **Provincial Visitor Information Centre** ⊠ *237 Shore Rd.* ☎ *902/245–2201* ⊙ *May–Oct.*

EXPLORING

Admiral Digby Museum. The town, county, and this museum are named for Britain's Rear Admiral Robert Digby, who during the American Revolution helped evacuate loyalists to Nova Scotia following the British surrender of New York City. You can learn a little bit about the admiral and a fair amount about Digby County history viewing the artifacts, paintings, and maps displayed here. ✉ *95 Montague Row* ☎ *902/245–6322* 🌐 *www.admuseum.ns.ca* 🎟 *By donation* 🕒 *Mid-June–late Aug., Mon.–Sat. 9–5; late Aug.–late Sept., Tues.–Fri. 9–noon and 1–4:30; late Sept.–mid-June, Thurs. and Fri. 1–4:30.*

WHERE TO EAT AND STAY

For expanded hotel reviews, visit Fodors.com.

$$ SEAFOOD 🍴 **Mariner's Landing.** Digby provides no shortage of opportunities for sampling fish-and-chips, but Mariner's Landing is the town's only seafood restaurant. A pleasant if low-frills affair, the dining area overlooks the harbor where the fishing fleet lands the catch you'll be eating. The friendly staff knows its way around seafood, including the famous Digby scallops, but can also direct you to the few nonseafood items on the menu, not to mention the delectable home-style desserts. The wine list favors local vintages, some of them worth a try. **■ TIP→ The seafood chowder here is satisfyingly creamy, with lobster, scallops, and other fresh seafood, and not too much potato.** [$] *Average main: C$14* ✉ *100 Water St.* ☎ *902/245–1821* 🕒 *Closed Oct.–Apr.*

$$$ RESORT FAMILY 🏨 **Digby Pines Golf Resort and Spa.** Complete with walking trails, lavish gardens, and Annapolis Basin views, this casually elegant 300-acre property offers myriad comforts. **Pros:** kids under seven eat free; no charge for Digby shuttle service. **Cons:** nearest beach is small, rocky, and across the road. [$] *Rooms from: C$185* ✉ *103 Shore Rd.* ☎ *902/245–2511, 800/667–4637* 🌐 *www.digbypines.ca* 🛏 *84 rooms, 6 suites, 31 cottages* 🕒 *Closed mid-Oct.–May* 🍽 *Multiple meal plans.*

SPORTS AND THE OUTDOORS

Fundy Adventures. Based in Gulliver's Cove, about 18 km (11 miles) from Digby, this company organizes clam digging, periwinkle picking, dulse harvesting, lobster hauling, and other tasty activities (C$66–C$111). ✉ *679 Gulliver's Cove Rd., off Hwy. 217* ☎ *902/245–4388* 🌐 *www.fundyadventures.com.*

Fundy Complex. If you want to get out on the water, drop by the complex to rent a kayak (from C$39) or board a whale-watching boat (C$48). ✉ *34 Water St.* ☎ *902/245–4950, 866/445–4950* 🌐 *www.fundyrestaurant.com.*

LONG ISLAND AND BRIER ISLAND

About 46 km (40 miles) southwest of Digby.

You don't just stumble across these islands—reaching them requires a commitment. Maybe Nova Scotian nature lovers are betting on that so they can keep this place all to themselves. You see, Long Island and Brier Island are surrounded by water rich in plankton, which attracts a variety of whales along with harbor porpoises, seals, and abundant sea birds.

GETTING HERE AND AROUND

First, follow Highway 217 down to the end of Digby Neck, a narrow peninsula separating St. Mary's Bay and the Bay of Fundy, to the hamlet of East Ferry. From there hop a five-minute ferry for Tiverton, Long Island. If you're carrying on to Brier Island, take a second, eight-minute ferry ride onward from Freeport, Long Island, to Westport. Brier Island Ferry links the two islands. Ferries must scuttle sideways to fight the ferocious Fundy tidal streams coursing through the narrow gaps. They operate hourly, year-round, at a cost of C$5 for each ferry (cash only) for the round-trip for car and passengers.

ESSENTIALS

Ferry Contact **Brier Island Ferry** ☎ *902/839–2302.*

WHERE TO EAT AND STAY

For expanded hotel reviews, visit Fodors.com.

$ HOTEL 🏨 **Brier Island Lodge and Restaurant.** Atop a bluff at Nova Scotia's most westerly point, this three-building complex commands a panoramic view of the Bay of Fundy. **Pros:** whale-watching tours; on-site gift shop. **Cons:** motel-quality rooms; main lodge rooms lack ocean views; shaky Internet connection; breakfast not included in off-season. [$] *Rooms from: C$89* ✉ *557 Water St., Westport* ☎ *902/839–2300, 800/662–8355* 🌐 *www.brierisland.com* 🛏 *40 rooms* 🕓 *Closed Nov.–Apr.* 🍴 *Multiple meal plans.*

SPORTS AND THE OUTDOORS

Brier Island Whale and Seabird Cruises. Of several operators of seasonal boat tours, this is best. On thrice-daily trips, from early June until mid-October, you travel out of Westport with researchers who collect data for international organizations. The fare is C$50, a portion of which funds further research. The same company also offers adrenaline-fueled Zodiac excursions (C$59) five times daily from mid-May through mid-October. ✉ *223 Water St., Westport* ☎ *902/839–2995, 800/656–3660* 🌐 *www.brierislandwhalewatch.com.*

Mariner Cruises Whale & Seabird Tours. Narration by an onboard naturalist makes this operator's cruises (from 2½ to 4½ hours; C$49) a solid choice. Boats depart Westport daily from mid-June to mid-October. ✉ *325 Water St., Westport* ☎ *902/839–2346, 800/239–2189* 🌐 *www.novascotiawhalewatching.ca.*

Ocean Explorations Whale Cruises. Tom Goodwin, a marine and wildlife biologist, conducts well-regarded trips (C$59) in fast-paced, open-top Zodiacs to view whales and other marine life. ✉ *Hwy. 217, opposite old ferry wharf, Tiverton* ☎ *902/839–2417, 877/654–2341* 🌐 *www.oceanexplorations.ca.*

ANNAPOLIS ROYAL

37 km (23 miles) northeast of Digby.

Fodor's Choice ★

Annapolis Royal's history spans nearly four centuries, and the town's bucolic appearance today belies its turbulent past. One of Canada's oldest settlements, it was founded by the French in 1605, destroyed by the British in 1613, rebuilt by the French as the main town of Acadia, and then fought over for the better part of a century. Finally, in 1710, New England colonists claimed the town and renamed it in honor of Queen Anne. There are approximately 150 historic sites and heritage buildings here, including the privately owned DeGannes-Cosby House, the oldest wooden house in Canada (built in 1708), which happens to sit on St. George, Canada's oldest street.

As if it didn't have enough history on its own, Annapolis Royal is also the ideal starting point for excursions to Port Royal, the place where European settlement of Canada began.

GETTING HERE AND AROUND

There is no public transportation to Annapolis Royal. To drive here take the Evangeline Trail or Highway 101 to Exit 22. If you are traveling from the east, Highway 201 is also an option.

ESSENTIALS

Visitor Information Annapolis Royal Visitor Information Centre ✉ *204 Prince Albert Rd.* ☎ *902/532–5454* ⊕ *www.annapolisroyal.com* ⊙ *Mid-May–mid-Oct.*

Historical Association of Annapolis Royal. Because Annapolis Royal flip-flopped between the French and English so many times, the past here is a complicated affair, but the members of the historical association are happy to walk you through it. They've developed a series of high-season strolls led by guides dressed in typical 18th-century fashion. This is an entertaining way to learn more about the historic significance and cultural heritage of the region—and with most of the strolls priced at C$7, they're a bargain. Options include daytime tours of the National Historic District and sites associated with the Acadian Experience, and in July and August there's an Acadian Candlelight tour (C$12.50) on Monday nights. Reservations for tours aren't necessary, but call or check the website to find out when they occur. ■ TIP→ **The wildly popular Candlelight Graveyard Tour (C$7) of Canada's oldest English cemetery (at Fort St Anne) takes place at 9:30 pm several times a week from early June through mid-October.** The association has put together a self-guided walk pamphlet for visitors who'd rather wander independently. ☎ *902/532–3035* ⊕ *www.tourannapolisroyal.com.*

FAMILY
Fodor's Choice ★

Port Royal National Historic Site. Downriver from Annapolis Royal is this reconstruction of Sieur de Monts and Samuel de Champlain's fur-trading post. The French set up shop here in 1605—two years before the English established Jamestown—making this the first permanent European settlement north of Florida. Port Royal also set other New World records, claiming the first tended crops, the first staged play, the first social club, and the first water mill. Unfortunately, it didn't have the first fire department: the original fortress burnt down within a decade.

At this suitably weathered replica, which is ringed by a log palisade, you're free to poke around the forge, inspect the trading post, pull up a chair at the dining table, or simply watch costumed interpreters perform traditional tasks in the courtyard. Children can play dress-up, too, donning period outfits and wooden sabot shoes. ⊹ *Hwy. 1 to Granville Ferry, then left 10.5 km (6.5 miles), following signs for Port Royal* ☎ *902/532–2898, 902/532–2321* ⊕ *www.pc.gc.ca* ✆ *C$3.90* ☉ *Late June–early Sept., daily 9–5:30; mid-May–late June and early Sept.–mid-Oct., Sun.–Thurs. 9–5:30; grounds open year-round.*

Annapolis Royal Historic Gardens. Like everything else in this town, the plants here are a blast from the past—17 heritage-themed acres represent different eras and include a glorious Victorian garden, a knot garden, a typical Acadian house garden, and a 2,000-bush rose collection with about 250 varieties. ✉ *441 St. George St.* ☎ *902/532–7018* ⊕ *www.historicgardens.com* ✆ *C$10* ☉ *Mid-May–mid-Oct., daily 9–8.*

farmers' market. On Saturday mornings from mid-May through mid-October and on Wednesdays from 10 to 2 in July and August, the best place in Annapolis Royal to stock up on picnic supplies is the farmers' market, which sets up on lower St. George Street next to Ye Olde Towne Pub. Expect artisanal bread, cured meats, homemade sweets, and preserves, plus fresh Annapolis Valley produce. Local craftsmen attend, too, and there's live entertainment. Most vendors only accept cash. ✉ *178 St. George St.* ☎ *902/245–4824* ⊕ *www.annapolisroyalfarmersmarket.com.*

Fort Anne National Historic Site. Gazing over the grassy knolls, it's hard to believe that this fort qualifies as the "most attacked spot in Canadian history" or that those knolls are actually nearly 400-year-old earthwork ramparts built up, in part, with rubble and blood. First fortified in 1629, the site preserves what is left of the fourth military edifice to be erected here, an early-18th-century gunpowder magazine and officers' quarters. The latter now houses a small museum, and anyone who believes a picture is worth 1,000 words should be sure to see the massive Heritage Tapestry displayed inside. Its four meticulously detailed panels depict four centuries of local history and as many local cultures. Special events at the fort include reenactments and Mi'Kmaq cultural presentations. ✉ *323 St. George St.* ☎ *902/532–2397 June–Sept., 902/532–2321 Oct.–May* ⊕ *www.pc.gc.ca* ✆ *Grounds free, museum C$3.90* ☉ *Grounds daily dawn–dusk; museum July and Aug., daily 9:30–5:30, June and Sept., Sun.–Thurs. 9:30–5:30. Guided tours by appointment.*

FAMILY **Upper Clements Parks.** A theme park with rides and an adventure park where you can test your skills and stamina clambering through the treetops are the stars here, all in a setting of apple orchards, green lawns, and beautiful trees. The theme park has 50-odd rides and attractions, many of which are kiddy classics such as mini planes and trains and an old-fashioned carousel. More action-oriented guests can brave the wooden Tree Topper Roller Coaster (the highest ride in Atlantic Canada) or zoom above the property on a 91-meter (300-foot) zip line, then splash out on the park's 70-meter (230-foot) waterslide. The park also has horseback-riding trails and a BMX bike course. ✉ *2931 Hwy. 1, Evangeline Trail, 5 km (3 miles) southwest of Annapolis Royal*

☎ *902/532–7557, 888/248–4567* 🌐 *www.upperclementsparks.com* 🎟 *Theme Park C$27.50 including unlimited rides, Adventure Park $29.50, zip line C$7.50* ⏲ *Mid-June–early Sept., daily 11–7.*

WHERE TO EAT

For expanded hotel reviews, visit Fodors.com.

$$ CANADIAN 🍴 **Ye Olde Towne Pub.** Any eatery that puts the words "ye olde" in front of its name makes gourmets understandably suspicious, but this place isn't aimed at them anyway. The substantial lunches and dinners served at this merry, low-key pub are a hit with locals who appreciate the good homemade fare, including the always excellent apple crisp. Diners sometimes spill out of the 1884 brick building and onto the patio, which is adjacent to a square where the farmers' market takes place. In a town short on nightlife, it's also a good place for postdinner lounging. [$] *Average main: C$14* ✉ *9–11 Church St.* ☎ *902/532–2244.*

WHERE TO STAY

$$ B&B/INN 🏨 **The Bailey House.** This blissful B&B, in an immaculately restored Georgian home on North America's oldest streetscape, does everything right—and it's on the waterfront. **Pros:** only B&B in town on the water; comfy feather-topped beds; lovely garden. **Cons:** late check-in (4 pm); no air-conditioning. [$] *Rooms from: C$135* ✉ *150 St. George St.* ☎ *902/532–1285, 877/532–1285* 🌐 *www.baileyhouse.ca* 🛏 *4 rooms, 1 suite* 🍽 *Breakfast.*

$ B&B/INN 🏨 **Bread and Roses Inn.** This historic Queen Anne–style mansion in the heart of town retains many original architectural details, such as soaring windows and mahogany and black walnut moldings. **Pros:** stunning public areas; some rooms are über romantic; two rooms have river view. **Cons:** room sizes vary; third floor has only 2.5-meter (8-foot) ceilings. [$] *Rooms from: C$119* ✉ *82 Victoria St.* ☎ *902/532–5727, 888/899–0551 reservations only* 🌐 *www.breadandroses.ns.ca* 🛏 *9 rooms* ⏲ *Closed Nov.–Mar.* 🍽 *Breakfast.*

$ B&B/INN 🏨 **Hillsdale House Inn.** Princes, kings, and prime ministers have all visited this historic 1859 property, which is convenient to the town's attractions and restaurants yet shielded from the downtown bustle. **Pros:** pet-friendly; impeccably clean. **Cons:** some bathrooms have a shower but no tub; air-conditioning in third-floor and some second-floor rooms only. [$] *Rooms from: C$117* ✉ *519 George St.* ☎ *902/532–2345, 877/839–2821* 🌐 *www.hillsdalehouseinn.ca* 🛏 *13 rooms* 🍽 *Breakfast.*

$$ B&B/INN 🏨 **Queen Anne Inn.** A beautiful Victorian building that's rimmed with gardens may not be out of the ordinary in Annapolis Royal, but what really distinguishes this inn is the consistent quality of the guest rooms, all generously proportioned and handsomely decorated. **Pros:** family-friendly; in-room extras include fluffy bathrobes. **Cons:** dinner served Wednesday to Sunday only; inn closed off-season. [$] *Rooms from: C$129* ✉ *494 St. George St.* ☎ *902/532–7850, 877/536–0403* 🌐 *www.queenanneinn.ns.ca* 🛏 *10 rooms, 2 suites* ⏲ *Closed late Oct.–early May* 🍽 *Breakfast.*

2

NIGHTLIFE AND THE ARTS

King's Theatre. Drama, concerts, comedy, and independent films are among the offerings at this intimate but up-to-date venue that opened in 1921 as a movie house. ⌧ *209 St. George St., Chester* ☎ *902/532–7704* ⊕ *www.kingstheatre.ca.*

SHOPPING

Catfish Moon Studio. Whimsical earthenware made on-site is sold here, as well as fun local crafts and folk art. ⌧ *170 St. George St.* ☎ *902/532–3055, 888/378–3899* ⊕ *www.catfishmoon.com.*

Lucky Rabbit Pottery. Classic porcelain pieces decorated with contemporary designs are the specialty here. From October through April the shop is open by chance or by appointment. ⌧ *15 Church St.* ☎ *902/532–0928* ⊕ *www.luckyrabbitpottery.ca.*

WOLFVILLE

114 km (71 miles) east of Annapolis Royal.

Settled in the 1760s by New Englanders, Wolfville is a fetching college town with ornate Victorian homes (some of which have been converted into B&Bs), a lively arts scene, and several fine restaurants. The natural setting is impressive, too: after all, the fields here are fertile enough to support a thriving wine industry.

GETTING HERE AND AROUND

At the time of writing there is no public transportation to Wolfville, but Maritime Bus is planning to begin a daily service in the near future, with bus stops at Acadia University (Horton Avenue) and the Mud Creek Mini Mart (Skyway Avenue). ⇨ *See the Planning section for contact information.* The Evangeline Trail runs right through town, and Highway 101 runs along the southern edge—take Exit 10 or Exit 11.

ESSENTIALS

Visitor Information Wolfville Visitor Information Centre ⌧ *11 Willow Ave.* ☎ *902/542–7000, 877/999–7117* ⊕ *www.wolfville.ca* ☉ *May–Oct.*

EXPLORING

TOP ATTRACTIONS

Fodor'sChoice
★
Domaine de Grand Pré. With award-winning vintages and sigh-inducing Fundy views, a stop Domaine de Grand Pré is doubly pleasing. From May through October, vineyard tours and tastings are offered three times daily. They take about 45 minutes, but you'll likely want to linger on this picturesque 10-acre property, so plan to have a meal at Le Caveau Restaurant or sip a glass of wine under the pergola. ⌧ *11611 Hwy. 1, 3 km (2 miles) east of Wolfville* ☎ *902/542–1753, 866/479–4637* ⊕ *www.grandprewines.com* ☙ *Tour and tasting C$7* ☉ *Wine shop early Jan.–Apr., weekends noon–5; May–Oct., Mon.–Sat. 10–6, Sun. 11–6; Nov. and Dec., Wed.–Sun. 11–5. Restaurant Mar.–Oct., lunch and dinner; Nov. and Dec., Tues.–Sat. dinner only.*

Grand Pré National Historic Site. Added to UNESCO's list of World Heritage Sites in 2012, this site commemorates the expulsion of the Acadians by the British in 1755. The tragic story is retold at the visitor center through artifacts and an innovative multimedia presentation that depicts *Le Grand Dérangement* from both a civilian and military perspective. The latter is shown in a wraparound theater that's modeled on a ship's interior. A bronze statue of Evangeline, the title character of Longfellow's tear-jerking epic poem, stands outside a memorial stone church that contains Acadian genealogical records. The manicured grounds have a garden, a duck pond, and, appropriately enough, French weeping willows. ⊠ *Grand Pré Rd., off Hwy. 1 (Evangeline Trail) 5 km (3 miles) east of Wolfville, Grand Pré* ☎ *902/542–3631, 866/542–3631* ⊕ *www.grand-pre.com* ⊠ *C$7.80* ⊙ *Late June–early Sept., daily 9–5; mid-May–late June and early Sept.–mid-Oct., Tues.–Sat. 9–5; grounds open year-round.*

OFF THE BEATEN PATH

Hall's Harbour. You'll see one of the best natural harbors on the upper Bay of Fundy and some of the highest tides *anywhere* in Hall's Harbour, a small community about 30 km (18 miles) northwest of Wolfville via Kentville and Highway 359. Go for a walk on a gravel beach bordered by cliffs, try sea kayaking, or seek out the artisans whose studios open here during summer months. The small Red Fishhouse Museum, with local artifacts, is open in summer. ☎ *902/678–7001* ⊕ *www. hallsharbour.org.*

Hall's Harbour Lobster Pound & Restaurant. If you're in the neighborhood during lobster season, this site is well worth a visit. It's one of the largest lobster-holding facilities in Canada, storing live lobsters in temperature-controlled pounds until they can be packed and shipped to international destinations. ■ TIP→ **You can pick out a lobster and have it prepared in the "cook shack" and delivered to you in the waterfront dining room. Or buy a live one to go.** ⊠ *1157 West Halls Harbour Rd., Hall's Harbour* ☎ *902/679–5299* ⊕ *www.hallsharbourlobster.com* ⊙ *Mid-May–June, daily noon–7; July–Sept., daily 11:30–9.*

WORTH NOTING

Acadia University Art Gallery. Temporary exhibitions here are devoted to established and up-and-coming artists, and there's a permanent collection strong on Maritime and Inuit art, works on paper, and works by women artists. It amounts to more than 1,700 works, though not all are on display. ⊠ *Beveridge Arts Centre, 10 Highland Ave., at Main St.* ☎ *902/585–1373* ⊕ *gallery.acadiau.ca* ⊠ *Free* ⊙ *Tues.–Sun. noon–4.*

Harriet Irving Botanical Gardens. These 6-acre gardens are devoted mainly to indigenous plants from the Acadian Forest Region. Nine native habitats are displayed, and there's also a medicinal and food garden, a beautiful walled garden, and a conservatory. ⊠ *32 University Ave., entry through K.C. Irving Environmental Science Centre* ☎ *902/585–5242* ⊕ *botanicalgardens.acadiau.ca* ⊠ *Free* ⊙ *Daily dawn–dusk, weather permitting; conservatory 8 am–10 pm.*

Robie Tufts Nature Centre. Many Wolfvillians will tell you that the best show in town is watching swifts—aerobatic birds that fly in spectacular formation—descend on the Tuft center's oversized chimney at dusk on summer evenings. The venue is named in honor of the late ornithologist, author, and long-time resident who published *Birds of Nova Scotia* in 1961. The illustrated tome is still considered the bible for birders in the province, and he had lots of material to work with because Nova Scotia, being located on the Atlantic flyway, is an important staging point for migratory species. ■ TIP→ **The Nova Scotia Bird Society (902/852–2077, nsbs.chebucto.org) has information about birding here and elsewhere in the province.** ✉ *117 Front St.*

WHERE TO EAT AND STAY

For expanded hotel reviews, visit Fodors.com.

$$$$ MODERN CANADIAN 🍴 **Front and Central.** Chef David Smart has brought the small-plate dining concept to Wolfville, and each of his tiny tasters is a culinary gem. Scallops, for instance, might come with pea puree, shiitake mushrooms, pickled pearl onions, nasturtium, and crispy prosciutto; accompanying three ounces of fried buttermilk chicken might be pickled-peach puree, cornbread, blue-cheese dressing, watermelon radishes, pickled celery, and pea shoots. Portions are small, so if you arrive with a heavy appetite the cost can mount up before you feel full. Warm tones, contemporary furnishings, and original art on the walls lend the dining room an urban-chic feel. [$] *Average main: C$40* ✉ *117 Front St., at Central* ☎ *902/542–0588, 866/542–0588* 🌐 *www.frontandcentral.com* 🕓 *Closed Mon. and occasionally for private functions.*

$$ B&B/INN 🏨 **Blomidon Inn.** Teak and mahogany furnishings, marble fireplaces, Victorian-style wallpaper, and a painted ceiling mural all add to the ambience at this 1887 sea captain's mansion. **Pros:** complimentary afternoon tea; 14 rooms have Jacuzzis and propane fireplaces; the standalone Perth Cottage offers maximum privacy. **Cons:** dinner reservations recommended even for guests; room sizes vary; only a cold breakfast buffet. [$] *Rooms from: C$139* ✉ *195 Main St.* ☎ *902/542–2291, 800/565–2291* 🌐 *www.blomidon.ns.ca* 🛏 *26 rooms, 2 suites, 1 cottage, 4 apartments* 🍽 *Multiple meal plans.*

$ B&B/INN 🏨 **Farmhouse Inn Bed and Breakfast.** In a pleasant shipbuilding village amid lovely countryside, this 1860 B&B is perfect for outdoor enthusiasts. **Pros:** surrounded by good hiking country; open year-round. **Cons:** you have to pay in advance; removed from Wolfville's restaurants; two-night minimum on certain dates. [$] *Rooms from: C$119* ✉ *9757 Main St., 15 km (10 miles) north of Wolfville, Canning* ☎ *902/582–7900, 800/928–4346* 🌐 *www.farmhouseinn.ca* 🛏 *2 rooms, 4 suites* 🍽 *Breakfast.*

$$ B&B/INN 🏨 **Tattingstone Inn.** Set back from the street amid more than an acre of gardens, this inn has an interesting history and many exceptional features including the pool and the delightful conservatory, where delicious breakfasts are served. **Pros:** Jacuzzi tubs in some rooms; pleasant atmosphere; peaceful. **Cons:** a bit of a walk to downtown. [$] *Rooms from: C$128* ✉ *620 Main St.* ☎ *902/542–7696, 800/565–7696* 🌐 *www.tattingstone.ns.ca* 🛏 *9 rooms* 🍽 *Breakfast.*

$ B&B/INN 🏨 **Victoria's Historic Inn & Carriage House.** A 2.5-meter (8-foot) stained-glass window imported from Britain more than a century ago sets the decorative mood at this elegant 1893 mansion. **Pros:** some rooms have fireplaces, balconies, or both; friendly, efficient staff. **Cons:** a few rooms are overdecorated. [$] *Rooms from: C$109* ✉ *600 Main St.* ☎ *902/542–5744, 800/556–5744* 🌐 *www.victoriashistoricinn.com* 🛏 *15 rooms, 1 suite* 🍽 *Breakfast.*

SPORTS AND THE OUTDOORS

Blomidon Provincial Park. This park on the shores of the Minas Basin has four main trails that collectively cover 14 km (9 miles). The beach is accessible at low tide, but be sure to check the tide tables; the water comes back in quite rapidly. ■**TIP**➔ **The 1.6-km (1-mile) Lookoff Trail yields especially fine cliff-top vistas.** ✉ *3138 Pereau Rd., off Hwy. 101, 31 km (19 miles) north of Wolfville, Cape Blomidon* ☎ *902/582–7319* ⊕ *www.novascotiaparks.ca* ✉ *No charge for day use* ⊙ *Mid-May– early Sept.*

WINDSOR

25 km (16 miles) southeast of Wolfville.

Windsor has much in common with Bridgewater on the South Shore in that both are historic towns that have evolved into regional service centers. One marker of Windsor's history is King's-Edgehill School. Founded in 1788, it is the oldest independent school in the British Commonwealth. The countryside around Windsor is pretty, particularly in autumn, and Haligonians often make the 66-km (41-mile) drive to the "Gateway of the Annapolis Valley" for its Pumpkin Festival.

GETTING HERE AND AROUND

When driving from east or west, take Exit 6 off Highway 101.

ESSENTIALS

Visitor Information Windsor Visitor Information Centre ✉ *Colonial Rd., north off Hwy. 101, Exit 6* ☎ *902/798–2690* ⊙ *Mid-May–mid-Oct.*

EXPLORING

TOP ATTRACTIONS

Haliburton House Museum. This was once home to Judge Thomas Chandler Haliburton (1796–1865), a lawyer, politician, historian, and, above all, humorist. Hugely popular in his own day, Haliburton inspired Mark Twain and put Nova Scotia on the literary map. Thomas Haliburton is also remembered for making the first recorded reference to hockey—the sport that was "born" here in the early 1800s. Fittingly, the **Windsor Hockey Heritage Centre** (☎ *902/798–1800,* ⊕ *www. birthplaceofhockey.com/museum*) resides at Haliburton House, and several rooms contain items from the collection. These include antique skates, hand-carved sticks, wooden pucks, trophies, team uniforms, and photographs. ✉ *414 Clifton Ave.* ☎ *902/798–2915* ⊕ *haliburton-house.novascotia.ca* ✉ *C$4, includes Windsor Hockey Heritage Centre* ⊙ *June–early Oct., Mon.–Sat. 10–5, Sun. 1–5.*

FAMILY   **Mermaid Theatre of Nova Scotia.** Puppets and performers retell classic and contemporary children's stories here. The troupe's home base is the 400-seat MIPAC (Mermaid Imperial Performing Arts Centre) adjacent to its Gerrish Street headquarters, but catching a show can be tricky because of the hectic worldwide touring schedule. If you can't time your trip to coincide with a play date, you can still marvel at Mermaid's props and puppets, as several floors filled with them are open for public viewing. ✉ *132 Gerrish St.* ☎ *902/798–5841* ⊕ *www.mermaidtheatre.ns.ca* ✉ *By donation* ⊙ *Year-round, weekdays 9–4.*

OFF THE BEATEN PATH

Uniacke Estate Museum Park. This country mansion was built in about 1815 for Richard John Uniacke, attorney general and advocate general to the Admiralty court during the War of 1812. Now a provincial museum, the Georgian-style house is preserved in its original condition, right down to the antique furnishings. Seven walking trails wend through the large lakeside property. There are picnic tables and a small tearoom on-site. ⚠ **The access road is gated, and the gates are locked at dusk.** ✉ *758 Hwy. 1, 30 km (19 miles) east of Windsor, Mt. Uniacke* ☎ *902/866–0032* 🌐 *uniacke.novascotia.ca* 🎫 *Museum C$4* 🕒 *June–early Oct., Mon.–Sat. 9:30–5, Sun. 11–5.*

WORTH NOTING

Fort Edward. Despite a devastating fire in 1897, some evidence of Windsor's earliest days remains at Fort Edward, which, dating from 1750, is the oldest blockhouse in Canada. ✉ *Fort Edward St.* ☎ *902/532–2321, 902/798–4706* 🌐 *www.pc.gc.ca.*

Sainte Famille Winery. Visits to the family-owned Sainte Famille Winery in Falmouth, 5 km (3 miles) west of Windsor, combine ecological history with the intricacies of growing grapes and aging wine. Tasting is done in the gift shop, where bottles are sold at bargain prices. The best time to come is at the end of the season when Sainte Famille hosts its annual Harvest Wine Fest. The one-day event features food, entertainment, and a competitive Grape Stomp. Even the kids' category is hotly contested. ✉ *11 Dudley Park La.* ☎ *902/798–8311, 800/565–0993* 🌐 *www.st-famille.com* 🎫 *Tours and tastings C$3.50–C$8.50* 🕒 *Tours June–Sept., daily at 10 and 2. Shop Mon.–Sat. 9–5 (also Sun. noon–5 Apr.–Dec.).*

WHERE TO EAT AND STAY

$$ ECLECTIC

🍴 **Cocoa Pesto Bistro.** A warm welcome and elegant surroundings provide a great first impression here, but it's the delicious, fresh, *and* health-conscious cuisine that lingers in memory. The menu changes seasonally, but might include pecan-crusted salmon or sweet- and dry-rub pork ribs straight from an apple-wood smoker. The bistro's rooms have a minimalist look that nicely balances the heritage building's original architectural features, and a patio provides outside dining in summer. [$] *Average main: C$14* ✉ *494 King St.* ☎ *902/472–3300* 🌐 *www.cocoapesto.com* 🕒 *No lunch; no brunch weekdays.*

$ B&B/INN

🏨 **Clockmakers Inn.** A distinctive 1894 building houses this appealing inn on the Evangeline Trail, just outside downtown, that provides a range of services and room styles. **Pros:** family-friendly; garden playground; two bicycles available for guest use. **Cons:** no elevator, though staff will help with luggage. [$] *Rooms from: C$119* ✉ *1399 King St.* ☎ *902/792–2573, 866/778–3600* 🌐 *www.theclockmakersinn.com* 🛏 *8 rooms* 🍽 *Breakfast.*

THE EASTERN SHORE AND NORTHERN NOVA SCOTIA

From the rugged Atlantic coastline to the wave-ravaged rim of the Bay of Fundy and the gentle shores of Northumberland Strait, the area east and north of Halifax is characterized by contrasts. The road toward Cape Breton meanders past thinly populated fishing villages and thick forests, whereas attractive towns and sandy beaches border Northumberland Strait. The Fundy Shore, meanwhile, scores points for dramatic scenery—expect steep cliffs harboring prehistoric fossils and intense tides that draw back to reveal the muddy sea floor.

This region has three excellent driving routes. The 316-km (196-mile) Sunrise Trail wends its way along Northumberland Strait, from the wild Tantramar Marsh in Amherst (on the New Brunswick border) to the thriving college town of Antigonish. The 315-km (195-mile) Marine Drive travels through romantic seaside villages and the living-history museum in Sherbrooke. Highlights on the 365-km (226-mile) Glooscap Trail include a majestic lighthouse at Cape d'Or and the notable fossil finds in Joggins. Any one leg could be done comfortably in two days from Halifax with a single overnight along the way.

SHERBROOKE AND SHERBROOKE VILLAGE

187 km (122 miles) northeast of Halifax.

Established by the French in the middle of the 17th century, this little town prospered briefly on the back of a gold rush in the late 19th century, and it's something of a thrill to know that 80% of Sherbrooke's gold is still buried underfoot. Today, however, it's better known for the Atlantic salmon that rush up St. Mary's River (though you can't fish for them) and for the excellent Sherbrooke Village open-air museum. The town makes a good base for exploring the rugged coastline.

GETTING HERE AND AROUND

There's no public transportation to Sherbrooke. From Halifax, drive east on Highway 107, then Trunk 7 E, via Musquodoboit Harbour and Sheet Harbour. If you're coming from the Northumberland Shore, head for New Glasgow and take Highway 347 south, turning onto Trunk 7 W for the last 20 km (12 miles) or so.

EXPLORING

FAMILY

Fodor'sChoice

★

Sherbrooke Village. Most visitors come to Sherbrooke to see this living-history museum, set within the contemporary town. It contains more than two dozen restored buildings (including an operating water-powered sawmill) that re-create life during the town's heyday. Between 1860 and 1914, this was a prime shipbuilding, lumbering, and gold-rush center. These days, costumed interpreters and artisans recapture the bustle by demonstrating blacksmithing, weaving, wood turning, soap making, and similar skills. Special events, such as old-fashioned Christmas and courthouse concerts, are held throughout the year. ⊠ *42 Main St., Hwy. 7, Sherbrooke* ☎ *902/522–2400, 888/743–7845* ⊕ *sherbrookevillage. novascotia.ca* ⊡ *C$10.75* ⊙ *June–late Sept., daily 9:30–5; Christmas celebrations last weekend in Nov.*

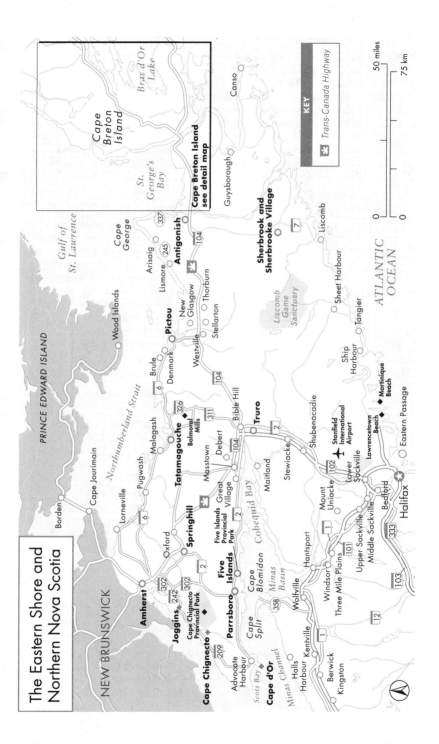

The Eastern Shore and Northern Nova Scotia

PRINCE EDWARD ISLAND

NEW BRUNSWICK

Gulf of St. Laurence

Northumberland Strait

Bras d'Or Lake

Cape Breton Island

St. George's Bay

Cape Breton Island see detail map

KEY

✈ Trans-Canada Highway

ATLANTIC OCEAN

Wood Islands

Borden

Cape Jourimain

Lorneville

Pugwash

Oxford

Malagash

Brule

Denmark

Cape George

Arisaig

Lismore

245

Pictou

New Glasgow

Westville

Stellarton

Thorburn

337

Antigonish

104

Guysborough

Canso

Sherbrook and Sherbrooke Village

7

Liscomb

Liscomb Game Sanctuary

Sheet Harbour

Tangier

Ship Harbour

Amherst

302

242

302

2

Springhill

Joggins

Cape Chignecto Provincial Park

Cape Chignecto

209

Advocate Harbour

Halls Harbour

Scots Bay

Minas Channel

Cape d'Or

Parrsboro

Five Islands

Cape Split

Cape Blomidon

Minas Basin

Five Islands Provincial Park

Great Village

Tatamagouche

326

Balmoral Mills

Masstown

Debert

311

Bible Hill

Truro

104

2

104

Cobequid Bay

Maitland

Shubenacadie

Stewiacke

Mount Uniacke

Stanfield International Airport

✈

102

Lower Sackville

Upper Sackville

Middle Sackville

Bedford

333

Halifax

103

12

Berwick

Kingston

Kentville

Wolfville

Hantsport

Windsor

Three Mile Plains

358

1

101

Lawrencetown Beach

◆ Martinique Beach

Eastern Passage

6

6

2

50 miles

75 km

BEACHES

OFF THE BEATEN PATH

Port Bickerton Lighthouse Beach Park. Hiking trails and a boardwalk lead to a sandy beach here, but the park's main attraction is its two lighthouses, which share the lofty bluff above. One is still working; the other, built in the early 1920s, houses the Nova Scotia Lighthouse Interpretive Centre, which recounts the history, lore, and vital importance of the province's lights. **Amenities:** parking (free); toilets. **Best for:** walking. ✉ *640 Lighthouse Rd., off Hwy 211, about 32 km (20 miles) east of Sherbrooke, Port Bickerton* 🌐 *www.portbickertonlighthouse.ca* 🎫 *Beach free, lighthouse site C$3* 🕒 *Beach daily, lighthouse site mid-June–mid-Sept., daily 9–5.*

WHERE TO STAY

For expanded hotel reviews, visit Fodors.com.

$$ RESORT FAMILY

🏨 **Liscombe Lodge Resort.** In a superb natural setting, with a choice of lodge rooms or secluded chalets and cottages, this place pairs an away-from-it-all location with a wide range of activities. **Pros:** fun packages and free experiential programs; Camp Adventure and other activities for kids; complimentary use of boats. **Cons:** rooms could use a redo; better suited to families than singles; large wedding parties can sometimes affect the atmosphere. [$] *Rooms from: C$165* ✉ *2884 Hwy. 7, 27 km (17 miles) southwest of Sherbrooke on Hwy. 7, Liscomb Mills* ☎ *902/779–2307, 800/665–6343* 🌐 *www.liscombelodge.ca* 🛏 *29 rooms, 1 suite, 38 cottages* 🕒 *Closed mid-Oct.–Apr.* 🍴 *Multiple meal plans.*

ANTIGONISH

61 km (38 miles) north of Sherbrooke; 115 km (71 miles) east of Truro; 55 km (34 miles) west of the Canso Causeway.

Pretty Antigonish, on the main route to Cape Breton Island, is home to St. Francis Xavier University, a center for Gaelic studies and the first coeducational Catholic institution to graduate women. The campus also has several cultural attractions.

GETTING HERE AND AROUND

At the time of writing there's no public transportation to Antigonish, but Maritime Bus is planning to establish a daily route, so it's worth checking to see if this has happened. ⇨ *See Planning section for contact information.* Driving couldn't be easier—the town is right on the Trans-Canada Highway (Highway 104). Coming up from Sherbrooke, you'd need Nova Scotia Trunk 7 E.

ESSENTIALS

Visitor Information **Antigonish Visitor Information Centre** ✉ *Antigonish Mall Complex, Church St., off Hwy. 104, Exit 33 N* ☎ *902/863–4921* 🌐 *antigonishcounty.ns.ca/vic.htm* 🕒 *May–Sept.*

EXPLORING

art gallery. St. Francis Xavier University's campus art gallery mounts a dozen exhibits of mostly contemporary works each year and hosts talks with regional and other artists. ✉ *Bloomfield Centre 103, West St., off Hwy. 104* ☎ *902/863–3300* 🌐 *sites.stfx.ca/artgallery.*

Surf's Up Down East

Being sparsely developed, the Eastern Shore—which starts on the fringes of Halifax and covers more than 200 km (125 miles) of coast—has few residents and even fewer tourist attractions. But, oh boy, does it have beaches! Two of the best are Lawrencetown and Martinique. About 27 km (17 miles) and 57 km (35 miles), respectively, from downtown Halifax, both strands are designated provincial parks and have lifeguards on duty in season to supervise swimming. Yet it's not so much swimmers as surfers that these beautiful, wave-blasted beaches attract.

Summer is prime time here, especially when north-tracking hurricanes churn up the Atlantic, so if you've already got surf gear all you have to do before hitting the water is check the local surf forecast at ⊕ *magicseaweed.com*. Otherwise, there are several outfitters who rent or sell boards and wet suits (you'll want a suit because the water is cold).

Happy Dudes Surf Emporium (☎ *902/827–4962* ⊕ *www.happydudes.ca*) has two locations—one at Martinique (✉ *2137 E. Petpeswick Rd., East Petpeswick*) and the other 3 km (2 miles) east of Lawrencetown Beach

(✉ *4891 Hwy. 207, Three Fathom Harbour*). In addition, a mobile outlet is typically parked right at Lawrencetown when the surf is up. Groups of three or more can get 3½ hours of lessons for C$50 per person, plus equipment rental; private lessons cost C$120 per person, or C$60 each for two people.

Also close to Lawrencetown Beach is the **Kannon Beach Surf Shop** (✉ *4144 Lawrencetown Rd., East Lawrencetown* ☎ *902/471–0025* ⊕ *www.kannonbeach.com*). The shop, in the basement of MacDonald House, also offers lessons, with equipment included, starting at C$95—and you get to keep the equipment for the rest of the day. Rentals cost C$40 per day for a board and a wet suit, including boots and gloves.

At the same location as Kannon, **One Life Surf School** (☎ *902/880–7873* ⊕ *www.onelifesurf.com*) is run by—but not exclusively for—women. Lessons start at C$70 per person for groups or C$100 for an individual. Equipment is included.

For more information and event listings, visit the website for the Surfing Association of Nova Scotia (⊕ *www.surfns.com*).

Bauer Theatre. During the school year, the Bauer is home to Theatre Antigonish, a nonprofit community company that presents classic and contemporary works. ✉ *St. Francis Xavier University, West St., off Hwy. 104* ☎ *902/867–3333* ⊕ *sites.stfx.ca/theatreantigonish*.

WHERE TO EAT AND STAY
For expanded hotel reviews, visit Fodors.com.

$$
ECLECTIC
FAMILY

✕**Gabrieau's Bistro.** Gabrieau's has earned a place in Antigonish hearts with its pleasant interior and an epicurean yet affordable menu that includes seafood, pasta, gourmet pizzas, and various vegetarian dishes. There are luscious desserts, and the wine list impresses, too. If the weather is nice, take a seat on the sunny patio and watch the town go by. To learn how to duplicate your favorite dish, you can take one of the public cooking classes conducted in the separate, open-kitchen Hawthorne Room. $ *Average main: C$20* ✉ *350 Main St.* ☎ *902/863–1925* ⊕ *www.gabrieaus.com* ⊙ *Closed Sun. No lunch Sat.*

$$

B&B/INN

▦ **Antigonish Victorian Inn.** Turn-of-the-century Victorian style—but with modern amenities—reigns at this beautifully restored turreted mansion. **Pros:** just a short walk from the town center; open year-round; delicious hot breakfast. **Cons:** not all options have en suite bathrooms; room size varies widely. $ *Rooms from: C$130* ✉ *149 Main St.* ☎ *902/863–1103, 800/706–5558* ⊕ *www.antigonishvictorianinn.ca* ⤳ *10 rooms, 2 apartments* ❧ *Breakfast.*

SPORTS AND THE OUTDOORS

Antigonish Landing Trail. A 4.8-km (3-mile) walking trail along the shoreline of Antigonish Harbour borders a large tidal marsh and wildlife sanctuary teeming with ospreys, bald eagles, and other birds. ■**TIP➜ To find the trailhead, park at the Antigonish Heritage Museum, on East Main Street, then cross the railroad tracks and bear right on Adam Street.** ✉ *Trailhead at end of Adam St.*

SHOPPING

Lyghtesome Gallery. The gallery sells paintings, sculptures, prints, drawings, and other works by Nova Scotian artists, at reasonable prices. ✉ *166 Main St.* ☎ *902/863–5804* ⊕ *www.lyghtesome.ns.ca.*

The Made in Nova Scotia Store. For the town's most comprehensive selection of crafts, natural products, and incredible edibles, drop by this store, which represents more than 100 regional artisans. ✉ *324 Main St.* ☎ *902/867–2642* ⊕ *www.themadeinnovascotiastore.com.*

PICTOU

74 km (46 miles) northwest of Antigonish; 66 km (41 miles) northeast of Truro.

Many people come to Pictou for the sole purpose of catching the ferry onward to Prince Edward Island (it departs from Caribou, just minutes away), but the town itself is lovely, with a revitalized waterfront centered on a very different vessel. In 1773 an aging cargo ship named the *Hector* arrived here carrying the initial load of Scottish Highlanders, making Pictou "The Birthplace of New Scotland." Each year in mid-August, the quay is the focal point for the weekend-long **Hector Festival,** which celebrates the Scots' arrival. Held in early July to mark the close of this region's fishing season, the raucous **Pictou Lobster Carnival** features lobster-boat races, trap-hauling contests, and, of course, a chance to eat the tasty crustaceans.

GETTING HERE AND AROUND

The Wood Islands Ferry from Prince Edward Island will land you in Pictou, but that's the only public transportation there is. The ferry runs from May through late December, with a minimum of three sailings a day, and up to nine in peak season. The fare for a vehicle, including passengers, is C$67.50; walk-on passengers pay C$17. Driving to Pictou is via the Trans-Canada Highway (Highway 104), branching onto Highway 106 for the last stretch.

ESSENTIALS

Visitor Information **Pictou Visitor Information Centre** ✉ *350 West River Rd., at Rotary Club of Pictou* ☎ *902/485–7044* 🕓 *May–mid-Dec.*

EXPLORING

Hector Heritage Quay. A 34-meter (110-foot) fully rigged replica of the *Hector* is moored here, and you can sometimes see maintenance work in progress. The handsome post-and-beam interpretive center recounts the story of the first hardy pioneers (33 families plus 25 unmarried men) who arrived aboard the original vessel in 1773, and the flood of Scots who followed them. The site also has working blacksmith, rigger, and carpentry shops. ✉ *33 Caladh Ave.* ☎ *902/485–4371* 🌐 *shiphector.com* 🎟 *C$7* 🕓 *Mid-May–June and Sept.–mid-Oct., daily 11–5; July and Aug., daily 9–7.*

Nova Scotia Museum of Industry. Your own job may be the last thing you want to think about while vacationing, but if you're curious about those the industrious locals have traditionally held, Stellarton, just 20 km (12 miles) from Pictou, is worth a detour for this museum that brings our industrial heritage to life. Like factory and mine workers of old, you can punch in with a time card and then get straight to work. Hands-on exhibits will show you how to hook a rag mat, print a bookmark, operate a steam engine, or pack chocolates into a moving box on an assembly line. Interactive computer exhibits explore multimedia as a tool of industry, and some 30,000 industrial artifacts are on display, including Canada's oldest steam locomotives. ✉ *147 N. Foord St., off Hwy. 104, Exit 24* ☎ *902/755–5425* 🌐 *museumofindustry.novascotia.ca* 🎟 *C$8.65* 🕓 *May and June, Mon.–Sat. 9–5, Sun. 1–5; July–Oct., Mon.–Sat. 9–5, Sun. 10–5; Nov.–Apr., weekdays 9–5.*

BEACHES

Melmerby Beach Provincial Park. One of Nova Scotia's most popular beaches, Melmerby has a boardwalk and some of the warmest water north of the Carolinas. Beaches straddle both the inner and outer edges of this horseshoe of land, the inner portion a glorious stretch of white sand. Swimming is safe here unless winds are high, when strong currents develop. The supervised area (in July and August) is clearly marked. ⚠ **Beware of poison ivy in the sand dunes and, between mid-July and early August, jellyfish in the water.** **Amenities:** food and drink; lifeguards; parking; showers; toilets. **Best for:** swimming. ✉ *6380 Little Harbour Rd., about 30 km (18 miles) east of Pictou* 🌐 *www.parks.gov.ns.ca.*

WHERE TO STAY

For expanded hotel reviews, visit Fodors.com.

$ B&B/INN 🏨 **Auberge Walker Inn.** A registered Heritage Property built in the 1860s, this centrally located inn is a block from the waterfront. **Pros:** some rooms have water views; suite has kitchenette and private entry. **Cons:** lots of stairs but no elevator; only a cold breakfast buffet included. [$] *Rooms from: C$89* ✉ *78 Coleraine St.* ☎ *902/485–1433, 800/370–5553* 🌐 *www.walkerinn.com* 🛏 *10 rooms, 1 suite* 🕓 *Closed mid-Nov.–mid-May* 🍴 *Breakfast.*

NIGHTLIFE AND THE ARTS

DeCoste Entertainment Centre. The center presents a summer-long program of concerts, pipe bands, Highland dancing, and ceilidhs with Gaelic music and dance. Past headliners have included acts ranging from k.d. lang to the Scottish Symphony Orchestra. ⊠ *85 Water St.* ☎ *902/485–8848, 800/353–5338* ⊕ *decostecentre.ca.*

SHOPPING

Grohmann Knives. You can see handcrafted Grohmann knives displayed at the Museum of Modern Art in New York—but you can buy them at the factory outlet store here. Prices are discounted and free factory tours usually take place on weekdays from 9 to 11:30 and 1:30 to 3:30. ⊠ *116 Water St.* ☎ *902/485–4224, 888/756–4837* ⊕ *www. grohmannknives.com.*

Pictou County Weekend Market. Craftspeople sell quality goods at this lively waterfront market that takes place on weekends between 10 and 5 from mid-June through mid-September. ⊠ *66 Caladh Ave.* ☎ *902/485–6329* ⊕ *www.pictouweekendmarket.com.*

Water Street Studios. This artisans' co-op sells hand-dyed and natural yarns, felted woolen items, and knits, along with weaving, blankets, pottery, stained glass, jewelry, and woodwork. ⊠ *110 Water St.* ☎ *902/485–8398.*

SPORTS AND THE OUTDOORS

Jitney Trail. The Jitney is a 5-km (3-mile) water's-edge route around Pictou Harbour that puts you in sight of marine life and working wharves. Hikers and bikers frequent it. ⊕ *www.trails.gov.ns.ca.*

Pictou Island Charters. The charter company operates ferry service (C$5) between Caribou and Pictou Island and conducts six-hour, tip-to-tip vehicle tours (C$50) of the island on Thursday and Friday in July and August. ☎ *902/921–1033, 902/497–5974 tour reservations* ⊕ *www. pictouislandcharters.ca.*

TATAMAGOUCHE

54 km (33½ miles) west of Pictou.

Though it only has about a thousand residents, tiny Tatamagouche is a force to be reckoned with. Canada's second-largest Oktoberfest (☎ *800/895–1177* ⊕ *www.nsoktoberfest.ca*)—a boisterous event complete with sausages, schnitzel, and frothy steins of beer—takes place here each fall. Summer brings strawberry and blueberry festivals, lobster, and chowder suppers. Within a 10-minute drive of Tatamagouche you have the opportunity to visit two historic mills.

GETTING HERE AND AROUND

There is no public transportation to Tatamagouche. If you're driving on the Trans-Canada Highway (Highway 104), go north at Truro via Highway 311; heading west from Pictou or east from Amherst, Highway 6 along the coast is the way to go.

EXPLORING

Balmoral Grist Mill. Built in 1874, this is one of the few water-powered mills still operating in Nova Scotia, now serving as the centerpiece of a small museum. You can observe flour-milling demonstrations and walk the site's 1-km (½-mile) trail. ⊠ *660 Matheson Brook Rd., 14 km (8½ miles) southeast of Tatamagouche via Hwy. 311, Balmoral Mills* ☎ *902/657–3016, 902/424–7398* ⊕ *balmoralgristmill. novascotia.ca* 🖾 *C$4* ⊙ *June–early Oct., Tues.–Sat. 10–5, Sun. 1–5.*

Jost Vineyards. The Jost winery produces wines from an astonishing number of varietals, consistently winning awards for its ice wine, a sweet affair made from grapes left on the vines until frost has "iced" them. You can taste wines year-round at the store here, and take winery tours from mid-June to mid-September. ⊠ *48 Vintage La., 17 km (11 miles) northwest of Tatamagouche via Hwy. 311, Malagash* ☎ *902/257–2636, 800/565–4567* ⊕ *www. jostwine.com* 🖾 *Tours and tastings free* ⊙ *Store mid-June–mid-Sept., daily 9–6, mid-Sept.–mid-June, daily 9–5. Tours mid-June–mid-Sept., daily at noon and 3.*

Margaret Fawcett Norrie Heritage Centre. Creamery Square is the hub of activity in Tatamagouche, and this waterfront heritage center recently developed on the square has gathered together several museums that were previously dotted around town. Located in a former dairy facility, the center appropriately includes the **Creamery Museum,** with butter-making equipment and related displays. The **Sunrise Trail Museum** traces Tatamagouche's Mi'Kmaq, Acadian, French, and Scottish roots through interactive displays. The **Anna Swan Museum** relates the story of local giantess Anna Swan (1846–88), who grew to the height of 7 feet 11½ inches. Finally, the **Brule Fossil Centre** preserves 290-million-year-old fossil tracks that were discovered nearby in 1994. Demonstrations on boatbuilding and butter making are regularly staged. This is also the site of a Saturday-morning farmers' market from February through December. ⊠ *39 Creamery Rd.* ☎ *902/657–3449* ⊕ *www. creamerysquare.ca* 🖾 *C$5, free Sat. 9–10 am* ⊙ *Mid-May–mid-Oct., Sun.–Fri. 10–6, Sat. 9–6.*

The Sutherland Steam Mill Museum. Dating from 1894, this mill participated in the transition from water to steam power. Steam engines allowed greater flexibility about location—mills no longer *had* to be near a river or other water source—and provided more raw power to run factory machinery. Workers at the Sutherland mill manufactured useful items ranging from carriages and sleds to old-time wooden bathtubs. Interesting demonstrations and hands-on activities take place in

---

THE GIANT ANNA SWAN

Anna Swan, born near Tatamagouche in 1846, weighed 18 pounds and was 27 inches long at birth, was 4 feet 6 inches when she was four years old, and 6 feet 2 inches by the time she was 10. The supersized Swan joined P. T. Barnum's museum when she was 7 feet 2 inches, but continued to grow for several more years until she reached her full height of 7 feet 11½ inches. She married another famously tall person: Martin Van Buren Bates, who is believed to have been at least 7 feet 9 inches tall.

July and August. ✉ *3169 Denmark Station Rd., off Hwy. 326, Denmark* ☎ *902/657–3365* ⊕ *sutherlandsteammill.novascotia.ca* ⊡ *C$4* ⊙ *June–early Oct., Tues.–Sat. 10–5, Sun. 1–5.*

WHERE TO STAY

For expanded hotel reviews, visit Fodors.com.

$$
B&B/INN
🚂 **Train Station Inn.** Guests at this ingeniously restored inn can sleep in an 1887 train station or one of nine beautifully converted cabooses parked on the tracks outside. **Pros:** the Trans-Canada Trail runs alongside the property; close to the water; memorable gift shop. **Cons:** air-conditioning in railcars only; often booked well in advance. $ *Rooms from: C$130* ✉ *21 Station Rd.* ☎ *902/657–3222, 888/724–5233* ⊕ *www.trainstation. ca* ⇥ *9 rooms, 1 suite* ⊙ *Closed Nov.–Apr.* ⦿ *Multiple meal plans.*

SPORTS AND THE OUTDOORS

The Butter Trail. Named for the creamery it backs onto, this is part of the Trans-Canada Trail system. The 26-km (16-mile) multiuse path follows the reclaimed rail bed that the Train Station Inn's cabooses once traversed. ⊕ *www.trails.gov.ns.ca.*

SHOPPING

Sara Bonnyman Pottery. Here you can watch the shop's namesake potter herself at work. The studio is open daily (except Sunday) in July and August, and informal tours are given in the afternoons. The rest of the year, the gallery is open by appointment and by chance. Visitors are also welcome to explore the large gardens. ✉ *Hwy. 246, RR 2, 326 Maple Ave. (Hwy. 246), 1.5 km (1 mile) uphill from post office* ☎ *902/657–3215* ⊕ *www.sarabonnymanpottery.com.*

SPRINGHILL

75 km (46½ miles) west of Tatamagouche.

If you're not going to be visiting Cape Breton, Springhill (on Highway 2) is worth a stop because it gives you a second chance to sample Nova Scotia's music-and-mining combo. This town was both the birthplace of acclaimed songstress Anne Murray and, before that, home to the ill-fated coal mine immortalized in "The Ballad of Springhill" (aka "Springhill Mining Disaster") by Peggy Seeger and Ewen McColl.

GETTING HERE AND AROUND

There is no public transportation to Springhill. By road, it's just west of the Trans-Canada Highway (Highway 104) between Oxford and Amherst; take Exit 5 onto Highway 142.

EXPLORING

Anne Murray Centre. The likable Springhill-born, part-Acadian pop singer spread her tiny wings and flew away to worldwide fame and fortune, but she still celebrates her roots—and her hometown pays tribute to her illustrious career—at this repository of costumes, gold records, photographs, and other artifacts. ■TIP➔ **Diehard fans can record a (virtual) duet with Murray, providing instant bragging rights to having performed with a partner who has sold more than 50 million records to date.** ✉ *36 Main St.* ☎ *902/597–8614* ⊕ *www.annemurraycentre.com* ⊡ *C$7* ⊙ *Mid-May–mid-Oct., daily 9–4:30.*

Springhill Miners Museum. The site of several tragedies, the Springhill coalfield gained international attention in 1958 when an earthquake created a "bump" that trapped mineworkers underground (75 of them died), but today at this museum you can descend into a mine under safer circumstances. Some of the guides are retired miners who provide firsthand accounts of their working days. Children under five are not admitted. ⊠ *145 Black River Rd., off Hwy. 2* ☎ *902/597–3449* ⌨ *C$7* ⊗ *Mid-May–mid-Oct., daily 9–5.*

AMHERST

33 km (21 miles) northwest of Springhill.

Amherst is a quaint, quiet town with a central location, but from the mid-1800s to the early 1900s it was a bustling center of industry and influence. From Amherst, Nova Scotia's Sunrise Trail heads toward Northumberland Strait, and the Glooscap Trail runs west through fossil country. Amherst is a mere 7 km (4 miles) from New Brunswick and 55 km (34 miles) from the Confederation Bridge, which connects the Maritime mainland to Prince Edward Island.

GETTING HERE AND AROUND

Maritime Bus provides daily service from Halifax to Amherst, where the bus stop is at the Circle K on South Albion Street. It takes a little over three hours and the fare is C$38.75 one way. Maritime also operates bus service from Fredericton (C$46; four hours) and Moncton (C$14.25; one hour). Amherst is on the Trans-Canada Highway (Highway 104), just south of the Nova Scotia–New Brunswick border; take Exit 3 or Exit 4. The town itself has no public transit system.

ESSENTIALS

Visitor Information Amherst Visitor Information Centre ⊠ *90 Cumberland Loop* ☎ *902/667–0787* ⊕ *www.amherst.ca/visitors.*

EXPLORING

Joggins Fossil Centre. On the Glooscap Trail, 35 km (22 miles) southwest of Amherst and 70 km (43 miles) northeast of Cape Chignecto, Joggins is famous for Coal Age fossils that were embedded in sandstone, then uncovered through erosion caused by Fundy's surging tides. You can spy them outside, in the sea cliffs, or inside the center. Opened in 2008—the same year Joggins was named a UNESCO World Heritage Site—this striking museum has a large, well-curated collection of specimens dating back some 300 million years, along with interesting displays outlining the region's geological and archaeological history. ■ **TIP→ The admission fee includes a half-hour guided beach tour; two-hour guided cliffs tours take place daily in peak months; and an in-depth four-hour tour occurs monthly.** ⊠ *100 Main St., Joggins* ☎ *902/251–2727, 888/932–9766* ⊕ *www.jogginsfossilcliffs.net* ⌨ *C$10.50, includes a 30-minute tour of the beach; C$25, includes 1½–2-hr tour (reservations essential); C$55, includes 4-hr guided tour and lunch (reservations essential)* ⊗ *Late Apr., May, Sept., and Oct., daily 10–4; June–Aug., daily 9:30–5:30; rest of yr by appointment.*

Tantramar Marshes. Spanning the Nova Scotia–New Brunswick border, the Tantramar Marshes stretch from Amherst up to Sackville and are alive with incredible birdlife and other wildlife. The name comes from the French *tintamarre* (meaning din or hubbub) because of the racket made by vast flocks of wildfowl. Said to be the world's largest marsh, the Tantramar is a migratory route for hundreds of thousands of birds and a breeding ground for more than 100 species.

WHERE TO STAY

For expanded hotel reviews, visit Fodors.com.

$ B&B/INN **Amherst Shore Country Inn.** With a 183-meter (600-foot) private beach and 20 acres of lawns and gardens overlooking Northumberland Strait, this inn on the Sunrise Trail Coastal Route has an interesting range of lodging options. **Pros:** tranquil location; outstanding dining; friendly hosts. **Cons:** most accommodations are away from the inn; breakfast is not included. [$] *Rooms from: C$109* ✉ *Hwy. 366 (Tyndal Rd.), 32 km (20 miles) northeast of Amherst, Lorneville* ☎ *902/661–4800, 800/661–2724* 🌐 *www.ascinn.ns.ca* 🛏 *4 rooms, 4 suites, 3 cottages* 🕒 *Closed weekdays Nov.–May* 🍴 *No meals.*

$$ B&B/INN **The Regent Bed & Breakfast.** Set peacefully back from the street, this picturesque 1898 Georgian house stands out for its grandeur, and the hosts are extremely welcoming and helpful. **Pros:** open year-round; luxurious linens; innkeepers will take guests sightseeing upon request. **Cons:** there's not that much to see in Amherst. [$] *Rooms from: C$120* ✉ *175 E. Victoria St.* ☎ *902/667–7676, 866/661–2861* 🌐 *www.theregent.ca* 🛏 *4 rooms* 🍴 *Breakfast.*

CAPE CHIGNECTO AND CAPE D'OR

105 km (65 miles) southwest of Amherst.

Two imposing promontories—Cape Chignecto and Cape d'Or—reach into the Bay of Fundy near Chignecto Bay.

GETTING HERE AND AROUND

There is no public transportation to the capes. From the Trans-Canada Highway (Highway 104) at Amherst, you need to head southwest via highways 302, 242, and 209. Highway 209 loops around a peninsula, with turnoffs for both capes.

EXPLORING

Advocate Harbour. This little fishing community is set on a Bay of Fundy natural harbor that loses all its water at low tide. A delightful coastal walk here follows the top of an Acadian dike that was built by settlers in the 1700s to reclaim farmland from the sea. Nearby is rocky Advocate Beach, noted for its monumental supply of tide-cast driftwood, which stretches for about 5 km (3 miles) east from Cape Chignecto.

Age of Sail Heritage Museum. Exhibits spread out over six buildings trace the history of the Fundy region's shipbuilding and lumbering industries, and the museum has an archive and genealogical-research area. The Wind and Wave Building is shaped to resemble an inverted half-model of a ship. You can also view a restored Methodist church, a blacksmith shop, a boathouse, and a lighthouse. A cute café serves light meals—chowder, lobster rolls, sandwiches, and the like. ✉ *8334 Hwy. 209, Port Greville* ☎ *902/348–2030* 🌐 *www.ageofsailmuseum.ca* 🎟 *C$5* ⏲ *Late May–mid-Oct., daily 10–6.*

Cape Chignecto Provincial Park. Miles of untouched coastline, more than 10,000 acres of old-growth forest harboring deer, moose, and eagles, and a variety of unique geological features are preserved in Nova Scotia's largest provincial park. It's circumnavigated by a 51-km (31-mile) hiking trail along rugged cliffs that rise 185 meters (600 feet) above the bay. Wilderness cabins and campsites are available. ✉ *1108 W. Advocate Rd., off Hwy. 209, Advocate Harbour* ☎ *902/392–2085, 902/254–3241 off-season* 🌐 *www.novascotiaparks.ca* 🎟 *Free* ⏲ *Mid-May–early Sept., Mon.–Sat. 8–6, Sun. 8–5; early Sept.–mid-Oct., daily 8–4:30; Eatonville day use area late June–mid-Oct., daily 8–8.*

Fodor's Choice ★ **Cape d'Or** (*Cape of Gold*). The explorer Samuel de Champlain poetically, but inaccurately, named Cape d'Or—there's copper in these hills, not gold. The region was actively mined a century ago, and at nearby Horseshoe Cove you may still find nuggets of almost pure copper on the beach, along with amethysts and other semiprecious stones. Cape d'Or's hiking trails border the cliff edge above the Dory Rips, a turbulent meeting of currents from the Minas Basin and the Bay of Fundy punctuated by a fine lighthouse.

WHERE TO EAT AND STAY

For expanded hotel reviews, visit Fodors.com.

$$ CANADIAN 🍴 **Wild Caraway Restaurant & Café.** The young proprietors of this eatery are enthusiastic about using local products in their cuisine. Casual but quality options like lobster rolls, fish cakes, quiche, and a daily pasta are served at lunch. Dinners are more sophisticated and might include pan-fried halibut, local scallops, and a 10-ounce rib eye. Brunch is served on Sundays only, starting at 9 am. The 1860s building housing the restaurant has windows that overlook the wharf. There are also two basic guest rooms (C$90, breakfast included) on the top floor, with a shared bathroom, for overnight stays. [$] *Average main: C$20* ✉ *3721 Hwy. 209, Advocate Harbour* ☎ *902/392–2889* 🌐 *www.wildcaraway.com* ⏲ *Closed Tues. and Wed. Call for off-season hrs.*

$ RENTAL 🏨 **Driftwood Park Retreat.** Five modern chalets are steps from the Fundy shore at this eco-friendly property. **Pros:** private balconies with a great view and a barbecue; free laundry room. **Cons:** there's not much else around; Wi-Fi only available in the office; TVs are available but must be requested. [$] *Rooms from: C$115* ✉ *47 Driftwood La., Advocate Harbour* ☎ *902/392–2008, 866/810–0110* 🌐 *www.driftwoodparkretreat.com* 🛏 *5 cottages* ⏲ *Closed mid-Nov.–Mar.* 🍽 *No meals.*

$ B&B/INN 🏨 **The Lighthouse on Cape d'Or.** Before automation, two lighthouse keepers manned the light on rocky Cape d'Or, and their cottages have been transformed into a small inn with unparalleled views of the Minas Basin. **Pros:** cool concept; warm hosts. **Cons:** difficult access; breakfast not included; no credit cards accepted. [$] *Rooms from: C$90* ✉ *Off Hwy. 209, 6 km (4 miles) from Advocate Harbour, Cape d'Or* ☎ *902/670–0534* 🌐 *www.capedor.ca* 🛏 *4 rooms* 💳 *No credit cards* ⏲ *Closed Nov.–Apr.* 🍽 *No meals.*

$ **Reid's Century Farm Tourist Home.**
B&B/INN Nestled between Cape d'Or and
Cape Chignecto, this is a working
cattle farm where you can enjoy
the bucolic pleasures of country
life or take a short drive to the
Fundy shore. **Pros:** rooms have coffeemakers; cottages have propane
barbecues. **Cons:** remote location;
bathrooms have shower but no
tub; no breakfast served. $ *Rooms
from: C$65* ⊠ *1391 W. Advocate
Rd., West Advocate* ☎ *902/392–
2592* ⊕ *www.reidstouristhome.ca*
↝ *3 rooms, 2 cottages* ⊘ *Closed
Oct.–May* ⦿ *No meals.*

SPORTS AND THE OUTDOORS

NovaShores Adventures. These kayak
tours explore the unspoiled coast
of Cape Chignecto on the Bay of
Fundy daily from mid-May through September. Prices for a day tour
are C$95, or C$125 including a lobster dinner on the beach; two- and
three-day options are also available. ⊠ *37 School La., Advocate Harbour* ☎ *902/392–276, 866/638–4118* ⊕ *www.novashores.com.*

> ### THE MYSTERY OF THE MARY CELESTE
>
> The *Mary Celeste*, originally
> christened the *Amazon*, was built
> on Spencer's Island in 1861. Its
> first captain died on the ship's
> maiden voyage and the boat was
> renamed. In 1872 the ship set
> sail for Europe carrying a cargo
> of wine and liquor. Less than a
> month later it was discovered
> abandoned at sea, all sails set
> and undamaged but without a
> trace of the crew and passengers.
> A cairn at Spencer's Island Beach
> (across from the Beach House
> Restaurant on Highway 209) com-
> memorates the vessel.

PARRSBORO

55 km (34 miles) east of Cape d'Or.

Parrsboro, the main town on the north shore of the Minas Basin, is a
hot spot for rock hounds and fossil hunters.

GETTING HERE AND AROUND

There is no public transportation to Parrsboro. By road, it's on Highway
2, which can be accessed from the Trans-Canada Highway (Highway
104) near Amherst, Springhill, or Truro.

EXPLORING
TOP ATTRACTIONS

FAMILY **Fundy Geological Museum.** Not far from the Minas Basin, where some
of the oldest dinosaur fossils in Canada have been found, this museum
showcases 200-million-year-old specimens alongside other mineral,
plant, and animal relics. The opportunity to peer into a working geology lab and see bright new interactive exhibits (like the Bay of Fundy
Time Machine) give this museum real kid appeal. ■TIP→ **On Fridays
and Saturdays in July and August, the curator leads fascinating two- to
four-hour field trips through the surrounding area, but you need your own
transportation because most don't start at the museum.** ⊠ *162 Two Island
Rd.* ☎ *902/254–3814* ⊕ *fundygeological.novascotia.ca* ⊠ *C$8, C$18
including admission and curatorial field trip* ⊘ *June–mid-Oct., daily
9:30–5:30; mid-Oct.–May, hrs vary, call ahead.*

WORTH NOTING

Minas Basin. The cliffs that rim the Minas Basin are washed by the world's highest tides twice daily: the result is a wealth of plant and animal fossils revealed in the rocks or carried down to the shore.

Nova Scotia Gem and Mineral Show. The combination of fossils and semiprecious stones makes Parrsboro a natural place to hold this show during the third weekend of August. In addition to dozens of exhibitors, the event includes themed demonstrations and geological field trips. Experts are on hand to identify any treasures you turn up. ✉ *Lions Arena, King St. and Western Ave.* 📞 *902/254–3814 Fundy Geological Museum.*

Ottawa House-by-the-Sea Museum. Although fossils have become Parrsboro's claim to fame, this harbor town was also a major shipping and shipbuilding port, and its history is chronicled here. The house, which overlooks the Bay of Fundy, is the only surviving building from a 1700s settlement. It was later the summer home of Sir Charles Tupper (1821–1915), a former premier of Nova Scotia and briefly the prime minister of Canada. Those with roots in Nova Scotia can research their ancestors in the genealogical archives. ✉ *1155 Whitehall Rd., 3 km (2 miles) south of downtown* 📞 *902/254–2376* ⊕ *www.ottawahousemuseum.ca* 💲 *C\$2* ⊗ *Late May–mid-Sept. or early Oct., daily 10–6.*

FAMILY **Parrsboro Rock and Mineral Shop and Museum.** The world's smallest dinosaur footprints, along with rare minerals, rocks, and fossils, are displayed at Eldon George's shop and museum. George, a goldsmith, lapidary, and wood-carver, sells his work in his shop and hosts tours for fossil and mineral collectors. ✉ *349 Whitehall Rd.* 📞 *902/254–2981* 💲 *Donations accepted* ⊗ *May–Oct., daily 10–6.*

Partridge Island. Semiprecious stones such as amethyst, quartz, and stilbite can be found at Partridge Island, 1 km (½ mile) offshore and connected to the mainland by an isthmus.

WHERE TO STAY

For expanded hotel reviews, visit Fodors.com.

$ 🏠 **Gillespie House Inn.** Colorful gardens border the driveway leading
B&B/INN up to this 1890 home that is convenient to Parrsboro but also a great choice for active visitors—the hosts can organize golfing, kayaking, and hiking experiences for you. **Pros:** impeccable rooms; customized packages available; eco-friendly, including some solar power. **Cons:** complimentary continental breakfast is the only meal served; no elevator. 💲 *Rooms from: C\$119* ✉ *358 Main St.* 📞 *902/254–3196, 877/901–3196* ⊕ *www.gillespiehouseinn.com* 🛏 *7 rooms* ⊗ *Closed Nov.–Apr.* ⑩ *Breakfast.*

$ 🏠 **Maple Inn, Parrsboro.** Two Italianate homes built in 1893 have been
B&B/INN combined to form this charming inn within walking distance of downtown Parrsboro and the waterfront. **Pros:** full breakfast included; RBC Rewards points can be redeemed here. **Cons:** no elevator; potential floral-wallpaper overload. 💲 *Rooms from: C\$99* ✉ *2358 Western Ave.* 📞 *902/254–3735, 877/627–5346* ⊕ *www.mapleinn.ca* 🛏 *6 rooms, 2 suites* ⊗ *Closed Nov.–Apr.* ⑩ *Breakfast.*

$ B&B/INN 🏨 **Parrsboro Mansion Inn.** Although this 1880 home, set far back on a 4-acre lawn, presents an imposing face, it's bright and modern inside. **Pros:** German breakfast buffet; host is a certified massage therapist with an on-site treatment room; heated pool. **Cons:** old-style small-screen TVs; one-week minimum stay from mid-October to mid-June. [$] *Rooms from: C$120* ✉ *3916 Eastern Ave.* ☎ *902/254–2585, 866/354–2585* 🌐 *www.parrsboromansion.com* 🛏 *3 rooms, 1 suite* 🍴 *Breakfast.*

NIGHTLIFE AND THE ARTS

Ship's Company Theatre. Top-notch plays, comedy, and a concert series are presented from July through September at this three-stage facility. At its heart is the *Kipawo,* a former Minas Basin ferry that was transformed into the original floating theater in the 1980s. ✉ *18 Lower Main St.* ☎ *902/254–2003, 800/565–7469* 🌐 *www.shipscompany.com.*

SPORTS AND THE OUTDOORS

Pegasus Paragliding. For an aerial view of the water, take one of the tandem flights (C$150) conducted by this company based along the Diligent River. ✉ *9874 Hwy. 209, Diligent River* ☎ *902/254–2972 summer only, 403/493–0609 year-round* 🌐 *www.pegasusparagliding.com.*

FIVE ISLANDS

25 km (15½ miles) east of Parrsboro.

Located between Parrsboro and Truro, Five Islands is one of the most scenic areas along Highway 2. According to Mi'Kmaq legend, these islands were created when the god Glooscap threw handfuls of sod at Beaver, who had mocked and betrayed him.

GETTING HERE AND AROUND

There is no public transportation to Five Islands. Highway 2 can be accessed off the Trans-Canadian Highway (Highway 104).

EXPLORING

Cobequid Interpretation Centre. The geology, history, and culture of the Five Islands area are interpreted here with pictures, videos, and panels, and you can get a sweeping view of the countryside and the impressive tides from the World War II observation tower. ■ **TIP→ Cobequid is home base for the Kenomee Hiking and Walking Trails, where hikers traverse varied landscapes ranging from forested valleys to coast and cliffs.** ✉ *3248 Hwy. 2, Economy* ☎ *902/647–2600* 🎟 *By donation* 🕒 *Mid-to-late June and Sept.–mid-Oct., daily 9–5; July and Aug., daily 9–6.*

BEACHES

Five Islands Provincial Park. On the shore of Minas Basin, the park has a beach for combing, trails for hiking, and mud flats for clam digging. Interpretive displays reveal the area's intriguing geology—semiprecious stones, Jurassic-period dinosaur bones, and fossils can all be found within the park's 1,500 acres. You can learn about geology and other topics, among them astronomy, rock hounding, and tidal pool exploration, during complimentary programs offered during high season (check the website). Because the water recedes nearly a mile at ebb tide you can walk on the ocean floor, though you'll have to run back mighty fast when the tide turns. That's precisely the goal of participants in the **Not Since Moses 10K Race** (⊕ *www.notsincemoses. com*), a mid-August event of (almost) biblical proportions. **Amenities:** parking (free); showers; toilets. **Best for:** swimming; walking. ✉ *618 Bentley Rd., Hwy. 2* ☎ *902/254–2980* ⊕ *www.novascotiaparks.ca* ✉ *Free* ☉ *Park accessible year-round; services open mid-June–mid-Oct., daily dawn–dusk.*

TRURO

91 km (57 miles) east of Parrsboro.

Truro's central location places it on many travelers' routes: this is rightly called "The Hub of Nova Scotia" because if you're driving down the Trans-Canada Highway you'll have to pass by. Within Truro itself, watch for the Tree Sculptures, a creative tribute to trees killed by the dreaded Dutch elm disease. Artists have been transforming the dead trees into handsome sculptures of historical figures, wildlife, and cultural icons. There's a large farmers' market every Saturday from mid-May to the end of October.

GETTING HERE AND AROUND
Truro is on the Trans-Canada Highway (Highway 104).

EXPLORING
River Breeze Farm. For up-close appreciation of local produce, this farm has pick-your-own strawberry and raspberry fields in summer and Atlantic Canada's largest corn maze in the fall. The place turns decidedly scary for Halloween, when "Fear Farm" is haunted by gruesome characters (real live actors) in the maze and a haunted house. ✉ *660 Onslow Rd., Upper Onslow, off Hwy. 102, Exit 14A* ☎ *902/895–5138* ⊕ *www.riverbreeze.info* ✉ *Berry picking price varies. Corn Maze C$10. Fear Farm: Haunted House C$14, Haunted Maze C$14, combined ticket C$20* ☉ *Berry picking July–early Sept. 8:30–4 (days vary, check website or call). Corn Maze mid-Sept.–mid-Oct. weekends noon–5 (last entry 3:30). Fear Farm every Fri. and Sat. in Oct. 7:30–9:30.*

FAMILY **Victoria Park.** At 400 acres, this park on the edge of downtown is Truro's biggest asset, with wooded hiking trails, a winding stream, two waterfalls, public tennis courts, and an outdoor (heated) pool that becomes a skating rink in the winter. Even if you're not staying in Truro, this park can be a good pit stop for car-weary travelers: kids especially will enjoy the pool, picnic pavilion, and playground. ✉ *Park Rd., off Brunswick St.* ☎ *902/893–6078 off-season, 902/895–7078 during season* ⊕ *www. truro.ca/vic-park.html* ✉ *Park free, pool C$10* ☉ *Daily dawn–dusk.*

WHERE TO EAT AND STAY
For expanded hotel reviews, visit Fodors.com.

$$ ✕ **Bistro 22.** Rich farmland fringes Truro, and chef Dennis Pierce knows
CONTEMPORARY how to make the most of the fabulous produce grown around here. His
Fodor's Choice 32-seat eatery has an upscale-casual ambience and a small but mighty
★ menu. Salads, sandwiches, and whole-grain pizzas topped with fresh ingredients dominate at lunch, while dinner includes meatier options such as pork stuffed with locally made Gouda and served with seasonal vegetables. Desserts, always made in-house, come generously

portioned. $ *Average main: C$17* ⊠ *16 Inglis Pl.* ☎ *902/843–4123* ⊕ *www.bistro22.ca* ⊘ *Closed Sun. and Mon. No dinner Tues. and Wed.*

$
HOTEL
FAMILY
☷ **Holiday Inn Hotel & Conference Centre.** A reliable choice in a town not meant for lingering, the Holiday Inn has clean and comfy rooms and bonuses such as a heated indoor pool, a fitness center, and free in-room Wi-Fi. **Pros:** downtown location; appeals to families and pet owners. **Cons:** standard, rather charmless rooms. $ *Rooms from: C$119* ⊠ *437 Prince St.* ☎ *902/895–1651, 866/863–3351* ⊕ *www.hitrurohotel.com* ⇥ *114 rooms* ⏍*Multiple meal plans.*

$
B&B/INN
☷ **Suncatcher Bed and Breakfast.** Rooms at this modest B&B are cheerful and bright: ditto for owner Ruth Mailloux, who knows the province from stem to stern and will happily advise you about itineraries and attractions. **Pros:** knowledgeable host; two-day stained glass workshops available by reservation. **Cons:** 6½ km (4 miles) from Truro; can be difficult to find. $ *Rooms from: C$115* ⊠ *25 Wile Crest Ave., North River* ☎ *902/893–7169, 877/203–6032* ⊕ *www.suncatcherbnb.com* ⇥ *2 rooms* ⏍*Breakfast.*

SPORTS AND THE OUTDOORS

Shubenacadie River Adventure Tours. On these adrenaline-inducing three-hour Zodiac inflatable-boat trips (C$85), you ride the waves created by the famous Fundy tides as the waters surge upstream. ■**TIP**➡ **The intensity of the tides determines the intensity of your ride; call or check the company's website to find out when your trip will be (relatively) mellow or fierce.** ⊠ *10061 Hwy. 215, South Maitland* ☎ *902/261–2222, 888/878–8687* ⊕ *www.shubie.com.*

Fodor'sChoice
★
Shubenacadie River Runners. Riding the white water churned up as the Fundy Tidal Bore rushes into Nova Scotia's largest river is an adventure you won't soon forget. With Shubenacadie River Runners you can confront the waves head-on in a self-bailing Zodiac. Tide conditions and time of day let you choose mildly turbulent or ultrawild rides. A full day of rafting costs C$80–C$90 and includes a steak barbecue; a half day costs C$60–C$70 and includes hot drinks. ⊠ *8681 Hwy. 215, Maitland* ☎ *902/261–2770, 800/856–5061* ⊕ *tidalborerafting.webs.com.*

Tidal Bore Rafting Park. When the world's highest tides rush up the Shubenacadie River, these rafts rush upstream, too, crossing eight sets of rapids along the way. You can either take the two-hour one-way trip (C$70) or precede that with a scenic two-hour float downstream (C$95 round-trip). Tours operate from May through October. ⊠ *12215 Hwy. 215, 14 km (9 miles) north of Shubenacadie, Urbania* ☎ *902/758–4032, 800/565–7238* ⊕ *www.raftingcanada.ca.*

SHOPPING

Saltscapes. Atlantic Canada's lifestyle magazine *Saltscapes* opened this retail outlet on Highway 102 just outside Truro—if you're Halifax-bound, you can't miss it. Maple syrup, maritime-music CDs, crafts, clothing, and other regional products share shelf space at this pseudo general store. A 170-seat restaurant that focuses on East Coast comfort food, including dishes from recipes published in the magazine, also does business here. ⊠ *Truro Power Centre, 25 Treaty Trail, off Hwy. 102, Exit 13A* ☎ *902/843–6700* ⊕ *www.saltscapesrestaurant.com.*

FAMILY
Fodor'sChoice
★
Sugar Moon Farm Maple Products & Pancake House. This sugar camp, store, and pancake house in the Cobequid Mountains, about 30 km (19 miles) north of Truro off Highway 311, is Nova Scotia's only year-round maple destination. Daily in the summer and on weekends the rest of the year you can tour the working facility and hike the sugar woods. In spring, when the sap is running, you can also watch demonstrations. Afterward, tuck into whole-grain buttermilk pancakes and waffles with maple syrup, local sausage, fresh biscuits, maple baked beans, and organic coffee at the lodge. Multiple times per year, a guest chef prepares a gourmet dinner (C$69) that cleverly incorporates maple products. At the store, you can buy your own sweet souvenirs, among them maple syrup, maple cream, maple candy, and maple butter. ✉ *221 Alex MacDonald Rd., Earltown* ☎ *902/657–3348, 866/816–2753* ⊕ *www.sugarmoon.ca.*

Thrown Together Pottery and Art. The owner's clay creations are sold here alongside works by many other local artisans. The shop is closed on Sundays and Mondays, and from January through March is open only by chance on Tuesdays and Wednesdays. ✉ *37 King St.* ☎ *902/895–9309* ⊕ *www.throwntogetherpottery.com.*

CAPE BRETON ISLAND

Fodor'sChoice
★
There isn't much new in the northeastern corner of Nova Scotia and that's precisely the point; Cape Breton Island's reputation rests on simple pleasures and heartfelt hospitality. This rugged terrain made the Highland Scots, who settled here in the 18th century, feel right at home and their influence remains obvious: North America's first single-malt whiskey distillery is on Cape Breton, as is its only college devoted to Gaelic language, arts, and culture.

GETTING HERE AND AROUND

To reach Cape Breton Island, you can drive from mainland Nova Scotia via the Canso Causeway; take a Marine Atlantic ferry from Newfoundland; or fly into Sydney's J.A. Douglas McCurdy Airport. The island itself has five convenient, camera-ready driving routes—and since these collectively cover about 710 km (440 miles), you should allow five days to explore. Enter by way of the causeway on Highway 104. Turning left at the rotary, take Highway 19 (the Ceilidh Trail), which winds along the hillside through fields and glens for 107 km (67 miles) before meeting the west end of the fabled Cabot Trail. Alternately, from the causeway you could follow the Bras d'Or Lakes Scenic Drive, which loops along lesser known roads of central Cape Breton and around the massive lake that lent the route its name; or veer east on the linked Fleur-de-Lis/Marconi Trail, which takes you to the must-see Fortress of Louisbourg and then onward to Sydney (Cape Breton's main city). Note that driving in this direction also puts your vehicle on the waterside for most of the trail making it easier to pull over for photo ops.

ESSENTIALS

Visitor Information Port Hastings Visitor Information Centre
✉ *96 Hwy. 4, Port Hastings* ☎ *902/625–4201* ☉ *May–Dec.* **Tourism Cape Breton** ☎ *902/563–4636, 888/562–9848* ⊕ *www.cbisland.com.*

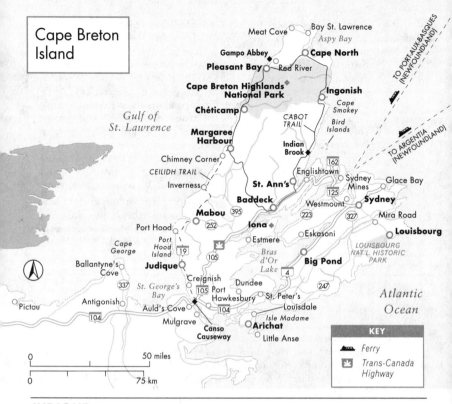

Cape Breton Island

Meat Cove   Bay St. Lawrence
             Aspy Bay
  Gampo Abbey   Cape North
Pleasant Bay   Red River
Cape Breton Highlands
    National Park   Ingonish
       Chéticamp   Cape
                              Smokey
Gulf of   CABOT   Bird
St. Lawrence   TRAIL   Islands
       Margaree
       Harbour   Indian
  Chimney Corner   Brook
CEILIDH TRAIL   162
  Inverness   Englishtown
              St. Ann's   Sydney   Glace Bay
         Baddeck   Mines
                        125
  Mabou   395   Westmount   Sydney
                   223   327
Port Hood   252   Iona   Mira Road
                                    Louisbourg
  Cape   Port   Eskasoni LOUISBOURG
 George Hood 19 105 *Bras*   NAT'L. HISTORIC
       Island   d'Or Big Pond PARK
Ballantyne's Judique *Lake*   4
   Cove   337 *St. George's* Dundee
 Antigonish   *Bay* 105 Port St. Peter's *Atlantic*
         Auld's Cove Hawkesbury Louisdale *Ocean*
 Pictou   104   104
              Mulgrave Canso *Isle Madame*
                     Causeway Arichat
                          Little Anse

KEY
Ferry
Trans-Canada Highway

0   50 miles

0   75 km

JUDIQUE

30 km (18 miles) north of the Canso Causeway; 75 km (47 miles) northeast of Antigonish.

Like so many Cape Breton communities, Judique is only a little clutch of buildings with Highway 19 running straight through as the main street. Nevertheless, the presence of **the Celtic Music Interpretive Centre** makes Judique an essential destination for anyone interested in the island music scene. Need some fresh air before getting back in the car and continuing up the Ceilidh Trail? The coastal area around Judique is good for hiking (a portion of the Trans-Canada Trail threads through) as well as swimming. For an offshore experience, consider taking a tour out of Little Judique Harbour.

GETTING HERE AND AROUND

There is no public transportation to Judique. By road, it's on the Ceilidh Trail (Highway 19)—a left turn at the traffic circle over the Canso Causeway.

EXPLORING

Celtic Music Interpretive Centre. Packed with exhibits detailing the fine points of fiddling, the center also has an archive with classic recordings and oral history interviews. Visitors eager to pick up a bow can play along to a video tutorial. If you'd rather just get an earful, that's no problem. In summer, daily except Sunday, musical demonstrations (C$12, admission to exhibits included) take place about a dozen times, and the center's dining room hosts lunchtime ceilidhs (free for the entertainment but not the lunch) from 11:30 to 1 and on Sunday afternoons starting at 3 (C$8). Wednesday-evening ceilidhs (C$6) run from July through mid-October. **TIP→ The adjacent Buddy McMaster School of Fiddling offers weeklong courses during October's Celtic Colours International Festival.** ✉ *5471 Hwy. 19, Judique* ☎ *902/787–2708* 🌐 *www.celticmusiccentre.com* 🎫 *C$6* 🕒 *Late May–mid-Oct., Mon.–Sat. 9–5, Sun. 11–6:30.*

2

MABOU

28 km (17 miles) northeast of Judique.

The village of Mabou is very Scottish (Gaelic-language signs attest to it), and the residents' respect for tradition is apparent in everything from the down-home meals they serve to the music they so exuberantly play; arguably the best place to sample both is at the Red Shoe.

GETTING HERE AND AROUND

There is no public transportation to Mabou. It's on the Ceilidh Trail.

EXPLORING

The best touring in the Mabou area is along the hiking trails that riddle the hills here. ⇨ *See Sports and the Outdoors, below.*

BEACHES

West Mabou Beach Provincial Park. A wide sweep of sandy beach backed by a dune system is the standout feature of this 530-acre park on Mabou Harbour. The only public-access beach in the area, it also has a fish-pond, a picnic area, and change rooms, but its status as a protected natural environment prevents any further development and preserves its peaceful quality. **TIP→ Behind the beach are 12-km (7.5-miles) of hiking trails, through agricultural land and marshes, that have fine views.** **Amenities:** parking (free); toilets. **Best for:** swimming; walking. ✉ *1757 Little Mabou Rd., off Hwy. 19* 🌐 *www.novascotiaparks.ca.*

WHERE TO EAT AND STAY

For expanded hotel reviews, visit Fodors.com.

$$$ CANADIAN 🍴 **Mull Café & Deli.** It's doubtful you'll drive by this informal restaurant on Mabou's main thoroughfare without seeing a parking lot full of cars. Owned by the proprietors of the Duncreigan Country Inn, it's a popular hangout for Cape Bretoners but also draws "come from away" diners thanks to its long lunchtime menu of hearty salads, creamy chowders, deep-fried seafood plates, and homemade desserts. After 5 (all day on Sunday) the dinner menu goes more upscale with dishes like scallops in white-wine and cream sauce, and lemon-chicken supreme. **TIP→ At peak times, reservations are recommended. The café displays local artwork, making this a pleasant place to linger, but for those in a rush there's a take-out deli counter.** [$] *Average main: C$22* ✉ *11630 Hwy. 19* ☎ *902/945–2244* 🌐 *www.mullcafe.com.*

CLOSE UP

The Music of Cape Breton

Weaned on old-time Scottish tunes, Cape Breton Island's traditional musicians are among the world's finest—and there's a widely held belief (in Scotland, too) that here the music has been preserved in a purer form than in the old country itself. In summer you can hear these musicians play at festivals, concerts, and, of course, ceilidhs (pronounced KAY-lees). The word, Gaelic for "visit," derives from the days when folks would gather in a neighbor's kitchen for music, stories, and step dancing. Today ceilidhs have evolved into public events that visitors are welcome to join. Bulletin boards, newspapers, and visitor information centers are a good source for listings. Inverness Country, which encompasses the Ceilidh Trail and is the epicenter of activity, has its own ceilidh lineup online at 🌐 *www.invernessco.com.* Any night of the week in peak season you'll also be able to attend a square dance somewhere in Inverness County. Propelled by virtuoso fiddling, locals of every age whirl through taxing "square sets," shaking the floor and rattling the rafters in the process. The highlight of the musical calendar is undoubtedly the Celtic Colours International Festival, held every October at the height of the island's spectacular fall-colors season. It gathers together Celtic musicians, singers, and dancers from around the corner and around the world for concerts and ceilidhs across the region.

$$ CANADIAN FAMILY Fodor's Choice ★

🍴 **Red Shoe.** More than a mere pub, this Cape Breton institution has evolved into an attraction in its own right, in part because it is owned by four of the Rankins, Canada's most celebrated singing siblings. There's music here every night, and sometimes during the day, and the "Shoe" is a magnet for the finest fiddlers and step dancers. As for the food, expect the usual pub favorites: fish-and-chips, pulled-pork sandwiches, grilled salmon, stuffed chicken, and mussels steamed in ale, garlic, and bacon. [$] *Average main: C$19* ✉ *11573 Hwy. 19* ☎ *902/945–2996* 🌐 *www.redshoepub.com* ⏲ *Closed mid-Oct.–May.*

$$ B&B/INN

🏨 **Duncreigan Country Inn.** With its harborside deck and peaceful location, the inn provides a great place to unwind after a day spent exploring Cape Breton. **Pros:** full buffet breakfast included; open year-round. **Cons:** no restaurant on-site; trees block some harbor views. [$] *Rooms from: C$135* ✉ *11409 Hwy. 19* ☎ *902/945–2207, 800/840–2207 for reservations* 🌐 *www.duncreigan.ca* 🛏 *7 rooms, 1 suite* 🍽 *Breakfast.*

$$ B&B/INN

🏨 **Glenora Inn & Distillery.** North America's first single-malt whiskey distillery adjoins this whitewashed inn north of Mabou, so if you stay here it'll be easy to sample a wee dram of Glenora's own Glen Breton Rare. **Pros:** unique atmosphere; sylvan property bisected by a brook. **Cons:** rooms could use a refresh; road to chalets is tricky to negotiate at night. [$] *Rooms from: C$169* ✉ *13727 Hwy. 19, Glenville* ☎ *902/258–2262, 800/839–0491* 🌐 *www.glenoradistillery.com* 🛏 *9 rooms, 6 chalets* ⏲ *Closed Nov.–mid-May* 🍽 *Multiple meal plans.*

2

NIGHTLIFE

Strathespey Place. Concerts, plays, and musicals are presented at this arts center that is also a venue for the annual Celtic Colours Festival. ⊠ *11156 Hwy. 19* ☎ *902/945–5300* ⊕ *www.strathspeyplace.com.*

SPORTS AND THE OUTDOORS

Fodor's Choice ★

Cabot Links. As Canada's only true links course, designed by Rod Whitman and opened in 2012, Cabot Links has caused much excitement among players and golf media alike, and with good reason. Set along the rugged Cape Breton seashore near Inverness, it is both challenging and stunningly scenic, and comes with superb lodging and dining options as well. ■ TIP➔ **This is a walking-only course, so no buggy rentals.** ⊠ *15933 Central Ave., 22 km (14 miles) north of Mabou on Cabot Trail, Inverness* ☎ *902/258–4653, 855/652–2268* ⊕ *www.cabotlinks. com* ⅄. *Course: 18 holes. 6942 yds. Par 72. Green Fee: C$130/C$150* ⊗ *Mid-May–mid-Nov.* ⌐ *Facilities: putting green, pull carts, caddies, rental clubs, pro shop, restaurant, bar.*

Mabou Highlands. The Cape Mabou Trail Club maintains 35 km (21 miles) of nature trails, 14 in total, on this mountain range. Gaelic-speaking immigrants from Scotland settled this region of plunging cliffs, isolated beaches, rising mountains, and glens, meadows, and hardwood forests, and some of the trails follow tracks made by carts traveling to and from the pioneer settlements. Today the area is so hauntingly quiet that you might halfway expect to meet the *sidhe,* the Scottish fairies, capering on the hillsides. ■ TIP➔ **Trail maps can be purchased from local retailers or online.**

MARGAREE HARBOUR

53 km (33 miles) north of Mabou.

Aside from pleasant pastimes like hillside hiking and saltwater swimming (Whale Cove and Chimney Corner are the local's top picks for the latter), the Margaree area promises world-class fly-fishing. Margaree Harbour not only marks the point where the Ceilidh Trail joins the Cabot Trail, it also sits at the mouth of the Margaree River: a designated Canadian Heritage River known for legendary salmon runs.

GETTING HERE AND AROUND

There is no public transportation to Margaree Harbour. It's just north of where the Ceilidh Trail meets the Cabot Trail, so is accessible cross-country from Baddeck as well as up the coast.

EXPLORING

Margaree Salmon Museum. Exhibits at this unassuming museum are proudly old-school, which seems fitting because they're housed in a former one-room schoolhouse. On display are all manner of fishing tackle, photographs, hand-tied flies, and other memorabilia related to salmon angling on the Margaree. Visitors can watch videos, study models of the river, and peek into the fish tank. ⊠ *60 E. Big Intervale Rd., Northeast Margaree* ☎ *902/248–2848* ⊴ *C$2* ⊗ *Mid-June–mid-Oct., daily 9–5.*

WHERE TO STAY

For expanded hotel reviews, visit Fodors.com.

$$ B&B/INN **Normaway Inn and Cabins.** Set on 500 acres in the Margaree Valley, this inn has rooms full of country character, hiking trails on the doorstep, and it rings with the sound of live traditional music from top Cape Breton fiddlers. **Pros:** bucolic site; central to island touring loops; own landing strip. **Cons:** isn't luxurious, and doesn't aspire to be. *$ Rooms from: C$159 ✉ 691 Egypt Rd. ☎ 902/248–2987, 800/565–9463 🌐 www.thenormawayinn.com 🛏 9 rooms, 3 suites, 15 cabins ⏲ Closed Nov.–May; cabins available off-season by arrangement 🍴 Multiple meal plans.*

SPORTS AND THE OUTDOORS

The Margaree has two fishing seasons: the early summer run, which opens annually on June 1, and the fall run, from mid-September through October, which coincides with the peak foliage period. Salmon-fishing licenses cost about C$62 per week for anglers who don't live in Nova Scotia. In Margaree, they're available from LeBlanc's Store, Ingraham's Irving & Convenience Store, and the Big Intervale Fishing Lodge.

Margaree Salmon Association. The association is heavily involved in salmon conservation and habitat restoration, and has put together a pamphlet, available on its website, outlining Margaree River fishing etiquette. In addition to the fishing advice, the pamphlet lists the names and contact information of guides who know the river well and can help you catch that trophy-size salmon. The guides typically charge C$200 per day. *☎ 902/248–2578 🌐 www.margareesalmon.org.*

CHÉTICAMP

25 km (16 miles) north of Margaree Harbour.

In Chéticamp, an Acadian enclave for more than 200 years, Francophone culture and traditions are still very much alive. That's why the Gaelic-inflected lilt in locals' voices is replaced by a distinct French accent. (You might be greeted in French but can respond in English—most residents are bilingual.) Size is another distinguishing factor because, with population of about 4,000, Chéticamp feels like a major metropolis compared to other western shore communities. The landscape is different, too. Poised between mountains and sea, Chéticamp stands exposed on a wide lip of flat land below a range of bald green hills, behind which lies the high plateau of the Cape Breton Highlands. Commercial fishing is the town's raison d'être, but rug hooking is its main claim to fame, a fact reflected in local attractions and shops. So pause to peruse them before racing into the adjacent national park.

GETTING HERE AND AROUND

There is no public transportation to Chéticamp. By road, it's on the Cabot Trail just south of the Cape Breton Highlands National Park.

ESSENTIALS

Visitor Information **Chéticamp Visitor Information Centre** *✉ Les Trois Pignons, 15584 Cabot Trail, Mahone Bay ☎ 902/224–2642 🌐 www.cheticamp.ca ⏲ Mid-May–mid-Oct.*

2

EXPLORING

Les Trois Pignons Cultural Center. The center, which contains the Elizabeth LeFort Gallery, displays samples of the rugs, tapestries, and related artifacts that helped make Chéticamp the World Rug Hooking Capital. Born in 1914, Elizabeth LeFort created more than 300 tapestries, some of which have hung in the Vatican, the White House, and Buckingham Palace. (One standout depicting U.S. presidents is made from seven miles of yarn!) Les Trois Pignons is also an Acadian cultural and genealogical information center. ✉ *15584 Cabot Trail Rd.* ☎ *902/224–2642* 🌐 *www.lestroispignons.com* 🎫 *C$5* 🕒 *July and Aug., daily 9–7; mid-May–June and Sept.–mid-Oct., daily 9–5; mid-Oct.–mid-May by appointment.*

WHERE TO EAT AND STAY

For expanded hotel reviews, visit Fodors.com.

$$ CANADIAN 🍴 **Le Gabriel Restaurant and Lounge.** Casual Le Gabriel's—you can't miss its large lighthouse entranceway—offers simple but substantial fare that includes North American standards and traditional Acadian favorites. The latter include *tourtière* (meat pie with a crispy crust) and *fricot* (a hearty stew with potatoes, pork bits, chives, and beef or chicken). Fresh fish dishes are popular, too, with snow crab and lobster available in season. Lighter fare includes hot and cold sandwiches, wraps, soups, and fish-and-chips. The menu and opening hours are more limited in the off-season. The lounge has billiard tables, and there's live music on most Saturday nights. [$] *Average main: C$19* ✉ *15424 Cabot Trail Rd.* ☎ *902/224–3685* 🌐 *www.legabriel.com.*

$$ RENTAL 🏨 **Cabot Trail Sea & Golf Chalets.** Linked to Le Portage Golf Club by a private pathway, these ocean-side chalets work well for golfers and anyone wanting more than a mere hotel room. **Pros:** discounted weekly rates; great golfing. **Cons:** books quickly; no meals available. [$] *Rooms from: C$159* ✉ *71 Fraser Doucet La.* ☎ *902/224–1777, 877/224–1777* 🌐 *www.seagolfchalets.com* 🛏 *12 chalets, 1 suite* 🕒 *Closed mid-Oct.–mid-May* 🍽 *No meals.*

$ B&B/INN 🏨 **Chéticamp Outfitters' Inn Bed & Breakfast.** Clean, cozy rooms overlook the ocean, mountains, and valley at this inn, and there's a top-floor patio along the length of the cedar house that takes full advantage of the view. **Pros:** walking distance to beach; breakfast includes memorable blueberry muffins. **Cons:** three rooms have shared bathrooms; most rooms lack televisions. [$] *Rooms from: C$85* ✉ *13938 Cabot Trail Rd.* ☎📠 *902/224–2776* 🌐 *www.cheticampns.com/cheticampoutfitters* 🛏 *6 rooms, 1 chalet* 🕒 *Closed Dec.–mid-Apr.* 🍽 *Breakfast.*

SPORTS AND THE OUTDOORS

On whale-watch cruises departing from Chéticamp's government wharf, you can see minkes, humpbacks, and finbacks in their natural environment.

Captain Zodiac Whale Cruise. The operators of these cruises aboard Zodiac vessels are so confident you'll spot a whale—finbacks, humpbacks, minkes, and pilots are the ones most sighted—that they'll refund your money if you don't. Trips (C$49) take place daily from May through October. ☎ *902/224–1088, 877/232–2522* 🌐 *www.novascotiawhales.com.*

Le Portage Golf Club. The beautiful but formidable holes at Le Portage overlook the Gulf of St. Lawrence. Course designers Robert and David Moote incorporated 60 sand bunkers, which together with the area's heavy winds provide no end to challenges no matter what your skill level. ⊠ *15580 Cabot Trail Rd.* ☎ *902/224–3338, 888/618–5558* ⊕ *www.leportagegolfclub.com* ⌁ *Course: 18 holes. 6777 yds. Par 72. Green Fee: C$39/C$59* ☉ *Mid-Apr.–Oct.* ☞ *Facilities: driving range, putting green, golf carts, pull carts, rental clubs, pro shop, lessons, restaurant, bar.*

Little Pond Stables. Daily horseback rides travel along wooded trails, beaches, and foothill paths. Tours (from C$30 to C$60) last between 30 and 90 minutes and set out at 9 am, noon, 3, and 5:30. Other activities include pony rides (C$1 per minute or C$25 for 30 minutes), wagon rides, and winter sleigh rides. ⊠ *103 LaPointe Rd., 5 km (3 miles) north of Chéticamp, off Cabot Trail, Petit Etang* ☎ *902/224–3858, 888/250–6799* ⊕ *www.horsebackcapebreton.com.*

Whale Cruisers Ltd. This outfit runs three-hour tours (C$40.25) aboard a 13-meter (42-foot) vessel two or three times daily from mid-May through mid-October. ⊠ *Government Wharf, Main St.* ☎ *902/224–3376, 800/813–3376* ⊕ *www.whalecruisers.com.*

SHOPPING

Chéticamp Hooked Rugs Coopérative Artisanale. Supplied by nearly 75 happy "hookers," as they delight in calling themselves, the co-op is renowned for its splendid handmade rugs. For those traveling light, it also sells small items such as hooked coasters. ⊠ *15067 Cabot Trail* ☎ *902/224–2170* ⊕ *www.cheticamphookedrugs.com* ☉ *June–late Oct.*

CAPE BRETON HIGHLANDS NATIONAL PARK

5 km (3 miles) north of Chéticamp; 108 km (67 miles) north of Ingonish.

GETTING HERE AND AROUND

There is no public transportation to the park. The Cabot Trail loops around it, past the western entrance, at Chéticamp, and the eastern one, at Ingonish.

EXPLORING

Cape Breton Highlands National Park. A 950-square-km (366-square-mile) wilderness of wooded valleys, barren plateaus, and steep cliffs, Cape Breton Highlands National Park stretches across northern Cape Breton from the gulf shore to the Atlantic. High-altitude bogs here are home to wild orchids and other unique flora. For animal lovers there's much to see as well, including moose, eagles, deer, bears, foxes, bobcats, and coyotes. Your chances of spotting wildlife naturally improve if you venture off the main road and hike one of the 25 trails at dusk or dawn. Be advised, though, that it's illegal to feed or approach any animal in the park and all should be observed from a safe distance.

⚠ **For your safety, never hike isolated trails alone. Even motorists must remain alert, particularly when driving in moose zones, which are marked by highway signs. Moose sometimes claim the road as their own, and things won't end well if you hit an animal weighing 1,200 pounds.**

A permit or pass is required for entering sections of the Cabot Trail within the national park and for use of the facilities such as exhibits, hiking trails, and picnic areas; there are additional fees for camping, fishing, and golf. Full details are available at the gateway information centers. ⊠ *Entrances on Cabot Trail near Chéticamp and Ingonish, 37639 Cabot Trail, Ingonish* ☎ *902/224–2306, 902/224–3814 bookstore* ⊕ *www.parkscanada.ca* 🎟 *C$7.80* ⊙ *Park year-round, daily dawn–dusk. Visitor centers mid-May–mid-Oct., daily 9–5 (8:30–7 in peak season).*

PLEASANT BAY

41 km (26 miles) north of Chéticamp.

Pleasant Bay is, well, pleasant, and because it's about halfway around the Cabot Trail, it's a convenient place to stop. Local fishermen catch lobster in spring and snow crab in summer. The water yields much bigger creatures, too, and it could be said that whales here outnumber people. Of course, that isn't hard considering the population is just about 350.

GETTING HERE AND AROUND

There is no public transportation to Pleasant Bay. By road, it's on the Cabot Trail just as it emerges from the northwest boundary of the Cape Breton Highlands National Park.

EXPLORING

FAMILY **Whale Interpretive Centre.** Visitors who like to stay on dry land while observing sea life should stop by the center. Using zoom scopes on the whale-spotting deck, you may catch a close-up glimpse of the many different species that often frolic just off-shore. Exhibits and models inside the center's modern structure explain the unique world of whales. ⊠ *104 Harbour Rd., Pleasant Bay* ☎ *902/224–1411* 🎟 *C$5* ⊙ *June–mid-Oct., daily 9–5.*

SPORTS AND THE OUTDOORS

WHALE-
WATCHING **Captain Mark's Whale & Seal Cruise.** Sightings are guaranteed on tours, from June through mid-September, aboard inflatable boats (C$44) or a 42-foot research vessel (C$35). Well-trained guides and researchers from Dalhousie University narrate the tours on the research vessel. ⊠ *Harbour Rd., off Cabot Trail, Pleasant Bay* ☎ *902/224–1316, 888/754–5112* ⊕ *www.whaleandsealcruise.com.*

Fiddlin' Whale Tours. Captain Stan MacKinnon adds music to the whale-watching mix, so you can enjoy his traditional Cape Breton fiddling as you scan the waves for whales (C$40, plus C$2 for parking). This may seem like a bizarre pairing, but apparently whales respond to the pitch and sometimes contribute their own songs. An on-board hydrophone helps you hear them. ⊠ *Harbour Rd., off Cabot Trail, Pleasant Bay* ☎ *902/383–2340, 866/688–2424* ⊕ *www.fiddlinwhaletours.com.*

CAPE NORTH

30 km (19 miles) east of Pleasant Bay.

This is where explorer Giovanni Caboto (aka John Cabot) made land in 1497. Not only does Cape North still feel like a new discovery, it also provides access to locales that are even more remote, like Bay St. Lawrence and Meat Cove.

GETTING HERE AND AROUND

There is no public transportation to Cape North. By road, it's at the northernmost point on the Cabot Trail.

BEACHES

Cabot's Landing Provincial Park. This long, sandy beach remains untouched by modern development, other than the picnic tables on the adjoining grassland. It's a great place for beachcombing and pondering the journeys of First Nations boatmen who once set out from here to paddle to Newfoundland. A cairn in the park, commemorating the purported arrival of John Cabot from England in 1497, offers further historical insights, but the jaw-dropping views of Aspy Bay and the surrounding wilderness area provide the best reasons to come here. **Amenities:** parking (free). **Best for:** solitude; walking. ✉ *1904 Bay St. Lawrence Rd., 2 km (1 mile) north of Four Mile Beach Inn* 🌐 *parks.gov.ns.ca* 🎟 *Free* 🕓 *Daily, mid-May–mid-Oct.*

WHERE TO STAY

For expanded hotel reviews, visit Fodors.com.

$ B&B/INN 🏨 **Four Mile Beach Inn.** Views of Aspy Bay and the ridge of the highland mountains are fantastic from this large 19th-century house near Cabot's Landing. **Pros:** breakfast buffet included; knowledgeable hosts. **Cons:** smallish rooms; two have shared bathrooms, and one has a bathroom across the corridor. [$] *Rooms from: C$99* ✉ *1528 Bay St. Lawrence Rd., Sugarloaf* ☎ *902/383–2282 June–Oct., 877/602–3737, 902/422–7450 mid-Oct.–mid-May* 🌐 *www.fourmilebeachinn.com* 🛏 *7 rooms, 1 apartment* 🕓 *Closed mid-Oct.–mid-May (season varies)* 🍴 *Breakfast.*

SPORTS AND THE OUTDOORS

Captain Cox's Whale Watch. Several tours (C$45) in a speedy Zodiac set out daily from July to mid-September from Bay St. Lawrence Wharf. Tours last between 2 and 2½ hours, and if you don't see a whale, you get another trip for free. ✉ *Bay St. Lawrence Rd., off Cabot Trail* ☎ *902/383–2981, 888/346–5556* 🌐 *www.whalewatching-novascotia.com.*

Eagle North. Based in Dingwall, which neighbors Cape North, this outfitter offers kayak tours (from C$45) as well as boat and bike rentals (from C$15 and C$10 per hour respectively), from May through October. ✉ *299 Shore Rd., South Harbour, Dingwall* ☎ *902/383–2552, 888/616–1689* 🌐 *www.kayakingcapebreton.ca.*

Oshan Whale Watch. The C$30 charge for a 2½-hour trip on a working lobster boat is a bargain, and if you don't sight a whale, you get another trip free. ✉ *3384 Bay St. Lawrence Rd.* ☎ *902/383–2883, 877/383–2883* 🌐 *www.oshan.ca.*

INGONISH

35 km (22 miles) southeast of Cape North.

The western gateway to the Cabot Trail, Ingonish is one of the leading vacation destinations on Cape Breton, largely because it's home to the much-touted Keltic Lodge Resort and adjacent Highland Links golf course. The spot is actually comprised of five villages—Ingonish proper, Ingonish Centre, Ingonish Beach, Ingonish Harbour, and Ingonish Ferry. Poised on two bays and divided by a long narrow peninsula, all together they cover about 16 km (10 miles).

GETTING HERE AND AROUND

There is no public transportation to Ingonish. By road, it lies on the eastern section of the Cabot Trail.

EXPLORING

Cape Smokey Provincial Park. The park that caps the 300-meter (984-foot) Cape Smokey Peak has a challenging coastal trail that is breathtaking in more ways than one. Hiking it takes about four hours. ☒ *40301 Cabot Trail Rd., Ingonish Ferry* ⊕ *parks.gov.ns.ca* ⊠ *Free* ☉ *Daily mid-May–early Oct.*

WHERE TO STAY

For expanded hotel reviews, visit Fodors.com.

$$$$
RESORT
FAMILY
🖼 **Keltic Lodge Resort and Spa.** Spread across the sea cliffs, this resort has glorious views of Cape Smokey and the surrounding highlands. **Pros:** breakfast is included; lots to do. **Cons:** rooms vary in size; Inn at Keltic rooms could use a makeover. $ *Rooms from: C$267* ☒ *383 Keltic Inn Rd., Middle Head Peninsula, Ingonish Beach* ☎ *902/285–2880, 800/565–0444* ⊕ *www.signatureresorts.com* 🗝 *72 rooms, 2 suites, 10 cottages* ☉ *Closed Nov.–Apr.* ⦿ *Multiple meal plans.*

$$
B&B/INN
🖼 **Lantern Hill & Hollow.** Hearing the surf is no problem at this intimate property because the six cottages are just steps from a private 3-km (2-mile) beach that is ideal for quick dips and nightly bonfires; firewood and beach toys are supplied. **Pros:** gorgeous property; convenient location. **Cons:** no meals provided; self-catering has only light housekeeping. $ *Rooms from: C$170* ☒ *36845 Cabot Trail, Ingonish Beach* ☎ *902/285–2010, 888/663–0225* ⊕ *www.lanternhillandhollow. com* 🗝 *3 suites, 6 cottages* ☉ *Closed mid-Oct.–late May* ⦿ *No meals.*

SPORTS AND THE OUTDOORS

Highlands Links. Perennially ranked as one of Canada's top courses, Highlands was designed by Stanley Thompson, who dubbed it "the mountains and ocean" course. ☒ *Cape Breton Highlands National Park, 247 Keltic Inn Rd., Ingonish Beach* ☎ *902/285–2600, 800/441–1118* ⊕ *www.highlandslinksgolf.com* 🏌 *Course: 18 holes. 6592 yds. Par 72. Green Fee: C$79/C$105* ☉ *Mid-May–late Oct.* ☞ *Facilities: putting green, golf carts, pull carts, rental clubs, pro shop, lessons, restaurant, bar.*

ST. ANN'S BAY AND AROUND

Extends for 65 km (40 miles) from Ingonish south to St. Ann's.

Continuing down the Cabot Trail from Ingonish, you'll skirt St. Ann's Bay where communities are of the blink-and-you'll-miss-it variety. Other North America's only Gaelic college, there are few actual attractions, but there are fun outdoor opportunities and some of Atlantic Canada's most distinctive shops.

GETTING HERE AND AROUND

There is no public transportation to the St. Ann's Bay area. By road, approach from the north on the Cabot Trail; from the south take the Trans-Canada Highway (Highway 105, aka "Mabel and Alexander Graham Bell Way") north from Baddeck, then turn onto Highway 312 and continue through Englishtown.

EXPLORING

Gaelic College of Celtic Arts and Crafts. Being home to direct descendants of the Gaelic pioneers, St. Ann's Bay is a logical site for this college, established in 1938 with a mission to promote and preserve the settlers' heritage. And mission accomplished, because today the campus provides a crash course in Gaelic culture. Weeklong summer-school courses—as well as occasional weekend workshops—focus on topics such as bagpiping and fiddling. The college hosts a Wednesday-evening ceilidh in summer and in fall is a key site for the Celtic Colours festival. ✉ *51779 Cabot Trail Rd., St. Ann's* ☎ *902/295–3411* 🌐 *www.gaeliccollege.edu* 🎫 *Great Hall of the Clans C$8* 🕒 *June and Sept., weekdays 9–5; July and Aug., daily 9–5.*

OFF THE BEATEN PATH

When you reach the Barachois River Bridge, you can stay on the Cabot Trail as it turns inland or choose a coastal route (the 312) that goes onward to Jersey Cove. From there you can take a ferry across St. Ann's Bay to Englishtown; then follow Highway 105 into Baddeck. Weather permitting, the ferry operates 24/7 year-round. Although you save minimal driving time (about 15 minutes) the two-minute trip is pretty and the one-way fare a mere C$5 per car.

WHERE TO STAY

For expanded hotel reviews, visit Fodors.com.

$$ B&B/INN 🏨 **Chanterelle Country Inn & Cottages.** You don't have to be a fan of the namesake mushroom to fall for this hilltop property on 100 acres, much of which is a wildlife preserve. **Pros:** natural soaps made especially for the inn; green credentials include some solar power and organic gardening; culinary and activity-based packages include golfing, kayaking, and mushroom-picking. **Cons:** three-day minimum stay in cottages; TVs and phones for inn rooms must be requested; rooms strictly fragrance-free, so don't unpack the perfume. [$] *Rooms from: C$145* ✉ *48678 Cabot Trail Rd., North River Bridge* ☎ *902/929–2263, 866/277–0577* 🌐 *www.chanterelleinn.com* 🛏 *8 rooms, 1 suite, 3 cottages* 🕒 *Inn by appointment only Nov.–Apr.* 🍴 *Multiple meal plans.*

$$ B&B/INN 🏨 **English Country Garden Bed & Breakfast.** Well positioned for those wishing to explore the bay area, this 37-acre lakefront property is itself ideal for strolling, though at the end of the day there's a lot to draw you indoors.

Pros: no stairs; reduced rates for extended stays; romance packages. **Cons:** spotty satellite TV coverage; very rural. $ *Rooms from: C$145* ✉ *45478 Cabot Trail Rd., Indian Brook* ☎ *866/929–2721, 902/929–2721* ⊕ *englishcountrygardenbb.ca* ⇦ *5 suites, 1 cottage* ⏐◎⏐ *Breakfast.*

SPORTS AND THE OUTDOORS

North River Kayak Tours. Half-day (C$64) and full-day (C$109) guided excursions are conducted from mid-May to mid-October by this outfitter. A light lunch is included in the former, and full-day tours include a hot lunch cooked on the beach. Basic rentals are also available. ■ **TIP→ Aspiring songwriters—no experience required—can take the Songwriting Kayaker Tour (C$249), including a full day of kayaking, a night's stay at a B&B, a songwriting lesson from an East Coast Music Award–nominated musician, and a copy of the tune you create.** ✉ *644 Murray Rd., 40 km (25 miles) northeast of Baddeck via Cabot Trail, North River Bridge* ☎ *902/929–2628, 888/865–2925* ⊕ *www.northriverkayak.com.*

SHOPPING

Gaelic College of Celtic Arts and Crafts Gift Shop. Filled with Celtic and clan-related items—crafts, books, clothing, and music—this shop has a custom kilt maker on-site. ✉ *51779 Cabot Trail Rd., St. Ann's* ☎ *902/295–3411* ⊕ *www.gaeliccollege.edu/craft-shop.*

Glass Artisans Studio & Gallery. Gorgeous glassware—be it stained, painted, blown, or fused—is sold here. ✉ *45054 Cabot Trail, North Shore* ☎ *902/929–2585, 888/262–6435* ⊕ *www.glassartisans.ca.*

Iron Art & Photographs. In addition to the metal sculptures with engaging and elegant forms, this gallery features photographic art and craft items. ✉ *48084 Cabot Trail Rd., Tarbot* ☎ *902/929–2821* ⊕ *www.ironart.ca.*

Leatherworks. Purses, pet collars, and even old-fashioned leather fire buckets are the specialties here. ✉ *45808 Cabot Trail Rd., Indian Brook* ☎ *902/929–2414* ⊕ *www.leather-works.ca.*

Piper Pewter. Much of the lead-free pewter giftware created here is inspired by Celtic designs. ✉ *46112 Cabot Trail, Indian Brook* ☎ *902/929–2227* ⊕ *www.piperpewter.com.*

Sew Inclined. Need a new outfit, or something to top off the one you're wearing? Fashions and theatrical, handmade hats in almost every imaginable style and fabric, crafted by milliner and costume designer Barbara Longva, are sold here from May through November. ✉ *41819 Cabot Trail, Wreck Cove* ☎ *902/929–2259, 902/929–2050* ⊕ *www.sewinclined.ca.*

Singing Pebbles Pottery. Teapots, mugs, and other pieces of fine, functional pottery are made on-site here and supplied to several craft galleries. If you'd like to visit the potter at her studio it's best to call before visiting because opening hours are not fixed. ✉ *42164 Cabot Trail Rd., Wreck Cove* ☎ *902/929–2399* ⊕ *www.singingpebbles.ca* ⊗ *By appointment.*

Wildfire Pottery. Cool clay creations, many of them in the shape of area animals, are the specialty here. The shop's operating hours are sporadic. ✉ *44429 Cabot Trail, North Shore* ☎ *902/929–2315* ⊕ *www.wildfirepottery.ca.*

Woodsmiths Studio. Wooden bowls, boxes, toys, and trinkets are made on-site here. The studio is closed on weekends and from mid-October to mid-May. ⊠ *44556 Cabot Trail Rd., Englishtown* ☎ *902/929–2111* ⊕ *www.woodsmithstudio.com.*

BADDECK

20 km (12 miles) southwest of St. Ann's.

Baddeck has enough down-to-earth amenities (like a grocery store) to make it a service center, and enough charm to make it a tourist destination. The population is only about 1,000 residents but the town's larger-than-usual concentration of lodgings, restaurants, and shops attracts motorists who are ending (or starting) a Cabot Trail trek. Boaters also come to explore Bras d'Or Lake. The most competitive among them raise anchor during Regatta Week, Baddeck's main event, which begins the first Sunday in August at the Bras d'Or Yacht Club (☎ *902/295–2107* ⊕ *www.brasdoryachtclub.ca*).

GETTING HERE AND AROUND

Maritime Bus serves Baddeck. The journey from Halifax takes about 5½ hours and costs C$63.50 one-way; the time from Truro is just under four hours and the fare is C$49. Call for other routes (⇨ *See Planning, above, for contact information*). Baddeck is on the Trans-Canada Highway (Highway 105).

ESSENTIALS

Visitor Information Baddeck Visitor Information Centre ⊠ *454 Chebucto St.* ☎ *902/295–1911* ⊕ *www.visitbaddeck.com* ☉ *June–mid-Oct.*

EXPLORING

FAMILY **Alexander Graham Bell National Historic Site.** This site pays homage to Bell's many inventions and humanitarian work. Inside the main building, films, photos, artifacts, and models provide a window into his ideas for creating telephones, man-carrying kites, airplanes, and a record-setting hydrofoil boat (a full scale replica of which dominates one exhibit hall). A kid's corner hosts demos and hands-on activities for aspiring young inventors. ⊠ *559 Chebucto St.* ☎ *902/295–2069* ⊕ *www.pc.gc.ca* ⊠ *C$7.80* ☉ *July–early Sept., daily 9–5; May and June and early Sept.–mid-Oct., Wed.–Sun. 9–5; Nov.–Apr., by appointment.*

Bras d'Or Lakes and Watershed Interpretive Centre. Occupying a former post office dating from 1885, this small interpretive center takes an ecological look at the body of water—some 965 km (600 miles) around—that cuts Cape Breton in two. In addition to the wildlife displays, there are maps and brochures aimed at helping visitors get the best out of the UNESCO Biosphere Reserve. ⊠ *532 Chebucto St.* ☎ *902/295–1675* ⊕ *brasdorpreservation.ca* ⊠ *By donation* ☉ *June–Aug., daily 9–7; call for off-season hrs.*

Usige Bàn Falls Provincial Park. The focal point of this park, 14.5 km (9 miles) north of Baddeck, is a forested 1.5-km (1-mile) round-trip trail to a much-photographed waterfall (*usige* is Gaelic for "water"). ⊠ *715 N. Branch Rd., Baddeck Forks* ⊕ *parks.gov.ns.ca* ⊠ *Free* ☉ *Daily mid-May–mid-Oct.*

Wagmatcook Culture & Heritage Centre. The center spotlights the ancient history and rich traditions of the native Mi'Kmaq people, with aboriginal guides providing interpretations and cultural entertainment. The restaurant here serves traditional foods (such as moose and eel), as well as more contemporary fare, and a crafts shop sells items made by members of this First Nations community. ✉ *10765 Hwy. 105, 16 km (10 miles) west of Baddeck* ☎ *902/295–1542, 866/295–2999* 🌐 *www.wagmatcook.com* 🎟 *Free (fees for some services); donations are welcome* 🕒 *May–Oct., daily 11–4; Nov.–Apr., weekdays 9–4 (hrs are flexible, so check first).*

WHERE TO EAT AND STAY

For expanded hotel reviews, visit Fodors.com.

$$$ SEAFOOD 🍴 **Baddeck Lobster Suppers.** For superfresh seafood overlooking Bras d'Or Lake, head for this former legion hall. It can seat 100 diners inside, and more on the deck, but it gets busy, particularly when a tour bus unloads (though these are by reservation only so you can call to check whether one is expected). There are just three options on the menu—lobster, planked salmon, and grilled steak—each served with unlimited mussels, seafood chowder, homemade rolls and biscuits, desserts, and nonalcoholic beverages (yes, all of these items are unlimited). Unlike some similar spots, this one is fully licensed so you can wash all that down with a cold brew. [$] *Average main: C$30* ✉ *17 Ross St.* ☎ *902/295–3307* 🌐 *www.baddecklobstersuppers.ca* 🕒 *Closed Nov.–May. No lunch.*

$ B&B/INN 🏨 **Baddeck Heritage House.** Since town sites are within walking distance, this 1860s B&B serves as a good base for touring, but just relaxing on the sunny deck, with views of the Bras d'Or Lakes, is a pleasant pastime, too. **Pros:** attentive, eco-conscious owners. **Cons:** small-ish rooms; the friendly family cat may make allergies flare. [$] *Rooms from: C$110* ✉ *121 Twining St.* ☎ *902/295–3219, 877/223–1112* 🌐 *www.baddeckheritagehouse.ca* 🛏 *4 rooms* 🕒 *Closed late Oct.–early May* 🍽 *Breakfast.*

$$$ B&B/INN 🏨 **Castle Moffett.** Though not a historic property (it was erected in 1992), this "castle" is enticingly regal and sits on 200 acres of grounds overlooking Bras d'Or Lake. **Pros:** the property is stunning in fall; suites are spacious. **Cons:** very pricey; some multinight minimum stay requirements; dining room has only one sitting at 7 pm. [$] *Rooms from: C$199* ✉ *11980 Hwy. 105, 19 km (12 miles) from Baddeck, Bucklaw* ☎ *902/756–9070, 888/756–9070* 🌐 *castlemoffett.com* 🛏 *6 rooms, 3 suites* 🕒 *Closed Nov.–Apr.* 🍽 *Multiple meal plans.*

$$ RESORT FAMILY 🏨 **Inverary Resort.** This 11-acre lakeside resort has idyllic views, lots of sporting opportunities, and a range of options, including cottages, suites, and rooms in a 1850 lodge or a modern building. **Pros:** very family-friendly; walking distance to town. **Cons:** breakfast not included; though open year-round, there are reduced services November through May. [$] *Rooms from: C$159* ✉ *368 Shore Rd.* ☎ *902/295–3500, 800/565–5660* 🌐 *www.capebretonresorts.com* 🛏 *129 rooms, 5 cottages* 🍽 *No meals.*

NIGHTLIFE AND THE ARTS

The Baddeck Gathering Ceilidhs. Featuring traditional music and dancing, ceilidhs (pronounced *kay-lees*) are held at St. Michael's Parish Hall every evening in July and August, starting at 7:30. The hall opens at

5 for ticket sales, or you can be sure to get in by phoning ahead for a reservation. The cost is C$10. ✉ *480 Chebucto St.* ☎ *902/295–0971* ⊕ *www.baddeckgathering.com.*

SPORTS AND THE OUTDOORS

GOLF

Bell Bay Golf Club. In addition to panoramic views from nearly all its holes, the club has a highly regarded golf school and one of the largest practice facilities in Eastern Canada. Thomas McBroom, responsible for several dozen courses in Canada, along with some in Europe and the Caribbean, designed Bell Bay. ✉ *761 Hwy. 205* ☎ *902/295–1333, 800/565–3077* ⊕ *www.bellbaygolfclub.com* ⚐ *Course: 18 holes, 7037 yds. Par 72. Green Fee: C$70/C$85* ⊗ *Mid-May–Oct.* ⚐ *Facilities: driving range, putting green, pitching area, golf carts, pull carts, rental clubs, pro shop, golf academy/lessons, restaurant, bar.*

BOAT TOURS

Amoeba Sailing Tours. Take a tour aboard a sleek schooner (C$25), lasting from 90 minutes to 2 hours, which views bald eagles and the Bell Estate. Trips depart daily at 11, 2, and 4:30 from June to mid-October, with an extra sailing at 6:30 pm in July and August. ✉ *Baddeck Wharf* ☎ *902/295–2481, 902/295–1426* ⊕ *www.amoebasailingtours.com.*

Donelda's Puffin Boat Tours. The Bird Islands, 2 km (1 mile) from the entrance to Bras d'Or Lake, are the breeding grounds for Atlantic puffins, as well as other seabirds and gray seals. To see them, sign up for one of these narrated nature cruises (C$38). From mid-May to late September, boats depart daily from Englishtown, about 28 km (17 miles) northeast of Baddeck. ✉ *1099 Hwy. 312, just before Englishtown Ferry, Englishtown* ☎ *902/929–2563, 877/278–3346* ⊕ *www.puffinboattours.ca.*

Paddle Dog. Easy 90-minute to 2-hour guided kayak tours on Bras d'Or Lake are offered three times daily in July and August (C$44). ✉ *22 Water St.* ☎ *902/929–2628* ⊕ *www.paddledog.ca.*

OFF THE BEATEN PATH

Iona, 77 km (48 miles) south of Baddeck, is admittedly off the beaten path. To reach Iona from Baddeck, follow Highway 105 to Exit 6, which leads to Little Narrows, then board a cable ferry for the two-minute ride to the Iona Peninsula (C$5; 24 hours a day, year-round). If you're big on Gaelic culture, a visit to the living history museum there will be ample reward.

Highland Village Museum. The 40-acre "village" is set high on a mountainside with a spectacular view of Bras d'Or Lake and narrow Barra Strait. Its 11 historical buildings (among them a forge, a school, a church, and a barn filled with heritage breeds of livestock) were assembled from all over the province to depict the Highland Scots' way of life, from their origins in the Hebrides to the present day. Costumed animators who tackle daily chores lend the village a further touch of authenticity and are always on the ready to give an impromptu Gaelic lesson. Interactive programs include games and activities for children. There's a gift shop on-site as well as a Genealogy and Family History Center (open by appointment) that may be of interest to anyone with Cape Breton blood in their veins. ✉ *4119 Hwy. 223* ☎ *902/725–2272, 866/442–3542* ⊕ *highlandvillage.novascotia.ca* ⚐ *C$11* ⊗ *June–mid-Oct., daily 10–5; gift shop year-round, weekdays 9–5.*

SYDNEY

62 km (39 miles) northeast of Iona; 77 km (48 miles) east of Baddeck.

If you come directly to Cape Breton via plane, ferry, or cruise ship, Sydney is where you'll land. If you're seeking anything resembling an urban experience, it's also where you'll want to stay: after all, this is the island's sole city. Moreover, it offers convenient access to popular attractions in the region—like the Miner's Museum in nearby Glace Bay (named for the *glace,* or ice, that filled its harbor in winter), the Fortress at Louisbourg, and beautiful Bras d'Or Lake.

GETTING HERE AND AROUND

Sydney is on the Marconi Trail, one of the province's main driving routes, and it has Cape Breton's only real airport. There are year-round air connections via Halifax on Air Canada/Jazz and seasonal ones (from May through October) via Toronto on WestJet. Scheduled flights to the French-held islands of St-Pierre and Miquelon also run. Marine Atlantic operates ferries between Newfoundland and North Sydney, about 20 km (12 miles) north, year-round.

TOURS

The Old Sydney Society, which operates Cossit House and trio of other restored building-cum-museums (Jost House, St. Patrick's Church, and the Cape Breton Centre for Heritage and Science), organizes 90-minute Ghost Walks through the historic North End on Tuesday and Wednesday evenings in July and August. Tours cost C$10 (refreshments included) and start at 7 pm; reservations required.

Tour Contact Old Sydney Society ⊠ *The Lyceum, 225 George St.* ☎ *902/539–1572* ⊕ *www.oldsydney.com.*

ESSENTIALS

Visitor Information Sydney Visitor Information Centre ⊠ *20 Keltic Dr.* ☎ *902/539–9876* ⊕ *www.sydney.capebretonisland.com* ⊘ *June–mid-Oct.* **North Sydney Visitor Information Centre** ⊠ *293 Rear Commercial St., North Sydney* ☎ *902/794–2989* ⊘ *July and Aug.*

EXPLORING

Cape Breton Miners' Museum. Here you can learn about the difficult lives of the local men whose job it was to extract coal from undersea collieries. After perusing the exhibits, you can don a hard hat and descend into the damp, claustrophobic recesses of a shaft beneath the museum with a retired miner who'll recount his own experiences toiling in the bowels of the earth. The 15-acre property also includes a replica village that gives you a sense of workers' home life, and it has a theater where the Men of the Deeps choir, a world-renowned group of working and retired miners, performs in summer. ⊠ *42 Birkley St., Quarry Point, 19 km (12 miles) east of Sydney, Glace Bay* ☎ *902/849–4522* ⊕ *www.minersmuseum.com* ☒ *Museum C$6, museum and mine tour C$12* ⊘ *July and Aug., daily 10–6 (until 7 on Tues.); Sept. and Oct., daily 10–6; Nov.–May, weekdays 9–4.*

Cossit House. Built in 1787, this unpretentious wooden building was originally home to Reverend Ranna Cossit—Cape Breton's first protestant minister—his wife Thankful, and their 10 children. Now faithfully restored and occupied by costumed interpreters, the North End residence is furnished with period pieces based on Cossit's own inventory. ⊠ *75 Charlotte St.* ☎ *902/539–7973* ⊕ *cossithouse.novascotia.ca* 🖾 *C$2* ⊙ *June–mid-Oct., Tues.–Sat. 10–5, Sun. 1–5.*

Marconi National Historic Site. On a spectacular headland, this site commemorates the spot at Table Head where, in 1902, Guglielmo Marconi built four tall wooden towers and beamed the first official wireless messages across the Atlantic Ocean. An interpretive trail leads to the foundations of the original towers and transmitter buildings. The visitor center has large models of the towers as well as artifacts and photographs chronicling the radio pioneer's life and work. ⊠ *15 Timmerman St., 23 km (14 miles) northeast of Sydney; follow signs from Hwy. 255, Glace Bay* ☎ *902/295–2069, 902/842–2530 summer* ⊕ *www.pc.gc.ca* 🖾 *Free (C$2.50 donation suggested)* ⊙ *Open July–early Sept., daily 10–6.*

Sydney Mines Heritage Museum and Cape Breton Fossil Centre. Two affiliated facilities across the harbor from Sydney proper chronicle the area's prehistoric and more recent pasts. The mines museum, which occupies a small converted train station, surveys area history but focuses on Sydney's coal-mining connection. Displays at the fossil center include 300-million-year-old specimens from the Sydney Coal Fields. ■TIP➔ **The fossil center's curator leads two-hour fossil-hunting field trips, by reservation, on Tuesdays and Thursdays at 10 am; you'll need your own transportation to the trip's starting point.** ⊠ *159 Legatto St., Sydney Mines* ☎ *902/544–0992* ⊕ *www.cbfossil.org* 🖾 *Museum C$6, field trip C$11* ⊙ *June–mid-Oct., Tues.–Sat. 9–5.*

WHERE TO EAT AND STAY

For expanded hotel reviews, visit Fodors.com.

$$$
CONTEMPORARY

✕ **Flavor Downtown.** In a city where deep fryers reign supreme, this small bistro-style eatery is a welcome find. The haddock is poached, the scallops seared, the prawns tossed in pesto sauce—and the absence of greasy batter means Flavor's flavors shine through. The menu is a broad one: homemade pastas are popular, as are the inventive sandwiches and all-day breakfast items. There are several gluten-free, vegan, and vegetarian options, too (a rarity in these parts), plus a Paleo Menu, providing low-carb, low-sugar, zero-gluten, high-protein meals (a rarity anywhere). Brunch is served on Saturday, and you can eat outside on the patio in summer. Another branch, Flavor 19, is at the Lingan Golf Course. $ *Average main: C$23* ⊠ *16 Pitt St.* ☎ *902/562–6611* ⊕ *www.cbflavor. com* ⊙ *Closed Sun.*

$$$
CONTEMPORARY

✕ **Governor's Pub and Eatery.** Sydney's first mayor, Walter Crowe, once lived in this Victorian home, built in the late 1800s. The restaurant, with hardwood floors, a fireplace, and high ceilings, is known for fresh seafood and hand-cut steaks, though there are lighter options such as salads, wraps, and burgers. Both the restaurant and the pub upstairs have large patios that overlook Sydney Harbour. On most nights the atmosphere is bustling and lively, with locals and travelers mixing over a pint, and there's regular live entertainment. The desserts are all homemade. $ *Average main: C$25* ⊠ *233 Esplanade* ☎ *902/562–7646* ⊕ *governorseatery.com* ⊙ *No brunch weekdays.*

$$ HOTEL **Cambridge Suites Hotel.** You can put yourself in the center of Sydney's waterfront action by staying at this comfortable all-suites hotel. **Pros:** free continental breakfast buffet; pet friendly. **Cons:** other people's pets are sometimes audible; conventional room style. [$] *Rooms from: C$139* ✉ *380 Esplanade* ☎ *902/562–6500, 800/565–9466* 🌐 *www.cambridgesuitessydney.com* 🛏 *147 suites* 🍴 *Multiple meal plans.*

NIGHTLIFE AND THE ARTS

Cape Breton University. The area's leading cultural institution, the university includes the 337-seat Boardmore Playhouse and the CBU Art Gallery (the only public gallery on the island). ✉ *1250 Grand Lake Rd.* ☎ *902/539–5300, 888/959–9995, 902/563–1652 box office* 🌐 *www.cbu.ca.*

Joan Harriss Cruise Pavilion. More than just a port for the many cruise ships that dock here each year, the pavilion is a popular entertainment venue, too. Its main stage and lighthouse stage host many musical acts, especially during events like Sydney's nine-day mid-summer Action Week (🌐 *www.actionweek.com*) and the nine-day Celtic Colours International Festival (🌐 *www.celtic-colours.com*), at venues all over Cape Breton. Even if you're not arriving by ship, the pavilion is easy enough to find: just look for the 18-meter (60-foot fiddle that towers outside it. ✉ *74 Esplanade* ☎ *902/564–9775* 🌐 *www.sydneyport.ca.*

CASINO

Casino Nova Scotia. At the casino you can try your luck at slot machines, test your skill at gaming tables, or simply settle in to enjoy the live entertainment—assuming you're at least 19 years old, the legal drinking age in Nova Scotia. ✉ *525 George St.* ☎ *902/563–7777, 866/334–1114* 🌐 *www.casinonovascotia.com.*

SPORTS AND THE OUTDOORS

Peterfield Provincial Park. Take a hike through history at this park on the south arm of Sydney Harbour. Initially developed as the private domain of David Matthews, a onetime mayor of New York City who remained loyal to the crown during the War of Independence, its 56 acres are laced with trails. ✉ *1126 Westmount Rd., off Hwy. 239, Westmount* ☎ *902/662–3030 Nova Scotia Provincial Parks* 🌐 *www.novascotiaparks.ca* 🎟 *Free* 🕒 *Mid-May–mid-Oct.*

SHOPPING

The Cape Breton Centre for Craft and Design. Showcasing the work of traditional and cutting-edge Cape Breton artisans in its airy second-floor gallery, the center, which houses on-site studios for pottery, weaving, and glass- and jewelry-making, also hosts hands-on workshops that are open to craft aficionados. The center is closed on Sunday. ✉ *322 Charlotte St.* ☎ *902/270–7491* 🌐 *www.capebretoncraft.com.*

Harbourside Boutiques. Top island retailers—among them Hattie's Heirlooms, the Cape Breton Curiosity Shop, Man of War Gallery, and Tastes of Cape Breton—are represented at Harbourside Boutiques in the Joan Harriss Cruise Pavilion. They're only open seasonally, though, sometimes daily in high season, sometimes just when cruise ships are in port. ✉ *74 Esplanade* ☎ *902/564–9775* 🌐 *www.sydneyport.ca.*

LOUISBOURG

53 km (33 miles) south of Glace Bay.

Though best known as the home of the largest historical reconstruction in North America, Louisbourg is also an important fishing community with a lovely harborfront. There are a number of good places to stay here, too.

GETTING HERE AND AROUND

There is no public transportation to Louisbourg. By road it's about a two-hour drive from the Canso Causeway, via Highway 125 then (at Exit 8) Route 22.

ESSENTIALS

Visitor Information **Louisbourg Visitor Information Centre** ✉ *7495 Main St.* ☎ *902/733–2321* 🌐 *www.louisbourgtourism.com* 🕐 *Mid-June–mid-Oct.*

EXPLORING

FAMILY Fodor's Choice ★ **Fortress of Louisbourg National Historic Site.** This may be Cape Breton's most remarkable attraction. From June through mid-October, costumed interpreters convincingly re-create the activities of the original inhabitants, so you can watch a military drill, see nails and lace being made, or dine in the town's three inns on food prepared from 18th-century recipes. Free guided tours are given in high season and events available at extra cost—including themed dinner theaters (C$48), a Murder Mystery Tour (C$27), and archaeological programs—make a visit here even more memorable. On the other hand, an off-season visit, without all these activities, can paint a more compelling picture of life in the fort 300 years ago. ■ TIP → **Plan on spending most or all of a day here, and bring a warm sweater or jacket—Louisbourg tends to be chilly at any time of year.** ✉ *265 Parks Service Rd.* ☎ *902/733–2280* 🌐 *www.fortressoflouisbourg.ca* 🎟 *C$17.60, guided tour C$3.90* 🕐 *Mid-May–mid-Oct., daily 9:30–5; mid-Oct.–mid-May, weekdays 9:30–4.*

WHERE TO EAT AND STAY

For expanded hotel reviews, visit Fodors.com.

$$ CANADIAN FAMILY 🍴 **Grubstake Restaurant.** *Coquilles St. Jacques* (scallops with mushrooms in a white wine–cream sauce), seafood pasta, and shrimp-and-scallop flambé are popular dishes at this 120-seat restaurant. Although seafood is the specialty, the baked Chicken Royale with mushrooms and the country-style barbecue pork are also excellent. The cocktail lounge is a great place to relax with a drink and meet some locals. Service is friendly and laid-back—though this sometimes translates into slow. Desserts are made on-site. [$] *Average main: C$18* ✉ *7499 Main St.* ☎ *902/733–2308* 🌐 *www.grubstake.ca* 🕐 *Closed Nov.–June.*

$ B&B/INN 🏨 **Cranberry Cove Inn.** This cozy cranberry-hued house, built in 1904, overlooks the harbor and is just a short drive from the Fortress of Louisbourg. **Pros:** cooked breakfast included; impeccable rooms. **Cons:** no elevator for three-story building; Wi-Fi is spotty in some rooms. [$] *Rooms from: C$105* ✉ *12 Wolfe St.* ☎ *902/733–2171, 800/929–0222* 🌐 *www.cranberrycoveinn.com* 🛏 *7 rooms* 🕐 *Closed mid-Oct.–mid-May* 🍽 *Breakfast.*

$ ⌂ **Louisbourg Harbour Inn Bed & Breakfast.** The central location of this
B&B/INN grand, former sea-captain's residence means it's just a few minutes'
walk to the Louisbourg Playhouse, Main Street, and the harbor.
Pros: cooked breakfast included; lovely views. **Cons:** no elevator for
three-story building; several rooms are small; two-night minimum for
the best room; children not accommodated. **$** *Rooms from: C$120*
✉ *9 Lower Warren St.* ☎ *902/733–3222, 888/888–8466* ⊕ *www.
louisbourgharbourinn.com* ⤳ *7 rooms* ⊘ *Closed early Oct.–early
June* ⦿ *Breakfast.*

$ ⌂ **Point of View Suites.** This modern hotel, built to resemble an oversize
HOTEL beach house, is the closest property to the Fortress of Louisbourg and
the only one in town that is on the water. **Pros:** private pebble beach;
knowledgeable owners who grew up in the area. **Cons:** nonocean-
view units overlook an RV lot; limited restaurant menu off-season.
$ *Rooms from: C$125* ✉ *15 Commercial St. Extension* ☎ *902/733–
2080, 888/374–8439* ⊕ *www.louisbourgpointofview.com* ⤳ *19 rooms*
⊘ *Closed mid-Oct.–mid-May* ⦿ *No meals.*

NIGHTLIFE AND THE ARTS

Louisbourg Playhouse. You can take in traditional Cape Breton music
and other entertainments nightly at the Louisbourg Playhouse, a 17th-
century-style theater that was modeled after Shakespeare's Globe.
Originally constructed as part of the Disney movie set for *Squanto: A
Warrior's Tale,* the venue was donated to the community in 1994 after
filming wrapped. ✉ *11 Aberdeen St.* ☎ *902/733–2996, 888/733–2787*
⊕ *www.louisbourgplayhouse.com* ⊘ *Mid-June–mid-Oct., nightly at 8.*

SPORTS AND THE OUTDOORS

BOATING

Rising Tide Expeditions. You can dip into the past with a full-day kayaking
excursion called "Fortress of Louisbourg: Paddle Through Time" for
C$135 from May through October. Other packages combine kayak-
ing with hiking or yoga. ✉ *8806 Gabarus Hwy., 55 km (34 miles)
from Louisbourg (by road) via Hwy. 327, Gabarus* ☎ *902/884–2884,
877/884–2884* ⊕ *www.risingtideexpeditions.ca.*

BIG POND

50 km (31 miles) west of Louisbourg.

This tiny community consists of a few houses dotted along the highway,
and a famous tea room.

GETTING HERE AND AROUND

There is no public transportation to Big Pond, which is off Route 4.

EXPLORING

Rita's Tea Room. Most people come to Big Pond to visit the home of
the late singer-songwriter Rita MacNeil, who died in 2013. Rita lived
with her children in this former one-room schoolhouse and opened
the tearoom in 1986. The building has been expanded to accommodate the multitude of visitors who arrive to sample Rita's Tea Room
Blend Tea, which is served along with light meals and tasty baked
goods. You can visit a display room of Rita's awards and photographs

and browse the gift shop. ✉ *8077 Hwy. 4* ☎ *902/828–2667* ⊕ *www.ritamacneil.com/tearoom.html* ✆ *Late June–mid-Oct., daily 10–5 (gift shop open June 1).*

ARICHAT

62 km (38 miles) southwest of Big Pond.

Arichat is the principal village on Isle Madame: the largest island in a 44-square-km (17-square-mile) archipelago of the same name, which sits at Cape Breton's southernmost tip. Known for its friendly Acadian culture and many secluded coves and inlets, Arichat has a deep harbor that made it an important fishing, shipbuilding, and trading center during the 19th century. Some fine old buildings from that period still remain. The two cannons overlooking the harbor were installed after John Paul Jones sacked the village during the American Revolution.

GETTING HERE AND AROUND

To get here from Big Pond, take Route 4 to Highway 320, which leads through Poulamon and D'Escousse before bridging Lennox Passage. Highway 206 meanders through the low hills to a maze of land and water at West Arichat. Together, the two routes encircle the island, meeting at Arichat.

One of the best ways to experience Isle Madame is by foot. Try Cape Auguet Eco-Trail, an 8.5-km (5-mile) hiking trail that extends from Boudreauville to Mackerel Cove and follows the rocky coastline overlooking Chedabucto Bay. Another good half-day hike leads to Gros Nez, the "large nose" that juts into the sea. The island also lends itself to biking, as most roads glide gently along the shore.

EXPLORING

Notre Dame de l'Assomption. Arichat was once the seat of the local Catholic diocese, and this church, built in 1837, retains the grandeur of its former status as a cathedral. The bishop's palace is now a law office. ■ **TIP**➜ **Brochures containing a self-guided tour can be found at the back of the church.** ✉ *2292 Hwy. 206* ☎ *902/226–2109* ✉ *Free* ✆ *Dawn–dusk. Mass, year-round Sun. 9:15 am.*

LeNoir Forge Museum. This restored 18th-century French blacksmith shop occupies a handsome stone structure on the waterfront. In its 19th-century heyday, it supplied parts to local shipbuilders. ✉ *712 Veterans Memorial Dr., off Hwy. 206* ☎ *902/226–9364* ✉ *Free, donations welcome* ✆ *Early June–Sept. 1, Mon.–Sat. 10–5, Sun. noon–5.*

3

NEW BRUNSWICK

WELCOME TO NEW BRUNSWICK

TOP REASONS TO GO

★ Go Whale-Watching: Double the fun of the Bay of Fundy by getting out onto the water to view several types of whale, plus seals, porpoises, and sea birds.

★ Experience Acadian Culture: Attractions such as Le Pays de la Sagouine or Acadian Historical Village on the Acadian Coastal Drive portray the French heritage of the region. Hear the distinctive accent at Dieppe Farmers' Market.

★ Eat Well: Enjoy freshly caught salmon, scallops, and lobster, in addition to fresh-picked fiddlehead ferns and dulse, Acadian poutine, and buffalo steaks.

★ Take a Hike: New Brunswick's provincial and national parks have amazing hiking trails and plenty of great spots to contemplate the gorgeous scenery or watch birds from an ocean cliff.

★ Go for a Swim: New Brunswick is blessed with beaches, rivers, and lakes; you can choose from water that's cold or warm, fresh or salty, on long sandy shores or in intimate coves.

1 Saint John. The port city of Saint John has become a vibrant urban destination, with a revitalized waterfront, an eclectic restaurant scene, lively nightlife and festivals, fun street art, and one of Canada's loveliest city parks. There's plenty of history, too, from first-class museums and historic sites to streets lined with 19th-century homes.

2 The Fundy Coast. Boasting some of the highest tides in the world, the Bay of Fundy is a diverse region with dramatic coastlines, tiny fishing villages, charming islands, and rocky beaches perfect for treasure hunting. Time seems to stand still here, and life is laid-back and informal. The city of Moncton, billed as the "crossroads of the Maritimes" or "Hub City," is an increasingly worthwhile place to visit, with fun attractions for the kids.

3 The Acadian Coast and St. John River Valley. A highlight of this region is French Acadian culture with its distinct foods, music, and festivals. Unlike the Bay of Fundy, the water on the Acadian Coast is downright balmy, and the selection of beaches can be mind-boggling. Much of the St. John River—more than 500 km (310 miles) of it—meanders through cities, townships, and charming villages. Pastoral farmland accompanies you most of the way.

GETTING ORIENTED

New Brunswick has it all: a mighty river (and many other impressive waterways), coastal waters with dramatically high tides on the Fundy shore, forests that sweep for miles, and mountain ranges perfect for activities like hiking and skiing. Most of all, this province has people who are exceptionally friendly. You'll find activities and attractions to suit every age and taste and then some.

Baie des Chaleurs

Miscou Island
Caraquet
Lamèque
Acadian ◆ Historical Village
Shippagan
Bathurst
Tracadie-Sheila

8   11   *Gulf of St Lawrence*

Miramichi City
Neguac

11   *Kouchibouguac National Park*

Richibucto
126
Bouctouche
Le Pays de la Sagouine

PRINCE EDWARD ISLAND
NEW BRUNSWICK

Shediac
11

Moncton   2   Memramcook
2   Dorchester   Sackville
Sussex   Hopewell Cape   NOVA SCOTIA
1   104
Fundy National Park   Alma
2
St. Martins

Bay of Fundy

0   50 mi
0   50 km

4 Fredericton. A gracious, small city bisected by the wide St. John River and spreading up the gentle slopes of its valley, Fredericton is the capital of New Brunswick and home to two fine universities. It has a historic core, arts and culture, and great shopping.

Updated by
Penny Phenix

Stunning scenery, vast forests, and world-class attractions characterize New Brunswick. Topping the list is the Bay of Fundy, shortlisted (but sadly not selected) to be one of the "New 7 Wonders of Nature," with the highest tides in the world, marine life that includes several species of whales, stretches of wilderness coastline, and charming harbor villages.

Add to this national and international historic sites, national parks teeming with wildlife, great beaches, vibrant towns and cities, and a thriving diversity of cultures, and you might wonder how the population can remain so utterly laid-back, but that's just another facet of New Brunswick's charm. The province is an old place in New World terms, and the remains of a turbulent past are still evident in some of its quiet nooks. Near Moncton, for instance, wild strawberries perfume the air of the grassy slopes of Fort Beauséjour, where, in 1755, one of the last battles for possession of Acadia took place, with the English finally overcoming the French. Other areas of the province were settled by the British; by Loyalists, American colonists who chose to live under British rule after the American Revolution; and by Irish immigrants, many seeking to avoid the famine in their home country. If you stay in both Acadian and Loyalist regions, a trip to New Brunswick can seem like two vacations in one.

For every gesture in the provincial landscape as grand as the giant rock formations carved by the Bay of Fundy tides at Hopewell Hill, there is one as subtle as the gifted touch of a sculptor in a studio. For every experience as colorful as the mountains of lobster served at Shediac's annual Lobster Festival, there is another as low-key as the gentle waves of the Baie des Chaleurs. New Brunswick is the luxury of an inn with five stars and the tranquillity of camping under a million.

At the heart of New Brunswick is the forest, which covers 85% of the province—nearly all its interior. The forest contributes to the economy, defines the landscape, and delights hikers, anglers, campers, and bird-watchers, but New Brunswick's soul is the sea. The biggest of Canada's three Maritime provinces, New Brunswick is largely surrounded by coastline. The warm waters of the Baie des Chaleurs, Gulf of St. Lawrence, and Northumberland Strait lure swimmers to their sandy beaches, and the chilly Bay of Fundy, with its monumental tides, draws breaching whales, whale-watchers, and kayakers.

PLANNING

WHEN TO GO

Each season brings unique reasons to travel to New Brunswick. Winter means skiing, snowmobiling, skating on public rinks, and cozy dinners. Spring is the time for canoeing the inland rivers, fishing, picking fiddleheads, and watching the province come alive.

Summer is peak tourist season, and Parlee Beach attracts thousands of sun worshippers. The resort towns of Fundy, including Alma, St. Andrews, and St. George, get busy, too. It's a good time to trek up to the lighthouse at Cape Enrage. Summer festivals abound, and the province's two national parks, Fundy and Kouchibouguac, are filled with nature lovers.

Fall means country fairs, harvest suppers, and incredibly beautiful scenic drives to enjoy autumn foliage. Fall colors are at their peak from late September through mid- to late October. The Autumn Foliage Colours Line (☎ 800/268–3255) provides daily updates on which drives are best.

FESTIVALS

Fodor's Choice
★

Harvest Jazz and Blues Festival. Hundreds (literally) of world-class musicians perform at around 30 venues in downtown Fredericton over six days in early September, encompassing many genres of jazz, blues, rock, and more. ⊠ *Fredericton* ☎ *506/454–2583 for information, 888/622–5837 for tickets* ⊕ *www.harvestjazzandblues.com.*

Irish Festival. In early July Miramichi celebrates everything Irish with four days of music, dancing, workshops, food, and drink in various locations. ⊠ *Miramichi City* ☎ *506/778–8810* ⊕ *www.canadasirishfest.com.*

New Brunswick Highland Games and Scottish Festival. The grounds of the riverside Government House is the venue for this long-established late-July festival, one of the best of its kind in North America. In addition to the competitive games, pipe bands, traditional music, and dancing, it features a 5-km kilted run. ⊠ *51 Woodstock Rd., Fredericton* ☎ *506/452–9244, 888/368–4444* ⊕ *www.highlandgames.ca.*

New Brunswick Summer Music Festival. For about 10 days in August, various venues around Fredericton host some of Canada's finest classical musicians, including at some free concerts in the cathedral on Officer's Square. ⊠ *Fredericton* ☎ *506/458–7836* ⊕ *nbsummermusicfestival.ca.*

Shediac Lobster Festival. The "lobster capital of the world" and home to the world's largest lobster further celebrates the crustacean with a five-day festival in mid-July. Events and entertainment include concerts, a parade, a midway, and lobster-eating competitions. ⊠ *Belliveau Ave., Shediac* ☎ *506/532–1122* ⊕ *www.shediaclobsterfestival.ca.*

PLANNING YOUR TIME

A good way to tour New Brunswick is to follow one of the five scenic drives into which the province is divided: The River Valley Scenic Drive follows more than 500 km (310 miles) of road along the St. John River; the Fundy Coastal Drive has potential views of whales and wildlife in the region of the Bay of Fundy; the Acadian Coastal Drive offers sandy beaches, picturesque villages, and vibrant culture; the Miramichi River Route is home to salmon fishing and folk festivals; and the Appalachian

Range Route has serene mountain vistas and beautiful bays. The Fundy Coast is perhaps the most popular area, and many prefer to spend more time here than in Saint John. Overnight in Alma, the little town that services Fundy National Park, or in Moncton, which has some good restaurants and shopping and fun amusements for children.

GETTING HERE AND AROUND

AIR TRAVEL

New Brunswick has three major airports: Saint John Airport, about 15 minutes east of downtown Saint John; Greater Moncton International Airport, about 10 minutes east of downtown Moncton; and Fredericton Airport, 10 minutes east of that city's downtown.

BOAT AND FERRY TRAVEL

Bay Ferries Ltd. runs from Saint John, New Brunswick, to Digby, Nova Scotia, and back once or twice a day, depending on the season. Passenger fares are C$43 per adult, C$86 for a car, and C$161–C$672 for a motorhome or car with trailer (depending on length), plus a C$20 fuel surcharge for the three-hour, one-way trip July through September. Off-season rates are cheaper.

The year-round 20-minute ferry crossing from Letete, on mainland New Brunswick, to Deer Island is a free service operated by the government of New Brunswick. From Deer Island, East Coast Ferries Ltd. runs services to Campobello, New Brunswick, and Eastport, Maine, from late June to mid-September. On the Campobello route, the fares are C$16 for a car and driver, C$3 for each adult passenger. The crossing takes about 40 minutes. On the Eastport route, the fares are C$13 for a car and driver and C$3 for each adult passenger. On both routes a fuel surcharge of C$4 is also applied, and cards are not accepted.

Coastal Transport has up to seven crossings per day from Blacks Harbour to Grand Manan late June through early September and four crossings per day the rest of the year. Round-trip fares, payable on the Grand Manan side, are C$32.55 for a car and C$10.90 for an adult. A one-way crossing takes about 1½ hours.

Contacts Bay Ferries Ltd. ⊠ *170 Digby Ferry Rd., off Lancaster St., Saint John* ☎ *506/694-7777, 866/7775-8291* ⊕ *www.nfl-bay.com.* **Coastal Transport** ☎ *506/662-3724, 855/882-1978* ⊕ *www.coastaltransport.ca.* **East Coast Ferries Ltd.** ☎ *506/747-2159, 877/747-2159* ⊕ *www.eastcoastferriesltd.com.*

BUS TRAVEL

Maritime Bus runs buses within the province and to destinations in Nova Scotia and Prince Edward Island. A relatively new company, their coverage is expanding so it's worth checking.

Contacts Maritime Bus ☎ *800/575-1807* ⊕ *www.maritimebus.com.*

CAR TRAVEL

New Brunswick is the largest of the Atlantic provinces, covering nearly 78,000 square km (30,000 square miles): around 320 km (200 miles) north to south and 240 km (150 miles) east to west. Unless you plan to fly into one of the hubs and stay there for your visit, you'd be wise to have a car. There's a good selection of car-rental agencies, but book early for July and August (and be aware that debit cards are not accepted); call or visit the websites to search for pick-up and drop-off locations throughout the province (bear in mind that rentals from airports carry a surcharge).

From Québec, the Trans-Canada Highway (Route 2, marked by a maple leaf) enters New Brunswick at St-Jacques and follows the St. John River through Fredericton and on to Moncton and the Nova Scotia border. From Maine, Interstate 95 crosses at Houlton to Woodstock, New Brunswick, where it connects with the Trans-Canada Highway. Those traveling up the coast of Maine on Route 1 cross at Calais to St. Stephen, New Brunswick. New Brunswick's Route 1 extends through Saint John and Sussex to join the Trans-Canada Highway near Moncton.

Route 7 joins Saint John and Fredericton. Fredericton is connected to Miramichi City by Route 8. Route 15 links Moncton to the eastern coast and to Route 11, which follows the coast north to Miramichi, around the Acadian Peninsula, and up to Campbellton.

DRIVING TIPS Watch out for moose, deer, black bears, porcupines, and raccoons, especially at night. Although major highways have moose and deer fences, many of the secondary roads do not, and twilight is an especially dangerous time for wildlife entering the roads. Reduce speed at night.

TRAIN TRAVEL

Train travel options in New Brunswick are limited: VIA Rail offers a thrice-weekly passenger service from Campbellton, Miramichi, and Moncton to Montréal and Halifax, with request stops at a number of smaller towns along the route (though none of them feature in this book). There is no train service to the cities of Saint John or Fredericton.

RESTAURANTS

You can eat extremely well in New Brunswick, with many restaurants sourcing top-quality ingredients from local farmers, fishermen, and artisan producers. At the top end are some of Canada's finest restaurants, such as the outstanding Windjammer in Moncton's Delta Beauséjour Hotel, Little Louis' Oyster Bar, also in Moncton, and The Blue Door in Fredericton. St. Andrews by-the-Sea has long been a culinary hot spot, while gastro-pubs are gaining ground throughout the province. At the other end of the scale, if you want to try some authentic Acadian food, there's a little paper-plate diner in Shediac, Le Menu Acadien, that cooks up *poutine rappé* (boiled potato dumpling with meat filling), *fricôt* (stew), and other delicacies according to grandma's recipes.

Prices in the reviews are the average cost of a main course at dinner or, if dinner is not served, at lunch.

HOTELS

Just about every kind of lodging experience is available in New Brunswick, including a plethora of high-end bed-and-breakfasts, rental properties, and a smattering of boutique hotels. When it comes to chain hotels, the Delta group is the cream of the crop, offering high standards of accommodations, superb restaurants, well-trained staff, and attractive room rates. In peak season rooms are snapped up quickly, particularly in the best bed-and-breakfasts, so it's wise to book as far in advance as possible. Outside peak season many of the bed-and-breakfasts and rental properties are closed, although those in the cities tend to stay open year-round.

Prices in the reviews are the lowest cost of a standard double room in high season. For expanded hotel reviews, facilities, and current deals, visit Fodors.com.

TOURS AND VISITOR INFORMATION

Whale-watching, sea kayaking, bird-watching, scuba diving, garden touring, river cruising, golfing, fishing, skiing, and snowmobiling are just a few of New Brunswick's alluring experiences. Bicycling in particular is a great way to tour New Brunswick. Two favorite biking areas in the province are the 33 km (20 miles) of country roads on Grand Manan Island (you can rent bikes from Adventure High; ⇨ *See the Grand Manan listings*) and the Quoddy Loop, which goes around Passamaquoddy Bay and the western mouth of the Bay of Fundy.

Baymount Outdoor Adventures operates bicycle tours for large groups along the Fundy shore near Hopewell Cape, and Off-Kilter Bike Tours organize fixed and customized excursions around St. Andrews by-the-Sea. B&Bs frequently have bicycles for rent, and Tourism New Brunswick has listings and free cycling maps.

Contacts Adventure High. Experienced guides lead kayaking tours in the Bay of Fundy, and packages that include a lobster dinner on the beach, cabin rentals, kayaking, and yoga, are also offered. You can rent bikes here, too. ✉ *83 Rte. 776, Grand Manan* ☎ *800/732–5492, 506/662–3563* ⊕ *www.adventurehigh. com.* **Baymount Outdoor Adventures.** This outfitter leads sea kayaking tours at Hopwell Rocks, and caving, hiking, and mountain-biking tours in the Bay of Fundy biosphere reserve. ☎ *506/734–2660, 877/601–2660* ⊕ *www. baymountadventures.com.* **Golf New Brunswick.** A resource for more than 20 golf courses in the province, all with carts and clubs to rent. ☎ *877/833–4662* ⊕ *www.golfnb.com.* **New Brunswick Trails Council** ☎ *506/459–1931, 800/526–7070* ⊕ *www.sentiernbtrail.com.* **Tourism New Brunswick** ☎ *800/561–0123* ⊕ *www.tourismnewbrunswick.ca.* **Uncorked Tours.** Escorted tours to New Brunswick wineries (with tastings), follow scenic routes and include visits to artisan studios. Tours are usually half- or full-days, but can be customized. ✉ *Arranged pickups, Saint John* ☎ *506/324–4644* ⊕ *www.UncorkedNB.com.*

SAINT JOHN

Like any seaport worth its salt, Saint John is a welcoming place but, more than that, it is fast transforming into a sophisticated urban destination worthy of the increasing number of cruise ships that dock at its revitalized waterfront. Such is the demand that a second cruise terminal opened in 2012, just two years after the first one, and 2013 will see the two-millionth cruise passenger disembark. All the comings and goings over the centuries have exposed Saint Johners to a wide variety of cultures and ideas, creating a characterful Maritime city with a vibrant artistic community. Visitors will discover rich and diverse cultural products in its urban core, including a plethora of art galleries and antiques shops in uptown.

NEW BRUNSWICK ITINERARIES

IF YOU HAVE 4 DAYS

Start in **Saint John,** steeped in English and Irish traditions and rich in history and art. The resort town of **St. Andrews by-the-Sea** is an hour's drive west and has plenty of art, crafts, history, nature, and seafood. Whale-watching tours leave from the wharf, and the outstanding **Kingsbrae Horticultural Garden** invites lingering. Spend a day and a night, then backtrack through Saint John, taking Route 1 then Route 111 to St. Martins and the **Fundy Trail Parkway.** Loop north then, via Route 111, to rejoin Route 1 just east of Sussex, and take Route 114 to **Fundy National Park,** spending the night, perhaps, in Alma. Route 915, east of the park, hugs the coast. At **Cape Enrage** you can visit a working lighthouse and enjoy a cup of seafood chowder. There are lots of things to do around **Hopewell Cape,** where the Fundy tides have sculpted gigantic rocks into flowerpot formations that turn into islands at high tide. Finish the trip with **Moncton,** a microcosm of New Brunswick culture and just an hour's drive from Fundy National Park.

IF YOU HAVE 7 DAYS

Add an Acadian Coast experience to the four-day tour above. Head north from **Moncton** and explore the area around **Shediac,** famous for its lobsters and Parlee Beach. Just beyond is **Bouctouche,** where visitors can walk for free for miles on a boardwalk over the dunes, and the make-believe land of Le Pays de la Sagouine, which pays tribute to Acadian author Antonine Maillet and La Sagouine, the charwoman character she created. Another 50 km (31 miles) north is **Kouchibouguac**

National Park, with protected beaches, forests, and peat bogs. The coastal drive from the park to **Miramichi City,** about 75 km (47 miles), passes through several bustling fishing villages. Most of the communities are Acadian, but as you approach Miramichi City, English dominates again. A stopover here positions you perfectly to begin your exploration of the Acadian Peninsula. It's only about 120 km (74 miles) from Miramichi City to **Caraquet,** where the Acadian Historical Village is a careful re-creation of traditional Acadian way of life.

IF YOU HAVE 10 DAYS

Follow the 7-day itinerary above. From **Caraquet** plan at least half a day to drive across the top of New Brunswick (Route 134 along the coast and Route 17 inland through the forest) to the St. John River valley. Begin your explorations among the flowers and the music of the New Brunswick Botanical Gardens in St-Jacques, outside **Edmundston.** The drive from here to Fredericton is about 275 km (171 miles) of panoramic pastoral and river scenery, including a dramatic gorge and waterfall at **Grand Falls,** the longest covered bridge in the world at Hartland, and historic Woodstock, New Brunswick's first town. **Kings Landing Historical Settlement,** near Fredericton, is a faithful depiction of life on the river in the 19th century. With its Gothic cathedral, Victorian architecture, museums, and riverfront pathways, **Fredericton** is a great stopping place and the seat of the province's government. The drive from Fredericton back to Saint John on Route 102 is just over 100 km (62 miles).

3

Barbour's
General
Store **4**

Carleton Martello
Tower **15**

Cherry
Brook Zoo **7**

Irving Nature
Park **16**

King Street **13**

King's
Square **10**

Loyalist Burial
Ground **9**

Loyalist
House **5**

Market Slip **2**

New
Brunswick
Museum **3**

Prince William
Street **14**

Reversing
Rapids **1**

Rockwood
Park **8**

Saint John
City Market ... **12**

Stone
Church **6**

Trinity
Church **11**

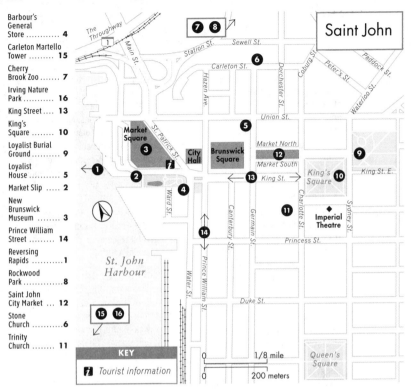

Industry and salt air have combined to give parts of Saint John a weather-beaten quality, but you'll also find lovingly restored 19th-century wooden and redbrick homes as well as modern office buildings, hotels, and shops.

The St. John River, its Reversing Rapids, and Saint John Harbour divide the city into eastern and western districts. The historic downtown area (locally known as "uptown") is on the east side, where an ambitious urban-renewal program started in the early 1980s has transformed the downtown waterfront. Older properties have been converted into trendy restaurants and shops, while glittering new apartment and condo buildings will take full advantage of the spectacular view across the bay. Harbour Passage, a redbrick walking and cycling path with benches and lots of interpretive information, begins downtown at Market Square and winds along the waterfront all the way to the Reversing Rapids. A shuttle boat between Market Square and the falls means you have to walk only one way. On the lower west side, painted-wood homes with flat roofs—characteristic of Atlantic Canadian seaports—slope to the harbor. Industrial activity is prominent on the west side, which has stately older homes on huge lots.

Regardless of the weather, Saint John is a delightful city to explore, as so many of its key downtown attractions are linked by enclosed overhead pedways known as the "Inside Connection."

GETTING HERE AND AROUND

Saint John airport receives flights from Halifax, Montréal, and Toronto, all of which provide connections to international flights. There is no rail service, and no long-distance bus service to the city. If you arrive in the downtown area by car, park and proceed on foot for full enjoyment. If it's just a day trip, you might consider using Saint John Transit's Parcobus park-and-ride service, but bear in mind that some city sights, such as Rockwood Park and the Cherry Brook Zoo or Irving Nature Park, are beyond the downtown area and you might need your car. Additionally, Saint John Transit offers two-hour sightseeing bus tours of historic areas from June to October on days when a cruise ship is in port, with two departures daily at 10 am and 12:30 pm. Times may be adjusted to suit cruise ship arrival times, but the tours are not restricted to cruise passengers. The pick-up and drop-off point is just up the street from the cruise ship terminal. Tickets, which can be purchased from the driver (cash only), cost C$20 for adults.

Rockwood Park Stables has a four-passenger horse-drawn carriage (C$80 per hour) and four 14-passenger trollies (C$226 per hour, including tour guide) for tours around the historic city center.

ESSENTIALS

Tour Information Rockwood Park Stables. Activities here include trail rides through the park, carriage tours of uptown Saint John, pony rentals, and riding lessons. ☎ *506/633–7659, 506/642–3222* ⊕ *www.horsesinsaintjohn.com.* **Saint John Transit** ☎ *506/658–4700* ⊕ *www.saintjohntransit.com.*

Visitor Information Tourism Saint John ☎ *506/658–2990, 866/463–8639* ⊕ *www.tourismsaintjohn.com.* **Visitor Information Centre** ✉ *Shoppes of City Hall, 15 Market Sq.* ☎ *506/658–2855, 866/463–8639* ⊕ *discoversaintjohn.com* ✉ *Barbour's General Store, 10 Market Sq.* ☎ *506/632–6813* ☉ *May–Oct.* ✉ *200 Bridge Rd.* ☎ *506/658–2937* ✉ *1509 Saint John Throughway W (eastbound)* ☎ *506/658–2940.*

EXPLORING

TOP ATTRACTIONS

FAMILY **Cherry Brook Zoo.** Snow leopards, Siberian tigers, and other exotic species are highlights of this 35-acre zoo with pleasant woodland trails, a waterfowl habitat with a boardwalk and floating gazebo, and an Aboriginal Medicine Wheel and Garden. There's an Awareness and Discover Center, where displays highlight the ongoing problem of poaching of endangered species and show more than 100 items seized by Canadian officials. The zoo also has a monkey house, a miniature golf course, and the Vanished Kingdom Park, a display that focuses on extinct animals. ✉ *901 Foster Thurston Dr., Rockwood Park* ☎ *506/634–1440* ⊕ *www.cherrybrookzoo.com* ✉ *$10.50; mini-golf $5.50* ☉ *Daily, June–early Sept. 10–8; spring and fall 10–5; winter 10–4:30.*

CLOSE UP

Walking Tour of Downtown Saint John

Saint John is a city on hills, and **King Street,** its main street, slopes steeply to the harbor. A system of escalators, elevators, and skywalks inside buildings allows you to climb to the top and take in some of the more memorable spots without effort, though you can also walk outside. A year-round information center is located about halfway in the Shoppes of City Hall.

Start at the foot of King, at **Market Slip.** This is where the Loyalists landed in 1783 and is the site of **Barbour's General Store** and the Little Red Schoolhouse. At Market Square, restored waterfront buildings house historical exhibits, shops, restaurants, and cafés. Also here are the Saint John Regional Library, a year-round visitor information center, a replica of the *Marco Polo* ship, and the fine **New Brunswick Museum.**

From the second level of Market Square, a skywalk crosses St. Patrick Street and an escalator takes you up into the City Hall shopping concourse. Here, you can branch off to Harbour Station, with its busy schedule of concerts, sporting events, and trade shows. Once you're through City Hall, another skywalk takes you across Chipman Hill and into the Brunswick Square complex of shops and offices, adjoining the city's largest hotel, the Delta Brunswick. To visit historic **Loyalist House,** exit onto Germain Street and turn left; it's on the corner at the top of the hill. Continue on for a block to see the venerable **Stone Church.** In the **Saint John City Market,** across from Brunswick Square, make sure to look up at the ceiling, which resembles the inverted hull of a ship. The oldest market in North America, constructed in 1875–76, it's also a great place to stop for lunch. When you leave by the door at the top of the market, you're near the head of King Street and right across Charlotte Street from **King's Square.** Take a walk through the square, past the statues and bandstand, to Sydney Street. Notice the walkways in the shape of the Union Jack Flag. Cross Sydney and you're in the **Loyalist Burial Ground.** Make your way back to Sydney Street and head south, turning right on King's Square South, where you can catch a glimpse of the handsome Imperial Theatre. Follow King's Square South and cross Charlotte Street to reach the back door of historic **Trinity Church.**

Finally, make your way back to King Street and walk down the hill toward the water. **Prince William Street** is at the foot of the hill, just steps from where you began at Market Slip. Turn left for antiques shops, galleries, restaurants, and historic architecture.

TIMING: Allow the better part of a day for this walk if you include a few hours for the New Brunswick Museum and some time for shopping. On Sunday the indoor walkways are open but the City Market is closed.

Irving Nature Park. The ecosystems of the southern New Brunswick coast are preserved in this lovely 600-acre park on a peninsula close to downtown. Roads and eight walking trails (up to several miles long) make bird- and nature-watching easy. Many shorebirds breed here, and it's a staging site on the flight path of shorebirds migrating between the Arctic and South America. Stop at the information kiosk just inside the entrance for a naturalist's notebook, a guide to what you'll find in the park, season by season. Tours are available, special events include off-season moonlight showshoeing, and it's an excellent spot for picnicking. Motor vehicles are excluded on Saturday before noon. ☒ *Sand Cove Rd.* ✥ *From downtown take Rte. 1 west to Exit 119A (Catherwood Rd.) south; follow Sand Cove Rd. 4.5 km (3 miles)* ☎ *506/653–7367* ✉ *Free* ☉ *May–early Sept., daily 8–8; early Sept.–mid-Oct., daily 8–6.*

Loyalist Burial Ground. Established soon after the United Empire Loyalists arrived in 1783, the cemetery closed in 1848 and was sadly neglected until 1995, when the Irving family restored it as a gift to the people of Saint John. Now, brick and granite walkways lead from the memorial gates through the restored gravestones and crypts amid shady trees and flowers. A highlight of the grounds is a magnificent beaver-pond fountain created to depict the hard work and tenacious spirit of the city's founders and those who followed them. ☒ *Sydney St., between King and E. Union Sts.* ✉ *Free* ☉ *Daily 24 hrs.*

Market Slip. The waterfront area at the foot of King Street is where the Loyalists landed in 1783. Today it's a lively and appealing area—the site of Market Square, the Hilton Saint John Hotel (⇨ *See Where to Stay*), restaurants, pubs, and a venue for festivals and street performers—but it still conveys a sense of the city's Maritime heritage. There's access to the Harbour Passage Trail, and a floating wharf accommodates boating visitors to the city and those waiting for the tides to sail up the St. John River.

FAMILY
Fodor's Choice
★

New Brunswick Museum. Imaginative and engaging in its approach, the provincial museum has fascinating displays covering the history, geology, and culture of New Brunswick. The popular whale exhibit includes Delilah, a full-size young right whale skeleton, suspended from the ceiling. You can also watch the phenomenal Bay of Fundy tides rise and fall in a glass tidal tube connected to the harbor and find out why the Stonehammer Geopark has global importance. There is a large and outstanding collection of artwork in the galleries, and the Family Discovery Gallery has fun and educational games for all ages. ☒ *1 Market Sq.* ☎ *506/643–2300, 888/268–9595* ⊕ *www.nbm-mnb.ca* ✉ *$8, $7 Nov.–mid-May* ☉ *Mid-May–Oct., weekdays 9–5 (to 9 pm Thurs.), Sat. 10–5, Sun. noon–5; Nov.–mid-May closed Mon.*

Reversing Rapids. The strong Fundy tides rise higher than the water level of the river, so twice daily, at the Reversing Rapids, the tidewater pushes the river water back upstream. When the tide ebbs, the river once again pours over the rock ledges and the rapids appear to reverse themselves. To learn more about the phenomenon, watch the film shown at the Reversing Rapids Visitor Information Center. Jet-boat tours provide a wild ride as well as a closer (and wetter) look, or you can get an overhead view from a zip-line tour. A pulp mill on the bank is not so scenic, but multimillion-dollar upgrades to pollution controls have eliminated any unpleasant odors. ■TIP→ It takes time to appreciate the Reversing Rapids fully; you need to visit at high, slack, and low tides. Check with any visitor information office for these times to help you plan. ⊠ *200 Bridge Rd.* ☎ *506/658-2937* ☒ *Free* ☉ *Daily dawn–dusk; visitor center mid-May–mid-Oct., daily 9–6 (also mid- to end Oct. on days when cruise ship in port); jet-boat tours early June–early Oct., daily 10–5 (weather permitting).*

FAMILY   **Rockwood Park.** Encompassing 2,200 acres, this is one of the largest urban parks in Canada and is also one of the dozen or so highlighted elements of the Stonehammer Geopark, designated as such by UNESCO for its geological importance. There are 55 hiking trails through the forest, 13 lakes, several sandy beaches, a campground, a golf course with an aquatic driving range, the Cherry Brook Zoo, horseback riding, events, concerts, and a unique play park for people of all ages. The Interpretation Centre organizes guided nature walks and has trail maps and information on events. ⊠ *142 Lake Dr. S, off Mt. Pleasant Ave.* ☎ *506/658-2883* ⊕ *www.rockwoodpark.ca* ☒ *Free* ☉ *Daily 8 am–dusk.*

Fodor's Choice   **Saint John City Market.** The inverted ship's hull ceiling of this handsome
★   market—the oldest continuously operating market in North America (1876)—occupies a city block between Germain and Charlotte streets. Its temptations include both live and fresh-cooked lobsters, great cheeses, dulse, fresh produce, and tasty, inexpensive snacks, along with plenty of souvenir and crafts items made by resident artists. ⊠ *47 Charlotte St.* ☎ *506/658-2820* ⊕ *www.sjcitymarket.ca* ☉ *Weekdays 7:30–6, Sat. 7:30–5.*

WORTH NOTING

Barbour's General Store. This authentic 19th-century country shop was relocated from Sheffield, New Brunswick, in 1967 and opened in the heart of the city as a museum commemorating the local family business that became Canada's leading producer of tea, spices, and nut butter. Now operating near the site where Barbour's factory once stood, it contains some 2,000 artifacts dating back to the 1860s, and also doubles as a retail outlet, visitor information center, and tea room. ⊠ *10 Market Sq.* ☎ *506/642-2242* ☒ *Free* ☉ *Early June–Oct. 30, daily 9–6.*

Carleton Martello Tower. The four-level tower, a great place from which to survey the harbor and Partridge Island, was built during the War of 1812 as a precaution against an American attack. Guides tell you about the spartan life of a soldier living in the stone fort, and an audiovisual presentation outlines its role in the defense of Saint John during World War II. ■TIP→ The Sunday afternoon "Saint John Privateers" program in July and August, included in admission fee and available in English and French, brings the era to life for families with children ages 6 to 11 (call to reserve space). ⊠ *454 Whipple St.* ☎ *506/636-4011* ⊕ *www.pc.gc.ca* ☒ *$3.90* ☉ *Late June–early Sept., daily 10–5:30.*

King Street. The steepest, shortest main street in Canada, lined with solid Victorian redbrick buildings, is filled with a variety of shops, eateries, and businesses.

King's Square. Laid out in a Union Jack pattern, this green refuge has a two-story bandstand and a number of monuments. The mass of metal on the ground in the northeast corner is actually a great lump of melted tools from a neighboring hardware store that burned down in Saint John's Great Fire of 1877, in which hundreds of buildings were destroyed. ✉ *Between Charlotte and Sydney Sts.*

Loyalist House. The former home of the Merritt family, wealthy Loyalist merchants, this imposing Georgian structure with eight fireplaces was built in 1817 and is furnished with authentic period pieces, including a working piano organ and kitchen equipment. ✉ *120 Union St.* ☎ *506/652–3590* 🌐 *www.loyalisthouse.com* 🎟 *$5* 🕘 *Loyalist Day (May 18)–Aug. 31, Mon.–Sat. 9–5 (also Sept. and Oct. on days when cruise ship in port).*

Prince William Street. South of King Street near Market Slip, this street is full of historic bank and business buildings that now hold shops, galleries, and restaurants; it's emerging as a dining destination. The lamp known as the Three Sisters, at the foot of Prince William Street, was erected in 1848 to guide ships into the harbor. Next to it is a replica of the Celtic cross on nearby Partridge Island, where many immigrants landed and were quarantined.

Stone Church. The first stone church in the city was built for the garrison posted at nearby Fort Howe of stone brought from England as ships' ballast. ✉ *87 Carleton St.* ☎ *506/634–1474* 🎟 *By donation* 🕘 *July and Aug., Tues., Wed., and Fri. 8:30–3:30.*

Trinity Church. The present church dates from 1880, when it was rebuilt after the Great Fire. Inside, over the west door, is a coat of arms—a symbol of the monarchy—rescued from the council chamber in Boston by a British colonel during the American Revolution. It was deemed a worthy refugee and given a place of honor in the church. Guided tours are available during July and August, and there's a self-guiding tour at other times. ✉ *115 Charlotte St.* ☎ *506/693–8558* 🎟 *Free; donations accepted* 🕘 *July and Aug., weekdays 9–4; Sat. 10–3, Sun. noon–3; Sept.–June, weekdays 9–noon and 1–3.*

WHERE TO EAT

$$$ SEAFOOD

🍴 **Billy's Seafood Company.** It's a restaurant, it's an oyster bar, it's a fish market, and it's lots of fun, too, with jazzy background music and amusing fish paintings on the walls. The fresh fish selection is impressive, and everything is cooked to perfection. The huge pesto scallops are always a hit, as is the grilled halibut with blueberry balsamic vinegar. Local lore says that this is where cedar-planked salmon originated, and it's delicious. Dining outside is a treat on a nice day, and you can get live and cooked lobsters packed to go. [$] *Average main: C$25* ✉ *Saint John City Market, 49–51 Charlotte St., Downtown* ☎ *506/672–3474, 888/933–3474* 🌐 *www.billysseafood.com.*

TASTES OF NEW BRUNSWICK

Cast your line just about anywhere in New Brunswick and you'll find some kind of fish-and-chips. Seafood is plentiful all year (lobsters, oysters, crabs, mussels, clams, scallops, and salmon) and prepared in as many ways as there are chefs. Try snacking on dulse, a dried purple seaweed as salty as potato chips and as compelling as peanuts.

A spring delicacy is fiddleheads—emerging ferns that look like the curl at the end of a violin neck. These emerald gems are picked along riverbanks, then boiled and sprinkled with lemon juice, butter, salt, and pepper.

The beers of choice are Moosehead, brewed in Saint John, Alexander Keith's (a Nova Scotia brewery) and, of course, the various Molson brews. A number of local breweries—notably Picaroons, based in Fredericton, and Moncton's Pump House Brewery—are also popular. New Brunswick also has 14 wineries so ask what's available in stores and restaurants. A good introduction would be to take one of the Uncorked Tours out of Saint John, which specialize in local wineries and artisan breweries.

New Brunswick's maple products are sought the world over, and chocolates made by Ganong Brothers of St. Stephen, who have been in the candy business for a century and a quarter, are a popular treat.

$$ THAI

🍴 **Lemongrass Thai Fare.** Sitting proudly within Saint John's culinary hot spot of Market Square, Lemongrass offers tasty Thai cuisine in its stylish restaurant and out on the heated three-tier patio. Thai stir-fries, noodle dishes, and curries, many featuring ginger and coconut, share the menu with both mild and fiery Indian dishes. The signature pad thai is the hottest (literally) item. The lunch menu is a great value. There's a pub, with live music, at the same location. [$] *Average main: C$18* ✉ *1 Market Sq., Downtown* ☎ *506/657–8424* 🌐 *lemongrass-saintjohn.com.*

$$$ BRITISH Fodor's Choice ★

🍴 **Saint John Ale House.** The gastropub concept has been fully embraced here, making it one of the best places to eat in the city—and it couldn't have a better location, with a great patio overlooking the downtown waterfront. Drawing on supplies from local farmers, fishermen, and food producers, the menu presents "progressive pub food." This might include sautéed trout with wilted greens, lamb shank with vegetables and mint oil, or a tender, 30-day dry-aged steak with bone marrow and truffle jus; even the fish-and-chips and cheeseburgers have a gourmet touch. The mind-boggling beer menu includes local microbrews. There's live entertainment Wednesday through Saturday. [$] *Average main: C$21* ✉ *1 Market Sq., Downtown* ☎ *506/657–2337* 🌐 *www.saintjohnalehouse.com.*

$$ LATIN AMERICAN

🍴 **Taco Pica.** This modest restaurant is a slice of home for the former Guatemalan refugees, now proud Canadian citizens, who run it as a worker's co-op. The atmosphere is colorful—ornamental parrots rule in the dining room—and the recipes are authentically seasoned with garlic, mint, coriander seeds, and cilantro. The *pepian* (beef stew) and the garlic shrimp are standout options on a menu that ranges from vegetarian quesadillas to Tequila Cactus Pork. There's regular live entertainment, including flamenco every Friday and occasional salsa nights. $ *Average main: C$17* ⊠ *96 Germain St., Downtown* ☎ *506/633–8492* ☾ *Closed Sun.*

$$$
DELI

✕**Urban Deli.** Cool yet pleasingly unpretentious, this downtown eatery gets rave reviews from an eclectic mix of businesspeople, shoppers, students, and city visitors. The daytime menu features classic deli fare, including sandwiches piled high with meat smoked on the premises, hearty soups, imaginative salads, and comfort food such as mac and cheese and ribs. Wednesday through Saturday, from 5 pm, Italian food is on offer. There's a great Saturday breakfast menu, too, including champagne or vodka cocktails. If you have to stand in line, be assured it's worth the wait. $ *Average main: C$26* ⊠ *68 King St., Downtown* ☎ *506/652–3354* ⊕ *www.urbandeli.ca* ☾ *Closed Sun. No dinner Mon. and Tues. No breakfast weekdays.*

WHERE TO STAY

For expanded hotel reviews, visit Fodors.com.

$$
HOTEL

Delta Brunswick Hotel. Right in the heart of the city, this hotel is within the Brunswick Square complex of shops and services and linked to other shopping and entertainment venues by an indoor walkway, making it perfect for a winter visit. **Pros:** friendly and helpful staff; near all downtown attractions. **Cons:** most rooms only have a street view. $ *Rooms from: C$149* ⊠ *39 King St.* ☎ *506/648–1981* ⊕ *www.deltahotels.ca* ⤶ *254 rooms* ⦿ *Multiple meal plans.*

$$
HOTEL

Hilton Saint John. The Hilton is sleek and stylish, with spacious rooms and a great city-center waterfront location. **Pros:** close to Harbour Station and the conference center; more than half of the rooms have harbor views, and city views are good, too; spacious rooms. **Cons:** atmosphere can be affected by conventioneers. $ *Rooms from: C$129* ⊠ *1 Market Sq.* ☎ *506/693–8484, 800/561–8282 in Canada* ⊕ *www.hilton.com* ⤶ *179 rooms, 18 suites* ⦿ *Multiple meal plans.*

$
B&B/INN

Homeport Historic Bed & Breakfast Inn. Graceful arches, fine antiques, Italian marble fireplaces, Oriental carpets, and a Maritime theme distinguish this pair of mansions overlooking the harbor. **Pros:** hospitable, well-versed owners; great sense of history; close to downtown and the Reversing Rapids. **Cons:** the amazing view is sometimes obscured by fog. $ *Rooms from: C$110* ⊠ *80 Douglas Ave.* ☎ *506/672–7255, 888/678–7678* ⊕ *www.homeport.nb.ca* ⤶ *6 rooms, 4 suites* ⦿ *Breakfast.*

$
B&B/INN

Shadow Lawn Inn. In an affluent suburb with tree-lined streets, palatial homes, tennis, golf, and a yacht club, this inn fits right in with its clapboards, columns, and antiques. **Pros:** great food; hospitable service. **Cons:** the location means a ride into town if you want to go out at night. $ *Rooms from: C$120* ⊠ *3180 Rothesay Rd., 12 km (7 miles) northeast of Saint John, Rothesay* ☎ *506/847–7539, 800/561–4166* ⊕ *www.shadowlawninn.com* ⤶ *9 rooms, 2 suites* ⦿ *Breakfast.*

NIGHTLIFE AND THE ARTS

THE ARTS

Imperial Theatre. Saint John's theater, opera, ballet, and symphony productions take place at this beautifully restored 1913 vaudeville arena. Tours ($2) are available from May through August during regular business hours, or by appointment September through April. ⊠ *24 King's Sq. S* ☎ *506/674–4100* ⊕ *www.imperialtheatre.nb.ca.*

Saint John Arts Centre. Several galleries here display the work of local artists and artisans. ⊠ *20 Peel Pl.* ☎ *506/633–4870* ⊕ *www. saintjohnartscentre.com* ☉ *Tues.–Sat. 9–5.*

NIGHTLIFE

Harbour Station. Musical and other types of performances take place at this hockey arena. ⊠ *99 Station St.* ☎ *506/657–1234, 800/267–2800* ⊕ *www.harbourstation.ca.*

O'Leary's Pub. In the downtown historic district, this pub specializes in old-time Irish fun complete with Celtic performers on off-season Tuesdays; on Wednesday, Brent Mason, a well-known neofolk artist, starts the evening and then turns the mike over to the audience, and Thursday to Saturday it's mostly live classic rock bands, starting at 10 pm. ⊠ *46 Princess St.* ☎ *506/634–7135* ⊕ *www.olearyspub.com.*

SPORTS AND THE OUTDOORS

Reversing Falls Jet Boat. The falls may have been rebranded as the Reversing Rapids, but this boat company hangs on to the former name. It offers two types of boat rides (C$43.95 each). On the 20-minute thrill ride into the heart of the rapids be prepared for a wild time and don't think for a second that the yellow slickers they supply will keep you dry—having a change of clothes in your car is an excellent idea. Size restrictions apply to the jet boat, and times depend on the tides. There's also a more sedate one-hour sightseeing tour, with informed commentary, along the rapids and up the river. ⊠ *100 Fallsview Ave.* ☎ *506/634–8987, 888/634–8987* ⊕ *www.jetboatrides.com* ☉ *Early June–early Oct.*

Saint John Adventures. Five zip lines ($60 plus tax) let you zoom down the cliffs and across the Reversing Rapids. ⊠ *50 Fallsview Ave.* ☎ *506/634–9477, 877/634–9477* ⊕ *www.saintjohnadventures.ca* ☉ *Late May–Oct., daily 9–dusk.*

SHOPPING

Brunswick Square. This large mall is connected to the city's "Inside Connection" covered walkway and contains more than 60 top-quality boutiques on three floors. The complex also includes a parking garage, offices, and the Delta Brunswick Hotel *(⇨ See Where to Stay).* ⊠ *King and Germain Sts.* ☎ *506/658–1000* ⊕ *www.brunswicksquare.ca.*

Handworks Gallery. Some of the best professional crafts and fine art made in New Brunswick are carried by this gallery, which represents more than 80 Saint John artists and artisans. The historic building was the home of 19th-century painter, J.C. Miles. ✉ *12 King St.* ☎ *506/652–9787* ⊕ *www.handworks.ca.*

Fodor's Choice
★

Peter Buckland Gallery. Art expert and writer Peter Buckland carries contemporary paintings, drawings, and sculpture by Canadian artists in his exceptional gallery—one of the finest private galleries in the province. In 2012, Peter received the Queen's Diamond Jubilee Medal for his contribution to the arts. ✉ *35 Duke St.* ☎ *506/693–9721* ⊘ *Thurs. and Fri. 10–5, Sat. 10–4, or by appointment.*

Trinity Galleries. Fine art from Canadian artists, including some based in the Maritimes, is on show here, along with sculpture and craft work. ✉ *128 Germain St.* ☎ *506/634–1611, 506/721–1476 for after hrs appointments* ⊕ *www.trinitygalleries.ca* ⊘ *Tues.–Fri. 10–3, Sat. 10–4 or by appointment.*

EN ROUTE

New River Beach. Unlike most Bay of Fundy beaches, this one is sandy and great for swimming, especially if you wait until the tide is coming in. The sun warms the sand at low tide, and the sand warms the water as it comes in. It's part of the New River Beach Provincial Park ($8 vehicle entrance fee) that also has a boardwalk through a bog, a playground, interpretive programs, hiking trails, kayak rentals, and camping. ✉ *New River Beach Rd., Lepreau, off Hwy. 1, 50 km (30 miles) west of Saint John* ☎ *506/755–4078.*

THE FUNDY COAST

Bordering the chilly and powerful tidal Bay of Fundy, where the world's most extreme tides rise and fall twice daily, is some of New Brunswick's most dramatic coastline. This area extends from the border town of St. Stephen and the lovely resort village of St. Andrews, past tiny fishing villages and rocky coves, through Saint John, and on through Fundy National Park and beyond. A vast area, encompassing inland areas and the coastline, is now designated the Stonehammer Geopark, with a dozen specific sites illustrating remarkable geological features formed over billions of years. The Fundy Islands—Grand Manan Island, Deer Island, and Campobello—are havens of peace that have lured harried mainlanders for generations. Some of the impressive 50-km (31-mile) stretch of coastline between St. Martins and Fundy National Park can be viewed from the Fundy Trail Parkway.

Fundy Trail Parkway. Starting from just outside St. Martins, this gloriously scenic coastal roadway has opened up a cliff-top wilderness area with a 16-km (10-mile) network of walking, hiking, and biking trails (bike rentals are available at C$11 per hour). There are viewpoints along the way, and footpaths and steps lead down to beaches and river estuaries. There's an interpretive center and suspension bridge at Big Salmon River, and on the other side of the bridge serious hikers can embark on the 41-km (24-mile) Fundy Footpath. ☎ *506/833–2019, 866/386–3987* ⊕ *www.fundytrailparkway.com* ✉ *C$5.50, guided walks C$4.50* ⊘ *Mid-May–mid-Oct. vehicle access 6 am–8 pm, Big Salmon River Interpretive Centre 8–8; mid-Oct.–mid-May foot and bike trails only.*

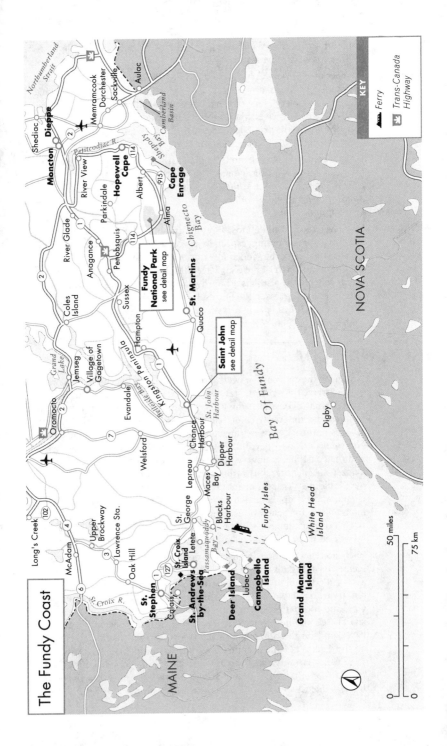

The Fundy Coast

MAINE

NOVA SCOTIA

Bay Of Fundy

Northumberland Strait

Cumberland Basin

Chignecto Bay

Shepody Bay

Petitcodiac R.

Grand Lake

Belleisle Bay

Kingston Peninsula

St. John Harbour

St. Croix R.

Passamaquoddy Bay

Fundy Isles

Long's Creek

McAdam

Upper Brockway

Lawrence Sta.

Oak Hill

Welsford

Evandale

Village of Gagetown

Jemseg

Oromocto

Coles Island

River Glade

Anagance

River View

Sussex

Hampton

Parkindale

Penobsquis

Albert

Alma

St. Martins

Quaco

Chance Harbour

Dipper Harbour

Maces Bay

Lepreau

St. George

Blacks Harbour

Letete

St. Croix Island

St. Andrews by-the-Sea

St. Stephen

Calais

Deer Island

Lubec

Campobello Island

Grand Manan Island

White Head Island

Digby

Moncton

Dieppe

Shediac

Memramcook

Dorchester

Sackville

Aulac

Hopewell Cape

Cape Enrage

Saint John
see detail map

Fundy National Park
see detail map

2

2

1

1

114

915

114

7

102

4

3

6

127

KEY

Ferry

Trans-Canada Highway

0   50 miles

0   75 km

ST. STEPHEN

113 km (70 miles) west of Saint John.

The elegant Ganong factory-outlet chocolate and candy store dominates the main street of St. Stephen, across the St. Croix River from Calais, Maine, and the small town is a mecca for chocoholics. Indeed, St. Stephen is known as "Chocolate Town." The Ganong brothers first opened a small grocery store in 1873 but soon began specializing in chocolate and candy making. Over the years, many chocolate-related innovations occurred here, including the production of the first chocolate candy bar with nuts in North America and the introduction of the heart-shaped box of chocolates (originally produced for Christmas but now a long-standing symbol of Valentine's Day). In early August "choctails," chocolate puddings, cakes, and all things chocolate are served during the Chocolate Festival, when you might see the "Chocolate Mousse" on menus about town.

GETTING HERE AND AROUND

From Saint John take Route 1 west. From the U.S., the town is right up against the U.S. border at Calais, Maine. There is no public transportation to or within the town, but once there, it's easy to explore on foot.

ESSENTIALS

Visitor Information Charlotte Coastal Region Visitor Information Centre ⊠ *5 King St., corner Milltown Blvd.* ☎ *506/466-4858* ⊕ *www.charlottecoastalregion.ca* ⊘ *Mid-June–Sept. (closed Sun. June and Sept.).* **Provincial Visitor Information Centre** ⊠ *5 King St., corner Milltown Blvd.* ☎ *506/466-7390* ⊘ *Late May–early Oct., daily.*

EXPLORING

FAMILY **Chocolate Museum.** Behind Ganong Chocolatier, this museum explores the sweet history of candy making with hand-dipping videos, a collection of antique chocolate boxes, and hands-on exhibits. A Heritage Chocolate Walk includes a guided tour of the museum and a stroll around town, pointing out buildings associated with the chocolate industry here. There are occasional activities for children, and a chocolate festival in early August. Happily, after all those tempting displays, there's a year-round retail outlet on-site in which to buy a few treats. ⊠ *73 Milltown Blvd.* ☎ *506/466-7848* ⊕ *www.chocolatemuseum.ca* ⊠ *C$7, Heritage Walk C$13* ⊘ *July and Aug., Mon.–Sat. 9:30–6:30, Sun. 11–3; May, June, and Sept., weekdays 10–4, Sat. 11–3; Mar., Apr., Oct., and Nov., weekdays 10–4. Heritage Walk June–Aug., Mon.–Sat. at 10 and 2.*

EN
ROUTE

St. Croix Island International Historic Site. The island where explorers Samuel de Champlain and Pierre Dugua, Sieur de Monts, spent their first harsh winter in North America in 1604 can be seen from this interpretive park at Bayside, on Route 127, about 23 km (14 miles) from St. Stephen. The memorial triptych was installed here in 2004 to mark the 400th anniversary and a self-guiding trail explains its significance. ⊕ *www.pc.gc.ca/eng/lhn-nhs/nb/stcroix/index.aspx.*

ST. ANDREWS BY-THE-SEA

31 km (19 miles) southeast of St. Stephen.

Fodor's Choice ★ A designated National Historic District on Passamaquoddy Bay, St. Andrews by-the-Sea is one of North America's prettiest resort towns. It has long been a summer retreat of the affluent, and mansions ring the town. Of the town's 550 buildings, 280 were erected before 1880, and 14 of those have survived from the 1700s. Some Loyalists even brought their homes with them piece by piece from Castine, Maine, across the bay, when the American Revolution didn't go their way. Pick up a walking-tour map at the visitor information center and follow it through the pleasant streets. Water Street, by the harbor, has eateries, gift and crafts shops, and artists' studios. The harbor has a cluster of whale-watching boats and outfitters for other activities.

GETTING HERE AND AROUND

There is no public transportation to St. Andrews by-the-Sea and it's about 100 km (60 miles) west of Saint John via Highway 1 then Route 127. Once there, the Water Street and harbor area is delightfully walkable, but a car would be needed to get to some of the attractions.

ESSENTIALS

Visitor Information St. Andrews ⊠ *24 Reed Ave., St. Andrews* ☎ *506/529–3556, 800/563–7397* ⊕ *standrewsbythesea.ca* ⊗ *Mid-May–mid-Oct., daily 9–5 (to 7 July and Aug.).*

EXPLORING

TOP ATTRACTIONS

FAMILY **Fundy Discovery Aquarium.** In a superb building that opened in 2011, this excellent aquarium is at the Huntsman Ocean Sciences Center, established more than a century ago. Marine exhibits include a huge tidal exhibit, teeming touch tanks, rare lobsters, sturgeon, and some very entertaining harbor seals (fed at 11 and 4 daily), as well as free movies and slide shows. ⊠ *1 Lower Campus Rd.* ☎ *506/529–1200* ⊕ *www.huntsmanmarine.ca* ⊠ *$12.39* ⊗ *Daily 10–5.*

FAMILY Fodor's Choice ★ **Kingsbrae Garden.** Nearly 2,500 varieties of trees, shrubs, and plants cover the 27 acres of woodland trails and many theme gardens here. One of Canada's most spectacular public gardens, it includes a garden specially designed for touch and smell, a rose garden, a bird and butterfly garden, and a gravel garden. A children's fantasy garden offers child-centered activities, and there are daily programs for kids under 12 (1:30 in July and August). Canada's first Wollemi pine, named Pericles, is a big attraction, as is the opportunity to participate in a ladybug release program every morning at 10:30. A Sculpture Garden features works by Don Pell and from the Beaverbrook collection, and Kingsbrae also has an art gallery, a café, and a new fine-dining restaurant, Savour in the Garden (⇨ *See Where to Eat*). ⊠ *220 King St.* ☎ *506/529–3335, 866/566–8687* ⊕ *www.kingsbraegarden.com* ⊠ *$16; guided tours $3* ⊗ *Mid-May–mid-Oct., daily 9–8.*

WORTH NOTING

Charlotte County Courthouse and Old Gaol. Active since 1840 and a National Historic Site since 1983, the courthouse is an exceptionally fine example of 19th-century Greek Revival architecture. The adjacent Old Gaol, on the other hand, is a grim reminder of the conditions that awaited local wrongdoers. The courthouse is also the home of Charlotte County Archives, whose volunteers offer free tours of the courthouse and the Old Gaol (June to September). ⊠ *123 Frederick St.* ☎ *506/529–4248* ⊕ *www.ccarchives.ca.*

Greenock Church. A remark was made at an 1822 dinner party about the "poor" Presbyterians not having a church of their own. As a result, Captain Christopher Scott, who took exception to the slur, spared no expense on this building, which is decorated with a carving of a green oak tree in honor of Scott's birthplace, Greenock in Scotland. ⊠ *146 Montague St.*

Ross Memorial Museum. A U.S couple who had a summer home in St. Andrews for 40 years established this museum. The Rosses donated the trappings of that home and an extensive collection of 19th-century New Brunswick furniture and decorative artwork to the town and purchased this 1824 Georgian mansion to house them. The Christmas Open House in late November and early December is a popular event. ⊠ *188 Montague St.* ☎ *506/529–5124* ⊕ *www.rossmemorialmuseum.ca* ✉ *By donation; $3 for off-season visits by appointment* ⊙ *Late May–early Oct., Mon.–Sat. 10–4:30, or by appointment.*

OFF THE BEATEN PATH

Ministers Island. This huge island estate, once completely self-sufficient, was the summer home of Sir William Van Horne, chairman of the Canadian Pacific Railway from 1899 to 1915. In summer, you can access the island by car, by bike, or on foot at low tide and by shuttle boat at high tide. Tours of the property include Covenhoven, Sir William's 50-room summer home; a tidal swimming pool; a livestock barn; a cottage; an old windmill; and the 1790 Minister's House from which the island takes its name. ■ TIP→ **If you drive, walk, or bike over, be sure to leave the island before the tide comes in or you will be stuck for another six hours. Check the tide schedule in the paper or call ahead.** ⊠ *Via Bar Rd., off Rte. 127, 5 km (3 miles) north of St. Andrews* ☎ *506/529–5081 for tour information* ⊕ *www.ministersisland.net* ✉ *$15 (cash only), includes boat and guided tour* ⊙ *Mid-May–mid-Oct., daily; times vary according to tides.*

WHERE TO EAT

$$

SEAFOOD

✕ **The Gables.** A relaxing meal on the outdoor deck of this friendly harborside eatery is the perfect way to end a day of whale-watching or craft shopping. The lobster club sandwich is a favorite, and in addition to seafood, there are steaks and other nonfish dishes on the menu. The hearty seafood chowder will warm the heart and soul on a foggy Fundy night, and homemade desserts top off the experience. The outdoor patio and deck offer breathtaking views of the harbor, and if the winds come up, there are warm fleece blankets available. [$] *Average main: C$19* ✉ *143 Water St.* ☎ *506/529–3440* 🕒 *Closed Nov.–Mar.*

$$ MODERN CANADIAN
🍴 **Niger Reef Tea House.** Overlooking the bay, with seating inside or out on a rustic deck, this 1926 former meeting house (of the Imperial Order of the Daughters of the Empire) is where red-seal chef David Peterson works his magic with locally sourced ingredients. Everything is top quality, from the simple but expertly produced lunchtime options—seafood chowder, sandwiches, frittata—to imaginative offerings on the select dinner menu. These might include traditional cedar-planked salmon with a ginger glaze, or lamb shanks braised in tomato-and-red-wine sauce. The splendid restored mural was painted by American artist Lucille Douglass (1877–1935). Arrive early for dinner; the Tea House closes at 8 pm, and as it's very popular with locals, reservations are recommended. [$] *Average main: C$19* ✉ *1 Joes Point Rd.* ☎ *506/529–8005* 🌐 *www.nigerreefteahouse.com* 🕒 *Closed Nov.–May.*

$$$$ MODERN CANADIAN Fodor's Choice ★
🍴 **Savour in the Garden.** One of New Brunswick's most exciting young chefs, Alex Haun, has returned to the place where his love of the culinary arts was nurtured—he worked at Kingsbrae's Garden Café at the age of 13. Now, still only in his twenties, the 12-time culinary Gold Medal winner is providing light healthy meals to garden visitors during the day, and creating a seriously special dining experience on Thursday, Friday, and Saturday evenings. Creative tasting menus—consisting of three or six courses—are based on available fresh local ingredients. One recent dish, Six Wings to Fly, featured duck ragout, seared quail breast and braised leg, partridge terrine, roasted potato shell, mushroom demiglace, sautéed carrots, sugar snap peas, chanterelles, and beet ketchup—yes, that's just one dish. Reservations are recommended for dinner. [$] *Average main: C$45* ✉ *220 King St.* ☎ *506/529–3335, 866/566–8687* 🌐 *www.kingsbraegarden.com* 🕒 *No dinner Sun.–Wed.*

WHERE TO STAY

For expanded hotel reviews, visit Fodors.com.

$$$ RESORT Fodor's Choice ★
🏨 **The Algonquin Resort.** One of Canada's iconic resorts, in one of New Brunswick's most delightful towns, the Algonquin reopened in 2013 after a complete and meticulous restoration. **Pros:** personal service; luxurious surroundings; includes a top-class golf course; indoor pool has a three-story waterslide. **Cons:** a bit of a walk from the waterfront hub (but there's a free shuttle). [$] *Rooms from: C$199* ✉ *184 Adolphus St.* ☎ *506/529–8823, 855/529–8693* 🌐 *algonquinresort.com* 🛏 *220 rooms, 13 suites* 🍽 *No meals.*

$$$$ HOTEL Fodor's Choice ★
🏨 **Kingsbrae Arms.** Expect excellent service from the hosts and staff at this restored 1897 estate, where eclectic antiques fill the rooms, and pampering touches include plush robes and daily afternoon tea. **Pros:** lovely grounds; close to Kingsbrae Garden; delicious local food prepared by creative chef. **Cons:** in winter the only meal offered is breakfast. [$] *Rooms from: C$329* ✉ *219 King St.* ☎ *506/529–1897* 🌐 *www.kingsbrae.com* 🛏 *8 suites, 2 rooms* 🍽 *Breakfast.*

$ B&B/INN **Montague Rose B&B.** In a good location, two blocks back from the harbor, this lovely French empire–style home offers a warm welcome and individually styled, comfortable bedrooms. **Pros:** friendly hosts; good location close to all downtown attractions. **Cons:** bathrooms have either a shower or a tub, so specify which you would prefer; fixed time for breakfast. [$] *Rooms from: C$125* ✉ *258 Montague St.* ☎ *506/529–8963, 888/529–8963* 🌐 *www.themontaguerose.com* 🛏 *4 rooms* 🍴 *Breakfast.*

$ HOTEL **Rossmount Inn Hotel Restaurant & Bar.** Surrounded by 87 acres at the base of Chamcook Mountain, this inn is renowned for hospitality and outstanding food and is particularly convenient for visiting Ministers Island. **Pros:** impeccable surroundings and details; amazing dinners. **Cons:** some rooms are very small; stairways steep. [$] *Rooms from: C$125* ✉ *4599 Rte. 127* ☎ *506/529–3351* 🌐 *www.rossmountinn.com* 🛏 *18 rooms* 🕓 *Closed Jan.–Easter* 🍴 *Multiple meal plans.*

$$ B&B/INN **Treadwell Inn.** This is one of the best locations in town, with gardens stretching to the water's edge and the harbor just two short blocks away. **Pros:** great views; good value; spacious rooms; shops and restaurants nearby. **Cons:** fills up fast; two-night minimum stay for the balcony rooms overlooking the bay; 14-day cancellation policy. [$] *Rooms from: C$149* ✉ *129 Water St.* ☎ *506/529–1011, 888/529–1011* 🌐 *www.treadwellinn.com* 🛏 *7 rooms* 🍴 *Multiple meal plans.*

SPORTS AND THE OUTDOORS

Off-Kilter Bike Tours. Two-hour, full-day, and multiday bike tours include the loan of a helmet and a kilt—yes, the Scottish garment. Owner Kurt Gumushel's father, a tailor, originally made the lightweight custom kilts for a particular group of mountain bikers, and the idea caught on. Tours cost C$60 for two hours, C$200 for a full day, including lunch and snacks. ✉ *18 King St.* ☎ *506/466–8388* 🌐 *www.offkilterbike.com.*

Sunbury Shores Arts & Nature Centre. Art workshops in drawing, etching, painting, pottery, and many other media are offered in conjunction with environmental excursions. ✉ *139 Water St.* ☎ *506/529–3386.*

DIVING **Navy Island Dive.** In addition to equipment rentals, this company runs dive trips to view the wonderful marine life of the Bay of Fundy. Tuition is also offered. ✉ *15 William St.* ☎ *506/529–4555* 🌐 *www.navyislanddive.nb.ca.*

FAMILY **Tall Ship Whale Adventures.** The *Jolly Breeze* is an elegant vessel for whale-watching, and particularly good for families. In addition to watching the whales, children can dress in pirate costume, have their faces painted, steer the ship, hoist sails, learn a sea shanty, and dabble in the marine touch tank. Breakfast is included on morning sailings, hot soup is served on later sailings, and there's a licensed bar on board. The adult price is C$55. ✉ *4 King St.* ☎ *506/529–8116.*

GOLF **Algonquin Golf Club.** On the shores of Passamaquoddy Bay, this is a beautifully landscaped 18-hole, par-72, 6,908-yard signature course designed by Thomas McBroom. The holes on the back 9—especially the 12th—have beautiful sea views, as does the Clubhouse Grill. Part of the Algonquin resort, it's also open to nonguests and has a "traditional golf" dress code. Green fees range from C$35 to C$85, depending on the season, and there are clubs and carts to rent. ⊠ *Off Rte. 127* ☎ *506/529–8165* ⊕ *algonquinresort.com/golf* ⚓ *Daily, May–Oct.*

KAYAKING Whale and nature cruises and kayak tours all begin at the town wharf.

Eastern Outdoors. Single and double kayaks and mountain bikes are available for rent, as well as lessons, tours around Navy Island, and white-water kayaking. ⊠ *165 Water St.* ☎ *506/529–4662, 800/565–2925* ⊕ *www.easternoutdoors.com.*

WHALE-
WATCHING
Fundy Tide Runners. A 24-foot Zodiac will zip you out into the bay to search for whales, seals, and marine birds. ⊠ *16 King St.* ☎ *506/529–4481* ⊕ *www.fundytiderunners.com.*

Quoddy Link Marine. Whale and wildlife tours ($58) are offered, late June to late October, on a powered catamaran that takes up to 47 passengers. ⊠ *6 King St.* ☎ *506/529–2600, 877/688–2600* ⊕ *www. quoddylinkmarine.com.*

SHOPPING

Crocker Hill Store/Steven Smith Designs. Owner-artist Stephen Smith is inspired by nature, and his art—on framed prints, T-shirts, tote bags, and note cards—majors on local birdlife. Call to check opening hours in winter. ⊠ *45 King St.* ☎ *506/529–4303, 888/255–4251* ⊕ *www. crockerhill.com.*

Garden by the Sea. This aromatic shop specializes in all-natural body products made in New Brunswick, including Bay of Fundy sea salts and ecoflowers, as well as fresh flowers and 130 varieties of ethical, fair trade and organic teas. ⊠ *217 Water St.* ☎ *506/529–8905.*

Oven Head Salmon Smokers. Regulations no longer allow tours of the smokehouse, but the friendly owners will explain the process of producing some of New Brunswick's best cold-smoked salmon and salmon jerky, and you can buy the finished product. You'll also see it for sale in local grocery stores and on the menu at many regional restaurants. ⊠ *101 Oven Head Rd., off Hwy. 1, Exit 45, Bethel* ☎ *506/755–2507, 877/955–2507* ⊕ *www.ovenheadsmokers.com.*

Serendipin' Art. Fine art, hand-blown glass, hand-painted silks, jewelry, and other crafts by more than 100 New Brunswick artists are sold here, and the second gallery next door has works produced elsewhere in the Maritimes. ⊠ *168–170 Water St.* ☎ *506/529–3327, 866/470–5500* ⊕ *www.serendipinart.ca* ⊙ *May–Oct., daily; Nov.–Apr., call to check hrs.*

Toose's. Owner Pam Vincent's sense of style is reflected in the artsy, sometimes quirky, range of gifts, jewelry, greetings cards, homewares, and irresistible chocolate truffles in this upscale boutique. There's another one just like it in the town of Quispamsis. ⊠ *147 Water St.* ☎ *506/529–4040* ⊙ *Closed Jan.–May.*

3

GRAND MANAN ISLAND

48 km (30 miles) east of St. Andrews by-the-Sea to Blacks Harbour, then 1½ hrs by car ferry.

Grand Manan, the largest of the three Fundy Islands, is also the farthest from the mainland. You might see whales, seals, or the occasional puffin on the way over. Circular herring weirs dot the island's coastal waters, and fish sheds and smokehouses lie beside long wharfs that reach out to bobbing fishing boats. Place names are evocative: Swallowtail, Southern Head, Seven Days Work, and Dark Harbour. It's easy to get around; only about 32 km (20 miles) of road lead from the lighthouse at Southern Head to the one at North Head. John James Audubon, that human encyclopedia of birds, visited the island in 1831, attracted by the more than 240 species of seabirds that nest here. The puffin may be the island's symbol, but whales are the stars. Giant finbacks, right whales, minkes, and humpbacks feed in the rich waters. With only 2,700 residents, it may seem remote and quiet, but there is plenty to do including birding, kayaking, whale-watching, and beachcombing. You can visit lighthouses, hike a heritage trail, visit the Whale and Seabird Research Station, or just hang around the busy wharves and chat with the fishermen. A day trip is possible, but you'll wish you had planned to stay at least one night.

GETTING HERE AND AROUND

Ferry service to Grand Manan is provided by **Coastal Transport,** which leaves the mainland from Blacks Harbour, off Route 1, and docks at North Head on Grand Manan Island. Plan to be at the ferry early as it operates on a first-come, first-served basis. Rates are C$32.55 for a car, excluding the driver, and C$10.90 for adults, payable on return passage from Grand Manan.

Coastal Transport ☎ *506/662–3724, 855/882–1978* 🌐 *www.coastaltransport.ca.*

EXPLORING

Adventure High. Kayaking tours on the Bay of Fundy range from two hours to weeklong trips, and some include a lobster dinner on the beach. You can rent bicycles here, too. ☎ *800/732–5492, 506/662–3563* 🌐 *www.adventurehigh.com.*

WHERE TO STAY

For expanded hotel reviews, visit Fodors.com.

$$ B&B/INN 🏨 **Inn at Whale Cove.** The main inn building here dates back to 1816 and has a shared living room with a fireplace and library. **Pros:** great rustic feel; lovely property for wandering. **Cons:** restaurant not open all year. [$] *Rooms from: C$145* ✉ *26 Whale Cottage Rd., off Whistle Rd., Grand Manan* ☎ *506/662–3181* 🌐 *www.whalecovecottages.ca* 🛏 *3 rooms, 5 cottages, 1 apartment* 🍴 *Multiple meal plans.*

$ B&B/INN 🏨 **Marathon Inn.** This mansion on 10 acres of grounds has been an inn since 1871; built by a sea captain, it sits on a hill with lovely views over the harbor. **Pros:** good food; pleasant hosts; discounts available on kayaking and whale-watching trips; free Wi-Fi and long-distance calls within North America. **Cons:** rooms vary in size. [$] *Rooms from: C$89* ✉ *19 Marathon La., North Head, Grand*

Manan ☎ *506/662–8488, 888/662–8488* ⊕ *www.marathoninn.com*
🔁 *23 rooms* ⦿ *Multiple meal plans.*

SPORTS AND THE OUTDOORS

WHALE-
WATCHING
A whale-watching cruise from Grand Manan takes you well out into the bay. Dress warmly, but some boats have winter jackets, hats, and mittens on board for those who don't heed this advice.

Sea Watch Tours. Interpreters on these tours are very knowledgeable about the birds you might encounter on your cruise, as well as about the whales. They also offer trips to Machias Seal Island to view Atlantic puffins. Trips (C$65–C$90) are four to five hours, late June through late September. ✉ *Breakwater Rd., Seal Cove, Grand Manan* ☎ *877/662–8552, 506/662–8552* ⊕ *www.seawatchtours.com.*

Seascape Kayak Tours. Seascape Kayak Tours in St. Andrews-by-the-Sea provides visitors with high quality sea-kayaking experiences and responsible adventure tourism. Seascape has received international recognition for its sustainable tourism practices. ☎ *506/747–1884, 866/747–1884* ⊕ *www.seascapekayaktours.com.*

Whales-n-Sails Adventures. Board a 60-foot sailboat to visit the whales, with narration by a marine biologist. Trips ($65, including tax and hot drinks) are four to five hours long and set out three times daily, at 11:30 and 4, late June through mid-September. Bird-watching charters are also available. ✉ *Grand Manan* ☎ *506/662–1999, 888/994–4044* ⊕ *www.whales-n-sails.com.*

DEER ISLAND

52 km (32 miles) east of St. Andrews by-the-Sea to Letete, 30 minutes by free ferry from Letete.

One of the pleasures of Deer Island is walking around the fishing wharves like those at Chocolate Cove. Exploring the island takes only a few hours; it's a mere 12 km (7 miles) long, varying in width from almost 5 km (3 miles) to a few hundred feet at some points.

GETTING HERE AND AROUND

From Saint John travel west on Highway 1 and take the Saint George exit, then take Route 172 south, a total distance of about 85 km (53 miles). The ferry runs every 30 minutes from 6:30 am to 5 pm, then hourly, with the last one back to the mainland leaving at 10 pm. There is no public transportation or bike rental on the island, so all but avid hikers will need a car.

EXPLORING

Deer Point. A walk through this small nature park is always pleasant, and a great way to pass the time while waiting for the ferry to Campobello Island. Just a few feet offshore in the Western Passage, the **Old Sow,** the second-largest whirlpool in the world, is visible, but its intensity depends on the state of the tide. The water is always highly active, though, and porpoises can often be seen. ✉ *Deer Island* ⊕ *www.deerislandpointpark.com.*

WHERE TO EAT AND STAY

For expanded hotel reviews, visit Fodors.com.

$$$ SEAFOOD 🍴 **45th Parallel Restaurant.** Seafood is an integral part of the home cooking at this casual and friendly motel restaurant. The lobster roll is renowned but you won't go wrong with other country diner options like fresh pan fried haddock or scallops. Old-fashioned chicken dinners—baked chicken, stuffing, real gravy, mashed potatoes, veggies, and cranberry sauce—are served here, too. Soup, sides, and tea or coffee are included in the price. Flowers surround the restaurant, and its dining terrace overlooks Passamaquoddy Bay. [$] *Average main: C$21* ✉ *941 Hwy. 772, Fairhaven* ☎ *506/747–2222 year-round, 506/747–2231 May–Oct.* ⏲ *Closed Nov.–Mar. and weekdays Apr., May, and Oct.*

$ RENTAL 🏨 **Sunset Beach Cottage & Suites.** Since this is right above a secluded cove, you can watch the porpoises and bald eagles during the day, and in the evening enjoy a rare East Coast treat—watching an ocean sunset from the pool or hot tub. **Pros:** peaceful and relaxing; friendly, helpful owners. **Cons:** a bit of a slope up the path from the beach. [$] *Rooms from: C$80* ✉ *21 Cedar Grove Rd., Fairhaven, Deer Island* ☎ *506/747–2972, 888/576–9990* 🌐 *www.cottageandsuites.com* 🛏 *5 suites, 1 cottage* ⏲ *Closed Nov.–Apr.* 🍽 *No meals.*

SPORTS AND THE OUTDOORS

Seascape Kayak Tours. Quality sea-kayaking experiences and responsible adventure tourism are provided May to October by this outfitter, which has received international recognition for its sustainable tourism practices. Half-day and full-day tours, and two-hour sunset paddles usually include sightings of wildlife, including seals, porpoises, whales, and bald eagles. ✉ *40 N.W. Harbour Branch Rd., Richardson, Deer Island* ☎ *506/747–1884, 866/747–1884* 🌐 *www.seascapekayaktours.com.*

CAMPOBELLO ISLAND

40 minutes by ferry (June to September) from Deer Island; 90 km (56 miles) southeast of St. Stephen via bridge from Lubec, Maine.

Fodor's Choice ★ Neatly manicured, preening itself in the bay, Campobello Island has always had a special appeal for the wealthy and the famous.

GETTING HERE AND AROUND

From Saint John, follow the directions for Deer Island (above). Once on Deer Island, drive 12 km (7 miles) to its southern tip for the East Coast Ferries service to Campobello (C$16 for car and driver, C$3 for each adult passenger, and C$4 fuel surcharge), a journey of around 30 minutes. Ferries from Deer Island run hourly from 8:30 am to 6:30 pm. The company also runs a ferry from Eastport, Maine, to Campobello (C$13 for car and driver, C$3 for each adult passenger, and a C$4 fuel surcharge). Once there, a car is essential.

The ferry from Campobello to Deer Island departs on the hour, every hour, until 7 pm.

East Coast Ferries Ltd. ☎ *506/747–2159, 877/747–2159* 🌐 *www.eastcoastferriesltd.com.*

EXPLORING

Herring Cove Provincial Park. The 425-hectare (1,049-acre) park has camping, a restaurant, a 9-hole, par-36 Geoffrey Cornish golf course, a sandy beach, and six hiking trails, one of which follows a logging trail once used by the Roosevelts. ✉ *Welshpool, Campobello* ☎ *506/752–7010, 800/561–0123.*

Roosevelt Campobello International Park. The 34-room rustic summer cottage of the family of President Franklin Delano Roosevelt is now part of a nature preserve, Roosevelt Campobello International Park, a joint project of the Canadian and U.S. governments. The miles of trails here make for pleasant strolling. Roosevelt's boyhood summer home was also the setting for the 1960 movie *Sunrise at Campobello.* Twice-daily Tea with Eleanor events include a talk about her life on the island. As an alternative to the ferry from Deer Island, drive across the border into Maine from St. Stephen, go down Route 1, and take Route 189 to Lubec, Maine, then cross the bridge to the island. ✉ *Roosevelt Park Rd., Campobello* ☎ *506/752–2922, 877/851–6663* 🌐 *fdr.net* 🎟 *Free* 🕓 *House and visitor center late May–mid-Oct., daily 10–6 ADT (9–5 EDT). Grounds year-round, daily dawn–dusk.*

WHERE TO STAY

For expanded hotel reviews, visit Fodors.com.

$ RENTAL 🏨 **An Island Chalet.** With stunning coastal views from their windows and front porches, and beds for four people, these log cottages (in spite of the singular name, there are five of them) offer great value. **Pros:** close to the FDR Bridge and Roosevelt-Campobello International Park; plenty of space for the price; a real bargain for a party of four. **Cons:** cell phone reception can be unreliable; beach rather difficult to reach. [$] *Rooms from: C$125* ✉ *115 Narrows Rd., Welshpool, Campobello* ☎ *506/752–2971* 🌐 *www.anislandchalet.com* 🛏 *5 cottages* 🍴 *No meals.*

$ B&B/INN 🏨 **The Owen House.** With glorious sea views, this 1835 house is full of antiques and original artwork by the owner, Joyce Morrell. **Pros:** a really peaceful haven, free of everyday distractions; many original features; the library next door has Wi-Fi. **Cons:** two rooms share a bathroom; the only TV is set up for video; not everyone likes a communal breakfast table. [$] *Rooms from: C$110* ✉ *11 Welshpool St., Welshpool, Campobello* ☎ *506/752–2977* 🌐 *www.owenhouse.ca* 🛏 *9 rooms* 🍴 *Breakfast.*

ST. MARTINS

54 km (34 miles) east of Saint John.

The fishing village of St. Martins has a rich shipbuilding heritage, whispering caves, miles of lovely beaches, spectacular tides, and a cluster of covered bridges, as well as several heritage inns and a couple of restaurants right on the beach. It's also the gateway to the spectacular Fundy Trail Parkway.

GETTING HERE AND AROUND

There is no public transportation to St. Martins. From Saint John drive north on Route 1, then head east on Route 111, past the airport, following signs for St. Martins. Coming from the Trans-Canada Highway (Route 2), exit onto Route 1 or Route 10; both will get you to Route 111, signposted St. Martins.

ESSENTIALS

Visitor Information Visitor Information Center ✉ *424 Main St. (in lighthouse at harbor)* ☎ *506/833–2006* ⊕ *www.stmartinscanada.com* ⊙ *June–Sept., daily.*

3

EXPLORING

Fundy Trail Parkway. The scenic drive portion of the Fundy Trail Parkway extends to an interpretive center at Salmon River, and will eventually go all the way to the Fundy National Park. The road closely parallels the cycling-walking Fundy Trail along the shore. There are lots of places to park and many accessible scenic lookouts. The 41-km (24-mile) Fundy Footpath, for expert hikers, already continues through to the national park. The parkway portion operates mid-May through mid-October. ☎ *506/833–2019* ⊕ *www.fundytrailparkway.com* ✉ *$5.50.*

WHERE TO STAY

For expanded hotel reviews, visit Fodors.com.

$
B&B/INN
St. Martins Country Inn. High on a hill overlooking the Bay of Fundy, the appeal of this restored sea captain's home comes from both its Victorian interiors and the accomplished cuisine on offer. **Pros:** breakfast available until 11; good food. **Cons:** some rooms are small; decoration may seem a little too "busy" to some. $ *Rooms from: C$110* ✉ *303 Main St.* ☎ *506/833–4534, 800/565–5257* ⊕ *www.stmartinscountryinn. ca* ✍ *16 rooms* ⊙ *Multiple meal plans.*

$
B&B/INN
Tidal Watch Inn. This luxurious property is just where the highest tides in the world sweep in and out each day, a mere 150 feet away! **Pros:** comfortable decor and atmosphere; good food. **Cons:** some rooms are in newer additions; not all rooms have good views; Wi-Fi not reliable in some rooms. $ *Rooms from: C$110* ✉ *16 Beach St.* ☎ *888/833–4772* ⊕ *www.tidalwatchinn.ca* ✍ *15 rooms, 2 cottages* ⊙ *Multiple meal plans.*

$
Weslan Inn. Fireplaces, antiques, and lots of floral prints give the rooms and the suite in this former sea captain's home an English country feel. Overlooking the bay or the lovely gardens, rooms have queen-size beds, and three have Jacuzzi baths. Breakfast is served in your room or in the dining room. **Pros:** true country charm in decor and service. **Cons:** watch out for mosquitoes on the lawn in the evenings. $ *Rooms from: C$122* ✉ *45 Main St.* ☎ *506/833–2351* ⊕ *www.weslaninn.com* ✍ *3 rooms, 1 suite* ⊙ *Breakfast.*

SPORTS AND THE OUTDOORS

SKIING
Poley Mountain Resort. Poley Mountain Resort has more than 100 skiable acres with a 660-foot vertical drop from a 910-foot summit, and five ski lifts. There are more than 30 trails, a snowboard park, and night skiing is also available. The season usually runs December through April. ✉ *69 Poley Mountain Rd., 13 km (8 miles) southeast of Sussex off Waterford Rd., Sussex* ☎ *506/433–7653* ⊕ *www.poleymountain.com.*

FUNDY NATIONAL PARK

135 km (84 miles) northeast of Saint John.

GETTING HERE AND AROUND

Fundy National Park is bisected by Route 114, which loops down from just east of Sussex, leaves the park at Alma, and follows the coast, via Riverview, to Moncton. From the Trans-Canada Highway (Route 2), exit onto Route 10 to Sussex, take Route 1 east for a short distance (signposted Moncton) before exiting onto Route 114 south. There are a number of parking places within the park.

EXPLORING

Alma. The small seaside town of Alma services Fundy National Park with motels, restaurants that serve good lobster, and a bakery that sells sublime sticky buns. There's plenty to do around here—from bird-watching and kayaking to horseback riding. ⊕ *www.villageofalma.ca.*

Fundy National Park. This incredible 206-square-km (80-square-mile) park is a microcosm of New Brunswick's inland and coastal climates, and was recently designated a Dark Sky Preserve by the Royal Astronomical Society of Canada, in recognition of its superb night skies free of light pollution. Park naturalists offer several programs each day, including beach walks and hikes to explore the park's unique climatic conditions and the fascinating evolution evident in the forests. The park has 100 km (60 miles) of varied hiking and mountain-biking trails, camping, golf, tennis, a heated Bay of Fundy saltwater pool, and a playground. Among the most scenic of the trails is Laverty Falls, a 2.5-km (1.5-mile) trail that takes you on an ascent through hardwood forests to the beautiful Laverty waterfall and arrives at the old Shepody Road. At Third Vault Falls, a 3.7-km (2.3-mile) trail starting from the Laverty Auto Trail Parking Lot, hikers emerge at the falls and can take a refreshing dip in the pool. On the way to the Coppermine Trail, a hike to an abandoned mine at Point Wolfe, visitors wind around a steep curve and through a bright-red covered bridge, a favorite spot for photographers. In the evening there are interactive programs in the amphitheater and campfires. The more than 600 campsites range from full-service to wilderness, and yurts and "oTENTik" accommodations—a combination of tent and cabin—are also available. ⊠ *Rte. 114* ☎ *506/887–6000* ⊕ *www.pc.gc.ca* 🖼 *$7.80* ☉ *Visitor Reception Centre and campgrounds closed mid-Oct.–mid-May.*

WHERE TO STAY

For expanded hotel reviews, visit Fodors.com.

$$
B&B/INN   🖼 **Falcon Ridge Inn.** Perched high above the village and the ocean, every window (and there are many) in this modern property affords a spectacular view and eliminates any need for air-conditioning. **Pros:** amazing view of the fishing boats of Alma and shale cliffs of Fundy; full breakfast served at individual tables. **Cons:** Fundy fog can unexpectedly block the vista; you can walk to the village, it's a steep slope back up. 🖼 *Rooms from: C$130* ⊠ *24 Falcon Ridge Dr.* ☎ *506/887–1110, 888/321–9090* ⊕ *www.falconridgeinn.nb.ca* 🍽 *4 rooms* ⧉⧉ *Breakfast.*

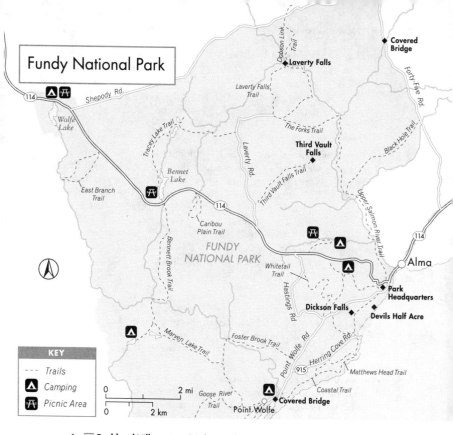

Fundy National Park

Fundy National Park

KEY
- - - Trails
▲ Camping
🎪 Picnic Area

0 ——— 2 mi

0 ——— 2 km

$

$ 🏠 **Parkland Village Inn.** Right on the water, next to the fishermen's wharf
B&B/INN in the heart of the bustling village, this long-established inn also has
a very good restaurant. **Pros:** view of the Bay of Fundy is extraordinary; nine of the guest rooms overlook the bay. **Cons:** can be hard to
get a room or table in peak season; breakfast not included in July and
August rates. **$** *Rooms from: C$120 ✉ 8601 Main St. ☎ 506/887–
2313, 866/668–4337 ⊕ www.parklandvillageinn.com ⤴ 10 rooms, 5
suites ⊘ Closed Nov.–Apr. ⫶⊙⫶ Multiple meal plans.*

SPORTS AND THE OUTDOORS

BIRD- **Mary's Point.** Every summer the bit of shoreline at Mary's Point draws
WATCHING tens of thousands of migrating birds, including semipalmated sandpip-
ers and other shorebirds. The area, now a bird sanctuary and interpretive center, is near Riverside-Albert. ✉ *Follow signs off Rte. 915.*

GOLF **Fundy National Park Golf Club.** This is one of the province's most beautiful
and challenging 9-hole courses, near cliffs overlooking the restless Bay
of Fundy. ✉ *Fundy National Park near Alma entrance ☎ 506/887–2970.*

HORSEBACK **Broadleaf Guest Ranch.** Horseback trail rides through lowland marshes
RIDING or along the beach start at $20 for half an hour and rise to $150 for a
six-hour excursion with lunch. Various combinations of riding, cycling,
canoeing, and rock climbing are also offered. ✉ *5526 Rte. 114, Hopewell
Hill ☎ 506/882–2349, 800/226–5405 ⊕ www.broadleafranch.com.*

SEA KAYAKING   **Baymount Outdoor Adventures.** Sea kayaking around the Hopewell Rocks can be arranged here, as well as hiking and biking. ⌧ *Hopewell Cape* ☏ *506/734–2660, 877/601–2660* ⊕ *www.baymountadventures.com.*

FreshAir Adventure. Bay of Fundy sea-kayaking excursions last from two hours to three days. Guides, instruction, and equipment are provided. ⌧ *16 Fundy View Dr.* ☏ *506/887–2249, 800/545–0020* ⊕ *www. freshairadventure.com.*

Baymount Outdoor Adventures. Baymount Outdoor Adventures has interpreters who lead expeditions into the White Caves near the Bay of Fundy. Note that caving is fun but strenuous and not for the claustrophobic. These excursions require crawling on cave floors and slithering through narrow openings. Baymount also arranges hikes, biking, and sea kayaking at Hopewell Rocks. Make reservations for all activities. ⌧ *Hillsborough* ☏ *506/734–2660* ⊕ *www.baymountadventures.com.*

EN
ROUTE   Along routes 915 and 114 from Alma to Moncton are dozens of talented artists and craftspeople, many of whom open their studios and galleries to visitors. Visitor information centers have information and maps.

SHOPPING

Albert County Clay Company. In a large converted community hall Judy Tait makes beautiful and stylish pottery from local clay, imprinted with the forms of leaves and wildflowers. ⌧ *900 Albert Mines Rd., off Rte. 114 near Hopewell, Curryville* ☏ *506/734–2851* ⊕ *www. albertcountyclayco.com.*

An Artist's Garden. Many of owner Karin Bach's wildlife clay sculptures are on display in a lovely organic garden outside, and the gallery contains more of her pottery and paintings, along with works by other local artists and artisans. ⌧ *Rte. 915, between Alma and Riverside-Albert* ☏ *506/882–2166.*

Kindred Spirits Stained Glass Studio ⌧ *2831 Main St., Hillsborough* ☏ *506/734–2342.*

Studio on the Marsh. In a perfect setting for wildlife art, this studio sells prints by the late Lars Larsen. His New Brunswick scenes in particular make excellent souvenirs. ⌧ *255 Marys Point Rd., off Rte. 915, Harvey-Albert* ☏ *506/882–2917* ⊕ *www.studioonthemarsh.com.*

Wendy Johnston's Pottery. Contemporary, functional, brightly colored pieces with abstract designs are produced here and the Art Effects Fine Craft Gallery represents more than 45 Maritimes artists. Call to check opening hours in the off-season. ⌧ *3923 Rte. 114, Hopewell Cape* ☏ *506/734–2046* ⊕ *www.wendyjohnstonpottery.com.*

CAPE ENRAGE

15 km (9 miles) east of Alma.

Cape Enrage juts more than 7 km (4½ miles) out into the bay, with a 6-km (4-mile) driftwood-cluttered beach, a lighthouse, and spectacular views, as well as an adventure center with a restaurant.

3

GETTING HERE AND AROUND

Just east of Alma, Route 915 branches right off Route 114, following a scenic route through Waterside. Look for a right turn on a minor road to Cape Enrage. Coming from the Hopewell Rocks end of the bay, Route 915 forks left off Route 114 at Riverside-Albert, and the Cape Enrage road is a left turn. There is an admission charge of C$4.50 mid-May–mid-October.

ESSENTIALS

Cape Enrage Interpretive Center ⊠ *650 Cape Enrage Rd., Waterside* ☎ *506/887–2273, 888/423–5454* ⊕ *www.capeenrage.ca.*

EXPLORING

Cape Enrage Adventures. Activities includes rappelling, rock-climbing, and zip-lining, and prices, which start at C$45 for 3 zip-line runs, include admission to the cape. The zip line is usually open daily, but reservations are required for other activities. A restaurant and a gift shop are on-site. ⊠ *650 Cape Enrage Rd., off Rte. 915* ☎ *506/887–2273, 888/423–5454* ⊕ *www.capeenrage.ca.*

HOPEWELL CAPE

40 km (25 miles) northeast of Alma.

The coastal road (Route 114) from Alma to Moncton winds through covered bridges and along rocky coasts.

GETTING HERE AND AROUND

Hopewell Cape is about 47 km (29 miles) south of Moncton, via Riverview, on Route 114. It is 190 km (118 miles) from Saint John, via Route 1 toward Moncton. Just beyond Sussex, take Exit 211 onto Route 114 and continue through Fundy National Park, Alma, and Riverside-Albert.

EXPLORING

FAMILY

Fodor'sChoice

★

Hopewell Rocks. These famous "giant flowerpots" have been carved by the Bay of Fundy tides. They're topped with vegetation and form tiny islands at high tide, while low tide reveals the entire columns and you can descend to the exposed seabed for closer study. There are also trails, an interactive visitor center, a café-restaurant, a gift shop, and a children's play area. Guided tours are available. It's about a 15-minute walk from the visitor center to the rocks, but there's also a shuttle service (C$2 each way). ⚠ **The tide comes in very quickly, so check tide tables, keep an eye on your watch, and exit the beach with time to spare.** ⊠ *131 Discovery Rd.* ☎ *877/734–3429* ⊕ *www.thehopewellrocks.ca* 🚍 *$9 (valid for 2 consecutive days)* ☾ *Mid-June–mid-Aug., daily 8–8; mid-Aug.–early Sept., daily 9–7; mid-May–mid-June and early Sept.–mid-Oct., daily 9–5. Visitors may enter park on foot in off-season, but no facilities are open.*

WHERE TO STAY

For expanded hotel reviews, visit Fodors.com.

$　　**Florentine Manor Heritage Inn.** With beautiful antique furniture and
B&B/INN　handmade quilts on the beds, this restored shipbuilder's house is a
haven for honeymooners and romantics, and the Fundy Coast is close
by. **Pros:** comfortably decorated, but not overstuffed rooms; abundant
bird life; good breakfasts. **Cons:** minimum two-night stay. $ *Rooms
from: C$119* ✉ *356 Rte. 915, Harvey on the Bay* ☎ *506/882–2271,
800/665–2271* ⊕ *www.florentinemanor.com* ☞ *8 rooms* ⦿ *Breakfast.*

$　　**Innisfree Bed and Breakfast.** An 1847 farmhouse just minutes from
B&B/INN　Hopewell Rocks now provides stylish and comfortable accommodations in rooms furnished with antiques and quilts. **Pros:** closest bed-
and-breakfast to Hopewell Rocks; friendly, helpful hosts; mountain
bikes for rent. **Cons:** may be too quiet for some. $ *Rooms from: C$120*
✉ *4270 Hwy. 114* ☎ *506/734–3510* ⊕ *www.innisfreebandb.com* ☞ *5
rooms, 1 suite* ⦿ *Breakfast.*

SHOPPING

Farm Life Studio. Normand Brandford's paintings and prints reflect his
affinity with farm animals—some living examples of the subject matter look on from the surrounding pastures—as well as local wildlife,
landscapes, and nostalgic scenes. ✉ *474 Albert Mines Rd., Albert Mines*
☎ *506/734–3493* ⊗ *Closed mid-Oct.–May; sometimes closed Mon.*

MONCTON AND DIEPPE

80 km (50 miles) northeast of Alma.

Metro Moncton—the second largest city in Atlantic Canada (after
Halifax, Nova Scotia)—is an attractive, welcoming city, with several
family-friendly attractions. There is an ongoing calendar of festivals
throughout the year.

An agreeable, lively place, and home to two universities, Moncton is
often called the Gateway to Acadia because of its equal mix of English
and French and its proximity to the Acadian shore, though it also has
a large Irish population and a growing Korean community. Moncton
has a renovated downtown with unique shops and restaurants and such
beautiful flowers that it has won national "Communities in Bloom"
awards. It is also beginning to make the most of its downtown riverside,
with a park and boardwalk.

The twin cities of Moncton and Dieppe—the join is almost
imperceptible—are considered the shopping mecca of Atlantic Canada.
Moncton's big chain stores are mostly strung out along Mountain Road
and the Trinity Power Centre, while Dieppe is home to the Champlain
Place shopping mall, a good Saturday farmers' market, and other retail
opportunities.

Two natural attractions are the main draws here: the Tidal Bore and
the Magnetic Hill, though you might be disappointed if you've read
too much about either of them. Nevertheless, it's worth experiencing
Magnetic Hill, and the city has a program underway to restore the Tidal
Bore to its former glory, diminished over the years by riverbank erosion.

GETTING HERE AND AROUND

Moncton is one of the few places in the province accessible by rail, on VIA Rail's Montréal—Halifax route known as "The Ocean." It also has one of the province's major airports. By road, the Trans-Canada Highway (Route 2) loops around the city, with several exit points.

Moncton has an excellent bus system, operated by Codiac Transit; the fare is C$2, or you can buy a 10-trip pass for C$18 or a 20-day pass for C$34.50, available from the bus station at 140 Millennium Boulevard or Shoppers Drug Marts (✉ *535 Edinburgh Dr. or 860 Mountain Rd.*). Free transfers are available from the driver if you need to change buses to get to a single destination. Buses are equipped with bike racks, so you can bike and ride to different destinations.

Roads to Sea offers day tours of the city and of some of the province's natural wonders.

ESSENTIALS

Bus Information Acadian Lines ☎ 800/567–5151 ⊕ www.acadianbus.com. **Codiac Transit** ☎ 506/857–2008 ⊕ www.codiactranspo.ca.

Tour Information Roads to Sea. Guided tours run May through October and include Bay of Fundy nature tours, the Acadian coast, and the City of Moncton. ☎ 506/850–7623, 877/850–7623 ⊕ www.roadstosea.com.

Visitor Information Moncton Tourism ☎ 800/363–4558, 506/853–3540 ⊕ www.tourism.moncton.ca.

EXPLORING
TOP ATTRACTIONS

FAMILY **Crystal Palace.** A stop here is virtually guaranteed to win beleaguered parents adoring looks from their children. With more than a dozen indoor rides and attractions, including miniature golf, laser tag, a climbing wall, and an arcade, this is a popular vacation spot for families and especially convenient if you stay at the adjacent Ramada *(⇨ See Where to Stay)*. Rides include a wave swinger and a low-rise bullet roller coaster. Height and weight restrictions apply. ✉ *499 Paul St., across from Champlain Pl., Dieppe* ☎ *506/859–4386, 877/856–4386* ⊕ *www.crystalpalace.ca* 🎫 *Tickets start at C$2.85, with various multiride options, up to C$77.60 pass for family of four for one day; miniature golf, climbing wall, or laser center C$6.90* ⊗ *Mid-June–early Sept., daily 10–9; Sept.–mid-June, Mon.–Thurs. noon–8, Fri. noon–9, Sat. 10–9, Sun. 10–8.*

FAMILY **Magic Mountain Water Park.** An excellent water theme park, adjacent to Magnetic Hill, Magic Mountain includes a huge wave pool, thrill-ride body slides, and gentler fun including a Splashpad and Puddle Jumpers Pond. ✉ *2875 Mountain Rd., off Trans-Canada Hwy. Exit 450 on outskirts of Moncton* ☎ *506/857–9283, 800/331–9283 in Canada* ⊕ *www.magicmountain.ca* 🎫 *$27* ⊗ *Mid–late June and mid-Aug.–early Sept., daily 10–6; July–mid-Aug., daily 10–7 (mini-golf until 10 pm all season).*

FAMILY **Magnetic Hill.** A bizarre optical illusion has been attracting visitors since Fodor's Choice the days of horse-drawn wagons. If you park your car in neutral at the ★ designated spot, you seem to be coasting uphill without power. Don't be tempted to turn the vehicle around; the effect is most pronounced when you are going backward. Get out and try it on foot and it seems harder to walk downhill than up. There are shops and a restaurant within the attached Wharf Village. ⊠ *North of Moncton off Trans-Canada Hwy. Exit 450 (Mountain Rd.); watch for signs* ☎ *506/384–9527* ⊕ *www.magnetichill.com* ☒ *$5* ⊙ *Mid-May–mid-Oct., daily 8–5 (to 7 July and Aug.).*

FAMILY **Magnetic Hill Zoo.** Celebrating its 60th year in 2013, this is the largest zoo in Atlantic Canada, covering 40 acres and housing 575 animals. There's no shortage of exotic species, including lemurs, lions and other big cats, zebras, and ostrich, and around 80 bird species are represented, both indigenous and exotic. A tropical house has reptiles, amphibians, birds, and primates, and at Old MacDonald's Barnyard, children can pet domestic animals or ride a pony in summer. ■TIP➜ **Check feeding times on the way in.** ⊠ *125 Magic Mountain Rd., off Trans-Canada Hwy. Exit 450 on outskirts of Moncton* ☎ *506/877-7718* ⊕ *www. moncton.ca/zoo* ☒ *$13 late June–early Sept.; $10 mid-May–late June and early Sept.–late Oct.; $6.75 mid-Apr.–mid-May* ⊙ *Mid-Apr.–mid-May, daily 10–4; mid-May–late June and early Sept.–late Oct., daily 10–7; late June–early Sept., daily 9–7.*

Resurgo Place. Incorporating the Moncton Museum, the new Transportation Discovery Museum, and the restored Free Meeting House, this complex—named after the city motto, meaning "I rise again"—is a fine introduction to Moncton's past. It will reopen in 2014 with a stunning new entrance and extended exhibition areas. The **Moncton Museum** has a comprehensive range of exhibits that trace the city's history and development from the days of the Mi'Kmaq people to the present day. The **Transportation Discovery Museum** is largely interactive, with displays that reflect Moncton's importance as transportation hub of the Atlantic Provinces. The beautiful, omni-denominational **Free Meeting House**, built in 1821, is the city's longest-standing building with the oldest burial ground. ⊠ *20 Mountain Rd.* ☎ *506/856–4383* ⊕ *www. moncton.ca* ☒ *Call for details* ⊙ *Call for hrs.*

Riverfront Park. The 5 km (3 miles) of multiuse trail along the banks of the Petitcodiac River are a delight for walkers, joggers, and bicyclers. Bore Park is a good place from which to view the Tidal Bore. ⊠ *Assomption Blvd.*

Fodor's Choice **Tidal Bore and Riverfront Park.** A multimillion-dollar restoration program
★ has made the **Tidal Bore** once again one of Moncton's prime natural attractions and robbed it of its former nickname, the "total bore," coined after the construction of a causeway upstream reduced it to a trickle. Now, when the world's highest tides come in on the Bay of Fundy, the surge of water pushes far upstream on the Petitcodiac River, reversing the flow with a wall of water that raises the level by about 7½ meters (roughly 25 feet) and fills the river to its banks. It is an incredible sight, particularly when tides are at their highest—a recent occurrence brought surfers from all over the world to ride the bore upstream. Bore Park on Main Street is the best vantage point, with terraced seating and, in summer, an introductory talk; viewing times are posted. The park is part of the larger **Riverfront Park**, with 5 km (3 miles) of multiuse trails along the banks of the river. ⚠ **Surfing, or entering the water at all, is extremely dangerous because of the deep, soft mud that lines the river.**

WORTH NOTING

Aberdeen Cultural Centre. The halls of the Aberdeen Cultural Centre, a converted schoolhouse home to theater and dance companies, a framing shop, artists' ateliers, and several galleries, ring with music and chatter. **Galerie 12** represents leading contemporary Acadian artists. **Galerie Sans Nom** is an artist-run co-op supporting avant-garde artists from throughout Canada. The artist-run **IMAGO Inc.** is the only print-production shop in the province. Guided tours are available by appointment. ✉ *140 Botsford St.* ☎ *506/857–9597* 🌐 *www.centreculturelaberdeen.ca* 🎟 *Free* 🕓 *Weekdays 10–4.*

Acadian Museum. On the campus of the University of Moncton, this museum has a remarkable collection of artifacts reflecting 300 years of Acadian life in the Maritimes. There's also a fine gallery showcasing contemporary art by local and national artists. ✉ *Clement-Cormier Bldg., 405 University Ave.* ☎ *506/858–4088* 🌐 *www.umoncton.ca/umcm-maum* 🎟 *$4* 🕓 *June–Sept., weekdays 10–5, weekends 1–5; Oct.–May, Tues.–Fri. 1–4:30, weekends 1–4.*

Free Meeting House. The 1821 Free Meeting House, a simple and austere National Historic Site operated by the Moncton Museum, is one of the city's oldest standing buildings. It was built as a gathering place for all religious denominations without their own places of worship. ✉ *100 Steadman St.* ☎ *506/856–4383* 🎟 *Donations accepted* 🕓 *Mon.–Sat. 9–4:30, Sun. 1–5.*

Lutz Mountain Heritage Museum. Within a restored 1883 meeting house, just north of Moncton, you'll find genealogical records of the area's non-Acadian pioneer settlers from as far back as 1766. With more than 3,000 artifacts, there's plenty to see. ✉ *3143 Mountain Rd.* ☎ *506/384–7719* 🌐 *www.lutzmtnheritage.ca* 🎟 *$2 suggested donation* 🕓 *Mid-June–mid-Sept., Mon.–Sat. 9–5; rest of yr by appointment.*

WHERE TO EAT

$ ECLECTIC

🍴 **Café Archibald.** This is a great little place for a quick bite or bistro meal in pleasant surroundings at any time of the day—breakfast is served from 7 am and it's open until 11 pm (midnight on Friday and Saturday). Fresh pastries are baked every morning and the open kitchen serves very good crêpes, pizzas, salads, sandwiches, and desserts. There's a huge range of coffees and teas as well as wine and beer. There's another branch in Dieppe at 216 Chemin Gauvin. [$] *Average main: C$10* ✉ *221 Mountain Rd.* ☎ *506/853–8819* 🌐 *www.cafearchibald.com.*

$$$$ MODERN FRENCH Fodor's Choice ★

🍴 **Little Louis' Oyster Bar.** In an unlikely location on a predominantly industrial street, this restaurant is a real find, so don't be deterred by the unpromising exterior. Oysters are, of course, a highlight here, but there is much more to Chef Pierre Richard's Modern French menu, with complex but perfectly balanced creations based on beef, lamb, and poultry, in addition to seafood. There's also a daily tasting menu with or without wine pairings. Desserts to leave you speechless include crème brûlée with a basket of fruit and ice-wine pearls, and a much heralded mini-meringue pie with maple. A first-rate wine list and impeccable service complete the experience. [$] *Average main: C$40* ✉ *245 Collishaw St.* ☎ *506/855–2022* 🌐 *www.littlelouis.ca* 🕓 *No lunch.*

$$ 🍴 **Pastalli Italian Cucina.** Seafood, steaks, lamb, and veal share the menu with pasta and pizzas at this upbeat Italian resto where old-world flavors are showcased in a friendly setting. The large portions and the bread bar are almost as popular as the World Wine Cellar. Reservations are advisable. [$] *Average main: C$17* ✉ *611 Main St.* ☎ *506/383–1050* 🌐 *www.pastalli.com.*

ITALIAN

$$$ 🍴 **Pisces by Gaston.** Seafood of all types is the obvious star of the creative menu here. Local catches go into dishes such as hazelnut-crusted halibut, lobster linguine carbonara, and baked stuffed lobster. Nonseafood options are limited to a few steak or chicken dishes. Casual elegance is the theme. Sadly, the restaurant doesn't make full use of its fine riverside location, fronting the busy road rather than the Petitcodiac River (and twice-daily tidal bore) at the back, but the food more than compensates. [$] *Average main: C$30* ✉ *300 Main St.* ☎ *506/854–0444* 🌐 *www.piscesbygaston.com* ⏲ *No lunch weekends.*

SEAFOOD

$$$ 🍴 **St James' Gate.** Named after the Guinness brewery in Dublin, this is by no means the standard idea of an Irish-theme pub. It is as authentic a re-creation of an ancient vaulted stone cellar as you will find, providing an atmospheric location to enjoy the accomplished cooking of head chef Emanuel Brison. The menu is strong on local seafood, such as halibut baked with a pistachio crust and curry maple glaze. Meat dishes are equally delicious, and the menu includes snacks, lighter meals, and pub favorites. There's a central, dark-wood bar, a street-side patio, and live music five nights a week. Upstairs is a chic 10-room boutique hotel (⇨ *See Where to Stay*). [$] *Average main: C$24* ✉ *14 Church St.* ☎ *506/388–4283* 🌐 *www.stjamesmoncton.com* ⏲ *No dinner Sun.*

ECLECTIC

$$$$ 🍴 **Windjammer.** One of Canada's finest restaurants, the richly elegant Windjammer, in the Delta Beauséjour Hotel *(⇨ See Where to Stay)* offers a memorable, pampering dining experience. It's modeled after the opulent luxury liners of the early 1900s, with lots of dark wood and brass, nautical paintings, and ship models, and creates an equally rarified atmosphere without being stuffy. The staff is attentive, knowledgeable, and friendly. Executive chef Stefan Mueller's menus include the "100 Mile Menu," featuring ingredients from land and sea sourced within 100 miles, including some vegetables, herbs, and edible flowers from the hotel's roof garden, which also supplies honey from its working beehives. An exceptional choice of seafood includes oysters and caviar appetizers, and a main-course platter featuring scallops, salmon, smoked sturgeon, halibut, mussels, and oysters in a light citrus broth. Meat choices include delicious Lamb Three Ways (pan seared, grilled, and in a sausage), châteaubriand for two, and filet mignon flambéed at your table. Amuses bouche, palate cleansers, delectable desserts, and a superb wine list (including local wines) complete the experience. [$] *Average main: C$45* ✉ *Delta Beauséjour Hotel, 750 Main St.* ☎ *506/877–7137* 🌐 *www.deltahotels.com* ✍ *Reservations essential* ⏲ *Closed Sun.*

INTERNATIONAL

Fodor's Choice ★

WHERE TO STAY

For expanded hotel reviews, visit Fodors.com.

$$ HOTEL **Château Moncton Hotel & Suites.** Alongside the Petitcodiac River, this modern hotel has a great view of the tidal bore, an extensive riverfront trail right out back, and is close to downtown businesses, shopping malls, restaurants, and movie theaters. **Pros:** convenient location; pleasant atmosphere; good-size rooms; hot and cold buffet breakfast included in the price. **Cons:** geared to business travelers; no restaurant on-site. [$] *Rooms from: C$145* ✉ *100 Main St.* ☎ *506/870–4444, 800/576–4040* 🌐 *www.chateaumoncton.ca* 🛏 *93 rooms, 12 suites* 🍴 *Breakfast.*

$ HOTEL Fodor's Choice ★ **Delta Beauséjour.** In a great downtown location, this is one of Moncton's finest and friendliest hotels, catering not only to business travelers, but also to families—particularly since a 38-meter (125-foot) indoor waterslide was added to the pool area. **Pros:** right in the hub of downtown shopping, restaurants, and businesses; some rooms overlook the river, with good tidal bore viewing. **Cons:** computer room is quite small. [$] *Rooms from: C$109* ✉ *750 Main St.* ☎ *506/854–4344, 888/351–7666* 🌐 *www.deltahotels.com* 🛏 *298 rooms, 6 suites* 🍴 *No meals.*

$$ HOTEL **Hotel St. James.** Moncton's first boutique hotel is in the heart of downtown, just off Main Street, and has chic and spacious rooms above a highly regarded pub-restaurant. **Pros:** good central location; stylish design; very comfortable; continental breakfast included. **Cons:** travel light—there's no elevator and everything, including reception, is upstairs. [$] *Rooms from: C$159* ✉ *14 Church St.* ☎ *888/782–1414* 🌐 *stjamesgatecanada.com* 🛏 *8 rooms, 1 suite* 🍴 *Breakfast.*

$ B&B/INN **Magnetic Hill Winery and B&B.** On Lutz Mountain, with a panoramic view over Moncton, this delightful bed-and-breakfast offers warm and friendly personal service from a winemaking family. **Pros:** price includes wine tastings and a bottle of wine; near Magnetic Hill and ancillary attractions. **Cons:** some distance out of town. [$] *Rooms from: C$119* ✉ *860 Front Mountain Rd.* ✣ *North of Hwy. 2, Exit 450. After turning off Mountain Rd. onto Front Mountain Rd., ignore Magnetic Hill B&B on left; Winery B&B is little farther on right.* ☎ *506/384–9463* 🌐 *www.magnetichillwinery.com* 🛏 *2 rooms* 🍴 *Breakfast.*

$$ HOTEL FAMILY **Ramada Plaza Crystal Palace.** Attached to the Crystal Palace indoor amusement complex, this hotel has a tropical-looking indoor pool at its heart and is popular with families. **Pros:** good service; kids love it. **Cons:** can feel overrun with children; themed rooms are cute, but some are not particularly spacious; pool aroma and humidity issues in some rooms. [$] *Rooms from: C$165* ✉ *499 Paul St., Dieppe* ☎ *506/858–8584, 800/561–7108* 🌐 *www.crystalpalacehotel.com* 🛏 *115 rooms, 21 suites* 🍴 *Multiple meal plans.*

NIGHTLIFE AND THE ARTS

Casino New Brunswick. Opened in 2010, the casino offers gaming tables and slots, an adjacent hotel, a restaurant, a pub, and a large, state-of-the-art concert hall with a lineup that has recently included Steve Earle, Howie Mandel, and Dwight Yoakam. The casino is open from 7 am to 3 am (24 hours on weekends), with table games from noon. ✉ *21 Casino Dr.* ☎ *506/859–7770, 877/859–7775* 🌐 *www.casinonb.ca.*

3

iRock. A young crowd comes for DJs playing loud dance music into the early hours on Thursday, Friday, and Saturday nights from 10. Friday is Ladies Night. ✉ *415 Elmwood Dr.* ☎ *506/384–4324* ⊕ *www. irockmoncton.ca.*

Navigators Pub. An antidote to the trendy Rouge next door, Navigators Pub is a no-frills downtown watering hole offering Acadian reggae on Monday and rock on Tuesday through Thursday and Sunday. It has a particularly nice (and sheltered) patio. ✉ *191 Robinson Court* ☎ *506/854–8427 bar, 506/871–5370 office* ⊕ *www.navspub.ca.*

The Old Triangle Irish Alehouse. A good re-creation of the quintessential Dublin pub, this place has a buzzing atmosphere, good food, and live music Wednesday through Saturday—some Irish, some easy listening. ✉ *751 Main St.* ☎ *506/384–7474* ⊕ *www.oldtriangle.com.*

Pump House Brewery. In addition to the house brews, you can enjoy live music Saturday nights. The pub is also a venue for the HubCap Comedy Festival in February. ✉ *5 Orange La.* ☎ *506/855–2337* ⊕ *www. pumphousebrewery.ca.*

SPORTS AND THE OUTDOORS

The Moncton area is home to two of New Brunswick's four signature golf courses.

Fox Creek Golf Club. This is an exceptional 6,065-yard course and a 9,000-square-foot clubhouse with a restaurant and pro shop. It's fast becoming famous for its architectural and natural beauty. The green fee is C$79, and club and cart rentals are C$40 each. There's a strict dress code. ✉ *200 Golf St., Dieppe* ☎ *506/859–4653, 888/257–4222* ⊕ *www.foxcreekgolfclub.ca.*

Royal Oaks Golf Club. An 18-hole, 7,103-yard, par-72 PGA Championship course, this was the first Canadian course designed by the U.S. golf course architect Rees Jones. The C$80 green fee goes down to C$55 for twilight hours, club rentals are C$40, and a power cart is C$20 per person. Call to check the dress code. ✉ *401 Royal Oaks Blvd., off Elmwood Dr.* ☎ *506/388–6257* ⊕ *www.royaloaks.ca.*

TreeGO Moncton. Children and adults can clamber through the treetops of Centennial Park, negotiating swinging rope-suspended logs, rope ladders, and zip lines, all while safely harnessed. Parents can watch their kids' progress from the ground. Adults embark on four courses, each more challenging than the last. Check the website for tips on suitable clothing and footwear. ✉ *Centennial Park, 811 St. George Blvd.* ☎ *506/388–4646, 877/707–4646* ⊕ *www.treegomoncton.com* ✉ *$36* ☻ *May–mid-Oct., 9:30–5 (reservations required).*

SHOPPING

Dieppe's Champlain Place shopping mall and Moncton's downtown boutiques and big box stores on the outskirts make the twin cities one of New Brunswick's major shopping destinations—a lot of people come over from Prince Edward Island to shop here, too. There's also quite a network of secondhand clothing stores—the Frenchy's chain is outstanding—with some amazing designer bargains. Farmers' markets in both cities and Moncton's Artisan Village focus on quality foods, arts, and crafts from local producers.

Fodor's Choice **Artisan Village.** Downtown Moncton's Artisan Village is an ambitious
★ and exciting transformation of a former bus depot/car dealership into an open-concept gallery and community of artists and craftspeople, the only one of its kind in the Maritimes. Metal artist Shane Myers is the visionary at the forefront of the ongoing project, which houses and represents some of the province's finest artisans. ✉ *465 Main St.* ☎ *506/388–9000* ⊕ *www.artisanvillage.ca.*

Champlain Place. This huge mall has more than 150 stores. ✉ *477 Paul St., Dieppe* ☎ *506/855–6255* ⊕ *www.champlainplace.com.*

Dieppe Market. Every Saturday, from 7 am to 1:30 pm, this market brims with fresh produce, baked goods, ethnic cuisine, crafts, and live music. There's also an "Express Market" on Friday from 1 to 6 pm. ✉ *232 Acadie Ave., Dieppe* ☎ *506/854–8557* ⊕ *www.marchedieppemarket.com.*

Marché Moncton Market. The market buzzes on Saturdays from 7 to 2, with around 130 vendors selling fresh produce, meat and deli foods, baked goods, and crafts. Vendors serve delicious ethnic lunches here Monday through Saturday. ✉ *120 Westmorland St.* ☎ *506/389–5969* ⊕ *www.marchemonctonmarket.ca.*

THE ACADIAN COAST

History and nature meet on the Tantramar salt marshes east of Moncton. Bounded by the upper reaches of the Bay of Fundy, the province of Nova Scotia, and the Northumberland Strait, the region is rich in history and culture. The inspiration for Canadian artists such as Alex Colville and of poets from Sir Charles G. D. Roberts to Douglas Lochhead, the marshes provide a highly productive wetland habitat, and the region is among North America's major migratory bird routes.

The white sands and gentle tides of the Northumberland Strait and Baie des Chaleurs are in stunning contrast to the rocky cliffs and powerful tides of the Bay of Fundy. Along the Acadian Coast the water is warm, the sand is fine, and the food delicious. Many people here find their livelihood in the forests, in the mines, and on the sea, and along the Acadian Peninsula working wharves are an attraction within themselves.

DORCHESTER AND MEMRAMCOOK

Memramcook is 24 km (15 miles) southeast of Moncton. Dorchester is 14 km (9 miles) south of Memramcook.

Memramcook and Dorchester are on opposite sides of a marsh, each surrounded by gentle, rolling landscape filled with colorful native grasses. Acadian roots run deep in Memramcook, while Dorchester was a center of British culture and industry long before the Loyalists landed and is home to some of the province's oldest buildings.

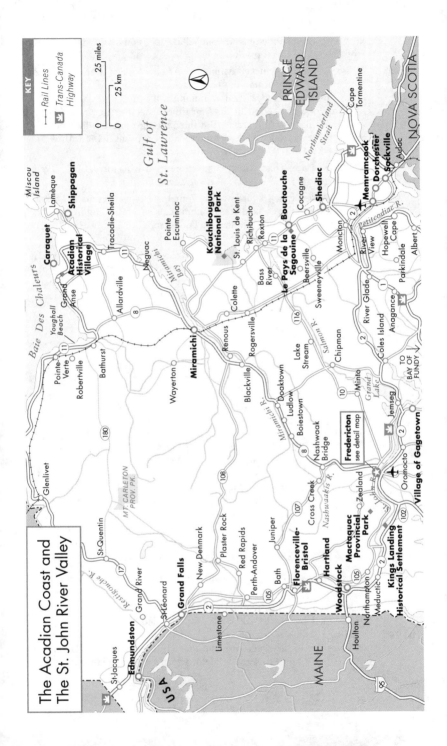

The Acadian Coast and The St. John River Valley

KEY

⊣—⊢ Rail Lines

🛪 Trans-Canada Highway

0 — 25 miles
0 — 25 km

Gulf of St. Lawrence

PRINCE EDWARD ISLAND

NOVA SCOTIA

Northumberland Strait

Cape Tormentine

Aulac
Sackville
Dorchester
Memramcook

Shediac
Cocagne
Bouctouche

Baie Des Chaleurs

Miscou Island
Lamèque
Shippagan
Caraquet
Acadian Historical Village
Youghall Beach
Pointe Verte
Tracadie-Sheila
Grand Anse
Neguac
Allardville

Pointe Escuminac

Kouchibouguac National Park
St. Louis de Kent
Richibucto
Rexton
Le Pays de la Sagouine
Bass River
Beersville
Sweeneyville

Miramichi Bay

Colette
Renous
Rogersville

Moncton
Petitcodiac R.
River View
Hopewell Cape
Parkindale
Albert
Hopewell

Robertville
Bathurst
Pointe Verte

Wayerton

Miramichi
Blackville
Doaktown
Ludlow
Boiestown

Lake Stream
Salmon R.
Chipman
Minto
Grand Lake
Jemseg
Coles Island
Anagance
River Glade

TO BAY OF FUNDY

Glenlivet

St-Quentin

MT. CARLETON PROV. PK.

New Denmark
Plaster Rock
Red Rapids
Perth-Andover
Juniper
Bath

Cross Creek
Nashwaak R.
Nashwaak Bridge

Fredericton
see detail map

Oromocto

Village of Gagetown

Zealand
Mactaquac Provincial Park
Kings Landing Historical Settlement

Restigouche R.
St-Jacques
Edmundston
Grand River
St-Léonard
Grand Falls
Limestone

MAINE
Houlton
Northampton
Meductic
Woodstock
Hartland
Florenceville-Bristol

USA

St. John R.

95

GETTING HERE AND AROUND

Memramcook and Dorchester are 24 km (15 miles) and 38 km (24 miles) southeast of Moncton via Route 106 through Dieppe. From the Trans-Canada Highway (Route 2), take Exit 488 for Memramcook and Exit 482 (Renaissance Street) for Dorchester. Route 106 (Royal Road) links the two towns.

ESSENTIALS

Visitor Information Center ✉ *Keillor House Museum, 4974 Main St., Dorchester* ☎ *506/379–6633* 🌐 *www.dorchester.ca* 🕒 *Tues.–Sat. 10–5, Sun. noon–5.*

Visitor Information Center ✉ *480 Centrale St., Memramcook* ☎ *506/758–9808* 🌐 *www.memramcook.com* 🕒 *June–mid-Oct., daily 9–5.*

EXPLORING

Keillor House and St. James Museum. An early Regency stone house built in 1813, Keillor House contains thousands of artifacts relating to mid-19th-century life, and docents are in costume. Its Coach House contains a fascinating collection of artifacts from the Dorchester Penitentiary. Just a minute away on foot is the St. James Museum. This former church building now contains the Beachkirk Collection of equipment used in the manufacturing of textiles, including antique looms. You can sometimes see demonstrations of carding, spinning, and weaving, and there are also blacksmiths' and carpenters' tools. ✉ *4974 Main St., Dorchester* ☎ *506/379–6633 mid-June–mid-Sept.* 🌐 *www.keillorhousemuseum.com* 🎫 *C$3* 🕒 *June–mid-Sept., Tues.–Sat. 10–5, Sun. noon–5.*

Monument Lefebvre National Historic Site. Commemorating the survival of the Acadians and celebrating the renaissance of Acadian culture, this monument is in the original home of St. Joseph's College, the first degree-granting French-language institution in Atlantic Canada, founded by Father Camille Lefebvre in 1864. A permanent interactive exhibit,"Reflections of a Journey—the Odyssey of the Acadian People," provides an excellent overview, and guided tours are available. ✉ *480 Central St., Memramcook* ☎ *506/758–9808* 🌐 *www.pc.gc.ca* 🎫 *C$3.90* 🕒 *June–mid-Oct., daily 9–5; mid-Oct.–May, Mon.–Sat. 9–5.*

WHERE TO EAT

$$ CANADIAN 🍴 **Bell Inn Restaurant.** This restaurant on the village square in Dorchester was built in 1811 as a stagecoach stop and is reputed to be the oldest stone structure in New Brunswick. Wander through the three dining rooms while you wait for an old-fashioned, delicious roast turkey dinner or one of the other comfort-food selections. Soups, salads, sandwiches, breakfast items (though it doesn't open until 11 am), and light meals are also available all day, and the homemade desserts are particularly delectable. The inn is not licensed for alcohol. [$] *Average main: C$15* ✉ *3515 Cape Rd., off Rte. 106, Dorchester* ☎ *506/379–2580* 🌐 *www.bellinnrestaurant.com* 🕒 *Closed Dec.–Feb. and Mon. and Tues.*

SPORTS AND THE OUTDOORS

Johnson's Mills Shorebird Reserve. The beaches here are an internationally recognized staging area for migratory shorebirds such as semipalmated sandpipers, of which 80% of the world population stop here. Their numbers are most impressive in July and August, when a Nature Conservancy interpretive center is open to coincide with high tides. ⊠ *Rte. 935, about 8 km (5 miles) south, Dorchester* ☏ *506/379–6347 (July and Aug. only)* ⊕ *www.natureconservancy.ca.*

SACKVILLE

22 km (14 miles) southeast of Dorchester and Memramcook.

Sackville is an idyllic university town complete with a swan-filled pond. Its stately homes and ivy-clad university buildings are shaded by venerable trees, and there's a waterfowl park right in town. With a program of high-profile festivals and events, it all makes for a rich blend of history, culture, and nature.

GETTING HERE AND AROUND

Sackville has two exits (504 and 506) off the Trans-Canada Highway (Route 2), about 50 km (31 miles) south of Moncton and 17 km (10½ miles) north of Amherst, Nova Scotia.

ESSENTIALS

Visitor Information Center ⊠ *34 Mallard Dr.* ☏ *506/364–4967* ⊙ *May–Oct., daily 9–5 (to 6 June and Sept.; to 8 July and Aug.); Nov.–Dec., Mon.–Sat. 9–5.*

EXPLORING

Fort Beauséjour National Historic Site. Near the Nova Scotia border in Aulac and 12 km (7 miles) east of Sackville, the site holds the ruins of a star-shaped fort that played a part in the 18th-century struggle between the French and British. The Deportation of the Acadians began here. The fort has fine views of the marshes at the head of the Bay of Fundy, and the Visitor Center has a fascinating collection of artifacts and interpretive exhibits. ⊠ *111 Fort Beauséjour Rd., Aulac* ☏ *506/364–5080 late June–early Sept., 506/876–2443 early Sept.–late June* ⊕ *www.pc.gc. ca/beausejour* ⊠ *$3.90* ⊙ *Late June–early Sept., daily 9–5.*

Owens Art Gallery. The oldest art gallery in Canada, first opened to the public in 1895, is on the Mount Allison University campus. It houses 3,200 works of 19th- and 20th-century European, American, and Canadian artwork in its permanent collection, and there are usually rotating exhibits as well. ⊠ *61 York St.* ☏ *506/364–2574* ⊕ *www.mta.ca/owens* ⊠ *Free* ⊙ *Weekdays 10–5, weekends 1–5; hrs extended for exhibition openings and special events.*

Sackville Waterfowl Park. In the heart of the town, the park has more than 3 km (2 miles) of boardwalk and trails through 55 acres of wetlands that are home to some 160 species of birds and 200 species of plants. Throughout the marsh, viewing areas and interpretive signs reveal the rare waterfowl species that nest here. There's an interpretive center, and guided tours ($6, including info kit and a snack at the end) are available in French and English mid-May through late August. A self-guided tour is also available at the visitor center and some stores in downtown Sackville. ⊠ *34 Mallard Dr.* ☏ *506/364–4967 May–Aug.* ⊕ *www.sackville. com/visit/attractions/waterfowl* ⊠ *Free* ⊙ *May–Aug., daily 9–5.*

WHERE TO STAY

For expanded hotel reviews, visit Fodors.com.

$

B&B/INN

Fodor'sChoice

★

Marshlands Inn. A list of celebrity guests is displayed in the entrance hall of this grand and elegant inn, including Queen Elizabeth II, who stopped in for afternoon tea and left the signed portrait that now hangs on the upstairs landing. **Pros:** good food; friendly owners. **Cons:** one room has a nice claw-foot bath, but the encircling shower curtain tends to cling. $ *Rooms from: C$119* ⊠ *55 Bridge St.* ☎ *506/536–0170, 800/561–1266* ⊕ *www.marshlands.nb.ca* ↩ *17 rooms, 1 suite* ⦿| *Multiple meal plans.*

3

SPORTS AND THE OUTDOORS

Canadian Wildlife Service. Without a doubt, bird-watching is the pastime of choice in this region, and these are the people to call for information. ⊠ *17 Waterfowl La.* ☎ *506/364–5044.*

Cape Jourimain Nature Centre. The National Wildlife Area here covers 1,800 acres of salt and brackish marshes and large numbers of waterfowl, shorebirds, and other species can be seen. The outstanding interpretive center includes a restaurant specializing in local fare and a boutique with nature art and fine crafts. You will also find a viewing tower, 13 km (8 miles) of trails, and daily programs. ■ **TIP→ This is the best location to photograph the striking architecture of the 13-km (8-mile) Confederation Bridge that links New Brunswick to Prince Edward Island.** ⊠ *5039 Rte. 16, at Exit 51, Bayfield* ☎ *866/538–2220, 506/538–2220* ⊕ *www.capejourimain.ca* ⊠ *Free (donations welcome)* ⦿ *Mid-May–late June, daily 9–6; late June–early Sept., daily 8–7.*

SHOPPING

Fog Forest Gallery. Small, friendly, and reputable, this commercial gallery represents Atlantic Canadian artists. It's closed on Sunday and Monday, except by appointment. ⊠ *14 Bridge St.* ☎ *506/536–9000* ⊕ *www.fogforestgallery.ca* ⦿ *Tues.–Sat.*

Sackville Harness Shop. Established in 1919, in what is said to be Sackville's oldest building, this is the only shop in North America that makes horse collars by hand, and it has a full range of tack and other equestrian products. If you don't have a horse, check out the Western boots, fine leather belts, wallets, bags, and jewelry. They also do shoe repairs. ⊠ *39 Main St.* ☎ *506/536–0642, 800/386–4888* ⊕ *www.sackvilleharness.com* ⦿ *Weekdays 8–5, Sat. 8–noon.*

SHEDIAC

25 km (16 miles) northeast of Moncton.

Shediac is the self-proclaimed Lobster Capital of the World, and it has a giant lobster sculpture to prove it. Beautiful Parlee Beach also draws people to this fishing village/resort town.

GETTING HERE AND AROUND

From Moncton, take Route 15 east to Exit 31B onto Route 11, then almost immediately exit onto Route 133 and follow signs into the town. The town is great for strolling, but a car is necessary to get to the beaches.

Acadian Culture

Culture is often defined by geographical boundaries, but Acadian culture defines Acadia because it isn't so much a place as it is an enduring French society. In New Brunswick it abides (although not exclusively) above an imaginary diagonal line drawn from Edmundston to Moncton. In the heartland you hear remnants of Norman-French (a dialect of old French), while around Moncton you're just as apt to hear a melodious Acadian dialect called Chiac, a tweedy kind of French with bits of English.

French settlers arrived in the early 1600s and brought with them an efficient system of dikes called *aboiteaux* that allowed them to farm the salt marshes around the head of the Bay of Fundy. In the 1700s they were joined by Jesuit missionaries who brought the music of Bach, Vivaldi, and Scarlatti, along with their zeal. In 1713 England took possession of the region, and authorities demanded that Acadians swear an oath to the English crown. Some did; others didn't. By 1755 it didn't seem to matter: only those who fled into the forests escaped Le Grand Dérangement—the Expulsion of the Acadians, mostly during the Seven Years' War—which dispersed them to Québec, the eastern seaboard, Louisiana (where they became known as Cajuns), France, and even as far as the Falkland Islands. It was a devastating event that probably should have eradicated French language and culture in the Maritimes, but it didn't. It did, however, profoundly affect Acadian expression—mobility remains a pervasive theme in the art, literature, and music of Acadian people.

Whether they were hiding deep in Maritime forests or living in exile,

Acadians clung tenaciously to their language and traditions. Within 10 years of their deportation, they began to return, building new communities along coasts and waterways in the northeastern part of the province, remote from English settlement. In the 1850s Acadians began to think "nationally." By 1884 there was an Acadian national anthem and a flag, essentially the French tricolor with a bright yellow star on the blue section.

The Acadian national holiday, on August 15, provides an official reason to celebrate Acadian culture. Le Festival Acadien de Caraquet stretches the celebration out for the two preceding weeks, with music and cultural events. Caraquet is also home to Théâtre Populaire d'Acadie, which mounts original productions for French communities throughout the Maritimes and encourages contemporary Acadian playwrights. Books by Acadian authors, including internationally renowned Antonine Maillet, circulate in Québec, France, and Belgium.

The earliest Acadian settlers made pine furniture that was elegant in its simplicity. Modern Acadian artisans continue to make functional things, such as pottery and baskets, beautiful. Handmade wooden spoons are doubly beautiful—in pairs they keep time for the music at kitchen parties, where Acadian families have traditionally sung their history around the kitchen fire. But it isn't necessary to have a party to enjoy "music de cuisine."

Clearly, the love of music endures: it rings clear in churches; the cotillion and quadrille are danced at soirees; and Acadian sopranos and jazz artists enjoy international renown.

—Ana Watts

3

ESSENTIALS

Visitor Information Center ✉ *229 Main St.* ☎ *506/532–7788* 🌐 *www.shediac.org* 🕒 *Mid-May–end Sept.*

EXPLORING

FAMILY Fodor's Choice ★

Parc de l'Aboiteau. On the western end of Cap-Pelé, the park has a fine, sandy beach as well as a boardwalk that runs through salt marshes where waterfowl nest. The beach complex includes a restaurant and lounge with live music in the evening. Cottages are available for rent year-round. ✉ *33 St-André Rd., Exit 53 off Rte. 15, Cap-Pelé* ☎ *506/577–2080, 506/577–2030 off season* 🌐 *www.cap-pele.com/aboiteau* 🎫 *$5 per vehicle* 🕒 *Beach mid-June–early Sept., daily dawn–dusk.*

FAMILY Fodor's Choice ★ **Parlee Beach.** The warmest salt water in Canada and a 3-km (2-mile) stretch of glistening sand has earned Parlee Beach the title of the best beach in Canada by several surveys. It is a popular vacation spot for families and plays host to beach-volleyball and touch-football tournaments; an annual sand-sculpture contest and a triathlon are held here as well. Summer services include canteens and a restaurant, changing rooms, and showers. ✉ *Exit 37 off Rte. 133* ☎ *506/533–3363* 🎫 *C$11 per vehicle* 🕒 *Services open mid-May–mid-Sept., daily 7 am–9 pm.*

WHERE TO EAT

$$ SEAFOOD 🍴 **The Green House on Main Restaurant.** Loaded with charm, artwork, and antiques, this upbeat restaurant is trendy despite its 19th-century building. Supplied by local farmers and food producers, they have a commitment to organic and natural foods, producing appetizers such as Cajun shrimp with prosciutto and cilantro cream, and inventive tuna steaks on the main course list. Naturally, there's lobster, too—this is Shediac, after all. Nonseafood dishes might include roasted pork loin or chicken wings. You can eat outside on the heated patio or upstairs in the intimate dining room. [$] *Average main: C$17* ✉ *406 Main St.* ☎ *506/533–7003* 🌐 *greenhouseonmain.ca.*

$ CANADIAN 🍴 **Le Menu Acadien.** Don't expect any frills here—it's a paper-plate diner and takeout, far removed from the touristy center of town—but if you want to taste some authentic Acadian dishes, try the *fricôt* (a hearty chicken soup), *poutine rappé* (a potato dumpling stuffed with ground pork), fish cakes, or traditional baked beans. All are expertly and freshly cooked to the owner's grandmother's recipes. You can also get fried clams, scallops, lobster rolls, and various other fast foods, all made from scratch with fresh ingredients. [$] *Average main: C$10* ✉ *55 Ohio Rd.* ✣ *From downtown Shediac drive east on Main St. and turn right at lights by Ultramar gas station* ☎ *506/532–6366* 🌐 *www.menuacadien.ca* 🕒 *Closed Jan.–May.*

WHERE TO STAY

For expanded hotel reviews, visit Fodors.com.

$ B&B/INN 🏨 **Auberge Inn Thyme.** A highlight of Shediac's downtown hub, this elegant heritage inn is full of character and enlivened by the friendly locals who frequent the coffee shop. **Pros:** lovely country inn feel; gracious hosts; spacious front porch. **Cons:** Room 7 can suffer from street noise; two bathrooms are not en suite and one has the tub in the bedroom. [$] *Rooms from: C$125* ✉ *310 Main St.* ☎ *506/532–6098, 877/466–8496* 🌐 *www.innthyme.com* 🛏 *7 rooms* 🕒 *Closed Nov.–Apr.* 🍽 *Breakfast.*

$ La Louisianne. Owned and run by two sisters from Alberta who fell in
B&B/INN love with the Maritimes, this 1914 home has been lovingly converted
to feature individually styled bedrooms, some with antique furnishings
and original features. **Pros:** generous four-course breakfasts, included
in the price, feature seasonal specialties. **Cons:** two rooms share a bath-
room; about a half-mile walk from downtown. $ *Rooms from: C$110*
⊠ *427 Main St.* ☎ *506/351–0505* ⊕ *www.lalouisianne.ca* ⤳ *5 rooms*
|◎| *Breakfast.*

$$$ Tait House. Set back from Shediac's main thoroughfare, this elegant
HOTEL and stately historic mansion is now an upscale boutique hotel with
Fodor'sChoice a fine restaurant. **Pros:** good food; pleasing combination of modern
★ amenities and antiques; reduction on room rate for evening diners.
Cons: only a continental breakfast is included in the price. $ *Rooms
from: C$189* ⊠ *293 Main St.* ☎ *506/532–4233, 888/532–4233* ⊕ *www.
maisontaithouse.com* ⤳ *9 rooms* |◎| *Multiple meal plans.*

BOUCTOUCHE

35 km (22 miles) north of Shediac.

This idyllic, bustling town on the sandy shores of Bouctouche Bay is
famous for pristine beauty and for Le Pays de la Sagouine, a theme park
based on an Acadian novel. The 12-km (7½-mile) dune of Bouctouche
is one of the few remaining on the east coast of North America and is
bordered by a 2-km (1¼-mile) boardwalk along the Irving Eco-Centre.

GETTING HERE AND AROUND
Bouctouche is 58 km (36 miles) northeast of Moncton via Route 15
east. From Route 15 take Exit 31B onto Route 11 north, then take Exit
32B for Bouctouche. A car is essential to reach all of the attractions.

ESSENTIALS
Visitor Information Center ⊠ *4 Acadie St.* ☎ *506/743–8811* ◷ *June–Sept.,
daily 9–6 (to 9 pm July and Aug.).*

EXPLORING

FAMILY **Irving Eco-Centre: La Dune de Bouctouche.** The center preserves a superb
example of a coastal ecosystem that protects the exceptionally fertile oyster
beds in Bouctouche Bay. Hiking trails and boardwalks to the beach make
it possible to explore sensitive areas without disrupting the environment of
one of the few remaining great dunes on the northwest coast of the Atlantic
Ocean. An outstanding interpretive center puts the ecosystem in perspec-
tive with nature exhibits, a film presentation, and a saltwater aquarium.
The staff regularly conducts guided walks. Swimming is allowed. ⊠ *1932
Rte. 475* ☎ *888/640–3300, 506/743–2600* ⊕ *www.irvingecocentre.com*
⊡ *Free* ◷ *Hiking trails and boardwalk daily dawn–dusk. Visitor center
early June–late Sept., daily 10–5 (to 6 pm July–early Sept.).*

FAMILY **Le Pays de la Sagouine.** La Sagouine is an old charwoman-philosopher
created by celebrated Acadian author Antonine Maillet, and this Acadian
culture theme park re-creates her world. It's a make-believe island com-
munity that comes to life (in French) in daylong musical and theatrical per-
formances, with dinner theater/musical evenings July through September.
There's also an English version on Sunday, mid-July through August. Tours

are available in English and French, and the Friday-night jam sessions are accessible to English-speaking visitors, too. ⊠ *57 rue Acadie, Exit 32 A or B off Hwy. 11* ☎ *506/743–1400, 800/561–9188* ⊕ *www.sagouine.com* ✉ *C$20, C$29 with Acadian Buffet, C$31 with Acadian Brunch, C$66 with dinner theater* ☉ *Late June–early Sept., daily 10–5:30.*

FAMILY **The Olivier Soapery.** An working artisan soapery, Olivier includes a museum with a fascinating array of bath-time memorabilia, from old bars of soap and soap-making equipment to tubs and basins. There's a skin-care art gallery, featuring paintings commissioned for soap labels throughout the years, and, naturally, plenty of soap is for sale. By far the best attraction, however, is the soap-making demonstration, several times a day. ⊠ *831 Rte. 505, 10 km (6 miles) north of Bouctouche, Ste-Anne-de-Kent* ☎ *506/743–8938, 800/775–5550* ⊕ *www.oliviersoaps. com* ✉ *Free* ☉ *Daily 9–5 (to 7:30 in summer).*

WHERE TO STAY
For expanded hotel reviews, visit Fodors.com.

$ 🏠 **Auberge le Vieux Presbytère de Bouctouche.** Near the water, this lovely
B&B/INN inn was formerly a rectory and then a retreat house complete with chapel (now a conference room). **Pros:** friendly staff; lovely grounds. **Cons:** rooms are rather old-fashioned; the inn is sometimes busy with weddings and conferences. 💲 *Rooms from: C$119* ⊠ *157 chemin du Couvent* ☎ *506/743–5568, 866/743–1880* ⊕ *www.vieuxpresbytere. nb.ca* ✍ *5 rooms, 5 suites, 3 apartments* ☉ *Closed Oct.–May* ⦿ *Multiple meal plans.*

KOUCHIBOUGUAC NATIONAL PARK

40 km (25 miles) north of Bouctouche; 100 km (62 miles) north of Moncton.

GETTING HERE AND AROUND
Kouchibouguac National Park is off Route 11. Take Exit 75 onto Route 117 and follow the signs. An alternative route is on the scenic Acadian Coastal Drive, following the starfish road signs.

EXPLORING

Fodor'sChoice **Kouchibouguac National Park.** The word Kouchibouguac (Kou-she-boo-
★ gwack) means "river of the long tides" in the Mi'Kmaq language, and this natural wilderness park consists of sandy beaches, dunes, bogs, salt marshes, lagoons, and freshwater, and is home to an abundance of birds. The visitor center (open mid-May–mid-October) features information and interpretive exhibits. Kellys Beach is supervised and has facilities. There are more than 60 km (37 miles) of trails for biking and hiking in summer and for cross-country skiing, snowshoeing, snow walking, and kick sledding in winter. The forests and peat bogs can be explored along 10 nature trails, each of which has a parking lot. There are lots of nature-interpretation programs, and you can canoe, kayak, and picnic or rent bikes and boats. Reserve ahead for one of the 311 campsites. ⊠ *Rte. 117, 60 km (37 miles) north of Bouctouche, off Hwy. 11* ☎ *506/876–2443* ⊕ *www.pc.gc.ca/kouchibouguac* ✉ *C$7.80 mid-June–early Sept.; C$3.90 Apr.–mid-June and early Sept.–Nov.*

MIRAMICHI

40 km (25 miles) north of Kouchibouguac; 150 km (93 miles) north of Moncton.

Celebrated for salmon rivers that reach into some of the province's richest forests, and the ebullient nature of its residents (Scottish, English, Irish, and a smattering of First Nations and French), this is a land of lumber kings, ghost stories, folklore, and festivals—celebrating the Irish in July, and folk songs and the Scottish in August. Sturdy wood homes dot the banks of Miramichi Bay. The city of Miramichi incorporates the former towns of Chatham and Newcastle and several small villages and is where the politician and British media mogul Lord Beaverbrook grew up and is buried.

Miramichi is 175 km (109 miles) northeast of Fredericton via Route 8 (also designated the scenic "Miramichi River Route"). From Moncton take Route 15 east then Route 11 north. A car is necessary to see all the attractions.

ESSENTIALS
Visitor Information Center ⊠ *199 King St.* ☎ *506/778–8444* ⊕ *www.discovermiramichi.com* ⊘ *Mid-June–end Aug.*

EXPLORING
TOP ATTRACTIONS
Beaubears Island. Formerly a thriving shipbuilding center, this is one of Miramichi's most interesting outdoor spots. Start at the museum-style interpretive center, with interactive audio-visual displays. A short boat trip will then take you to the island to see two historic sites, staffed by characters who love to share their colorful island stories and adventures. There are also guided tours and trips around the island in a 26-foot traditional canoe, and regular special events are another attraction. ⊠ *35 St. Patrick's Dr., Nelson* ☎ *506/622–8526* ⊕ *www.beaubearsisland.ca* 🎫 *Interpretive center C$5; tours C$10–C$23, canoe trip C$25* ⊘ *Mid-May–mid-June and late Aug.–mid-Oct., Mon.–Sat. 10–4, Sun noon–4; mid-June–late Aug., Mon.–Sat. 10–6, Sun. noon–8.*

Metepenagiag Heritage Park. Two important First Nations archaeological sites, the Augustine Mound and Oxbow national historic sites, are at the heart of this park, "Where Spirits Live"—where the Mi'Kmaq have lived for more than 3,000 years. In the museum, enthusiastic and knowledgeable staff are on hand to answer questions about the exhibits and there's a good film about the history of the site. Outside, there are a number of walking trails to explore, and events include drumming circles, traditional dancing, and the annual Pow Wow in June. ⊠ *2156 Micmac Rd., 36 km (22 miles) west of Miramichi, Red Bank* ☎ *506/836–6118, 888/380–3555* ⊕ *www.metpark.ca* 🎫 *C$8* ⊘ *May–Oct., daily 10–5.*

WORTH NOTING
Atlantic Salmon Museum. This museum provides a look at the endangered Atlantic salmon and at life in noted fishing camps along the rivers. It has an aquarium, displays of fishing equipment, and works of art. ⊠ *263 Main St., 80 km (50 miles) southwest of Miramichi City, Doaktown*

☎ 506/365–7787 🌐 *www.atlanticsalmonmuseum.com* 🎫 *C$5* ⏲ *Mid-Apr.–mid-Oct., Mon.–Wed. 9–5, Thurs.–Sat. 9–9, Sun. noon–9; may be closed Sun. early and late in season.*

FAMILY **Central New Brunswick Woodmen's Museum.** This 15-acre site has a 100-year-old trapper's cabin, a blacksmith shop, wheelwright shop, cookhouse/bunkhouse, and other exhibits pertaining to the woodman's way of life. A popular 10-passenger amusement train winds along 1½ km (1 mile) of woodland track. ✉ *6342 Rte. 8, 110 km (68 miles) southwest of Miramichi City, Boiestown* ☎ *506/369–7214* 🌐 *www.woodmensmuseum.com* 🎫 *C$6; guided tour C$2; train ride C$3* ⏲ *June–mid-Oct., daily 9:30–5.*

3

FAMILY **Ritchie Wharf Park.** This waterside public park recalls the area's former shipbuilding industry. It has a nautical-theme playground complete with a "Splash Pad" that sprays water from below and dumps it from buckets above. Shops sell local crafts, and there are several restaurants and docking facilities. An amphitheater showcases local entertainers on Sunday afternoons in summer. ✉ *Norton's La., Newcastle* 🎫 *Free* ⏲ *Park daily dawn–dusk. Shops mid-May–early Sept., daily 11–10.*

WHERE TO EAT AND STAY

For expanded hotel reviews, visit Fodors.com.

$$ CHINESE 🍴 **Cunard Restaurant.** With its Irish accent and lumberjack history, Miramichi is an unlikely place to find a great Chinese restaurant. The Cunard, however, has what it takes to make it anywhere, and has been pleasing locals and visitors since 1980. It is renowned for its Szechuan chicken and orange-glazed beef stir fry, and Canadian dishes also feature on the six-page menu. A small buffet is offered for Friday lunch and early evening on Sunday, but this is principally a table-service restaurant. Monday through Thursday lunch specials are a good value. Takeout is also available. [$] *Average main: C$15* ✉ *32 Cunard St.* ☎ *506/773–7107* 🌐 *www.cunardrestaurant.com.*

$ B&B/INN 🏨 **King George B&B.** In a listed historic building in the former town of Newcastle, a stylish blend of antique and modern furnishings provides upscale accommodations. **Pros:** within walking distance of the Ritchie Wharf boardwalk; evening meal can be arranged for late arrivals; multinight discounts available. **Cons:** rooms vary in size, the Princess Room, with twin beds, being quite compact. [$] *Rooms from: C$105* ✉ *561 King George Hwy.* ☎ *506/352–0557* 🌐 *kinggeorgebandb.com* 🛏 *3 rooms, 1 suite* 🍽 *Multiple meal plans.*

$$ RESORT 🏨 **Pond's Resort.** This property near the water offers a traditional fishing-camp experience with a few added luxuries. The lodge and cabins are surrounded by trees and overlook the world-famous Mirimachi salmon river. There's a golf course nearby, too. The Fiddlehead ($$) restaurant makes use of local produce in its innovative preparations. **Pros:** a fisherman's paradise and a haven from the modern world. **Cons:** a bit too rustic for some; the six lodge rooms share two bathrooms. [$] *Rooms from: C$149* ✉ *91 Porter Cove Rd., 100 km (62 mile) southwest of Miramichi City; follow signs on Rte. 8, Ludlow* ☎ *506/369–2612* 🌐 *www.pondsresort.com* 🛏 *6 rooms, 15 cabins* ⏲ *Closed mid-Oct.–mid-Apr.*

$ 🏨 **Rodd Miramichi River.** This riverside hotel in the downtown Chatham
HOTEL   area is convenient for business travelers and geared to vacationers'
needs with a range of special activity packages. **Pros:** good fishing
opportunities; next to a small riverside park. **Cons:** sometimes taken
over by business conventions and wedding parties. $ *Rooms from:
C$112* ✉ *1809 Water St.* ☎ *506/773–3111* ⊕ *www.roddvacations.com*
⤴ *76 rooms, 4 suites* ⦿ *No meals.*

SHIPPAGAN

37 km (23 miles) north of Tracadie-Sheila.

Shippagan is an important fishing and marine education center as well
as a bustling town with lots of amenities and the gateway to the idyllic
islands of Lamèque and Miscou.

GETTING HERE AND AROUND

Shippagan is about 110 km (68 miles) northeast of Miramichi via Route
11, taking Exit 217 onto Route 113 for the final 12 km (7½ miles).
The town is very walkable, but a car is necessary to get to the islands.

ESSENTIALS

Visitor Information Center ✉ *200 Hôtel-de-ville Ave.* ☎ *506/336–3900*
⊕ *www.shippagan.ca* ⊗ *Mid-June–late Aug.*

EXPLORING

FAMILY   **Aquarium and Marine Centre.** This wonderful aquarium has a serious side
and a fun side, with labs that are the backbone of marine research in
the province and more than 3,000 specimens to see in 31 indoor tanks,
outdoor touch tanks, and the Harbour Seal pool. Feeding time for the
seals (at 11 and 4) is always popular, as are the touch tanks, containing
such species as sea stars, clams, sea cucumbers, and rare blue lobsters.
Another exhibit illustrates the underwater world of the Acadian peninsula and how fishing is carried out there. ✉ *100 rue de l'Aquarium*
☎ *506/336–3013* ⊕ *www.aquariumnb.ca* 🎫 *C$8.50* ⊗ *Early June–late
Sept., daily 10–6.*

Île Miscou (Miscou Island). Accessible by bridge from Île Lamèque, Miscou
has white sandy beaches, and the dunes and lagoons are good places to
see migrating bird species. ⊕ *ilemiscouisland.webs.com.*

Ste-Cécile Church. Across a causeway from Shippagan is Île Lamèque and
Ste-Cécile Church. Although the church is plain on the outside, every
inch of it is decorated on the inside. Each July, the International Festival
of Baroque Music takes place here. ✉ *Rte. 113 at Petite-Rivière-de-l'Île.*

CARAQUET

40 km (25 miles) west of Shippagan.

Perched on Caraquet Bay, along the beautiful Baie des Chaleurs, with
Québec's Gaspé Peninsula beckoning across the inlet, Caraquet is rich
in French flavor and is the acknowledged Acadian cultural capital. Its
beaches are also a draw, and it has begun to attract the attention of the
cruise lines that ply the waters of the Atlantic Provinces.

GETTING HERE AND AROUND

Caraquet is 113 km (70 miles) north of Miramichi on Route 11. A car is necessary to get around its scattered attractions.

ESSENTIALS

Visitor Information Center ✉ *39 St-Pierre Blvd. W* ☎ *506/726–2676* 🌐 *www.caraquet.ca* 🕓 *Late May–late Sept..*

EXPLORING

Fodor's Choice ★ **Acadian Festival.** This two-week celebration of Acadian culture is held here in the first two weeks of August. In the Tintamarre, costumed participants parade noisily through the streets; the Blessing of the Fleet, a colorful and moving ceremony that's usually held on the first Sunday of the festival, eloquently expresses the importance of fishing to the Acadian economy and way of life. Alongside these events is a schedule of concerts, theater, storytelling, poetry, and visual arts. ☎ *506/727–2787* 🌐 *www.festivalacadien.ca.*

FAMILY **Acadian Historical Village.** A highlight of the Acadian Peninsula, the more than 40 restored buildings here re-create Acadian communities between 1770 and 1949. There are modest homes, a church, a school, and a village shop, as well as an industrial area that includes a lobster hatchery, a cooper, and a tinsmith shop. The bilingual staff tells fascinating stories and the demonstrations are great fun; visitors are invited to take part. For the full experience, you can enjoy dinner and entertainment during the evening and stay overnight in the grand Hôtel Château Albert, an authentic re-creation of a 1907 hotel—a chauffeured 1925 vehicle transports you and your luggage from the parking lot. ✉ *14311 Rte. 11, 10 km (6 miles) west of Caraquet, Rivière-du-Nord* ☎ *506/726–2600, 877/721–2200* 🌐 *www.villagehistoriqueacadien.com* 🎟 *C$17.50 (valid for 2 days); C$9 mid–late Sept.* 🕓 *Early June–mid-Sept., daily 10–6; mid-Sept.–late Sept., 1 tour daily at 10, by appointment.*

Pope's Museum. The Pope's Museum, 7 km (4 miles) outside Caraquet, is the only museum in North America dedicated to papal history. It celebrates the church's artistic and spiritual heritage with models of buildings such as St. Peter's Basilica and the cathedral in Florence. ✉ *184 Acadie St., Grand-Anse* ☎ *506/732–3003* 🎟 *$8* 🕓 *Late June–Aug. 31, daily 10–6 (last tour at 5).*

WHERE TO EAT AND STAY

For expanded hotel reviews, visit Fodors.com.

$ BISTRO 🍴 **Grains de Folie.** This artisan bakery-café is a great place to drop in for a quick bite, with an inviting aroma of fresh-baked bread and freshly brewed coffee to greet you. There's quick counter service for delicious soups, sandwiches, omelets, panini, pizzas, salads, and tempting pastries, with table-service breakfasts until 1 pm on weekends. There's also a deli counter with a great range of cheeses. Huge murals by a local artist cover the walls on both levels, a terrace is open in summer, and there's regular live entertainment. [$] *Average main: C$12* ✉ *171 blvd. St-Pierre W* ☎ *506/727–4001* 🌐 *www.grainsdefolie.ca* 🕓 *No dinner. Closed Mon. and Tues. Sept.–May.*

$$$ HOTEL Fodor's Choice ★ **Hotel Paulin.** Caraquet is famous not only for lobsters, oysters, artisans, and festivals, but also for Hotel Paulin. **Pros:** personal service; excellent food. **Cons:** atmosphere can feel a bit stuffy. [$] *Rooms from: C$195 ✉ 143 blvd. St-Pierre W ☎ 506/727–9981, 866/727–9981 🌐 www.hotelpaulin.com 🛏 6 rooms, 6 suites 🍴 Multiple meal plans.*

$$$ FRENCH Fodor's Choice ★ **La Fine Grobe Sur Mer.** This is one of New Brunswick's finest restaurants, where you can savor owner/chef George Frachon's creations while gazing out over the sea through the wall of windows. Drawing on the culinary arts of his French homeland, Georges imparts an expert touch to such dishes as sautéed scallops with garlic and parsley, beef tenderloin, or Poulet à la Provençale, and his wine list is equally outstanding. Herbs and greens are home-grown and baguettes are baked in an outdoor oven. The dining room is casual and bright, with some interesting art and artifacts. Reservations are recommended. There are two bedrooms on the second floor for overnight stays. [$] *Average main: C$25 ✉ 289 rue Principal, 16 km (10 miles) north of Bathurst on Rte. 134, Nigadoo ☎ 506/783–3138 🌐 www.finegrobe.com ⏲ No lunch.*

SPORTS AND THE OUTDOORS

FAMILY **Sugarloaf Provincial Park.** Eight trails on the 507-foot drop at Sugarloaf Provincial Park accommodate skiers and snowboarders of all levels in winter and mountain bikers in summer; a chairlift operates in both seasons. There are also more than 25 km (16 miles) of bike trails, cross-country ski trails, hiking trails, a summer alpine slide, and other recreational amenities. Instruction and equipment rentals are available, including GPS for geocaching, there's a summer welcome center, and the lodge operates a lounge and restaurant year-round. ✉ *596 Val d'Amour Rd., 180 km (112 miles) northwest of Caraquet, Atholville ☎ 506/789–2366, 506/753–6825 for ski/snowboard rentals, 800/561–0123 for campsite reservations 🌐 parcsugarloafpark.ca 🎟 Bike park C$5 per ride, C$17 per half day, or C$25 full day. Alpine skiing/snowboarding C$14 evening, C$22–C$29 per day; cross-country skiing/snowshoeing season pass C$30–C$60 ⏲ Park gates daily 8–dusk. Bike park mid-June–Aug., Thurs.–Sat. 10–7:30, Sun. 10–5; Sept., weekends 10–5. Winter sports mid-Dec–Mar. (call for hrs).*

ST. JOHN RIVER VALLEY

The St. John River valley scenery is panoramic—gently rolling hills and sweeping forests, with just enough rocky gorges to keep it interesting. The native peoples (First Nations, French, English, Scots, and Danes) who live along the river ensure that its culture is equally intriguing. The St. John River forms 120 km (74 miles) of the border with Maine, then swings inland, eventually cutting through the heart of Fredericton and rolling down to the city of Saint John. Gentle hills of rich farmland and the blue sweep of the water make this a lovely area for driving. In the early 1800s the narrow wedge of land at the northern end of the valley was coveted by Québec, New Brunswick, and the United States. To settle the issue, New Brunswick governor Sir Thomas Carleton rolled dice with the governor of British North America in Québec City. Sir Thomas won—by one point. Settling the border with the Americans was more difficult; even the lumberjacks engaged in combat. Finally, in 1842, the British flag was hoisted over Madawaska County. One old-timer, tired of being asked to which country he belonged, replied, "I am a citizen of the Republic of Madawaska." So began the mythical republic, which exists today with its own flag (an eagle on a field of white) and a coat of arms.

EDMUNDSTON

275 km (171 miles) northwest of Fredericton.

Edmundston, the unofficial capital of Madawaska County, has always depended on the wealth of the deep forest around it—the legend of Paul Bunyan was born in these woods. Even today the town looks to the pulp mills of the Twin Rivers Paper Company as the major source of employment.

GETTING HERE AND AROUND

Edmundston is on the Trans-Canada Highway (Route 2) about 16 km (10 miles) southeast of the Québec border—Exit 18 is best for downtown—and just across the river from Madawaska, Maine. A car is necessary to visit the Botanical Garden, on the northern edge of the city.

ESSENTIALS

Visitor Information Edmundston–Madawaska Tourism ⊠ *121 Victoria St.* ☎ *506/737–1850, 866/737–6766* ⊕ *tourismedmundston.com.*

EXPLORING

Fodor's Choice ★ **Foire Brayonne.** The annual Foire Brayonne, held in Edmundston over the long weekend surrounding New Brunswick Day (beginning on the Wednesday before the first Monday in August), is one of the largest Francophone festivals outside of Québec. It's also one of the liveliest and most vibrant cultural events in New Brunswick, with concerts by acclaimed artists as well as local musicians and entertainers. ☎ *506/739–6608* ⊕ *www.foirebrayonne.com.*

FAMILY **New Brunswick Botanical Garden.** In the Edmunston suburb of St-Jacques, roses, rhododendrons, alpine flowers, and dozens of other annuals and perennials bloom in 10 gardens. Khronos: The Celestial Garden has an astronomical theme, complete with a contemporary stone circle. The music of Mozart, Handel, Bach, and Vivaldi often plays in the background. Two arboretums have coniferous and deciduous trees and shrubs. Mosaiculture plantings on metal frames placed throughout the gardens illustrate legends and cultural themes. Children (and adults) enjoy the living butterfly exhibit. ⊠ *15 Main St., St-Jacques* ☎ *506/737–4444* ⊕ *www.jardinnbgarden.com* ⊘ *$14, $6 for butterfly exhibit only* ⊘ *May, June, and Sept., daily 9–5; July and Aug., daily 9–8; also for special events for Halloween and Christmas.*

WHERE TO EAT AND STAY

For expanded hotel reviews, visit Fodors.com.

$$$ STEAKHOUSE ✕ **Chantal's Steak House.** You'll need directions to this out-of-the-way spot, but it's well worth seeking out. The interior is chic and stylish, the mother-and-daughter team who run it are friendly and efficient, and the

steak, seafood, and ribs are succulent. The strong French influence adds an interesting element to the food, which utilizes imported spices and fresh, locally sourced ingredients. It's a good place to try fiddleheads, too, particularly when paired with shrimp in a cassoulet. Round the meal off with a helping of the traditional *tarte au sucre* (sugar pie), which, in spite of the name, is not too sweet. If you want wine with the meal you'll need to bring your own. $ *Average main: C$23* ⊠ *721C Victoria St.* ☎ *506/735–8882* ⊕ *chantalsteakhouse.webnode.fr.*

$

B&B/INN

Auberge les Jardins Inn and Motel Brayon & Chalets. Fine French cuisine is the major attraction at this inn, although the guest rooms, decorated with woodland themes, are lovely. **Pros:** good food; peaceful despite the highway. **Cons:** not much else to do here; some distance from downtown. $ *Rooms from: C$119* ⊠ *60 rue Principal, St-Jacques* ☎ *506/739–5514, 800/630–8011* ⊕ *www.lesjardinsinn.com* ⟿ *30 rooms, 10 cottages* ⦿ *Multiple meal plans.*

$$

HOTEL

Four Points by Sheraton. Linked to both the convention center and the shopping mall in downtown Edmundston, Canada's first Four Points by Sheraton opened in 2013 after a complete remodeling of the former Clarion hotel building. **Pros:** very comfortable and well-equipped; friendly and helpful staff. **Cons:** no nice views; needs more luggage carts. $ *Rooms from: C$135* ⊠ *100 Rice St.* ☎ *506/739–7321, 800/576–4656* ⊕ *www.fourpoints.com/edmundston* ⟿ *95 rooms, 8 suites* ⦿ *Multiple meal plans.*

SPORTS AND THE OUTDOORS

Mont Farlagne. There are 21 trails for downhill skiing on a vertical drop of 600 feet, and is four lifts can handle 4,000 skiers per hour; there's night skiing on eight trails. Snowboarding, tube sliding, and a snow park with jumps and modules add to the fun. Equipment rentals and lessons are available, and there are a pro shop, a cafeteria, and a bar. ⊠ *360 Mont Farlagne Rd., St-Jacques* ☎ *506/739–7669* ⊕ *www.montfarlagne.com.*

GRAND FALLS

65 km (40 miles) southeast of Edmundston.

The St. John River rushes over a high cliff, squeezes through a narrow rocky gorge, and emerges as a wider river at the town of Grand Falls. The result is a magnificent cascade whose force has worn strange round wells in the rocky bed, some as large as 5 meters (16 feet) in circumference and 9 meters (30 feet) deep.

GETTING HERE AND AROUND

Grand Falls is just off the Trans-Canada Highway (Route 2), at Exit 77 or 79. From Edmundston an alternative (and about the same distance) is on Route 144, the River Valley Scenic Drive. There's not much to see in town, other than the falls and gorge, but it's an easy walk across the bridge along Broadway Boulevard to cafés and restaurants.

ESSENTIALS

Visitor Information La Rochelle Tourist Information Centre ⊠ *1 Chapel St.* ☎ *506/475–7766, 877/475–7769* ⊕ *www.grandfalls.com.* **Malabeam Tourist Information Center** ⊠ *25 Madawaska Rd.* ☎ *506/475–7788, 877/475–7769* ⊕ *www.grandfalls.com* ⊘ *Mid-May–June, daily 10–6; July and Aug., daily 9–9; Sept.–mid-Oct., daily 10–5.*

EXPLORING

Gorge Walk. Starting at the Malabeam Tourist Information Center, the walk covers the full length of the gorge and is dotted with interpretive panels and monuments. Nearby, you can descend the nearby 250 steps to the wells, holes worn in the rocks by the swirling water. Guided walking tours are also available. According to native legend, a young woman named Malabeam led her Mohawk captors to their deaths over the foaming cataract rather than guide them to her village. The bodies of the Mohawks were found the following day, but Malabeam was not found. The view over the gorge from the center is breathtaking, particularly at snow-melt time or after heavy rain. ⊠ *25 Madawaska Rd.* ☎ *506/475–7788 information center* 🎫 *Walk free; steps to wells C$5; guided walks C$4 or C$8, depending on length* ⊘ *Gorge walk daily dawn–dusk, steps to wells and guided tours daily 10–6.*

Grand Falls Museum. Pioneer and early Victorian artifacts are the basis of a collection that includes memorabilia of Ron Turcotte, the jockey who rode Secretariat to Triple Crown victory in 1973, and the balance beam used by daredevil Van Morrell, who crossed the falls on a tightrope in 1904. ⊠ *68 Madawaska Rd., Suite 100* ☎ *506/473–5265* 🎫 *Free; donations accepted* ⊘ *July and Aug., weekdays 10–5.*

Open Sky Adventures. This outfitter operates a pontoon boat at the lower end of the gorge, offering a fascinating perspective of the cliffs and wells, from May through October; rides are C$25. Zip-lining, repelling, and kayaking are also offered. ⊠ *16087 Rte. 105* ☎ *506/473–4803, 506/477–9799* ⊕ *www.openskyadventures.com.*

FLORENCEVILLE-BRISTOL

81 km (50 miles) south of Grand Falls.

The title, "French Fry Capitol of the World" does nothing to convey how pretty Florenceville is, with its Main Street running right along the riverside, but there's no getting away from the fact that it's also the home of McCain's. The main factory is north of town, various ancillary buildings are dotted around, and vast potato fields spread out in all directions. Upstream, the incorporated twin-town of Bristol has a railroad heritage and one of the best restaurants in the province.

GETTING HERE AND AROUND

Both towns are right on the River Valley Scenic Route (Route 105), with the Trans-Canada highway running parallel at a discreet distance. There's no public transportation, but driving and parking are easy, and exploration is best done on foot.

ESSENTIALS

Visitor Information **Florenceville-Bristol Visitor Information Centre** ✉ *Potato World, 385 Centreville Rd., Florenceville-Bristol* ☎ *506/392–1955* 🌐 *www.florencevillebristol.ca.*

EXPLORING

Andrew and Laura McCain Gallery. This lively gallery hosts an eclectic series of exhibitions each year, showcasing Atlantic Canadian artists working in traditional and experimental media, as well as art and craft workshops, seasonal festivals, and children's events. ✉ *8 McCain St., Unit 1, Florenceville* ☎ *506/392–6769* 🌐 *www.mccainartgallery.com* 🎟 *Free* 🕒 *Mon.–Sat. 10:30–5 (to 8 pm Thurs.).*

WHERE TO EAT AND STAY

For expanded hotel reviews, visit Fodors.com.

$$$ MODERN CANADIAN Fodor's Choice ★

🍴 **Fresh Fine Dining.** Gourmet restaurants rarely show up in such unlikely locations as this—a restored 1930s Canadian Pacific railcar in a small New Brunswick town—and even if you're not traveling the St. John River route, it's well worth a detour (reservations advised). The menu is well-balanced, with dishes such as pan-roasted breast of pheasant, fanned on fresh fruit, with local cheddar cheese and apple cider risotto. Most exciting, though, is to opt for the "Chef's Choice"—just say what you *don't* like and he'll create something specially for you (and even if every diner in the place takes this option, no two will get the same dish). Railroad buffs will also enjoy the displays at the adjacent Shogomoc Railway site. [$] *Average main: C$28* ✉ *9189 Main St., Florenceville-Bristol* ☎ *506/392–6000* 🌐 *www.freshfinedining.com* 🕒 *Closed Sun. No lunch.*

$ RENTAL

🏨 **Shamrock Suites.** In a converted 19th-century home, the elegant suites have been designed to suit business and leisure travelers for short or long stays, with access to fully equipped kitchens and laundry areas. **Pros:** lovely setting, on 6 acres of heritage gardens; high levels of comfort and good amenities; continental breakfast included; well placed for those with business at McCain's. **Cons:** two of the rooms share a bathroom and TV. [$] *Rooms from: C$105* ✉ *8 Curtis Rd., Florenceville-Bristol* ☎ *506/392–8801, 506/391–5274 cell* 🌐 *www.shamrocksuites.ca* 🛏 *5 rooms* 🍽 *Breakfast.*

HARTLAND

19 km (12 miles) south of Florenceville-Bristol.

Hartland is best known for having the longest covered bridge in the world, still carrying traffic across the wide St. John River. A sleepy little town for much of the year, it is deluged with bus-loads of camera-toting tourists in summer. You can also visit the Covered Bridge Potato Chip company, just across the highway, for a tour and tasting of the still warm chips straight off the production line.

GETTING HERE AND AROUND

The town is on Route 105 (the River Valley Scenic Route), and has an exit off the Trans-Canada highway, which runs a short distance to the east. There's no public transportation.

ESSENTIALS

Visitor Information Hartland Visitor Information Centre ✉ *365 Main St., beside bridge, Hartland* ☎ *506/375-4075* 🌐 *www.town.hartland.nb.ca* 🕒 *May–Oct.*

EXPLORING

Longest Covered Bridge. New Brunswick has its fair share of superlatives, but this may be the most surprising. In what is otherwise a rather sleepy little town, the St. John River is spanned by the longest covered bridge in the world—391 meters (1,282 feet) long. A national and provincial historic site, it opened in 1901. It's still used by traffic crossing the river between Routes 103 and 105, and you can walk across on the safely separated pedestrian walkway that was added in 1945. ⚠ **If you want to drive across (maximum height is 13 feet 9 inches; maximum weight 10 tons), there's only room for traffic going one way at a time, and there are no traffic lights; you just stop to check whether anything's coming the other way and wait your turn if necessary (turn headlights on).** ✉ *Hartland.*

WHERE TO EAT AND STAY

For expanded hotel reviews, visit Fodors.com.

$$$ MODERN CANADIAN Fodor's Choice ★

🍴 **Jeremiah's.** Just across the road from the world's longest covered bridge, this fine restaurant occupies a stunning renovation of an 1892 church. Original features have been matched with chic modern fittings and color schemes, and there's an excellent boardroom downstairs for meetings or private parties. Lunchtime offerings (served 11 am to 5 pm) include freshly made soups, salads, sandwiches, and light meals, while the evening menu features such dishes as seafood risotto with fennel, lemon-and-tomato beurre blanc, Portuguese Steak-on-a-Stone, or pork tenderloin painted with lavender honey, over bacon, vegetables, and hash. Reservations are required for dinner. The lunch menu runs all day on Sunday. [$] *Average main: C$30* ✉ *362 Main St., Hartland* ☎ *506/375-8200* 🌐 *jeremiahs.ca* 🕒 *Closed Mon. No dinner Tues. Off-season opening limited; call to check.*

$ B&B/INN

🏨 **Covered Bridge B&B.** High above the St. John River, near the world's longest covered bridge and the River Valley Scenic Drive, this superior bed-and-breakfast has exceptionally spacious rooms and top-notch modern bathrooms, some with whirlpool tubs. **Pros:** friendly and helpful owners; children welcome; special rates for longer off-season stays. **Cons:** a few unexpected steps to watch out for; one bathroom, though private, is not en suite. [$] *Rooms from: C$105* ✉ *2651 Rte. 103, Somerville* ☎ *506/324-0939* 🌐 *www.coveredbridgebandb.ca* 🛏 *5 rooms* 🍽 *Breakfast.*

WOODSTOCK

93 km (58 miles) northwest of Fredericton.

New Brunswick's first incorporated town (in 1856), Woodstock still preserves many fine old buildings on its leafy streets, and a self-guiding walking-tour leaflet is available from the visitor information center. A focal point of the town is the meeting of its two rivers, the St. John and the Meduxnekeag, with riverside walks, a nature reserve, a floating dock in summer, and a small marina. The big celebrations are Old Home Week and the Dooryard Arts Festival, both in August. Other than that, it's a laid-back town with a kind of understated charm.

GETTING HERE AND AROUND

Woodstock is off the Trans-Canada Highway (Route 2) at exits 188 and 185. Coming from the U.S., Interstate 95 becomes Route 95 as it crosses the U.S. border at Houlton, Maine, and continues the short distance to Woodstock. Downtown is easily explored on foot, though it's quite an uphill trudge to some of the finest old residential streets, and a car is necessary to visit the Old Court House in Upper Woodstock.

ESSENTIALS

Visitor Information Provincial Visitor Information Centre ✉ *109 Richmond Corner, Tourist Bureau Rd., Woodstock* ☎ *506/325–4427* 🕒 *Late May–early Oct., daily 9–6 (to 7 pm July and Aug.).*

Connell House. A fine example of Greek Revival architecture, this is the former home of Honorable Charles Connell (1810–73), a politician active in many areas of public life, but perhaps best remembered for putting his own image on the 5-cent stamp instead of that of the queen when he was Postmaster General. The largely restored house, home to the Carleton County Historical Society, contains fine furniture, artifacts, musical instruments, and the Tappan Adney Room, honoring the man who is credited with saving the birchbark canoe. His grave is in the Upper Woodstock Cemetery. Temporary exhibitions and occasional concerts are added attractions. ✉ *128 Connell St., Woodstock* ☎ *506/328–9706* 🌐 *www.cchs-nb.ca* 🎫 *C$5* 🕒 *July and Aug., Tues.–Sat. 10–6, Sat. 10–6, Sun. and Mon. by appointment; Sept.–June, Tues.–Fri. 9–4:30.*

Old County Court House. Dating from 1833, this splendid galleried former court house has been restored after years of neglect and misuse and was opened to the public by H.R.H. Princess Anne in 1986. Guided tours are available in summer and occasional special events include an annual Christmas concert. ✉ *19 Court St., Upper Woodstock, Woodstock* ☎ *506/328–9706* 🌐 *www.cchs-nb.ca* 🎫 *$2 donation requested* 🕒 *July and Aug., Tues.–Sat. 10–6, Sun. and Mon. by appointment.*

WHERE TO EAT AND STAY

For expanded hotel reviews, visit Fodors.com.

$$ GERMAN 🍴 **Heino's German Cuisine.** Renowned across the Maritimes and across the border, this authentic German restaurant is in the rather unlikely setting of an out-of-town motel, the John Gyles Motor Inn. Heino has been running both since 1971, and serves up satisfying portions of dishes such as sauerbraten (succulent marinated beef), German-style pot roast with herb gravy, various schnitzels, and seven kinds of sausage. The Heino Platter, in two sizes (neither of them small), is a good option, offering tastings of several main course dishes. There are also "Canadian" steak, burger, and seafood choices and delectable desserts. Reservations recommended. [$] *Average main: C$15* ✉ *1182 Rte. 165, Fredericton* ✣ *15 km (9 miles) south of Woodstock via Rte. 165, or just off Exit 200 of Hwy. 2* ☎ *506/328–6622, 866/381–8800* 🌐 *www.johngylesmotorinnltd.ca.*

$$ HOTEL **Best Western Plus Woodstock Hotel & Conference Centre.** Conveniently located just off the Trans-Canada Highway and Highway 550, 95 miles from the U.S. border at Houlton, this hotel is largely business oriented, but is somewhat more stylish than many modern chain hotels. **Pros:** convenient for the highway; nice indoor pool. **Cons:** no restaurant; out of walking distance to downtown. [$] *Rooms from: C$130* ✉ *123 Gallop Court, Woodstock* ☎ *506/328–2378, 888/580–1188 reservations* 🌐 *www.bestwesternwoodstock.com* 🛏 *87 rooms, 18 suites* 🍴 *Breakfast.*

KINGS LANDING HISTORICAL SETTLEMENT

72 km (45 miles) east of Woodstock; 30 km (19 miles) west of Fredericton.

GETTING HERE AND AROUND

There's no public transportation to King's Landing. By car, it's just off the Trans-Canada Highway (Route 2), but the River Valley Scenic Drive is a more pleasant option; it's well signposted from both.

EXPLORING

Kings Landing Historical Settlement. When the Mactaquac Dam was created in the 1960s, a number of historically important buildings were saved and moved to a new shore. Restored and furnished, they created a living-history museum in the form of a typical Loyalist settlement of 1790 to 1900. The winding country lanes and meticulously restored homes are populated with costumed docents who accurately portray the society and lifestyles of the era. It's interesting to compare the life of the wealthy owner of the sawmill to that of an immigrant farmer. Various "Heritage Workshops" allow visitors to try 19th-century trades, including processing wool and preparing herbal remedies from the plants in the lanes and gardens, and summer camps encourage children to dress in period costume, attend a one-room schoolhouse, and learn the chores, games, and mannerisms of 19th-century youth. There are daily productions in the theater, barn dances, and strolling musicians. Hearty meals and heritage ales are served at the Kings Head Inn. ✉ *5804 Rte. 102, Exit 253 off Trans-Canada (Hwy. 2), Prince William* ☎ *506/363–4999* 🌐 *kingslanding.nb.ca* 🎟 *C$15.71* 🕒 *Early June–mid-Oct., daily 10–5.*

MACTAQUAC PROVINCIAL PARK

25 km (16 miles) west of Fredericton.

GETTING HERE AND AROUND

The park is on Route 105, west of Fredericton and off the Trans-Canada Highway (Route 2) at Exit 258, via Routes 102 then 105. There are two main entrances: on the northern edge opposite the intersection of Routes 105 and 615, and midway down the western side off Route 105 near the golf course. A third, southern entrance only leads to Walinaik Cove marina.

EXPLORING

Mactaquac Provincial Park. Surrounding the giant pond created by the Mactaquac Hydroelectric Dam on the St. John River is Mactaquac Provincial Park. Its facilities include an 18-hole championship golf course, two beaches, two marinas (one for powerboats and one for sailboats), supervised crafts activities, myriad nature and hiking trails, and a restaurant. There are also guided walks on summer Wednesdays through a nature reserve to beaver ponds. Reservations are advised for the 300 campsites in summer, but winter is fun, too; there are lots of trails for cross-country skiing and snowshoeing, and sleigh rides are available by appointment. The toboggan hills and skating/ice hockey ponds are even lighted in the evening. There's a TreeGO attraction (*506/363–4440; www.treegomactaquac.ca*) in the adjacent Centennial Park. ✉ *1265 Rte. 105, Mactaquac* ☎ *506/363–4747* 💲 *C$8 per vehicle, mid-May–mid-Oct.; no entrance fee in winter* ⊙ *Daily 8 am–dusk; overnight camping mid-May–mid-Oct.*

FREDERICTON

The small inland city of Fredericton, on a broad point of land jutting into the St. John River, is a gracious and beautiful place that feels more like a large village. It's especially interesting to visit if history is your passion.

Fredericton's predecessor, the early French settlement of Ste. Anne's Point, was established in 1642 during the reign of the French governor Joseph Robineau de Villebon, who made his headquarters at the junction of the Nashwaak and St. John rivers. Settled by Loyalists and named for Frederick, second son of George III, the city serves as the seat of government for New Brunswick's 754,000 residents. Wealthy and scholarly Loyalists set out to create a gracious and beautiful place, and even before the establishment of the University of New Brunswick, in 1785, the town served as a center for liberal arts and sciences.

Fredericton was the first city in Canada to offer free Wi-Fi throughout downtown. To learn more check out ⊕ *www.fred-ezone.ca.*

GETTING HERE AND AROUND

Fredericton is a little way north of the Trans-Canada Highway (Route 2), with four exits to choose from. Coming from the west, Exit 280 onto Route 8 is best; from the east take Exit 294 onto Route 7. Fredericton has an excellent bus service, operating Monday to Saturday 6:15 am to 11 pm; fares are C$2.25 or 10 trips for C$20, and exact change is required.

Downtown Queen Street runs parallel to the river and has several historic sights and attractions. Most major sights are within walking distance of one another. Bike rentals are available from Savage's on King Street and Radical Edge on Westmorland, and the city has a network of trails through parks and along the river. Dressed in 18th-century costumes, actors from the Calithumpians Theatre Company conduct free historical walks three times a day, from Canada Day (July 1) to Labor Day. The tours start at City Hall at 10 am, 2:30 pm, and 5 pm and last about an hour. After dark, actors lead a Haunted Hike (C$14) through historic neighborhoods and ghostly graveyards. Check at the City Hall Visitor Information Centre for details.

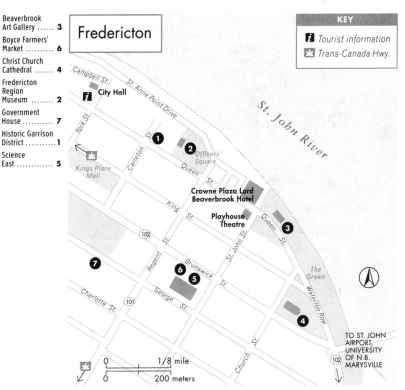

Beaverbrook
Art Gallery **3**

Boyce Farmers'
Market **6**

Christ Church
Cathedral **4**

Fredericton
Region
Museum **2**

Government
House **7**

Historic Garrison
District **1**

Science
East **5**

Fredericton

KEY

ℹ *Tourist information*

⬇ *Trans-Canada Hwy.*

ESSENTIALS

Bike Rentals Radical Edge ✉ *129 Westmorland St.* ☎ *506/459–1448*
⊕ *radicaledge.ca.* **Savage's** ✉ *441 King St.* ☎ *506/457–7452*
⊕ *www.sbcoutlet.com.*

Tour Information Calithumpians Theatre Company. Haunted Hikes are
conducted Monday through Saturday, departing from the Coach House
(796a Queen Street) at 9:15 pm. ☎ *506/457–1975* ⊕ *www.calithumpians.com.*

Visitor Information City Hall Visitor Information Centre
✉ *397 Queen St.* ☎ *506/460–2129 May–Oct., 506/460–2041 Nov.–late Apr.*
⊕ *www.tourismfredericton.ca* ⊗ *May–Oct. (in off-season visit tourism office at
11 Carleton St.).* **Fredericton Tourism** ✉ *11 Carleton St.* ☎ *506/460–2041,
888/888–4768* ⊕ *www.tourismfredericton.ca.* **Visitor Information Center**
✉ *Tilley House, 69 Front St., Village of Gagetown* ☎ *506/488–2966.*

EXPLORING
TOP ATTRACTIONS

Fodor's Choice
★

Beaverbrook Art Gallery. A lasting gift of the late Lord Beaverbrook, born
and raised in New Brunswick before building his U.K. media empire, this
gallery could hold its head high in the company of some of the smaller
European galleries. It contains a significant collection of Canadian, American, and British masterworks that rivals many major Canadian galleries.

Salvador Dalí's gigantic painting *Santiago el Grande* has always been the star, but a rotation of avant-garde Canadian paintings now shares pride of place. The McCain "gallery-within-a-gallery" is devoted to the finest Atlantic Canadian artists. From 2013 to 2016, 75 important works will not be on view here—as part of the "Masterworks of the Beaverbrook Art Gallery" exhibition, they will be touring North American galleries. ⊠ *703 Queen St.* ☎ *506/458–8545 administration, 506/458–2028 reception* ⊕ *www.beaverbrookartgallery.org* 🖃 *C$10* ⊙ *Tues.–Sat. 10–5 (to 9 Thurs.), Sun. and holidays noon–5.*

> **FREDERICTON ARTS**
>
> The **Downtown Fredericton Culture Crawl** takes place the first Thursday of every month, from June to September. During the festival, you can visit around 15 of the art galleries, craft studios, and shops in the downtown area, all within walking distance of each other (all stay open until 8 pm). It's free, and maps are available at City Hall Visitor Information Centre.

FAMILY
Fodor's Choice
★

Historic Garrison District. The restored buildings of this British and Canadian post, which extends two blocks along Queen Street, include soldiers' barracks, a guardhouse, and a cell block. This is a National Historic Site and one of New Brunswick's top attractions. Local artisans operate studios in the casemates below the soldiers' barracks in Barracks Square. In July and August free guided tours run throughout the day, and there are regular outdoor concerts in **Officers' Square.** Redcoat soldiers have long stood guard in Officers' Square, and a formal changing-of-the-guard ceremony takes place July and August at 11 am and 4 pm daily, with an additional ceremony at 7 pm on Tuesday and Thursday. It's even possible for children (ages 4 to 12) to live a soldier's life for a while: each summer at 1:15 (or 11:15 for the French version), would-be redcoats get their own uniforms, practice drilling, and take part in a "mission" ($8 per person). The square hosts a number of festivals, there's nightly entertainment in summer, and on Sunday evenings in July and August, free classic movies are shown under the stars in Barracks Square at approximately 9 pm. ⊠ *Queen St. at Carleton St.* ☎ *506/460–2129* 🖃 *Free* ⊙ *Daily 24 hrs.*

WORTH NOTING

Boyce Farmers' Market. It's hard to miss this Saturday-morning market because of the crowds. It's one of the finest markets in Canada, the building and surrounding space housing more than 250 local suppliers offering lots of local meat and produce, cheeses, baked goods, maple syrup, crafts, and seasonal items such as wreaths. The market sells good ready-to-eat food as well, from German sausages to tasty samosas. ⊠ *665 George St.* ☎ *506/451–1815* ⊕ *frederictonfarmersmarket.ca* ⊙ *Sat. 6 am–1 pm.*

Christ Church Cathedral. This gray stone building, completed in 1853, is an excellent example of decorated neo-Gothic architecture. The cathedral's design was based on an English medieval architectural style, and the cathedral became a model for many American churches. Inside is some fine carved marble and a clock known as "Big Ben's little brother"—it was the prototype for London's famous timepiece, designed by Lord Grimthorpe. ⊠ *168 Church St.* ☎ *506/450–8500* 🖃 *Free* ⊙ *Self-guided* *tours weekdays 9–6, Sat. 10–6, Sun. between services. Guided tours July and Aug., weekdays 9–6, Sat. 10–6, Sun. 1–5.*

OFF THE BEATEN PATH

Marysville. A National Historic District, Marysville is one of Canada's best-preserved examples of a 19th-century mill town. Its architecture and social history are amazing and can be appreciated with the help of a self-guided walking-tour booklet available at the Fredericton Regional Museum. Marysville itself is on the north side of the St. John River, about 10 km (6 miles) from downtown Fredericton via Route 8.

FAMILY **Fredericton Region Museum.** The Officers' Quarters in the Historic Garrison District house a museum that presents a living picture of the community from the time when only First Nations peoples inhabited the area through the Acadian and Loyalist days to the immediate past. Its World War I trench puts you in the thick of battle, and the shellacked remains of the giant Coleman Frog, a Fredericton legend, still inspire controversy. There is also an artists' co-op store featuring locally produced art and crafts. ■TIP➜ If you're visiting outside the summer months, wear warm clothing—the historic site has no heating or insulation. ✉ Officers' Sq., 571 Queen St. ☎ 506/455–6041 ⊕ www.frederictonregionmuseum.com ✆ C$5 ☉ July–early Sept., Mon.–Sat. 10–5, Sun. noon–5; Apr.–June and early Sept.–Nov., Tues.–Sat. 1–4 or by appointment; Dec.–Mar. by appointment.

Government House. This imposing 1828 Palladian mansion on the south bank of the St. John River has been restored as the official residence and office for New Brunswick's lieutenant governor. A hands-on interpretive center spans 12,000 years of history. Guided tours take in elegantly restored state rooms and art galleries. The 11-acre grounds, once a 17th-century Acadian settlement, borders an early Maliseet burial ground. It's also the venue for a number of festivals and other events every year. ✉ 51 Woodstock Rd. ☎ 506/453–2505 ⊕ www.gnb.ca/lg ✆ Free ☉ Mid-June–early Sept., weekdays 10–5, weekends noon–5 (last tour at 4); early Sept.–mid-June, weekdays 10–4 by appointment.

FAMILY **Science East.** This hands-on science center, in the former York County Jail, is all about family fun, with more than 150 hands-on exhibits on its three floors. You can test your reflexes in the Batak Reaction Tester, have fun with flying machines in the wind tunnel, set off the rocket launcher, walk into a giant kaleidoscope, create a mini-tornado, and explore the museum in the dungeon. The Hurricane Simulator is a current favorite. There's a giant pirate ship in the outdoor playground. ✉ 668 Brunswick St. ☎ 506/457–2340 ⊕ www.scienceeast.nb.ca ✆ C$8 ☉ June–Aug., Mon.–Sat. 10–5, Sun. noon–4; Sept.–May, weekdays noon–5, Sat. 10–5.

WHERE TO EAT

$$$

INTERNATIONAL

Fodor'sChoice

★

✕ **The Blue Door.** Well-deserved accolades keep pouring in for this excellent restaurant where the concept is upscale global cuisine made with local and organic ingredients, some provided by local farmers. It's also New Brunswick's only Oceanwise restaurant, promising that all the seafood served comes from sustainable stock. The food is inventive and consistently good, from home-baked specialty breads to succulent steaks cooked with local artisan beer, and the tamarind-chili Arctic char comes highly recommended. The surroundings are stylish, intimate, and nicely unpretentious, and the friendly servers are knowledgeable and engagingly enthusiastic about the food. [$] *Average main: C$23* ✉ *100 Regent St., at King St.* ☎ *506/455–2583* 🌐 *www.thebluedoor.ca* 🕒 *Closed Sun. No lunch Sat. and Mon.*

$$$ ECLECTIC 🍴 **Brewbaker's.** Downtown Fredericton's most popular casual lunch and dinner spot has a cool urban interior, highlighted by cleverly lit walls of empty bottles and stained glass windows from an old church. The rooftop garden patio is so popular that they've added another, a boon in inclement weather. The open kitchen on the main floor greets you with enticing aromas from bubbling pots of pasta sauces. Fabulous salads accompany authentic pastas and thin-crust wood-oven pizzas, and steak and seafood are also hot menu items. [$] *Average main: C$21* ✉ *546 King St.* ☎ *506/459–0067* 🕒 *No lunch Sun.*

$$$ SEAFOOD 🍴 **[catch] Urban Grill.** The new restaurant in the Delta Fredericton Hotel (⇨ *See Where to Stay*) is already making waves in the local restaurant scene. Majoring in seafood (hence the name), the kitchen turns out delicious, expertly constructed dishes like salmon marinated in soy sauce, whiskey, and maple brown sugar and cooked on a cedar plank, and tender lobster linguini with Canadian goat cheese. Nonfish dishes might include mesquite grilled ribs with apple-maple sauce or a coconut curry pad Thai. The staff is friendly, knowledgeable, and enthusiastic, and a great view of the St. John River almost (but not quite) draws your eye away from the food. [$] *Average main: C$21* ✉ *225 Woodstock Rd.* ☎ *506/478–4251* 🌐 *www.deltahotels.com/Hotels/Delta-Fredericton.*

$$$ MEDITERRANEAN 🍴 **The Palate Restaurant & Café.** Artwork by local artists enhances the colorful interior, and the open kitchen gives a view of the enthusiastic chefs in action. The menu leans toward Mediterranean and Western European, adding a few exotic touches and interesting combinations of flavors, as in a Thai coconut chicken soup, a richly flavored pork tenderloin with smoked paprika, and lemon meringue salmon, with lemon, Parmesan and chive aioli. The vegetarian option might be a tofu "meat loaf" with baked sweet potato and roasted onion sauce. The lunch menu focuses on creative sandwiches, panini, stir-fries, and salads and is significantly less expensive than dinner. [$] *Average main: C$22* ✉ *462 Queen St.* ☎ *506/450–7911* 🌐 *www.thepalate.com* 🕒 *Closed Sun. No brunch weekdays.*

WHERE TO STAY

For expanded hotel reviews, visit Fodors.com.

$ B&B/INN Fodor's Choice ★ 🏨 **Carriage House Inn.** Originally the 1875 home of Fredericton's mayor, this beautiful pre-Victorian mansion—a Provincial Historic Site—is as authentic as they come, and the welcome couldn't be warmer. **Pros:** excellent location near everything, but on a quiet and stately street; fabulous breakfast; accommodating and friendly hosts. **Cons:** perhaps not for those who favor a more modern style. [$] *Rooms from: C$119* ✉ *230 University Ave.* ☎ *506/452–9924, 800/267–6068* 🌐 *www.carriagehouse-inn.net* 🛏 *10 rooms, 1 suite* 🍽 *Breakfast.*

$$ 🏨 **Crowne Plaza Lord Beaverbrook Hotel.** This historic hotel has a great
HOTEL   location, overlooking the river at the back, fronting some of the city's
most important landmarks, and an easy walk to downtown attractions. **Pros:** has the comfort and amenities you'd expect from a large
chain hotel; convenient location; own parking lot. **Cons:** some rooms
are small; corridors to some areas are a bit of a warren; some restaurant menus are overpriced. $ Rooms from: C$150 ⊠ 659 Queen St.
☎ 506/455–3371, 866/444–1946 ⊕ www.cpfredericton.com ⇆ 155
rooms, 13 suites ❣❢ Multiple meal plans.

$$ 🏨 **Delta Fredericton Hotel.** The Delta group's recently redesigned Atlantic
RESORT   flagship is a chic urban resort where the super-friendly staff create a lively
Fodor'sChoice modern atmosphere. **Pros:** high levels of comfort; lots of amenities; enthu-
★   siastic staff; wonderful riverside location. **Cons:** outside the downtown
area. $ Rooms from: C$159 ⊠ 225 Woodstock Rd. ☎ 506/457–7000
⊕ www.deltahotels.com ⇆ 202 rooms, 20 suites ❣❢ Some meals.

$ 🏨 **Riverside Resort and Conference Centre.** Overlooking the Mactaquac
RESORT   Headpond, this hotel has a relaxed, country atmosphere and 35 acres of
FAMILY   lovely grounds with walking trails, a children's playground, and a boat
dock. **Pros:** comfortable, affordable family accommodations; activities,
including skiing and golf packages, can be arranged; environmentally
friendly water treatment plant. **Cons:** outside of Fredericton; exterior
could do with a paint job. $ Rooms from: C$109 ⊠ 35 Mactaquac
Rd., off Rte. 102, 12 km (7 miles) west of Fredericton, French Village ☎ 506/363–5111, 800/561–5111 ⊕ www.riversidefredericton.com
⇆ 82 rooms, 4 suites, 6 cottages ❣❢ Multiple meal plans.

NIGHTLIFE AND THE ARTS

THE ARTS
Calithumpians Theatre Company. The Calithumpians Theatre Company
has free outdoor performances daily in summer (12:15 weekdays, 2
weekends) in Officers' Square, and an evening Haunted Hike ($14;
July–early September, Monday–Saturday 9:15 pm) ambles through
a historic neighborhood and ghostly graveyards. It sets out from the
Coach House at 796a Queen Street. ☎ 506/457–1975.

Fodor'sChoice   **Harvest Jazz and Blues Festival.** This major weeklong annual festival takes
★   place during the second full week of September, with big-name headlin-
ers and others playing in 27 venues all over downtown. ⊠ 81 Regent
St. ☎ 506/455–4523, 888/622–5837 ⊕ www.harvestjazzandblues.com.

Fodor'sChoice   **Playhouse.** A wide range of entertainment is staged at this fine theater
★   next door to the provincial legislature, from comedy and concerts to
cultural performances by Symphony New Brunswick, Theatre New
Brunswick, and traveling ballet and dance companies. ⊠ 686 Queen St.
☎ 506/458–8344, 866/884–5800 ⊕ www.theplayhouse.ca.

NIGHTLIFE
Fredericton has a lively nightlife, with lots of live music in downtown
pubs, especially on weekends. King Street and Piper's Lane, off the 300
block of King Street, have a number of spots.

The Capital Complex. An eclectic collection of live bands, covering all genres, plays at the Capital Bar; Wilser's Room pub has live entertainment and a monthly comedy club; and the complex also includes the Phoenix dance club. Bands and DJs feature on Thursday to Saturday nights; Wilser's Room entertainment is on Tuesday and Wednesday. ⊠ *362 Queen St.* ☎ *506/459–3558* ⊕ *thecapitalcomplex.com.*

Dolan's Pub. Owned by drummer Barry Hughes, this is a great place to see live rock and blues bands from all over Eastern Canada on Thursday, Friday, and Saturday nights. It also has a first-rate rock/blues open mike session on Wednesday. St. Patrick's Day here is a wild daylong party. ⊠ *349 King St.* ☎ *506/454–7474* ⊕ *www.dolanspub.ca.*

Isaac's Way. This is a great place to relax and enjoy comfort food with a twist and view local art (for sale) on the walls, but most of all it's a popular evening gathering place that's big on community spirit. ⊠ *649 Queen St.* ☎ *506/472–7937.*

Lunar Rogue. An old-world pub atmosphere and a globally ranked whiskey bar (more than 400 brands) are the main attractions here, with live music Saturday night except in summer. ⊠ *625 King St.* ☎ *506/450–2065* ⊕ *www.lunarrogue.com.*

SPORTS AND THE OUTDOORS

CANOEING AND KAYAKING

Small Craft Aquatic Center. Shells, canoes, and kayaks can be rented by the hour or day, and the center also arranges guided tours and instruction. It's open daily from noon, mid-June through early September. ⊠ *63 Brunswick St.* ☎ *506/460–2260.*

GOLF

Kingswood Park. An 18-hole, par-72 championship course and a 9-hole executive course designed by Cooke-Huxham International take pride of place here. (Nongolfing members of the family will appreciate the Kingswood Entertainment Centre, with indoor play facilities, a bowling alley, skating rink, and arcade games.) ⊠ *31 Kingswood Park* ☎ *506/443–3333, 800/423–5969* ⊕ *www.kingswoodpark.ca* 🏌 *9 am–dusk.*

SKIING

Many of Fredericton's 70 km (44 miles) of walking trails, especially those along the river and in Odell and Wilmot parks, are groomed for cross-country skiing.

Ski Crabbe Mountain. The 18 trails here have a vertical drop of 263 meters (853 feet), and amenities include snowboard and ski rentals, a ski shop, instruction, a skating pond, cross-country skiing, babysitting, and a lounge and restaurant. ■ TIP→ **Check the website for details of half-price offers and special events.** ⊠ *50 Crabbe Mountain Rd., 55 km (34 miles) west of Fredericton, Central Hainesville* ☎ *506/463–8311 select 300 for Snow Phone, 902/896–1205* ⊕ *www.crabbemountain. com* ▭ *Lift tickets C$30 night, C$35 half-day, C$40 full day; lift ticket plus equipment rental C$55 full day* ☉ *Sept.–mid-Apr., Mon. and Tues. 9–4:30 (to 9 during school holidays), Wed.–Sun. 9–9; call Snow Phone to check as hrs are subject to weather conditions.*

WALKING

Fredericton has a fine network of walking trails, one of which follows the river from the Green past the Victorian mansions on Waterloo Row, behind the Beaverbrook Art Gallery, and along the riverbank to the Sheraton.

Visitor Information Center. Get your trail maps here. ⊠ *City Hall, 397 Queen St. at York St.* ☎ *506/460–2129* ⊕ *www.tourismfredericton.ca.*

SHOPPING

3

Aitkens Pewter. The owners of this shop design, produce, and sell pewter jewelry and belt buckles, goblets, candlesticks, and other home decor pieces. They also have stores in Saint John and Halifax. ⊠ *408 Queen St.* ☎ *506/453–9474, 800/567–4416* ⊕ *www.aitkenspewter.com.*

Botinicals. Crafts and paintings by 63 artists—most resident in New Brunswick—are sold here. ⊠ *610 Queen St.* ☎ *506/454–6101, 877/450–6101* ⊕ *botinicalsgiftshop.com* ⊙ *Closed Sun.*

Carrington & Co. This gift shop in the Delta hotel is a gem, packed full of quality crafts and clothes, including Tilley Endurables. ⊠ *225 Woodstock Rd.* ☎ *506/450–8415.*

Eloise. This women's fashion boutique specializes in Canadian clothing lines. ⊠ *69 York St.* ☎ *506/453–7715* ⊕ *eloiseltd.com.*

Endeavours and ThinkPlay. Artistic endeavors are catered to here, with all kinds of art and craft supplies and stationery, funky toys, and games that appeal to all ages. ⊠ *412 Queen St.* ☎ *506/455–4278, 800/565–0422* ⊕ *www.artstuff.ca.*

Gallery 78. In a distinctive historic house, the oldest private gallery in New Brunswick has original works by nearly 80 Atlantic Canadian artists. ⊠ *796 Queen St.* ☎ *506/454–5192, 888/883–8322* ⊕ *www.gallery78.com.*

River Valley Crafts and Artist Studios. Pottery, jewelry, paintings, and other crafts are made and sold in this shop in the converted soldiers' barracks of the Historic Garrison District, and there's a schedule of art and craft demonstrations. ⊠ *Barracks Sq., 485 Queen St., corner of Carleton St.* ☎ *506/460–2837.*

Urban Almanac General Store. An eclectic collection of household gifts, furniture, loose-leaf teas, gadgets, and gizmos of exemplary design will keep you browsing here. ⊠ *75 York St.* ☎ *506/450–4334* ⊕ *www.urbanalmanac.com.*

VILLAGE OF GAGETOWN

50 km (31 miles) southeast of Fredericton.

Fodor's Choice ★ The historic riverside Village of Gagetown—not to be confused with the Gagetown military base at Oromocto—bustles in summer, when artists welcome visitors, many of whom arrive by boat and tie up at the marina, to their studios and galleries. It also has several small restaurants with interesting menus.

GETTING HERE AND AROUND

If you're driving from Fredericton, the Trans-Canada Highway (Route 2) is fast and direct, leaving at Exit 330, signposted "Village of/de Gagetown"(do not follow the earlier signs for "Gagetown," which lead to the military base). Route 102 from Fredericton is the scenic option. Once there, the village is great for strolling.

EXPLORING

Queens County Museum. Expanding by leaps and bounds, the museum's original building, **Tilley House** (a National Historic Site), was the birthplace of Sir Leonard Tilley, one of the Fathers of Confederation. It displays Loyalist and First Nations artifacts, early-20th-century medical equipment, Victorian glassware, and more. The nearby **Queens County Courthouse** (16 Courthouse Road) is part of the museum and has archival material and courthouse furniture as well as changing exhibits. The third site is **Flower House** in Cambridge Narrow (2270 Lower Cambridge Road), built in 1818 by artist Anthony Flower. It relates his family history and contains a collection of his art, alongside works by other New Brunswick artists. ✉ *69 Front St., Village of Gagetown* ☎ *506/488–2483 seasonal* 🌐 *www.queenscountyheritage.com* 🎟 *C$3, C$5 for two buildings, C$7 for all three buildings* 🕒 *Mid-June–mid-Sept., daily 10–5; May, Oct., and Nov. by appointment.*

WHERE TO EAT AND STAY

For expanded hotel reviews, visit Fodors.com.

$$ INTERNATIONAL 🍴 **Creek View Restaurant.** On a corner just one block back from Front Street, this charming little restaurant serves country cuisine in a pleasant atmosphere, with outdoor seating in summer. The wide-ranging menu—the same at lunch and dinner—is strong on seafood and comfort food, and caters well to kids and gluten-averse diners. Breakfast is available until 1 pm on weekends. There's regular entertainment, with cover charges ranging from C$10 to C$18, depending on who's playing. It closes at 7 pm early in the week; call to check opening hours outside the summer season. [$] *Average main: C$13* ✉ *38 Tilley Rd.* ☎ *506/488–9806* 🌐 *www.thecreekviewrestaurant.com.*

$ B&B/INN 🏨 **Step-Aside B&B.** In the heart of the village, this waterfront heritage B&B overlooking the marina is renowned for its hospitality. **Pros:** delicious full breakfast and taxes included in the price; friendly and knowledgeable owners. **Cons:** bathrooms in the original house are private but not en suite. [$] *Rooms from: C$100* ✉ *58 Front St.* ☎ *506/488–1808* 🛏 *4 rooms* 🕒 *Closed Jan.–Apr.* 🍽 *Breakfast.*

SHOPPING

Grimross Crafts. This lovely art and crafts store represents 25 local craftspeople. It's open daily in summer, but closed mid-October to mid-June, except for the last week in November during the village's "Christmas in the Village" event. ✉ *64 Front St.* ☎ *506/488–2832.*

Juggler's Cove. This studio-gallery features pottery and paintings. ✉ *27 Front St.* ☎ *506/488–2574.*

PRINCE EDWARD ISLAND

WELCOME TO PRINCE EDWARD ISLAND

TOP REASONS TO GO

★ **Overdose on Anne:** The orphan nobody wanted has been adopted by the world. She's everywhere on the Island, but Cavendish's Green Gables farmhouse is ground zero.

★ **Get Beached:** Been there? Dune this. The most jaded, jet-setting beach bum will still be dazzled by the parabolic dunes at Prince Edward Island National Park in Greenwich.

★ **Go Golfing:** A concentration of championship courses—among them the Links at Crowbush Cove, Dundarave, and Brudenell River—make PEI a top choice for golfers.

★ **Cycle the Confederation Trail:** Even "I haven't ridden a bike in ages" types can cover the stunning 10-km (6-mile) waterside stretch between Morell and St. Peter's Bay.

★ **Enjoy Fresh Seafood:** Forget the frozen fish sticks of your childhood. The local seafood here—whether served in a classy restaurant or community hall—is sensational.

1 Charlottetown. PEI's historic capital city has urban amenities and a small-town vibe. Centrally located, it makes an excellent base for exploring the Island.

2 Central Coastal Drive. This 198-km (123-mile) circuit encompasses Green Gables, Prince Edward Island National Park, and the less-touristed Red Sands Shore.

QUEBEC

4

GETTING ORIENTED

Erosion and time have gnawed Prince Edward Island into a ragged crescent, with deep inlets and tidal streams that divide the province into three nearly equal parts, known locally by their county names (from east to west) of Kings, Queens, and Prince. The Island is 195 km (121 miles) long and ranges in width from 6 km (4 miles) to 61¼ km (38 miles). Despite the gentle hills in the eastern and central regions of Prince Edward Island, the land never rises to a height of more than 152 meters (500 feet) above sea level. To the west, from Summerside to North Cape, the terrain is flatter.

North Lake

Prince Edward
Island National Park

Greenwich P.E.I.
National Park

East Point

Basin Head **3**

Morell

2

16

Souris

2

Port-la-Joye-
Fort Amherst **1**

4

CHARLOTTETOWN

3

Georgetown

Orwell

Montague

*Gulf of
St Lawrence*

Pownal
Bay

4

Pinette

Northumberland Strait

High Island

~-·- **PRINCE EDWARD ISLAND** -·~
NOVA SCOTIA

3 **Points East Coastal Drive.** Lovely lighthouses and great golf courses plus fishing ports, hidden coves, singing sands, and fun festivals are all highlights here.

4 **North Cape Coastal Drive.** Anchored by Summerside (the Island's second largest city), this region includes a distinctive coastline and farm-filled interior.

Updated
by Susan
MacCallum-
Whitcomb

Prince Edward Island is a camera-ready landmass marked by verdant patchwork fields that stretch out beneath an endless cobalt sky to meet sandy white beaches and the surrounding sea. But it's so much more than just another pretty place. Like the water temperature in summer, people here are remarkably warm. Their heartfelt hospitality and slow-paced lifestyle entice visitors to return year after year.

Colonized by France in 1603, Prince Edward Island (or Île Saint-Jean, as it was then called) was handed over to Britain under the Treaty of Paris in 1763. Tensions steadily increased as absentee British governors and proprietors failed to take an active interest in the area's growth; nevertheless, the development of fisheries and agriculture in the early 19th century strengthened the local economy. Soon settlement increased, and those willing to take a chance on the Island prospered.

As relations between emboldened tenants and their distant landlords continued to worsen, heated talk about uniting with other colonies in British North America began. (The Civil War, then raging in the United States, made the idea of forging a peaceable alliance all the more appealing.) So in 1864, the Island's capital city hosted the Charlottetown Conference, a milestone in this nation's history, which ultimately led to the creation of the Dominion of Canada in 1867.

Despite this political alliance, it took another 130 years—and almost 13 km (8 miles) of concrete—for Prince Edward Island to be *physically* linked with the rest of the country. When the Confederation Bridge opened between Borden-Carleton and Cape Jourimain, New Brunswick, in 1997, traditionalists feared it would destroy PEI's tranquillity. (As you explore the villages and fishing ports, it's easy to see why they cherish it so.) Yet outside the tourist hub of Cavendish, the Island still seems like an oasis of peace in an increasingly busy world.

In summer, thanks to the relatively shallow Gulf of St. Lawrence and circulating Gulf Stream, Prince Edward Island beaches have the warmest saltwater north of the Carolinas. (Temperatures can reach 70°F in July and August.) Factor in sandy strands and the result is fine swimming conditions. Best of all, the Island's 1,760-km (1,100-mile) coast means a beach is always close by. Basin Head Beach, near Souris, has miles of singing sands. Often less populated, and with fine ocean sunsets, is West Point. At Greenwich, near St. Peter's Bay, a boardwalk stroll brings you to an endless empty beach.

PLANNING

WHEN TO GO

PEI is generally considered a summer destination—in July and August the beaches have the warmest water north of the Carolinas—but don't overlook the shoulder seasons. May, June, September, and October usually have fine weather and few visitors. In late spring those famous farm fields look especially green, and bright wildflowers blanket the roadsides. Autumn, too, is multihued thanks to the changing fall foliage. If white is your color, come in winter for cross-country skiing, snowmobiling, and ice skating. Bear in mind that many sights and services close in mid-October; however, you won't have any problem finding food, lodging, and fun things to do year-round in Charlottetown.

FESTIVALS AND EVENTS

June through mid-October, the calendar is crowded with events—many of them arts-oriented. Summerside, Georgetown, and Victoria-by-the-Sea also host their own summer theater festivals. Different musical genres are represented, too, and sporting events are prevalent. Witness eating as an extreme sport at numerous over-the-top seafood festivals.

Charlottetown Festival. PEI's marquee theatrical event is the Charlottetown Festival, where *Anne of Green Gables—The Musical* takes center stage. ⊠ *Nova Scotia* ☎ *902/628–1864, 800/565–0278* ⊕ *www.charlottetownfestival.com.*

PEI International Shellfish Festival. Democratic as always, Charlottetown plays no favorites with seafood during the PEI International Shellfish Festival in September. It promises all kinds of seafood galore (some of it prepared by celebrity guest chefs) along with fishing excursions, cooking demos, and other themed events. ⊠ *Charlottetown* ☎ *866/955–2003* ⊕ *peishellfish.com.*

PEI Jazz & Blues Festival. The capital gets jazzed up in August for the PEI Jazz & Blues Festival. ⊠ *Charlottetown* ☎ *902/894–7131* ⊕ *www.jazzandblues.ca.*

Summerside Lobster Carnival. Summerside holds a weeklong Lobster Carnival every July. ⊠ *Summerside* ☎ *902/724–4925* ⊕ *www.summersidelobstercarnival.ca.*

Tyne Valley Oyster Festival. Tyne Valley, an attractive Prince County community, hosts an Oyster Festival in August complete with fried oyster suppers and oyster chowder competitions. ⊠ *Tyne Valley* ☎ *902/432–9415* ⊕ *www.tynevalleyoysterfestival.ca.*

PLANNING YOUR TIME

Covering 5,656 square km (2,184 square miles) PEI is roughly the size of Delaware; and the fact that its area is small is a big advantage for visitors. First timers will want to concentrate on the central section, which includes not only the capital city (Charlottetown), but also the province's most popular beaches, key portions of the Confederation Trail, plus must-see Anne sites. *(⇨ To learn more about the irrepressible character L.M. Montgomery introduced in 1908, see the "Who Is Anne, anyway?" box.)* If you've already covered those bases, travel west or east to enjoy the quiet charms of the adjoining regions.

GETTING HERE AND AROUND

AIR TRAVEL

Scheduled air service operates in and out of Charlottetown Airport (YYG), 5 km (3 miles) north of the capital. Air Canada runs direct service year-round from Halifax, Montreal, Ottawa, and Toronto. WestJet provides year-round service from Toronto. Delta has nonstop flights to Charlottetown, but only from mid-June to mid-September. At the airport you can rent a car or grab a cab for the C$12 drive into town.

Air Canada ☎ 888/247–2262 ⊕ www.aircanada.ca. **Charlottetown Airport** ☎ 902/566–7997 ⊕ www.flypei.com. **Delta Airlines** ☎ 800/221–1212, 800/241–4141 ⊕ www.delta.com. **WestJet** ☎ 888/937–8538 ⊕ www.westjet.com.

BUS TRAVEL

Maritime Bus offers daily scheduled service to Borden-Carleton, Charlottetown, and Summerside. Mini-bus service to Borden-Carleton, Charlottetown, Summerside, and select destinations is available from Halifax through PEI Express Shuttle or Advanced Shuttle Service.

Advanced Shuttle Service ☎ 902/888–3353, 877/886–3322 ⊕ www.advancedshuttle.ca. **Maritime Bus** ☎ 800/575–1807 ⊕ www.maritimebus.com. **PEI Express Shuttle** ☎ 902/462–8177, 877/877–1771 ⊕ www.peishuttle.com.

CAR OR MOTORCYCLE TRAVEL

Due to limited public transport, having your own wheels is almost a necessity on the Island. Motorists can come via the 13-km (8-mile) Confederation Bridge, which connects Cape Jourimain, New Brunswick, with Borden-Carleton, PEI. The crossing takes about 10 minutes, and the toll is C$17.75 for motorcycles, C$44.50 for cars and, for larger vehicles, C$7.25 per each additional axle. On the island, there are more than 3,700 km (2,300 miles) of paved road, including three scenic drives: North Cape Coastal Drive, Central Coastal Drive, and Points East Coastal Drive. Designated Heritage Roads offer an old-fashioned alternative. Surfaced with red clay (the local soil base) and often arched with a canopy of trees, they meander through rural, undeveloped areas where you're likely to see lots of wildflowers and birds. A four-wheel-drive vehicle isn't necessary, but in spring and inclement weather the mud can get quite deep, making narrow, unpaved roads impassable. A highway map of the province is available from Tourism PEI and at visitor centers on the Island.

■ TIP→ Don't get too excited about crossing over to the Island without purchasing a ferry ticket or paying the bridge toll. Fares are only collected when you leave PEI—giving you further incentive to stay.

Confederation Bridge ☎ 902/437–7300, 888/437–6565 ⊕ www.confederationbridge.com.

FERRY TRAVEL

Weather permitting, Northumberland Ferries sails between Wood Islands, PEI, and Caribou, Nova Scotia, from May to late December. The crossing takes about 75 minutes, and there are three to nine per day depending on the season. Round-trip rates vary with the length of vehicle; those up to 6 meters (20 feet) long cost C$67.50 and those up to 15.25 meters (50 feet) long cost C$109. Foot passengers are charged C$17, cyclists C$20, and motorcyclists C$40. Fuel surcharges (C$5 for passenger vehicles at the time of writing) must also be added in.

Northumberland Ferries ☎ *877/762-7245* ⊕ *www.ferries.ca.*

RESTAURANTS

From humble mom-and-pop spots and creative cafés that give classic dishes a contemporary twist, to splurge-worthy bastions of fine dining, there is no shortage of places to eat on Prince Edward Island. In Charlottetown especially (where innovative options like Terre Rouge Bistro Marche are being added to the mix) the restaurant scene is booming. The ambience tends to be casual across the board, and reservations are seldom necessary—though at popular waterfront fish shacks, you may be in for a lengthy lineup.

Prices in the reviews are the average cost of a main course at dinner or, if dinner is not served, at lunch.

HOTELS

Full-service resorts, boutique hotels, vintage motels, and waterside vacation rentals are just some of your lodging options on PEI. Beyond the capital, inns and B&Bs—sometimes with cottage colonies attached—dominate and, design-wise, almost all of them favor the historic and traditional over the hip and trendy. Whatever you choose, it's wise to book three to six months in advance—either directly or through the province's online reservation system (⊕ *www.tourismpei.com/pei-online-reservations*)—if you are planning to arrive in July or August. Note that all accommodations here are nonsmoking and precious few have elevators.

Prices in the reviews are the lowest cost of a standard double room in high season. For expanded hotel reviews, facilities, and current deals, visit Fodors.com.

TOURS

Coach tour companies (a number of which cater to the Anne-obsessed Japanese market) do offer PEI itineraries. But since exploring quiet nooks and crannies is one of the chief delights here, traveling aboard a big bus can defeat the purpose. One popular alternative is to sign on for a bike tour of the 357-km (222-mile) Confederation Trail, which extends almost the complete length of the Island, from Tignish to Elmira. The trail's gentle grade makes pedaling comparatively easy; moreover, outfits like Eastwind Cycle and Freewheeling Adventures help you cover it in style by providing multiday inn-to-inn trips complete

---

EXPERIENCE REQUIRED

Prince Edward Island may be a Lilliputian place with a laid-back atmosphere but it has a very sophisticated tourism sector that has bundled the best of the island under the "Authentic PEI Experiences" banner. Eager to haul a lobster trap or tour a potato farm? No problem. Prefer to paint a watercolor or turn PEI's signature red clay into a piece of pottery? Consider it done. How about trying your hand at fiddling or deep-sea fishing? Those too can be arranged. Click ⊕ *www.tourismpei.com/pei-experiences* for complete listings.

4

with luggage transfers and van support. If you're more interested in day tours, biking, boating, and fishing excursions are readily available, as are culture-oriented outings. ⇨ *For other unique options, see our "Experience Required" box.*

Eastwind Cycle ☎ *902/471–4424, 866/447–7468* ⊕ *www.eastwindcycle.com.* **Freewheeling Adventures** ☎ *902/857–3600, 800/672–0775* ⊕ *www.freewheeling.ca.*

VISITOR INFORMATION

Well-staffed, well-stocked visitor information centers are strategically positioned throughout PEI. Provincially operated ones can be found at the island's main points of entry (Borden-Carleton, near the Confederation Bridge; Wood Islands, at the ferry terminal; and Charlottetown, at the airport) as well as in Cavendish, Souris, and West Prince: ⊕ *www.tourismpei.com/pei-visitor-information* has complete details. Municipally run centers are located in Charlottetown, Summerside, and St. Peter's. For help with advance planning, click PEI's official tourism website (⊕ *www.tourismpei.com*) or call the office (☎ *800/463–4734*) to order a free printed copy of the comprehensive Island Visitor's Guide.

CHARLOTTETOWN

Designated as the Island capital in 1765, Charlottetown is both PEI's oldest and largest urban center. However, since the whole "metropolitan" area only has a population of about 65,000, a pleasing small-town atmosphere remains. The city is a winner appearance-wise as well. Peppered with gingerbread-clad homes, converted warehouses, striking churches, and monumental government buildings, Charlottetown's core seems relatively unchanged from its 19th-century heyday when it hosted the conference that led to the formation of Canada. The city is understandably proud of its role as the "Birthplace of Confederation" and, in summer, downtown streets are dotted with people dressed as personages from the past who'll regale you with tales about the Confederation debate.

GETTING HERE AND AROUND

The city center is compact, so walking is the way to go. If you drive in for a day of sightseeing, you can park at an on-street meter or in garages like those on Pownal, Queen, and Fitzroy streets. Alternately, you can rent a bike at **Outer Limit Sports, Go Wheelin Bike Rentals,** or **MacQueen's Bike Shop.** Rentals start around C$25 per day. **Trius Transit** also operates trolley-style buses as part of a public-private partnership (some cover the surrounding communities of Cornwall and Stratford, too). Most have their hub downtown at the Confederation Centre of the Arts, and the fare is C$2.25 in exact change. Prefer a guided tour? **Confederation Players'** costumed interpreters lead C$15 walks in July and August. A ghostly evening version is also available. The amphibious **Harbour Hippo** offers 55-minute land-and-sea tours (C$26), June through September, from its headquarters at Prince Street Wharf, near Founders' Hall; while a sister vehicle, dubbed the

PRINCE EDWARD ISLAND ITINERARIES

IF YOU HAVE 3 DAYS

Begin your Island escape by crossing the Confederation Bridge from the mainland to Borden-Carleton. The PEI section of the Trans-Canada Highway begins here and continues through Charlottetown to the Wood Islands Ferry Terminal. Following it, make your first stop 22 km (14 miles) east in **Victoria**, one of the Island's quaintest little communities. Proceeding on to **Charlottetown**, you'll have time to see key city sights and catch a performance of *Anne of Green Gables—The Musical* at the Confederation Centre before bedtime. On Day 2 make the 39-km (24-mile) cross-Island drive to the **Green Gables Shore**—aka northern Queens County—for the quintessential PEI sun-and-sand experience. Landing in **Cavendish**, you can lounge on the beach (or take advantage of the educational programming) in Prince Edward Island National Park; make a pilgrimage to the Green Gables farmhouse (Anne's fictional home); then indulge in some cheesy but fun amusements along the Route 6 strip, otherwise known as Cavendish Road. On Day 3, veer 91 km (57 miles) east to **Georgetown** in Kings County. Take a stroll through this classic waterside town, then sign on for one of the up-close seafood encounters run locally by Tranquility Cove Adventures. From Georgetown, it's a 41-km (26-mile) drive south to **Wood Islands,** where you can catch a ferry back to the mainland. Just keep in mind that from May to early November, the last one leaves at 8 pm. Note that this route can essentially be done in reverse if you're entering the Island by way of the Northumberland Strait boat.

IF YOU HAVE 5 DAYS

Stick to the above itinerary but leave an extra day to pursue your passion in both Queens County and Kings County. In the former that might mean investigating more Anne-related sites or sussing out PEI's other famous export—oysters. In the latter, it might mean looking at lighthouses or cycling an especially nice section of the Confederation Trail. Beach bumming and golfing opportunities also abound in each.

IF YOU HAVE 7 DAYS

Since PEI is so small, you can see it all. Travelers who want comprehensive coverage can spend their additional two days exploring Prince County to the west: **Summerside** (the Island's second city) and windy **North Cape** are well worth a look, as is the rich, agricultural area inland. An alternative, though, is to stop driving and just drink it all in. Prince Edward Island is an ideal place to decompress. So simply park yourself somewhere—anywhere—and give yourself permission to genuinely relax.

Hippopotabus, takes visitors through town on an open-top double decker bus (C$17). **Prince Edward Tours** (a Gray Line affiliate) runs conventional 75-minute city bus tours (C$19), as well as half- and full-day tours to the Green Gables Shore (C$59 and C$79 respectively). On-the-water excursions are also available through the company.

ESSENTIALS

Confederation Players Walking Tours. Costumed guides from the Confederation Players troupe lead history-themed walks in July and August as part of the Charlottetown Festival. English-language tours depart Founders' Hall at 11 and 3, Monday to Saturday. A ghostly evening version is also available at 8, Tuesday to Saturday. Tours last 60 to 90 minutes and cost C$15. ☎ 800/565–0278 ⊕ *www.charlottetownfestival.com.*

Go Wheelin Bike Rentals ⊠ 6 Prince St. ☎ 902/566–5259, 877/286–6532 ⊕ www.gowheelinpei.com. **Harbour Hippo** ☎ 902/628–8687 ⊕ www. harbourhippo.com. **MacQueen's Bike Shop** ⊠ 430 Queen St. ☎ 902/368–2453, 800/969–2822 ⊕ www.macqueens.com. **Outer Limit Sports** ⊠ 330 University Ave. ☎ 902/569–5690 ⊕ ols.ca. **Prince Edward Tours** ☎ 902/566–5466, 877/286–6532 ⊕ princeedwardtours.com. **Trius Transit** ☎ 902/566–9962 ⊕ www.triustransit.ca.

EXPLORING

TOP ATTRACTIONS

FAMILY **Beaconsfield Historic House.** Designed by W.C. Harris in 1877 for shipbuilder James Peake Jr., this gracious mansion-*cum*-museum near the entrance to Victoria Park is one of the Island's finest historic homes. The 11 furnished rooms have rich architectural details and accents (imagine ornate plaster moldings and imported chandeliers)—little wonder the once-wealthy Peake went bankrupt soon after his house was completed. Having taken a tour of the first and second floors, pause to enjoy a view of Charlottetown Harbour from the veranda. An on-site bookstore has a variety of Island publications, and special events (such as musical performances and history-themed lectures) are held year-round. A carriage house on the grounds also hosts a children's festival on weekday mornings, mid-July through late-August. ⊠ 2 Kent St. ☎ 902/368–6603 ⊕ www.peimuseum.com ⊒ $5 ☉ July and Aug., daily 10–5; Sept.–June, call for hrs.

Boardwalk. Charlottetown's boardwalk extends from Confederation Landing to Victoria Park, wending its way along the water past historic sites and leafy picnic spots, providing views of sailboats and cruise ships en route. As an added bonus, it's lit at night for romantic strolls.

FAMILY
Fodor's Choice
★
Confederation Centre of the Arts. With a 1,100-seat main stage theater, a 1,000-seat outdoor amphitheater, and several studio stages, this blocklong building—opened in 1964 to mark the centennial of the Charlottetown Conference—is the Island's leading cultural venue. Each year, from late-June through September, it hosts the famous **Charlottetown Festival** (☎ 902/628–1864 or 800/565–0278, ⊕ *www.charlottetownfestival.com*), which includes *Anne of Green Gables—The Musical*, plus concerts, comedy acts, and other theatrical productions. Weather permitting, the festival offers free lunchtime performances in the amphitheater and on the plaza every day except Sunday. Off-season, a dynamic mix of touring and local productions, choral concerts, and special events is also scheduled. Visitors planning to take advantage of any of these will find that the Centre's bar and bistro, Mavor's ($$$), makes a convenient spot for preshow dining. Also on-site: a provincial

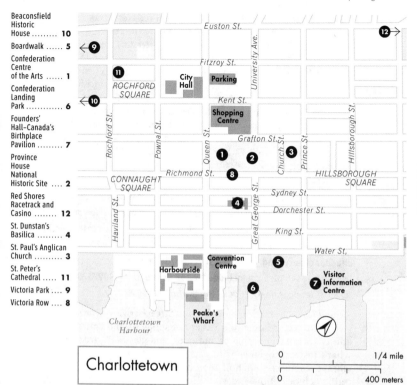

Beaconsfield Historic House **10**

Boardwalk **5**

Confederation Centre of the Arts **1**

Confederation Landing Park **6**

Founders' Hall–Canada's Birthplace Pavilion **7**

Province House National Historic Site **2**

Red Shores Racetrack and Casino **12**

St. Dunstan's Basilica **4**

St. Paul's Anglican Church **3**

St. Peter's Cathedral **11**

Victoria Park **9**

Victoria Row **8**

Charlottetown

0   1/4 mile

0   400 meters

art gallery and public library. The former (which has more than 15,000 works in its collection) holds year-round exhibits showcasing Canadian art. The latter, being cool and quiet, offers a welcome break from vacation craziness. ⊠ *145 Richmond St.* ☎ *902/566–1267, 800/565–0278* ⊕ *www.confederationcentre.com* ☺ *Gallery: mid-May–June, daily 9–5; July and Aug., Mon.–Sat., 9–8, Sun, 9–5; Sept.–mid-Oct., daily 9–5; mid-Oct.–mid-May, Wed.–Sat. 11–5, Sun. 1–5. Library: Mon., Fri., and Sat. 10–5, Tues.–Thurs. 10–9 (10–8 in summer), Sun. 1–5.*

FAMILY **Founders' Hall–Canada's Birthplace Pavilion.** The state-of-the-art exhibits and multimedia displays at this 21,000-square-foot interpretive center on the Historic Charlottetown Waterfront merge high tech with history. A case in point: the "Time Travel Tunnel," which transports visitors back to the Charlottetown Conference of 1864, eventually returning them to the present day with a greater understanding of how Canada came together as a country. In addition to its own gift shop, Founders' Hall has a civic visitor information center where you can get maps, brochures, and advice, as well as a kiosk where you can book tours and purchase theater tickets. ⊠ *6 Price St.* ☎ *902/368–1864, 800/955–1864* ⊕ *www.foundershall.ca* ⊠ *$9.50* ☺ *May, daily 9–5; June, daily 8:30–6; July and Aug., daily 8:30–7; Sept., daily 8:30–5; Oct., daily 9–4; last admission 1 hr before closing.*

Province House National Historic Site. This three-story neoclassical sandstone structure, completed in 1847 to house the colonial government, is a designated National Historic Site and remains the seat of the Provincial Legislature. Period rooms, now restored to their 1860s appearance, include the Confederation Chamber where representatives of the 19th-century British colonies originally gathered. A short film explains the significance of their meeting; and, in summer, there are themed interpretive programs available weekdays from 9 to 5. July through September, starting at 9:30 pm, the PEI Sound and Light Show (which focuses on Confederation and the Island) is projected onto the front of the building as well. ⊠ *165 Richmond St.* ☎ *902/566-7626* ⊕ *www. assembly.pe.ca* ⊠ *By donation* ⊗ *Mid-Oct.–May, weekdays 9–5; June–mid-Oct., daily 9–5.*

NEED A BREAK? **Cows Creamery Factory.** Just outside of Charlottetown, the Cows Creamery Factory offers 30-minute tours that teach you everything you need to know about ice cream production. Following a film (shown in the "Milky Whey Theater"), you can watch staff make waffle cones, whimsical T-shirts, cheddar cheese, and, of course, that award-winning ice cream. Happily, lick-worthy samples are included. ⊠ *397 Capital Dr.* ☎ *902/628-3614* ⊠ *$5* ⊗ *Tours: June–Oct., daily (on the half hr) 10–5.*

Fodor's Choice ★ **Victoria Row.** The section of Richmond Street between Queen and Great George streets is home to a variety of shops (Island crafts, art, hand-knitted sweaters, chocolates, antiques, and glassware are just some of what's inside), together with eateries, cafés, and a dance club. This vibrant, compact stretch of road really comes alive in summer, when traffic is blocked off and you'll frequently see musicians perform at lunchtime or in the evenings. For more shopping, head around the corner to Queen Street or Water Street.

WORTH NOTING

Confederation Landing Park. This waterfront recreation area at the bottom of Great George Street occupies the site where the Fathers of Confederation famously landed in 1864. Walkways and park benches offer plenty of opportunities to survey the activity of the harbor, with the added attraction of banks and banks of wild rose bushes behind. During summer, performers in period costume stroll about the area re-creating the events that led up to Canadian Confederation. Occasionally, the park also doubles as a venue for Canadian acts like Nickelback or Cirque du Soleil. **Peake's Wharf,** right next to it, has casual restaurants and bars, souvenir and crafts shops, and a marina where boat tours can be arranged. It hosts its own outdoor concert series in peak months. Featuring local talent, the free shows start at 2:30 and 6:30 daily. ⊠ *Water St. between Queen and Hillsborough Sts.* ⊠ *Free* ⊗ *Daily dawn–dusk.*

Red Shores Racetrack and Casino. Since 1880 this track at the eastern end of the city has been the home of a sport dear to islanders—harness racing. (No, they don't race harnesses. They race horses harnessed to tippy, two-wheeled carriages called sulkies.) An on-site theater simulcasts racing from other tracks, while slot machines and Texas Hold'em provide further gambling options. If you'd rather save your dollars for

CLOSE UP

A Good Walk

Start your walk at the **Confederation Centre of the Arts** on Richmond Street, in the heart of downtown. Housing the provincial art gallery and a public library, it's also home to the **Charlottetown Festival**. Next door, the **Province House National Historic Site** is where the first meeting to discuss federal union took place. Turn onto Great George Street, dipping into **St. Dunstan's Basilica**, a Roman Catholic Church notable for its twin Gothic spires. Then continue down Great George to the water, where you can enjoy lunch at a wharf-side restaurant or a picnic in **Confederation Landing Park**. Next, follow the boardwalk to **Founders'** Hall. After going inside for a crash course in Canadian history, head back to Province House and explore the shops of **Victoria Row** before investigating what Queen Street has to offer in the way of pubs and restaurants. Many visitors will be happy to call it a day there. But if you have the time (and attention span) for one further sight, venture west to visit one of the finest 19th-century residential buildings in the city: **Beaconsfield Historic House**.

TIMING: The downtown area can be explored on foot in a few hours, but the wealth of sights and harbor views warrants a full day.

---

dinner, there is excellent dining at the Top of the Park Dining Room ($$–$$$) too. In August, during **Old Home Week** (☎ 902/629–6623, ⊕ www.oldhomeweekpei.com), Eastern Canada's best harness horses converge here for 10 days of races. Old Home Week also brings the provincial agricultural exhibition and a family-friendly midway to Red Shores. ✉ 21 Exhibition Dr. ☎ 902/620–4222, 877/620–4222 ⊕ www.redshores.ca ✆ Free ☉ Mon.–Thurs. 11 am–midnight, Fri. and Sat. 11 am–2 am, Sun. noon–midnight; races Apr.–Jan., schedule varies.

St. Dunstan's Basilica. One of Canada's largest churches, St. Dunstan's, is the seat of the Roman Catholic diocese on the Island. The church is known for its fine Italian carvings and twin Gothic spires. ✉ 45 Great George St. ☎ 902/894–3486 ⊕ www.stdunstans.pe.ca ☉ Weekdays 9–5. Services weekdays at noon, Sat. at 9 and 5, Sun. at 10:30 and 5.

St. Paul's Anglican Church. Erected in 1896, this is actually the third church building on the same site. The first was erected in 1769, making this parish the Island's oldest. Large sandstone blocks give it a heavy exterior. However, the interior seems to soar heavenward, largely because of the vaulted ceilings: a common architectural feature of churches designed by W.C. "Willy" Harris. It seats only 450 but appears much larger. Harris is reputed to be the Island's finest architect, and St. Paul's will give you an idea why. Some of the stained glass dates back to the 19th century. ✉ 101 Prince St. ☎ 902/892–1691 ⊕ www.stpaulschurch.ca ☉ Weekdays 9–5; Sun. services at 8 and 10 am.

St. Peter's Cathedral. The glorious murals adorning this Anglican edifice's **All Souls' Chapel** were painted by artist Robert Harris, and the chapel itself was designed in 1888 by his brother W.C. Harris, the most celebrated Island architect. (It is attached to the side of the cathedral. If it isn't open, just ask.) Within the main sanctuary, free summer organ recitals are given Thursdays at noon. ✉ *Rochford Sq., All Souls' Lane and Rochford St.* ☎ *902/566–2102* 🌐 *www.stpeter.org/cathedra.html* 🕒 *Weekdays 9–5; Sun. morning services at 8 and 10:30 (10 in summer).*

FAMILY **Victoria Park.** At the southern tip of the city, overlooking Charlottetown Harbour, sit 40 serene acres that provide the perfect place to stroll, picnic, or cool off on a hot day. Next to the park, on a hill between groves of white birches, is the white Georgian-style **Government House.** Built in 1834 as the official residence for Lieutenant Governors (the Queen's provincial representatives), it's open weekdays in July and August from 10 to 4 for free guided tours. The collection of antique cannons that still "guard" the city's waterfront is a play area for children, though there is also an actual playground, a pool open daily in summer from 11 to 8, and a water-play area at the northwest entrance to the park. Runners and walkers can take advantage of woodland trails and a boardwalk that edges the harbor. ✉ *Lower Kent St.* ☎ *902/368–1025* 🕒 *Daily sunrise–sunset.*

WHERE TO EAT

$ CAFÉ 🍴 **Beanz Espresso Bar.** This hip-with-a-heart café is an excellent spot for hearty sandwiches, plus soups, salads, and, of course, coffee. Just remember to save room for the sweets: Beanz' inexpensive squares, bars and cakes taste like they came right out of an *Anne of Green Gables* church social. (Bakers who can prepare these old-school recipes are a dying breed!) Come daily for breakfast, lunch, or a *very* early dinner. The café closes at 6 Monday to Saturday, 4 on Sunday. [$] *Average main: C$8* ✉ *38 University Ave.* ☎ *902/892–8797* 🌐 *beanzespressobar.com.*

$$$ SEAFOOD 🍴 **Claddagh Oyster House.** Urban decor meets rural delicacies at this upscale restaurant, which occupies a handsome brick building downtown. Not surprisingly, given the name and location, seafood is a specialty here—the local oysters, mussels, and lobsters are all memorable. But there are alternatives for vegetarian and meat-loving locavores (think risotto made with market veggies or grilled PEI striploin served with roasted PEI potatoes). It's a popular spot for tourists and residents alike, and the service is friendly. Upstairs, the Olde Dublin Pub ($$) has pub grub, ample ale, and live music on the Guinness Stage seven nights a week from mid-June to mid-September. [$] *Average main: C$27* ✉ *131 Sydney St.* ☎ *902/892–9661* 🌐 *www.claddaghoysterhouse.com.*

$ DESSERT 🍴 **Cows Ice Cream.** Using a family recipe, fresh milk from Prince Edward Island cows is carefully combined with other fine, natural ingredients to create more than 32 flavors of premium ice cream that should be slowly savored (ideally in a handmade waffle cone). Cows outlets are open seasonally on Route 6 in Cavendish, in Gateway Village at the approach to the Confederation Bridge, and on board the PEI–Nova Scotia passenger ferry, *The Confederation.* ✉ *150 Queen St.* ☎ *902/892–6969* ✉ *Peake's Wharf* ☎ *902/566–4886* 🌐 *www.cows.ca.*

$$$ ECLECTIC 🍴 **Daniel-Brenan Brickhouse.** Opened in 2011 in a converted warehouse downtown, this is the sort of place that could pull a trendy crowd based solely on its decor, but the open kitchen also delivers. Local ingredients

are used to create dishes with international appeal (think Thai chicken curry, Provençal-style bouillabaisse, or lobster poutine). The restaurant has a solid wine list, and classic desserts like berry cobbler and crème brûlée for sweet-toothed diners. Dietary purists, meanwhile, will be pleased by the number of vegan, vegetarian, and gluten-free offerings. $ *Average main: C$22* ⊠ *125 Sydney St.* ☎ *902/566–4620* ⊕ *daniel-brenanbrickhouse.com* ⊘ *No lunch Sun.*

$$

SEAFOOD

✕ **Fishbones Oyster Bar & Seafood Grill.** Fishbones, on pedestrianized Victoria Row right behind the Confederation Centre of the Arts, is a good choice for pre- or post-theater dining. Although focused on fish, the menu is broad enough to include quality options for non–seafood fans, and the service is at once efficient and friendly. Prices are reasonable, too. But the setting—whether under the giant faux tree inside or on the patio outside, where diners are often serenaded by live jazz music—will still make you feel like you're having a proper night out. $ *Average main: C$20* ⊠ *136 Richmond St.* ☎ *902/628–6569* ⊕ *www.fishbones. ca* ⊘ *Late Sept.–late May.*

$$

SEAFOOD

✕ **The Gahan House Pub & Brewery.** PEI's original microbrewery, housed in an 1880 brick building downtown, clearly takes pride in its products. Seven handcrafted ales (and one wickedly good root beer) are prominently displayed on the upstairs menu, and tours of the downstairs brewing operation ($9, samples included) are given in summer. Beer reappears in several dishes as well, including the signature brown-bag fish-and-chips with honey wheat ale–battered haddock and pulled pork sandwiches accented with IPA barbeque sauce. But even teetotalers will appreciate that the food here is always tasty, affordable, and well presented. $ *Average main: C$13* ⊠ *126 Sydney St.* ☎ *902/626–2337* ⊕ *www.gahan.ca* ⊘ *Tours in July and Aug. only, Sun.–Thurs. at 5 and 7.*

$

CAFÉ

✕ **Leonhard's.** Alexandra and Axel Leonhard have gone from humble beginnings selling homemade bread at a local farmers' market to running a full-fledged café where food is made from scratch without additives, preservatives, or artificial flavorings. The room is bright and cheerful, and the devoted clientele keeps coming back for breakfast, casseroles, hearty gluten-free soups, sandwiches, and delicious desserts. Organic teas and freshly roasted coffee are served as well. With only six tables inside (and a couple more on the street in summer), you may have to wait for a seat or grab something to go. In any case, come early: Leonhard's closes at 5. $ *Average main: C$9* ⊠ *42 University Ave.* ☎ *902/367–3621* ⊕ *www.leonhards.ca* ⊘ *Closed Sun.*

$$$

CONTEMPORARY

Fodor's Choice

★

✕ **Lot 30.** Acclaimed chef Gordon Bailey has one basic agenda at his restaurant—to serve stand-out meals inspired by quality produce, meat, and seafood from PEI and Maritime sources. He tailors his menu to what's available that day, but notable dishes have included a lobster salad appetizer with citrus vanilla vinaigrette and mains such as duck breast with potato gnocchi, maple-braised pork belly with perogies, and seared scallops with Thai black rice. The sophisticated dining room is spacious yet spare, and the atmosphere is lively. $ *Average main: C$30* ⊠ *151 Kent St.* ☎ *902/629–3030* ⊕ *lot30restaurant.ca* ⊘ *No lunch. Closed Mon. Sept.–June. Closed Jan.*

$$$ CANADIAN 🍴 **The Lucy Maud Dining Room.** Chefs at this restaurant, part of the acclaimed Culinary Institute of Canada, are second-year students working under the supervision of master-chef instructors; service is provided by hospitality students. It's an opportunity to enjoy ambitious dishes that combine local ingredients with international influences. The institute's dining room could use some freshening up, but nothing can detract from the view of the water out its large windows. Although dinner is served year-round, lunch is offered only from mid-October to mid-May. [$] *Average main: C$26* ✉ *4 Sydney St.* ☎ *902/894–6868* 🌐 *www.hollandcollege.com/culinary-institute-of-canada/lucy-maud-dining-room* ✍ *Reservations essential* ⏲ *Closed mid-May–early June and Sept.–mid-Oct. Closed Sun., Mon., and holidays.*

$$ CANADIAN 🍴 **The Pilot House.** In the 19th-century Roger's Hardware building, this restaurant has both fine dining and casual fare. Old wooden beams, brick columns, and a unique bar top made of black granite inlaid with bird's-eye maple make the place cozy. A pub menu ($$) concentrates largely on classic sandwiches and creative pizzas, while quality PEI-raised beef and fresh seafood dominate the dinner menu ($$$). [$] *Average main: C$20* ✉ *70 Grafton St.* ☎ *902/894–4800* 🌐 *thepilothouse.ca* ⏲ *Closed Sun.*

$$$$ STEAKHOUSE 🍴 **Sims Corner Steakhouse and Oyster Bar.** Chef Kyle Panton's farm-to-plate focus helped him earn accolades from the Prince Edward Island Restaurant Association, while the custom-cut, Island-raised beef he prepares (it's aged 45 days for richer taste) has helped him earn kudos from patrons. Seafood selections start with a wide range of oysters at the raw bar, and divine desserts are made in-house. All can be washed down with an award-winning selection of Old and New World wines. Earthy colors, brick walls, exposed beams, and plush booths encourage you to linger indoors, but there is also a pleasant patio for warm-weather dining. [$] *Average main: C$40* ✉ *86 Queen St.* ☎ *902/894–7467* 🌐 *www.simscorner.ca.*

$$$ ITALIAN 🍴 **Sirenella Ristorante.** Northern Italian cuisine and unfailingly good service make Sirenella one of Charlotteville's top restaurant choices. The menu, which changes twice a year, has something for everyone. Owner Italo Marzari handpicks the Italian wines on the list, and noteworthy mains—like the excellent *vitello pizzaiola* (veal in a sauce of white wine, capers, garlic, and oregano, topped with *bocconcini* cheese and tomato sauce)—are complemented by a range of handmade pastas. [$] *Average main: C$23* ✉ *83 Water St.* ☎ *902/628–2271* 🌐 *www.sirenella.ca* ⏲ *Closed Sun.; no lunch Sat.*

$ VEGETARIAN 🍴 **Splendid Essence.** Sharing a pretty house with a Buddhist prayer hall, this little eatery serves vegetarian fare with Asian flair. Aside from the expected noodles, dumplings, and stir fries, Splendid Essence has a fine selection of hot and cold teas, which you can enjoy outdoors on the porch in fine weather. [$] *Average main: C$12* ✉ *186 Prince St.* ☎ *902/566–4991* ⏲ *Closed Sun.*

$$$ BISTRO 🍴 **Terre Rouge Bistro Marche.** Occupying a heritage brick-and-stone structure, this new bistro gives Charlottetown's dining scene a French twist. The menu changes frequently, but the farm-to-table focus never wavers. Expect house-cured charcuterie, artisanal cheeses, plus favorite French

ENJOYING SHELLFISH

Prince Edward Island shellfish has a reputation for being among the world's best. Mollusks and crustaceans are harvested all along the coast, so you can spot fishermen in shallow boats scooping up oysters with what look like giant salad servers. Moreover, you can see rows of buoys in bays and estuaries holding up lines covered with mussels, plus solo buoys securing the lobster traps that wait to be hauled offshore. Obviously, you'll see shellfish on almost every Island menu, too, as well as on many activity rosters: tour operators are taking increasing numbers of visitors out to trap, haul, tong, and shuck. Shellfish also pops up on festival calendars.

4

dishes (including foie gras, steak frites, duck confit, and roasted marrow bones—all beautifully plated). And for dessert? *Mais oui,* macarons! There's also an on-site "marché" with goodies to go; and if you need an early morning fix, coffee and fresh pastries are available from 8 am. $ *Average main: C$21* ⊠ *72 Queen St.* ☎ *902/892–4032* ⊕ *terrerouge-pei.com* ☽ *Closed Sun. and Mon. in winter.*

WHERE TO STAY

For expanded hotel reviews, visit Fodors.com.

$$$ **Delta Prince Edward.** Adjoining the Prince Edward Island Convention Centre and positioned next to Peake's Wharf, this high-rise hotel occupies an ideal spot from which to explore the waterfront and historic downtown on foot. **Pros:** modern, fresh lobby area; upper category rooms have Jacuzzis; elevator; free Wi-Fi. **Cons:** some rooms look dated (makeovers were slated at press time); parking costs C$17 per day. $ *Rooms from: C$244* ⊠ *18 Queen St.* ☎ *902/566–2222, 866/894–1203* ⊕ *www.deltaprinceedward.com* ↪ *202 rooms, 8 suites* ⦿ *No meals.*

HOTEL

$$$ **Dundee Arms Inn.** A 1903 Queen Anne mansion and modern annex (actually a surprisingly stylish 1960s motel) make up this attractive inn just minutes from downtown. **Pros:** relaxed setting; free Wi-Fi; in-room perks include fluffy robes and Paya Organic bath products. **Cons:** rooms vary widely in size and quality; breakfast not included. $ *Rooms from: C$185* ⊠ *200 Pownal St.* ☎ *902/892–2496, 877/638–6333* ⊕ *www.eden.travel/dundee* ↪ *18 rooms, 4 suites.*

B&B/INN

$$$ **Elmwood Heritage Inn.** Tranquil is the key term to describe this 1889 inn, which sits at the end of a tree-lined lane in a residential neighborhood. **Pros:** an acre of grounds; in-room mod cons like iPod docks and flat-screen TVs; free Wi-Fi. **Cons:** rather flowery for some tastes; a 15-minute walk to downtown. $ *Rooms from: C$209* ⊠ *121 N. River Rd.* ☎ *902/368–3310, 877/933–3310* ⊕ *www.elmwoodinn.pe.ca* ↪ *5 rooms, 3 suites* ⦿ *Breakfast.*

B&B/INN

$$$ B&B/INN Fodor's Choice ★ 🏨 **Fairholm National Historic Inn.** The Fairholm, a designated National Historic Site, is the primo Maritime example of the architectural Picturesque movement. **Pros:** lovely gardens; attractive packages and specials offered; free Wi-Fi. **Cons:** lots of wallpaper; not for those seeking big-hotel amenities. [$] *Rooms from: C$180* ✉ *230 Prince St.* ☎ *902/892–5022, 888/573–5022* 🌐 *www.fairholminn.com* 🛏 *7 rooms* 🍴 *Breakfast.*

$$$ HOTEL Fodor's Choice ★ 🏨 **The Great George.** This centrally located boutique hotel is fashioned out of 15 heritage buildings. **Pros:** excellent staff; comfy beds topped with duvets and premium linens; free Wi-Fi and access to hotel gym. **Cons:** street noise is sometimes audible on the Great George side. [$] *Rooms from: C$224* ✉ *58 Great George St.* ☎ *902/892–0606, 800/361–1118* 🌐 *www.thegreatgeorge.com* 🛏 *34 rooms, 22 suites, 4 condos* 🍴 *Breakfast.*

$$$$ HOTEL 🏨 **The Holman Grand Hotel.** Sitting atop the Confederation Court Mall, the 10-story structure's upper floors provide sensational views; bottom ones, connected to both the mall and Confederation Centre of the Arts, offer indoor access to city amenities. **Pros:** elevator; some suites have kitchenettes; all rooms have mini-refrigerators and Keurig coffeemakers; free Wi-Fi. **Cons:** standard rooms have spa-worthy showers but no tubs; comparatively pricey. [$] *Rooms from: C$260* ✉ *123 Grafton St.* ☎ *902/367–7777, 877/455–4726* 🌐 *www.theholmangrand.com* 🛏 *62 rooms, 18 suites.*

$$ HOTEL 🏨 **The Hotel on Pownal.** Guests were impressed when this one-time motel morphed into a contemporary, budget-conscious lodging option in 2010—and the Hotel on Pownal has lived up to its early promise. **Pros:** new gym; free Wi-Fi and buffet breakfast; free coffee, tea, and home-baked treats available 24/7. **Cons:** no elevator; no on-site restaurant; no views. [$] *Rooms from: C$153* ✉ *146 Pownal St.* ☎ *902/892–1217, 800/268–6261* 🌐 *thehotelonpownal.com* 🛏 *40 rooms, 5 suites* 🍴 *Breakfast.*

$$$ B&B/INN 🏨 **Shipwright Inn B&B.** The name of this cottage-y 1860s inn is a nod to the first owner's occupation, and its charming accommodations further attest to his seafaring ways (the Captain's Quarters, the Navigator's Retreat. **Pros:** downtown location with pretty garden; some rooms have balconies and fireplaces. **Cons:** minimalists may find the number of knickknacks disconcerting; five rooms are in a 1996 addition. [$] *Rooms from: C$189* ✉ *51 Fitzroy St.* ☎ *902/368–1905, 888/306–9966* 🌐 *www.shipwrightinn.com* 🛏 *8 rooms, 1 apartment* 🍴 *Breakfast.*

CROSSROADS

The intersection of Richmond Street and Great George Street is frequently—although you can never predict when—the place to see all manner of old and new conveyances: modern buses, elegant horse-drawn carriages, open-top double-decker buses, traditional trolleys, and even amphibious vehicles are all used to get around this historic city.

NIGHTLIFE AND THE ARTS

For complete and current listings of entertainment events check *The Buzz*; you can pick up a free copy at most hotels, restaurants, and newsstands or view it online at ⊕ *www.buzzon.com.*

THE ARTS

Benevolent Irish Society Hall. The Benevolent Irish Society Hall stages Friday night ceilidhs with Celtic dancing, fiddling, and a few stories thrown in for good measure, mid-May through October. ✉ *582 N. River Rd.* ☎ *902/892–2367* ⊕ *benevolentirishsocietyofpei.com.*

Feast Dinner Theatre. Atlantic Canada's longest-running dinner theater specializes in fun, fluffy musicals. Watch lively shows while chowing down on a buffet meal from late-June through August. ✉ *Rodd Charlottetown Hotel, 75 Kent St.* ☎ *902/629–2321* ⊕ *www.roddvacations.com/feast.*

The Guild. The Guild, one of Charlottetown's major cultural centers, hosts plays, performances, and a variety of exhibits throughout the year. ✉ *111 Queen St.* ☎ *902/620–3333, 866/774–0717* ⊕ *www.theguildpei.com.*

NIGHTLIFE

Globe World Flavours. Prim Anne fans may not approve, but, after hours on Saturday, Globe World Flavours (a Victoria Row eatery) morphs into a dance club. More sedate entertainment is offered most other evenings. ✉ *132 Richmond St.* ☎ *902/370–4040* ⊕ *www.dinedrinkdance.ca.*

St. James Gate Pub. Known for its plentiful pub fare and convivial crowd, the St. James Gate also features live local music on Friday and Saturday nights, making it a great place to eat, drink, and be merry. ✉ *129 Kent St.* ☎ *902/892–4283* ⊕ *www.stjamesgatepei.com.*

SPORTS AND THE OUTDOORS

GOLF

Clyde River Golf and Country Club. The club is a 27-hole facility with linked 9- and 18-hole courses, located about 10 minutes west of Charlottetown. Part of the scenery includes pretty farmland and the Clyde River itself. The club, its pro shop, and restaurant are open May through October. ✉ *384 Clyde River Rd., Rte. 247, RR #2, Clyde River* ☎ *902/675–2585* ⊕ *www.clyderivergolf.ca.*

Fox Meadow Golf and Country Club. This 18-hole club is a mere five minutes southeast of the city. Its challenging par-72 championship course, designed by Rob Heaslip, overlooks Charlottetown Harbour and the community of Stratford. ✉ *167 Kinlock Rd., Stratford* ☎ *902/569–4653, 877/569–8337* ⊕ *www.foxmeadow.pe.ca.*

WATER SPORTS

Peake's Wharf Boat Tours. June to mid-September, Peake's Wharf Boat Tours operates assorted cruises—sunset and seal-watching ones among them—aboard a 14-meter (45-foot) vessel. Prices start at $25 for a 70-minute trip. ✉ *1 Great George St., Peake's Wharf* ☎ *902/566–4458* ⊕ *www.peakeswharfboattours.com.*

Saga Sailing Adventures. May to October, you can sail away on a sloop courtesy of Saga Sailing Adventures. The 2½-hour outings are priced at $110. Charter tours are also available. ⊠ *Charlottetown Yacht Club, 1 Pownal St.* ☎ *902/672–1222* ⊕ *www.sagasailing.com.*

Top Notch Charters. Top Notch Charters offers fun, informative lobster fishing excursions for $45 ($80 with a lobster dinner included) in July and August. ⊠ *2 Prince St.* ☎ *902/626–6689* ⊕ *www.markscharters.com.*

> **SILLY HAT SYNDROME**
>
> A curious affliction seems to strike vacationers in certain locales. In Disney destinations it compels them to don mouse ears; in Caribbean resorts, it manifests itself through the wearing of colorful knit caps with dangling faux dreadlocks. In PEI, you will know you're in the midst of an outbreak when you see otherwise sane people sporting beribboned straw boaters with red *à la Anne* braids attached.

SHOPPING

The most interesting shops in Charlottetown are on Peake's Wharf, in Confederation Court Mall (off Queen Street), along Victoria Row (the section of Richmond Street between Queen and Great George streets), and on Water Street. There are also factory outlet stores along the Trans-Canada Highway at North River Causeway near the western entrance to the city, next to Cows Creamery.

Anne of Green Gables Chocolates. This local chocolatier fittingly sells old-fashioned chocolates, peanut brittle, and assorted candy—all made here. (For a double dose of local flavor, try chocolate-coated PEI potato chips.) Sweet treats for those who can't get enough of the Island's sweetest fictional orphan are available at this location year-round. Other outlets in Avonlea Village, Gateway Village and on the Cavendish Boardwalk open seasonally. ⊠ *100 Queen St.* ☎ *902/368–3131* ⊕ *www.annechocolates.com.*

Charlottetown Farmers' Market. Along with the expected array of local produce, artisanal cheeses, organic meats and tasty baked goods, you'll find a fine array of Island-made crafts. The market runs from 9 until 2 on Saturdays year-round as well as on Wednesdays, July through early October. ⊠ *100 Belvedere Ave.* ☎ *902/626–3373* ⊕ *charlottetownfarmersmarket.weebly.com.*

Moonsnail Soapworks and Aromatherapy. The vegetable-based soaps sold here are hand-crafted and scented with essential oils. The expanding inventory also includes sublime bath and body-care products, and a pet-care line. ⊠ *85 Water St.* ☎ *902/892–7627, 888/771–7627* ⊕ *www.moonsnailsoapworks.com.*

Northern Watters Knitwear. This shop carries its own line of chill-chasing knitted sweaters and a wide range of other Island-made products. ⊠ *150 Richmond St.* ☎ *902/566–5850, 800/565–9665* ⊕ *www.nwknitwear.com.*

Pilar Shephard Art Gallery. This gallery has earned a name for quality Maritime, Canadian, Inuit, and international art. Antiques and Canadian-designed jewelry are also sold on-site. ⊠ *82 Great George St.* ☎ *902/892–1953* ⊕ *www.pilarshephard.com.*

CENTRAL COASTAL DRIVE

The 198-km (123-mile) Central Coastal Drive heads northeast on Route 2 out of Charlottetown and continues, with a left turn onto Route 6, to the north shore. Route 6 takes you by classic fishing communities and the striking strands of Prince Edward Island National Park before depositing you in *Anne of Green Gables* country. (The section around Cavendish is cluttered with commercial tourist tat. If you look beyond the fast-food outlets and tacky gift shops, however, you can still find unspoiled beauty.) This beach-blessed section alone—newly christened the Green Gables Shore—has enough in the way of attractions, amusements, and outdoor opportunities to satisfy many vacationers. Yet it's worth traveling south, too, following the coast to the quieter Red Sands Shore on the other side of the Island, passing rolling farmland and oyster-filled Malpeque Bay en route. Considering that visitors who come to the Island via the Confederation Bridge land smack in the middle of this shore, it seems ironic that its red headlands remain relatively undiscovered. Historic sites, villages harking back to Victorian days, and a distinctive sandstone coastline are here to explore.

PRINCE EDWARD ISLAND NATIONAL PARK

24 km (15 miles) north of Charlottetown.

Fodor's Choice
★ **Prince Edward Island National Park.** Prince Edward Island National Park has been touched with nature's boldest brushstrokes—sky and sea meet red sandstone cliffs, woodlands, wetlands, rolling dunes, and long stretches of sand. The original portion, a narrow strip of protected coast, extends for 40 km (25 miles) along the north shore of the Island from Cavendish to Dalvay. A separate adjunct sits about 24 km (15 miles) farther east on the Greenwich Peninsula. (⇨ *For details on the latter, see Greenwich section.*)

There are several entrances to the park system off routes 6, 13, and 313. Start your visit at Cavendish Grove, which occupies the former site of a 16-hectare amusement park off Route 6. Pull in at the Welcome Centre; then take a pleasant 1-km (½-mile) stroll to Cavendish Beach. The beach itself is supervised in summer, and the way down to it is lined with maple trees, which seems fitting here in the "Cradle of Confederation." A relaxing alternative is to picnic in the titular grove, accompanied by a soundtrack of songbirds and honking Canada geese who call the nearby pond home. A full slate of cultural and ecological interpretive programs aimed at all ages is also available. More active types can bike, hike, or (in winter) cross-country ski on the park's scenic trails. If you'd rather be out on the water, kayak and canoeing opportunities abound. ⊠ *Cavendish* ☎ *902/672–6350* ⊕ *www.pc.gc.ca* ⊠ *C$7.80 July and Aug.; C$3.90 other times* ☉ *Mid-May–mid-Oct., daily dawn–dusk; full services July and Aug. only.*

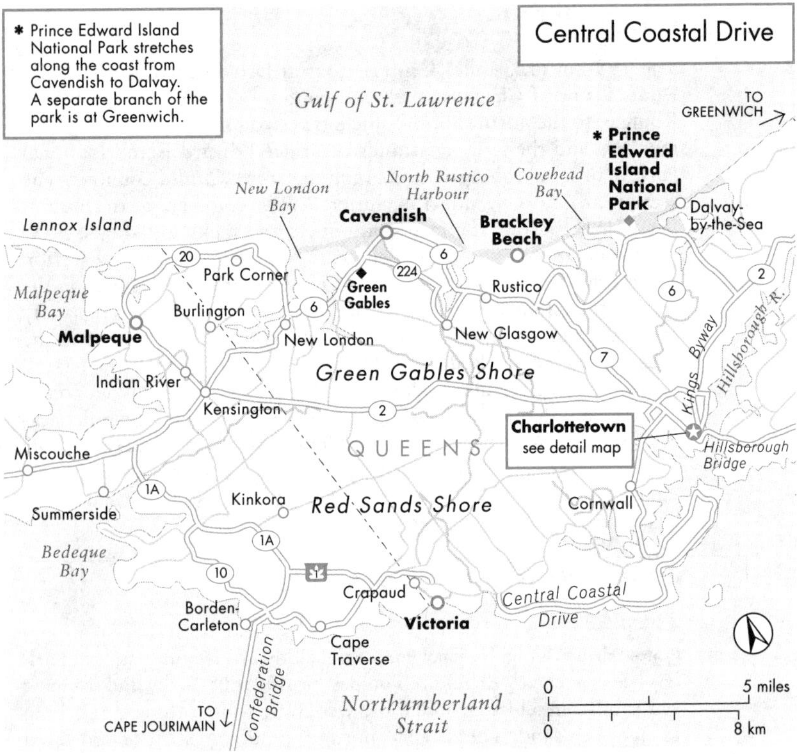
Central Coastal Drive
* Prince Edward Island National Park stretches along the coast from Cavendish to Dalvay. A separate branch of the park is at Greenwich.
Gulf of St. Lawrence
TO GREENWICH
* Prince Edward Island National Park
Dalvay-by-the-Sea
North Rustico Harbour
Covehead Bay
New London Bay
Cavendish
Brackley Beach
Lennox Island
Park Corner
Green Gables
Rustico
Malpeque Bay
Burlington
Malpeque
New London
New Glasgow
Green Gables Shore
Indian River
Kensington
Kings Byway
Hillsborough R.
Charlottetown
see detail map
Hillsborough Bridge
Miscouche
QUEENS
Summerside
Kinkora
Red Sands Shore
Cornwall
Bedeque Bay
Crapaud
Central Coastal Drive
Borden-Carleton
Victoria
Cape Traverse
Confederation Bridge
TO CAPE JOURIMAIN
Northumberland Strait
0
5 miles
0
8 km

WHERE TO EAT AND STAY

For expanded hotel reviews, visit Fodors.com.

$$ SEAFOOD Fodor's Choice ★ 🍴 **Richard's Fresh Seafood.** This down-home dockside eatery serves common fare in an uncommonly good way. Befitting its location, the seafood is *very* fresh. Expect lobster rolls, scallop sandwiches, steamed clams, and such served with fries that are twice-cooked for added crispness, plus homemade sauces and slaws. If you'd rather cook up your own fishy feast, the adjacent fish market sells everything you'll need. [$] *Average main: C$15* ✉ *9 Wharf Rd., Covehead Bay* ☎ *902/672–3030* 🌐 *www.richardsfreshseafood.com* ⏲ *Closed Oct.–May.*

$$$$ B&B/INN 🏨 **Dalvay-by-the-Sea.** Built in 1895 as the summer retreat for a U.S. oil tycoon, this sprawling Queen Anne Revival "cottage" on the east edge of Prince Edward Island National Park is filled with antique furnishings, giving guest rooms a lovely period look. **Pros:** vintage vibe; 100 meters (328 feet) from the beach; free Wi-Fi. **Cons:** no air-conditioning; no TVs in guest rooms; no kitchens in chalets. [$] *Rooms from: C$269* ✉ *16 Cottage Crescent, just off Rte. 6, near Dalvay Beach, Stanhope* ☎ *902/672–2048, 888/366–2955* 🌐 *www.dalvaybythesea.com* 🛏 *26 rooms, 8 chalets* ⏲ *Closed mid-Oct.–May.*

SPORTS AND THE OUTDOORS

BIKING **Dalvay Bike Rentals.** The resort Dalvay-by-the-Sea rents bikes suitable for all members of the family to guests and nonguests alike. Rates are $9 per hour, $26 per day. ⊠ *Rte. 6, near Dalvay Beach, Stanhope* ☎ *902/672–2048* ⊕ *www.dalvaybythesea.com.*

FISHING **Richard's Deep-Sea Fishing.** Captain Richard Watts takes eager anglers out on his 13.5-meter (45-foot) boat three times per day in summer. Fishing gear is supplied and whatever you catch will be cleaned and filleted. ⊠ *5 Wharf Rd., Covehead Bay* ☎ *902/672–2376.*

GOLF **Stanhope Golf and Country Club.** The 18 holes of the links-style, par-72 course at Stanhope Golf and Country Club are among the most challenging and scenic on the Island. Ocean breezes help. The course is a couple of miles west of Dalvay, along Covehead Bay. ⊠ *Off Rte. 6, 2961 Bay Shore Rd., Stanhope* ☎ *902/672–2842, 888/672–2842* ⊕ *www.stanhopegolfclub.com.*

BRACKLEY BEACH

15 km (9 miles) north of Charlottetown.

Brackley Beach abuts Prince Edward Island National Park, so park access is easy and sand is in ample supply. Because this is more a chunk of coastline than an actual community, Brackley Beach offers considerably fewer amenities than neighboring Cavendish. Activities here are refreshingly simple. Water sports, for example, tend to be the nonmotorized kind, and gentle pursuits like bird-watching are popular (area waterways attract many migratory species). Nevertheless, lodgings such as Shaw's have been in business for generations, so clearly there is enough here to warrant guests' return.

GETTING HERE AND AROUND

Lying along Route 15, just north of Route 6, Brackley Beach is meant for motorists.

WHERE TO EAT AND STAY

For expanded hotel reviews, visit Fodors.com.

$$$
ECLECTIC
Fodor's Choice
★

✕ **The Dunes Café.** Sharing a property with the Dunes Studio Gallery (⇨ *See Shopping*), this café has wood ceilings that soar above the indoor dining room and a deck overlooking the dunes and marshlands of Covehead Bay. Like the view, the food is amazing, showcasing local ingredients with an international twist. Your main, for example, might be a Mediterranean rack of lamb or lobster pad thai. The eclectic menu is also offered in the lounge and on a patio that sits above vibrant gardens. ⓢ *Average main: C$25* ⊠ *3622 Brackley Point Rd., Rte. 15* ☎ *902/672–1883* ⊕ *www.dunesgallery.com* ⊘ *Closed Oct.–May.*

$$$
B&B/INN

🏠 **Barachois Inn.** Rustico, just below Brackley Beach, is one of the oldest communities on the Island—and this 1880 inn's Victorian elegance blends right in with the historic surroundings. **Pros:** themed packages available; thoughtful hosts; free Wi-Fi; on-site gym. **Cons:** pretty far from civilization; gable ceilings not great for tall guests. ⓢ *Rooms from: C$235* ⊠ *2193 Church Rd., Rte. 243, off Rte. 6, 8 km (5 miles) west of Brackley Beach, Rustico* ☎ *902/963–2194, 800/963–2194* ⊕ *www. barachoisinn.com* ⤶ *4 rooms, 4 suites* ⦶ *Breakfast.*

$$ RESORT FAMILY **Shaw's Hotel and Cottages.** Canada's oldest family-operated inn has been winning a faithful following since opening in 1860. **Pros:** next to the national park; free kayaks and canoes; laundry facilities. **Cons:** there may be mosquitoes in the air or jellyfish in the water; a/c in deluxe inn rooms only. [$] *Rooms from: C$160* ✉ *99 Apple Tree Rd., Rte. 15* ☎ *902/672–2022* 🌐 *www.shawshotel.ca* 🛏 *15 rooms, 3 suites, 25 cottages* ⏲ *Closed early Oct.–May; some cottages open in shoulder months* 🍴 *Breakfast.*

NIGHTLIFE AND THE ARTS

Brackley Drive-In Theatre. Brackley Drive-In Theatre gives visitors in this neck of the woods a reason to stay up past dark. It shows a pair of first-run flicks nightly from mid-May to mid-September. Onion rings and other classic snacks from the canteen complement the experience. ✉ *3164 Brackley Point Rd., Rte. 15* ☎ *902/672–3333* 🌐 *drivein.ca* 🎟 *$10 per person, cash only.*

Howes Hall Gallery. Howes Hall Gallery specializes in original paintings and primitive hooked mats. There is an exhibit space in back, and the artist/owners give occasional summer classes that allow artsy vacationers to hone their own skills. ✉ *3421 Brackley Point Rd., Rte. 15* ☎ *902/672–4111* 🌐 *www.howeshallgallery.com* ⏲ *Closed Oct.–mid-June.*

SPORTS AND THE OUTDOORS

Northshore Rentals. Run by Shaw's Hotel, this shop can equip you with kayaks, canoes, and bicycles. Per hour rates are $12, $11, and $6.50 respectively. ✉ *Rte. 15 at Shaw's Hotel* ☎ *902/672–2022.*

SHOPPING

The Dunes Studio Gallery. This gallery sells an array of cool Canadian-made goods. Choose between pottery (you can watch it being crafted on-site), Island art, clothing with as unmistakable Indonesian influence, funky furniture, fine jewelry, contemporary glassware and other one-of-a-kind items. ✉ *3622 Brackley Point Rd., Rte. 15* ☎ *902/672–2586* 🌐 *www.dunesgallery.com* ⏲ *Closed Oct.–May.*

The Great Canadian Soap Co. Time to come clean! The Great Canadian Soap Co. produces dozens of types of goat's milk soap at its home base in Brackley Beach. (That explains the gamboling goats you'll encounter near the shop.) Other all-natural bath and beauty products are available as well. ✉ *4224 Portage Rd., Rte. 6* ☎ *800/793–1644* 🌐 *www.greatcanadiansoap.com.*

CAVENDISH

21 km (13 miles) west of Brackley Beach.

Cavendish is the most visited Island community after Charlottetown. The proximity of Prince Edward Island National Park, with its promise of summertime sun and sand, is one reason for the heavy influx of vacationers. The crop of amusement park–style attractions that has sprung up on Route 6 as a counterpoint to the pristine park is another. However, it all began with *Anne of Green Gables.* Thousands of Anne-ites flock to the Cavendish area every year to visit the homes associated with

Lucy Maud Montgomery, who was born and buried in the area, and to explore the places so lovingly described in her books.

GETTING HERE AND AROUND

Most visitors drive themselves to Cavendish. Prince Edward Tours offers four-hour outings to the area from Charlottetown on Tuesday, Wednesday, Friday, and Sunday, mid-June to late September. Tours depart from Founders' Hall and cost C$59 per person.

Prince Edward Tours ⊠ *Charlotte-town* ☎ *902/566–5466, 877/286–6532* ⊕ *princeedwardtours.com.*

EXPLORING

TOP ATTRACTIONS

FAMILY **Avonlea—Village of Anne of Green Gables.** At Avonlea, purpose-built structures have been combined with heritage ones—among them a schoolhouse where L.M. Montgomery once taught—to convincingly re-create Anne's fictional hometown. Blissed-out devotees can sip raspberry cordial and take in the scene as strolling actors bring favorite scenes to life. For everyone else, activities like spoon-playing lessons, wagon rides, and old-fashioned sack races still ensure a fun day out. ⊠ *8779 Rte. 6* ☎ *902/963–3050* ⊕ *www. avonlea.ca* ⊠ *$19.30; $7.02 in Sept. for limited program* ☉ *Mid-June–Aug., daily 10–5; first wks of Sept., daily 10–4.*

Gardens of Hope. Need a break from those Cavendish crowds? Gardens of Hope, part of the PEI Preserve Company property, is about 8 km (5 miles) south of town beside the Island's most beautiful river valley. The garden itself covers more than 12 acres. With 2 km (1 miles) of walking trails that thread past fountains and groomed flower beds, then through natural woodland, it provides ample opportunity for quiet contemplation. ⊠ *2841 New Glasgow Rd., off Rte. 13, New Glasgow* ☎ *902/964–4300, 800/565–5267* ⊕ *preservecompany.com/gardens-of-hope* ⊠ *By donation* ☉ *Dawn–dusk.*

FAMILY
Fodor's Choice
★
Green Gables. Green Gables, ½ km (¼ mile) west of Lucy Maud Montgomery's Cavendish Home, is the green-and-white 19th-century farmhouse that served as the inspiration for the Cuthbert place in *Anne of Green Gables.* The house, outbuildings, and grounds, all of which belonged to cousins of the author's grandfather, re-create some of the settings found in the book. The same goes for short walking trails dubbed the Haunted Wood and Lovers Lane/Balsam Hollow. If you're well acquainted with the novel you'll spy lots of evocative details on-site (say, a broken slate or amethyst brooch). If not, watching an introductory film in the Visitor Centre will help you get up to speed. An audio-visual presentation on Montgomery's life shares space with a café in the barn nearby. This National Historic Site has been part of

WHAT'S IN A NAME?

Prince Edward Island was named for the fourth son of King George III (the monarch who lost America in the War of Independence). A rather run-of-the-mill royal, Edward seemed destined to be little more than a historical footnote until he was saved from obscurity by Britain's convoluted rules of succession. Because none of Edward's older siblings had living heirs (at least not legitimate ones), his daughter took the throne by default when she was just 18 years old. Her name? Victoria.

4

Who is Anne, Anyway?

In Lucy Maud Montgomery's 1908 novel, Marilla Cuthbert and her brother Matthew live on a PEI farm. Getting on in years, the pair decides to adopt an orphan boy to help out with the chores. It's with some surprise, then, that Matthew comes back from the train station with a feisty, 11-year-old, redheaded *girl.* But it's not long before Anne—her adventures and mishaps and friends—becomes an essential part of Marilla and Matthew's lives. An immediate hit, the book made Anne an essential part of readers' lives as well. Even Mark Twain, who called her "the dearest and most lovable child in fiction since the immortal Alice [in Wonderland]," was smitten.

Montgomery went on to write a total of eight volumes in the series. In 1985, the original was made into a two-part TV movie, which was a huge success, airing first on the CBC in Canada and then on PBS in the United States. That was followed by a series that ran from 1990 to 1996. Anne has also become a stage staple thanks to theatrical productions like *Anne of Green Gables—The Musical* (a must-see at the Confederation Centre in Charlottetown) and *Anne and Gilbert* (a melodious sequel that debuted in 2005). Of course, for the millions of modern-day Anne fans, Cavendish is hallowed ground because the top Green Gables sites and experiences are all in the area. These include **Green Gables**, the **Site of Lucy Maud Montgomery's Cavendish Home, Avonlea—Village of Anne of Green Gables**, the **Lucy Maud Montgomery Birthplace**, and the **Anne of Green Gables Museum at Silver Bush.**

Prince Edward Island National Park since 1937 and hosts daily events throughout July and August such as guided tours, puppet shows, and old-fashioned games. ⊠ *8619 Rte. 6* ☎ *902/963–7874* ⊕ *www.pc.gc. ca/lhn-nhs/pe/greengables/index.aspx* ⊠ *C$7.80* ⊙ *July and Aug., daily 9–5; Sept. and Oct., Tues.–Sat. 9–5.*

Lucy Maud Montgomery Birthplace. The Lucy Maud Montgomery Birthplace is a cottage-y white house with green trim overlooking New London Harbour, 11 km (7 miles) southwest of Cavendish. The *Anne* author was born here in 1874, and the interior has been furnished with antiques to conjure up that era. Among memorabilia on display are a replica of Montgomery's wedding gown and personal scrapbooks filled with many of her poems and stories. ⊠ *Junction of Rtes. 6 and 20* ☎ *902/886–2099* ⊠ *$4* ⊙ *Late May–early Oct., daily 9–5.*

Site of Lucy Maud Montgomery's Cavendish Home. The Site of Lucy Maud Montgomery's Cavendish Home is where the writer lived with her maternal grandparents after the untimely death of her mother. Though the foundation of the house where Montgomery wrote *Anne of Green Gables* is all that remains, the homestead's fields and old apple-tree gardens are lovely. A bookstore and small museum are also on the property, which is operated by descendants of the family and is a National Historic Site of Canada. ⊠ *8521 Rte. 6* ☎ *902/963–2231* ⊕ *www.peisland. com/lmm* ⊠ *$4* ⊙ *Mid-May–mid-Oct., daily 10–5.*

WORTH NOTING

FAMILY **Ripley's Believe It or Not!.** Looking for a rainy day activity? Kids can ogle the oddities and artifacts at the local Ripley's Believe It or Not! outpost from June to September. ⊠ *8863 Rte. 6* ☏ *902/963–2242* ⊕ *www.ripleyspei.com.*

FAMILY **Sandspit.** The largest amusement park on PEI kicks things up a notch with midway rides and go-kart tracks that appeal to tots and tweens alike. Single-ride coupons and park passes are available. ⊠ *8986 Rte. 6* ☏ *877/963–3939, 902/963–3939* ⊕ *www.sandspit.com* ☉ *Mid-June–early Sept.*

FAMILY **Shining Waters Family Fun Park.** Topping the list of irresistibly cheesy amusements operating seasonally along the Route 6 tourist corridor is Shining Waters Family Fun Park. Open from mid-June to early September, it has waterslides, a kiddy splash pool, pseudo–pirate ship, petting zoo, and more. ⊠ *8885 Rte. 6* ☏ *877/963–3939, 902/963–3939* ⊕ *www.shiningwaterspei.com.*

WHERE TO EAT

$$ ✕ **Café on the Clyde at Prince Edward Island Preserve Company.** One of
CANADIAN the best spots on the Island to stop for a bite, this café has wonderful desserts and an extensive tea list. The dining room, with a soaring ceiling and two walls of windows looking over the Clyde River, opens for breakfast, lunch, and dinner. Everything served is noted for freshness—even the ice cream is homemade. Particularly praiseworthy items include the savory potato pie with maple-bacon cream and not-too-sweet raspberry cream cheese pie. A popular shop sells gourmet products and preserves made on-site. $ *Average main: C$17* ⊠ *2841 New Glasgow Rd., off Rte. 13, New Glasgow* ☏ *902/964–4300, 800/565–5267* ⊕ *preservecompany.com* ☉ *Closed mid-Oct.–late May.*

$$$ ✕ **New Glasgow Lobster Suppers.** Established in 1958, New Glasgow Lob-
SEAFOOD ster Suppers brings fresh lobster direct from a pound on the premises
FAMILY to your plate. Scallops, roast beef, salmon, chicken, haddock, ham,
Fodor's Choice even a vegetarian dish are other choices if you've already had your fill
★ of crustaceans. All come with fresh rolls, steamed mussels, seafood chowder, salads, homemade desserts, and beverages. Whew. Bar service is available, as is a separate children's menu. The bustling dining area can seat up to 500 guests at one time, and it often fills up. But because turnover is fast, there isn't usually a long wait. $ *Average main: C$27* ⊠ *604 Rte. 258, off Rte. 13, New Glasgow* ☏ *902/964–2870* ⊕ *www. peilobstersuppers.com* ☉ *No lunch. Closed mid-Oct.–late May.*

WHERE TO STAY

Accommodations in the Cavendish area are often booked a year in advance for July and most of August. If you're late in planning, don't despair—hotels in Charlottetown and elsewhere in the central region are still within easy driving distance of "Anne's Land."

For expanded hotel reviews, visit Fodors.com.

$ ⌂ **Bay Vista Motel and Cottage.** This straightforward, spotlessly clean
FAMILY motel has real family appeal. **Pros:** friendly staff; picnic area with shared-use barbecues; free Wi-Fi; laundry facilities. **Cons:** looks like a motel inside and out. $ *Rooms from: C$115* ⊠ *9517 Rte. 6* ☏ *902/963–2225, 800/846–0601* ⊕ *www.bayvista.ca* ➷ *31 rooms, 2 suites, 1 cottage* ☉ *Closed late Sept.–early June* ⦿ *Breakfast.*

THE CONFEDERATION TRAIL

In the 1980s, new life was given to the ground once covered by the Prince Edward Island Railway, when the abandoned track was converted into a recreational route dubbed the Confederation Trail. Gorgeous, well groomed, and generally flat, its 357 km (222 miles) are ideal for hiking and, above all, biking. Serious cyclists can race through it in 17 hours. But most pedal pushers opt for a more leisurely pace that allows them to stop and smell the lupines. If you're short on time, rent a bike from any cycle shop and just do a single section. Plum-color access gates are near roadways at many points, and food and lodging are available at villages along the way. Tourism PEI (🌐 *www.tourismpei.com*) provides details on rental locations and touring tips, plus a free "Confederation Trail Cycling Guide" that includes maps and itinerary highlights. Just a heads-up: helmets are compulsory in PEI for drivers and passengers, regardless of age.

$$ FAMILY 🏨 **Cavendish Country Inn and Cottages.** The family atmosphere of this 9-acre cottage complex is a big draw for some folks; there are several playgrounds on-site, as well as a pair of pools, fire pits, and outdoor games (complimentary movies help on rainy days). **Pros:** choice of accommodations for the budget-conscious; free Wi-Fi; laundry facilities. **Cons:** no a/c; dated decor; if you want a quieter holiday, this isn't the place. [$] *Rooms from: C$150* ✉ *8405 Cavendish Rd., Rte. 6* ☎ *902/963–2181, 800/454–4853* 🌐 *www.cavendishpei.com* 🛏 *11 rooms, 35 cottages* 🕓 *Closed late Oct.–mid-May* 🍴 *No meals.*

$$ B&B/INN 🏨 **Kindred Spirits Country Inn and Cottages.** Named in a nod to Anne, this lovely 6-acre property is just a short walk from Green Gables. **Pros:** helpful staff; National Park passes provided; free Wi-Fi; laundry facilities. **Cons:** decor a bit twee for some tastes; breakfast not included in cottage rates. [$] *Rooms from: C$170* ✉ *Memory La. off Rte. 6* ☎ *902/963–2434, 800/461–1755* 🌐 *www.kindredspirits.ca* 🛏 *25 rooms, 20 cottages* 🕓 *Closed late Oct.–mid-May* 🍴 *Breakfast.*

SPORTS AND THE OUTDOORS

GOLF **Andersons Creek Golf Club.** The 18-hole, par-72 Andersons Creek Golf Club, just southwest of Cavendish, was designed by Graham Cooke. Proud of the game's Scottish roots, the championship course employs its own bagpiper. ✉ *68 Rte. 240, Stanley Bridge* ☎ *902/886–2222, 866/886–4422* 🌐 *www.andersonscreek.com.*

Eagles Glenn Golf Course. Graham Cooke was the designer behind the par-72 Eagles Glenn Golf Course, which has 18 walkable holes, in a stunning setting. This championship course, along with its practice facility and club house, is open May through October. ✉ *374 Eagles Glenn Blvd., Rte. 6* ☎ *902/963–3600, 866/963–3600* 🌐 *www.eaglesglenn.com.*

Glasgow Hills Resort and Golf Club. The 18-hole, par-72 Glasgow Hills Resort and Golf Club, about five minutes southeast of Cavendish, wins high praise for its challenging Les Furber–designed layout and killer clubhouse views. ✉ *98 Glasgow Hills Dr., New Glasgow* ☎ *866/621–2200* 🌐 *www.glasgowhills.com.*

Green Gables Golf Course. This classic Stanley Thompson–designed course was restored by Thomas McBroom in 2007. The result reflects many of Thompson's original features. With great views and ocean breezes tickling your shot, it's a good choice for both aspiring and avid golfers. The clubhouse lounge serves refreshments and light meals. The 18-hole, par-72 course opens for play May through October. ⊠ *8727 Rte. 6* ☎ *902/963–4653, 888/870–5454* ⊕ *www.greengablesgolf.com.*

Inn at the Pier. Inn at the Pier lets you splash out in rented kayaks or Jet Skis. Parasailing rides and deep-sea fishing trips can also be arranged. ⊠ *9796 Rte. 6* ☎ *902/886–3126, 877/886–7437* ⊕ *www.innatthepier. com/watersports.*

MALPEQUE

Malpeque is 32 km (20 miles) west of Cavendish.

There are two good reasons why motorists make the drive to Malpeque. Some do it to cram in one last Anne shrine—specifically Silver Bush at Park Corner. Others continue westward to stuff themselves full of oysters. Named for the bay from which many are drawn, the Malpeque variety has had a huge cachet since earning the "best in show" title at the 1900 Paris World's Fair. Eating them is a time-honored tradition. The same goes for harvesting them: traditional methods are still employed (tongs are used, not dredgers) despite the fact that Prince Edward Island sells about 300,000 tons of oysters annually.

GETTING HERE AND AROUND
Malpeque is best accessed—and appreciated—by car. To reach it, veer off Route 6 at New London onto Route 20.

EN ROUTE Just north of Darnley (on Route 20, about halfway between Park Corner and Malpeque) lies a long beach with a number of sandstone caves at the end. Darnley Beach does not have developed facilities and is often almost entirely deserted except for the seabirds—so it's perfect for those seeking a "castaway" experience.

EXPLORING
FAMILY **Anne of Green Gables Museum at Silver Bush.** The Anne of Green Gables Museum at Silver Bush was once home to Lucy Maud Montgomery's aunt and uncle. The writer also lived here for a time and was married in the parlor in 1911—in fact, that room serves as a wedding venue for modern-day couples. Inside the house, which is still owned by Montgomery descendants, are mementos such as photographs and a quilt Montgomery worked on. The site includes a gift shop jam-packed with licensed Anne of Green Gables goodies, and there is a Matthew Cuthbert look-alike on hand to take visitors on buggy rides around the pastoral 110-acre property. Trip lengths vary with rates starting at $5. ⊠ *4542 Rte. 20, Park Corner* ☎ *902/886–2884, 800/665–2663* ⊕ *www.annemuseum.com* ⊠ *$5* ☉ *May and Oct., daily 11–4; June and Sept., daily 10–4; July and Aug., daily 9–5; off-season by appointment.*

Cabot Beach Provincial Park. In addition to a popular campground, 360-acre Cabot Beach Provincial Park has fine day-use facilities—particularly for families. In summer, the sandy beach is supervised, plus there's a playground and children's programming. Naturalist-led walks are also available. ✉ *449 King St., Rte. 20, Malpeque* ☎ *902/836–8945, 877/445–4938* 🎟 *Free for day use* ⏲ *June–mid Sept., daily dawn–dusk.*

St. Mary's Church. Built in 1902 by Island architect W. H. Harris, this church hosts performances by visiting artists from mid-June to mid-September as part of the Indian River Festival of Music. The church has very good acoustics plus a beautiful pastoral setting, and the concerts here are often broadcast nationally by the Canadian Broadcasting Corporation. ✉ *Rte. 104, 1374 Hamilton Rd., 6 km (3.5 miles) south of Malpeque, Indian River* ☎ *902/836–4933, 866/856–3733* 🌐 *www.indianriverfestival.com* 🎟 *$10–$45.*

WHERE TO EAT AND STAY

For expanded hotel reviews, visit Fodors.com.

$$ SEAFOOD 🍴 **Malpeque Oyster Barn.** If it's oysters you're after, here's where to get 'em! You'll be hard pressed to find fresher bivalves; after all, you can see their beds right outside the window of this casual wharf-side eatery. Nor will you find plumper, sweeter ones. Oysters can be prepared several ways, but purists should just order a dozen unadorned (with a cold beer as an accompaniment), then slurp away. Chowder, steamed mussels, lobster rolls, and similar fare appear on the menu as well, and there is a retail outlet in case you want to take some seafood home. [$] *Average main: C$18* ✉ *Malpeque Wharf Rd., Rte. 20, Malpeque* ☎ *902/836–3999* ⏲ *Sept.–June.*

$$ B&B/INN 🏨 **Noble House.** Staying at this cheery yellow heritage farmhouse with its welcoming front porch and gingerbread trim, you might feel like you have stepped into a Norman Rockwell painting—save for the fact that, back in the day, guests wouldn't have been able to book into well-equipped rooms that pair period charm with contemporary amenities like Jacuzzi tubs, cable TV, and high-speed Internet. **Pros:** close to Cabot Beach and Indian River Festival concerts; off-season rates available mid-September to mid-June. **Cons:** no a/c; resident pets may not appeal to those with allergies. [$] *Rooms from: C$155* ✉ *187 Taylor Rd., RR #1, Malpeque* ☎ *902/836–4380* 🌐 *www.bbcanada.com/5051.html* 🛏 *3 rooms* 🍽 *Breakfast.*

SPORTS AND THE OUTDOORS

Dale's Deep Sea Adventures. Daily fishing trips leave from Malpeque Harbour (beside Cabot Beach Provincial Park) from July to early September. The $45 price includes all equipment, and Dale will clean what you catch. ✉ *Rte. 20, Malpeque* ☎ *902/836–3393* 🌐 *www.kata.pe.ca/attract/dalesdeepsea.*

Malpeque Bay Kayak Tours. Malpeque is a French corruption of the Mi'Kmaq word for "big water." You can go out and explore it in summer with Malpeque Bay Kayak Tours. Informative, half-day interpretive trips cost $55. The company also rents kayaks, stand-up paddleboards, and—for on-shore adventures—bicycles. ✉ *Rte. 20, Malpeque* ☎ *902/836–3784, 866/582–3383* 🌐 *www.peikayak.ca.*

A Bridge Too Far?

Gephyrophobiacs (people with an extreme fear of bridges) had best avoid the Confederation Bridge. Linking Borden-Carleton to Cape Jourimain, New Brunswick, it is the longest in the world spanning ice-covered water. But for anyone else intent on driving to or from PEI, the so-called fixed link is the way to go. Even if you're merely passing by while doing the Central Coastal circuit, this 13-km (8-mile) engineering marvel is worth a look. To construct it, massive concrete pillars—each 65 feet across and 180 feet high—were sunk into waters more than 110 feet deep. The cost? A cool billion.

First-time traversers invariably want to stop on the bridge itself to take a picture. Don't—it's illegal. You must maintain a speed of 80 kph (50 mph). The best angles are from the Prince Edward Island side anyway. For an up-close perspective, pull into Gateway Village at the foot of the bridge. In addition to a 3-acre park where you can take in the bridge view, it has a plethora of souvenir shops where you can buy postcards of said view.

4

VICTORIA

22 km (14 miles) east of Borden-Carleton.

Cross country from the Green Gables Shore is the Red Sands Shore where charming, understated villages await. The jewel in this coastal crown is Victoria. Known locally as Victoria-by-the-Sea, it is, well, Victorian . . . and by the sea. It's also peaceful, lovingly preserved, and popular with artsy types who come to escape the hectic pace of modern life. Browse the shops; admire the architecture; then kick back on a nearby beach that's washed by the warm waters of Northumberland Strait.

GETTING HERE AND AROUND

Victoria—sitting just off the Trans-Canada Highway, 22 km (14 miles) east of the Confederation Bridge—is most easily reached by car. When you arrive in the village, park by the wharf and set out on foot. It's only two blocks wide and two blocks long, so you won't get lost.

WHERE TO EAT AND STAY

For expanded hotel reviews, visit Fodors.com.

$$ ✕ **Landmark Café.** This quirky, memorabilia-filled eatery has soups, sal-
CAFÉ ads, sandwiches, and a killer daily quiche. But it's the fresh seafood that really stands out. Try Eugene's Cajun-style shrimp and scallops, or go back to basics with what may be the Island's best chowder. You can count on friendly service, too. Like so many places on PEI, this one is family owned and operated—and it shows. The caveat is that the little Landmark fills up quickly, so having reservations (or patience) helps. 🟏 *Average main: C$15* ✉ *12 Main St.* ☎ *902/658–2286* ⊕ *www. landmarkcafe.ca* ☉ *Closed Oct.–May.*

$ ▥ **Orient Hotel Bed and Breakfast.** Cozy guest rooms and suites that are
B&B/INN individually decorated lend this vintage B&B a comforting grand-ma's-house vibe. **Pros:** some rooms have water views; lovely hosts; free Wi-Fi and bicycle storage. **Cons:** some rooms are small; no

air-conditioning. [$] *Rooms from: C$100* ✉ *34 Main St.* ☎ *902/658–2503, 800/565–6743* 🌐 *www.theorienthotel.com* 🛏 *4 rooms, 3 suites* 🕒 *Closed Oct.–May* 🍴 *Breakfast.*

$ B&B/INN 🏨 **Victoria Village Inn and Restaurant.** Guest rooms in this three-story Victorian—built for a sea captain in the 1880s—are basic in terms of decor, but they have lovely "bones" (note the original plank floors and tall sash windows). **Pros:** common living room with TV and board games; free Wi-Fi; open year-round. **Cons:** some rooms are small; no TVs and no air-conditioning. [$] *Rooms from: C$100* ✉ *22 Howard St.* ☎ *902/658–2483, 866/658–2483* 🌐 *www.victoriavillageinn.com* 🛏 *3 rooms, 1 suite* 🍴 *Breakfast.*

NIGHTLIFE AND THE ARTS

Victoria Playhouse. Offering a renowned professional program that celebrates Canadian theater and music, this place may only have 150 seats but it has big talent and huge heart. Between late June and mid-September, the circa-1914 venue mounts three different plays plus assorted concerts. ✉ *Howard and Main Sts.* ☎ *902/658–2025, 800/925–2025* 🌐 *www.victoriaplayhouse.com.*

SPORTS AND THE OUTDOORS

By-the-Sea Kayaking. June through September, By-the-Sea Kayaking runs paddling tours—among them ones with clam-digging included. Kayaks as well as bicycles are also available for rent. ✉ *Victoria Wharf* ☎ *902/658–2572, 877/879–2572* 🌐 *www.bytheseakayaking.ca.*

SHOPPING

Island Chocolates. A family-run chocolate factory in a 19th-century store, Island Chocolates sells sweets handmade with Belgian chocolate, fresh fruit, nuts, and liqueurs. Espresso, teas, and other decadent desserts are also available, and there is a nice deck to sit on while you munch. Willy Wonka wannabes will enjoy the chocolate-making workshops ($35) held on Wednesdays and Sundays. ✉ *7 Main St.* ☎ *902/658–2320* 🌐 *www.islandchocolates.ca* 🕒 *Closed mid-Sept.–mid-June.*

POINTS EAST COASTAL DRIVE

For 375 km (233 miles), the Points East Coastal Drive traces the shoreline of tranquil Kings County on the east end of PEI. The route passes forests, farms, fishing villages, and (in early summer, at least) fields of blue, white, pink, and purple lupines that slope down to red cliffs and blue sea. Championship golf courses are also in abundant supply. Ditto for lighthouses and long beaches; among these, Basin Head and the Greenwich section of Prince Edward Island National Park stand out. Accessible by car from other parts of the province, the Points East Coastal Drive can also be reached via ferry from Nova Scotia.

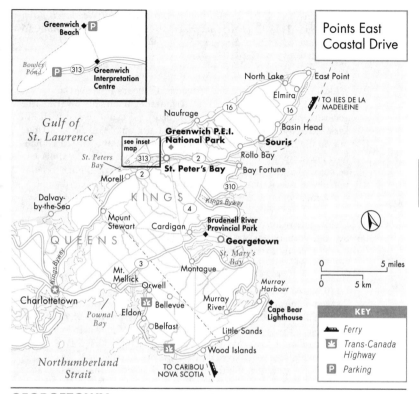

Points East
Coastal Drive

4

GEORGETOWN

52 km (32 miles) northeast of Charlottetown.

The pint-sized capital of Kings County, at the tip of a peninsula jutting into Cardigan Bay, was a major shipbuilding center in the 19th century. Thanks to its location—and early settlers' vocation—the town has both wraparound sea views and a collection of charming, Victorian-era buildings. Georgetown is also a mere five minutes from Brudenell River Provincial Park (the county's largest such facility).

GETTING HERE AND AROUND

Georgetown is a drive-to destination. To get here from Charlottetown or the Wood Islands Ferry, follow the signs for the well-marked Points East Coastal Drive. Alternately, you can save time by cutting cross-country from Charlottetown on Route 3.

EXPLORING

FAMILY **Roma at Three Rivers.** This National Historic Site, about 2 km (1 mile) outside of Georgetown, commemorates the trading post French merchant Jean Pierre Roma established here in 1732. Costumed staffers offer interpretive programs and guided tours daily (there are trails with informational panels if you'd prefer to explore independently). Heritage lunches with sustaining soup and brick-oven bread are also served on-site. ✉ *505 Roma Point Rd., off Rte. 319, Brudenell Point* ☎ *902/838–3413* 🌐 *www.roma3rivers.com* 🎫 *By donation (min.C$5 recommended)* 🕒 *Late June–late Sept., daily 10–6.*

WHERE TO EAT AND STAY

For expanded hotel reviews, visit Fodors.com.

$$$ SEAFOOD 🍴 **Clamdiggers Beach House and Restaurant.** In theory you could come here and just gorge on the waterfront restaurant's namesake bivalves (the generous platter of whole, hand-breaded fried clams served with PEI fries and house-made coleslaw is always a hit). But if you did you'd miss out on the fresh crab cakes, and the seafood stew, and the seared halibut. There are lots of options for meat lovers, too. All of the above can be enjoyed either inside the bright, beach house–style dining room or outside on a deck that sits a mere 8 meters (26 feet) from Cardigan Bay. [$] *Average main: C$24* ✉ *7 West St., Georgetown* ☎ *902/652–2466* 🌐 *www.clamdiggers.ca* 🕒 *Closed Oct.–May.*

$ B&B/INN 🏨 **Georgetown Inn.** The mantra for guests at the Georgetown Inn could be "eat, sleep, repeat" because it offers both quiet, country-style accommodations and exceptional dining experiences. **Pros:** peacefulness personified; free Wi-Fi; friendly staff. **Cons:** dinner reservations essential; sloped ceilings reduce headroom in third-floor lodgings. [$] *Rooms from: C$115* ✉ *62 Richmond St., Georgetown* ☎ *902/652–2511, 877/641–2414* 🌐 *www.peigeorgetownhistoricinn.com* 🛏 *8 rooms* 🍽 *Breakfast.*

$$$ RESORT 🏨 **Rodd Brudenell River.** If you've come to eastern PEI to golf, this resort is *the* place to stay because the provincial park that shares its name is home to (count 'em) two 18-hole championship courses. **Pros:** many rooms and all cottages have private decks or balconies; half the cottages have fireplaces and full kitchens. **Cons:** tired decor; fine dining ($$$) available late June to mid-September only. [$] *Rooms from: C$189* ✉ *86 Dewars La., Brudenell River Provincial Park, Georgetown* ☎ *902/652–2332, 800/565–7633* 🌐 *www.roddvacations.com* 🛏 *67 rooms, 32 hotel suites, 32 cottage suites* 🕒 *Closed Nov.–Apr.*

NIGHTLIFE AND THE ARTS

Kings Playhouse. In summer months, the Kings Playhouse stages lighthearted comedies on Sunday and Wednesday evenings. On Tuesdays, the venue is turned over to fiddlers and dancers during the weekly ceilidh. ✉ *65 Grafton St., Georgetown* ☎ *902/652–2053, 888/346–5666* 🌐 *www.kingsplayhouse.com.*

SPORTS AND THE OUTDOORS

Brudenell River Golf Course. The 18-hole, par-72 Brudenell River Golf Course is one of the best in the country and arguably the most popular on the Island. ✉ *82 Dewars Ln., Brudenell River Provincial Park, Georgetown* ☎ *800/235–8909* 🌐 *peisfinestgolf.com.*

Brudenell River Provincial Park. From late June to late August, the park promises interpretative programs, plus a wealth of outdoor opportunities—including boating, hiking, and supervised swimming. Two championship golf courses (Brudenell River and Dundarave) are the icing on its proverbial cake. ✉ *283 Brudenell Island Blvd., Rte. 3, Georgetown* ☎ *902/652–8966, 877/445–4938.*

Dundarave Golf Course. With its striking red sandstone bunkers, the 18-hole Dundarave Golf Course is Brundenell River's beautiful younger sister. ✉ *82 Dewars La., Brudenell River Provincial Park, Georgetown* ☎ *800/235–8909* ⊕ *peisfinestgolf.com.*

Outside Expeditions. July through early September, Outside Expeditions offers both kayak rentals and kayak tours at its Brudenell River Provincial Park location. The latter includes everything from easy 90-minute paddles ($39) appropriate for any level of expertise to six-hour seal-watching excursions ($120). Rental bikes and stand-up paddleboards are also available. ✉ *283 Brudenell Island Blvd., Rte. 3, Brudenell River Provincial Park, Georgetown* ☎ *902/902-652–2434, 800/207–3899* ⊕ *www.getoutside.com.*

Tranquility Cove Adventures. One way to experience PEI like a native is to sign up with Tranquility Cove Adventures for a few hours of clam digging or deep-sea fishing from mid-June through September. The fun, informative outings cost $98 and $55 respectively. ✉ *1 Kent St., Georgetown Wharf, Georgetown* ☎ *902/969-7184* ⊕ *www.tcapei.com.*

SOURIS

Souris is 46 km (29 miles) northeast of Georgetown.

A pretty town perched on the water, Souris (pronounced "Surrey") gives easy access to PEI's essential sights and sounds. The seascape includes harbors, lighthouses, and bountiful beaches. There's music in the salt air too, thanks to the seasonal ceilidhs and outdoor concerts Souris hosts (the events calendar at ⊕ *www.sourispei.com* has full details). You'll hear more five minutes away in Rollo Bay, which holds the PEI Bluegrass and Old Time Music Festival (☎ *902/566-2641* ⊕ *peibluegrass. tripod.com*) in early July and the Rollo Bay Fiddle Festival mid-month (☎ *902/687-2584* ⊕ *www.rollobayfiddlefest.ca*).

GETTING HERE AND AROUND
The East Connection Shuttle (☎ *902/892-6760*) carries passengers on request from Charlottetown to Souris and other Kings County communities. The fare is approximately C$85 one-way. You'll want your own vehicle, however, to properly see outlying areas. To drive yours here from Georgetown, follow signs for the Points East Coastal Drive or veer a little inland to Route 4, which merges with Route 2 near Fortune.

EXPLORING
FAMILY **Basin Head Provincial Park.** Located 13 km (8 miles) east of Souris, this park is noted for an expanse of exquisite silvery sand that's backed by grassy dunes. The beach (accessible via a boardwalk and supervised in peak months) no longer qualifies as a secret. But it's still well worth visiting—and not only because it's one of the Island's most beautiful. If you scuff your feet in the sand here, you can hear it squeak and squawk. The so-called singing sand is a rare phenomenon produced by the sand's high silicia content.

On a beach-top bluff inside the park, you'll also find the small **Basin Head Fisheries Museum** (☎ *902/357–7233,* 🌐 *www.peimuseum.com, $4, early June–Oct., daily 9–5*), which depicts the ever-changing nature of PEI's inshore fishing industry through artifacts, exhibits, and dioramas. ✉ *336 Basin Head Rd., off Rte. 16* ☎ *902/357–7230, 877/445–4938* 🌐 *www.tourismpei.com/provincial-park/basin-head.*

Myriad View Artisan Distillery. The Myriad View Artisan Distillery in Rollo Bay, just west of Souris, handcrafts spirited spirits—like Strait Vodka and Dandelion 'Shine. Complimentary tours and tastings are offered May through September and products can be purchased on-site. ✉ *1336 Rte. 2, Rollo Bay* ☎ *902/687–1281* 🌐 *www.straitshine.com.*

Prince Edward Distillery. A must-see for tippling tourists is the Prince Edward Distillery, north of Souris. Its premium vodka proves that more than french fries and chips can be made from those famous PEI potatos. Take a 25-minute tour that's followed by a tasting ($10); then buy some liquid souvenirs to take home. ✉ *9984 Rte. 16, Hermanville* ☎ *902/687–2586, 877/510–9669* 🌐 *www.princeedwarddistillery.com.*

WHERE TO EAT AND STAY

For expanded hotel reviews, visit Fodors.com.

$$ 🍴 **21 Breakwater Restaurant.** A welcome addition to a town where dining options are thin, this new eatery overlooking Colville Bay stays true to its rural roots yet presents a menu with some international élan (witness the mussels in lime butter or the herby fish-and-chips that are baked Portuguese-style). The pretty deck offers diners the option to eat *plein air*, and there's a separate children's menu. [$] *Average main: C$16* ✉ *21 Breakwater St.* ☎ *902/687–2556* ⏲ *Closed Sun.*

$ CANADIAN 🍴 **Sheltered Harbour Café & Pub.** Like its former roadside digs, Sheltered Harbour's new, larger location in Souris is frequented mostly by locals. Basic fare—picture clams, scallops, and other seafood, plus burger platters and down-home roast turkey dinners—is served in large portions at reasonable prices. If you're gearing up for a long day at the shore, fill up here first with a hearty breakfast. [$] *Average main: C$11* ✉ *41 Breakwater St.* ☎ *902/687–1997* 🌐 *www.shelteredharbour.com* ⏲ *Closed Mon., Jan.–June.*

$$$ B&B/INN 🏨 **Inn at Bay Fortune.** This 1913 inn was built by Elmer Blaney Harris (whose play *Johnny Belinda* was inspired by PEI events) and later owned by actress Colleen Dewhurst (who played Marilla in the *Anne of Green Gables* series), but today regular Joes can book into their gorgeous gabled retreat and six-room addition. **Pros:** bikes and kayaks on-site; many rooms have fireplaces and some have balconies; free Wi-Fi. **Cons:** mosquitoes can be bothersome; not directly on the beach. [$] *Rooms from: C$200* ✉ *758 Rte. 310, off Rte. 2, 10 minutes west of Souris, Bay Fortune* ☎ *902/687–3745, 888/687–3745* 🌐 *www.innatbayfortune.com* 🛏 *11 rooms, 6 suites, 2 cottages* ⏲ *Closed early Oct.–late May* 🍽 *Breakfast.*

$$$ B&B/INN 🏨 **Inn at Spry Point.** Inn at Bay Fortune's sister property hugs the end of a 110-acre peninsula a few kilometers east, so you benefit from both an attractive shoreline and a 1-km (½-mile) sandy beach. **Pros:** ocean sounds lull you to sleep; comfy beds; free Wi-Fi. **Cons:** relatively remote;

no TV; breakfast is complimentary but lunch and dinner aren't served on-site. $ *Rooms from: C$230* ⊠ *Spry Point Rd., off Rte. 310, Little Pond* ☎ *902/583–2400, 888/687–3745* ⊕ *www.innatsprypoint.com* ↪ *15 rooms* ☉ *Closed early Oct.–mid-June* ⦿ *Breakfast.*

SPORTS AND THE OUTDOORS

Paradise on the Sea Adventures. This outfitter will lead you on a seafood hunt, involving snorkeling for bar clams with a little mackerel fishing and a lot of eating thrown in for good measure. Full-day tours cost C$105. Bluefin tuna charters are also offered. ⊠ *118 Breakwater St., Souris Marina* ☎ *902/969–7727* ⊕ *peitunafishing.ca.*

ST. PETER'S BAY

28 km (17 miles) northwest of Souris.

St. Peter's Bay won the location lottery—as least that's what folks who love quiet, outdoorsy destinations think. The nearby Greenwich portion of Prince Edward Island National Park has dunes that draw beachgoers, hikers, and bird-watchers (so many avian species flock here that the park runs themed programs). If you'd rather pursue a different kind of birdie, the Links at Crowbush Cove are a short drive west. St. Peter's Bay, meanwhile, provides a sublime backdrop for cycling. On the waterside leg of the Confederation Trail between the village and Morell, you pedal past idyllic coves dotted with boats and buoys.

GETTING HERE AND AROUND

Driving independently is the best way to get here. From Souris continue along the Points East Coastal Drive or take a cross-country shortcut on Route 2. Alternately, the East Connection Shuttle (☎ *902/892–6760*) will bring you here from Charlottetown; expect to pay about C$70 one-way.

EXPLORING

The Points East Coastal area is rich for lighthouse lovers. PEI has more than 50 of the navigational aids, but many of the highlights (literally) are right here. For further details, grab a copy of the themed brochure produced by the PEI Lighthouse Society.

Fodor's Choice ★ **Greenwich (P.E.I. National Park).** The west end of the Greenwich peninsula, known for its superior beach and shifting sand dunes, was federally protected in 1998 when a 6-km (3.5-mile) section was incorporated into Prince Edward Island National Park. Because the dunes are still moving, gradually burying the nearby woods, here and there bleached tree bits thrust up through the sand like wooden skeletons. The road in ends at an interpretive center (open early June to mid-September) where displays, hands-on activities, and themed programs teach visitors about the ecology of this unique land formation. Walking trails let you follow the progression from forest to dune to beach, and include a photogenic boardwalk over Bowley Pond. Due to the delicate nature of the dune system, you're required to stay on designated paths and refrain from touching flora. Changing facilities and a picnic area can be found at the beach itself, which is supervised from late July to late August. ⊠ *Rte. 313, 6 km (4 miles) west of St. Peters*

Bay ☎ *902/672–6350* 🌐 *www.pc.gc.ca* 🎟 *C$7.80 July and Aug.; C$3.90 other times* 🕓 *Mid-May–mid-Oct., daily dawn–dusk; full services July and Aug. only.*

Panmure Head Lighthouse. Marking the entrance to Georgetown Harbour, it stands more than 18.5 meters (60 feet) tall. You can ascend to the top in July and August; then catch your breath browsing the on-site gift shop ✉ *62 Lighthouse Rd., Rte. 347, Panmure Island* ☎ *902/393–4444* 🎟 *C$4.*

Point Prim Lighthouse. Erected in 1845, Point Prim is PEI's oldest light. Daily tours run from mid-June to mid-September. ✉ *2147 Point Prim Rd., Rte. 209, 11 km (7.5 miles) west of Belfast, Belfast* ☎ *902/659–2768* 🌐 *www.pointprimlighthouse.com* 🎟 *C$3.50.*

WORD OF MOUTH

"A pastoral scene of endless green rolling hills with an ocean background soothes the soul. You see that at every turn in PEI, along with beautiful beaches and family attractions. Add some great eating places with food fresh from the ground and the ocean, quiet paths for walking and cycling, and the occasional bit of city entertainment and you have a place I want to visit year after year."

—cynthia_jane

Wood Islands Lighthouse. This lighthouse, by the ferry terminal, is open from early June to late September. Inside you'll find exhibits on local history and marine lore—like the Phantom Ship of Northumberland Strait. ✉ *173 Lighthouse Rd., Rte. 1, Wood Islands* ☎ *902/962–3110* 🌐 *www.woodislandslighthouse.com* 🎟 *C$6.*

WHERE TO EAT AND STAY

For expanded hotel reviews, visit Fodors.com.

$ SEAFOOD 🍴 **Rick's Fish 'n' Chips and Seafood House.** Rick's french fries are fresh-cut, his haddock fresh-caught—and together they make one of the Island's top fish-and-chip platters. Also on the menu at this spartan spot: deep-fried clams, scallop burgers, marinated mussels, and oysters on the half-shell. The standard burger and wings selection is available for those who aren't seafood fans, and there are homemade pizzas, too. Service is friendly, but you might have to wait a bit during peak hours for a seat inside or a picnic table outside. [$] *Average main: C$9* ✉ *5544 Rte. 2, St. Peters* ☎ *902/961–3438* 🌐 *www.ricksfishnchips.com* ✍ *Reservations not accepted* 🕓 *Closed Oct.–mid-May.*

$$$ B&B/INN 🏨 **The Inn at St. Peters.** One of the province's best-positioned inns occupies 13 idyllic acres minutes from the Greenwich park. **Pros:** attentive service; free Wi-Fi; rooms' perks include sofas, fireplaces, DVD players, and mini-refrigerators. **Cons:** relatively pricey for PEI. [$] *Rooms from: C$245* ✉ *1668 Greenwich Rd., off Rte. 313, St. Peters Bay* ☎ *902/961–2135, 800/818–0925* 🌐 *www.innatstpeters.com* 🛏 *16 suites* 🕓 *Late May–early Oct.* 🍽 *Breakfast.*

NIGHTLIFE AND THE ARTS

St. Peters Courthouse Theatre. In summer, local musical acts perform and amateur actors mount plays several times a week at the St. Peters Courthouse Theatre. Logically enough, the venue is a restored courthouse that dates back to 1874. Expect to pay C$10–C$15 per ticket. ✉ *5697 Rte. 2, St. Peters* ☎ *902/961–3636, 902/961–3004 Oct.–May* ⊕ *www. courthousetheatre.com.*

SPORTS AND THE OUTDOORS

The Links at Crowbush Cove. Talk about a sand trap. Designed by Thomas McBroom, the Links at Crowbush Cove is an 18-hole, par-72 Scottish-style course with dune views. ✉ *710 Canavoy Rd., Rte. 350, between West St. Peters and Morell, Lakeside* ☎ *800/235–8909* ⊕ *peisfinestgolf.com.*

Plover Bike Rentals. Plover Bike Rentals has cycles and accessories, including tag-along kid carriers. Open mid-May to mid-October (daily in peak season, weekdays only in shoulder season), its rates start at C$25 for a half-day. ✉ *15465 Northside Rd., junction of Rte. 2 and Rte. 16, St. Peters* ☎ *902/367–7900* ⊕ *www.stpetersbay.com/rentals.*

OFF THE
BEATEN
PATH

East Point Lighthouse. Ships from many nations have been wrecked on the reef running northeast from East Point Lighthouse. Guided tours of the towering 1867 edifice are offered mid-June through Labor Day. Books about life at sea, as well as local crafts, are available at the on-site gift shop. Because of the erosion, caution should be used when approaching the high cliffs overlooking the ocean here. ✉ *Lighthouse Rd., off Rte. 16, East Point* ☎ *902/357–2106* ⊕ *www.eastpointlighthouse.com* 🖼 *C$5.*

NORTH CAPE COASTAL DRIVE

Prince County's 350-km (217-mile) North Cape Coastal Drive winds along the west coast of the Island, through very old, very small villages that still adhere to a traditional way of life. Fishermen plowing boats through choppy seas and farmers driving tractors through fields of rich, red soil are common sights. (The potatoes the latter grow prove Anne and oysters aren't the Island's only major exports!) You may be tempted to stay on the straight, flat Route 2 most of the way. But to see all that "Up West" has to offer take Route 14 to West Point and continue north along Northumberland Strait, returning along the Gulf of St. Lawrence via Route 12.

SUMMERSIDE

71 km (44 miles) west of Charlottetown.

Summerside, the second-largest city on PEI, has an attractive waterfront with a beach and boardwalk in the west end. It has a fine collection of heritage homes, too, many of them erected around the turn of the 20th century when Summerside was the headquarters of a virtual gold rush based on silver fox ranching (a small municipal museum tells that tale). Today fishing and potato processing are more profitable enterprises— though good fish-and-chips spots are curiously in short supply. Happily, lobster is plentiful in early July during the 10-day **Summerside Lobster Carnival.**

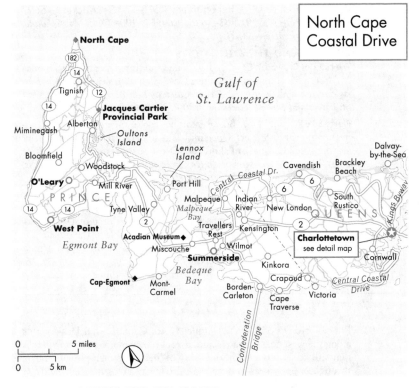

North Cape
Coastal Drive

North Cape

182

14

Tignish 12

14

Jacques Cartier
Provincial Park

Miminegash

Alberton

Oultons
Island

Gulf of
St. Lawrence

Bloomfield

Woodstock

Lennox
Island

Dalvay-
by-the-Sea

O'Leary

Mill River

Port Hill

Central Coastal Dr.

Cavendish

Brackley
Beach

PRINCE

Tyne Valley

2

Malpeque

Malpeque
Bay

Indian
River

New London

South
Rustico

6

6

14

14

West Point

Acadian Museum◆

Travellers
Rest

Kensington

QUEENS

2

Kings Byway

Egmont Bay

Miscouche

Wilmot

Summerside

Charlottetown
see detail map

Cornwall

Cap-Egmont ◆

Mont-
Carmel

Bedeque
Bay

Kinkora

Crapaud

Central Coastal
Drive

Borden-
Carleton

Cape
Traverse

Victoria

Confederation Bridge

0 ——— 5 miles

0 ——— 5 km

GETTING HERE AND AROUND

Summerside can be accessed by car, bus, or shuttle. Once here, you're best off exploring on foot. Biking is another option: the Confederation Trail passes through the city, and the former railway station makes an excellent starting point for cycling excursions.

EXPLORING

TOP ATTRACTIONS

Spinnakers' Landing. Spinnakers' Landing, the cornerstone of Summerside's waterfront revitalization project, is a collection of cheery little structures that are linked by a boardwalk and designed to evoke a seaside fishing village. The development offers a good blend of shopping, history, and entertainment; plus you can climb a lighthouse lookout for panoramic views of Bedeque Bay and the city. In summer, weather permitting, there's often free weekend entertainment (usually starting at 6 pm) on the outdoor stage over the water. ✉ *150 Harbour Dr.* ☎ *902/436–6692* ⊕ *www.spinnakerslanding.com* ⏰ *Mid-June–mid-Sept.; shops open daily 9:30–5:30 (9:30–9 in July and Aug.).*

Wyatt House Museum. Built in 1867 (the year Canada was "born"), the restored, heirloom-filled home of a prominent local family feels like a Summerside time capsule. Guided interpretive tours last about 50 minutes. The entry fee also admits you to another of the Wyatt Heritage

Properties: the Lefurgey Cultural Centre at 205 Prince Street. ✉ *85 Spring St.* ☎ *902/432–1327* 🎟 *C$10* 🕓 *July and Aug., Mon.–Sat. 10–5; June and Sept, weekdays 10–5; off-season tours by appointment.*

WORTH NOTING

Acadian Museum (*Musée Acadien*). Many descendants of PEI's first French settlers still live in the Miscouche area, 10 km (6 miles) northwest of Summerside, and the Acadian Museum commemorates their history. This National Historic Site includes a permanent exhibition on Acadian life as well as an audiovisual presentation outlining the story of Island Acadians from the early 1700s onward. A genealogical center, heritage walking trail, and themed gift shop are also on-site. ✉ *23 Main Dr. E, Rte. 2, Miscouche* ☎ *902/432–2880* 🌐 *www.museeacadien.org* 🎟 *C$4.50* 🕓 *July and Aug., daily 9:30–7; Sept.–June, weekdays 9:30–5, Sun. 1–4.*

4

Bishop's Machine Shop. Once part of a foundry complex, this old-fashioned machine shop houses an interesting collection of tools and gadgets. ✉ *101 Water St.* ☎ *902/432–1296* 🎟 *By donation* 🕓 *July and Aug., Mon.–Sat., 10–4; June and Sept. by appt.*

Eptek Art and Culture Centre. On the waterfront, Eptek Art and Culture Centre has rotating exhibits of PEI history and fine arts on display in the main gallery: the variety of the exhibitions is one of the center's hallmarks. ✉ *130 Harbour Dr.* ☎ *902/888–8373* 🌐 *www.peimuseum.com* 🎟 *By donation* 🕓 *June and Sept., weekdays 9–4, Sun. noon–4; July and Aug., Mon.–Sat. 9–5, Sun. noon–5; Oct.–May, Tues.–Fri. 10–4, Sun. noon–4.*

International Fox Museum and Hall of Fame. Housed in a 1911 armory, the International Fox Museum and Hall of Fame recounts the days when fox fur was the height of fashion—and fox "farming" was a thriving Summerside industry. ✉ *33 Summer St.* ☎ *902/432–1296* 🌐 *culture-summerside.com/international-fox-museum/* 🎟 *By donation* 🕓 *July and Aug., Mon.–Sat. 10–4; June and Sept. by appointment*

Summerside Lobster Carnival. In July Summerside celebrates the 10-day Summerside Lobster Carnival, with livestock exhibitions, harness racing, fiddling contests, and, of course, lobster suppers. ☎ *902/724–4925* 🌐 *www.summersidelobstercarnival.ca.*

WHERE TO EAT AND STAY

For expanded hotel reviews, visit Fodors.com.

$$ CANADIAN 🍴 **The Deckhouse Pub & Eatery.** Summerside hardly qualifies as a foodie haven, so your best picks are places that keep it simple. The Deckhouse delivers on that front; generous portions of traditional pub grub are supplemented by a range of tasty seafood dishes (try the chowder). Its location right at Spinnakers' Landing means that water views are an added bonus. Live music, performed on Friday and Saturday evenings, is another. The downside is that it's only open in the summer months. [$] *Average main: C$15* ✉ *150 Harbour Dr.* ☎ *902/436–0660* 🕓 *Early Sept.–mid-June.*

$ CAFÉ 🍴 **Samuel's Coffeehouse.** Along with the requisite lattes and cappuccinos, Samuel's Coffeehouse serves homemade soups, bagel sandwiches, paninis, and such inside a handsome 1895 building. Tempting baked goods are also available. [$] *Average main: C$7* ✉ *4 Queen St.* ☎ *902/724–2300* 🌐 *samuelscoffeehouse.ca.*

$ RESORT 🏨 **Clark's Sunny Isle Motel.** PEI may be one of the last places in Canada where motels are plentiful and worth recommending, and Clark's Sunny Isle is a case in point. **Pros:** well-tended 20-acre property includes a walking trail to the water; each room has a mini-refrigerator, high-definition LCD TV, and free Wi-Fi. **Cons:** free continental breakfast only served in May and October; basic decor. [$] *Rooms from: C$84* ✉ *720 Water St. E* ☎ *902/436–5665, 877/682–6824* 🌐 *www.sunnyislemotel.com* 🛏 *21 rooms* 🕓 *Closed Nov.–Apr.* 🍴 *Breakfast.*

NIGHTLIFE AND THE ARTS

College of Piping and Celtic Performing Arts of Canada. The College of Piping and Celtic Performing Arts of Canada hosts an energetic revue—featuring more than 30 bagpipers, Highland dancers, step dancers, and fiddlers—three nights a week in July and August. During the same months, mini-concerts also run three times daily, and the C$5 tab can be credited toward the price of evening show tickets. ✉ *619 Water St. E* ☎ *902/436–5377, 877/224–7473* 🌐 *www.collegeofpiping.com.*

Feast Dinner Theatre. At Feast Dinner Theatre, musical comedy is served up with a buffet meal Tuesday through Saturday, from mid-June until the end of August. ✉ *Brothers 2 Restaurant, 618 Water St.* ☎ *902/436–7674* 🌐 *www.brothers2.ca.*

Harbourfront Theatre. Sharing space with the Eptek Art and Culture Centre (but accessed through a different entrance), the 527-seat Harbourfront Theatre stages dramatic and musical productions year-round. Touring musicians routinely drop by, too. ✉ *124 Harbour Dr.* ☎ *902/888–2500, 800/708–6505* 🌐 *www.harbourfronttheatre.com.*

SPORTS AND THE OUTDOORS

PEI Segway Tours. PEI Segway Tours puts a different spin on two-wheeling fun. One- and two-hour tours ($39 and $69 respectively) depart daily from the Spinnakers' Landing Lighthouse. ✉ *150 Harbor Dr.* ☎ *902/436–1883* 🌐 *www.peisegway.com.*

Two Fish Bike Co. If you are interested in cycling the Summerside section of the Confederation Trail, Two Fish Bike Co. has all the rental equipment you'll need. It costs C$35 for a full day. ✉ *368 Water St.* ☎ *902/303–4362* 🌐 *www.peibikerentals.ca.*

O'LEARY

37 km (23 miles) northwest of Summerside.

Central Prince County is composed of a loose network of small communities set amid green fields. In the tradition of their forebears, most residents are farmers, and those in O'Leary are no exception. In terms of preferred crops, the potato is big here—literally. A giant fiberglass one that looms outside the PEI Potato Museum is the town's distinguishing feature. After eating potatoes prepared every possible way, you can work off the calories in nearby Mill River Provincial Park with golfing and other outdoor activities.

CLOSE UP

Club Hopping—Island Style

Great golf clubs are par for the course on PEI, where green gables and green fields are complemented by challenging golf greens. There are more than 30 courses, both 9- and 18-hole, open to the public from May through October, with top choices including—from west to east—Mill River, Andersons Creek, Eagles Glenn, Green Gables, Glasgow Hills, Stanhope, Fox Meadow, Links at Crowbush Cove, Brudenell River, and Dundarave. All are within a 45-minute drive of one another, which means ambitious golfers can play 27 or 36 holes a day. Contact Golf PEI (☎ *866/465-3734* 🌐 *www.golfpei.ca*) for details on courses, events, and play-and-stay packages, or to book tee times.

GETTING HERE AND AROUND

You'll need a car to explore O'Leary and the surrounding area. To get here from Summerside, follow Route 2 west; then transfer onto Route 142.

EXPLORING

PEI Potato Museum. The potato is one terrific tuber: that's the message delivered by the PEI Potato Museum. Earnest and intriguing, it has exhibits devoted to "The Amazing Potato," displays of antique potato-farming equipment, a Potato Hall of Fame, even a gift shop selling potato-themed goods. The museum also runs fun add-on tours, which include a guided spin through the facility, plus a trip out to a potato farm, a potato fudge-making lesson, and a lunch of (you guessed it) potato-based dishes. ✉ *1 Dewar La.* ☎ *902/859–2039, 800/565–3457 for tours* 🌐 *www.peipotatomuseum.com* 🎟 *$8 for museum, $49 for tours* 🕒 *Mid-May–mid-Oct., Mon.–Sat. 9–5, Sun. 1–5.*

WHERE TO STAY

For expanded hotel reviews, visit Fodors.com.

$$ RESORT 🏨 **Rodd Mill River.** Since full-blown resorts are so rare in this portion of the province, Rodd Mill River provides a welcome change of pace, with amenities that range from spa facilities and tennis courts to an indoor pool with a curling 27-meter (90-foot) waterslide. **Pros:** good base for exploring western PEI; golf packages are frequently available. **Cons:** dated decor, some public areas could be refreshed. [$] *Rooms from: C$156* ✉ *Rte. 136, 5 km (3 miles) east of O'Leary, 180 Mill River Resort Rd., Woodstock* ☎ *902/859–3555, 800/565–7633* 🌐 *www.roddvacations.com* 🛏 *80 rooms, 10 suites* 🕒 *Closed Nov.–Jan. and Apr.* 🍴 *Some meals.*

SPORTS AND THE OUTDOORS

Mill River Golf Course. The 18-hole, par-72 Mill River Golf Course is among the most scenic and challenging in eastern Canada. It has been the site of several championship tournaments, and a season of the golf reality show *The Big Break* was filmed here. Book in advance.

✉ *180 Mill River Resort Rd., off Rte. 2, Mill River Provincial Park, Woodstock* ☎ *800/235–8909* ⊕ *peisfinestgolf.com* ⊗ *Closed late Oct.– early May.*

SHOPPING

MacAusland's Woollen Mills. The MacAusland's Woollen Mills, 5 km (3 miles) west of O'Leary, has been producing its famous MacAusland 100% pure virgin wool blankets since 1932. ✉ *Rte. 2, Bloomfield* ☎ *902/859– 3005, 877/859–3005* ⊕ *www.macauslandswoollenmills.com.*

WEST POINT

24 km (15 miles) south of O'Leary.

West Point, on the southern tip of the western shore, may be tiny (there are only about 700 residents), but it is home to PEI's tallest functioning lighthouse. After admiring the handsome structure, you can stroll the 1,500-meter (4,921-foot) beachfront boardwalk; then cool off with a swim at Cedar Dunes Provincial Park.

GETTING HERE AND AROUND

Easily accessible by car from O'Leary via Rte. 14, West Point is usually viewed as a day trip. The presence of the West Point Lighthouse Inn, however, gives lighthouse-loving motorists an incentive to stay overnight.

EXPLORING

FAMILY **West Point Lighthouse Museum.** Built in 1875, lit in 1876, manned until Fodor's Choice 1963, and still operating today, the West Point Lighthouse is a certifiable ★ PEI icon. A gracefully tapered shape and eye-popping black-and-white stripes make the 21-meter (69-foot) structure very photogenic. Inside, displays and assorted artifacts relating to lighthouses province-wide make it educational too. Be sure to climb the 72 steps to the top for panoramic views. Beautiful any time of day, they are especially glorious at sunset because the lighthouse faces west. ✉ *364 Cedar Dunes Park Rd., Rte. 14* ☎ *902/859–3605, 800/764–6854* ⊕ *www.westpointlighthouse. com* ☑ *$3.50* ⊗ *Late May–early Oct., daily 9–9.*

WHERE TO STAY

For expanded hotel reviews, visit Fodors.com.

$$ 🏠 **West Point Lighthouse Inn.** Few people can say they've spent the night
B&B/INN in a lighthouse—or at least in a guest room adjacent to one—so take the opportunity when you're here. **Pros:** unique lodgings; original rooms full of character; some pets allowed. **Cons:** dearth of area dining options; books quickly; lighthouse equals bright flashing light. 🖇 *Rooms from: C$160* ✉ *364 Cedar Dunes Park Rd., Rte. 14* ☎ *902/859–3605, 800/764–6854* ⊕ *www.westpointlighthouse.com* 🛏 *13 rooms* ⊗ *Closed mid-Sept.–mid-June* ⦿ *Breakfast.*

SPORTS AND THE OUTDOORS

Cedar Dunes Provincial Park. Cedar Dunes Provincial Park, which encompasses the lighthouse site, boasts blissful beaches and supervised swimming in summer. Recreational programs—including guided walks of the park's nature trails—are also available seasonally. ✉ *265 Cedar Dunes Park Rd., Rte. 14* ☎ *902/859–8785, 877/445–4938.*

NORTH CAPE

47 km (29 miles) north of O'Leary.

Mother Nature meets modern technology at PEI's northwest tip. The Gulf of St. Lawrence and Northumberland Strait converge at North Cape's reef (the longest rock reef in North America) creating a popular hangout for seals, seabirds, and other forms of marine life. But it's the wind sweeping over the water that makes this place really stand out. Scores of windmills—some of them 80 meters (262 feet) high—dot the site. Part of the Atlantic Wind Test Site and Wind Farm, they were built to make the "Gentle Island" even greener.

GETTING HERE AND AROUND

North Cape is another drive-to destination. To reach it, take Route 14 along the Strait or Route 12 along the Gulf.

EXPLORING

North Cape Wind Energy Interpretive Centre. The North Cape Wind Energy Interpretive Centre has exhibits that explain how turbine technology channels wind power to produce "clean" electricity for Islanders. It also includes a few displays pertaining to local history and a touch tank with lobster, crabs, and starfish that kids will enjoy. (A staff member will lift one out so you can get a real feel for these aquatic creatures.) ✉ *21817 Rte. 12* ☎ *902/882–2991* 🌐 *www.northcape.ca* 🎫 *$5.70* 🕒 *July and Aug., daily 9–8; May, June, Sept., and Oct., daily 10–6.*

WHERE TO EAT AND STAY

For expanded hotel reviews, visit Fodors.com.

$$ SEAFOOD 🍴 **The Boat Shop Steak & Seafood Restaurant.** This attractive spot occupies a converted boat builder's workshop—which explains not only its waterfront location but its oversized windows and soaring ceiling. Fine, fresh seafood, not surprisingly, dominates the menu. (Time your visit right and you may be able to see fishermen unloading the catch of the day or graceful blue herons angling for their own dinner.) Traditional homemade desserts like blueberry bread pudding and sticky date cake are another highlight. Patio seating is available on fine days. [$] *Average main: C$20* ✉ *296 Rte. 152, 33 km (21 miles) south of North Cape, Northport* ☎ *902/853–4905* 🌐 *www.northportpier.ca* 🕒 *Closed mid-Sept.–early June.*

$$ SEAFOOD 🍴 **Wind & Reef Restaurant.** Dining options are few and far between in this remote corner of PEI, so it's a blessing that the airy eatery above the North Cape Wind Energy Interpretative Centre offers more than mere sustenance. The Island seafood—including oysters, mussels, and lobster—is fresh and well prepared. Service is unfailingly friendly. The restaurant's panoramic windows, providing views of the water and (at low tide) the reef, are an added bonus. [$] *Average main: C$20* ✉ *21817 Rte. 12* ☎ *902/882–3535* 🕒 *Closed Oct.–May.*

$ B&B/INN 🏨 **La Petite France B&B.** Built in the 1890s, this heritage home with its plentiful gables and pretty bay windows has a classic Island look. *joie de vivrecroque-monsieur***Pros:** attentive hosts; near a popular biking trail head; free Wi-Fi. **Cons:** two rooms share a bathroom; the largest room is in a new addition. [$] *Rooms from: C$100* ✉ *441 Church St.,*

Alberton ☎ *902/853–3975* 🌐 *www.lapetitefrance-pei.com* 🛏 *4 rooms* ⏲ *Closed Nov.–Apr.* 🍴 *Breakfast.*

$$ B&B/INN 🏨 **Northport Pier Inn.** Conveniences like air-conditioning and Wi-Fi set this spot a notch above many rural inns, but it's the view that guests really rave about. **Pros:** restaurant and marina next door; roomy kitchenette suites work well for families. **Cons:** decor is basic; during lobster season (May and June) early morning harbor traffic might disturb light sleepers. [$] *Rooms from: C$138* ✉ *298 Rte. 152, 33 km (21 miles) south of North Cape, Northport* ☎ *902/853–4520, 855/887–4520* 🌐 *www.northportpier.ca* 🛏 *12 rooms, 2 suites* ⏲ *Closed Oct.–May* 🍴 *Breakfast.*

SPORTS AND THE OUTDOORS

Black Marsh Nature Trail. One of the best ways to see North Cape's natural and manmade assets is by hiking the Black Marsh Nature Trail. The 5.5-km (3.5-mile) return path extends past tidal pools, whirring windmills, and the Cape's 1908 lighthouse to a pretty bog crossed via a boardwalk. ✉ *21817 Rte. 12.*

Jacques Cartier Provincial Park. Jacques Cartier Provincial Park, south of North Cape, was named for the famed French explorer who came ashore nearby in 1534. In July and August, you can take naturalist-led hikes on park trails or swim on the supervised Gulf of St. Lawrence beach. ✉ *16448 Rte. 12, Kildare Capes* ☎ *902/853–8632, 877/445–4938.*

Matthews Deep Sea Fishing & Ocean Adventures. Matthews Deep Sea Fishing & Ocean Adventures offers C$40 fishing trips (sometimes with bird- and whale-watching on the side) out of Northport from July to mid-September. Bay cruises and beach picnics are other options. ✉ *265 Rte. 152, Northport* ☎ *902/853–7943* 🌐 *www.matthewsdeepseafishing.ca.*

NEWFOUNDLAND AND LABRADOR

WELCOME TO NEWFOUNDLAND AND LABRADOR

TOP REASONS TO GO

★ **Appreciate the Rugged Beauty of Gros Morne National Park:** Magnificent mountains, fine hiking, sweeping vistas, quaint lighthouses, hidden fjords, and the deep blue sea are just some of the reasons people flock to this park.

★ **Meet the People:** You'll never get lost here because the people go out of their way to help visitors. These are some of the nicest, friendliest folks you're likely to meet.

★ **See the Wildlife:** Whales, puffins, caribou, and moose. Whale-watching boat tours. Bird sanctuaries and ecological reserves. Thirty-three million seabirds can't be wrong.

★ **Spot Icebergs:** Newfoundland is one of the easiest places to see these 10,000-year-old beauties of the ocean. See them from St. Anthony to St. John's.

★ **Eat Amazing Fish Dishes:** Crab cakes, seafood chowder, lobster, shrimp, and cod, cod, cod: au gratin, panfried, or in the traditional Newfoundland dish of fish and *brewis* (pronounced "bruise"), a meal of cod and hard-tack (hard bread).

1 **St John's.** The capital of Newfoundland is usually the starting point for visits to the province.

2 **Avalon Peninsula.** This picturesque region is home to about half of Newfoundland's population. Cape Spear National Historic Site is the easternmost point in North America.

3 **Eastern Newfoundland.** The Bonavista Peninsula has history and archaeological artifacts; the Burin Peninsula is more about stark landscapes. Clarenville, halfway between the two, is a good base for exploring, though not much of a destination in itself. Terra Nova was Newfoundland's first National Park.

4 **Gander and around.**
Gander is known for its airport and aviation history; it's mostly a good base for exploring fishing villages like Twillingate as well as Fogo Island, which is becoming known for its artists' studios.

5 **Western Newfoundland.** The wild and rugged Great North Peninsula is home to two UNESCO World Heritage Sites (Gros Morne National Park and L'Anse aux Meadows), and the west coast is famed for its Atlantic salmon fishing, Long Range Mountains, winter sports, and the hub of the west coast: Corner Brook.

GETTING ORIENTED

The province includes the island of Newfoundland and Labrador; the latter is on the mainland, bordering Québec. Most airlines fly in to the provincial capital of St. John's (not to be confused with the city of Saint John, in New Brunswick), on the Avalon Peninsula, making it the logical starting point for visitors to Newfoundland. Farther west is the Burin Peninsula, and to the north are the Bonavista Peninsula and Notre Dame Bay. On the west side of Newfoundland, the Northern Peninsula stretches up toward Labrador; Corner Brook is a good starting point for exploring the mountains. In Newfoundland, you'll do much of your driving on Route 1, the Trans-Canada Highway, which goes east–west from St. John's to Port aux Basques.

Updated by
Penny Phenix

Magnificent mountains, sweeping vistas, wooden houses perched on rocky sea cliffs, hidden fjords, and the deep blue sea. Newfoundland, or "the Rock" as the island is sometimes affectionately called, lures visitors with the promise of dramatic landscapes, incredible hiking and outdoor experiences, and the warmth of the people. Canada starts here, from the east, on the island of Newfoundland in the North Atlantic. Labrador, to the northwest, is on the mainland bordering Québec. Along the province's nearly 17,699 km (11,000 miles) of coastline, humpback whales feed near shore, millions of seabirds nest, and 10,000-year-old icebergs drift by fishing villages.

On the east coast of Canada, the province of Newfoundland and Labrador, as it is officially called, is a bit of a contradiction in terms: it's the youngest province—it joined the Confederation in 1949—but its European timeline stretches back to AD 1000, when Vikings made first landfall on the Great Northern Peninsula. They assembled a sod hut village at what is now L'Anse aux Meadows National Historic Site, calling their new home Vinland. They stayed less than 10 years and then disappeared into the mists of history. As early as the Vikings were, they were actually preceded by the Maritime Archaic people who lived in the region as long ago as 6,000 years. L'Anse Amour, a 7,500-year-old burial ground in southern Labrador, is the oldest-known cemetery in North America.

When explorer John Cabot arrived at Bonavista from England in 1497, he reported an ocean so full of fish they could be caught in a basket lowered over the side of a boat. Within a decade, St. John's had become a crowded harbor. Soon, fishing boats from France, England, Spain, and Portugal vied for a chance to catch Newfoundland's lucrative cod, which would shape the province's history.

At one time, 700 outports dotted Newfoundland's coast, devoted to the world's most plentiful fish. Today, only about 400 of these settlements survive. By 1992, cod had become so scarce from overfishing that the federal government called a moratorium, throwing thousands out of work. The cod have not yet returned, forcing generations of people to retrain for other industries or leave, and the fishing industry has since diversified into other species, mainly shrimp and crab. The development of one of the world's richest and largest nickel deposits at Voisey's Bay in northern Labrador, near Nain, holds hope for new prosperity, as does the growing offshore oil and gas industry.

Despite Newfoundland and Labrador's more than 50 years as a Canadian province, its people remain resolutely independent and maintain a unique language and lifestyle. E. Annie Proulx's Pulitzer Prize–winning novel *The Shipping News* (1993) brought the province to the world's attention, and Newfoundland writers such as Wayne Johnston (*The Colony of Unrequited Dreams, The Navigator of New York*), Michael Crummey (*River Thieves, Galore*), and Lisa Moore (*February*) continue to introduce international audiences to the province.

Visitors to Newfoundland find themselves straddling the centuries. Old Irish, French, and English accents and customs still exist in small towns and outports despite television and the Internet, but the cities of St. John's in the east and Corner Brook to the west are very much part of the 21st century. Wherever you travel in the province, you're sure to meet some of the warmest, wittiest people in North America. Strangers have always been welcome in Newfoundland.

PLANNING

WHEN TO GO

Seasons vary dramatically in Newfoundland and Labrador. Most tourists visit between June and September, when the bogs and meadows turn into a colorful riot of wildflowers and greenery and the province is alive with festivals, fairs, and concerts. Daytime temperatures hover between 20°C (68°F) and 25°C (77°F). In spring, icebergs float down from the north, and in late spring, whales arrive to hunt for food along the coast, staying until August. Fall is also popular: the weather is usually fine, hills and meadows are loaded with berries, and the woods are alive with moose, caribou, partridge, and rabbits. In winter, ski hills attract downhillers and snowboarders, forest trails hum with snowmobiles, and cross-country ski trails in various communities and provincial and national parks are oases of quiet.

This rocky island perched on the edge of the cold North Atlantic Ocean might be the only place in the world where you can have four seasons in one day and where the saying "If you don't like the weather out your front door, go look out the back door" rings true. St. John's is a weather champion in Canada. It holds the distinctions of being the foggiest, snowiest, wettest, windiest, and cloudiest of all major Canadian cities.

When packing for the trip, remember it's all about layers in Newfoundland. You'll need shorts and short-sleeve shirts for when it's warm and sunny. Pack a fleece jacket or a hoodie in case the temperature drops. A windbreaker might be the most important piece of clothing; you'll need it to keep the chill out when the winds are up. To top off your ensemble, you'll need rain gear, like a slicker. Throw in a pair of gloves, too. May the sun shine on your holidays, but if it doesn't, you'll be dressed for it.

FESTIVALS

Newfoundlanders love a party, and from the cities to the smallest towns they celebrate their history and unique culture with festivals and events throughout the summer. "Soirees" and "times"—big parties and small parties—offer a combination of traditional music, recitation, comedy, and local food.

Buskers Festival. For three days in early August magicians, circus artists, comedians, and other street performers entertain on three stages in downtown St. John's. ⊠ *St. John's* ⊕ *downtownstjohns.com.*

Fish, Fun & Folk Festival. During the last full week in July, the town of Twillingate hosts this festival where you can enjoy fish cooked every possible way while listening to folk musicians perform. ⊠ *Twillingate* ⊕ *www.fishfunfolkfestival.com.*

George Street Festival. George Street in St. John's is famous for its live-music pubs, and for six days at the beginning of August the entire street becomes an open-air party, with big-name bands taking the main stage. ⊠ *St. John's* ⊕ *www.georgestreetlive.ca.*

Gros Morne Summer Music. Live music is presented from mid-July to late August at venues that include locations in Corner Brook, Woody Point, and Norris Point. The main focus is classical, but you might also hear jazz or traditional sounds by international artists. ☎ *709/639–7293* ⊕ *www.gmsm.ca.*

Gros Morne Theatre Festival. First-rate summer entertainment is provided from May through mid-September by this festival in Cow Head, at the northern end of Gros Morne National Park. Most productions are dramas, though there are some comedies and musical performances based on local stories and songs. ⊕ *www.theatrenewfoundland.com.*

Iceberg Festival. St. Anthony celebrates the annual iceberg migration with 10 days of boat trips, cultural activities, iceberg-wine tastings, and other events. ⊠ *St. Anthony* ⊕ *theicebergfestival.ca.*

Miawpukek Annual Pow Wow. In early July the Miawpukek First Nations celebrate their "traditions, culture, and spiritualism" with dancing, singing, drumming, art and crafts displays, feasts, and ceremonies. ⊠ *Conne River* ⊕ *www.mfngov.ca.*

Newfoundland and Labrador Folk Festival. The province's biggest traditional-music festival takes place in St. John's in early August. ☎ *709/576–8508, 866/576–8508* ⊕ *www.nlfolk.com.*

Stephenville Theatre Festival. Held in July and August, this festival presents mostly musicals, some new, some familiar. ⊠ *129 Montana Ave., Stephenville* ☎ *709/643–4982, 709/643–4553 box office* ⊕ *www.stephenvilletheatrefestival.com.*

Trails, Tales & Tunes. In mid-May picturesque Norris Point, in the Gros Morne National Park, hosts events that include concerts and kitchen parties, art exhibits, storytelling, culinary events, guided walks and hikes, and trail riding on bicycles. ⊠ *Norris Point* ⊕ *www.trailstalestunes.ca.*

PLANNING YOUR TIME

Many visitors to Newfoundland and Labrador arrive in St. John's, the provincial capital and a great place get a sense of the regions centuries of history. Spend a few days touring downtown, including Water Street, the oldest street in North America. Less than an hour's drive south of St. John's you can see whales, icebergs, and huge seabird colonies at Bay Bulls. You can also take a side trip to Cape St. Mary's, one of the best places in the world to see gannets up close—you can walk to within 10 meters of their nests!

Those with more time often drive across the island. Twillingate, 444 km (276 miles) from St. John's (a five-hour journey), is an especially scenic destination, and Fogo Island is gaining acclaim as for its unique artists' studios and artists-in-residence programs. The ferry to Fogo Island takes about an hour each way. With a visually stunning coastline and settlements such as picturesque Trinity, you could enjoy a marvelous three-day interlude touring the Bonavista Peninsula in eastern Newfoundland.

Allow at least three days to appreciate western Newfoundland's dramatic mountains and rugged shoreline. One fly-and-drive option is through Deer Lake airport. An alternative would be to take the car ferry from Nova Scotia, which arrives in Port aux Basques, on the southern coast. Corner Brook, this region's main city, makes a fine base for exploring the picturesque Bay of Islands. You won't want to miss the glacier-carved fjords and magnificent mountains at Gros Morne National Park, a UNESCO World Heritage Site. Take a boat tour, go hiking or sea kayaking, and visit an interpretation center to learn more about what you've seen. Many people spend at least a couple of days here—if you're a hiker, you could easily spend a week exploring the multitude of trails. Farther up the Peninsula at L'Anse aux Meadows National Historic Park, another UNESCO World Heritage Site, you can visit the only authenticated Viking settlement in North America.

> **ZONE DEFENSE**
>
> Newfoundland has its own time zone—Newfoundland Standard Time—a half hour ahead of the rest of Labrador and the other Atlantic provinces. When time zones were established, the Dominion of Newfoundland was an independent country with its own time zone. The government tried to make the province conform to Atlantic Standard Time in 1963, 14 years after it became part of Canada, but the measure was quashed by public outcry, so Newfoundlanders remain the first people in Canada to welcome the New Year.

GETTING HERE AND AROUND

AIR TRAVEL

The province's main airport is St. John's International Airport, and another international airport is at Gander, farther west. Domestic airports are at Stephenville, Deer Lake, and St. Anthony. ■TIP→ **If you plan to fly in and rent a car, book as far in advance as possible; rental vehicles are in limited supply, and in peak season they go quickly.**

BOAT AND FERRY TRAVEL

Marine Atlantic operates a car ferry from North Sydney, Nova Scotia, to Port aux Basques, Newfoundland (crossing time is six hours), and, from June through September, from North Sydney to Argentia (crossing time from 12 to 14 hours).

Contacts Marine Atlantic ☎ 902/794–5254, 800/341–7981 ⊕ www.marine-atlantic.ca.

CAR TRAVEL

Newfoundland has an excellent highway system, and most secondary roads are paved, but some are winding, which will require you to moderate your speed. Bear this in mind when deciding how far to travel in a day. Also remember that summer is road-mending season and speed limits are reduced to 50 kph (31 mph) in construction areas. With time out for a meal, it takes about 11 hours to drive along the Trans-Canada Highway (Route 1) from Port aux Basques to St. John's. The trip from Corner Brook to St. Anthony, at the northernmost tip of the island, takes about five hours. Driving from St. John's to Grand Bank, on the Burin Peninsula, takes about four hours. If you're heading for the southern coast of the Avalon Peninsula, pick up Route 10 just south of St. John's and follow it toward Trepassey.

■TIP➡ More than 110,000 moose live in Newfoundland, and most highways run through their habitats. If possible, avoid night driving, as most moose-related vehicle accidents (about 700 a year) happen between dusk and dawn. Watch for vehicles that slow down or stop on the side of the road: the driver may have spotted a moose. Pay attention to the caution signs indicating where moose cross frequently.

In winter, some highways close during and after severe snowstorms. Year-round, the Department of Transportation's website has up-to-date information on road conditions and closures. The website of the province's tourism board has a handy Scenic Touring Routes page listing itineraries—categorized by region and then by areas of interest—all over Newfoundland.

Contacts **Department of Transportation & Works** ☎ *709/635–4100 Western Region, 709/292–4300 in Grand Falls–Windsor and Central Newfoundland, 709/466–4132 Eastern Region, 709/729–2382 Avalon Region, 709/533–2801 Terra Nova National Park* ⊕ *www.roads.gov.nl.ca.* **Scenic Touring Routes** ⊕ *www.newfoundlandlabrador.com/placestogo/scenictouringroutes.*

OUTDOOR ACTIVITIES AND TOURS

Fishing the unpolluted waters of Newfoundland is an angler's dream, and many outfitters are available to make the dream come true. The website of the Newfoundland & Labrador Outfitters Association contains a list of members, with contact details and online links.

Many provincial parks and both of the national parks have hiking and nature trails, and coastal and forest trails radiate out from most small communities. The East Coast Trail, on the Avalon Peninsula, covers 540 km (336 miles) of coastline, passing through two dozen communities and along cliff tops that provide ideal lookouts for icebergs and seabirds. The East Coast Trail Association has details. Gros Morne Adventures runs guided day and multiday hikes in Gros Morne National Park.

Local operators offer sea kayaking, ocean diving, canoeing, wildlife viewing, mountain biking, white-water rafting, hiking, and interpretive walks in summer. In winter, snowmobiling expeditions are popular. In spring and early summer, a favored activity is iceberg watching. Maxxim Vacations in St. John's organizes packaged adventure and cultural tours. McCarthy's Party in St. John's arranges guided bus tours, learning vacations, and charter services. The luxurious Tucka-more Lodge, in Main Brook, on the Great Northern Peninsula, is a base for winter snowmobile excursions and for viewing caribou, seabird colonies, whales, and icebergs. Wildland Tours in St. John's operates weeklong guided tours to view wildlife and visit historically and culturally significant sites.

Outfitters East Coast Trail Association ☎ *709/738–4453*
⊕ *www.eastcoasttrail.ca.* **Gros Morne Adventures** ☎ *709/458–2722*
⊕ *www.grosmorneadventures.com.* **Newfoundland & Labrador Outfitters Association** ☎ *709/639–5926, 866/470–6562* ⊕ *www.nloa.ca.*

Tour Operators Maxxim Vacations ☎ *709/754–6666, 800/567–6666*
⊕ *www.maxximvacations.com.* **McCarthy's Party** ☎ *709/579–4444,*
888/660–6060 ⊕ *www.mccarthysparty.com.* **Newfoundland and Labrador Tourism** ☎ *709/729–2830, 800/563–6353* ⊕ *www.newfoundlandlabrador.com/ thingstodo.* **Tuckamore Lodge** ☎ *709/865–6361, 888/865–6361*
⊕ *www.tuckamorelodge.com/tour-packages-cat.htm.* **Wildland Tours**
☎ *709/722–3123, 888/615–8279* ⊕ *www.wildlands.com.*

RESTAURANTS

People who know a little about eating out in Newfoundland will tell you all about cod, the staple for centuries and still a firm favorite. More sophisticated diners, though, will make sure you're aware of the top-quality ingredients grown here and the world-class chefs who have revolutionized the St. John's culinary scene: Chris Chafe at Magnum and Stein's, Jeremy Charles at Raymond's, Todd Perrin (a past final-ist in the Canada's Top Chef contest) at the Chef's Inn B&B, and the inspirational Roary MacPherson, the executive chef at the Sheraton Hotel and an enthusiastic promoter of island cuisine. Towns outside St. John's might lack its concentration of excellence, but talented chefs live and work beyond the capital, many of them committed to using fresh local and organic ingredients. Some unique dining experiences unfold as well, among them the Great Viking Feast, staged by Light-keepers Seafood Restaurant in St. Anthony, at which diners tuck in to moose stew in a sod hut.

Unlike elsewhere in Atlantic Canada, you'll find moose meat on res-taurant menus here. It's very lean, very tasty, somewhat similar to beef, and certainly worth ordering if you get the chance.

Prices in the reviews are the average cost of a main course at dinner or, if dinner is not served, at lunch.

HOTELS

Most hotels in Newfoundland are casual, friendly, and with the kind of amenities, standards, and rooms styles you'd expect elsewhere in North America. Wi-Fi is widespread, and you won't have to search hard to find a room with a view. Recognizable brands, Sheraton, Mar-riott, Ramada, and Holiday Inn among them, do business in St. John's, in historic buildings or standard modern structures. Lodgings outside the city are more varied. You'll find motels, timber-frame lodges, inns comprised of one or more heritage houses, and all kinds of rental properties. There's also the unique Fogo Island Inn, a cutting-edge architectural marvel atop a rugged cliff on a remote offshore island (⇨ *See Change Islands and Fogo Islands, below*).

Prices in the reviews are the lowest cost of a standard double room in high season. For expanded hotel reviews, facilities, and current deals, visit Fodors.com.

Contacts Newfoundland & Labrador Tourism ☎ *709/729–2830, 800/563–6353* ⊕ *www.newfoundlandlabrador.com/wheretostay.*

ST. JOHN'S, NEWFOUNDLAND

Old meets new in the province's capital (metro-area population a little more than 200,000), with modern office buildings surrounded by heritage shops and colorful row houses. St. John's mixes English and Irish influences, Victorian architecture and modern convenience, and traditional music and rock and roll into a heady brew. The arts scene is lively, but overall the city moves at a relaxed pace.

For centuries, Newfoundland was the largest supplier of salt cod in the world, and St. John's Harbour was the center of the trade. As early as 1627, the merchants of Water Street—then known as the Lower Path—were doing a thriving business buying fish, selling goods, and supplying alcohol to soldiers and sailors.

The city of St. John's encircles St. John's Harbour, expanding past the hilly, narrow streets of old St. John's. Downtown has the most history and character. The city was destroyed by fire many times, and much of its row housing was erected following the last major blaze, known as the Great Fire, in 1892. Heritage houses on Waterford Bridge Road, winding west from the harbor along the Waterford River, and on Rennies Mill Road and Circular Road to the east (backing onto Bannerman Park) were originally the homes of sea captains and merchants. Duckworth Street and Water Street, which run parallel to the harbor, are where to find the shops and restaurants, but take a trip down the narrow lanes and paths as you get farther from the harbor to get the best sense of the city's history.

Signal Hill in the east end, with its distinctive Cabot Tower, is the city's most prominent landmark. The hill rises up from the Narrows, the appropriately named entrance to St. John's Harbour. Standing at Cape Spear and looking back towards St. John's you will see Cabot Tower (and Signal Hill) but you'll scarcely believe there's a city there, because the entrance to the port is narrow and almost hidden.

GETTING HERE AND AROUND

The only direct way to get to St. John's is to fly in (⇨ *See Planning*) or arrive by cruise ship. The nearest ferry route from the mainland docks at Argentia, about an hour's drive from the city. From the airport, it's a 15-minute taxi ride to downtown. There are no public transit routes or private shuttle buses between the downtown and the airport. Cabs are exclusively operated by City Wide Taxi, with fixed rates to certain hotels, ranging from C$12.50 to C$30. For other destinations, fares are metered, with a C$5 basic charge.

NEWFOUNDLAND ITINERARIES

IF YOU HAVE 3 DAYS

Pick either the west or east coast of Newfoundland. On the west coast, after arriving by overnight ferry at **Port aux Basques,** detour off the Trans-Canada Highway (Route 1) through St. Andrews to explore the **Codroy Valley** and **Cape Anguille** before continuing north to **Gros Morne National Park.** Drive over the Tablelands to **Trout River,** then stay overnight in Woody Point. On Day 2, hike up **Gros Morne Mountain** or take the shorter, easier walk to **Western Brook Pond** for the boat trip. Spend the night at Rocky Harbour or Norris Point. On Day 3, drive to **Corner Brook** and explore the scenic **Bay of Islands,** then make your way back to Port aux Basques for the overnight ferry.

On the east coast, the ferry docks at Argentia. Explore the Avalon Peninsula, beginning in **St. John's,** where you should spend your first night. The next day visit **Cape Spear,** the most easterly point in North America, and the **Witless Bay Ecological Reserve,** where you can see whales, seabirds, and icebergs. Drive through **Placentia** and spend Day 3 at **Cape St. Mary's Ecological Reserve,** known for its gannets and dramatic coastal scenery. The drive from St. John's to Cape St. Mary's takes about 2½ hours each way. If you don't want to drive back to St. John's the same day, stay overnight at the Bird Island Resort in St. Brides.

IF YOU HAVE 6 DAYS

Spend your first day in **St. John's** and stay overnight there. The next day, visit **Cape Spear** and the **Witless Bay Ecological Reserve.** Spend the night in **Placentia,** and on Day 3 visit **Cape St. Mary's Ecological Reserve** before heading to picturesque **Trinity.** Explore the town and stay overnight there. On Day 4 take the Rugged Beauty Boat Tour, then drive up to **Cape Bonavista.** Stay there, and on Day 5 visit **Terra Nova National Park.** Spend the night at **Clarenville,** getting up on the sixth day to explore the picturesque villages on Conception Bay's north shore, including **Cupids** and **Harbour Grace,** before returning to St. Johns.

IF YOU HAVE 9 DAYS

After spending your first day and night in **St. John's,** head for the Bonavista Peninsula and picturesque **Trinity** on Day 2. Spend the night in Trinity, then continue north to visit **Terra Nova National Park** and continue to **Twillingate,** renowned for icebergs and whale-watching. Next, head for **Gros Morne National Park** for Days 4 and 5, then return east on Day 6 to spend the night in **Clarenville.** On Day 7 drive down to **Cape St. Mary's Ecological Reserve.** Overnight in **Placentia,** then head for **Cape Spear** and the **Witless Bay Ecological Reserve,** before spending the final day back in St John's.

5

Metrobus Transit operates more than 20 bus routes (C$2.25 per ride) in St. John's. The transit company also operates a "step-on, step-off" trolley (seasonal) serving downtown, major hotels, and visitor attractions for a flat fee of C$5 per day for individuals or C$20 for a family. You can also purchase a single trolley trip for C$2.25. For rides within the city, taxis carry a flag rate of C$3.25, with increments of C$0.25 for every 0.166 km and C$0.25 for each 30 seconds of stop time. Downtown is walkable, but you'll want a car to explore farther afield because public-transit options are few (or none).

Taxi and Bus Contacts City Wide Taxi ☎ *709/722-7777*
⊕ *www.citywidetaxi.ca.* **Metrobus Transit** ☎ *709/722-9400*
⊕ *www.metrobustransit.ca.*

TOURS

An alternative to driving yourself around is to take a sightseeing jaunt with a local guide, who can offer an insider's perspective. One specialized walking tour is the St. John's Haunted Hikes, in which the Reverend Thomas Wickam Jarvis, played by actor Dale Jarvis, leads several different and very popular walking tours of city sites linked to hauntings and urban legends; on summer evenings, the tours (C$10–C$15) begin at the west entrance of the Anglican Cathedral on Church Hill at 9:30 pm. Look for the crowd of people standing in the dark. The ToursByLocals website has links to accredited St. John's guides who lead walking and other tours for cruise-ship passengers and other visitors.

Contacts St. John's Haunted Hike ☎ *709/685-3444* ⊕ *www.hauntedhike.com.*
ToursByLocals ⊕ *www.toursbylocals.com/St-Johns-Newfoundland-Tours.*

VISITOR INFORMATION

Visitor Information Centre ✉ *348 Water St.* ☎ *709/570-2038*
⊕ *www.stjohns.ca* ⏲ *Oct.–Apr., weekdays 9–4:30; May–early Oct., daily 9–4.*

EXPLORING

TOP ATTRACTIONS

Basilica Cathedral of St. John the Baptist. Consecrated in 1855 after 14 years of construction, this Romanesque-style Roman Catholic cathedral holds a commanding position above Military Road, overlooking the older section of the city and the harbor. The Irish sculptor John Hogan carved the sanctuary's centerpiece, *The Dead Christ,* out of Carrara marble in the mid-19th century. Also note the many stained-glass windows, side altars, and statuary. A museum with vestments and religious objects is next door in the Episcopal Library of the Bishop's Palace. ✉ *200 Military Rd.* ☎ *709/754-2170* ⊕ *www.thebasilica.ca* 🏛 *Museum C$2* ⏲ *Museum mid-June–Aug., Mon.–Sat. 10–4, Sun. 1–4; Sept.–mid-June, daily 8–3.*

Colonial Building. This columned building erected between 1847 and 1850 was the seat of the Newfoundland government from the 1850s until 1960, when the legislature moved to its current home, the Confederation Building, in the north end of the city. The limestone for the building was imported from Cork, Ireland. It is closed for renovations until 2015. ✉ *Military and Bannerman Rds.*

St. John's

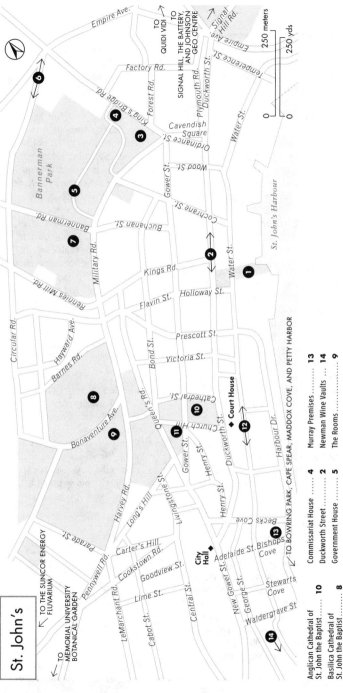

TO THE SUNCOR ENERGY FLUVARIUM →

TO MEMORIAL UNIVERSITY BOTANICAL GARDEN →

Empire Ave.

TO QUIDI VIDI →

TO SIGNAL HILL, THE BATTERY, AND JOHNSON GEO CENTRE →

Signal Hill Rd.

Empire Ave.

Temperence St.

Factory Rd.

Forest Rd.

King's Bridge Rd.

Plymouth Rd.

Duckworth St.

Cavendish Square

Ordnance St.

Water St.

250 meters

250 yds

Bannerman Park

Gower St.

Wood St.

Cochrane St.

Buchanan St.

Military Rd.

Bannerman Rd.

Rennies Mill Rd.

Kings Rd.

Water St.

St. John's Harbour

Circular Rd.

Hayward Ave.

Flavin St.

Holloway St.

Barnes Rd.

Prescott St.

Victoria St.

Bond St.

♦ Court House

Queen's Rd.

Cathedral St.

Church Hill

Duckworth St.

Harbour Dr.

Bonaventure Ave.

Gower St.

Henry St.

Harvey Rd.

Long's Hill

Livingstone St.

Henry St.

Becks Cove

TO BOWRING PARK, CAPE SPEAR, MADDOX COVE, AND PETTY HARBOR

Parade St.

Carter's Hill

Cookstown Rd.

Pennywell Rd.

Goodview St.

♦ City Hall

Adelaide St.

Bishops Cove

LeMarchant Rd.

Lime St.

Central St.

New Gower St.

George St.

Stewarts Cove

Cabot St.

Waldergrave St.

Anglican Cathedral of St. John the Baptist...... **10**

Basilica Cathedral of St. John the Baptist...... **8**

Circular Road **6**

Colonial Building **7**

Commissariat House **4**

Duckworth Street **2**

Government House **5**

Gower Street United Church **6**

Harbourside Park **1**

Murray Premises **13**

Newman Wine Vaults ... **14**

The Rooms **9**

St. Thomas Anglican (Old Garrison) Church **3**

Water Street **12**

CLOSE UP

A Good Walk

Begin at **Harbourside Park,** on Water Street, where Gilbert planted the staff of England and claimed Newfoundland. When you leave, turn left on Water Street, right on Holloway Street, and then right onto **Duckworth Street.** The east end of this street is full of crafts shops and other stores. After walking east for five blocks, turn left onto Ordnance Street, one of several streets that recall St. John's military past. Cross Military Road to **St. Thomas Anglican (Old Garrison) Church,** built in the 1830s as a place of worship for British soldiers.

Turn left as you leave St. Thomas and walk up King's Bridge Road. The first building on the left is **Commissariat House,** an officer's house restored to the style of the 1830s and one of the oldest buildings in the province. North of here, a shady lane on the left leads to the gardens of **Government House**. **Circular Road,** where the business elite moved after a fire destroyed much of the town in 1846, is north of Government House. Back on Military Road, cross Bannerman Road to the **Colonial Building,** the former seat of government. Walk west on Military Road. The Roman Catholic **Basilica Cathedral of St. John the Baptist** is on the right. Cross Bonaventure Avenue as you leave the Basilica to visit the **Rooms,** the province's one-stop shop for arts, culture, and heritage and the home of the provincial archives, museum, and art gallery. As you leave the Rooms, turn right down Garrison Hill, so named because it once led to Fort Townshend, now home to fire and police stations. Cross Queen's Road and walk down Cathedral Street to Gower Street and the Gothic Revival

Anglican Cathedral of St. John the Baptist. The entrance is on the west side on Church Hill. **Gower Street United Church** is directly across from the cathedral on the west side of Church Hill. Continue to the bottom of Church Hill to see the Duckworth Street **Court House,** with its four different turrets. Exit the courthouse and turn right; then go down the long set of steps to **Water Street,** one of the oldest commercial streets in North America. Turn right to reach the **Murray Premises,** a restored mercantile complex with boutiques, a science center, offices, restaurants, a coffee bar, and a wine cellar. Exit Murray Premises, take a left on Water Street, and continue to the last stop, the historic **Newman Wine Vaults,** at 436 Water Street, just west of the corner of Water and Springdale streets, where for 200 years the legendary Newman's Port has been aged.

Downtown St. John's is compact but hilly. The walk avoids major uphill climbs. Expect to spend up to a full day visiting these sights, depending on how long you stay at each location and the number of stores you take in along the way. This walk is best undertaken from spring to fall.

Duckworth Street. Once called the Upper Path, this has been the "second street" of St. John's for centuries, Water Street being the main street. Stretching from the bottom of Signal Hill in the east to near City Hall in the west, Duckworth Street has restaurants, bars, antiques and crafts shops, and lawyers' offices. A few blocks east of City Hall, the late 19th-century **Court House** has an eccentric appearance: each of its four turrets is in a different style. It's not possible to go inside, but the exterior is worth a look. Lanes and stairways from Duckworth Street lead down to Water Street and up to higher elevations.

Government House. The lieutenant governor—the queen's representative in Newfoundland—lives at Government House. Myth has it that the moat around the 1830s structure was designed to keep out snakes, though Newfoundland is among the few regions in the world (along with Ireland and New Zealand) where there are none. The house, so the story goes, was originally intended for the governor of a warmer colony, where serpents might be a problem, but in fact the moat was designed to allow more light into the basement rooms. House tours (free), usually on Tuesday and Thursday mornings, can be arranged by appointment; the marvelous garden you can explore on your own. ⊠ *50 Military Rd.* ☎ *709/729–4494, 709/729–4738 tour reservations* ⊕ *www.govhouse.nl.ca* ☐ *Free* ☉ *Weekdays 8:30–5, garden open daily.*

Gower Street United Church. This 1896 church has a redbrick facade, green turrets, 50 stained-glass windows, and a massive pipe organ. The church itself is on a sort of concrete island, the lone occupant of a small tract of land surrounded by four streets. ⊠ *99 Queen's Rd., at Gower St.* ☎ *709/753–7286* ⊕ *www.gowerunited.ca* ☐ *Free* ☉ *Sept.– May, weekdays 9–4; July and Aug., weekdays 9–noon; tours available year-round during office hrs or by appointment.*

Harbourside Park. This is the spot where Sir Humphrey Gilbert claimed Newfoundland for Britain in 1583, much to the amusement of the French, Spanish, and Portuguese fishermen in port at the time. They thought him a fool, a judgment borne out a few days later when he ran his ship aground and drowned. The small park is a good vantage point to watch the boats come and go and a nice spot to stop for a rest, but the larger parks have more green space and are better for picnics. The area down here where the harbor-pilot boat is docked is known as the Queen's Wharf. ⊠ *Water St. E.*

FAMILY

Fodor'sChoice

★

The Rooms. An eye-catching feature of the cityscape since 2005, this lively space celebrating the arts and cultures of Newfoundland and Labrador has a design inspired by traditional "fishing rooms," shacks by the waterside where fishing families would process their catch. Exhibits in the Connections Gallery, the Husky Energy Gallery, and the Elinor Gill Ratcliffe Gallery explore the region's cultural heritage, while the Provincial Art Gallery presents contemporary and older works from the permanent art collection and mounts temporary art exhibitions. Displays at the Provincial Archives include historical photos and documents. The Rooms hosts many family-oriented activities— summer events for children include art and crafts, Inuit games, nature projects, and creative workshops. The facility's observation deck has awe-inspiring views over St. John's. ■TIP→ **The fourth-floor Rooms Café serves tasty seafood dishes; on Wednesday nights it's open for dinner and is a great place to watch the sun set or the fog creep in over the city.** ⊠ 9 *Bonaventure Ave.* ☎ *709/757–8000* ⊕ *www.therooms.ca* ⊠ *C$7.50 (includes guided tours), free Wed. 6–9 pm and first Sat. of each month (Nov.–May); special exhibits extra* ⊙ *June–mid-Oct., Mon.–Sat. 10–5 (to 9 Wed.), Sun. noon–5; mid-Oct.–May, Tues.–Sat. 10–5 (to 9 Wed.), Sun. noon–5. Archives closed Sun. yr-round. Guided tours Wed., Fri., and Sun. at 2 and 3:30.*

Water Street. Originally called the Lower Path, Water Street has been the site of businesses since at least the 1620s. The older architecture resembles that of seaports in southwest England and Ireland.

WORTH NOTING

Anglican Cathedral of St. John the Baptist. Designed by Sir George Gilbert Scott, this fine example of Gothic Revival architecture was erected in the mid-1800s, with major additions in the 1880s, but it had to be rebuilt after the 1892 fire. Free lunchtime organ recitals take place on Wednesday afternoons at 1:15. In July and August, you can slip into the crypt for a cup of tea and homemade scones, tea biscuits, and cookies (C$8). Tea service, run by the women of the parish, operates from 2:30 to 4:30 pm on weekdays except Wednesdays, when it starts at 2. ⊠ *16 Church Hill* ☎ *709/726–5677* ⊕ *www.stjohnsanglicancathedral. org* ⊠ *Free* ⊙ *Tours July and Aug., weekdays 10–noon and 2–4, Sat. 10–noon, Sun. after 11 am service.*

Circular Road. After the devastating fire of 1846, the business elite of St. John's moved to Circular Road. The street contains some very fine Victorian houses and shade trees.

Commissariat House. The residence and office of the British garrison's supply officer in the 1830s has been restored to reflect that era. Interpreters sometimes dress in period costume, and the videos and labels are engaging and informative. ⊠ *King's Bridge Rd. and Military Rd.* ☎ *709/729–6730, 709/729–0592* ⊕ *www.seethesites.ca* ⊠ *C$6* ⊙ *Mid-May–mid-Oct., daily 9:30–5:30.*

Murray Premises. One of the oldest buildings in St. John's, the Murray Premises dates from only 1846; the last (and worst) time the city was destroyed by fire was in 1892. This restored warehouse now houses shops, offices, and restaurants. ⊠ *5 Beck's Cove.*

Newman Wine Vaults. This 200-year-old building with stone barrel vaults is where the renowned Newman's Port was aged. According to legend, a Newman and Company vessel loaded with port wine was driven off course by pirates in 1679 and forced to winter in St. John's. Upon its return to London, the cargo was found to have improved in flavor, and after that the company continued to send port to be matured in these wine cellars. The vaults are now a historic site, with guides who interpret the province's long and unique association with port. ■TIP→ **You can purchase more than 20 different brands of port on-site.** ⊠ *436 Water St.* ☎ *709/739–7870* ⊕ *www.seethesights.ca* ⊠ *C$6* ⊙ *July and Aug., Wed.–Sun. 1–5, or by appointment.*

St. Thomas Anglican (Old Garrison) Church. English soldiers used to worship at this black-wood church, the oldest in the city, during the early and mid-1800s. ⊠ *8 Military Rd.* ☎ *709/576–6632, 709/576-6641* ⊕ *www.st-thomaschurch.com* 🔁 *Free* ⊙ *June–Aug., weekdays 9–2; call for off-season hrs.*

GREATER ST. JOHN'S

A number of must-see attractions can be found a short drive from the downtown core of St. John's. When you stand with your back to the ocean at Cape Spear National Historic Site—the easternmost point of North America—the entire population of the continent is to your west. Cape Spear and the historic property with Hill National Historic Site are excellent places to see icebergs and whales in spring and early summer. Plan to spend a full day exploring Greater St. John's to give yourself some time at each spot.

EXPLORING

TOP ATTRACTIONS

The Battery. This tiny fishing village perches precariously at the base of steep cliffs between Signal Hill and St. John's Harbour. Narrow lanes snake around the houses, so it's a good place to get out of the car and walk.

Fodor's Choice ★ **Cape Spear National Historic Site.** At the easternmost point of land on the continent, songbirds begin chirping in the dim light of dawn, and whales (in early summer) feed directly below the cliffs, providing an unforgettable start to the day. From April through July, you might see icebergs floating by. **Cape Spear Lighthouse,** Newfoundland's oldest such beacon, has been lovingly restored to its original form and furnishings. There's a small, well-stocked souvenir kiosk in the parking lot for those who don't want to or are unable to climb the path to the main gift shop. ⊠ *Cape Spear Dr./Rte. 11* ☎ *709/772–5367* ⊕ *www.pc.gc.ca* 🔁 *Site free, lighthouse C$3.90, C$6.30 for same-day access with Signal Hill* ⊙ *Site daily dawn–dusk; lighthouse mid-May–mid-June, Wed.–Sun. 9–5; mid-June–Sept., daily 10–6; Sept.–mid-Oct., Wed.–Sun. 9–5. Visitor Interpretation Centre and Heritage Gift Shop mid-May–late June, daily 10–6; late June–mid-Oct, daily 8:30–8:30.*

FAMILY **Johnson GEO CENTRE.** Built deep into the earth with only the entryway protruding aboveground, this geological shrine is literally embedded in Signal Hill, itself made up of 550-million-year-old rocks. (The province's oldest rocks date back 3.87 billion years.) There are exhibits about how Earth was made and on the solar system. "The Titanic Story," a multimedia exhibition includes fascinating artifacts and video footage from the wreck site. Step on an oil platform in the ExxonMobil Oil & Gas Gallery and learn about how oil and gas are formed. Kids 5 and up love the 3D Earth and Space Theatre. ⊠ *175 Signal Hill Rd.* ☎ *709/737–7880, 866/868–7625* ⊕ *www.geocentre.ca* 🔁 *$12* ⊙ *Daily 9:30–5.*

Memorial University Botanical Garden. The gardens at this 110-acre natural area include rock gardens, a Newfoundland historic-plants bed, peat and woodland beds, an alpine house, a medicinal garden, a native plant collection, a vegetable garden, a crevice garden, a shade garden, a dried-flower garden, and a compost demonstration garden. There are also five pleasant walking trails. You can see scores of rhododendron varieties here, as well as many kinds of butterflies and the rare hummingbird hawkmoth. Guided walks are available with advance notice for groups of 10 or more. ■ TIP→ **The nature trails and gardens are closed to the public from November through April, but the gift shop remains open.** ✉ *C.A. Pippy Park, 306 Mt. Scio Rd.* ☎ *709/864–8590* 🌐 *www.mun.ca/botgarden* *C$7, C$5 off-season* ⏲ *May–Oct., daily 10–5; Nov., daily 10–4.*

NEED A BREAK?

The Garden Cafe. On the grounds of the Memorial University Botanical Garden, this café has many teas to choose from, along with fresh-baked scones, soups, salads, and sandwiches. The menu changes daily and includes vegetarian and vegan choices. ■ TIP→ **The restaurant will pack a picnic lunch for you.** ✉ ***306 Mt. Scio Rd.*** ☎ ***709/753–0173*** ⏲ ***May–Oct., daily 10:30–4:30.***

Quidi Vidi. No one knows the origin of the name of this fishing village, one of the oldest parts of St. John's. The town is best explored on foot, as the roads are narrow and make driving difficult. The inlet, known as the Gut, is a traditional outport in the middle of a modern city, making it a contrast worth seeing. It's also a good place to catch sea-run brown trout in the spring. ✥ *Take first right off Kings Bridge Rd. (at Sheraton Hotel Newfoundland) onto Forest Rd., which heads into village.*

FAMILY
Fodor's Choice ★

Signal Hill National Historic Site. In spite of its height, Signal Hill was difficult to defend: throughout the 1600s and 1700s it changed hands with every attacking French, English, and Dutch force. In 1762, this was the site of the final battle between the French and British in the Seven Years' War (usually called the French and Indian War in the United States). A wooden palisade encircles the summit of the hill, indicating the boundaries of the old fortifications. In July and August, cadets in 19th-century British uniform perform a tattoo of military drills and music. En route to the hill is the **Visitor Center,** with exhibits describing the history of St. John's. There's also a café.

Cabot Tower, at the top of Signal Hill, was constructed in 1897 to commemorate the 400th anniversary of explorer John Cabot's landing in Newfoundland. In 1901 Guglielmo Marconi received the first transatlantic-wire transmission near here, and today you can visit the Marconi exhibit on the top floor. The drive to the tower along Signal Hill Road affords fine harbor, ocean, and city views, as does the tower itself. Walking trails take you to the base of the hill and closer to the ocean. Dress warmly; it's always windy. ✉ *Signal Hill Rd.* ☎ *709/772–5367* 🌐 *www.pc.gc.ca* *Site and tower free; visitor center C$3.90, C$6.30 to include same-day visit to Cape Spear* ⏲ *Site daily dawn–dusk. Cabot Tower mid-May–Aug., daily 10–8; Sept.–Nov., daily 10–6. Visitor center mid-May–mid-Oct., daily 10–6; mid-Oct.–mid-May, weekdays 8:30–4:30.*

WORTH NOTING

Bowring Park. An expansive Victorian park west of downtown, Bowring resembles famous city parks of London, after which it was modeled. Dotting the grounds are ponds and rustic bridges; the statue of Peter Pan just inside the east gate was cast from the same mold as the one in Kensington

Park in London. The wealthy Bowring family, which made its money in trade and shipping, donated the park, which in 2014 celebrates its 100th anniversary. ✉ *305 Waterford Bridge Rd.* ☎ *709/364–1531* 🌐 *www.bowringpark.com* 🎟 *Free* ⏱ *Daily dawn–dusk.*

Maddox Cove and Petty Harbour. These neighboring fishing villages lie along the coast between Cape Spear and Route 10. The wharves and sturdy seaside sheds, especially those in Petty Harbour, hearken back to a time not long ago when the fishery was paramount in the economy and lives of the residents. An arts and heritage festival takes place here in late August. 🌐 *www.pettyharbourmaddoxcove.ca.*

> **DAY AT THE RACES**
>
> If you're in St. John's on the first Wednesday of August, head down to Quidi Vidi Lake and experience the Royal St. John's Regatta (🌐 *www.stjohnsregatta.org*), the oldest continuous sporting event in North America. The fixed-seat rowing shells hold a crew of six and the coxswain. The town shuts down for this garden party/reunion/sporting event that draws more than 30,000 people. If the winds are high, the holiday's off, shops open, and the regatta moves to Thursday, Friday, or whenever the weather clears.

FAMILY **The Suncor Energy Fluvarium.** A tributary of a nearby river was diverted here so visitors could see the life that inhabits it from under water. See into the river through nine large windows at the only public facility of its kind in North America. In season you can observe spawning brown and brook trout in their natural habitat. There are also tanks housing other fish and amphibians, and exhibits relating to the aquatic environment. ■ TIP→ **Feeding time for the fish, frogs, and eels is at 4 pm daily.** ✉ *C.A. Pippy Park, 5 Nagle's Pl.* ☎ *709/754–3474* 🌐 *fluvarium.ca* 🎟 *C$7* ⏱ *July and Aug., weekdays 9–5, weekends 10–5; Sept.–June, weekdays 9–4:30, weekends noon–4:30.*

WHERE TO EAT

$$$$ CANADIAN 🍴 **Bacalao.** The four rooms of this old house in St. John's have been converted into cozy dining rooms, all with fireplaces. Bacalao, pronounced "back-allow," is salt cod, a staple for Newfoundlanders and the Mediterraneans who came to fish here, and a variation of it is featured every night. Other nouvelle-Newfoundland options include moose and caribou dishes, and mussels in Quidi Vidi Iceberg beer. Everything, including desserts, is prepared from scratch, using local ingredients wherever possible. Even the washroom soap is locally made. ■ TIP→ **In addition to global wines, you can also sample local vintages here, among them the distinctive Lady of the Woods, made from birch sap.** [$] *Average main: C$32* ✉ *65 LeMerchant Rd.* ☎ *709/579–6565* 🌐 *www.bacalaocuisine.ca* ✍ *Reservations essential* ⏱ *Closed Mon.*

$$$$ SEAFOOD Fodor's Choice ★ 🍴 **Bianca.** This restaurant is known for its fine wines and its unique process for selecting them: patrons walk over to the racks and choose the one they want; the prices are on the bottles. If you don't know what you want, Bianca herself might be around to help. Her spacious restaurant, painted purple and brightened by a few well-chosen pieces of art,

fronts Water Street, and panels of sheer purple hang in the windows, providing privacy by day and offering an attractive, hazily surrealistic view of passers-by at night. Seafood is the specialty—blackened salmon with chorizo, shrimp, and mussels or lobster tagliatelle with a cognac-and-lobster reduction, for instance—but the menu always includes other options, such as rack of lamb with Moroccan spices and caramelized onions. $ *Average main: C$32* ✉ *171 Water St.* ☎ *709/726–9016* ⊕ *biancas.net* ⌖ *Reservations essential* ☾ *No lunch weekends.*

$$$$
AMERICAN

✕ **Blue on Water.** The trendy restaurant in the hotel of the same name makes organic synonymous with simple, tasty, and fresh. The menu specials include whatever is best at the market or from local farmers, fishermen, and other suppliers, and the herbs and vegetables are homegrown. A hint of strawberry and maple enlivens the foie gras; the flavors of potato-bacon pavé, rapini, blue cheese, and partridgeberry jus lend the elk medallion a soupçon of sophistication; and lobster might find itself jazzed up with goat cheese, scallion, truffle oil, and asparagus. The extensive wine list includes vintages from around the world. Soups, salads, sandwiches, and flatbreads are the lunch-menu staples, along with a few mains, such as pan-seared salmon and steak frites. $ *Average main: C$35* ✉ *319 Water St.* ☎ *709/754–2583, 877/431–2583* ⊕ *www.blueonwater.com.*

$$
SEAFOOD
FAMILY
Fodor's Choice
★

✕ **Ches's.** Since the 1950s, this restaurant has been serving fish-and-chips to a steady stream of customers from noon until after midnight. They come from all walks of life to sample the flaky fish fried in a batter whose recipe the owner keeps under lock and key (literally). Ches's decor is strictly laminated tabletops and plastic chairs, but the fish is hot, fresh, and delicious. From the sea you can also order shrimp, scallops, and salmon with chips, and there are wings, fried chicken, and burgers for those seeking a meal with origins on terra firma. Additional locations do business in St. John's and beyond. $ *Average main: C$13* ✉ *9 Freshwater Rd.* ☎ *709/722–4083* ✉ *655 Topsail Rd.* ☎ *709/368–9473* ✉ *29–33 Commonwealth Ave.* ☎ *709/364–6837* ✉ *8 Highland Dr.* ☎ *709/738–5022* ✉ *207 Kenmount Rd.* ☎ *709/576–7659* ⊕ *www.chessfishandchips.ca.*

$$
INDIAN
Fodor's Choice
★

✕ **India Gate.** Consistency and quality in service and food make this one of the busiest restaurants in St. John's for evening dining, takeout, or the popular weekday lunch buffet. Lunch turnover is high, and the buffet steamers are continuously replenished with steaming "rice pillow," mulligatawny soup, lamb, and vegetable korma. In the evening, you can choose a five-course dinner for two (C$50–C$60) or share options such as butter chicken or the exceptional prawns nilgiri (prawns in a rich sauce of spices and cashews). The presence of the owner on-site and the (recorded) sitar music add to the inviting atmosphere. Regulars have been known to spend an entire meal speculating on the secret behind the perfect rice. $ *Average main: C$20* ✉ *286 Duckworth St., Downtown* ☎ *709/753–6006* ⊕ *www.indiagatenl.com* ☾ *No lunch weekends; no buffet weekends.*

$
PAKISTANI

✕ **International Flavours.** This restaurant at the foot of Signal Hill may not look like much, but the home-style curry dishes are delicious and a good value. It's easy to miss, as there's almost no storefront, but worth persevering to find. There's only street parking, so the best idea is to combine your visit with a stroll through the Battery or reward yourself after a hike up to Cabot Tower. $ *Average main: C$11* ⊠ *4 Quidi Vidi Rd.* ☎ *709/738–4636* ⊗ *Closed Sun. and Mon.*

$ | CHINESE | ⨉**Magic Wok Eatery.** The chefs at the family-run Magic Wok prepare traditional Hong Kong–style Chinese dishes, along with "North American–style" ones for the less adventurous. The popular eatery occupies a spacious structure with containers of flowers and shrubs brightening the sidewalk out front. Prices are very reasonable, making this a magnet for couples, families, and groups of office workers or friends, who come for the beef, duck, and seafood, often flambéed at the table. Try Har Gaw (like a light, crispy won ton) for a crunchy starter, and almond chicken Gai Ding in a "bird's nest." ■ TIP→ **This is one of the few downtown restaurants that offer free parking.** $ *Average main: C$12* ⊠ *402–408 Water St.* ☎ *709/753–6907* ⊕ *www.magicwok.ca* ⊗ *Closed Mon. No lunch weekends.*

$$$$ | INTERNATIONAL | ⨉**Magnum & Steins.** Exposed stone walls, original paintings, and chic furnishings make for a serene dining atmosphere in this restored heritage building right downtown. The short but classic dinner menu features succulent steaks, pan-roasted chicken, Atlantic salmon, and New Zealand lamb, with interesting accompaniments such as garlic-fried spinach; bacon, onion, and rapini potato hash; and organic radish sprouts. The lunch and bar menus display some international influences (Asian duck-confit nachos and crispy coconut prawns, for example), and there's a lengthy international wine list with a decent selection available by the glass. $ *Average main: C$34* ⊠ *329 Duckworth St.* ☎ *709/576–6500* ⊕ *www.magnumandsteins.ca* ⊗ *No lunch weekends.*

$$$$ | CANADIAN | ⨉**Oppidan.** The Sheraton Hotel's main restaurant strikes just the right balance between formality and a relaxed atmosphere. The room's key elements are its big windows, which overlook the harbor, and a modern constant-flame fireplace. The friendly, unobtrusive service distracts neither from the views nor the expertly prepared cuisine. Regional specialties made from locally sourced ingredients include cod tongues with scrunchions (small pieces of deep-fried pork). Big chunks of scallops, lobster, and fish add heft to the delicious seafood chowder, and steaks are juicy and tender. In addition to lunch and dinner, an excellent hot and cold breakfast buffet is laid out until 1 pm. $ *Average main: C$35* ⊠ *115 Cavendish Sq.* ☎ *709/726–4980* ⊕ *www.starwoodhotels.com/sheraton.*

$ | VEGETARIAN | ⨉**The Sprout.** Local artists and craftspeople display their creations on the walls here, but works of art also arrive at your table in the form of salads, soups (including the Me-So Hungry Miso Soup), sandwiches (a house favorite being the Bravocado—cheese, avocado, and sprouts on homemade whole-grain bread), tapas, and mains. For excellent vegetarian fare, try the falafel platter, the black-bean burrito, or the organic-vegetable stir-fry, or perhaps a burger of the tofu, lentil, or chickpea ("Give Peas a Chance") variety. The vegan chocolate mousse is decadent. Gluten free options are also available. $ *Average main: C$12* ⊠ *364 Duckworth St.* ☎ *709/579–5485* ⊕ *thesproutrestaurant. com* ⌲ *Reservations not accepted* ⊗ *Closed Sun. No lunch Sat. No brunch weekdays.*

5

$$ ✕ **Sun Sushi and Bubble Tea Restaurant.** This is the place to enjoy squid
JAPANESE if you love it or to try it for the first time: the panfried delicacy with a
light soy glaze is tender and will forever separate the words "rubbery"
and "squid" in your mind. The dark wood tables are overlaid with
glass tops, and everything is spotless and bright. Most tables front
Duckworth Street, but you can also sit by the open kitchen area and
observe the concentration of cooks preparing an eel roll. Sun Sushi is
especially popular with a young crowd that enjoys the affordable tuna,
octopus, and battered shrimp with a sweet tempura sauce. $ *Aver-
age main: C$15* ⊠ *186 Duckworth St., Downtown* ☎ *709/726–8688*
⊕ *www.sunsushi.com* ⊘ *Closed Sun.*

WHERE TO STAY

For expanded hotel reviews, visit Fodors.com.

$$ ▦ **Blue on Water.** A modern boutique hotel with stylish contemporary
HOTEL interiors, Blue on Water is the essence of its name—a calm, comfortable
lodging with a whiff of the Atlantic when the windows are open. **Pros:**
spacious bathrooms; great restaurant and bar downstairs. **Cons:** street
noise can sometimes be heard in rooms. $ *Rooms from: C$159* ⊠ *319
Water St.* ☎ *709/754–2583* ⊕ *www.blueonwater.com* ⟿ *7 rooms, 5
suites* ⦿ *No meals.*

$$$ ▦ **Courtyard St. John's Newfoundland.** Business travelers in particular like
HOTEL this attractive Marriott property at the east end of Duckworth Street.
Pros: large and elegantly furnished business center; library; complimen-
tary valet parking; bar has harbor view. **Cons:** restaurant (Smitty's) is a
franchise; working harbor can be noisy. $ *Rooms from: C$219* ⊠ *131
Duckworth St.* ☎ *709/722–6636, 866/727–6636* ⊕ *www.marriott.com*
⟿ *81 rooms, 5 suites* ⦿ *No meals.*

$$$ ▦ **Delta St. John's.** Half the rooms in this popular downtown convention
HOTEL hotel overlook the harbor; the others look out on the city but tend to
be quieter (rooms facing New Gower Street have the best views). **Pros:**
floor-to-ceiling windows in guest rooms; fitness center includes squash
courts; next door to the Mile One entertainment complex. **Cons:** not
in the prettiest part of downtown. $ *Rooms from: C$229* ⊠ *120 New
Gower St.* ☎ *709/739–6404, 888/793–3582* ⊕ *www.deltahotels.com*
⟿ *373 rooms, 30 suites* ⦿ *Breakfast.*

$$$ ▦ **Holiday Inn—Government Centre.** The surprise at this chain hotel is the
HOTEL location: walking trails from the property meander around small lakes
and link with the Grand Concourse hiking trails. **Pros:** outdoor heated
pool in summer; easy to find from airport or Trans-Canada Highway.
Cons: a long walk to downtown; rooms are fine but nothing special;
restaurant is part of a chain. $ *Rooms from: C$199* ⊠ *180 Portugal
Cove Rd.* ☎ *709/722–0506, 800/933–0506* ⊕ *www.holidayinn.com*
⟿ *177 rooms, 75 suites* ⦿ *Breakfast.*

$$$ ▦ **Murray Premises Hotel.** Part of the Murray Premises National His-
HOTEL toric Site *(⇨ See Exploring)* near St. John's harborfront, this delight-
ful boutique hotel pairs original architectural features with luxurious
contemporary furnishings and amenities. **Pros:** historic character;
short (though sometimes uphill) walk to downtown attractions. **Cons:**

CLOSE UP

Newfoundland English

Newfoundland English is full of words brought to this rocky land centuries ago, when the fertile fishing grounds lured sailors and settlers from Britain, Ireland, and elsewhere in Europe. In the late 16th century, colonies of people came here with very little—except, of course, for their culture, in the form of words, sayings, and songs. Because of the province's relative isolation, accents remained strong and the archaic words took root to become Newfoundland English.

Listen for Newfoundland expressions for everything, from food terms like *scoff* (a big meal), *touton* (fried bread dough), and *duff* (a pudding), to words to describe the fickle weather, such as *leeward* (a threatening storm), *airsome* (bracing cold), and *mauzy* (foggy and damp). "The sun is splitting the rocks!" is something you might hear on a fine day.

A plethora of terms relate to the fishing industry: a *flake* is where you dry fish, perhaps after having caught them on your *dory*, a small rowboat. A *bedlamer* is a young seal. And, of course, there are plenty of words to describe all manner of people: a *gatcher* is a show-off and a *cuffer* tells tall tales.

A *drung* is a narrow road, a *scuff* is a dance, to *coopy* means to crouch down, and if you're going for a *twack*, you're window-shopping. If you're from *Upalong*, that means you're not from here.

To help develop an ear for the provincial dialects, pick up a copy of the *Dictionary of Newfoundland English* (🌐 *www.heritage.nf.ca/dictionary*), which contains more than 5,000 words. St. John's–based Twackwear (🌐 www.twackwear.com) preserves old Newfoundland words by printing them on T-shirts. In St. John's they can be found at the Downhome Shoppe & Gallery (✉ 103 Water St.), Wild Things (✉ 124 Water St.), or one of the Heritage Shops—at Signal Hill, Avalon Mall, and the Murray Premises.

soundproofing could be better. [$] *Rooms from: C$209* ✉ *5 Beck's Cove* ☎ *709/738–7773, 866/738–7773* 🌐 *www.murraypremiseshotel.com* 🛏 *69 rooms* 🍴 *Breakfast.*

$$ HOTEL 🏨 **Quality Hotel—Harbourview.** In the core of downtown, directly overlooking the harbor, this hotel has friendly staffers who immediately flash welcoming smiles when you enter the tiled, sand-color lobby. **Pros:** connecting rooms available; refrigerators available on request. **Cons:** harbor can be noisy; you have to hike a hill if you're walking from Water Street. [$] *Rooms from: C$175* ✉ *2 Hill O'Chips* ☎ *709/754–7788, 800/424–6423* 🌐 *www.choicehotels.ca* 🛏 *160 rooms* 🍴 *No meals.*

$$$$ HOTEL 🏨 **Sheraton Hotel Newfoundland.** Charming rooms overlook the harbor at this nine-story hotel where uniformed bellhops sometimes meet you at the door. **Pros:** heritage neighborhood; walking distance to Signal Hill and the Battery; spa and hair salon on-site. **Cons:** no indoor parking; restaurant overpriced. [$] *Rooms from: C$263* ✉ *115 Cavendish Sq.* ☎ *709/726–4980* 🌐 *www.starwoodhotels.com/sheraton* 🛏 *282 rooms, 19 suites* 🍴 *Breakfast.*

NIGHTLIFE AND THE ARTS

THE ARTS

Arts and Culture Centre. A 1,000-seat main theater is the focal point of this center, which also houses the St. John's Public Library. It's the site of musical and theatrical events from September through June. ⊠ *95 Allandale Rd.* ☎ *709/729–3650, 709/729–3900 box office* ⊕ *www. artsandculturecentre.com.*

Resource Centre for the Arts. An innovative theater with professional mainstage and experimental second-space productions year-round, the center has been the launching pad for the province's most successful theatrical exports. ⊠ *LSPU Hall, 3 Victoria St.* ☎ *709/753–4531* ⊕ *www.rca.nf.ca.*

NIGHTLIFE

The well-deserved reputation of St. John's as a party town has been several hundred years in the making. To become an "honorary Newfoundlander" visitors can take part in the screeching-in ceremony, which involves reciting the "Screechers Creed," kissing a cod, and knocking back a shot of Screech Rum.

George Street. The city's most famous street may be short and cobblestoned, but it is said to have more bars per capita than any other street in North America—25 total, as it happens. Trapper John's, to name one, has been named the fourth-greatest drinking establishment in the world by *Readers' Digest.* (It's also a great place to undertake the "Screeching In Ceremony.") Seasonal open-air festivals, which close off the street, include the George Street Festival in August, with big-name headliners. ⊕ *www.georgestreetlive.ca.*

O'Reilly's Pub. When Russell Crowe comes to town, he jams at O'Reilly's Pub, famous for its nightly live Irish and Newfoundland music. Starting times vary, but shows typically begin late. O'Reilly's also has a full pub-grub menu; the fish-and-chips is excellent. ⊠ *13 George St.* ☎ *709/722–3735, 866/307–3735* ⊕ *www.oreillyspub.com.*

Ship Pub. Traditionally this pub has served as the local arts watering hole and attracts a young, hip crowd. There's live music from Wednesday through Saturday year-round, with Wednesday a folk-music night. Good pub food is served between noon and 4 from Saturday through Tuesday; it's served until 8 from Wednesday through Friday. ⊠ *265 Duckworth St.* ☎ *709/753–3870.*

SPORTS AND THE OUTDOORS

HIKING

Grand Concourse. A well-developed, marked trail system, the Grand Concourse, crosses St. John's, Mount Pearl and Paradise, covering more than 120 km (75 miles). Some trails traverse river valleys, parks, and other open areas; others are sidewalk routes. Well-maintained trails encircle several lakes, including Long Pond and Quidi Vidi Lake, both of which are great for bird-watching. Detailed maps are available at tourist information centers and many hotels. ☎ *709/737–1077* ⊕ *www. grandconcourse.ca.*

SCUBA DIVING

The ocean around Newfoundland and Labrador rivals the Caribbean in clarity, though certainly not in temperature. There are thousands of known shipwreck sites. One, a sunken whaling ship, is only several feet from the shore of the Conception Bay community of Conception Harbour. The wrecked ship and a wealth of sea life can be explored with a snorkel and wet suit.

Ocean Quest. This outfitter leads ocean tours aboard Zodiacs and a 38-foot custom boat to popular scuba-diving sites, including the WWII shipwrecks off Bell Island and the Conception Bay whaling wrecks. Ocean Quest also organizes tours from Gros Morne National Park and Terra Nova National Park and seasonal Close Encounters tours to view icebergs, whales, and caves, and the company offers diving and other classes. Tours depart from the Foxtrap Marina. ⊠ *Head office and dive shop, 17 Stanley's Rd., Conception Bay South* ☎ 709/834–7234, 866/623–2664 ⊕ *www. oceanquestadventures.com.*

SEA KAYAKING

One of the best ways to explore the coastline is by kayak, which lets you visit sea caves and otherwise inaccessible beaches. There's also a very good chance you'll see whales, icebergs, and seabirds.

Stan Cook Sea Kayak Adventures. The guides at Stan Cook lead kayaking tours to world-famous sanctuaries, through waterfalls and into caves; in season you can paddle near whales and around icebergs. To provide the most time at the main destinations, participants on the two-hour (C$99) and 3½-hour (C$149) "Go and Tow" tours, which depart from Cape Broyle, kayak out to the ocean and return by motorized towboat. You can also combine kayaking with a hiking tour along the East Coast Trail (C$339), or just hike (C$69 half day, C$109 full day). Lunch is included on all tours. ⊠ *67 Circular Rd.* ☎ 709/579–6353, 888/747–6353 ⊕ *www.wildnfld.ca.*

WHALE-WATCHING

The east coast of Newfoundland, including the area around St. John's, provides spectacular whale-watching opportunities. Twenty-two species of dolphins and whales are visible along the coast—huge humpback whales weighing up to 30 tons come close to shore to feed in late spring and early summer. You may be able to spot icebergs and large flocks of nesting seabirds in addition to whales on many boat tours. For tour times and rates, visit the tour-company near Pier 7 in summer, or inquire at your hotel.

Iceberg Quest Ocean Tours. Expect to see whales, icebergs, and intensely beautiful scenery on two-hour fully narrated boat tours (C$60) to the most easterly points in North America. As the vessel heads out through the harbor narrows between Signal Hill and Fort Amherst on its way to Cape Spear, you'll be entertained with traditional and local music. From May through August, departures take place daily at 9:30, 1, 4, and 7. ⊠ *Pier 6, 135 Harbour Dr.* ☎ *709/722–1888, 866/720–1888* ⊕ *icebergquest.com.*

SHOPPING

ARTS AND CRAFTS

Christina Parker Gallery. The gallery specializes in works by local artists—paintings, sculptures, drawings, prints, and other media. ⊠ *50 Water St.* ☎ *709/753–0580* ⊕ *www.christinaparkergallery.com.*

Devon House Craft Centre. Serving as headquarters of the Craft Council of Newfoundland and Labrador, the center displays local works and showcases innovative designs. Check out the exhibits upstairs. ⊠ *59 Duckworth St.* ☎ *709/753–2749* ⊕ *www.craftcouncil.nl.ca.*

Downhome Shoppe and Gallery. With thousands of books, music, crafts, artwork, and souvenirs created by Newfoundlanders and Labradorians, this shop occupying two late-1850s buildings is a great place to pick up a homegrown memento. ⊠ *303 Water St.* ☎ *709/722–2970, 888/588–6353* ⊕ *www.shopdownhome.com.*

Eastern Edge Gallery. Artists that run this center present everything from paintings and drawings to performance and video art from emerging talents. The gallery, which opens at noon, is closed on Sundays and Mondays. ⊠ *72 Harbour Dr., between Clift's-Baird's Cove and Prescott St.* ☎ *709/739–1882* ⊕ *www.easternedge.ca.*

Emma Butler Gallery. Some of the province's more prominent and established artists show their works here. The gallery is closed on Sundays and Mondays, except by appointment. ⊠ *111 George St. W* ☎ *709/739–7111* ⊕ *www.emmabutler.com.*

The Lane Gallery. The gallery exhibits the well-composed seascapes, landscapes, and other photographs of Don Lane, a St. John's native. ⊠ *Sheraton Hotel Newfoundland, 115 Cavendish Sq., main lobby* ☎ *709/753–8946, 877/366–5263* ⊕ *www.lanegallery.com.*

Newfoundland Weavery. You'll find throws, prints, lamps, books, crafts, and other gift items here. ⊠ *177 Water St.* ☎ *709/753–0496.*

Quidi Vidi Village Plantation. Nine artists and artisans have their studios here, making this a perfect place to pick up original art and craftworks, including textiles, prints, pottery, stained glass, and jewelry. It's closed on Monday. ⊠ *10 Maple View Pl., Quidi Vidi* ☎ *709/570–2038* ⊕ *quidividivillageplantation.com.*

MUSIC

Fred's Records. The best selection of local recordings—about 1,000 individual titles—can be found at this independent store, along with other music. ⊠ *198 Duckworth St.* ☎ *709/753–9191* ⊕ *www.freds.nf.ca.*

O'Brien's Music Store. This shop bills itself as the oldest store on the oldest street in the oldest city in North America. It's worth a visit just to see the accordions, tin whistles, fiddles, ukuleles, and ugly sticks (traditional Newfoundland instruments made from discarded tools and household items) on display. The shop also stocks recorded music. ⊠ *278 Water St.* ☎ *709/753–8135* ⊕ *obriensmusic.com.*

CLOTHING AND GIFTS

Living Planet. Eco-friendly T-shirts designed by local artists are the specialty here. ⊠ *197 Water St.* ☎ *709/754–9300* ⊕ *www.living planet.ca.*

NONIA (*Newfoundland Outport Nursing and Industrial Association*). This nonprofit shop was founded in 1920 to raise money for public health services, with the proceeds from the sale of the homespun, hand-knit clothes used to hire nurses. Today it sells a variety of knits for all ages. ⊠ *286 Water St.* ☎ *709/753–8062, 877/753–8062.*

PINK, WHITE, AND GREEN

You won't be in St. John's long before you'll ask what's with the pink, white, and green? The tricolor flag flies from houses and buildings, and in souvenir shops the cheerful bands of color show up on rings, earrings, fleece, windbreakers, mittens, and aprons. To quote the song "The Flag of Newfoundland": "The pink the rose of England shows, the green St. Patrick's emblem bright, while in between a spotless sheen of Andrew's cross displays the white." The 19th-century flag has gained popularity in recent years as an affectionate symbol of the "secret nation."

AVALON PENINSULA

On the southern half of the Newfoundland peninsula, small Irish hamlets are separated by large tracts of wilderness. You can travel part of the peninsula's southern coast in one or two days, depending on how much time you have. Quaint towns line Route 10, and the natural sights are beautiful. La Manche and Chance Cove, both abandoned communities–turned–provincial parks, attest to the region's bounty of natural resources. At the intersection of routes 90 and 91 in Salmonier, you can head west and then south to Route 100 to Cape St. Mary's Ecological Reserve, or north toward Salmonier Nature Park and on to the towns on Conception Bay. Each of these routes takes about three hours. On the latter, Harbour Grace is a good place to stop; if you plan to travel on to Bay de Verde, at the northern tip of the peninsula, and down the other side of the peninsula on Route 80 along Trinity Bay, consider overnighting in the Harbour Grace–Carbonear area. Otherwise turn around and retrace your steps to Route 1.

WITLESS BAY ECOLOGICAL RESERVE

29 km (18 miles) south of St. John's.

GETTING HERE AND AROUND

The departure point for boat trips around the reserve is Bay Bulls, about 32 km (20 miles) south of St. John's via Route 10. Gatherall's *(⇨ See below)* provides shuttle-bus service from St. John's if you're taking one of the company's tours.

EXPLORING

Witless Bay Ecological Reserve. Four small islands and the water sur-rounding them make up the reserve, the summer home of millions of seabirds—puffins, murres, kittiwakes, razorbills, and guillemots. The birds and the humpback and minke whales that linger here before mov-ing north to their summer grounds in the Arctic feed on capelin (a fish that belongs to the smelt family) that swarm inshore to spawn.

In late spring and early summer, this is an excellent place to see icebergs, which can remain in Newfoundland's waters into June and sometimes July. The loud crack as an iceberg breaks apart can be heard from shore, but a boat gets you a closer look at these natural ice sculptures. Icebergs have spawned a lucrative business in Newfoundland beyond tourism. Iceberg water and iceberg vodka are now on the market, made from ice chipped from the 10,000-year-old bergs as they float by.

The best views of birds and icebergs are from the tour boats that oper-ate here (⇨ *See listings below*) and are the only way to visit the reserve. There is no public access to the islands themselves—only management staff and scientific researchers (with a permit) are allowed to land.
■ TIP➔ **If you're driving down from St. John's, allow about four hours: between 30 and 45 minutes each way for the drive, about 90 minutes for the boat trip, and a bit of time to spare.** ✛ *Take Pitts Memorial Dr. (Rte. 2) from downtown St. John's and turn right onto Goulds off-ramp, then left onto Rte. 10.*

SPORTS AND THE OUTDOORS

Gatherall's Puffin and Whale Watch. From early May to late September Gatherall's conducts six 90-minute trips (C$56) per day into the waters of Witless Bay Reserve on a high-speed catamaran. The catamaran is stable even in rough seas, so if you're the queasy type, this one might be right for you. Shuttle service (C$25 additional, round-trip) is available from hotels in St. John's. ⊠ *90 Northside Rd., Bay Bulls* ☎ *709/334–2887, 800/419–4253* ⊕ *www.gatheralls.com.*

O'Brien's Whale and Bird Tours. This company offers two-hour excur-sions (C$55) in a 100-passenger boat to view whales, icebergs, and seabirds. You can also board a 12-passenger boat for a 90-minute tour (C$85). ⊠ *22 Lower Rd., off Southside Rd., Bay Bulls* ☎ *709/753–4850, 877/639–4253* ⊕ *www.obriensboattours.com.*

▌ EN
ROUTE

Although there are many pretty hamlets along the way from Witless Bay to Ferryland on Route 10, **La Manche,** accessible only on foot, and **Brigus South** have especially attractive settings. La Manche is an aban-doned fishing community between Tors Cove and Cape Broyle. The former residents moved to other towns after a storm destroyed part of the community in 1966; a suspension bridge washed away by the storm's tides has since been rebuilt and is worth a visit. Brigus South is a fishing village with a strong traditional flavor whose name is derived from an old French word for "intrigue."

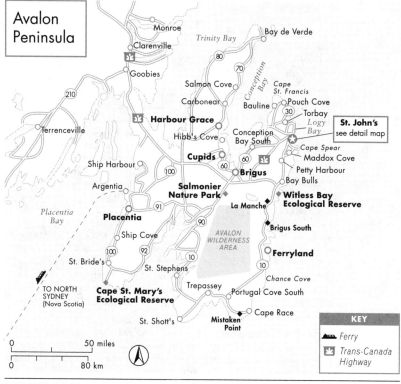

Avalon
Peninsula

Monroe
Trinity Bay
Bay de Verde
Clarenville
80
70
Goobies
Cape
Salmon Cove
St. Francis
210
Carbonear
Bauline
Pouch Cove
30
Torbay
Terrenceville
Harbour Grace
Hibb's Cove
Conception
Bay South
Logy
Bay
St. John's
see detail map
Cupids
60
Cape Spear
Maddox Cove
Ship Harbour
100
60
Brigus
Petty Harbour
Bay Bulls
Argentia
91
**Salmonier
Nature Park**
La Manche
**Witless Bay
Ecological Reserve**
Placentia
Bay
Placentia
90
AVALON
WILDERNESS
AREA
Brigus South
Ship Cove
Ferryland
100
92
10
St. Bride's
St. Stephens
10
Chance Cove
TO NORTH
SYDNEY
(Nova Scotia)
Trepassey
Portugal Cove South
**Cape St. Mary's
Ecological Reserve**
Cape Race
St. Shott's
Mistaken
Point

KEY
Ferry
Trans-Canada
Highway

0   50 miles
0   80 km

5

FERRYLAND

43½ km (27 miles) south of Witless Bay Ecological Reserve.

The main road into Ferryland hugs the coastline, where tiny bay houses dot the steep hills. Ferryland is one of the oldest European settlements in North America: the Englishman Sir George Calvert, later Lord Baltimore, settled it in 1620. Calvert didn't stay long on this cold windswept shore—he left for a warmer destination and is more commonly credited with founding Maryland. In the summer this is a great spot to whale-watch.

GETTING HERE AND AROUND

There is no public transportation to Ferryland, which is south of St. John's on Route 2 and then Route 10, a total of about 76 km (47 miles).

EXPLORING

FAMILY **Colony of Avalon.** A major ongoing archaeological dig at Ferryland has uncovered this early-17th-century colony founded by George Calvert, later Lord Baltimore. The highlights of a visit here include six dig sites, exhibits of artifacts uncovered at them, two period gardens, and a reconstructed 17th-century kitchen. You can watch the conservationists at work in their laboratory, examining and restoring newly discovered artifacts, and take in living-history demonstrations that provide a feel for colonial times. Absorbing guided tours often take place. ⊠ *Rte. 10* ☎ *709/432–3200, 877/326–5669* ⊕ *www.colonyofavalon.ca* ☒ *C$9.50 includes tour* ☉ *Early June–early Oct., daily 10–6.*

Ferryland Lighthouse. This historic lighthouse, built in 1871, now signals the spot for breathtaking views, worry-free picnics, and great food such as smoked salmon and ice-shrimp sandwiches, green salads, and gooseberry fools. You bring the appetite, and the lighthouse staff packs everything else— even the blanket. Bread is baked daily here; in fact everything is made on-site down to the desserts and freshly squeezed lemonade. Check the website for menus. Picnics start at C$25 per person (C$12 for children) and reservations are required. There must be romance in the shadow of the lighthouse, because it has become a popular destination for engagement proposals. ⊠ *Rte. 10* ☎ *709/363–7456* ⊕ *www.lighthousepicnics.ca* ☉ *Late May–late Sept., Wed.–Sun. 11:30–4:30.*

THE IRISH LOOP

The Irish Loop (Route 10) goes around the southern shore of the Avalon Peninsula below St. John's. The highway hugs the coastline and takes you into the heart of Irish Newfoundland—to Bay Bulls, Witless Bay, Ferryland, Aquaforte, Fermeuse, Portugal Cove South, Trepassey, and Salmonier. It's a world filled with whales, caribou, and seabirds. If you keep following the loop around you'll end up back in St. John's.

OFF THE BEATEN PATH

Mistaken Point Ecological Reserve. At 575 million years old, this is one of the most significant fossil sites in the world. Fossils of more than 20 species of ancient organisms are found in the mudstones here, and almost all of them represent extinct groups unknown in our modern world. Mistaken Point is 145 km (90 miles) south of St. John's via Route 10. Access to the fossils is by guided hike only. Tours are offered daily at 1 pm and begin at the Edge of Avalon Interpretive Centre in Portugal Cove South. Tours generally take from 3½ to 4 hours and include a 3-km (1.8-mile) one-way hike across the barrens towards the ocean to the fossil site. Call ahead to ensure availability and to check weather conditions.

■**TIP**➔ While you're here, travel 8 km (5 miles) farther along the road to **Cape Race Lighthouse,** the northeasternmost point in North America and most famous for receiving one of the first SOS messages from the *Titanic.* ⊠ *Off Rte. 10 about 16 km (10 miles) southeast of Portugal Cove South on minor roads, Portugal Cove South* ☎ *709/438–1012 reserve, 709/438–1100 lighthouse* ⊕ *www.env.gov.nl.ca* ☒ *Free* ☉ *May–mid-Oct.*

SALMONIER NATURE PARK

88 km (55 miles) northwest of Ferryland; 11 km (7 miles) south of the Trans-Canada Highway.

GETTING HERE AND AROUND

There is no public transportation to the park. By road, it's off the Trans-Canada Highway (Route 1). Take Exit 35 and drive south on Route 90.

EXPLORING

Salmonier Nature Park. Many indigenous animal species—including caribou, lynx, and otters—along with moose, which were introduced from New Brunswick a little more than a century ago, can be seen at this 3,460-acre wilderness area. An enclosed 100-acre exhibit allows up-close viewing. ⊠ *Salmonier Line/Rte. 90, 12 miles south of Trans-Canada Hwy. (Hwy. 1)* ☎ *709/229–7888* ⊕ *www.gov.nl.ca/snp* ☞ *Free* ☉ *Early June–early Sept., daily 10–6; early Sept.–mid-Oct., weekdays 10–4.*

EN ROUTE
Hawke Hills. From Salmonier Nature Park to Brigus, take Route 90, which passes through the scenic Hawke Hills before meeting up with the Trans-Canada Highway (Route 1). This reserve is the best representative of alpine barrens in Canada east of the Rockies. Turn off at Holyrood Junction (Route 62) and follow Route 70, which skirts Conception Bay, to get there.

BRIGUS

19 km (12 miles) north of the intersection of routes 1 and 70.

This compact historic village on Conception Bay is wonderfully walkable, with a public garden, winding lanes, and a teahouse. Brigus is best known as the birthplace of Captain Bob Bartlett, the famed Arctic explorer who accompanied Admiral Robert Peary on polar expeditions during the first decade of the 20th century.

GETTING HERE AND AROUND

There is no public transportation to Brigus. By road, leave the Trans-Canada Highway (Route 1) at Exit 31, drive north on Route 70 toward Conception Bay, and turn right onto the Conception Bay Highway (Route 60) for the last few kilometers. From St. John's, head southwest on Route 2 and pick up Route 60 heading west around the coast, a total of about 74 km (46 miles).

EXPLORING

Hawthorne Cottage. The home of the Arctic explorer Robert Bartlett is one of the few surviving examples of picturesque cottage style, with a veranda decorated with ornamental wooden fretwork. It dates from 1830 and is a national historic site. ■**TIP➡ During July and August a local troupe performs several vignettes about the town of Brigus and Bartlett's adventures. Look for postings for Live! On the Lawn Theatre (the performances take place outdoors).** ⊠ *South St. and Irishtown Rd.* ☎ *709/528–4004 May–Oct., 877/753–9262 off-season appointments* ⊕ *www.historicsites.ca* ☞ *C$5 (theater and house tour)* ☉ *May–Oct., daily 10–6, or by appointment.*

WHERE TO STAY

For expanded hotel reviews, visit Fodors.com.

$
B&B/INN
Brittoner Bed & Breakfast. This restored home dating to 1842 is in the heart of Brigus, near Hawthorne Cottage and hiking trails. **Pros:** on a pond; harbor view from some rooms; full hot breakfast. **Cons:** no credit cards accepted. $ *Rooms from: C$90* ⊠ *12 Water St.* ☎ *709/528–3412, 709/579–5995 Nov.–Apr.* 🛏 *3 rooms* ⊟ *No credit cards* ☉ *Closed Nov.–Apr.* ⦿ *Breakfast.*

CUPIDS

5 km (3 miles) northwest of Brigus.

Cupids is the oldest English colony in Canada, founded in 1610 by John Guy, to whom the town erected a monument in 1910. Nearby is a reproduction of the enormous Union Jack that flew during that 300th-anniversary celebration. When the wind snaps the flag, you can hear it half a mile away. Cupids recently celebrated its 400th anniversary, and the new Cupids Legacy Centre was built to house the many artifacts that have been found related to the archaeology of John Guy's settlement.

GETTING HERE AND AROUND

To get to Cupids, drive west from Brigus on Route 60 and turn right on Keatings Road.

EXPLORING

Cupids Legacy Centre & Museum. With interactive displays, interpretive tours, a shop, and an archaeological lab, this is a good place to get a glimpse of the English settlement founded here in 1610. The bright and modern museum traces 400 years of settlement in the area through interactive exhibits and a selection of the 153,000 artifacts recovered to date at the archaeological site. These include trade beads and the oldest coin found in Canada. You can visit the Plantation site dig nearby and see (and talk to) technicians at work in the laboratory. ⊠ *368 Seaforest Dr.* ☎ *709/528–1610* ⊕ *www.cupidslegacycentre.ca* 🖙 *C$8.50 for Legacy Centre only, C$6 for Plantation site only, C$14.50 for both* ☉ *June–Oct., daily 10–5; off-season by appointment.*

WHERE TO STAY

For expanded hotel reviews, visit Fodors.com.

$
B&B/INN
Skipper Ben's. This restored 1891 heritage home has wood ceilings and antique furnishings, and its three rooms are spacious. **Pros:** ocean views from deck and rooms; excellent meals; the sound of the sea will lull you to sleep at night. **Cons:** no private bathrooms; no air-conditioning; road runs between B&B and water. $ *Rooms from: C$79* ⊠ *408 Seaforest Dr.* ☎ *877/528–4436* ⊕ *www.skipperbens.com* 🛏 *3 rooms with shared bath* ⦿ *Breakfast.*

HARBOUR GRACE

21 km (13 miles) north of Cupids.

Harbour Grace, once the headquarters of 17th-century pirate Peter Easton, was a major commercial town in the 18th and 19th centuries. Beginning in 1919, the town was the departure point for many attempts to fly the Atlantic. Amelia Earhart left Harbour Grace in 1932 to become the first woman to fly solo across the Atlantic. The town has two fine churches and several registered historic houses.

GETTING HERE AND AROUND

Harbour Grace is off Route 75, which leaves the Trans-Canada Highway (Route 1) at Exit 31.

WHERE TO STAY

For expanded hotel reviews, visit Fodors.com.

$ | B&B/INN | 🖼 **Rothesay House Inn Bed & Breakfast.** The front of this charming provincial heritage building has a lovely harbor-view porch. **Pros:** local seasonal produce and seafood; engaging and helpful hosts; pretty garden. **Cons:** no air-conditioning; two resident dogs (could be a plus for animal lovers). 💲 *Rooms from: C$120* ✉ *34 Water St.* ☎ *709/596–2268, 877/596–2268* ⊕ *www.rothesay.com* 🛏 *4 rooms* 🍴 *Breakfast.*

PLACENTIA

48 km (30 miles) south of the Trans-Canada Highway.

Placentia was first settled by 16th-century Basque fishermen and was Newfoundland's French capital in the 1600s. The remains of an old fort built on a hill look out over Placentia and beyond, to the placid waters and wooded, steep hillsides of the inlet.

GETTING HERE AND AROUND

The Nova Scotia–Argentia ferry docks 7 km (4½ miles) north of Placentia. From the port head south to Route 100 and continue south to reach Placentia. From the Trans-Canada Highway (Route 1), take Route 100 south.

EXPLORING

Castle Hill National Historic Site. Just north of Placentia, Castle Hill is what remains of the French fortifications. The visitor center has a "Life at Plaisance" exhibit that shows the hardships endured by early English and French settlers. Performances of *Faces of Fort Royal,* a play about the French era, take place from mid-July to mid-August (call for times). There are hiking trails from the forts and many lookouts on-site. ✉ *Castle Hill Rd., off Rte. 100* ☎ *709/227–2401* ⊕ *www. historicplaces.ca* 🎫 *Site C$3.90, play by donation* 🕙 *June–early Oct., daily 10–6.*

WHERE TO STAY

For expanded hotel reviews, visit Fodors.com.

$ | HOTEL | 🖼 **Harold Hotel.** Convenient to the Argentia–Nova Scotia Ferry, just 5 km (3 miles) away, this hotel is in the heart of Placentia and a two-minute walk from the boardwalk and the ocean. **Pros:** smoke-free; minutes to ferry terminal; dining room is air-conditioned. **Cons:** no air-conditioning in guest rooms. [$] *Rooms from: C$89* ✉ *Main St., off Rte. 100* ☎ *709/227–2107* 🛏 *18 rooms* 🍴 *Multiple meal plans.*

$ B&B/INN Fodor's Choice ★ **Rosedale Manor Bed & Breakfast.** Gorgeous rooms at this 1893 waterfront heritage home far exceed what you'd expect for the low price, and tall guests will be happy with the Blueberry Room, with its extra-long bed. **Pros:** 1 km (½ mile) from Argentia Ferry; cordless phones available with free long distance. **Cons:** no elevator. [$] *Rooms from: C$99* ✉ *40 Orcan Dr.* ☎ *709/227–3613, 877/999–3613* 🌐 *www.rosedalemanor.ca* 🛏 *6 rooms* 🍴 *Breakfast.*

ROUTE 100: THE CAPE SHORE

The Cape Shore area, which includes Cape St. Mary's north to Argentia, is culturally and historically rich: the French settlers had their capital here in Placentia, and Irish influence is also strong in music and manner. Birders come to view the fabulous seabird colony at Cape St. Mary's. You can reach the Cape Shore, on the western side of the Avalon Peninsula, from Route 1 at its intersection with Route 100. The ferry from Nova Scotia docks in Argentia, near Placentia.

CAPE ST. MARY'S ECOLOGICAL RESERVE

65 km (40 miles) south of Placentia.

GETTING HERE AND AROUND

Public transit doesn't serve the cape. By road, it's about an hour from Placentia, south and then briefly east on Route 100 to Route 90 south. Alternatively, from Route 91 you can head south on Route 92 and then west on Route 100 to Route 90 south. A 1-km (½-mile) clifftop path leads from the reserve's parking lot to an observation point. The path is not suitable for wheelchairs or strollers.

EXPLORING

Fodor's Choice ★ **Cape St. Mary's Ecological Reserve.** The third-largest nesting colony of gannets in North America resides here, at the most accessible seabird colony on the continent. A paved road takes you within a mile of the colony. You can visit the interpretation center—guides are on-site in summer—and then walk to within 100 feet of nesting gannets, murres, black-billed kittiwakes, and razorbills. At busy times you may have to wait your turn at the observation point. Call the weather line to check on conditions before heading out. The reserve has some of the most dramatic coastal scenery in Newfoundland and is a good place to spot whales. **TIP→ Most birds visit from March through August. In July, August, and September the interpretation center presents local artists performing traditional music.** ✉ *Off Rte. 100, Cape St. Mary's* ☎ *709/277–1666 cell phone, 709/337–2473* 🌐 *www.env.gov.nl.ca* 🎟 *Free* ⏲ *Mid-May–June and Sept.–mid-Oct., daily 9–5; July and Aug., daily 8–7.*

WHERE TO STAY

For expanded hotel reviews, visit Fodors.com.

$ **Bird Island Resort.** The landscape around this lodging a half-hour
HOTEL drive from Cape St. Mary's has the dramatic touches one expects of
Newfoundland, but the facility itself feels more motel than resort.
Pros: basic but clean rooms; suites have decks and kitchenettes. **Cons:**
no restaurant; no air-conditioning. $ *Rooms from: C$89* ⊠ *Off Rte.
100, St. Bride's* ☎ *709/337–2450, 888/337–2450 NL only* ⊕ *www.
birdislandresort.com* ⤳ *15 rooms, 5 suites* ⦿| *No meals.*

$ **Capeway Motel & Efficiency Units.** This former convent, built in 1968, is
HOTEL about a 15-minute drive from the seabird sanctuary at Cape St. Mary's.
Pros: complimentary breakfast; well-equipped one- and two-bedroom
suites with kitchenettes; guest rooms have in-room tea/coffee. **Cons:**
plain decor. $ *Rooms from: C$89* ⊠ *11 Main St. (Rte. 100), St. Bride's*
☎ *709/337–2163, 866/337–2163* ⊕ *www.thecapeway.ca* ⤳ *2 rooms, 5
suites* ⦿| *Breakfast.*

EASTERN NEWFOUNDLAND

Eastern Newfoundland packs in plenty of history and fabulous natural
landscapes. The Bonavista Peninsula has archaeological artifacts; the
Burin Peninsula is more about stark landscapes. Clarenville, halfway
between the two, is a good base for exploring. Terra Nova was Newfoundland's first National Park.

CLARENVILLE

189 km (117 miles) northwest of St. John's.

Pleasant little Clarenville has a marina, a small bird sanctuary, and a monu-
ment commemorating the landing of the first transatlantic telephone cable.
The town makes a convenient base for several excursions: the Bonavista
Peninsula, with its Discovery Trail and the twin communities of Trinity and
Bonavista; Terra Nova National Park; and the Burin Peninsula.

GETTING HERE AND AROUND

No useful public transit serves Clarenville. To drive here from St. John's
by car, a two-hour trip, take the Trans-Canada Highway (Route 1) west
and then north.

ESSENTIALS

Visitor Information Clarenville Visitor Information Centre ⊠ *379 Trans-
Canada Hwy.* ☎ *709/466–3100.*

EXPLORING

Discovery Trail. If history and quaint towns appeal to you, follow this
trail, which begins in the east in Clarenville, on Route 230A, or from
the west at Port Blandford, on Route 233. It includes two gems: the
old town of Trinity, famed for its architecture and theater festival, and
Bonavista, one of John Cabot's reputed landing spots. The provincial tourism website (⊕ *www.newfoundlandlabrador.com*) has a more
detailed description. Clarenville itself is largely a departure point for
these more attractive destinations.

WHERE TO STAY

For expanded hotel reviews, visit Fodors.com.

$$ **Clarenville Inn.** Though it lacks style, this hotel on the Trans-Canada
HOTEL Highway has comfortable rooms, and the ones in the back have a view
of Clarenville and Random Sound. **Pros:** heated outdoor pool in sum-
mer; lounge with a patio. **Cons:** right on the highway. $ *Rooms from:*
C$135 ⊠ *134 Trans-Canada Hwy. (Rte. 1)* ☎ *709/466–7911, 877/466–*
7911 ⊕ *www.clarenvilleinn.ca* ⤳ *62 rooms, 1 suite* ⦿ *No meals.*

$ **St. Jude Hotel.** Ideally placed for touring the Bonavista Peninsula
HOTEL and Terra Nova National Park, this modern hotel has spacious and
comfortable rooms, and the ones at the front have good bay views.
Pros: friendly staff; restaurant has an outdoor patio; elevator. **Cons:**
construction-company parking lot near hotel. $ *Rooms from: C$125*
⊠ *247 Trans-Canada Hwy. (Rte. 1)* ☎ *709/466–1717, 800/563–7800*
⊕ *www.stjudehotel.com* ⤳ *60 rooms, 3 suites* ⦿ *No meals.*

SHOPPING

Mercer's Marine. Family-run Mercer's stocks marine gear and cloth-
ing, rainwear, outdoor apparel, rubber boots, warm clothing in case
you didn't pack enough, and knitting material in case you want to
make your own. The shop, which also sells just about everything
else, including kitchenware, is worth a stop if you're in the neighbor-
hood. ⊠ *210 Marine Dr.* ☎ *709/466–7430* ⊕ *www.mercersmarine.*
com ⊗ *Closed Sun.*

TERRA NOVA NATIONAL PARK

⟲ *24 km (15 miles) north of Clarenville.*

GETTING HERE AND AROUND

The park straddles the Trans-Canada Highway (Route 1). The southern
entrance is near Port Blandford, the northern one near Glovertown.

EXPLORING

Terra Nova National Park. Newfoundland's first national park, estab-
lished in 1957, offers natural beauty, dramatic Bonavista Bay coast-
line, rugged woods, and many outdoor activities. Moose, black bear,
and other wildlife roam freely in the forests and marshy bogs, pods of
whales play in the waters within view, and many species of birds inhabit
the cliffs and shores. Golfing, sea kayaking, fishing, and backcoun-
try camping and canoeing are among the activities the 400-square-km
(154-square-mile) park supports. You can arrange guided walks at the
visitor center, which has exhibits, a small shop, and a decent snack bar/
cafeteria. ■ TIP➜ **Coastal Connections** (*709/533–2196, www.coastalcon-
nections.ca*) conducts summer marine tours that leave from the visitor
center. ⊠ *Trans-Canada Hwy., Glovertown* ☎ *709/533–2801 National
Parks Service, 709/533–2942 Terra Nova National Park* ⊕ *www.pc.gc.
ca* ⊡ *C$5.80* ⊗ *Daily dawn–dusk. Visitor center July and Aug., daily
10–6; Sept.–mid-Oct., Thurs.–Mon. 10–4.*

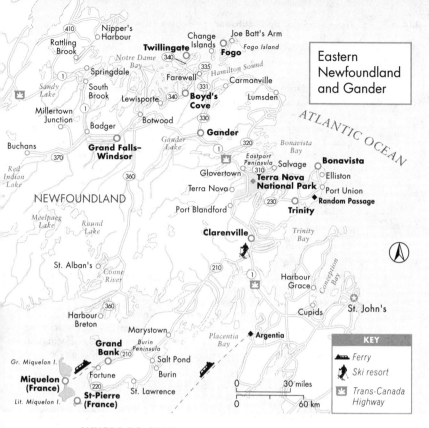

Eastern
Newfoundland
and Gander

KEY

🚂 Ferry

⛷ Ski resort

�× Trans-Canada Highway

WHERE TO STAY

For expanded hotel reviews, visit Fodors.com.

$ 　📷 **Freshwater Inn.** On a quiet cove on Freshwater Bay, this little inn has
B&B/INN 　large, well-equipped rooms and is a good base for visiting Terra Nova
　National Park, 25 km (15 miles) south. **Pros:** no stairs; owner is a
　licensed fishing guide for local salmon rivers and sea angling; owner can
　provide personalized walking tours. **Cons:** no choice at breakfast; no
　good restaurants nearby. ⑤ *Rooms from: C$125* ⊠ *Rte. 320, 10 km (6
　miles) northeast of Trans-Canada Hwy., Exit 24, Gambo* ☎ *709/674–
　5577, 877/674–5577* ⊕ *www.freshwaterinn.com* ⇱ *3 rooms* ⊗ *Closed
　Nov.–Apr.* ⓘ *Breakfast.*

$$ 　📷 **Terra Nova Resort and Golf Community.** This 220-acre oceanfront resort
RESORT 　near Terra Nova National Park combines big-city-hotel luxuries with
FAMILY 　the charm of a country inn—and it has two of the most beautiful golf
　courses in Canada. **Pros:** heated indoor/outdoor pool year-round; dining
　room overlooks Clode Sound. **Cons:** some rooms not air-conditioned;
　some rooms could use some renovations. ⑤ *Rooms from: C$126* ⊠ *Off
　Trans-Canada Hwy., Port Blandford* ☎ *709/543–2525, 709/543–2626
　golf reservations, 877/546–2525* ⊕ *www.terranovagolf.com* ⇱ *73
　rooms, 7 suites, 7 chalets* ⓘ *Multiple meal plans.*

OFF THE BEATEN PATH

The Eastport Peninsula. A short, pretty drive from Terra Nova National Park, part of it on a thin strip of road between two bodies of water, will take you to the Eastport Peninsula; take Route 310, at the northern boundary of the national park. There are two beautiful, sandy beaches—at Eastport and at Sandy Cove—and either is perfect to laze away an afternoon, or you can sightsee. The very old outport of Salvage and the small port of Happy Adventure are charming. B&Bs and cabins dot this agricultural peninsula, and the schedule of musical and literary festivals (⊕ *www.beachesheritagecentre.ca*) might convince you to stay a night or two. At Burnside, you can visit an archaeology center with Beothuk artifacts or take a boat ride to the Beaches, once the largest Beothuk settlement in Bonavista Bay (⊕ *www.burnsideheritage.ca*).

TRINITY

71 km (44 miles) northeast of Clarenville.

Fodor's Choice
★

Trinity is one of the jewels of Newfoundland. The village's ocean views, winding lanes, and snug houses are the main attractions, and several homes have been turned into museums and inns. In the 1700s, Trinity competed with St. John's as a center of culture and wealth. Its more contemporary claim to fame, however, is that its intricate harbor was a favorite anchorage for the British navy. The smallpox vaccine was introduced to North America here by a local rector. On West Street an information center with costumed interpreters is open daily mid-June through October.

GETTING HERE
To get here from Clarenville, take Route 230 to Route 239.

EXPLORING
Mercantile Premises. At this provincial historic site you can slip back in time more than a century to the era when mercantile families ruled tiny communities. Next door the counting house has been restored to the 1820s and the retail store to the 1900s. An interpretation center traces the history of the Trinity, once a hub of commerce. ⊠ *West St.* ☏ *709/464–2042* ⊕ *www.seethesites.ca* ⊡ *C$6* ⊗ *Mid-May–mid-Oct., daily 9:30–5.*

Skerwink Trail. About 9,000 people a year come to hike this historic footpath, a cliff walk with panoramic vistas of Trinity and the ocean. On the trail you'll see sandy beaches, sea stacks (giant protruding rocks that have slowly eroded over time), seabirds and, in season, whales, icebergs, and bald eagles. The 5.3-km (3¼-mile) walk, which begins across the harbor in Port Rexton–Trinity East, is not for the faint of heart—it takes about two hours and can be steep in places. There are benches along the way, though. ■ TIP→ **Trail maps are available at the visitor center in Southern Bay.** ⊠ *Off Rte. 230, Port Rexton* ☏ *709/466–3845* ⊕ *www. theskerwinktrail.com.*

WHERE TO EAT AND STAY
For expanded hotel reviews, visit Fodors.com.

$$
B&B/INN

⊞**Artisan Inn.** Six houses in the heart of Trinity make up this inn, two of which—the Campbell and Gover houses—are from the mid-1800s and are Registered Heritage Structures. **Pros:** owners are very friendly; all accommodations are in Historic Trinity; several choices within the set menus. **Cons:** no à la carte dining; no elevators; only a continental breakfast included, and not for the vacation home rentals. §*Rooms from: C$129* ⊠*49 High St.* ☎*709/464–3377, 877/464–7700* ⊕*www. trinityvacations.com* ↻*5 rooms, 1 suite, 4 vacation homes* ⊘*Closed Nov.–Apr.* ⏼*Breakfast.*

$
B&B/INN

Eriksen Premises. One of Trinity's heritage structures, this two-story mansard-style building with ocean views has been restored to its original elegance, but with modern comforts added. **Pros:** good location; large sitting room has cable TV, mini-refrigerator, and tea and coffee. **Cons:** no elevator; no air-conditioning; dining room very busy before theater shows. §*Rooms from: C$120* ⊠*8 West St., Trinity Bay* ☎*709/464–3698, 877/464–3698* ⊕*www.trinityexperience.com* ↻*6 rooms, 1 suite* ⊘*Closed mid-Oct.–Apr.* ⏼*Breakfast.*

$
B&B/INN
Fodor's Choice
★

Fishers' Loft Inn. These are without a doubt the best accommodations on the Bonavista Peninsula, with beautiful gardens and stunning views: whales sometimes swim among the small fishing boats in the harbor, within sight of the several 19th-century buildings that make up this spectacular hillside property, and icebergs drift by farther out in the bay. **Pros:** colorful kitchen gardens enrich the dining experience; gift shop with juried crafts; main-floor wheelchair-accessible rooms; parking at each building. **Cons:** no air-conditioning; only one dining option; some hillside walking between buildings. §*Rooms from: C$120* ⊠*Mill Rd., 15 km (9 miles) northeast of Trinity, Port Rexton* ☎*877/464–3240* ⊕*www. fishersloft.com* ↻*14 rooms, 7 suites* ⊘*Closed Nov.–Apr.* ⏼*No meals.*

$
RENTAL

Sherwood Suites. These affordable suites are spacious and have living rooms and private patios from which to enjoy ocean views. **Pros:** some units good for family of four; on-site laundry facilities; free Wi-Fi in all rooms; near Skerwink Trail; beautiful 20-acre property; several restaurants within a short drive. **Cons:** no restaurant; only a pay phone for guest use; no air-conditioning. §*Rooms from: C$79* ⊠*32–34 Rocky Hill Rd., Port Rexton* ☎☎*709/464–2130, 877/464–2133* ⊕*www.sherwoodsuites. com* ↻*4 rooms, 12 suites* ⊘*Closed Oct.–late May* ⏼*No meals.*

NIGHTLIFE AND THE ARTS

Rising Tide Theatre. Dinner theater, local dramas, comedies, and newly commissioned plays are performed from mid-June to mid-October as part of the Bight Festival at the Rising Tide Theatre. The theater company also presents the New-Founde-Land Trinity Pageant and conducts walking tours of lanes, roads, and historical sites. More theater than tour, with actors in period costume, the strolls take place on Wednesday and Saturday at 2. ⊠*40 West St.* ☎*709/464–3232, 888/464–3377* ⊕*www.risingtidetheatre.com.*

SPORTS AND THE OUTDOORS

Atlantic Adventures Charters and Tours. Sail on a 46-foot motorized sailboat for whale-watching or just cruising Trinity Bay. The boat generally departs daily at 10 and 2, except when the weather and charter bookings interfere. Tours (C$65) take two hours. Group charters (2½-hours) with a meal are available. ⊠*Departures from Dockside Marina* ☎*709/464–2133, 709/781–2255 off-season* ⊕*www.atlanticadventures.com.*

Fodor's Choice
★

Rugged Beauty Boat Tours. Experience much more than the rugged beauty of the glorious coastline on this excellent four-hour open-boat trip (C$70) with a knowledgeable skipper whose family has lived here for generations. You'll hear true stories about the lives of the fisherfolk, be moved by the compulsory evacuations that wrenched his and other families from their beloved homes, and enjoy some local humor, too. And you'll disembark for an informal cup of tea at the skipper's vacation cabin on a beautiful bay before heading back. This could be the best half-day of your entire Newfoundland trip. Tours on the skipper's 27-foot boat, which can accommodate 12 guests, take place from May to October. ⊠ *Rte. 239 at New Bonaventure, off Rte. 230* ☎ *709/464–3856* ⊕ *www.ruggedbeautyboattours.net.*

OFF THE BEATEN PATH

Random Passage. Drive along Route 239, until the end of the road at New Bonaventure, about 14 km (8½ miles) from Trinity, then walk a short way, and you'll reach the breathtaking cove now known as Random Passage. Bernice Morgan's novel of that name, set in early-19th-century Newfoundland, captured the imagination of readers, and in 2000, an internationally televised miniseries based on the book was filmed here at this constructed site. You can roam the church, a schoolroom, houses, and a fishing stage and flakes (where the fish is dried), or sit near the vegetable garden and enjoy the quiet beauty of the cove's meadows and pastures. There are guided one-hour site tours. From July to September, there's a Sunday afternoon reading/concert (Random Passage Series) with writers and musicians. The Old Schoolhouse tearoom (open from 9:30 to 4:30) serves homemade fish cakes, pea soup, and light lunches. ⊠ *On Rte. 239, off Rte. 230, New Bonaventure* ☎ *709/464–2233* ⊕ *www.randompassagesite.com* 🎫 *C$8* ⏱ *Mid-May–mid-Oct., daily 9:30–5:30 (last tour 4:30).*

BONAVISTA

28 km (17 miles) north of Trinity.

No one knows exactly where explorer John Cabot landed when he came to Atlantic Canada in 1497, but many believe, based on his descriptions of the newfound land, it was at Bonavista.

GETTING HERE AND AROUND

Public transit doesn't serve Bonavista. From Trinity drive north on Route 239 and continue north (turn right) on Route 230; from the Trans-Canada Highway, take the exit for Route 230A and join Route 230 north of George's Brook.

EXPLORING

Cape Bonavista Lighthouse. A provincial historic site on the point, about 1 km (½ mile) outside town, the lighthouse was built in 1843 and has been restored to the way it looked in 1870. Admission includes entry to the Mockbeggar Plantation. ☎ *709/468–7444* ⊕ *www.seethesites.ca* 🎫 *C$6 (Sun. free)* ⏱ *Mid-May–early Oct., daily 9:30–5:30.*

FAMILY **Mockbeggar Plantation.** The home of F. Gordon Bradley, a proponent of Confederation, has been restored to its 1939 appearance, the better to chronicle the days leading up to Newfoundland's becoming, a decade later, a province of Canada. The site's history goes much farther back, at least to the 1700s, when it was a fishery plantation. Interpreters describing this and subsequent eras lead tours of an early-18th-century fish store, a carpentry shop, and a cod-liver-oil factory. ✉ *Mockbeggar Rd., off Rte. 230* ☎ *709/468–7300* 🌐 *www.seethesites.ca* 🎟 *C$6, includes entry to Cape Bonavista Lighthouse* ⏲ *Mid-May–early Oct., daily 10–5:30.*

Ryan Premises National Historic Site. On the waterfront, this restored fish-merchant's property depicts the history of the commercial cod fishery that prospered here between 1869 and the 1950s. ✉ *Rte. 235, off Rte. 230* ☎ *709/468–1600* 🌐 *www.pc.gc.ca* 🎟 *C$3.90* ⏲ *Mid-May–mid-Oct., daily 10–6.*

WHERE TO STAY

For expanded hotel reviews, visit Fodors.com.

$$ B&B/INN 🏨 **The Harbour Quarters.** Overlooking Bonavista harbor, just a few steps from the Ryan Premises, this heritage property is a great place to drop anchor for the night. **Pros:** easy walk to everything; sunset view from restaurant and deck; smoke-free; elevator. **Cons:** on the main road; no lunch at restaurant during the off-season. [$] *Rooms from: C$155* ✉ *42 Campbell St.* ☎ *709/468–7982, 866/468–7982* 🌐 *www.harbourquarters.com* 🛏 *10 rooms, 1 suite* 🍴 *No meals.*

GRAND BANK

62 km (38 miles) west of Burin.

One of the loveliest communities in Newfoundland, Grand Bank has a fascinating history as an important fishing center. Because of trading patterns, the architecture here was influenced more by Halifax, Boston, and Bar Harbor, Maine, than by the rest of Newfoundland.

GETTING HERE AND AROUND

Grand Bank is on the Burin Peninsula Highway (Route 210), which winds south and then west down the Burin Peninsula.

EXPLORING

Provincial Seamen's Museum. An outpost of The Rooms in St. John's, this sail-shaped building contains a bright and lively museum celebrating the province's connection with both land and sea. Exhibits include boats, ship models, and artifacts from the 1800s to the present. ✉ *54 Marine Dr.* ☎ *709/832–1484* 🌐 *www.therooms.ca/psm* 🎟 *C$2.50* ⏲ *Mid-Apr.–early Oct., Mon.–Sat. 9–4:45, Sun. noon–4:45.*

ST-PIERRE AND MIQUELON

70-minute ferry ride from Fortune.

The islands of St-Pierre and Miquelon, France's only territory in North America, are but a ferry ride away from Newfoundland. Shopping and dining on French cuisine are both popular pastimes here. The bakeries open early, so there's always piping-hot fresh bread for breakfast, and bargain hunters can find reasonably priced wines from all over France. An interesting side trip via boat takes you to see seals, seabirds, and other wildlife, plus the huge sandbar (formed on the bones of shipwrecks) that now connects formerly separate Great and Little Miquelon.

GETTING HERE AND AROUND

You can fly to St-Pierre from St. John's, Halifax, Sydney, or Montréal with Air Saint Pierre, or you can take a ferry from Fortune, which is 10 km (6 miles) from Grand Bank. Visitors to the islands must carry proof of citizenship—all non-Canadians must have a passport, and Canadians should have a passport or a government-issued photo ID. Because of the ferry schedule, a trip to St-Pierre means an overnight stay in a hotel or a pension, the French equivalent of a B&B. If you're flying you'll need to stay longer—from St. John's flights (C$202.21 one-way, C$339.76 round-trip) are on Wednesday, Friday, and Sunday, and schedules don't allow for a one-day round-trip; the other departure points are seasonal. St-Pierre is on French time, a half hour ahead of Newfoundland, so make sure you adjust your watch for the ferry schedule. Once you arrive in St-Pierre everything is within a short taxi ride or walking distance.

Air Saint-Pierre. International flight service is provided between St. John's and the French island of St-Pierre, as well as domestic service between the islands of Miquelon and St-Pierre. ☎ *877/277–7765* 🌐 *www.airsaintpierre.com.*

ESSENTIALS

If you plan to stay here for any length of time, be aware that the electrical supply is the same as in France—220v, 50 Hz. Check for compatibility with you electronic equipment and carry adapters if necessary. For other information about traveling to and within the islands check with their tourist board.

Contacts St-Pierre and Miquelon Tourist Board ☎ *011–508/410–200* 🌐 *www.tourisme-saint-pierre-et-miquelon.com.*

EXPLORING

St-Pierre Tours. A passenger ferry operated by this company leaves Fortune (south of Grand Bank) daily from April to June and twice a day in July and August; the crossing takes 90 minutes. Call for schedule and rates. ✉ *Fortune* ☎ *709/832–2006, 800/563–2006* 🌐 *www.spmtours.com.*

WHERE TO EAT AND STAY

For expanded hotel reviews, visit Fodors.com.

$$$ FRENCH 🍴 **L'Atelier Gourmand.** French cuisine receives creative yet not overly complicated flourishes at this restaurant specializing in fresh seafood from the surrounding waters. This might include lobster grilled with garlic and anise, or crispy cod and chorizo in cream. For meat dishes there might be slow-cooked pork loin with Thai spices, or duck breast with raspberry vinaigrette, and there's sure to be a classic grilled steak. As might be expected, the wine list favors France. In fine weather you can dine on the outdoor patio. ■ **TIP→ Cash payments must be in euros or U.S. dollars.** [$] *Average main: C$27* ✉ *12 rue du 11 Novembre, St-Pierre, St-Pierre and Miquelon* ☎ *011–508/415–300* 🌐 *www.lateliergourmandspm.com.*

$$ HOTEL 🏨 **Hotel Robert.** Convenient to the ferry, this waterfront hotel used to accommodate Al Capone when he ran rum through St-Pierre during prohibition—you can see his hat in the mini Prohibition-era museum on-site. **Pros:** on the waterfront, a five-minute walk from ferry; rental

car available; ocean views from breakfast room. **Cons:** no elevator; no room service. $ *Rooms from: C$137* ✉ *2 rue du 11 Novembre, St-Pierre and Miquelon* ☎ *011–508/412–419* ⊕ *www.hotelrobert.com* ⤴ *40 rooms, 3 suites* ❙◎❙ *Breakfast.*

GANDER AND AROUND

Gander, in east-central Newfoundland, is known for its airport and its aviation history. North of it is Notre Dame Bay, an area of rugged coastline and equally rugged islands that was once the domain of the now extinct Beothuk tribe. Only the larger islands are currently inhabited. Before English settlers moved into the area in the late 18th and early 19th centuries, it was seasonally occupied by French fisherfolk. Local dialects preserve centuries-old words that have vanished elsewhere. The bay is swept by the cool Labrador Current, which carries icebergs south through Iceberg Alley; the coast is also a good whale-watching area.

GANDER

367 km (228 miles) north of Grand Bank; 331 km (207 miles) west of St. John's; 149 km (93 miles) west of Clarenville.

Gander, a busy town of 9,500 people, is notable for its aviation history. During World War II, the airport here, now called Gander International, was a major strategic air base because of its favorable weather and secure location. After the war, the airport became a hub for civilian travel. It gained some renown when planes destined for the U.S. were diverted here following the September 11, 2001, terrorist attacks. The movie Diverted told the heartwarming story. Today the airport is a major air-traffic-control center.

With its varied lodging options, Gander is a good base for travel in this part of the province, including to Twillingate, the town of Change Islands, and Fogo Island.

GETTING HERE AND AROUND

Gander is on the Trans-Canada Highway (Route 1). To get to Twillingate take Route 330 north to Route 331 north, eventually connecting to Route 340 to Twillingate. To visit Change Islands and Fogo Island depart Route 331 at Route 335 and head northeast. You can drive on causeways to Twillingate but will need to catch the ferry in Farewell to get to Change Islands and Fogo Island. If you fly into Gander's airport, book a rental car in advance, as supplies are limited.

Contacts Gander International Airport ✉ *1000 James Blvd.* ☎ *709/256–6666* ⊕ *www.ganderairport.com.*

EXPLORING

FAMILY **North Atlantic Aviation Museum.** Next to the visitor information center, this museum provides an expansive view of Gander's and Newfoundland's roles in aviation. In addition to viewing the aircraft collection (including a World War II–era Lockheed Hudson and a Voodoo fighter jet) and some photographs, you can climb into the cockpit of a real DC-3.

There's also a unique aviation gift shop. ✉ *135 Trans-Canada Hwy.* ☎ *709/256–2923* 🌐 *www.northatlanticaviationmuseum.com* 🎟 *C$6* 🕓 *June–mid-Sept., daily 9–7; mid-Sept.–May, weekdays 9–5.*

Silent Witness Memorial. The memorial marks the spot where, on December 12, 1985, an Arrow Air DC-8 carrying the 101st Airborne Division home for Christmas crashed, killing 256 American soldiers and civilian flight crew. The site lies off the highway a short distance on a rough gravel road, but it's a must-see. The setting, a clearing in the woods overlooking the grandeur of Gander Lake, is moving, and the memorial sculpture, of a boy and girl holding the hands of a peacekeeper, is poignantly rendered. ✉ *Eastern side of Trans-Canada Hwy., 4 km (2½ miles) from Gander.*

OFF THE BEATEN PATH

Change Islands and Fogo Island. Modernity arrived late here, and old expressions and accents still survive, so these outposts feel frozen in time. Change Islands (🌐 *www.changeislands.ca*), a town with outbuildings built on outcroppings and on stilts, is a nice place for a quiet walk. Fogo Island is known for its hiking trails, including Brimstone Head, one of the four corners of the earth according to the Flat Earth Society. More recently Fogo Island has begun to reinvent itself with many modern artist studios and arts-residency projects (🌐 *www.shorefast.org*). The town of **Tilting,** on Fogo's far end, is famous for its "vernacular" architecture—two-story houses with typically one of three floor plans. The Dwyer Fishing Premises won an award for preservation of the architectural heritage of Newfoundland and Labrador and is part of the Tilting National Historic Site (☎ *709/266–1320,* 🌐 *www.townoftilting.com*), along with the Lane House Museum, the Old Irish Cemetery, and Sandy Cove Park.

There are about a dozen places to stay on the island, including the four-room Foley's Place B&B in Tilting (☎ *709/658–7244 or 866/658–7244*) and Peg's Bed and Breakfast (☎ *709/266–7130*) in the community of Fogo. To get to Change Islands and Fogo Island you must take a ferry from Farewell, which is on Route 335 north of the Trans-Canada Highway. **Provincial Ferry Service** charges C$18.15 for a vehicle and driver from Farewell to Fogo; C$4.13 from Fogo to Change Islands, and C$7.15 from Change Islands to Farewell, with additional fees for other passengers. ☎ *855/621–3150 ferry service* 🌐 *www.tw.gov.nl.ca/ferryservices/schedules/c_fogo.html.*

WHERE TO EAT AND STAY

For expanded hotel reviews, visit Fodors.com.

$$$ BISTRO

🍴 **Bistro on Roe.** The concept here isn't complex, but it's well executed: creative cuisine, reasonable prices, friendly atmosphere. The combination of crisp white tablecloths and often whimsical local art mirrors the simple-yet-rich fare of owner-chef Alex Bracci and Jillian Hulan. Black Angus filet mignon in a bourbon and brown sugar sauce is the menu's star, but the kitchen performs wonders with dishes such as scallops with blueberries and a port-wine sauce, and pan-roasted salmon stuffed with spinach, dill, and cream cheese. With meatless entrées that might include handmade ravioli stuffed with butternut squash in a butter and pecan sauce, vegetarians won't feel slighted. [$] *Average main: C$26* ✉ *110 Roe Ave.* ☎ *709/651–4763* 🌐 *www.bistroonroe.com* 🕓 *Closed Sun. No lunch.*

$$$$ **Fogo Island Inn.** Everything about this place, perched on the very edge
B&B/INN of the continent, invites superlatives—stunning modern architecture and
interior design, breathtaking ocean views, exquisite cuisine, advanced
technology, and the ultimate in that famous Newfoundland hospitality. **Pros:** supremely peaceful; all meals, snacks, and gratuities included
in the price; high level of social integrity within the community. **Cons:**
very expensive; access sometimes affected by the weather. $ *Rooms
from: C$850 ⊠ Joe Batt's Arm, Fogo Island ☎ 709/658–3444 ⊕ www.
fogoislandinn.ca ⇨ 29 suites ❏ All meals.*

$$ **Hotel Gander.** You won't get lost finding this hotel right on the Trans-
HOTEL Canada Highway—a good stopover if you're traveling from coast to
coast, but also a destination for its golf packages. **Pros:** vehicles with
boat trailers can park easily; bright, cheerful dining room; bar has out-
side patio; children under 12 stay and eat for free. **Cons:** living room
in suites not air-conditioned; highway traffic makes front rooms noisy.
$ *Rooms from: C$139 ⊠ 100 Trans-Canada Hwy. ☎ 709/256–3931,
800/563–2988 ⊕ www.hotelgander.com ⇨ 147 rooms, 4 suites, 2 cot-
tages ❏ Multiple meal plans.*

BOYD'S COVE

71 km (44 miles) north of Gander.

Between 1650 and 1720, the Beothuks' main summer camp on the
northeast coast was at the site of what is now Boyd's Cove. The coast-
line in and near Boyd's Cove is somewhat sheltered by Twillingate
Island and New World Island, linked to the shore by short causeways.

GETTING HERE AND AROUND

From Gander head north on Route 330 to Gander Bay South and Har-
ris Point. Here, turn left onto Route 331 toward Twillingate, crossing
the causeway over Gander Bay, then swing right and continue north.

EXPLORING

Beothuk Interpretation Centre. Explore the lives of the Beothuks, an extinct
First Nations people who succumbed in the early 19th century to a com-
bination of disease and battle with European settlers. A 1.5-km (1-mile)
trail leads to the archaeological site that was inhabited from about 1650
to 1720, when pressure from settlers drove the Beothuks from this part
of the coast. Walk softly to feel "The Spirit of the Beothuk," represented
in a commanding bronze statue by Gerald Squires that stands almost hid-
den in the woods. ⊠ *Rte. 340 ☎ 709/656–3114, 800/563–6353 ⊕ www.
seethesites.ca ☜ $6 ☉ Mid-May–mid-Oct., daily 9:30–5.*

TWILLINGATE

41 km (25 miles) north of Boyd's Cove.

The inhabitants of this scenic old fishing village make their living from
the sea and have been doing so for nearly two centuries. Colorful
houses, rocky waterfront cliffs, local museums, and a nearby light-
house add to the town's appeal. One of the best places on the island to
see icebergs, Twillingate is known to the locals as Iceberg Alley. These
majestic and dangerous mountains of ice are awe inspiring to see when

they're grounded in early summer. With its range of lodging options, Twillingate makes a good base for exploring the surrounding region.

GETTING HERE AND AROUND

From Boyd's Cove, continue north on Route 340.

EXPLORING

Long Point Lighthouse. Among the few Newfoundland lighthouses you can climb (55 steps), this 1876 structure on a 300-foot cliff inspires gasps with its panoramic view—which include whales and icebergs at the right times of year. Groomed hiking trails begin at the base, and the nearby Long Point Centre has a fascinating collection of local artifacts. ✉ *Main St., Long Point* ☎ *709/884–1467* 🎟 *C$7* 🕒 *Mid-May–mid-Oct., daily (call for hrs).*

Prime Berth Twillingate Fishery & Heritage Centre. A "prime berth" was the term for the best fishing grounds in this area. Berths were allocated by annual lottery to local fishermen, whose livelihoods depended quite literally on the luck of the draw. This museum pays tribute to those fishermen and portrays their lifestyle. There's also a blacksmith shop, an aquarium, an observation tower, and a crafts studio. The facility's owner, David Boyd, aka Captain Dave, conducts boat trips to fish for lobster and cod or to watch whales and icebergs. ✉ *118 Main St.* ☎ *709/884–5925* 🌐 *www.primeberth.com* 🎟 *C$5; C$10 for guided tour* 🕒 *June–Sept., daily 10–5.*

WHERE TO EAT AND STAY

For expanded hotel reviews, visit Fodors.com.

$ CAFÉ 🍴 **Crow's Nest.** On the way to the Long Point Lighthouse, this friendly little café has a great ocean view and a deck from which to enjoy it—you might even see a passing whale or two if you're here in July or August. Light meals, including homemade soups, wraps, and chili, are served until 4 pm, or you can drop in for coffee and a delicious cinnamon bun. ■ TIP→ **This is a good place to pick up a bagged lunch before you hike or to replenish your energy upon your return.** [$] *Average main: C$8* ✉ *127 Main St., Crow Head* ☎ *709/893–2029* 🕒 *Closed Mon. in Aug., Mon. and Tues. in Sept. Limited opening rest of yr; call for details.*

$ HOTEL 🏨 **Anchor Inn.** Overlooking "iceberg alley," this hotel has a pleasant, welcoming atmosphere, and large, comfortable rooms, with either a queen-size bed or two doubles. **Pros:** great views; spacious rooms; friendly staff. **Cons:** breakfast is only included off-season; some needed improvements still to be made by new owners. [$] *Rooms from: C$120* ✉ *3 Path's End* ☎ *709/884–2777, 800/450–3950* 🌐 *anchorinntwillingate.com* 🛏 *14 rooms, 8 suites* 🕒 *Closed Jan.* 🍽 *Multiple meal plans.*

$ B&B/INN 🏨 **Paradise Bed & Breakfast.** Watch icebergs and whales from the deck of this modern, one-story home overlooking Twillingate Harbour. **Pros:** all rooms have private bathrooms; continental breakfast includes a hot item. **Cons:** no air-conditioning; two rooms have showers, not tubs; house doesn't reflect Twillingate history and heritage. [$] *Rooms from: C$90* ✉ *192 Main St.* ☎ *709/884–5683, 877/882–1999* 🌐 *www.capturegaia.com/paradiseb&b.html* 🛏 *3 rooms* 💳 *No credit cards* 🕒 *Closed mid-Oct.–mid-May* 🍽 *Breakfast.*

$ B&B/INN **Toulinguet Inn Bed & Breakfast.** In this 1920s-era home on the harbor front, rooms are old-fashioned, bright, and airy, and a second-story balcony looks out over the Atlantic Ocean. **Pros:** sunroom and balcony overlook the harbor; all rooms have private bath/shower; away from the highway. **Cons:** smoking permitted on balcony; no air-conditioning in rooms. [$] *Rooms from: C$95* ✉ *56 Main St.* ☎ *709/884–2080, 888/447–8687* 🛏 *4 rooms* ⏲ *Closed Oct.–mid-May* 🍴 *Breakfast.*

SPORTS AND THE OUTDOORS

Iceberg Man Tours. Owner Cecil Stockley's local nickname is "Iceberg Man," and he's been leading tours for more than 30 years. Two-hour cruises (C$50) take you out to see not only icebergs, but also whales and birds. Iceberg photography is the company's specialty, helping amateur photographers out to get that perfect shot. Tours depart at 9:30, 1, and 4, and sunset charters are available. The Iceberg Shop craft emporium on the harbor is under the same ownership. ☎ *709/884–2242, 800/611–2374* 🌐 *www.icebergtours.ca.*

Twillingate Adventure Tours. Two-hour guided cruises (C$50) on the M.V. *Daybreak* take you to see icebergs, whales, and seabirds. ✉ *128 Main St.* ☎ *709/884–5999, 888/447–8687* 🌐 *www.twillingateadventuretours.com.*

5

GRAND FALLS–WINDSOR

95 km (59 miles) from Gander.

This central Newfoundland town is an amalgamation of two towns that were joined in 1991. The papermaking town of Grand Falls was the quintessential company town, founded by British newspaper barons early in the 20th century, but the mill, which shipped newsprint all over the world, closed its doors in 2009. Windsor was once an important stop on the railway, but since its demise the city has foundered.

GETTING HERE AND AROUND

Grand Falls-Windsor is on the Trans-Canada Highway (Route 1), west of Gander and east of Deer Lake.

EXPLORING

A Logger's Life Provincial Museum. A division of the Rooms in St. John's, this museum portrays the hard lives of the workers who supplied wood for the paper mill in a logging camp that has been re-created to reflect the 1920s. ✉ *Off Rte. 1, Exit 17, 2 km (1 mile) west of Grand Falls–Windsor* ☎ *709/486–0492* 🌐 *www.therooms.ca/museum/prov_museums.asp* 🎫 *C$2.50, includes Mary March Provincial Museum* ⏲ *Mid-May–mid-Sept., Mon.–Sat. 9–4:45, Sun. noon–4:45.*

Mary March Provincial Museum. Demasduit, one of the last Beothuks, was given the European name Mary March, and displays at this museum named for her trace the lives and customs of aboriginal cultures in Newfoundland and Labrador. ✉ *24 St. Catherine's St.* ☎ *709/292–4522* 🌐 *www.therooms.ca/museum/prov_museums.asp* 🎫 *C$2.50, includes A Logger's Life Museum* ⏲ *Late Apr.–mid-Oct., Mon.–Sat. 9–4:45, Sun. noon–4:45.*

WHERE TO STAY

For expanded hotel reviews, visit Fodors.com.

$$ 🏨 **Mount Peyton Hotel.** This is a convenient choice, with a variety of
HOTEL lodging options, but make sure you get a room on the hotel side of the
highway—motel rooms are smaller, more down-at-the-heels, and cut off
from the hotel and restaurants. **Pros:** VIP suite is comfortable, with terry
bathrobes, easy chairs, and other extras; good local music on Friday
night at the pub, with no cover. **Cons:** front rooms very close to highway
traffic; smoking rooms still available. $ *Rooms from: C$135* ⊠ *214
Lincoln Rd.* ☎ *709/489–2251, 800/563–4894* ⊕ *www.mountpeyton.
com* ⌐ *101 hotel rooms, 31 motel rooms, 16 suites* 🍽 *No meals.*

WESTERN NEWFOUNDLAND

The Great Northern Peninsula is the northernmost visible extension
of the Appalachian Mountains. Its eastern side is rugged and sparsely
populated. The Viking Trail—Route 430 and its side roads—snakes
along its western coast through Gros Morne National Park, fjords,
sand dunes, and communities that have relied on lobster fishing for
generations. At the tip of the peninsula, the Vikings established the first
European settlement in North America a thousand years ago, but for
thousands of years before their arrival, the area was home to native
peoples who hunted, fished, and gathered berries and herbs.

Corner Brook boasts a fabulous natural setting on the Gulf of St. Law-
rence, ringed by mountains, and with plenty of green spaces within
its boundaries. It has good shopping and a lively arts scene, and the
nearby Humber River is world renowned for its salmon fishing. To
the south, the Port au Port Peninsula, west of Stephenville, shows the
French influence in Newfoundland, distinct from the farming valleys of
the southwest, which were settled by Scots. A ferry from Nova Scotia
docks at Port aux Basques in the far southwest corner.

DEER LAKE

208 km (129 miles) west of Grand Falls–Windsor.

Deer Lake was once just another small town on the Trans-Canada
Highway, but the opening of Gros Morne National Park in the early
1970s and the construction of Route 430, a first-class paved highway
passing right through to St. Anthony, changed all that.

GETTING HERE

Today, with an airport and car rentals available, Deer Lake is a good
starting point for a fly–drive vacation, and it's open all year. There are
connections from eastern and central Canada, and from St. John's.
From the airport there is a shuttle bus into Deer Lake (and Corner
Brook), as well as major car-rental outlets, but make early reservations
because stocks are limited.

ESSENTIALS

Visitor Information Deer Lake Visitor Information Centre ⊠ *60A Trans-Can-
ada Hwy.* ☎ *709/635–2202* ⊕ *www.town.deerlake.nf.ca.*

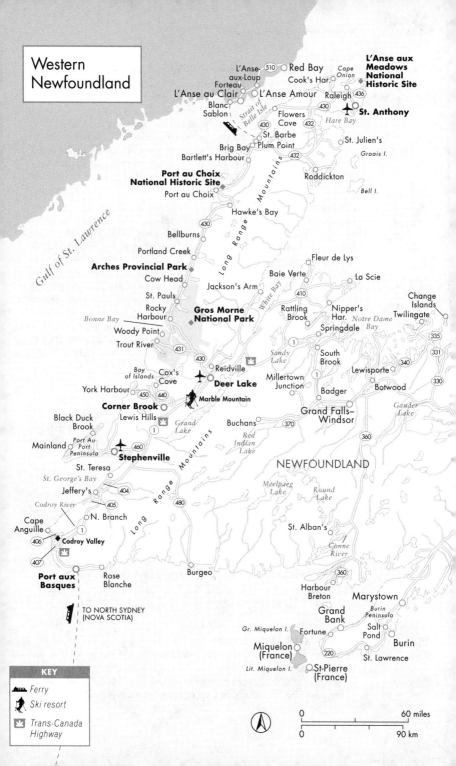

Western Newfoundland

L'Anse aux Meadows National Historic Site
Cape Onion
Red Bay
510
L'Anse-aux-Loup
Forteau
Cook's Har.
Raleigh
436
L'Anse au Clair
L'Anse Amour
St. Anthony
Blanc Sablon
430
Flowers Cove
432
Hare Bay
St. Barbe
Brig Bay
Plum Point
St. Julien's
Bartlett's Harbour
432
Groais I.
Port au Choix National Historic Site
Roddickton
Bell I.
Port au Choix
Hawke's Bay
430
Bellburns
Fleur de Lys
Portland Creek
Baie Verte
La Scie
Arches Provincial Park
Cow Head
Jackson's Arm
410
Change Islands
St. Pauls
Rattling Brook
Nipper's Har.
Twillingate
Rocky Harbour
Gros Morne National Park
Springdale
Notre Dame Bay
335
Bonne Bay
331
Woody Point
South Brook
Trout River
431
Sandy Lake
1
340
430
Reidville
Millertown Junction
Lewisporte
330
Cox's Cove
Deer Lake
Badger
Botwood
York Harbour
450
440
Marble Mountain
Gander Lake
Corner Brook
Lewis Hills
1
Grand Lake
Buchans
Grand Falls–Windsor
Black Duck Brook
370
Red Indian Lake
NEWFOUNDLAND
Mainland
Port Au Port Peninsula
460
Stephenville
St. Teresa
Meelpaeg Lake
Round Lake
St. George's Bay
Jeffery's
404
Codroy River
405
480
N. Branch
Cape Anguille
1
406
St. Alban's
Codroy Valley
407
Conne River
Port aux Basques
Rose Blanche
Burgeo
360
Harbour Breton
Marystown
TO NORTH SYDNEY (NOVA SCOTIA)
Grand Bank
Burin Peninsula
Salt Pond
Burin
Gr. Miquelon I.
Fortune
220
St. Lawrence
Miquelon (France)
St-Pierre (France)
Lit. Miquelon I.

KEY
- Ferry
- Ski resort
- Trans-Canada Highway

0   60 miles
0   90 km

EXPLORING

Long Range Mountains. Stretching all the way from the southwest coast to the Northern Peninsula, a distance of about 400 km (250 miles), the Long Range Mountains form the northernmost extent of the Appalachian Mountains. Their highest point, southwest of Corner Brook, is 814 meters (2,670 feet), and the range encompasses the Gros Morne National Park and several provincial parks. Jacques Cartier, who saw them in 1534 as he was exploring the area on behalf of France, noted that their shape reminded him of the long, rectangular-shaped farm buildings of his home village in France. Among the mountains, small villages are interspersed with rivers teeming with salmon and trout.

FAMILY **Newfoundland Insectarium.** An intriguing collection of live and preserved insects, spiders, and scorpions from six temperate zones is housed here, and there's a glass beehive with 10,000 honeybees. The greenhouse is home to hundreds of live tropical butterflies. A walking trail leads through woodland to the Humber River and Rocky Brook—you have a good chance of spotting beavers and muskrats from the viewing deck. Check out the gift shop, which sometimes stocks lollipops with edible dried scorpions inside. **TIP→ The Insectarium is a one-minute drive off the Trans-Canada Highway at Deer Lake; turn north onto Route 430, also signed here as Bonne Bay Road.** ✉ *2 Bonne Bay Rd., Reidville* ☎ *709/635–4545, 866/635–5454* 🌐 *www.nfinsectarium.com* 🎟 *C$12* 🕒 *July and Aug., daily 9–6; May, June, Sept., and Oct., weekdays 9–5, Sat. 10–5, Sun. noon–5.*

WHERE TO EAT AND STAY

For expanded hotel reviews, visit Fodors.com.

$ AMERICAN ✕ **Deer Lake Irving Big Stop.** Good home-cooked meals, burgers and fries, and healthy options like salads and salmon make this franchise eatery a welcome pit stop, as do the reassuringly clean washrooms. The adjacent convenience store sells gifts, souvenirs, some outdoor apparel, magazines, and basic motoring supplies. [$] *Average main: C$10* ✉ *Trans-Canada Highway (Rte. 1), Exit 16* ☎ *709/635–2129.*

$$ HOTEL 🏨 **Deer Lake Motel.** Recent renovations have perked up what was already a clean and comfortable motel, the nearest lodging to Gros Morne National Park. **Pros:** easy to find, at the junction of the Trans-Canada Highway and the Viking Trail (Highway 430). **Cons:** restaurant more like a coffee shop; highway traffic noisy; no elevator. [$] *Rooms from: C$139* ✉ *15 Trans-Canada Hwy.* ☎ *709/635–2108, 800/563–2144* 🌐 *www.deerlakemotel.com* 🛏 *55 rooms, 2 suites* 🍴 *No meals.*

GROS MORNE NATIONAL PARK

Fodor's Choice ★ *46 km (29 miles) north of Deer Lake.*

GETTING HERE AND AROUND

Traveling north from Deer Lake, the park's main entry point is just before the community of Wiltondale. Continue on Route 430 to Rocky Harbour for the main visitor center and Cow Head, at the northern end of the park. For the southern part of the park, turn left on Route 431.

EXPLORING

FAMILY **Bonne Bay Marine Station.** A visit here is a must, especially for kids, who often find themselves enthralled by the touch tank, the centerpiece of the 45-minute guided aquarium tours. In addition to experiencing sea stars, crabs, algae, and other marine life firsthand, participants also learn about the station's past and current research projects. ⊠ *1 Clarke's La., Norris Point* ☎ *709/458–2874, 709/458–2550* ⊕ *www.bonnebay. mun.ca* ⊠ *C$6.25* ⊙ *Mid-May–mid-Oct., daily 9–5.*

Discovery Centre. On the outskirts of Woody Point, a charming community of old houses and imported Lombardy poplars, this is the main center for interpreting the geology of Gros Morne National Park. Educational programs about natural history are conducted, and there's a craft shop. ■**TIP→ At the back of the center's parking lot is the fine Lookout Hills trail, a 5-km (3-mile) trek with outstanding views of Bonne Bay, Gros Morne Mountain, and the Tablelands.** ⊠ *Rte. 431, heading west toward Trout River* ☎ *709/458–2417* ⊙ *Mid-May–mid-Oct., daily 9–5 (to 6, mid-June–early Sept.).*

Green Gardens Trail. This spectacular 9-km (5.5-mile) round-trip hike starts at Long Pond—on Route 431, 3 km (2 miles) east of Trout River— passes through the Tablelands barrens, and descends sharply to a coastline of eroded cliffs and green meadows. Be prepared to do a bit of climbing on your return journey. A longer version of the trail includes a loop around Wallace Brook. ⚠ **Some parts of the cliff edges are undercut, so stick to the trail.** ⊠ *Rte. 431* ☎ *709/458–2417* ⊕ *www.pc.gc.ca.*

Gros Morne National Park. Because of its geological uniqueness and immense splendor, this park has been named a UNESCO World Heritage Site. Camping and hiking are popular recreations, and boat tours are available.

To see Gros Morne properly you should allow yourself at least two days, but most people, once they're here, would appreciate having a few more. Scenic **Bonne Bay,** a deep fjord, divides the park into distinct northern and southern sections.

The most popular attraction in the northern portion of Gros Morne is the boat tour of **Western Brook Pond.** You park at a lot on Route 430 and take a 45-minute walk to the boat dock through an interesting mix of bog and woods. Cliffs rise 2,000 feet on both sides of the gorge, and high waterfalls tumble over ancient rocks. Those in good shape can tackle the 16-km (10-mile) hike up **Gros Morne Mountain,** at 2,644 feet the second-highest peak in Newfoundland. Weather permitting, the reward for your effort is a unique Arctic landscape and spectacular views. The park's **northern coast** has an unusual mix of sand beaches, rock pools, and trails through tangled dwarf forests (called tuckamore forests locally). Sunsets seen from **Lobster Head Cove Lighthouse** are spectacular. In season you might spot whales here, and a visit to the lighthouse museum, devoted to the history of the area, is rewarding.

Woody Point, a community of old houses and imported Lombardy poplars, is in the southern part of the park, on Route 431. Rising behind it are the **Tablelands,** a unique rock massif that was raised from the earth's mantle through tectonic upheaval. Its rocks are toxic to most plant life and have weathered to a rusty brown color. The Tablelands provide a remarkable exposure of mantle rock, rarely seen at the earth's surface; it's the main reason Gros Morne National Park has received UNESCO World Heritage status. The small community of **Trout River** is at the western end of Route 431 on the Gulf of St. Lawrence. You pass the scenic Trout River pond on the way there. 🌐 *www.pc.gc.ca* 🎟 *C$9.80.*

Gros Morne Visitor's Centre. The thoughtful displays and videos about the park make this is a good place to familiarize yourself with the park and what it has to offer. ✉ *Rte. 430, Rocky Harbour* ☎ *709/458–2417, 709/458–2066* 🌐 *www.pc.gc.ca* 🕒 *Mid-May–late Oct., daily 9–5 (to 8 late June–early Sept.).*

LEAVE THE CAR BEHIND

You can drive to the pretty town of Woody Point, but why not leave the car behind and take a boat? Leave your wheels at Norris Point and take the water taxi (BonTours, ⇨ *See below for contact info).* The journey takes 15 minutes, and you'll probably see whales and kayakers out on the water. In Woody Point, you can have lunch and spend the day strolling or stay overnight. The water taxi leaves Norris Point at 9 am, 12:30 pm, and 5 pm daily and leaves Woody Point roughly half an hour later, mid-June through August (C$14 return).

WHERE TO EAT

$$$$ MODERN CANADIAN

🍴 **Black Spruce.** The short but enticing menu here reflects the kitchen team's expert touch and dedication to the concepts of sustainable farming and incorporating local ingredients. You could start with the particularly tasty seafood chowder with smoked bacon and crème fraîche, then move on to perfectly cooked beef tenderloin with champ, Stilton crust, and seasonal vegetables. For a fish dish, you'll have to wait and see what the local fishermen have just brought in. Desserts range from beautifully light to naughtily rich choices, the latter well represented by the figgy duff (a local pudding) served with molasses and Sea Buckthorn ice cream. TIP→ **Arrive before the sun goes down to enjoy the stunning view over Bonne Bay.** [$] *Average main: C$31* ✉ *Neddies Harbour Inn, 7 Beach Rd., Neddies Harbour, Norris Point* ☎ *709/458–3089* 🌐 *theblackspruce.ca* 🕒 *Closed Mon. and Nov.–Apr. Closed Tues. mid-Sept.–Oct.*

$$$ SEAFOOD

🍴 **Fisherman's Landing.** The wide-ranging menu at Fisherman's Landing includes plenty of seafood but pizza and other options as well. Both the food and the service here are reliable, which means that the place can get busy, but you can always browse the crafts shop upstairs until your table's ready. The restaurant is open from 6 am to 11 pm. ⇨ *See also Where to Stay.* [$] *Average main: C$25* ✉ *44 Main St., Rocky Harbour* ☎ *709/458–2060* 🌐 *www.fishermanslandinginn.com.*

$$$ CANADIAN Fodor's Choice ★

🍴 **Java Jack's Restaurant and Gallery.** The pleasures of this lively restaurant begin with a stroll past the meticulously kept organic garden, where you can see the herbs, peas, and other vegetables you'll enjoy inside. The dinner menu has many seafood options—the pan-seared scallops in mild mango curry are especially good—as well as meat dishes and vegan and vegetarian selections. The wines are well chosen and reasonably priced.

The restaurant doubles as a gallery; works by Atlantic Canadian artists (all for sale) decorate the walls. **TIP→ Stop in for a take-away bag lunch—perhaps a shredded-pork sandwich slathered with partridgeberry-honey mustard—for the boat trip to Western Brook Pond, or dine here and enjoy the splendid harbor views.** [$] *Average main: C$27* ✉ *88 Main St. N, Rocky Harbour* ☎ *709/458–3004* 🌐 *javajacks.ca* ✍ *Reservations not accepted* ⏲ *Closed Tues. and Oct.–mid-May.*

$$$ SEAFOOD 🍴 **Seaside Restaurant.** The chefs at this two-story restaurant overlooking the ocean prepare fresh seafood in traditional, innovative, Newfoundland style. A perfect meal might start with Northern scallops served on greens brightened with deep burgundy partridgeberries, followed by grilled shark. Cod tongues—a secret recipe—are popular and offered throughout the season, and the ocean catfish is also highly recommended. The boardwalk is delightful for a stroll before or after you eat, and you can watch the sunset from the upper deck. [$] *Average main: C$22* ✉ *Main St., Trout River* ☎ *709/451–3461* 🌐 *www.grosmorneescapes.com* ⏲ *Closed Oct.–late May.*

5

WHERE TO STAY

For expanded hotel reviews, visit Fodors.com.

$ B&B/INN 🏨 **Blanchard House.** Well located for visits to the southern section of Gros Morne National Park, this spotlessly clean 1904 heritage home has been renovated but retains its period character. **Pros:** some rooms have gorgeous bay windows; all rooms have private baths; one hot item daily with continental breakfast. **Cons:** no Internet access; three rooms have shower but no tub; beds are all standard double size. [$] *Rooms from: C$69* ✉ *12 Blanchard La., Woody Point* ☎ *709/451–3236, 877/951–3236* 🌐 *www.crockercabins.com* 🛏 *4 rooms* ⏲ *Closed early Oct.–late May* 🍽 *Breakfast.*

$$ HOTEL 🏨 **Fisherman's Landing Inn.** Although it's not on the water as the name implies, this is a spacious, bright, and well-maintained property. **Pros:** smoke-free; crafts shop off lobby; cross-country-skiing and snowshoeing winter packages. **Cons:** a bit overpriced; limited food and wine menu; 2-km (1¼-mile) walk from most other eateries; away from the waterfront. [$] *Rooms from: C$139* ✉ *2129 West Link Rd., Rocky Harbour* ☎ *709/458–2711, 866/458–2711* 🌐 *www.fishermanslandinginn.com* 🛏 *37 rooms, 3 suites* 🍽 *No meals.*

$$$ B&B/INN Fodor's Choice ★ 🏨 **Neddies Harbour Inn.** In a picture-perfect location overlooking beautiful Bonne Bay, this boutique-style inn has spacious rooms and a fine restaurant. **Pros:** perfect location; excellent breakfasts included in the price; hot tub, sauna, and fitness room. **Cons:** Breakfast service stops at 9 am. [$] *Rooms from: C$185* ✉ *7 Beach Rd., Neddies Harbour, Norris Point* ☎ *709/458–3089, 877/458–2929* 🌐 *theinn.ca* 🛏 *14 rooms, 1 suite, 4 cottages* ⏲ *Closed Nov.–Apr.* 🍽 *Breakfast.*

$$ HOTEL 🏨 **Ocean View Hotel.** Right on the water, this two-story hotel has good-size modern rooms and nightly entertainment in summer. **Pros:** near crafts stores and dining options; there's a small strand of beach across the street. **Cons:** open windows bring loud music from pub; pub accessible only with cover charge. [$] *Rooms from: C$149* ✉ *38–42 Main St., Rocky Harbour* ☎ *709/458–2730, 800/563–9887* 🌐 *www.theoceanview.ca* 🛏 *38 rooms, 5 suites* 🍽 *No meals.*

$$ B&B/INN **Sugar Hill Inn.** The inn is quiet and relaxing; large windows throughout the building let in lots of light, and the warm color schemes and natural wood on floors and ceilings adds character to the spacious, uncluttered guest rooms, most of which have a private deck. **Pros:** cedar-lined hot tub and sauna; water comes from a spring on the property. **Cons:** exterior doesn't suggest the quality inside. [$] *Rooms from: C$165* ✉ *115–129 Main St., Norris Point* ☎ *709/458–2147, 888/299–2147* 🌐 *www.sugarhillinn.nf.ca* 🛏 *5 rooms, 5 suites, 1 cottage* 🕒 *Closed Nov.–mid-May (except for group bookings)* 🍴 *Breakfast.*

$$ B&B/INN **Wildflowers Country Inn.** Set back from the main road on a property full of trees, this grand 80-year-old clapboard house overlooks the ocean. **Pros:** common room with a refrigerator; guided tours include back-country snowmobile tours in season. **Cons:** no air-conditioning; some rooms have shower, not bath. [$] *Rooms from: C$129* ✉ *108 Main St. N, Rocky Harbour* ☎ 📠 *709/458–3000, 888/811–7378* 🌐 *www.wildflowerscountryinn.ca* 🛏 *5 rooms, 1 cottage* 🍴 *Breakfast.*

NIGHTLIFE AND THE ARTS

Two major festivals, Gros Morne Summer Music and the Gros Morne Theatre Festival (⇨ *See Planning*) make for a lively arts scene during high season.

SPORTS AND THE OUTDOORS

BonTours. BonTours runs sightseeing boat tours of Western Brook Pond (C$53–C$65, depending on time of day) in Gros Morne National Park and on Bonne Bay (C$40) as well as a water taxi service (C$8 one-way or C$14 round-trip) between Norris Point and Woody Point. ✉ *42 Main St., Rocky Harbour* ☎ *709/458–2016, 888/458–2016* 🌐 *www.bontours.ca.*

Gros Morne Adventures. Sea kayaking on Bonne Bay in Gros Morne National Park is offered by this outfitter, as well as guided coastal and mountain hiking (C$125 for a full day) in the area. Guided sea kayaking tours start at C$55 for two hours, rising to C$125 for a half-day outing. Kayak rentals start at C$35 (single) and C$45 (double). ✉ *Clarkes Rd., Norris Point* ☎ *709/458–2722, 800/685–4624* 🌐 *www.grosmorneadventures.com.*

ARCHES PROVINCIAL PARK

20 km (12 miles) north of Gros Morne National Park.

GETTING HERE AND AROUND

Route 430 connects the Arches Provincial Park to Gros Morne National Park and Deer Lake in the south and St. Anthony in the north.

EXPLORING

The Arches Provincial Park. A geological curiosity, the park contains rock formations made millions of years ago by wave action and undersea currents. The succession of caves through a bed of dolomite was later raised above sea level by tectonic upheaval. **TIP→ This is a good place to stop for a picnic.** ✉ *Rte. 430, Portland Creek* ☎ *709/635–4520* 🌐 *www.env.gov.nl.ca* 🎟 *Free* 🕒 *Early June–mid-Oct.*

EN ROUTE

Port au Choix National Historic Site. The remains of Maritime Archaic and Dorset people have been found along this coast between the Arches Provincial Park and L'Anse aux Meadows, and this site has an interesting interpretation center with exhibits about what's been uncovered to date. **■ TIP→ Archaeologists digging in the area uncovered an ancient village. Ask at the center for directions to it.** ✉ *Point Riche Rd., west of Rte. 430 off Fisher Rd.; 94 km (58½ miles) north of Arches Provincial Park, Port au Choix* ☎ *709/458–2417, 709/861–3522* 🌐 *www.pc.gc.ca* 🎫 *C$3.90* 🕒 *June–mid-Oct., daily 9–6* 🕒 *Interpretation center closed mid-Sept.–mid-June.*

L'ANSE AUX MEADOWS NATIONAL HISTORIC SITE

295 km (183 miles) northeast of Arches Provincial Park.

GETTING HERE AND AROUND

Follow Route 430 north to Route 436 and continue north for 30 km (18½ miles) more.

Fodor's Choice ★

L'Anse aux Meadows National Historic Site. Around the year 1000, Vikings from Greenland and Iceland founded the first European settlement in North America, near the northern tip of Newfoundland. They arrived in the New World 500 years before Columbus but stayed only a few years and were forgotten for centuries. It was only in 1960 that the Norwegian team of Helge and Anne Stine Ingstad discovered the remains of the Viking settlement's long sod huts. Today L'Anse aux Meadows is a UNESCO World Heritage Site. Parks Canada has a fine visitor center and has reconstructed some of the huts to give you a sense of centuries past. An interpretation program introduces you to the food, clothing, and way of life of that time. Bilingual guides are available. ✉ *Rte. 436, St. Anthony* ☎ *709/623–2608* 🌐 *www.pc.gc.ca* 🎫 *C$11.70* 🕒 *June–early Oct., daily 9–6 (closes at 5 near beginning and end of season).*

FAMILY

Norstead. Two kilometers (1 mile) east of L'Anse aux Meadows is Norstead, a reconstruction of an 11th-century Viking port, with a chieftain's hall, church, and ax-throwing arena. Interpreters in period dress answer questions as they go about their Viking business. ✉ *Rte. 436, off Rte. 430, 40 km (25 miles) north of St. Anthony, St. Anthony* ☎ *709/623–2828, 877/620–2828* 🌐 *www.norstead.com* 🎫 *C$10* 🕒 *June–mid-Sept., daily 9–6.*

WHERE TO EAT

$$$ SEAFOOD Fodor's Choice ★

🍴 **Norseman Restaurant.** One of the attractions of this restaurant on the harborfront is that you can pick your own lobster from a crate. Other seafood on the menu includes fresh mussels, crab, and shrimp from the area; from the land there's sometimes caribou. The wine list and spirits list is extensive and smartly selected. The paintings, jewelry, and carvings on display are for sale, and in July and August there's live traditional music on Tuesday and Friday. [$] *Average main: C$25* ✉ *L'Anse aux Meadows* ✥ *Turn right at end of Rte. 436* ☎ *709/623–2370, 877/623–2018* 🌐 *www.valhalla-lodge.com/restaurant* 🕒 *Closed late Sept.–mid-May.*

WHERE TO STAY

For expanded hotel reviews, visit Fodors.com.

$$$$ B&B/INN **Quirpon Lighthouse Inn B&B.** This restored 1920s lighthouse is on a small—7 km (4 miles) by 1.5 km (1 mile)—island off Quirpon (pronounced kar-poon), on the northern tip of Newfoundland, and getting here is half the fun. **Pros:** indoor whale-watching station; package includes return boat trip and all meals; visit L'Anse aux Meadows by boat. **Cons:** the only option is the full package. [$] *Rooms from: C$350* ✉ *Rte. 436, off Rte. 430, about a 3½-hr drive north of Cow Head, Quirpon Island* ☎ *709/634–2285, 877/254–6586* 🌐 *www.linkumtours.com* 🛏 *9 rooms, 1 suite* 🕒 *Closed Oct.–Apr.* 🍴 *All meals.*

$ B&B/INN **Tickle Inn at Cape Onion.** This refurbished, century-old fisherman's house on the beach is probably the northernmost residence on the island of Newfoundland. **Pros:** close to Burnt Cape ecological reserve; optional four-course dinner reasonably priced ($25). **Cons:** meals served at one table with the owner hosting; small bedrooms; no rooms with private bath. [$] *Rooms from: C$85* ✉ *Cape Onion* ☎ *709/452–4321 June–Sept., 866/814–8567, 709/739–5503 Oct.–May* 🌐 *www.tickleinn.net* 🛏 *4 rooms with shared bath* 🕒 *Closed Oct.–May* 🍴 *Breakfast.*

$ B&B/INN Fodor's Choice ★ **Valhalla Lodge Bed & Breakfast.** On a hill overlooking "Iceberg Alley" 8 km (5 miles) from L'Anse aux Meadows, the Valhalla has quiet and brightly painted rooms with large windows, pine Scandinavian furniture, and handmade quilts. *The Shipping News,***Pros:** view of whales and icebergs (and occasionally the aurora borealis) from the lodge; sauna; sitting room with fireplace and patio. **Cons:** few services or restaurants within walking distance; some bathrooms small. [$] *Rooms from: C$113* ✉ *Rte. 436, Gunner's Cove* ☎ *709/623–2018, 877/623–2018, 709/754–3105 off-season* 🌐 *www.valhalla-lodge.com* 🛏 *5 rooms* 🕒 *Closed Oct.–Apr.* 🍴 *Breakfast.*

$ B&B/INN **Viking Nest/Viking Village Bed & Breakfast.** Thelma Hedderson owns and oversees these two B&Bs on the same property, both convenient for visits to the Viking settlement at L'Anse aux Meadows. **Pros:** proximity to L'Anse aux Meadows; en suite bathrooms in the Viking Village; full hot breakfast included. **Cons:** no elevator; two rooms at Nest share a bathroom; no air-conditioning. [$] *Rooms from: C$79* ✉ *Rte. 436, Hay Cove, L'Anse aux Meadows* ☎ *877/858–2238* 🌐 *www.vikingvillage.ca* 🛏 *9 rooms, 7 with bath* 🕒 *Viking Village closed Oct. 15–May 1* 🍴 *Breakfast.*

ST. ANTHONY

16 km (10 miles) south of L'Anse aux Meadows.

The northern part of the Great Northern Peninsula served as the setting for *The Shipping News,* E. Annie Proulx's 1993 Pulitzer Prize–winning novel. St. Anthony is built around a natural harbor on the eastern side of the Great Northern Peninsula, near its tip. If you take a trip out to the lighthouse, you may see an iceberg or two float by, and it's a good spot for whale-watching.

GETTING HERE AND AROUND

St. Anthony is the terminus of Route 430, and most travelers arrive via this highway. For variety, some return to St. John's or other destinations by heading south from St. Anthony on Route 432, which rejoins Route 430 near Plum Point, a drive of about 140 km (87 miles).

EXPLORING

Grenfell Historic Properties. A museum and a nearby museum and interpretation center document the life and inspirational work of the English-born doctor Wilfred Grenfell (later Sir Wilfred), who in the early 20th century provided much-needed medical services and transformed the lives of the people of this remote land. ✉ *4 Maraval Rd.* ☎ *709/454–4010* 🌐 *www.grenfell-properties.com* 🎟 *C$10* 🕒 *May–Sept., daily 9–8.*

WHERE TO EAT AND STAY

For expanded hotel reviews, visit Fodors.com.

$$$ SEAFOOD 🍴 **Lightkeepers Seafood Restaurant.** Good seafood and solid Canadian fare are served in this former lighthouse-keeper's home on a parkland site overlooking the ocean. Halibut, shrimp, crab, and cod are usually good bets, as is the seafood chowder. Watch whales and bergs (when they oblige) as you feast on bakeapple cheesecake for dessert. The owners also operate the raucous Great Viking Feast dinner theater, housed in a turf-roof building. [$] *Average main: C$22* ✉ *21 Fishing Point Rd.* ☎ *709/454–4900, 877/454–4900* 🌐 *www.lightkeepersvikingfeast.com* 🕒 *Closed Oct.–late May.*

$ HOTEL 🏨 **Hotel North.** The centrally located Hotel North might not be the most scenic spot in town, but it contains pleasant and comfortable rooms (also two self-contained cottages), all with Sealy Posturepedic mattresses. **Pros:** all rooms have mini-refrigerators and coffeemakers. **Cons:** parking for registration is congested; no landscaping. [$] *Rooms from: C$119* ✉ *19 West St.* ☎ *709/454–3300* 🌐 *www.hotelnorth.ca/three* 🛏 *46 rooms, 2 cabins* 🍽 *No meals.*

$$ B&B/INN 🏨 **Tuckamore Lodge & Country Inn.** About an hour from St. Anthony, this Scandinavian-style cedar lodge with a lofty ceiling is a luxurious base from which to explore the natural bounty of the area. **Pros:** outdoor wooden sauna; many on-site activities; canoes available; billiards table. **Cons:** meals served at communal tables; few dining options nearby. [$] *Rooms from: C$150* ✉ *1 Southwest Pond Rd., Main Brook* ☎ *709/865–6361, 888/865–6361* 🌐 *www.tuckamorelodge.com* 🛏 *9 rooms, 3 suites* 🍽 *Breakfast.*

SPORTS AND THE OUTDOORS

Northland Discovery Boat Tours. Specialized 2½-hour trips (C$58) aboard a custom-built vessel will take you to see whales, dolphins, icebergs, seabirds, and sea caves. A local naturalist always accompanies the tours, which take place from mid-May through mid-September. ✉ *Off West St., behind Grenfell Interpretation Centre* ☎ *709/454–3092, 877/632–3747* 🌐 *www.discovernorthland.com.*

SHOPPING

Grenfell Handicrafts. Training villagers to become self-sufficient in a harsh environment was one of the British missionary Wilfred Grenfell's aims, and a windproof cloth that they turned into well-made parkas came to be known as Grenfell cloth. Here you can purchase it in the form of mittens, coats, and tablecloths embroidered with motifs such as polar bears and dog teams. The shop also stocks other handicrafts, most of them locally made. ✉ *4 Maraval Rd.* ☎ *709/454–3576* 🌐 *www.grenfell-properties.com.*

CORNER BROOK

50 km (31 miles) southwest of Deer Lake.

Newfoundland's fourth-largest city, Corner Brook is the hub of the island's west coast. Hills fringe three sides of the city, which has dramatic views of the harbor and the Bay of Islands. The town is also home to a large paper mill and a branch of Memorial University. Captain James Cook, the British explorer, charted the coast in the 1760s, and a memorial to him overlooks the bay.

The town enjoys more clearly defined seasons than most of the rest of the island, and in summer it has many pretty gardens. The nearby Humber River is the best-known salmon river in the province, and there are many kilometers of well-maintained walking trails in the community.

GETTING HERE AND AROUND

Corner Brook is a convenient hub and point of departure for exploring the west coast. It's about a three-hour drive (allowing for traffic) from the Port aux Basques ferry. The north and south shores of the Bay of Islands have fine paved roads—Route 440 on the north shore and Route 450 on the south—and both are a scenic half-day drive from Corner Brook. Route 450 is especially lovely, and there are many well-developed hiking trails near the end of the road at Bottle Cove and Little Port. The town has two public bus routes. Bus fare is C$2.50 for one ride, C$11 for five.

EXPLORING

Newfoundland Emporium. Flossy, a huge and handsome Newfoundland dog, will greet you at the door of this store, which is crammed from wall to wall with Newfoundland-related stuff—reputedly more than 16,000 items. The main three-level store is full of books (including ones by Newfoundlanders and about Newfoundland, as well as volumes about ships and sailing), art, crafts, music, antique furniture, collectibles, and art. ✉ *11 Broadway* ☎ *709/634–9376.*

WHERE TO STAY

For expanded hotel reviews, visit Fodors.com.

$$ HOTEL 🏨 **Glynmill Inn.** Tucked away on a treed property with a pond and a walking trail, this well-built Tudor-style inn once housed the senior staff and visiting top brass of the local paper mill. **Pros:** quiet, pleasant setting; art gallery; Deer Lake airport shuttle service (C$22). **Cons:** hard to find from the highway; small windows in many rooms; older rooms not as nice as ones in newer wing. [$] *Rooms from: C$141* ✉ *1B Cobb La.* ☎ *709/634–5181, 800/563–4400 in Canada* 🌐 *www.steelehotels.com* 🛏 *55 rooms, 23 suites* 🍴 *No meals.*

$$$ RENTAL 🏨 **Marble Villa.** These spotless condo-style units are meant for skiers, but they're perfect for a quiet summertime break and as a base from which to make Bay of Islands and Gros Morne day trips. **Pros:** beautiful

property with pond and walking trails; kitchens with dishwashers and fireplaces in most units; spacious, comfortable rooms; packages include ziplining and ATV tours. **Cons:** cafeteria-style restaurant closed except during ski season; few eating options in area. [$] *Rooms from: C$189* ✉ *Dogwood Dr., off Rte. 1, Exit 8* ☎ *709/637–7666, 800/636–2725* 🌐 *www.skimarble.com* 🛏 *29 condos* 🍴 *No meals.*

SPORTS AND THE OUTDOORS

Crystal Waters Boat Tours. From May to early October, Crystal Waters conducts Bay of Islands cruises (C$40) at 10 am, 2 pm, and 6 pm, depending on demand. ✉ *Bay of Islands Yacht Club, Pikes Ave., off Griffin Dr.* ☎ *866/344–9808, 709/632–1094* 🌐 *www.crystalwatersboattours.com.*

STEPHENVILLE

82 km (51 miles) south of Corner Brook.

The former Harmon Air Force Base is in Stephenville, a town best known for its summer theater festival *(⇨ See Planning, above)*. To the west of town is the Port au Port Peninsula, which was largely settled by the French, who brought their way of life and language to this small corner of Newfoundland.

GETTING HERE AND AROUND

Stephenville is off the Trans-Canada Highway (Route 1). Take Exit 3, then drive southwest on Route 460 most of the way. After briefly heading southwest on Route 490, follow Minnesota Drive to get downtown.

EXPLORING

Port au Port Peninsula. A slender isthmus tethers this peninsula to the west coast. About 20 tiny communities retain a French and First Nations heritage, but other than that it's largely undeveloped, with a wilderness interior and a rocky coastline. There are superb ocean views from Cape St. George, and some rewarding hiking trails. ✣ *Drive west on Rte. 460 from Stephenville to Cape St. George, at southwestern extremity; continue north up peninsula's west side (Rte. 460 becomes Rte. 463 after about 15 km [9 miles]) and loop east back to Rte. 460. Turn left (east) to return to Stephenville.*

EN ROUTE

Codroy Valley. As you travel down the Trans-Canada Highway toward Port aux Basques, routes 404, 405, 406, and 407 bring you into the small Scottish communities of the Codroy Valley. Some of the most productive farms in the province are nestled in the valley against the backdrop of the Long Range Mountains, from which gales strong enough to stop traffic hurtle down to the coast. Locally known as Wreckhouse winds, they have overturned tractor trailers. The Codroy Valley is great for bird-watching, and the Grand Codroy River is ideal for kayaking. Walking trails, a golf course, and mountain hikes make the area an appealing stop for nature lovers. 🌐 *www.codroyvalley.com.*

PORT AUX BASQUES

166 km (103 miles) south of Stephenville.

In the 1500s and early 1600s there were seven Basque ports along Newfoundland's west coast and in southern Labrador; Port aux Basques was one of them and was given its name by the town's French successors. It's now the main ferry port connecting the island to Nova Scotia.

GETTING HERE AND AROUND

The ferry from Sydney, Nova Scotia, docks at Port aux Basques. By road, the town is at the western end of the Trans-Canada Highway (Route 1).

ESSENTIALS

Visitor Information **Port aux Basques Visitor Information Centre** ✉ *Trans-Canada Hwy.* ☎ *709/695–2262* 🌐 *www.portauxbasques.ca.*

EXPLORING

J. T. Cheeseman Provincial Park. If you are using the Port aux Basques ferry, this park 10 km (6 miles) from the port makes a good first or last stop, particularly if you're on a camping trip. Rich in natural flora, this is a nesting site for the piping plover. One of the hiking trails leads to waterfalls on Little Barachois River; another, with views of Table Mountain, includes fitness stations. The long, sandy Cape Ray Beach is good for swimming and sunbathing—its day-use area has picnic tables and fireplaces, and there are about a hundred campsites. ✉ *Trans-Canada Hwy. (Rte. 1)* ☎ *709/695–7222, 709/695–4520* 🌐 *www.nlcamping.ca* 🕒 *Mid-May–mid-Sept., daily.*

WHERE TO STAY

For expanded hotel reviews, visit Fodors.com.

$ HOTEL 🏨 **St. Christopher's Hotel.** A comfortable two-story hotel near the Nova Scotia ferry, St. Christopher's serves good food at reasonable prices. **Pros:** business center; local fare, such as moose stew, served in the restaurant; waterfront boardwalk close by. **Cons:** limited, overpriced wine list; noise from conventions, weddings, and visiting sports teams; airconditioners sometimes loud. [$] *Rooms from: C$120* ✉ *146 Caribou Rd.* ☎ *709/695–7034, 800/563–4779* 🌐 *www.stchrishotel.com* 🛏 *76 rooms, 7 suites* 🍴 *No meals.*

UNDERSTANDING NOVA SCOTIA AND ATLANTIC CANADA

BOOKS AND MOVIES

FRENCH VOCABULARY

BOOKS AND MOVIES

Books

Newfoundland and Labrador For contemporary fiction, pick up *The Shipping News,* the Pulitzer Prize–winning novel by E. Annie Proulx: it's an atmospheric and moving tale of fishing and family, set in Newfoundland (the author is American); the book is much better than the movie. Wayne Johnston is a native Newfoundlander and *The Colony of Unrequited Dreams* is a comic epic about the history of the province. His *Baltimore's Mansion* is a memoir depicting his childhood on the Avalon Peninsula. *The Day the World Came to Town: 9/11 in Gander,* by Jim DeFede, tells the story of the passengers on the 39 flights that were diverted and the townsfolk who pulled out all the stops to accommodate and feed them. The event was also the subject (somewhat fictionalized) of the 2009 TV movie *Diverted,* which was shot on location in the town. *The North Bay Narrative,* by Walter Staples (Peter E. Randall), is the true story of the evolution of a remote outpost into a bustling fishing town. *Random Passage,* by Bernice Morgan, is historical fiction about a family of early Newfoundland settlers arriving from England; it was a best seller and the basis for a television miniseries of the same name.

New Brunswick David Adams Richards is one of New Brunswick's best-known writers. His novels *Mercy Among the Children* and *Bay of Love and Sorrows,* both set in northern New Brunswick, explore bleak themes. Richards also wrote *Lines on the Water,* a tale of the fishing community on the Miramichi River. In Beth Powning's memoir *Home: Chronicle of a North Country Life* the author and her husband relocate from Connecticut to a farm near the Bay of Fundy. *Life on an Unfinished Border,* by Jacques Poitras, is about the history and establishment of the New Brunswick–Maine border, engagingly told through both personal and political stories of those living on either side.

Nova Scotia The sweeping novel *Fall on Your Knees,* by Ann-Marie MacDonald, takes place partly on Cape Breton Island; it was an Oprah's Book Club selection. Henry Wadsworth Longfellow's long poem *Evangeline* tells the story of lovers separated when the British deported the Acadians in 1755 and has inspired a number of tourist attractions in the province. *Island: The Complete Stories,* by Alistair MacLeod, is a collection of tales about everyday life in Nova Scotia. MacLeod's first novel, *No Great Mischief,* is the story of a Scottish family that builds a new life on Cape Breton.

Prince Edward Island It almost goes without saying that *Anne of Green Gables* is a must-read.

General Acadian culture is unique to this region, and Clive Doucet's *Notes from Exile: On Being Acadian* is a thoughtful memoir that explores what it means to be Acadian and incorporates the history of Acadie and the Acadians.

Movies

Rain, Drizzle, and Fog (1998) is a documentary about Newfoundland seen through the eyes of a "townie," or resident of St. John's. *The Shipping News* (2001), set in Newfoundland, was filmed primarily in Corner Brook, New Bonaventure, and Trinity, Newfoundland. Evidence of the TV mini-series *Random Passage,* based on the book of the same name (⇨ *See above*), lingers on in New Bonaventure, where the set was (unusually) left in place at the request of locals, and has become a tourist attraction. Trinity Bay was again used as a location for the English-language remake of the 2003 Québec comedy, *The Grand Seduction,* which premiered in 2013. The documentary *Ghosts of the Abyss* (2003) has excellent footage of the *Titanic,* which sank off the coast of Newfoundland. Canadian director James Cameron's *Titanic* (1997) was filmed partly in Halifax.

FRENCH VOCABULARY

	ENGLISH	FRENCH	PRONUNCIATION
BASICS			
	Yes/no	Oui/non	wee/nohn
	Please	S'il vous plaît	seel voo **play**
	Thank you	Merci	mair-**see**
	You're welcome	De rien	deh ree-**ehn**
	Excuse me, sorry	Pardon	pahr-**don**
	Good morning/ afternoon	Bonjour	bohn-**zhoor**
	Good evening	Bonsoir	bohn-**swahr**
	Good-bye	Au revoir	o ruh-**vwahr**
	Mr. (Sir)	Monsieur	muh-**syuh**
	Mrs. (Ma'am)	Madame	ma-**dam**
	Miss	Mademoiselle	mad-mwa-**zel**
	Pleased to meet you	Enchanté(e)	ohn-shahn-**tay**
	How are you?	Comment allez-vous?	kuh-mahn- tahl-ay **voo**
	Very well, thanks	Très bien, merci	tray bee-ehn, mair-**see**
	And you?	Et vous?	ay **voo**?
USEFUL PHRASES			
	Do you speak English?	Parlez-vous anglais?	par-lay **voo ahn**-glay
	I don't speak . . .	Je ne parle pas . . .	zhuh nuh parl pah
	French	français	frahn-**say**
	I don't understand	Je ne comprends pas	zhuh nuh kohm-**prahn** pah
	I understand	Je comprends	zhuh kohm-**prahn**
	I don't know	Je ne sais pas	zhuh nuh say **pah**
	What's your name?	Comment vous appelez-vous?	ko-mahn voo za-pell-ay-**voo**
	My name is . . .	Je m'appelle . . .	zhuh ma-**pell** . . .
	What time is it?	Quelle heure est-il?	kel air eh-**teel**
	How?	Comment?	ko-**mahn**
	When?	Quand?	kahn
	Yesterday	Hier	ee-air

ENGLISH	FRENCH	PRONUNCIATION
Today	Aujourd'hui	o-zhoor-**dwee**
Tomorrow	Demain	duh-**mehn**
Tonight	Ce soir	suh **swahr**
What is it?	Qu'est-ce que c'est?	kess-kuh-**say**
Why?	Pourquoi?	**poor**-kwa
Who?	Qui?	kee
Where is . . .	Où est . . .	oo ay
the train station?	la gare?	la gar
the subway station?	la station de métro?	la sta-**syon** duh may-**tro**
the bus stop?	l'arrêt de bus?	la-**ray** duh **booss**
the bank?	la banque?	la bahnk
the . . . hotel?	l'hôtel . . .?	lo-**tel**
the store?	le magasin?	luh ma-ga-**zehn**
the . . . museum?	le musée . . .?	luh mew-**zay**
the elevator?	l'ascenseur?	la-sahn-**seuhr**
the telephone?	le téléphone?	luh tay-lay-**phone**
Where are the restrooms?	Où sont les toilettes?	oo sohn lay twah-**let**
(men/women)	(hommes/femmes)	(**oh**-mm/**fah**-mm)
Here/there	Ici/là	ee-**see**/la
Left/right	A gauche/à droite	a goash/a dwaht
Straight ahead	Tout droit	too dwah
Is it near/far?	C'est près/loin?	say pray/lwehn
I'd like . . .	Je voudrais . . .	zhuh voo-**dray**
A room	une chambre	ewn **shahm**-bruh
I'd like to buy . . .	Je voudrais acheter . . .	zhuh voo-**dray** **ahsh**-tay
How much is it?	C'est combien?	say comb-bee-**ehn**
A little/a lot	Un peu/beaucoup	uhn peuh/bo-**koo**
More/less	Plus/moins	plu/mwehn
Enough/too (much)	Assez/trop	a-say/tro

ENGLISH	FRENCH	PRONUNCIATION

DINING OUT

ENGLISH	FRENCH	PRONUNCIATION
A bottle of . . .	une bouteille de . . .	ewn boo-**tay** duh
A cup of . . .	une tasse de . . .	ewn tass duh
A glass of . . .	un verre de . . .	uhn vair duh
Bill/check	l'addition	la-dee-see-**ohn**
Bread	du pain	dew pan
Breakfast	le petit-déjeuner	luh puh-**tee** day-zhuh-**nay**
Butter	du beurre	dew burr
Cocktail/aperitif	un apéritif	uhn ah-pay-ree-**teef**
Dinner	le dîner	luh dee-**nay**
Dish of the day	le plat du jour	luh plah dew **zhoor**
Enjoy!	Bon appétit!	bohn a-pay-**tee**
Fixed-price menu	le menu	luh may-**new**
Fork	une fourchette	ewn four-**shet**
I am diabetic	Je suis diabétique	zhuh swee dee-ah-bay-**teek**
I am vegetarian	Je suis végétarien(ne)	zhuh swee vay-zhay-ta-ree-**en**
I cannot eat . . .	Je ne peux pas manger de . . .	zhuh nuh **puh** pah mahn-**jay** deh
I'd like to order	Je voudrais commander	zhuh voo-**dray** ko-mahn-**day**
Is service/the tip included?	Est-ce que le service est compris?	ess kuh luh sair-**veess** ay comb-**pree**
It's good/bad	C'est bon/mauvais	say bohn/mo-**vay**
It's hot/cold	C'est chaud/froid	Say sho/frwah
Knife	un couteau	uhn koo-**toe**
Lunch	le déjeuner	luh day-zhuh-**nay**
Menu	la carte	la cart
Napkin	une serviette	ewn sair-vee-**et**
Pepper	du poivre	dew **pwah**-vruh
Plate	une assiette	ewn a-see-**et**

ENGLISH	FRENCH	PRONUNCIATION
Please give me . . .	Donnez-moi . . .	doe-nay-**mwah**
Salt	du sel	dew sell
Spoon	une cuillère	ewn kwee-air
Sugar	du sucre	dew **sook**-ruh
Wine list	la carte des vins	la **cart** day vehn

MENU GUIDE

FRENCH	ENGLISH

POISSONS/FRUITS DE MER (FISH/SEAFOOD)

FRENCH	ENGLISH
Anchois	Anchovies
Bar	Bass
Brandade de morue	Creamed salt cod
Brochet	Pike
Cabillaud/Morue	Fresh cod
Calmar	Squid
Coquilles St-Jacques	Scallops
Crevettes	Shrimp
Daurade	Sea bream
Écrevisses	Prawns/Crayfish
Harengs	Herring
Homard	Lobster
Huîtres	Oysters
Langoustine	Prawn/Lobster
Lotte	Monkfish
Moules	Mussels
Palourdes	Clams
Saumon	Salmon
Thon	Tuna
Truite	Trout

FRENCH	ENGLISH
VIANDE (MEAT)	
Agneau	Lamb
Boeuf	Beef
Boudin	Sausage
Boulettes de viande	Meatballs
Brochettes	Kebabs
Cassoulet	Casserole of white beans, meat
Châteaubriand	Double fillet steak
Choucroute garnie	Sausages with sauerkraut
Côtelettes	Chops
Côte/Côte de boeuf	Rib/T-bone steak
Côte/Côte de boeuf	Rib/T-bone steak
Entrecôte	Rib or rib-eye steak
Épaule	Shoulder
Escalope	Cutlet
Foie	Liver
Gigot	Leg
Porc	Pork
Ris de veau	Veal sweetbreads
Saucisses	Sausages
Selle	Saddle
Tournedos	Tenderloin of T-bone steak
Veau	Veal
METHODS OF PREPARATION	
Au four	Baked
Ballotine	Boned, stuffed, and rolled
Bien cuit	Well-done
Bleu	Very rare
Frit	Fried
Grillé	Grilled

FRENCH	ENGLISH
Rôti	Roast
Saignant	Rare

VOLAILLES/GIBIER (POULTRY/GAME)

Blanc de volaille	Chicken breast
Canard/Caneton	Duck/Duckling
Cerf/Chevreuil	Venison (red/roe)
Coq au vin	Chicken stewed in red wine
Dinde/Dindonneau	Turkey/Young turkey
Faisan	Pheasant
Lapin/Lièvre	Rabbit/Wild hare
Oie	Goose
Pintade/Pintadeau	Guinea fowl/Young guinea fowl
Poulet/Poussin	Chicken/Spring chicken
Poulet/Poussin	Chicken/Spring chicken

LÉGUMES (VEGETABLES)

Artichaut	Artichoke
Asperge	Asparagus
Aubergine	Eggplant
Champignons	Mushrooms
Chou-fleur	Cauliflower
Chou (rouge)	Cabbage (red)
Laitue	Lettuce
Oignons	Onions
Petits pois	Peas
Pomme de terre	Potato
Tomates	Tomatoes

TRAVEL SMART
NOVA SCOTIA AND
ATLANTIC CANADA

GETTING HERE AND AROUND

■ AIR TRAVEL

Flying time to Halifax is 1½ hours from Montréal, 2 hours from Boston, 2½ hours from New York, 4½ hours from Chicago (with connection), 8 hours from Los Angeles (with connection), and 6 hours from London. The flying time from Toronto to both Charlottetown and St. John's is about 3 hours; a flight from Montréal to St. John's is 2 hours. Visitors from New York can expect a 4-hour flight to St. John's, while Bostonians can expect a 3-hour trip to Newfoundland and Labrador's capital. Inside the Atlantic provinces, a jump from Halifax to Charlottetown or Moncton takes only about 30 minutes while a trip from Halifax to St. John's is about 90 minutes.

Departing passengers at all major airports must pay an airport-improvement fee (typically C$10–C$25) plus a security fee before boarding (up to C$14.25 for round-trip flights within Canada and C$24.25 for international ones), though these are usually rolled into the ticket price. All major, regional, and charter airlines that serve Atlantic Canada prohibit smoking, as do all Canadian airports.

Airlines and Airports Airline and Airport Links.com. Links to many of the world's airlines and airports.
⊕ *www.airlineandairportlinks.com.*

Airline-Security Issues Canadian Air Transport Security Authority ⊕ *www.catsa-acsta. gc.ca.* **Transportation Security Administration.** For answers to almost any question that might arise, check the websites of the Transportation Security Administration.
⊕ *www.tsa.gov.*

AIRPORTS

The largest airport in the area is Halifax Stanfield International Airport (YHZ). *For information about smaller airports, see the individual chapters.*

Information Halifax Stanfield International Airport ☎ *902/873–4422, 902/873–1223* ⊕ *www.hiaa.ca.*

FLIGHTS

Air Canada and its partner Air Canada Express (formerly Jazz) dominate the national airline industry, serving every major city in the region as well as many smaller centers. WestJet, the main competitor, serves select cities both within Atlantic Canada and elsewhere on the continent, while Porter Airlines, a comparative upstart, flies direct to Halifax from Ottawa, Montréal, and St. John's with connections to other locales. As for U.S.–based carriers, American Airlines, Delta, and United provide service to Halifax. European budget airlines, including Condor and Icelandair, also have service to Atlantic Canada on a seasonal basis.

Regional carriers like Provincial Airlines and Air Labrador connect remoter parts of Newfoundland and Labrador with destinations in Québec. Contact regional travel agencies for charter companies. Halifax's airport is 40 km (25 miles) northeast of downtown, and ground transportation takes 30 to 40 minutes, depending on traffic. If you're flying nonstop to the States at the end of your trip, remember that in addition to leaving time for the drive back to the airport you must also leave yourself sufficient time *in* the airport because air travelers are required to preclear U.S. customs before departing.

Information Air Canada ☎ *888/247– 2262* ⊕ *www.aircanada.ca.* **Air Labrador** ☎ *800/563–3042* ⊕ *www.airlabrador.com.* **American Airlines** ☎ *800/433–7300* ⊕ *www.aa.com.* **Condor Airlines** ☎ *866/960– 7915* ⊕ *www.condor.com.* **Delta Airlines** ☎ *800/221–1212 for U.S. reservations, 800/241–4141 for international reservations* ⊕ *www.delta.com.* **Icelandair** ☎ *800/223– 5500* ⊕ *www.icelandair.com.* **Porter Airlines** ☎ *888/619–8622* ⊕ *www.flyporter. com.* **Provincial Airlines** ☎ *800/563–2800*

⊕ *www.provincialairlines.com.* **United Airlines** ☎ *800/864–8331 for U.S. reservations, 800/538–2929 for international reservations* ⊕ *www.united.com.* **WestJet** ☎ *888/937–8538* ⊕ *www.westjet.com.*

▍BOAT TRAVEL

Car ferries provide essential transportation on the east coast of Canada, connecting Nova Scotia with New Brunswick, PEI, and Newfoundland.

Bay Ferries Ltd. sails the *Princess of Acadia* between Saint John, New Brunswick, and Digby year-round. There is at least one round-trip per day—typically two from mid-May through late October—and the crossing takes approximately three hours.

Weather permitting, from May through late December, Northumberland Ferries operates between Caribou, Nova Scotia, and Wood Islands, Prince Edward Island, making the 75-minute trip several times each day.

Marine Atlantic operates daily year-round between North Sydney and Port aux Basques, on the west coast of Newfoundland. Thrice-weekly service between North Sydney and Argentia, on Newfoundland's east coast, is offered from late June through mid-September. Reservations are required. ⇨ *For additional information about regional ferry service, see individual chapters.*

Information Bay Ferries, Ltd. ☎ *877/762–7245* ⊕ *www.ferries.ca.* **Marine Atlantic** ☎ *800/341–7981* ⊕ *www.marine-atlantic.ca.* **Northumberland Ferries** ☎ *877/762–7245* ⊕ *www.ferries.ca.*

▍BUS TRAVEL

If you don't have a car, you'll likely have to rely on bus travel in Atlantic Canada, especially when visiting the many out-of-the-way communities that don't have airports or rail lines. Buses usually depart and arrive only once a day from any given destination. Maritime Bus provides regional service throughout Nova Scotia, New Brunswick, and PEI. By connecting with Greyhound Lines you can also reach further flung destinations via Québec. Buses are quite comfortable, have clean bathrooms, and make occasional rest stops.

Bus terminals in major centers and even in many minor ones are usually efficient operations with service all week and agents on hand to handle ticket sales. In some less-trafficked spots, however, the bus station is simply a counter in a local convenience store, gas station, or snack bar. If you ask, the bus driver will usually stop anywhere on the route to let you off, even if it's not a designated terminal. There are a number of small, regional bus services, but connections are not always convenient.

Tickets may be purchased in advance, but—capacity-wise—it isn't usually necessary to do so.

Information Greyhound Canada ☎ *800/661–8747* ⊕ *www.greyhound.ca.* **Maritime Bus** ☎ *800/575–1807* ⊕ *www.maritimebus.com.*

▍CAR TRAVEL

Your own driver's license is acceptable in Atlantic Canada for up to three months, and the national highway system is excellent. It includes the Trans-Canada Highway, the longest in the world—running about 8,000 km (5,000 miles) from Victoria, British Columbia, to St. John's, Newfoundland, with ferries bridging coastal waters at each end.

FROM THE U.S.

Drivers must carry owner registration and proof of insurance coverage, which is compulsory in Canada. The Canadian Non-Resident Inter-Provincial Motor Vehicle Liability Insurance Card, available from any U.S. insurance company, is accepted as evidence of financial responsibility within the country. The minimum liability coverage in New Brunswick, Newfoundland and Labrador, and Prince Edward Island is C$200,000; in Nova Scotia, it's C$500,000. If you're driving a car that is not registered in your name, carry a letter from the owner that authorizes your use of the vehicle.

The U.S. Interstate Highway System leads directly into Canada along Interstate 95 from Maine to New Brunswick, and there are many smaller highway crossings between the two countries as well.

■ TIP→ Motorists crossing into Atlantic Canada from the U.S. can check border-wait times online; they're updated hourly. Click on "Border wait times" at ⊕ www.cbsa-asfc.gc.ca.

Information Insurance Bureau of Canada ☎ 902/429-2730, 800/565-7189 within Atlantic Canada ⊕ www.ibc.ca.

GASOLINE

Because Canada uses metric measurements, gasoline is always sold in liters with one gallon equaling about 3.8 liters. The cost is regulated by provincial governments and can change weekly, often by zone. (As of this writing, you can expect to pay C$1.31—or C$4.96 per gallon—in Halifax for mid-grade unleaded gas.) For up-to-date per-liter prices, check the individual governmental websites.

Contacts New Brunswick Energy and Utilities Board ⊕ www.nbeub.ca. **Newfoundland and Labrador Public Utilities Board** ⊕ www.pub.nf.ca. **Nova Scotia Utility and Review Board** ⊕ nsuarb.novascotia.ca. **Prince Edward Island Regulatory and Appeals Commission** ⊕ www.irac.pe.ca.

ROADSIDE EMERGENCIES

In case of an accident or emergency call 911. If you're a member of the American Automobile Association, you're automatically covered by the Canadian Automobile Association while traveling in Canada.

Emergency Services Canadian Automobile Association ☎ 800/222-4357, 800/561-8807 ⊕ www.caa.ca.

■ TIP→ Motorists should bear in mind that many roads in rural areas require attentive driving, as they are often narrow and don't always have a paved shoulder (sharply curving ones warrant special attention). That said, they're generally well surfaced and offer exquisite scenery.

RULES OF THE ROAD

Speed limits, always given in kilometers, vary from province to province, but are usually within the 90- to 110-kph range outside cities. (As a mile equals 1.6 km that translates into 50–68 mph.) Radar-detection devices are illegal, and speed limits are strictly enforced. Tickets start at C$75 but run into the hundreds depending how far over the limit you go.

By law, you are required to wear a seat belt. Children must also be properly restrained regardless of where they're seated. Those under 40 pounds must be strapped into approved child-safety seats. Even children over 40 pounds who are under age nine and less than 145 centimeters (57 inches) in height are legally required to use child seats. This rule does not apply, however, if you're visiting from outside Atlantic Canada and driving your own vehicle, provided it complies with the child-restraint safety laws of the province or country where the car is registered.

Drinking and driving (anything over .08 blood-alcohol level) is a criminal offense. In the Atlantic provinces, however, there are also serious penalties—including license suspension and vehicle confiscation—if you're found to have a .05 blood-alcohol level. Road-block checks are not unusual, especially on holiday weekends.

Another no-no is using a handheld cell phone while driving. All four provinces have banned the practice. Other regulations, such as those concerning headlight use and parking, differ from province to province. Some have a statutory requirement to drive with your headlights on for extended periods after dawn and before sunset. Parking rules are set by individual municipalities. In Halifax, tickets for violators are common and start at C$20.

❚ CRUISE SHIP TRAVEL

Every season, from mid-April through October, cruise ships sailing up from New England, and in some cases across the ocean from Europe, arrive in Atlantic Canadian waters. In terms of traffic, Halifax is hands down the most popular port of call, annually receiving more than 130 ships representing major lines such as Royal Caribbean, Holland America, Princess, Silversea, Carnival, Crystal, and Cunard.

Saint John (New Brunswick), Charlottetown (PEI), and Sydney (Nova Scotia) each receive about 75 cruise ship calls annually. Cruise ships are also an emerging element of the Newfoundland and Labrador tourism sector. Right now, the province plays host to a relatively small number of major lines, and they must first dock at either Corner Brook or St. John's, the only ports with customs officers; however, there are another 30-odd outports all over the province that attract smaller,

more intrepid operators like Adventure Canada or Lindblad Expeditions (a National Geographic Society partner).

Contacts Adventure Canada ⊕ www.adventurecanada.com. **Atlantic Canada Cruise Association** ⊕ www.atlanticcanadacruise.com. **Cruise Halifax** ⊕ www.cruisehalifax.ca. **Cruise Newfoundland and Labrador** ⊕ www.cruisenewfoundland.com. **Cruise Saint John** ⊕ www.cruisesaintjohn.com. **Historic Charlottetown Seaport.com** ⊕ www.historiccharlottetownseaport.com. **Lindblad Expeditions** ⊕ www.expeditions.com. **Port of Sydney** ⊕ portofsydney.ca.

❚ TRAIN TRAVEL

VIA Rail, Canada's Amtrak counterpart, provides transcontinental rail service to Atlantic Canada, but it's limited to an overnight Montréal-to-Halifax trip, called The Ocean, which runs three times per week. The train stops in a dozen Nova Scotian and New Brunswick towns along the way, among them Truro, Amherst, Moncton, and Miramichi. There are three service classes: Economy Class, featuring an upright seat with foot- and head-rest, is the least expensive; Sleeper Class, with a berth or bedroom cabin, is the middle-of-the-road option; and Sleeper Plus (offered from mid-June to mid-October) is an upgraded version of the latter that includes cabin accommodations, meals, access to the panoramic Park Car, complimentary educational activities, and pre-boarding privileges. You can expect to pay more than double for accommodations in Sleeper Plus over seats in Economy Class.

If you're planning to travel a lot by train, look into the Canrail pass. It enables you to take seven one-way trips anywhere in Canada over a 21-day period. During the high season (June to mid-October), a standard pass is C$1,008, plus applicable taxes. The low-season rate (valid mid-October through May) is C$630, plus taxes.

Information VIA Rail Canada ☎ 888/842–7245 ⊕ www.viarail.ca.

ESSENTIALS

▮ ACCOMMODATIONS

In Atlantic Canadian cities, you may choose between luxury hotels (whether business-class or boutique-y), moderately priced modern properties, and older ones with fewer conveniences but more charm. Options in smaller towns and in the countryside include large full-service resorts, small privately owned inns, bed-and-breakfasts, and a diminishing number of roadside motels.

Accommodations will generally cost more in summer than at other times (except those places, such as ski resorts, where winter is high season) and should be booked well in advance for peak periods. A special event or festival that coincides with your visit might fill every room for miles around. Inquire about special deals and packages when making reservations. Big-city hotels that cater to business travelers often offer weekend packages. Discounts are common when you book for a week or longer, and many urban hotels offer rooms at up to 40% off in winter.

The lodgings we list are the cream of the crop in each price range. We always list the facilities that are available, but we don't specify whether they cost extra. So when pricing accommodations, always ask what's included and what qualifies as an add-on. It's worth noting that most hotels allow children under a certain age to stay in their parents' room at no extra cost, yet some charge for them as extra adults; also ask about the cut-off age for discounts if you're traveling as a family.

Properties are assigned a price category based on the lowest nightly rack rate for a standard double room in high season (excluding holidays).

Most hotels and other lodgings require your credit card details before they will confirm your reservation. Whether you provide these online, over the phone, or even via fax, get confirmation in writing and have a copy of it handy when you check in.

Be sure you understand the hotel's cancellation policy. Some places allow you to cancel without any kind of penalty—even if you prepaid to secure a discounted rate—if you cancel at least 24 hours in advance. Others require you to cancel a week in advance or penalize you the cost of one night. Small inns and B&Bs are most likely to require you to cancel far in advance.

APARTMENT AND HOUSE RENTALS

Rental cottages are common in the Atlantic provinces, especially Nova Scotia and Prince Edward Island. Many of them are privately owned but only used by the family for a few weeks each summer. That leaves week after week available for rental potential, with most owners leaving the booking to an online agency or enterprising neighbor. Start your house hunting by visiting reliable commercial websites or search under "where to stay" at the official provincial tourism websites (⇨ See individual chapters).

Information HomeAway. With more than 850 Atlantic Canadian properties, this leads the pack. ⊕ www.homeaway.com. **Atlantic Canada Vacation Rentals.** A site that scores points for its wide geographic coverage—just look under "Stay" for listings. ⊕ www.atlanticcanada.worldweb.com.

BED-AND-BREAKFASTS AND INNS

Staying in smaller, more intimate spots is a wonderful way to meet people who are passionate about their communities and well versed in local events and history. Inns and B&Bs are both prevalent in Nova Scotia, particularly in the Annapolis Valley and the South Shore, where you can stay in the magnificent homes once occupied by ship builders, politicians, and other esteemed citizens. Prince Edward Island and New Brunswick also have a number of stately lodgings.

Information **B&B Canada.** This site helpfully divides each province into tourist regions. ⊕ *www.bbcanada.com.* **The Inns of Distinction of Prince Edward Island.** This offers a selection of carefully vetted Island options. ⊕ *www.innsofpei.com.* **Nova Scotia Bed & Breakfast Guide.** The Nova Scotia Bed & Breakfast Guide lists properties belonging to the provincial B&B association. ⊕ *www.nsbedandbreakfast.com.* **Select Inns of Atlantic Canada.** Covers inns, B&Bs, and boutique hotels in all four provinces. ⊕ *www.selectinns.ca.* **Unique Country Inns.** Heritage inns and other interesting accommodations in Nova Scotia are covered by Unique Country Inns. ⊕ *www.uniquecountryinns.com.*

International sites with a strong local lineup include **Bed & Breakfast.com** ⊕ *www.bedandbreakfast.com.*

HOTELS

Although Canada doesn't have a national government-run system for rating hotels, many have joined the voluntary Canada Select program, which assigns member properties one to five stars based on strict criteria. Most hotel rooms have air-conditioning, private baths with tubs and showers, and two double beds; all those we list have air-conditioning and private bath unless otherwise noted.

Information **Canada Select** ☎ *506/458–1995 in New Brunswick, 709/722–3133 in Newfoundland and Labrador, 902/406–4747 in Nova Scotia, 902/566–3501 in PEI* ⊕ *www.canadaselect.com.*

▌COMMUNICATIONS

INTERNET

Getting online in Atlantic Canada isn't a problem. Most hotels—as well as many inns and B&Bs—provide either a public computer, in-room broadband connections, or wireless capabilities to guests, although some only offer the last of these in the lobby or other common areas. It's also increasingly easy to find a coffee shop where you can surf while you sip, especially now that the ubiquitous Tim Hortons chain has introduced free Wi-Fi at countless outlets (to locate the closest one, click ⊕ *www.timhortons.com/ca/en/tools/wifi.html*). Airports and ferry terminals have also jumped on the wireless bandwagon, offering travelers an option for computer time while they wait for their next flight or boat ride.

PHONES

Phone numbers in Atlantic Canada have seven digits. In most cases, the prefix of phone numbers denotes a certain geographical area within the province you are calling. Area codes are three numbers and are as follows: for Prince Edward Island and Nova Scotia (902), New Brunswick (506), and Newfoundland and Labrador (709). Note that if you are placing a long-distance call—whether within a province, to another province, or to the U.S.—you must dial 1 first. If you're phoning another country, ⊕ *www.howtocallabroad.com* can guide you through the process.

LAND LINES

Calling from a hotel phone is almost always the most expensive option as lodgings usually add huge surcharges to all calls, particularly international ones. Calling cards help keep costs down but only if you purchase them locally. (They're readily available at grocery and drug stores as well as some convenience stores and gas stations.) Pay phones, which cost C25¢ for each call, are still quite common in airports, bus depots, and other such venues. They can be used to make long-distance calls either by phoning the operator ("0") to reverse the charges, by depositing several coins to pay for the first minute of talk, or by using credit or phone cards (some pay phones, especially in airports, are equipped to handle cards directly).

MOBILE PHONES

If you have a multiband phone (some countries use different frequencies from what's used in the United States) and your service provider uses the world-standard GSM network (as do AT&T and Verizon), you can probably use your phone abroad. Long-distance charges, however, can be steep—ditto for roaming fees (C$1 a minute is considered reasonable).

The good news is that there are several strategies for minimizing costs. If you're on a short trip, expect to call home frequently, or just want the convenience of keeping your usual cell number, simply request that your service provider temporarily add Canadian access to your existing plan before you cross the border. If you're mainly interested in making calls inside the region, save one of your old mobile phones (or buy a cheap one online), ask your provider to unlock it, and take it with you as a travel phone, buying a new SIM card with pay-as-you-go service in each destination. This way you'll have a local number and will be able take advantage of low local rates when making local calls. Renting a travel phone before you go through Cellular Abroad or Mobal and then installing a Canadian SIM card will achieve the same end.

However you proceed, bear in mind that it's typically cheaper to send a text message than to make a phone call, as text messages have a very low set fee (often less than C5¢).

■ TIP→ If you are carrying a laptop, tablet, or smartphone, downloading Skype software (⊕ www.skype.com) will enable you to make no- or low-cost calls anywhere in the world via the Internet.

Contacts Cellular Abroad. Cellular Abroad rents and sells GSM phones and sells SIM cards that work in many countries. ☎ 800/287-5072 ⊕ www.cellularabroad.com. **Mobal.** Mobal rents mobiles and sells GSM phones (starting at $29) that will operate in 170 countries. Per-call rates vary throughout the world. ☎ 888/888-9162 ⊕ www.mobal.com.

■ CUSTOMS AND DUTIES

You're always allowed to bring goods of a certain value back home without having to pay any duty or import tax, but there's a limit on the amount of duty-free tobacco and liquor you can return with, and some countries have separate limits for perfumes. For exact figures, check with your customs department. The values of so-called duty-free goods are included in these amounts. When you shop abroad, save all your receipts, as customs inspectors may ask to see them as well as the items you purchased. If the total value of your goods is more than the duty-free limit, you'll have to pay a tax (most often a flat percentage) on the value of everything beyond that limit.

U.S. Customs and Immigration (⇨ *Information in the U.S., below*) has preclearance services at international airports in Halifax, as well as Montréal, Toronto, Ottawa, Winnipeg, Calgary, Edmonton, Vancouver, and Victoria.

American and British visitors may bring the following items into Canada dutyfree: 200 cigarettes, 50 cigars, and 200 grams (7 ounces) of tobacco; 1.14 liters (40 imperial ounces) of liquor, 1.5 liters (53 imperial ounces) of wine, or 24 355-milliliter (12-ounce) bottles or cans of beer for personal consumption. Any alcohol and tobacco products in excess of these amounts are subject to duty, provincial fees, and taxes. You can also bring in gifts valued at C$60 or less without paying duty. Neither alcohol nor tobacco products qualify as gifts, and all gifts—regardless of their value— must be declared.

Cats and dogs must have a certificate issued by a licensed veterinarian that clearly identifies the animal and certifies that it has been vaccinated against rabies during the preceding 36 months. Guide dogs are allowed into Canada without restriction. Plant material must be declared and inspected as there may be restrictions on some live plants, bulbs, and seeds. With certain restrictions or prohibitions on some fruits and vegetables, visitors may bring food with them for their own use, providing the quantity is consistent with the duration of the visit.

Canada's firearms laws are significantly stricter than those in the United States. Only sporting rifles and shotguns may be imported, provided they are to be used for sporting, hunting, or competition while in the country. All firearms must be declared to Canadian Customs at the first point of entry. Failure to declare firearms will result in their seizure, and criminal charges may be made. Regulations require visitors to have a confirmed "Non-Resident Firearms Declaration" to bring any guns into Canada; a fee of C$25 applies, and the declaration (which acts like a temporary license) is valid for 60 days. For more information contact the Canadian Firearms Program.

Information in Canada Canada Border Services Agency ☎ *800/461–9999 within Canada, 506/636–5064 outside Canada* ⊕ *www.cbsa.gc.ca.* **Canadian Firearms Program** ☎ *800/731–4000* ⊕ *www.rcmp-grc.gc.ca.*

Information in U.S. U.S. Customs and Border Protection ☎ *877/227–5511* ⊕ *www.cbp.gov.*

▌EATING OUT

The Atlantic provinces are a preferred destination for seafood lovers. Excellent fish and shellfish are available in all types of dining establishments. The restaurants we list are the top picks in each price category.

MEALS AND MEALTIMES

Unless otherwise noted, the restaurants listed in this guide are open daily for lunch and dinner. Pubs generally serve food all day and into the wee hours of the night. The dinner meal at restaurants usually begins around 5 pm with seating through 9 or 10 pm.

RESERVATIONS AND DRESS

Regardless of where you are, it's a good idea to make a reservation if you can. We only mention them specifically when reservations are essential (in short, when there's no other way you'll ever get a table) or when they are not accepted. We mention dress only when men are required to wear a jacket or a jacket and tie.

SMOKING

Smoking in *all* indoor public places is prohibited in both New Brunswick and Newfoundland and Labrador. PEI is a little more lenient in that it allows smoking in certain designated areas (including some outdoor patios after 10 pm). Nova Scotia, on the other hand, has some of the country's toughest legislation. In addition to the public indoor ban, it has banned smoking in private cars when passengers under the age of 19 are present. It also requires stores selling tobacco products to stock them out of customers' view.

WINES, BEER, AND SPIRITS

Locally produced wines, ranging from young table wines to excellent vintages, are offered in most licensed restaurants and are well worth trying. Provincially owned liquor stores, as well as private outlets, are operated in Atlantic Canada. Stores selling alcohol are permitted to be open on Sundays (typically from noon or 1 until 5 pm). But provinces like Prince Edward Island allow certain outlets to open on that day in peak months only. Sundays aside, most liquor stores open at 10 am and close at 9 or 10 pm. For a list of government-operated stores (including private "agents" who sell beer through convenience stores in Newfoundland and Labrador), check out the website for each province.

▌ELECTRICITY

Canada uses the same voltage as the United States, so all of your electronics should make the transition without any fuss at all. No need for adapters.

▮ EMERGENCIES

The U.S. embassy—like all other foreign embassies—is in Ottawa, Ontario (the nation's capital). There are also seven U.S. consulates in Canada, including one in Halifax.

Foreign Consulates U.S. Consulate ⊠ *Suite 904, Purdy's Wharf Tower II, 1969 Upper Water St., Halifax, Nova Scotia* ☎ *902/429–2480* ⊕ *halifax.usconsulate.gov.* **U.S. Embassy** ⊠ *490 Sussex Dr., Ottawa, Ontario* ☎ *613/688–5335* ⊕ *canada.usembassy.gov.*

▮ HOURS OF OPERATION

Most banks are open Monday through Friday 10 to 5 or 6. All banks are closed on national holidays. Nearly all banks have automatic teller machines (ATMs) that are accessible around the clock.

Hours at museums vary, but most open at 10 or 11 and close in the evening. Many are closed on Monday; some stay open late one day a week, and admission is sometimes waived during those extended hours. Stores, shops, and supermarkets usually are open Monday through Saturday 9 to 6, and Sunday noon to 5, although in major cities supermarkets are often open 7:30 am to 11 pm, and some food stores are open 24 hours a day. Stores often stay open Thursday and Friday evenings, most shopping malls until 9 pm. Drugstores in major cities are often open until midnight, and convenience stores tend to be open until at least that time every day.

HOLIDAYS

Canadian national holidays are as follows: New Year's Day (January 1), Good Friday (late March or early April), Easter Monday (the Monday after Good Friday), Victoria Day (the first Monday preceding May 25), Canada Day (July 1), Labour Day (the first Monday in September), Thanksgiving (the second Monday in October), Remembrance Day (November 11), Christmas Day (December 25), and Boxing Day (December 26).

New Brunswick, much of Nova Scotia, and parts of PEI recognize the first Monday in August as another holiday, while Newfoundlanders and Labradorians, who love any excuse to party, also celebrate St. Patrick's Day (March 17), St. George's Day (April 23), Discovery Day (the Monday nearest to June 24), and Orangemen's Day (July 12).

▮ MONEY

ATMS AND BANKS

Your own bank will probably charge a fee for using ATMs abroad; the foreign bank you use may also charge a fee. Nevertheless, you'll usually get a better rate of exchange at an ATM than you will at a currency-exchange office or even when changing money in a bank. And extracting funds as you need them is a safer option than carrying around a large amount of cash. The easiest way to minimize transaction fees is by making withdrawals from ATMs affiliated with your home bank. Users of Cirrus or PLUS networks can locate them at ⊕ *www.mastercard.com/atmlocator* and ⊕ *www.visa.com/atms* respectively.

▮ TIP ➔ **PIN numbers with more than four digits are not recognized at ATMs in many countries. If yours has five or more, remember to change it before you leave.**

Most banks, gas stations, malls, and convenience stores have ATMs that are accessible round the clock.

CREDIT CARDS

American visitors should note that in Canada, as in Europe, chip-and-pin cards are now widely used; however, most venues that accept credit cards are still equipped to process transactions by the traditional swipe-and-sign method as well. It's a good idea to inform your credit-card company before you leave home. Otherwise, it might put a hold on your card owing to unusual activity—not a good thing halfway through your trip. Record all your credit-card numbers—along with the phone numbers to call if your cards are lost or stolen—in a safe place, so you're prepared should something go wrong. Both MasterCard and Visa have general numbers you can call (collect if you're abroad) if your card is lost, but you're better off phoning the number of your issuing bank, as MasterCard and Visa usually just transfer you to your bank anyway.

If you plan to use your credit card for cash advances, you'll need to apply for a PIN at least two weeks before your trip. Although it's usually cheaper (and safer) to use a credit card abroad for large purchases (so you can cancel payments or be reimbursed if there's a problem), note that some credit-card companies *and* the banks that issue them add substantial percentages to all foreign transactions, whether they're in a foreign currency or not. Check on these fees before leaving home, so there won't be any surprises when you get the bill.

■TIP➔ **Before you charge something, ask the merchant whether or not he or she plans to do a dynamic currency conversion (DCC). In such a transaction the credit-card processor (shop, restaurant, or hotel, not Visa or MasterCard) converts the currency and charges you in dollars. In most cases you'll pay the merchant a 3% fee for this service in addition to any credit-card company and issuing-bank foreign-transaction surcharges.**

Dynamic currency conversion programs are becoming increasingly widespread. Merchants who participate in them are supposed to ask whether you want to be charged in dollars or the local currency, but they don't always do so. And even if they do offer you a choice, they may well avoid mentioning the additional surcharges. The good news is that you *do* have a choice. You can avoid it entirely thanks to American Express; with its cards, DCC simply isn't an option.

Reporting Lost Cards American Express
☏ 800/297-8500 within U.S. or Canada, 336/393-1111 collect from abroad ⊕ www.americanexpress.com. **MasterCard**

☏ 800/627-8372 within U.S. or Canada, 636/722-7111 collect from abroad ⊕ www.mastercard.com. **Visa** ☏ 800/847-2911 within U.S. or Canada, 410/581-3836 collect from abroad ⊕ www.visa.com.

CURRENCY AND EXCHANGE

Throughout this book, unless otherwise stated, all prices are given in Canadian dollars.

U.S. dollars are accepted in much of Canada (especially in communities near the border), though you should expect to receive any change in Canadian currency. To get the most favorable exchange rate, convert at least some of your money into Canadian funds. Major U.S. credit cards are also accepted in most areas.

The units of currency in Canada are the Canadian dollar (C$) and the cent, in almost the same denominations as U.S. currency ($5, $10, $20, 5¢, 10¢, 25¢, etc.). Note that C$1 and C$2 coins are used in Canada instead of bills (these are known as a "loonie," because of the loon that appears on the coin, and a "toonie," respectively). The Royal Canadian Mint stopped distributing pennies in February 2013; however, you will still find some in circulation.

Prices throughout this guide are given for adults. Substantially reduced fees are almost always available for children, students, and senior citizens.

■ PASSPORTS AND VISAS

Citizens of the United States need a passport or other WHTI-compliant document to reenter their country when returning by air from Canada. Passports, passport cards, or other WHTI-compliant documents are also required for adults crossing the border by land or sea, though children under age 16 may continue to do so using only a U.S. birth certificate. Check with U.S Customs and Border Protection (⊕ *www.cbp.gov* or ⊕ *www.getyouhome.gov*) for full details.

Anyone under 18 who is either traveling alone or with only one parent should carry a signed and dated letter from both parents or from all legal guardians authorizing the trip. It's also a good idea to include a copy of the child's birth certificate, custody documents (if applicable), and death certificates of one or both parents (if applicable). Be aware that most airlines do not allow children under age five to travel independently. Air Canada is particularly strict: children must be at least eight years of age to fly unaccompanied and can only travel on nonstop flights. Citizens of the United States, United Kingdom, Australia, and New Zealand do not need visas to enter Canada for a period of six months or fewer. Visitors from numerous other countries are also exempt: see Citizenship and Immigration Canada's website (⊕ *www.cic.gc.ca*) for a complete list.

▌ TAXES

A goods and services tax (GST) of 5% applies on virtually every transaction in Canada except for the purchase of basic groceries. Newfoundland and Labrador and New Brunswick have a 13% single harmonized sales tax (HST), which combines the GST and the provincial sales tax. In PEI it is 14%, and in Nova Scotia it is 15%.

Information Canada Customs and Revenue Agency ☎ *800/267–6999 within Canada, 613/952–3741* ⊕ *www.ccra-adrc.gc.ca.*

▌ TIME

New Brunswick, Nova Scotia, and Prince Edward Island are on Atlantic time, which is (during daylight saving time) three hours earlier than Greenwich mean time (GMT) and one hour later than eastern daylight time (EDT). Newfoundland and Labrador are on Newfoundland time, which is –2:30 GMT and +1:30 EDT.

▌ TIPPING

Tips and service charges are not usually added to a bill in Canada. In general, tip 15% of the total bill (before tax). This goes for waiters and waitresses, barbers and hairdressers, and taxi drivers. Porters and doormen should get about C$2 a bag. For maid service, leave at least C$2 per person a day (C$3 in luxury hotels).

▌ TOURS

SPECIAL-INTEREST TOURS
The companies listed *below* offer multi-day tours. *Additional operators that run different-length trips are listed in each chapter either on the Planner page or with the specific community.*

ACTIVE ADVENTURES
Atlantic Canada Cycling organizes bike junkets in all four Atlantic provinces. **Backroads** offers two-wheel trips all over the globe, including Nova Scotia's Lighthouse Route and Bay of Fundy area. **Coastal Adventures** has sea kayaking options in Nova Scotia and Newfoundland based around themes such as icebergs and buried treasure. **Eastwind Cycle** specializes in custom bike tours in New Brunswick, Nova Scotia, and PEI. **Easy Rider Tours** celebrates pedal power with bike tours in PEI and Nova Scotia. **Freewheeling Adventures** arranges Atlantic Canadian holidays for bikers, hikers, paddlers, and yoga enthusiasts; multisport offerings for families are available, too. **Fresh Air Adventure** focuses on sea-kayaking trips in New Brunswick's fabled Bay of Fundy biosphere. **Ocean Quest**, one of Canada's premier adventure expedition planners, offers cool vacations in Newfoundland and Labrador that can include wreck diving and snorkeling with whales. **Pedal & Sea** specializes in guided and self-guided bike tours in Eastern Canada.

■TIP→ Most airlines accommodate bikes as luggage, provided they're dismantled and boxed.

Contacts **Atlantic Canada Cycling**
☎ *902/423-2453, 888/879-2453*
⊕ *www.atlanticcanadacycling.com.* **Back-roads** ☎ *510/527-1555, 800/462-2848*
⊕ *www.backroads.com.* **Coastal Adventures**
☎ *902/772-2774, 877/404-2774* ⊕ *www.coastaladventures.com.* **Eastwind Cycle**
☎ *902/471-4424, 866/447-7468* ⊕ *www.eastwindcycle.com.* **Easy Rider Tours**
☎ *978/463-6955, 800/488-8332* ⊕ *www.easyridertours.com.* **Freewheeling Adventures** ☎ *902/857-3600, 800/672-0775*
⊕ *www.freewheeling.ca.* **Fresh Air Adventure** ☎ *506/887-2224, 800/545-0020*
⊕ *www.freshairadventure.com.* **Ocean Quest**
☎ *709/834-7234, 866/623-2664* ⊕ *www.oceanquestadventures.com.* **Pedal & Sea Adventures** ☎ *877/777-5699* ⊕ *www.pedalandseaadventures.com.*

CULTURAL AND CULINARY TOURS

The escorted and self-guided trips that **Atlantic Tours, Collette Vacations,** and Maxxim Vacations run throughout the region typically serve up a hefty dose of local history. **Vision Atlantic Vacations** offers similar fare along with more specialized options: including a 16-night itinerary that showcases Newfoundland's lighthouses and legends. Gourmets will also appreciate the company's multiday food-focused trips, which might include visits to wineries, lobster pounds, apple orchards, and maple sugar farms. For those who'd prefer to learn how to prepare local delicacies themselves, Nova Scotia's **Trout Point Lodge** operates a highly regarded vacation cooking school at its wilderness resort.

Contacts **Atlantic Tours** ☎ *902/423-7172, 800/565-7173* ⊕ *www.ambassatours.com.* **Collette Vacations** ☎ *800/468-5955*
⊕ *www.collettevacations.ca.* **Maxxim Vacations** ☎ *709/754-6666, 800/567-6666*
⊕ *www.maxximvacations.com.* **Trout Point Lodge** ☎ *902/761-2142* ⊕ *www.troutpoint.com.* **Vision Atlantic Vacations**
☎ *709/686-1395, 877/847-4660* ⊕ *www.visionatlanticvacations.com.*

FISHING

Packages put together by the Big Intervale Fishing Lodge lure anglers to Cape Breton's Margaree, a Canadian Heritage River. Country Haven offers fishing tours on New Brunswick's salmon-rich Miramichi. Tony's Tuna Fishing bundles lodgings with personalized deep-sea fishing and hands-on lobstering experiences in PEI. Newfoundland's Tuckamore Lodge schedules fresh- and saltwater fly-fishing excursions, including ones for women only.

Contacts **Big Intervale Fishing Lodge**
☎ *902/248-2275* ⊕ *bigintervalelodge.com.* **Country Haven** ☎ *877/359-4665, 506/843-9010* ⊕ *www.miramichifish.com.*
Tony's Tuna Fishing ☎ *902/357-2207*
⊕ *www.tonystunafishing.com.* **Tuckamore Lodge** ☎ *888/865-6361* ⊕ *www.flyfishing-tuckamore.com.*

GOLF

Golf New Brunswick, Golf Newfoundland, Golf Nova Scotia, and **Golf PEI** provide info on courses and related vacation packages in their respective provinces. For a regional overview, visit **Golf Coastal Canada's** comprehensive website at ⊕ *www.golfcoastalcanada.ca.*

Contacts **Golf New Brunswick** ☎ *877/833-4662* ⊕ *www.golfnb.ca.* **Golf Newfoundland** ☎ *709/651-8717* ⊕ *www.golfnl.ca.*
Golf Nova Scotia ☎ *866/933-3217* ⊕ *www.golfnovascotia.com.* **Golf Prince Edward Island** ☎ *866/465-3734* ⊕ *www.golfpei.ca.*

▍VISITOR INFORMATION

Provincial tourism offices *(⇨ See individual chapters for details)* are an invaluable source of information, as is Parks Canada (⊕ *www.pc.gc.ca*).

INDEX

A

Aberdeen Cultural Centre, 157
Acadia University Art Gallery, 76
Acadian Coast (New Brunswick), 161–174
Acadian culture, 48, 166
Acadian Festival, 173
Acadian Historical Village, 173
Acadian Interpretive Centre and Museum, 68
Acadian Museum (Moncton), 157
Acadian Museum (Summerside), 231
Admiral Digby Museum, 70
Adventure High, 145
Adventure tours, 316–317
New Brunswick, 136, 145, 152, 153, 160, 177
Newfoundland and Labrador, 244–245, 283, 290
Novia Scotia, 70, 96
Prince Edward Island, 225, 227
Advocate Harbour, 90
Age of Sail Museum, 90–91
Air travel, 306–307
New Brunswick, 124
Newfoundland and Labrador, 243
Nova Scotia, 28
Prince Edward Island, 196
Alexander Graham Bell National Historic Site, 110
Alexander Keith's Nova Scotia Brewery, 37
Alma, 150
Amherst, 89–90
Amusement parks
New Brunswick, 155, 171
Nova Scotia, 73–74
Prince Edward Island, 217
Andrew and Laura McCain Gallery, 178
Anglican Cathedral of St. John the Baptist, 252
Anna Leonowens Gallery, 37
Anna Swan Museum, 87
Annapolis Royal, 72–75
Annapolis Royal Historic Gardens, 73
Annapolis Valley, 48–79
Anne Murray Centre, 88
Anne of Green Gables, 215–216, 219

Anne of Green Gables Museum at Silver Bush, 216, 219
Antigonish, 82–84
Apartment and house rentals, 33, 310
Aquarium and Marine Centre (Shippagan), 172
Aquariums, 140, 172, 255
Archelaus Smith Museum, 64
Arches Provincial Park, 290–291
Arichat, 118
Art gallery (Antigonish), 82
Art Gallery of Nova Scotia, 34
Art Gallery of Nova Scotia (Western Branch), 65
Artisan Village, 161
Atlantic Salmon Museum, 170–171
ATMs, 314
Avalon Peninsula (Newfoundland and Labrador), 263–271
Avonlea – Village of Anne of Green Gables, 215, 216

B

Baddeck, 110–112
Balmoral Grist Mill, 87
Banks, 314
Barbour's General Store, 132
Barrington Museums, 64
Barrington Woolen Mill, 64
Basilica Cathedral of St. John the Baptist, 248
Basin Head Provincial Park, 225–226
Basin Head Fisheries Museum, 226
Battery, The (St. John's), 253
Bauer Theatre, 83
Beaches, 18
New Brunswick, 137, 167, 169
Nova Scotia, 39, 61, 78, 82, 85, 94–95, 99, 106
Prince Edward Island, 213–214, 219–220, 225–226, 234
Beaconsfield Historic House, 200
Beothuk Interpretation Centre, 281
Beaubears Island, 170
Beaverbrook Art Gallery, 183–184
Bed and breakfasts, 310–311
Bianca ✕, 255–256
Bicycling

New Brunswick, 126, 143
Nova Scotia, 55, 58, 62, 106
Prince Edward Island, 213, 229, 232
Big and Little Tancook Islands, 52
Big Pond, 117–118
Bird-watching
New Brunswick, 126, 146, 151, 163–164, 165
Newfoundland and Labrador, 263–264, 270–271
Nova Scotia, 71, 76–77, 84, 91
Bishop's Machine Shop, 231
Bistro 22 ✕, 95–96
Black Loyalist Heritage Site, 63
Blue Door, The ✕, 185–186
Boardwalk (Charlottetown), 200
Boat and ferry travel, 307
New Brunswick, 124
Newfoundland and Labrador, 243, 288
Nova Scotia, 28–29
Prince Edward Island, 196–197
Boating and sailing
New Brunswick, 136, 146, 177
Newfoundland and Labrador, 275–276, 283, 290, 293, 295
Nova Scotia, 32–33, 51, 54, 58, 62, 65, 70, 71, 86, 96, 106, 112, 117
Prince Edward Island, 209–210
Bonavista, 276–277
Bonne Bay Marine Station, 287
Books about Nova Scotia, 298
Bouctouche, 168–169
Bowring Park, 254–255
Boyce Farmers' Market, 184
Boyd's Cove, 281
Brackley Beach, 213–214
Bras d'Or Lakes Interpretive Centre, 110
Bridgewater, 59
Brier Island, 70–71
Brigus, 267–268
Brigus South, 264
Brule Fossil Centre, 87
Buddy McMaster School of Fiddling, 99
Bus travel, 307
New Brunswick, 124
Nova Scotia, 28
Prince Edward Island, 196
Business hours, 314

C

Cabot Beach Provincial Park, 219–220
Cabot Links, 101
Cabot Tower, 254
Cabot Trail, 18
Cabot's Landing Provincial Park, 106
Campobello Island, 147–148
Canadian Museum of Immigration at Pier 21, 34
Candlelight Graveyard Tour, 72
Canoeing, 46, 62, 188
Cape Bonavista Lighthouse, 276
Cape Breton Highlands National Park, 104–105
Cape Breton Island (Nova Scotia), 97–118
Cape Breton Miners' Museum, 113
Cape Chignecto, 90–92
Cape Chignecto Provincial Park, 91
Cape d'Or, 90–92
Cape Enrage, 152–153
Cape Enrage Adventures, 153
Cape Forchu Lighthouse, 66
Cape North, 106
Cape Race Lighthouse, 266
Cape Sable Island, 64
Cape St. Mary's Ecological Reserve, 270–271
Cape Smokey Provincial Park, 107
Cape Spear Lighthouse, 253
Cape Spear National Historic Site, 253
Car travel, 307–309
New Brunswick, 124–125
Newfoundland and Labrador, 244
Nova Scotia, 28
Prince Edward Island, 196
Caraquet, 172–174
Carleton Martello Tower, 132
Carriage House Inn ⌂ , 186
Casinos
New Brunswick, 159
Nova Scotia, 45, 115
Prince Edward Island, 202–203
Castle Hill National Historic Site, 269
Cavendish, 214–219
Central Coastal Drive (Prince Edward Island), 18, 211–222
Celtic Colours International Festival, 99

Celtic Music Interpretive Centre, 98–99
Central New Brunswick Woodmen's Museum, 171
Change Islands, 280
Charlotte County Courthouse and Old Gaol, 141
Charlotte Lane Café ✕ , 64
Charlottetown (Prince Edward Island), 198–210
Charlottetown Festival, 200–201
Cherry Brook Zoo, 129
Ches's ✕ , 256
Chester, 52–53
Chéticamp, 102–104
Children, attractions for, 22, 272
Chocolate Museum, 139
Christ Church Cathedral, 184–185
Church Point (Point de l'Eglise), 67–69
Churches
New Brunswick, 133, 141, 156, 172, 184–185
Newfoundland and Labrador, 248, 251, 252, 253
Nova Scotia, 39, 68, 69, 118
Prince Edward Island, 203–204, 220
Circular Road (St. John's), 252
Clarenville, 271–272
Climate, 14
Cobequid Interpretation Centre, 94
Codroy Valley, 295
Colleges and universities, 108, 115
Colonial Building (St. John's), 248
Colony of Avalon (archaeological dig), 265–266
Commissariat House, 252
Confederation Bridge, 221
Confederation Centre of the Arts, 200–201
Confederation Landing Park, 202
Confederation Trail, 218
Connell House, 180
Corner Brook, 294–295
Cossit House, 113–114
Costs, 10
Court House (St. John's), 251
Covered bridges, 179
Crafts, 46
Creamery Museum, 87
Credit cards, 10, 314–315

Cruise travel, 309
Crystal Palace, 155
Cuisine, 20
New Brunswick, 134
Nova Scotia, 41
Prince Edward Island, 207
Cultural and culinary tours, 317
Cupids, 268
Cupids Legacy Centre & Museum, 268
Currency and exchange, 315
Customs and duties, 312–313

D

Deer Island, 146–147
Deer Lake, 284–286
Deer Point, 146
DeGarthe Memorial, 49
Delta Fredericton Hotel ⌂ , 187
DesBrisay Museum, 59
Dieppe, 154–161
Digby, 69–70
Dining, 10, 313. ⇨ See also under cities and provinces
Discounts and deals, 29
Discovery Centre, 287
Discovery Trail, 271
Domaine de Grand Pré (winery), 75
Dorchester, 161–164
Downtown Fredericton Culture Crawl, 184
Drives, 18
Duckworth Street (St. John's), 251
Dunes Café, The ✕ , 213
Duties, 312–313

E

East Point Lighthouse, 229
Eastern Newfoundland, 271–279
Eastern Shore (Nova Scotia), 80–97
Eastport Peninsula, 274
Edmundston, 175–176
Église Ste-Marie (St. Mary's Church; Nova Scotia), 68
Electricity, 313
Emergencies, 314
and car travel, 308
Eptek Arts and Culture Centre, 231

F

Faire Brayonne, 175
Fairholm National Historic Inn ⌂ , 208

Farmers' market (Annapolis Royal), 73

Ferry service. ⇨ *See* Boat and ferry travel

Ferryland, 265–266

Ferryland Lighthouse, 266

Festivals and seasonal events
New Brunswick, 123, 173, 175, 184, 187
Newfoundland and Labrador, 241–242, 255
Nova Scotia, 27, 69, 93, 99, 100
Prince Edward Island, 195, 200–201, 203, 229, 231

Firefighters Museum of Nova Scotia, 66

Fisheries Museum of the Atlantic, 56

Fishers' Loft Inn ⊠ , 275

Fishing, 18, 317
Nova Scotia, 58, 102
Prince Edward Island, 213, 220, 227, 236

Five Islands, 94–95

Five Islands Provincial Park, 94–95

Fleur de Sel ✕ , 56

Florenceville-Bristol, 177–178

Flower House, 190

Fogo Island, 280

Fort Anne National Historic Site, 73

Fort Beauséjour National Historic Site, 164

Fort Edward, 79

Fort Point Lighthouse Park, 59–60

Fortress of Louisbourg National Historic Site of Canada, 19, 116

Founders' Hall-Canada's Birthplace Pavilion, 201

Fredericton (New Brunswick), 182–190

Fredericton Region Museum, 185

Free Meeting House, 156, 157

French vocabulary, 299–304

Fresh Fine Dining ✕ , 178

Fundy Coast (New Brunswick), 137–161

Fundy Discovery Aquarium, 140

Fundy Geological Museum, 92

Fundy National Park, 150–152

Fundy Trail Parkway, 137, 149

G

Gaelic College of Celtic Arts and Crafts, 108

Gagetown, 189–190

Gander and environs, 279–284

Gardens
New Brunswick, 126, 140, 175
Newfoundland and Labrador, 253–254
Nova Scotia, 38, 73, 76
Prince Edward Island, 215

Gardens of Hope, 215

Georgetown, 223–225

Golf, 317
New Brunswick, 126, 143–144, 151, 160, 188
Nova Scotia, 46, 101, 104, 107, 112
Prince Edward Island, 209, 213, 218–219, 224–225, 229, 233–234

Gorge Walk, 177

Government House (Fredericton), 185

Government House (Halifax), 38

Government House (St. John's), 251

Gower Street United Church, 251

Grand Bank, 277

Grand Falls (New Brunswick), 176–177

Grand Falls Museum, 177

Grand Falls-Windsor (Newfoundland), 283–284

Grand Manan Island, 145–146

Grand Pré National Historic Site, 75–76

Great George, The ⊠ , 208

Greater St. John's, 253–263

Green Gables, 215–216

Green Gardens Trail, 287

Greenock Church, 141

Greenwich (P.E.I. National Park), 227–228

Grenfell Historic Properties, 293

Gros Morne Mountain, 287

Gros Morne National Park, 19, 286–290

Gros Morne Visitor's Centre, 288

H

Haliburton House Museum, 78

Halifax (Nova Scotia), 14, 31–48

Halifax Citadel National Historic Site, 34–35

Halifax Public Gardens, 38

Halifax Seaport Farmers' Market, 38, 47

Halifax Waterfront Boardwalk, 35–36

Hall's Harbour, 76

Hall's Harbour Lobster Pound & Restaurant, 76

Harbour Grace, 269

Harbourside Park, 251

Harriet Irving Botanical Gardens, 76

Hartland, 178–179

Harvest Jazz and Blues Festival, 123, 187

Hawke Hills, 267

Hawthorne Cottage, 267

Hector Heritage Quay, 85

Herring Cove Provincial Park, 148

Highland Village Museum, 19, 112

Hiking and walking
New Brunswick, 130, 177, 188
Newfoundland and Labrador, 260, 274
Nova Scotia, 36, 46–47, 99, 101, 115
Prince Edward Island, 203, 236

Historic Garrison District (Fredericton), 184

Historic Properties (Halifax), 36–37

Historical Association of Annapolis Royal, 72

Holidays, 314

Hopewell Cape, 153–154

Hopewell Rocks, 153

Horse racing, 202–203

Horseback riding, 47, 104, 151

Hotel Paulin ⊠ , 174

Hotels, 10, 311. ⇨ *See also* under cities and provinces
prices, 31, 126, 197, 246

House rentals, 33, 310

Houses and buildings, historic
New Brunswick, 133, 141, 163, 173, 180, 181, 185, 190
Newfoundland and Labrador, 248, 251, 252, 267, 274, 276–277
Nova Scotia, 36–37, 38, 60, 66, 78, 93, 113–114
Prince Edward Island, 200, 202, 215–216, 230–231

I

Icebergs, *283*
Île Miscou, *172*
India Gate ✕ , *256*
Ingonish, *107*
Inns, *310–311*
International Fox Museum and Hall of Fame, *231*
Internet, *311*
Iona, *112*
Irish Loop, *266*
Irving Eco-Centre: La Dune de Bouctouche (coastal ecosystem), *168*
Irving Nature Park, *131*

J

J.C. Williams Dory Shop, *63–64*
J.T. Cheeseman Provincial Park, *296*
Java Jack's Restaurant and Gallery ✕ , *288–289*
Jeremiah's ✕ , *179*
Joggins Fossil Center, *89*
Johnson GEO Centre, *253*
Jost Vineyards, *87*
Judique, *98–99*
Julien's Pâtisserie, Bakery & Café ✕ , *53*

K

Kayaking
New Brunswick, 126, 144, 145, 146, 147, 152, 188
Newfoundland and Labrador, 261, 290
Nova Scotia, 47, 51, 58, 62, 70, 92, 106, 109
Prince Edward Island, 220, 222, 225
Keillor House and St. James Museum, *163*
Kejimkujik National Park and Historic Site, *19, 61–62*
Kejimkujik National Park-Seaside, *60*
Killam Brothers Shipping Office, *66*
King Street (Saint John), *133*
Kings Landing Historical Settlement, *19, 181*
King's Square (Saint John), *133*
Kingsbrae Arms 🔲 , *142*
Kingsbrae Garden, *140*
Kouchibouquac National Park, *19, 169*

L

La Fine Grobe Sure Mer ✕ , *174*
La Manche, *264*
Labrador. ⇨ See Newfoundland and Labrador
Language, *21, 259, 299–304*
L'Anse aux Meadows National Historic Site, *19, 291–292*
Le Pays de la Sagouine, *168–169*
LeNoir Forge Museum, *118*
Les Trois Pignons Cultural Center, *103*
Lighthouses, *20*
Newfoundland and Labrador, 253, 266, 276, 281, 287
Nova Scotia, 59–60, 64, 66, 82
Prince Edward Island, 228, 229, 234
Little Louis's Oyster Bar ✕ , *157*
Liverpool, *59–61*
Lobster Head Cove Lighthouse, *287*
Lodging, *10, 310–311.*
⇨ *See also* under cities and provinces
Logger's Life Provincial Museum, *283*
Long Island, *70–71*
Long Point Lighthouse, *281*
Long Range Mountains, *286*
Longest Covered Bridge, *179*
Lot 30 ✕ , *205*
Louisbourg, *116–117*
Loyalist Burial Ground, *131*
Loyalist House, *133*
Lucy Maud Montgomery Birthplace, *216*
Lunenburg, *55–59*
Lunenburg Town Walking Tours, *56*
Lutz Mountain Heritage Museum, *157*

M

Mabou, *99–101*
Mabou Highlands, *101*
Mactaquac Provincial Park, *181–182*
Maddox Cove and Petty Harbour, *255*
Magic Mountain Water Park (theme park), *145*
Magnetic Hill, *155–156*
Magnetic Hill Zoo, *156*
Mahone Bay, *53–55*
Malpeque, *219–220*

Marconi National Historic Site, *114*
Margaree Harbour, *101–102*
Margaree Salmon Museum, *101*
Margaret Fawcett Norrie Heritage Centre, *87*
Maritime Museum of the Atlantic, *37*
Market Slip (Saint John), *131*
Marshlands Inn 🔲 , *165*
Mary Celeste (ship), *92*
Mary E. Black Gallery, *38*
Mary March Provincial Museum, *283*
Marysville, *185*
Memorial University Botanical Garden, *253–254*
Memramcock, *161–164*
Mercantile Premises, *274*
Mermaid Theatre of Nova Scotia, *78*
Metepenagiag Heritage Park, *170*
Minas Basin, *93*
Ministers Island, *141*
Miquelon, *277–279*
Miramichi, *170–172*
Miscou Island, *172*
Mistaken Point Ecological Reserve, *266*
Mockbeggar Plantation, *276–277*
Moncton, *154–161*
Moncton Museum, *156*
Money matters, *314–415*
Montgomery, Lucy Maud, *215–216*
Monument Lefebvre National Historic Site, *163*
Motorcycle travel, *196*
Movies about Nova Scotia, *298*
Murray Premises, *252*
Museums and galleries, *19*
New Brunswick, 131, 132, 136–137, 139, 141, 152, 156, 157, 161, 163, 164, 165, 170–171, 173, 177, 178, 180, 183–184, 185, 189, 190
Newfoundland and Labrador, 251–252, 253, 268, 274, 277, 279–280, 281, 283, 287, 288
Nova Scotia, 34–35, 37, 38–39, 52, 53, 56, 59, 60, 63–64, 65, 66, 68, 70, 72–73, 75–76, 78, 79, 82, 84, 85, 86, 87–89, 90–91, 92, 93, 94,

97, 98–99, 101, 103, 105,
109–110, 111, 112, 113,
114, 115, 118
Prince Edward Island, 200–
201, 214, 217, 219, 226,
230–231, 233, 234, 235
Music
New Brunswick, 123, 136, 187
Newfoundland and Labrador,
262–263
Nova Scotia, 69, 98–99, 100,
101, 111–112, 115
Prince Edward Island, 209, 232
Myriad View Artisan Distillery,
226

N

Neddis Harbour Inn 🖼 , 289
New Brunswick, 12, 120–190
Acadian Coast, 161–174
children, attractions for, 22
cuisine, 134
dining and lodging, 125–126,
133–135, 141–143, 145–146,
147, 148, 149, 150–151,
154, 157–159, 163, 164,
167–168, 169, 171–172,
173–174, 175–176, 178, 179,
180–181, 185–187, 190
festivals and seasonal events,
123, 173, 175, 184, 187
Fredericton, 182–190
Fundy Coast, 137–161
itinerary recommendations, 127
nightlife and the arts, 136,
159–160, 187–188
outdoor activities and sports,
136, 143–144, 146, 147,
149, 151–152, 160, 163–164,
174, 176, 188–189
prices, 125, 126
Saint John, 126–137
St. John River Valley, 174–182
shopping, 136–137, 144, 152,
154, 160–161, 164, 189, 190
timing the visit, 123–124
tours, 126, 130, 136, 143–144,
145, 146, 147, 152, 153, 160
168–169, 177, 184
transportation, 124–125
visitor information, 126
**New Brunswick Botanical Gar-
den,** 175
New Brunswick Museum, 131
New Glasgow Lobster Suppers
✕ , 217
New River Beach, 137
Newfoundland and Labrador,
12, 18, 238–296

Avalon Peninsula, 263–271
children, attractions for, 22, 272
dining and lodging, 245–246,
254, 255–259, 268, 269–270,
271, 272, 273, 274–275,
277, 278–279, 280–281,
282–283, 284, 286, 288–290,
291–292, 293, 294–295, 296
Eastern Newfoundland,
271–279
festivals and seasonal events,
241–242, 255
Gander and environs, 279–284
itinerary recommendations,
247, 250
language, 259
nightlife and the arts, 260,
275, 290
outdoor activities and sports,
244–245, 255, 260–262, 264,
274, 275–276, 283, 290,
293, 295
prices, 245, 246
St. John's, 14, 246–263
shopping, 262–263, 272,
293–294
time zone, 243
timing the visit, 241–243
tours, 244–245, 248, 261–262,
264, 275–276, 278, 281,
290, 293, 295
transportation, 243–244, 288
Western Newfoundland,
284–296
Newfoundland Emporium, 294
Newfoundland Insectarium,
286
Newman Wine Vaults, 252
Nightlife and the arts. ⇨ See
under cities and provinces
Norseman Restaurant ✕ , 291
Norstead, 291
**North Atlantic Aviation
Museum,** 279–280
North Cape, 235–236
North Cape Coastal Drive
(Prince Edward Island),
229–236
**North Cape Wind Energy Inter-
pretive Centre,** 235
Northern Nova Scotia, 80–97
Notre Dame de l'Assumption,
118
Nova Scotia, 12, 24–118
Cape Breton Island, 97–118
children, attractions for, 22
cuisine, 41
dining and lodging, 31, 33,
39–44, 51, 52–53, 54, 56–58,

61, 62, 64–65, 66–67, 68–69,
70, 71, 74, 77, 79, 83–84,
85, 88, 90, 91–92, 93–94,
95–96, 97, 99–100, 102, 103,
106, 107, 108–109, 111,
114–115, 116–118
discounts and deals, 29
Eastern Shore and Northern
Nova Scotia, 80–97
festivals and seasonal events,
27, 69, 93, 99, 100
Halifax, 14, 31–48
itinerary recommendations, 30
nightlife and the arts, 44–45,
53, 69, 75, 86, 94, 100, 101,
111–112, 115, 117
outdoor activities and sports,
29, 46–47, 51, 54–55, 58, 61,
62, 65, 70, 71, 78, 83, 84,
86, 88, 92, 94, 96, 99, 101,
102, 103–104, 105, 106,
107, 109, 112, 115, 117
prices, 31
shopping, 46, 47–48, 51, 53,
55, 58–59, 67, 86, 88, 93,
96–97, 104, 109–110, 115
South Shore and Annapolis Valley, 48–79
timing the visit, 27
tours, 29, 32–33, 36, 51, 54,
56, 59, 65, 71, 72, 84, 86,
88, 92, 96, 112, 113
transportation, 28–29
visitor information, 31
**Nova Scotia Gem and Mineral
Show,** 93
**Nova Scotia Museum of Indus-
try,** 85
**Nova Scotia Museum of Natu-
ral History,** 38–39

O

Old County Court House, 180
Old Gaol (St. Andrews by-the-
Sea), 141
Old Home Week, 203
Old Meeting House Museum
(Barrington), 64
Old Sow (whirlpool), 146
O'Leary, 232–234
Olivier Soapery, The, 169
Open Sky Adventures, 177
**Ottawa House-by-the-Sea
Museum,** 93
Outdoor activities and sports.
⇨ See under cities and
provinces
Owens Art Gallery, 164

P

P.E.I. National Park (Greenwich), 227–228
Panmure Head Lighthouse, 228
Paragliding, 94
Parc de l'Aboiteau, 167
Parks, 19
New Brunswick, 131, 132, 148, 150–152, 156, 167, 169, 170, 171, 174, 181–182
Newfoundland and Labrador, 251, 254–255, 267, 272–273, 286–291, 296
Nova Scotia, 39, 59–60, 61–62, 72–73, 75–78, 79, 82, 85, 91, 94–95, 99, 104–105, 106, 107, 110, 115
Prince Edward Island, 202, 211–213, 219–220, 224, 225–226, 234, 236
Parlee Beach, 167
Parrsboro, 92–94
Parrsboro Rock and Mineral Shop and Museum, 93
Partridge Island, 93
Passports and visas, 315–316
Peggy's Cove, 49–51
PEI Potato Museum, 233
Pelton-Fuller House, 66
Perkins House Museum, 60
Peter Buckland Gallery, 137
Petty Harbour, 255
Pictou, 84–86
Placentia, 269–270
Plane travel. ⇨ *See* Air travel
Playhouse (theater), 187
Pleasant Bay, 105
Point de l'Eglise (Church Point), 67–69
Point Pleasant Park, 39
Point Prim Lighthouse, 228
Points East Coastal Drive (Prince Edward Island), 222–229
Pope's Museum, 173
Port au Choix National Historic Site, 291
Port au Port Peninsula, 295
Port aux Basques, 296
Port Bickerton Lighthouse Beach Park, 82
Port Royal National Historic Site, 72–73
Press Gang, The ✕, 43
Prices
dining, 31, 125, 197, 245
lodging, 31, 126, 197, 246
New Brunswick, 125, 126

Newfoundland and Labrador, 245, 246
Nova Scotia, 31
Prince Edward Island, 197
Prime Berth Twillingate Fishery & Heritage Centre, 281
Prince Edward Distillery, 226
Prince Edward Island, 12, 192–236
Central Coastal Drive, 211–222
Charlottetown, 198–210
children, attractions for, 22
cuisine, 207
dining and lodging, 197, 202, 204–208, 212, 213–214, 217–218, 220, 221–222, 224, 226–227, 228, 231–232, 233, 235–236
festivals and seasonal events, 195, 200–201, 203, 229, 231
itinerary recommendations, 199
nightlife and the arts, 209, 214, 222, 224, 228–229, 232
North Cape Coastal Drive, 229–236
outdoor activities and sports, 202–203, 209–210, 213, 214, 218–219, 220, 222, 224–225, 227, 229, 232, 233–234, 236
Points East Coastal Drive, 222–229
prices, 197
shopping, 210, 214, 222, 234
timing the visit, 195
tours, 197–200, 203, 209–210, 225, 227, 232
transportation, 196–197
visitor information, 197, 198
Prince Edward Island National Park, 19, 211–213
Prince William Street (Saint John), 133
Province House National Historic Site, 202
Provinces, 15
Provincial Seamen's Museum, 277

Q

Queens County Courthouse, 190
Queens County Museum, 190
Quidi Vidi, 254, 255

R

Random Passage, 276
Rappelling, 153
Red Shoe ✕, 100

Red Shores Racetrack and Casino, 202–203
Rendez-vous de la Baie, 68
Restaurants, 10, 313. ⇨ *See also* under cities and provinces
prices, 31, 126, 197, 245
Resurgo Place, 156
Reversing Rapids, 18, 131–132
Richard's Fresh Seafood ✕, 212
Ripley's Believe It or Not!, 217
Rita's Tea Room, 117–118
Ritchie Wharf Park, 171
River Breeze Farm, 95
River Valley Scenic Drive, 18
Riverfront Park, 156
Robie Tufts Nature Center, 76–77
Rockwood Park, 132
Roma at Three Rivers, 223–224
Rooms, The, 251–252
Roosevelt Campobello International Park, 148
Rosedale Manor Bed & Breakfast ⊞, 270
Ross Farm Living Museum of Agriculture, 52
Ross Memorial Museum, 141
Rossignol Cultural Centre, 60
Ross-Thomson House & Store, 63
Royal St. John's Regatta, 255
Rugged Beauty Boat Tours, 276
Ryan Premises National Historic Site, 277

S

Sackville, 164–165
Sackville Waterfowl Park, 164
Sailing. ⇨ *See* Boating and sailing
St. Andrews by-the-Sea, 140–144
St. Ann's Bay, 108–110
St. Anthony, 292–294
St. Bernard Church, 69
St. Croix Island International Historic Site, 139
St. Dunstan's Basilica, 203
St. James Museum, 163
Saint John (New Brunswick), 126–137
Saint John Ale House ✕, 134
Saint John City Market, 132
St. John River Valley (New Brunswick), 174–182
St. John's (Newfoundland), 14, 246–263

St. Martins, *148–149*
St. Mary's Church (Église Ste-Marie; Nova Scotia), 68
St. Mary's Church (Prince Edward Island), 220
St. Paul's Anglican Church (Charlottetown), 203
St. Paul's Anglican Church (Halifax), 39
St. Peter's Bay, 227–229
St. Peter's Cathedral, 203–204
St-Pierre, 277–279
St. Stephen, 139
St. Thomas Anglican (Old Garrison) Church, 253
Sainte Famille Winery, 79
Ste-Cécile Church, 172
Salmonier Nature Park, 267
Sandspit (amusement park), 217
Savour in the Garden ✕, 142
Scenic drives, 18
Science East (Fredericton), 185
Scuba diving
New Brunswick, 126, 143
Newfoundland and Labrador, 261
Nova Scotia, 58
Seafood, 20
Seal Island Light Museum, 64
Segway tours, 232
Shediac, 165–168
Shelburne, 63–65
Shelburne County Museum, 63–64
Shelburne Museum Complex, 63–64
Sherbrooke and Sherbrooke Village, 80–82
Sherman Hines Museum of Photography, 60
Shining Waters Family Fun Park, 217
Shippagan, 172
Shopping. ➪ *See* under cities and provinces
Signal Hill National Historic Site, 254
Silent Witness Memorial, 280
Site of Lucy Maud Montgomery's Cavendish Home, 216
Skerwink Trail, 274
Skiing, 149, 174, 176, 188
Souris, 225–227
South Shore (Nova Scotia), 48–79
Spinnaker's Landing (Summerside), 230

Sports and outdoor activities. ➪ *See* under cities and provinces
Springhill, 88–89
Springhill Miners Museum, 89
Stargazers, programs for, 62
Stephenville, 295–296
Stone Church, 133
Sugar Moon Farm Maple Products and Pancake House ✕, 97
Summerside, 229–232
Summerside Lobster Carnival, 229, 231
Summerville Beach Provincial Park, 61
Suncor Energy Fluvarium, The, 255
Sunrise Trail Museum, 87
Surfing, 18, 61, 83
Sutherland Steam Mill Museum, 87–88
Swan, Anna, 87
Swimming, 47, 234
Swissair Memorial, 49, 51
Sydney, 113–115
Sydney Mines Heritage Museum and Fossil Centre, 114
Symbols, 10

T

Tablelands, *287–288*
Tait House ⊡, 168
Tantramar Marsh, 90
Tatamagouche, 86–88
Taxes, 316
Telephones, 311–312
Terra Nova National Park, 272–274
Theater
New Brunswick, 136, 187
Newfoundland and Labrador, 260, 275
Nova Scotia, 45, 53, 75, 78, 83, 94, 101, 115, 117
Prince Edward Island, 200–201, 209, 214, 222, 224, 228–229, 232
Thomas Raddall Provincial Park, 60
Tidal Bore and Riverfront Park, 156
Time zones, 243, 316
Timing the visit, 14
Tipping, 316
Titanic, 37
Tours and packages, 316–317
Train travel, 309

New Brunswick, 125
Nova Scotia, 29
Transportation Discovery Museum, 156
Trinity, 274–276
Trinity Church, 133
Trout Paint Lodge ⊡, 67
Trout River, 288
Truro, 95–97
Twillingate, 281–283

U

Uniacke Estate Museum Park, 79
Upper Clements Park (amusement park), 73–74
Usige Ban Falls Provincial Park, 110

V

Vacation rentals, 33, 310
Valhalla Lodge Bed & Breakfast ⊡, 292
Victoria, 221–222
Victoria Park (Charlottetown), 204
Victoria Park (Truro), 95
Victoria Row (Charlottetown), 202
Vikings, 291
Village of Gagetown, 189–190
Visas, 315–316
Visitor information, 317
Vocabulary, 299–304

W

Wagmatcook Culture & Heritage Centre, 111
Walking tours
New Brunswick, 130, 177
Newfoundland and Labrador, 248, 250
Nova Scotia, 36, 56, 59, 72, 84, 86, 88, 113
Prince Edward Island, 203
Water sports, 209–210
Water Street (St. John's), 252
Waterfalls, 18, 131–132, 136, 176–177
Weather, 14
West Mabou Beach Provincial Park, 99
West Point, 234
West Point Lighthouse Museum, 234
Western Brook Pond, 287
Western Counties Military Museum, 64

Western Newfoundland,
  284–296
Whale Interpretive Centre, 105
Whale watching
  New Brunswick, 126, 143,
    144, 146
  Newfoundland and Labrador,
    261–262, 264
  Nova Scotia, 58, 70, 71, 103,
    104, 105, 106
White-water rafting, 96
Wile Carding Mill Museum, 59

Windjammer ✕ , *158*
Windsor (Nova Scotia), *78–79*
Windsor Hockey Heritage
  Centre, *78*
Wineries, *75, 79, 87, 252*
Witless Bay Ecological Reserve,
  263–264
Wolfville, *75–78*
Wood Islands Lighthouse, *228*
Woodstock, *179–181*
Woody Point, *288*

Wyatt House Museum,
  230–231

Y

Yarmouth, *65–67*
Yarmouth County Museum &
  Archives, *66*

Z

Zip-line tours, *136, 160*
Zoos, *129, 156*

PHOTO CREDITS

NOTES

NOTES

NOTES

NOTES

NOTES

NOTES

NOTES

NOTES

Fodor's NOVA SCOTIA & ATLANTIC CANADA

Publisher: Amanda D'Acierno, *Senior Vice President*

Editorial: Arabella Bowen, *Editor in Chief*; Linda Cabasin, *Editorial Director*

Design: Fabrizio La Rocca, *Vice President, Creative Director*; Tina Malaney, *Associate Art Director*; Chie Ushio, *Senior Designer*; Ann McBride, *Production Designer*

Photography: Melanie Marin, *Associate Director of Photography*; Jessica Parkhill and Jennifer Romains, *Researchers*

Maps: Rebecca Baer, *Senior Map Editor*; Mark Stroud (Moon Street Cartography) and David Lindroth, *Cartographers*

Production: Linda Schmidt, *Managing Editor*; Evangelos Vasilakis, *Associate Managing Editor*; Angela L. McLean, *Senior Production Manager*

Sales: Jacqueline Lebow, *Sales Director*

Marketing & Publicity: Heather Dalton, *Marketing Director*; Katherine Fleming, *Senior Publicist*

Business & Operations: Susan Livingston, *Vice President, Strategic Business Planning*; Sue Daulton, *Vice President, Operations*

Fodors.com: Megan Bell, *Executive Director, Revenue & Business Development*; Yasmin Marinaro, *Senior Director, Marketing & Partnerships*

13th Edition

ISBN 978-0-8041-4203-8

ISSN 1558–8173

SPECIAL SALES

PRINTED IN THE UNITED STATES OF AMERICA

10 9 8 7 6 5 4 3

ABOUT OUR WRITERS

Having visited countless countries on six continents, frequent Fodor's contributor Susan MacCallum-Whitcomb can say with some certainty that Atlantic Canada is her favorite place on earth. Born and bred in New Brunswick, Susan has strong family ties to Prince Edward Island, and currently resides with her husband and two children in Nova Scotia—so she pretty much has the region covered. She updated the Experience, Prince Edward Island, and Travel Smart chapters for this edition.

Penny Phenix moved to New Brunswick in 2009, after a long association with the province through travel writing commissions and marriage to a New Brunswicker. She has written or contributed to many guidebooks, including *Spiral Guide Canada, Key Guide Canada, Essential Canada East,* and *Explorer Canada.* For this edition, she updated the Nova Scotia, New Brunswick, Newfoundland and Labrador, and Understanding Nova Scotia and Atlantic Canada chapters.